W9-CCC-941

McGraw-Hill Education

# SSAT/ISEE

## Fifth Edition

# McGraw-Hill Education

# SSAT/ISEE

## Fifth Edition

**Nicholas Falletta**

Foreword by Gregg W. M. Maloberti,
Dean of Admission, The Lawrenceville School

New York  Chicago  San Francisco  Athens  London  Madrid
Mexico City  Milan  New Delhi  Singapore  Sydney  Toronto

Copyright © 2019, 2016 by McGraw-Hill Education. All rights reserved. Printed in the United States of America. Except as permitted under the United States Copyright Act of 1976, no part of this publication may be reproduced or distributed in any form or by any means, or stored in a database or retrieval system, without the prior written permission of the publisher.

1 2 3 4 5 6 7 8 9   LHS   24 23 22 21 20 19

**Contributor**
**Dr. Janet E. Wall** contributed the mathematics review chapters and mathematics portions of the Practice Tests in this book.

ISBN      978-1-260-45803-9
MHID       1-260-45803-2

e-ISBN  978-1-260-45804-6
e-MHID      1-260-45804-0

SSAT is a registered trademark of The Enrollment Management Association, which was not involved in the production of, and does not endorse, this product.
ISEE is a registered trademark of ERB (Educational Records Bureau), which was not involved in the production of, and does not endorse, this product.

McGraw-Hill Education products are available at special quantity discounts to use as premiums and sales promotions or for use in corporate training programs. To contact a representative, please visit the Contact Us pages at www.mhprofessional.com.

# CONTENTS

## Part II Strategies for the Verbal, Reading, and Writing Sections

### Chapter 5 Strategies for Synonym Questions,  55

### Chapter 6 Strategies for Verbal Analogy Questions (SSAT Only),  65

### Chapter 7 Strategies for Sentence Completion Questions (ISEE Only),  77

### Chapter 8 Strategies for Reading Comprehension Questions,  91

### Chapter 9 Strategies for the Writing Section,  119

# Foreword: What to Expect at an Independent School

*Gregg W. M. Maloberti*
*Dean of Admission*
*The Lawrenceville School*

If you or your parents have purchased this book, then you are most likely hoping to be admitted to an independent school. This short introduction will tell you more about independent schools. You'll learn about some of the benefits and advantages that an independent school can offer you, and you'll find out some important facts about the admissions process.

## The Benefits of Attending an Independent School

When asked why they wish to attend an independent school, many students say they want to get a "better" education or to attend a "good" college. Parents often say they are looking for a school of the "highest" quality to give their children the "best" opportunity for success. Statements like these help explain how much students and parents value education, but they offer little insight into the advantages that independent schools offer their students.

By definition, independent schools exist as an alternative to public schools as well as to one another. Independent schools come in all shapes and sizes, coeducational and single sex, and day and boarding. They are free to specialize in anything and everything from academic rigor, to performing or fine arts, to character and leadership development, to helping students with learning disabilities. For you as a student, that means that you can choose an independent school that shares your values and allows you to focus on what is important to you. By choosing a school that has a mission and purpose closely aligned with your own principles, you can move closer to achieving your own goals.

**Faculty**   Above all, independent schools pride themselves on the quality of their faculty. Independent school teachers often boast degrees from top-flight academic institutions, years of classroom experience, and a commitment to educational research and curricular development. They have been involved with many cutting-edge programs that are reshaping American education. For example, it was at independent schools that the Harkness method of teaching, sometimes called the Conference Plan, was originally introduced in the 1930s. Prior to this innovation, nearly all instruction took place in the form of a lecture. Now it is commonplace to see students seated around oval or round tables actively discussing the day's lesson. The Advanced Placement Program, known better as the APs, was originally initiated in the 1950s through collaboration between three independent schools and three leading universities.

Many programs and schools that include outdoor leadership training and experiential learning can trace their roots back to faculty who were given support, resources, and encouragement by independent schools.

**Small Classes** One of the greatest benefits that you're likely to find in an independent school is the small class size. Independent schools create student-to-teacher ratios that enable small classes and greater personal interaction. In these classes, teachers are able to give students the kind of individual attention that promotes student achievement. When the classroom experience includes discussion, active participation, and debate, students are much more likely to be actively engaged in the learning process. Just imagine yourself in this kind of classroom: If you and your classmates know you will be called upon in class, you will be far more likely to arrive in class better prepared and more willing to engage in the lesson. Many independent school faculty value student participation so much that it becomes a factor in assessing performance and assigning grades.

Class size becomes even more important when you consider the total number of students each teacher meets with daily. If a teacher meets 5 classes of 30 students each day, there are 150 papers to mark every time a writing assignment is given. Independent schools typically keep class sizes small enough and teaching loads reasonable enough to accommodate regular review of student work. The National Association of Independent Schools (NAIS) reported that the average class size in their member schools was 15 and the average faculty-to-student ratio was 8.8:1. Teaching takes time and energy, and with fewer students and fewer sections, teachers not only perform better in their classrooms but also are able to meet with their students on an individual basis. Many schools reserve time during the school day when teachers are available to meet with their students in small groups or one-on-one. The chance to work individually with a teacher is just as important to a student who is in need of remedial attention as it is to a student who needs mentoring or enrichment.

**Student-Teacher Interaction** Independent school teachers often play a multitude of roles over the course of a school day. They may serve as teachers, coaches, academic advisers, or club sponsors, and in boarding schools they may be dormitory parents as well. While it sounds exhausting for the teachers, you as a student can benefit through interacting with teachers in a variety of places and situations. At nine o'clock in the morning, your teacher may be helping you as you struggle with a geometry proof, but at four in the afternoon, that same teacher may be coaching you in soccer as you score the winning goal. Situations like these that allow you to see and work with your teachers in a variety of situations help develop real relationships that can increase trust and communication. Few students can ever explain why, but they all know that they perform better for teachers that they like, and they like teachers who show an interest in them.

Some independent schools organize their dining halls to facilitate interactions between students and their teachers by offering family-style meals with a faculty member at the head of each table. Others create a casual environment where students and faculty can intermingle naturally. Regardless of the method, creating social situations outside the classroom helps students develop more natural and meaningful relationships with their teachers.

**Environmental Awareness**  Increasingly, independent schools are taking an interest in the environment. Many independent schools are large land holders, and simply holding onto their land, which can be thousands of acres in some cases, helps stem the tide of urban and suburban sprawl. Schools that preserve open space are contributing to wildlife preservation, green space, and clean water supplies. Many independent schools are developing aggressive recycling and smart purchasing programs to curb the flow of packaging and containers into the waste stream. For instance, many independent schools now lease computers, a practice which frees them from the expense of their disposal at the end of their use cycle. Leased computers are then returned to the manufacturer for recycling, reselling, or proper disposal. Faculty and students take an active role in developing and implementing environmentally sound practices at their schools. By involving the students directly in issues related to the environment, independent schools are developing the awareness and skills that will help their students become more environmentally responsible as adults.

**Sports**  Athletics play a major role in many independent schools. Competitive, intramural, and recreational sports are often offered as an alternative to traditional physical education. Great emphasis is placed on sportsmanship and fair play. Some independent school athletic leagues have rivalries that date back over a hundred years. Independent schools offer a uniquely wide range of sports options. In addition to American favorites such as football, basketball, baseball, and soccer, sports such as crew, squash, fencing, field hockey, and lacrosse are widely available.

**Student Diversity**  Independent schools have embraced diversity as a way of preparing their students for leadership roles in a rapidly changing global society. Initially, financial aid helped break through the economic barriers of affording tuition. Through concerted efforts at recruiting minority students, independent schools offer an experience in racial diversity that is approaching the current composition of American society. Since independent schools can freely cross municipal boundaries to draw students, they are able to overcome the obstacles of real estate prices and taxes that have kept public schools from becoming less homogeneous. Indeed, boarding schools can draw from any neighborhood in the country or the world.

Through affiliations with outreach programs such as the Albert G. Oliver Program, Prep for Prep, the White Foundation, NJ Seeds, the Boys and Girls Clubs of New York City, A Better Chance, and the Black Student Fund, independent day and boarding schools have been able to identify talented and motivated students from even the most impoverished schools in urban cities and rural America. Increasingly, independent schools are becoming attractive to the growing population of affluent minority families who wish to provide their children with the best educational opportunities.

According to the U.S. Department of Education, National Center for Educational Statistics, Private School Universe Survey, 1999–2000 and 2001–2002, there were 1,207,182 minority students in the total population of 5,341,513 private school students. This figure represents a 3.46 percent increase over the previous years. The trend is expected to continue as the population of the United States continues to change.

Independent schools are taking a leadership role in developing a multicultural approach to education. By recognizing and celebrating the racial, ethnic, religious, and cultural differences between their students, independent schools are building stronger communities by debunking stereotypes and building trust where there was once only fear and suspicion. Some independent schools are modifying their curricula to include perspectives that have not always been well represented, such as African-American literature and Asian history.

**Preparing for College**   In standardized testing, students at NAIS schools demonstrate consistently high results. According to data from the College Board for the 2003–2004 academic year, SAT scores of independent school students exceeded the national average by more than 150 points, continuing the trend since the NAIS began keeping records in 1975–1976. Independent school students achieved an average verbal score of 593 and a math score of 600, compared to the national average of 508 for verbal and 518 for math. In the SAT II subject tests, independent school students outscored the national mean in 16 of the 23 subject areas.

As college attendance dominates the list of reasons why most families choose independent schools, it is reassuring to report that NAIS data reports that 98.9 percent of their member schools' students graduated from high school in the academic year 2000–2001. In the same year, 94.3 percent of NAIS graduating seniors attended four-year colleges.

## Applying to an Independent School

When you apply for admission to an independent school, you are typically asked to visit the school, have some type of interview, take a standardized test, write an application, and submit supporting documents including a current transcript and teacher recommendations. The admission office at any school should be able to tell you exactly what is required and give you a schedule that includes any deadlines for testing or the submission of application materials, as well as the date by which you will be notified of whether or not you are accepted. Most schools follow a traditional cycle of inviting visits and interviews in the fall, collecting application materials in midwinter, and mailing decision letters in the early spring. Some schools have open admission year-round, while others may follow a rolling admission program throughout the year. Even the most selective schools sometimes have last-minute openings in the summer months.

**School Visits**   On a school visit, you may do nothing more than take a brief tour and have an interview with an admissions officer or a faculty member. On the other hand, the visit may be a full-day program during which you may be given a test and produce a writing sample. School visits may take many forms, including open houses, opportunities to visit classes, and individual tours. Most independent schools have fairly firm ideas about how they conduct their visits. Some schools are quite open to guests, encouraging you to pay a lengthy visit and participate fully in school activities. Keep in mind, though, that some schools receive hundreds or even thousands of visitors a year, and these schools must structure their tours in such a way that they do not interfere with the current students' normal school day. If there is a new visitor in a classroom every day, the dynamic between the teacher and the students is likely to be altered in some meaningful way. In almost all cases, once a school has accepted you, you will be invited to pay an extensive visit that will include time in the classroom.

Before you come for a visit, make sure you inquire about dress code. You'll feel more comfortable if you can present yourself in a manner similar to that of students enrolled at the school. Schools typically run on rather tight schedules with only 5 or 10 minutes between class periods, and guides, who may be students or faculty, typically give tours during a free class period or break in their schedule.

Try to be punctual so that your visit gets off to a good start and concludes without anyone feeling rushed or inconvenienced. If you have any special requests to meet with program directors, coaches, teachers, administrators, or other school personnel, make your requests in advance of your visit. Schools can be very accommodating, but the more notice they have of your expectations, the more likely they will be able to arrange an interesting visit. The most important thing to remember about visits to schools is that first impressions are lasting.

**Testing**   Like any examination at school, preparing for an entrance test such as the SSAT or the ISEE is an important activity. Even though there is no way to know exactly what will be on the test, understanding the kinds of questions that will be on the test and being familiar with the directions for each section will help you be more relaxed and confident on the day of the test.

Good testers come to the exam with an understanding of how the test is scored and have a strategy in mind for guessing. For instance, the SSAT gives one point for each correct answer and only takes away one-quarter point for each wrong answer. Given that information, making educated guesses between two answer choices after eliminating the others will likely help you increase your test score. This does not mean that guesses should be made in every instance, as those quarter-point penalties do add up. The message here is that guessing is part of the test-taking strategy and should be formulated well in advance of the test date.

Many students think that taking the test multiple times will increase their scores dramatically. Although students who take the test without adequate preparation, when in poor health, or under emotional duress may benefit from a second try, on average only about 10 percent of testers who use test preparation guides or attend a test preparation course in advance of taking the test improve their scores by 10 percent in subsequent test administrations. In most cases, improving your test scores by 10 percent will not likely significantly alter the admission decision for a given candidate.

Each school has it own philosophy about the importance of test scores and their use in the admission process. It is important to remember that even when a school provides the range or the average of the test scores of the admitted candidates, these ranges or averages should not be viewed as either minimum requirements or guarantees of admission. Admission committees typically consider more than just a candidate's test scores when making an admission decision.

**The Application**   Completing an application for admission should not become an onerous task or require substantial parental involvement. Many applications specifically request that the application be completed in the student's own handwriting. The application affords little opportunity for gamesmanship, and the goal should not be to win an essay contest for originality but instead to present a clear and accurate representation of your interests, talents, activities, and abilities. Experienced admission committees can quickly spot the contrived essay or the heavy hand of the parent as editor.

Both the SSAT and ISEE include a timed writing sample that will be collected during the test. That sample will be compared to other writing samples in your application, and while many students write better with more time or the use of a word processing computer program, wild discrepancies between the writing on the application and that in the writing sample rarely work to the advantage of the candidate.

Some candidates have been known to go to great lengths to create portfolios of their accomplishments, recordings of their musical performances, and even videos showcasing talents and experiences. Not all schools are interested in receiving such materials, and it is worthwhile to inquire as to how such materials may be viewed by the admission committee. On the other hand, schools that are interested in learning more about a candidate's abilities may have specific guidelines for submitting audition tapes, athletic highlight films, or artistic portfolios. You should inquire whether such materials may or may not be returned prior to submitting them. It is not advisable to submit anything that cannot be replaced if lost or damaged. Whenever possible, it is best to limit yourself to answering all the applicable questions and satisfying all the necessary requirements of an application. Exceeding these expectations may not always have the desired effect.

Candidates should be mindful of the fact that their current schools may have many documents to prepare for other students as well. Requests for transcripts and teacher recommendations should be made well in advance of the deadlines for submission. It is a generous courtesy to provide an envelope with postage addressed to the school. In most cases, the current school will send the materials directly to the admissions office. These materials are generally regarded as confidential, and you and your parents should not expect to see or review them once they have been completed.

The admission office will notify candidates when all the materials have arrived and the application is complete. Given the amount of paperwork involved in the process, many parents become quite anxious and make frequent and regular calls to both the school sending the documents and the admissions office receiving them. Until a reasonable amount of time has passed, these calls are not terribly welcome. Looking into these matters takes time away from the actual process of completing the forms or sorting and filing the documents once they arrive. Most schools will notify you of any missing credentials in a timely manner.

To ease the process of applying to multiple schools, many independent schools now receive some version of a common application or recommendation form. It is wise to consult each school about their policies and preferences regarding the use of such applications. While a growing number of schools accept common recommendations, they may not also accept the candidate statement portion of the common applications. An increasing number of schools are accepting online versions of applications through either their own or the SSAT website. These online applications often have web-based tracking systems that help candidates manage the application process.

Any candidate who is applying to multiple schools should consider using at least common recommendation forms as they are quite convenient for teachers who otherwise have to complete redundant paperwork. If you use a common application or any portion of a common application, be aware that additional forms or materials may be required. Schools that accept these common forms agree not to penalize candidates for availing themselves of these resources that help them complete the application process in a timely and efficient manner. Ultimately, admission committees are more concerned with the content of an application than with how it was completed or delivered.

## Affording an Independent School

Applying for financial aid adds another dimension to the application process, but it should not be viewed as a barrier to admission. Nearly all independent schools provide assistance for families who cannot afford the full tuition. While a few schools offer merit awards and loans, in most cases financial aid is awarded on the basis of need as determined by the School and Student Service for Financial Aid, a service of the National Association of Independent Schools (NAIS). Some schools will complete their own evaluations or may use the services of a similar organization.

Application forms for financial aid are available at most admissions offices and through the School and Student Service (SSS) website at sss.ets.org. According to the NAIS website, in the academic year 2004–2005, a total of $815.7 million in financial aid was awarded by the 956 member schools. At these same schools, an average of 18 percent of the student population received some financial aid in the form of grants, with an average award of $14,430 for boarding schools and $8,499 for day schools. While the vast majority of financial aid comes in the form of need-based awards, 317 NAIS member schools reported in 2004–2005 $24.8 million in merit awards, averaging $3,225 per award.

Since fewer than 5 percent of enrolled students receive merit awards, it is worthwhile to inquire about the particulars of a merit program before moving forward with the application process. Most schools either offer their own loan programs or have relationships with lending institutions that offer loans specifically designed to help parents finance the cost of an independent school tuition. Information about these programs is available from most admissions offices or the SSS website.

# Choosing an Independent School

Identifying and selecting a list of schools to consider may seem a daunting task. Your selection of day schools may be limited by distance or the realities of commuter traffic in your neighborhood, but the possibilities for boarding schools are virtually unlimited. There are many printed directories available in bookstores and libraries that will help both expand and, later, narrow your search.

**School and Other Websites** The Internet is a wonderful source of information as well. Most schools have invested in rather sophisticated websites that reveal as much if not more than traditional printed materials. In addition to describing the academic curriculum, the faculty and students, the athletic programs, the fine and performing arts programs, and the physical plant, many websites offer detailed information about the activities and events that shape the culture of the school. Most websites are brimming with pictures of events and performances as well as candid shots revealing the character of daily life.

The school's website is an excellent place to begin to gather information that will inform your visit to campus. It will give you an idea of questions to ask and some notions about what you might like to see on your tour or even people you would like to meet.

The National Association of Independent Schools collects data on nearly one thousand member schools each year. Most of their data are accessible to the general public at no cost through their website, http://www.nais.org. You can find statistical data on a variety of subjects, ranging from tuition, to class size, to SAT scores. These data represent the schools broadly, and while some reports designate both boarding and day schools, information on individual schools is not offered.

Two other associations do offer information about individual schools. The Enrollment Management Association manages a database of nearly six hundred of their member schools. At http://www.ssat.org, you can find detailed information about individual schools as well as contact information and a direct link to individual schools' websites. The Association of Boarding Schools (TABS) manages a database of over three hundred boarding schools, which includes a host of data that will help you differentiate one school from another. Also, Boarding-Schools.org offers a click-through service that connects you directly to individual school's websites.

It is worth noting that NAIS, SSAT, and TABS are credible sources that are managed by professional organizations to which independent schools belong and support. Each of these associations is a not-for-profit organization governed by a board made up of independent school educators and dedicates its mission to the promotion of independent schools.

**Directories** Additionally, there are several printed directories that have long served the promotion of independent schools. These include *Bunting and Lyon Private Independent Schools, Porter Sargent Handbook of Private Schools, Vincent Curtis Educational Register*, and *Peterson's Guide*. Most are available at libraries and bookstores. Some of these publications have accompanying websites, and none of them ranks schools.

As is often true on the Internet, there are less credible sources of information. Some of these sources even rank schools. This is a practice that is frowned upon by most schools and all the aforementioned professional associations. In today's consumer-minded society, too much emphasis is placed on ranking, and most educators do not believe that ranking schools helps students make a wise choice between schools.

Furthermore, it may be of interest to know that some of the websites that do rank schools accept payment for advertising those same schools. Their fee structures vary according to the amount of exposure a school wishes to receive, and the data on these websites are self-reported by the same fee-paying schools. You may notice that some schools are missing from these rankings because they have chosen to not support the practice of ranking and have not posted their information on these websites. As with all decisions, consider information from a wide range of sources and then make informed choices.

**School Accreditation**   One way to judge the quality of an independent school is to identify its accrediting body. Independent schools have the option of seeking accreditation from regional, national, and international accrediting organizations. The regional accrediting bodies include Middle States Association of Colleges and Schools (MSACS), New England Association of Colleges and Schools (NEACS), North Central Association of Colleges and Schools (NCACS), Northwest Association of Schools and Colleges (NASC), Southern Association of Colleges and Schools (SACS), and Western Association of Schools and Colleges (WASC). These are some of the same accrediting bodies that serve colleges and universities throughout the country. In order to receive accreditation, independent schools must complete an evaluation that is supervised by an accrediting organization. The process is designed to ensure that the independent schools hold themselves publicly accountable and operate in a manner that demonstrates that they meet acceptable standards of educational quality, professional competence, and fiscal responsibility. It is important to note that some schools that are not accredited may be in the process of becoming so. Independent schools complete the accreditation process on a schedule dictated by their accrediting body.

# PART I

# GETTING STARTED

# How to Use This Book

Both the SSAT and ISEE include many different types of questions, and your preparation time may be short. That is why it is important to use your study time wisely. This book provides strategies and practice for all test question types, and it has been organized to make your study program practical and efficient. It will help you:

- Familiarize yourself with the format and question types of the test you'll be taking.
- Review all the verbal and math skills you need for the test.
- Check your progress with Practice Sets at the end of each review chapter.
- Practice your test-taking skills using Practice Tests.

The following five-step study program has been designed to help you make the best use of this book.

## Step 1. Learn the Format of the Test You'll Be Taking

Read Chapter 2 of this book, titled "SSAT and ISEE: An Overview." In that chapter you will find charts illustrating the latest format of the test you will be taking. Note that the ISEE has different formats depending on which level of the test you take. You'll also find important information about how each test is scored.

Once you know the format of your test, you'll know what kinds of questions to expect. Then look at the Contents in this book. You'll see that Part II includes separate chapters for each of the verbal, reading, and writing question types on the two tests. You'll also see that one of these chapters is marked "SSAT Only" and another is marked "ISEE Only." The chapters that are not marked with these labels apply to both tests. Next, in Part III of this book you'll see that there are chapters reviewing math skills in five areas: arithmetic, algebra, geometry, data analysis/probability, and word problems. These chapters will help you prepare for the math sections of both tests. There is also a chapter on a particular math question type that appears only on the upper-level version of the ISEE: Quantitative Comparisons. By knowing the format of the test you'll be taking, you can pick which of these chapters you need to study. That way, you can focus your time and efforts on what you really need to know for your test.

Chapter 3, "Strategies for Top Scores," provides valuable suggestions to help you study smart. Chapter 4 provides valuable mind maps to help you visualize solutions.

## Step 2. Make a Study Schedule

It's important to allow yourself the time you will need to properly prepare for the SSAT or ISEE test that you'll be taking. Different students have different needs and different learning and study styles. For this reason, you'll find three charts below that provide study plans for 3 weeks, 6 weeks, and 10 weeks.

If you have the time, plan to spend at least two weeks or so working your way through Parts II and III of this book, which offer review and practice for the verbal and math question types. Then be sure to set aside enough time at the end of your schedule to take at least one or two of the Practice Tests at the end of the book. However, if you do not have much time before the test, you may want to shorten your review time and instead focus entirely on the Practice Tests.

### 10-Week Study Plan

|  | SSAT | ISEE |
|---|---|---|
| Week 1 | Chapters 1–4: Getting Started<br>Chapter 5: Synonyms | Chapters 1–4: Getting Started<br>Chapter 5: Synonyms |
| Week 2 | Chapter 6: Verbal Analogies | Chapter 7: Sentence Completion<br>Chapter 8: Reading Comprehension |
| Week 3 | Chapter 8: Reading Comprehension | Chapter 9: Writing |
| Week 4 | Chapter 9: Writing | Chapter 10: Arithmetic |
| Week 5 | Chapter 10: Arithmetic | Chapter 11: Algebra |
| Week 6 | Chapter 11: Algebra | Chapter 12: Geometry |
| Week 7 | Chapter 12: Geometry | Chapter 13: Data Analysis and Probability |
| Week 8 | Chapter 13: Data Analysis and Probability | Chapter 14: Word Problems |
| Week 9 | Chapter 14: Word Problems | Chapter 15: Quantitative Comparisons |
| Week 10 | Practice Tests | Practice Tests |

### 6-Week Study Plan

|  | SSAT | ISEE |
|---|---|---|
| Week 1 | Chapters 1–4: Getting Started<br>Chapter 5: Synonyms | Chapters 1–4: Getting Started<br>Chapter 5: Synonyms |
| Week 2 | Chapter 6: Verbal Analogies<br>Chapter 8: Reading Comprehension | Chapter 7: Sentence Completion<br>Chapter 8: Reading Comprehension |
| Week 3 | Chapter 9: Writing | Chapter 9: Writing |
| Week 4 | Chapter 10: Arithmetic<br>Chapter 11: Algebra | Chapter 10: Arithmetic<br>Chapter 11: Algebra<br>Chapter 12: Geometry |
| Week 5 | Chapter 12: Geometry<br>Chapter 13: Data Analysis and Probability<br>Chapter 14: Word Problems | Chapter 13: Data Analysis and Probability<br>Chapter 14: Word Problems<br>Chapter 15: Quantitative Comparisons |
| Week 6 | Practice Tests | Practice Tests |

|  | SSAT | ISEE |
|---|---|---|
| Week 1 | Chapters 1–4: Getting Started | Chapters 1–4: Getting Started |
|  | Chapter 5: Synonyms | Chapter 5: Synonyms |
|  | Chapter 6: Verbal Analogies | Chapter 7: Sentence Completion |
|  | Chapter 8: Reading Comprehension | Chapter 8: Reading Comprehension |
|  | Chapter 9: Writing | Chapter 9: Writing |
| Week 2 | Chapter 10: Arithmetic | Chapter 10: Arithmetic |
|  | Chapter 11: Algebra | Chapter 11: Algebra |
|  | Chapter 12: Geometry | Chapter 12: Geometry |
|  | Chapter 13: Data Analysis and Probability | Chapter 13: Data Analysis and Probability |
|  | Chapter 14: Word Problems | Chapter 14: Word Problems |
|  |  | Chapter 15: Quantitative Comparisons |
| Week 3 | Practice Tests | Practice Tests |

## Step 3. Study the Chapters on the Verbal, Reading, and Writing Question Types

Part II of this book provides detailed explanations and samples for all of the verbal, reading, and writing question types on the two tests. They will also give you strategies for answering the different question types. Use the appropriate study table to determine which chapters you'll want to study.

You do not need to work through these chapters in the order in which they appear. Skip around if you like, but make sure you read all the chapters covering the question types on the test you'll be taking. Each review chapter ends with a set of practice questions that you can use to see how well you have mastered the material. If you get a question wrong, go back and reread the chapter.

## Step 4. Study the Math Review Chapters

Part III of this book provides chapters reviewing all the math topics you'll need to know for either test: arithmetic, algebra, geometry, data analysis/probability, and word problems. No matter which test you're taking, you'll want to study all of these chapters very carefully. Each topic covered in these chapters is followed by an "On Your Own" set of practice questions. Use these questions to check how well you have mastered the material. If you get a question wrong, go back and reread the section covering that topic.

Chapter 15 in Part III covers a math question type called Quantitative Comparisons that appears only on the upper-level version of the ISEE. If you are taking that test, you'll want to study this chapter carefully. If you are not taking the upper-level ISEE, you can skip this chapter.

## Step 5. Take Practice Tests

Once you have completed your study and review for all of the question types on the test you'll be taking, get ready for the real exam by taking the Practice Test in either Part IV or Part V, whichever corresponds to the real test you'll be taking. If you are taking the middle-level or upper-level SSAT, you can practice with all three of the SSAT Practice Tests. If you are taking the ISEE, take the Practice Test that corresponds to the level of the real test you'll be taking. You might also want to take the other ISEE Practice Tests for additional practice with the test question types.

When you take each test, try to simulate actual test conditions. Sit in a quiet room, time yourself, and work through as much of the test as time allows. The tests are ideal for practice because they have been constructed to be as much like the real test as possible. The directions and practice questions are very much like those on the real test. You'll gain experience with the test format, and you'll learn to pace yourself so that you can earn the maximum number of points in the time allowed.

Follow the scoring instructions to rate your test performance. Each test will also serve as a review of the topics tested because complete explanations are provided for every question. The explanations can be found at the end of each test. If you get a question wrong, you'll want to review the explanation carefully. You may also want to go back to the chapter in this book that covers the question topic.

# SSAT and ISEE: An Overview

The SSAT (Secondary School Admission Test) and the ISEE (Independent School Entrance Examination) are the two most widely used admission tests at private schools in the United States. These tests help school administrators compare the academic abilities of students from a variety of elementary and presecondary schools.

The schools to which you are applying will tell you which test is required, but it is up to you to make your own arrangements for taking the exam and submitting your scores in a timely fashion. Both the SSAT and the ISEE test the same basic verbal, reading, and quantitative skills. This book examines both of these important private school admission tests in depth. It offers valuable tips and strategies for answering each question type and provides full-length sample exams to help you simulate actual test conditions at home. As any good test-taker will tell you, knowing what to expect is half the battle when it comes to earning top scores!

## What Is the SSAT?

The SSAT is a standardized test developed and administered by The Enrollment Management Association. Approximately 700 independent schools require SSAT scores as part of their admission process. The test is designed to measure verbal, math, and reading skills.

The SSAT is offered seven times a year—in November, December, January, February, March, April, and June. Complete information about the test and registration forms are available

- online at www.ssat.org.
- by phone at 609-683-4440.
- by mail at SSAT, CN 5339, Princeton, NJ 08543.

The SSAT is offered in two levels:

- Lower level for students in grades 5–7
- Upper level for students in grades 8–11

## What Is the Format of the SSAT?

The format of the test is the same for both the upper and lower levels.

Format of the SSAT

| Section | Questions | Time |
|---|---|---|
| Verbal<br>• Synonyms<br>• Verbal Analogies | 60 | 30 minutes |
| Quantitative I<br>• Arithmetic<br>• Elementary Algebra<br>• Geometry | 25 | 30 minutes |
| Reading Comprehension<br>• Humanities<br>• Social Studies<br>• Science | 40 | 40 minutes |
| Quantitative II<br>• Arithmetic<br>• Elementary Algebra<br>• Geometry | 25 | 30 minutes |
| Essay | 1 | 25 minutes |

All multiple-choice questions have five answer choices.

The multiple-choice sections may be administered in any order.

The essay may be administered either before or after the multiple-choice portion of the test. The essay is not scored, but a copy is sent to each school to which your SSAT scores are sent.

## How Is the SSAT Scored?

SSAT scores are computed by awarding 1 point for each correct answer and subtracting $\frac{1}{4}$ point for each incorrect answer. This calculation produces a Raw Score, which is then converted to a Scaled Score by the use of tables constructed specifically for each test.

On the lower-level test, verbal, quantitative, and reading scores are each reported on a scale of 440–710. Total scores are reported on a scale of 1320–2130.

On the upper-level test, verbal, quantitative, and reading scores are each reported on a scale of 500–800. Total scores are reported on a scale of 1500–2400.

On a recent test, median 50th percentile scores for reading, verbal, and quantitative sections were as shown below.

Lower-Level Median 50th Percentile Scores

| Grade | Reading | Verbal | Quantitative |
|---|---|---|---|
| 5 | 569 | 584 | 563 |
| 6 | 593 | 614 | 593 |
| 7 | 611 | 638 | 614 |

Upper-Level Median 50th Percentile Scores

| Grade | Reading | Verbal | Quantitative |
| --- | --- | --- | --- |
| 8 | 629 | 662 | 647 |
| 9 | 644 | 683 | 668 |
| 10 | 656 | 645 | 686 |
| 11 | 626 | 653 | 689 |

Two to three weeks after you take the test, a score report, along with a copy of your essay, will be sent to each school, educational consultant, and educational organization that you indicated on your registration form. Scores remain active for one academic year.

## What Is the ISEE?

Like the SSAT, the ISEE is a test of verbal, reading, quantitative, and writing skills designed for students seeking admission to private schools. The ISEE is developed by the ERB (Educational Records Bureau) and is administered worldwide at more than 400 Prometric testing centers.

The ISEE is offered on a variety of dates and in a variety of locations. For a complete listing of test dates and locations, check the *ISEE Student Guide*, which is available through the school to which you are applying or online at www.erbtest .org. The *Student Guide* also contains the registration materials you will need to sign up for the ISEE. You may register by mail, phone, fax, or online, but there is an additional charge for registering by phone or fax.

The ISEE has three levels:

- Lower level for students in grades 4 or 5 applying for grades 5 or 6.
- Middle level for students in grades 6 or 7 applying for grades 7 or 8.
- Upper level for students in grades 8 or above applying for grades 9–12.

Each level has the same five sections, but the levels vary slightly in format.

You may take the ISEE only once within a six-month period. It's important to note that you cannot take the ISEE for practice. It may be taken only for the purpose of submitting scores to a participating school as part of the admission process.

## What Is the Format of the ISEE?

The charts below show the format of the ISEE at the lower, middle, and upper levels.

## Lower Level for Candidates for Grades 5 and 6

| Test | Questions | Time |
|---|---|---|
| Verbal Reasoning<br>• Synonyms<br>• Sentence Completions | 34 | 20 minutes |
| Quantitative Reasoning<br>• Comprehension<br>• Interpretation/Application<br>• Higher-Order Thinking | 38 | 35 minutes |
| Reading Comprehension<br>• Humanities<br>• Science<br>• Social Studies | 25 | 25 minutes |
| Mathematics Achievement<br>• Knowledge and Skills<br>• Computation/Comprehension<br>• Applications | 30 | 30 minutes |
| Essay | 1 | 30 minutes |

## Middle Level for Candidates for Grades 7 and 8

| Test | Questions | Time |
|---|---|---|
| Verbal Reasoning<br>• Synonyms<br>• Sentence Completions | 40 | 20 minutes |
| Quantitative Reasoning<br>• Comprehension<br>• Interpretation/Application<br>• Higher-Order Thinking<br>• Quantitative Comparison | 37 | 25 minutes |
| Reading Comprehension<br>• Humanities<br>• Science<br>• Social Studies | 36 | 35 minutes |
| Mathematics Achievement<br>• Knowledge and Skills<br>• Computation/Comprehension<br>• Applications | 47 | 40 minutes |
| Essay | 1 | 30 minutes |

Upper Level for Candidates for Grades 9 to 12

| Test | Questions | Time |
|---|---|---|
| Verbal Reasoning<br>• Synonyms<br>• Sentence Completions | 40 | 20 minutes |
| Quantitative Reasoning<br>• Arithmetic/Algebra/Geometry<br>• Concepts/Understanding<br>• Applications/Higher-Order Thinking<br>• Quantitative Comparison | 37 | 35 minutes |
| Reading Comprehension<br>• Humanities<br>• Science<br>• Social Studies | 36 | 35 minutes |
| Mathematics Achievement<br>• Arithmetic/Algebra/Geometry<br>• Knowledge and Skills<br>• Computation/Comprehension<br>• Applications | 47 | 40 minutes |
| Essay | 1 | 30 minutes |

All multiple-choice questions have four answer choices.

The multiple-choice sections may be administered in any order.

The essay is always last. Like the SSAT essay, the ISEE essay is not scored, but a copy is sent to each school to which your ISEE scores are sent.

Because each level is given to students at more than one grade, you may find some questions are too difficult for you. Don't be concerned. Your score is compared only to the scores of other students in the same grade.

## How Is the ISEE Scored?

ISEE scores are computed by awarding 1 point for each correct answer. There is no deduction for incorrect answers, so the number of questions you answer correctly becomes your Raw Score. This Raw Score is then converted to a Scaled Score by the use of tables specifically constructed for each test.

On the middle-level test, verbal reasoning scores are reported on a scale of 763–922, quantitative reasoning scores are reported on a scale of 779–926, reading comprehension scores are reported on a scale of 759–929, and mathematics achievement scores are reported on a scale of 765–932.

In the upper-level test, verbal reasoning scores are reported on a scale of 750–950, quantitative reasoning scores are reported on a scale of 750–950, reading comprehension scores are reported on a scale of 750–950, and math achievement scores are reported on a scale of 800–950.

On a recent test, median 50th percentile scores for verbal reasoning, quantitative reasoning, reading comprehension, and mathematics ability were as shown below:

### Middle-Level Median 50th Percentile Scores

| Grade | Verbal Reasoning | Quantitative Reasoning | Reading Comprehension | Mathematics Achievement |
|---|---|---|---|---|
| 6 | 851 | 866 | 848 | 866 |
| 7 | 878 | 873 | 883 | 876 |

### Upper-Level Median 50th Percentile Scores

| Grade | Verbal Reasoning | Quantitative Reasoning | Reading Comprehension | Mathematics Achievement |
|---|---|---|---|---|
| 8 | 875 | 875 | 883 | 876 |
| 9 | 883 | 878 | 891 | 880 |
| 10 | 889 | 881 | 897 | 884 |

ISEE score reports include test scores and diagnostic information. They are sent out to schools and parents approximately 7 to 10 business days after testing. A copy of your essay is sent, along with your score report, to each school you indicated on your registration form.

# CHAPTER 3

# Strategies for Top Scores

When you take the SSAT or ISEE, you'll want to do everything you can to make sure you get your best possible score. That means studying right, building good problem-solving skills, and learning proven test-taking strategies. Here are some tips to help you do your best.

## Study Strategies

- **Get to know the format of the exam.** Use the Practice Tests in this book to familiarize yourself with the test format, which does not change from year to year. That way, you'll know exactly what to expect when you see the real thing on test day.
- **Get to know the test directions.** If you are familiar with the directions ahead of time, you won't have to waste valuable test time reading them and trying to understand them. The format and directions used in the practice exams in this book are modeled on the ones you'll see on the actual SSAT or ISEE.
- **Get to know what topics are covered.** Get to know what specific topics are covered on the exam. You'll find all of them in the strategy sections and practice exams in this book.
- **Study hard.** If possible, plan to study for at least an hour a day for two weeks before the test. You should be able to read all the strategy chapters in this book, work your way through the Practice Sets at the end of each chapter, and complete one or more Practice Tests during that time period. If you are pressed for time, focus on taking at least one Practice Test, reading the explanations, and then reviewing the question types that give you the most trouble.

## Math Problem-Solving Strategies

- **Solve math problems in whatever way is easiest for you.** There are usually several ways to solve a math problem and arrive at the correct answer. Do what is easiest for you. Remember that the SSAT and ISEE math questions are all multiple choice. That means that no one is going to be checking your work and judging you by which solution method you chose, so solve the problem any way you like.

- **Build good math problem-solving skills.** When you tackle SSAT or ISEE math questions, try to follow this three-step process:

  1. When you first read a question, make a list of the given values and variables and the units for the variables.
  2. Ask yourself, "What do I know and what do I need to find out?" The answers to those questions will help you figure out how to solve the problem.
  3. Solve the problem and see if the answer makes sense. For example, if you know that one variable should be much larger than another, make sure your answer reflects that relationship. You'll see how this works with many of the problems in this book.

- **Make sure you know what the question is asking.** The questions on the SSAT or ISEE are not deliberately designed to trick you, but it is still important that you look closely at each one to make sure you know what it is asking. Pay special attention to questions that include the word *NOT*. You may want to circle that word to make sure you take it into account as you choose your answer.

## General Test-Taking Strategies

- **Answer all the easy problems first, then tackle the harder ones.** Keep in mind that the longest sections on the SSAT and ISEE are only 40 minutes long. There isn't much time to spend trying to figure out the answers to harder questions, so skip them and come back to them later. There are two reasons why you should do this. The first reason is that every question counts the same in the scoring of the exam. That means that you are better off spending time answering the easier questions, where you are sure to pick up points. The second reason is that by answering the easier questions, you'll build your confidence and get into a helpful test-taking rhythm. Then when you go back to a question you skipped, you may find that it isn't as hard as you first thought.

- **Use the process of elimination.** Keep in mind that on the SSAT and ISEE, like any other multiple-choice test, the answer is right in front of you. Try eliminating answer choices that you know are incorrect. Often this can help you select the correct answer.

- **On the ISEE, guess if you have to.** On the ISEE, there is no penalty for wrong answers, so you have nothing to lose by guessing. If time is running out and there are questions you have not answered, you might pick up extra points by guessing answers to those questions.

- **On the SSAT, if you must guess, make an educated guess.** The SSAT has a one-quarter-point penalty for wrong answers to discourage random guessing. So if you have absolutely no idea how to answer a question, you are better off skipping it entirely. However, you may be able to eliminate one or more answer choices. If you can do that, you can increase your odds of guessing the correct answer. If you can make this kind of educated guess, go ahead. If you guess correctly, you'll earn another point.

## Tips for Test Day

- **Don't panic!** Once test day comes, you're as prepared as you're ever going to be, so there is no point in panicking. Use your energy to make sure that you are extra careful in answering questions and marking the answer sheet.

- **Be careful when marking your answer sheet.** Remember that the answer sheet is scored by a machine, so mark it carefully. Fill in answer ovals completely, erase thoroughly if you change your mind, and do not make any stray marks anywhere on the sheet. Also, make sure that the answer space you are marking matches the number of the question you are answering. If you skip a question, make sure that you skip the corresponding space on the answer sheet. Every 5 or 10 questions, check the question numbers and make sure that you are marking in the right spot. You may want to mark your answers in groups of 5 or 10 to make sure that you are marking the answer sheet correctly.

- **Watch the time.** Keep track of the time as you work your way through the test. Try to pace yourself so that you can tackle as many of the questions as possible within the time limit. Check yourself at 10- or 15-minute intervals using your watch or a timer.

- **Don't panic if time runs out.** If you've paced yourself carefully, you should have time to tackle all or most of the questions. If you do run out of time, however, don't panic. Make sure that you have marked your answer sheet for all the questions you have answered so far. **If you are taking the ISEE,** guess answers to any remaining questions. You have nothing to lose since there is no penalty on the ISEE for wrong answers. **If you are taking the SSAT,** however, do NOT mark answers to random guesses. Since there is a one-quarter-point penalty on the SSAT for wrong answers, you don't want to lose any credit!

- **Use extra time to check your work.** If you have time left over at the end of the test, go back and check your work. Make sure that you have marked the answer sheet correctly. Check any calculations you may have made to make sure that they are correct. Take another look at any questions you may have skipped. Resist the urge to second-guess your answers, however, as this may lead you to change an already correct answer to a wrong one.

# Mind Maps for Mastering Key Skills

The SSAT and ISEE are different tests, but both examinations evaluate your mastery of many of the same verbal, writing, and mathematical skills.

## What Are Mind Maps?

- The mind maps in this chapter present diagrams that visualize, or present mental pictures, of methods that will help you answer these questions correctly.
- Remember there is no one "correct" mind map for any skill.
- Create your own mind maps for other skills that you want to master.

## How Do I Use the Mind Maps in This Book?

Use the chart below to identify which mind maps to use with Chapters 5–13.

| Chapter | Use with Mind Map |
|---|---|
| 5 | 1: Synonyms |
| 6 | 2: Verbal Analogies |
| 7 | 3: Sentence Completion |
| 8 | 4: Main Idea |
| | 5: Details |
| | 6: Inferences |
| 9 | 7: Essay Writing |
| 10 and 11 | 8: Order of Operations |
| | 9: Factors |
| | 10: Multiples |
| | 11: Fractions and Mixed Numbers |
| | 12: Percents, Fractions, and Decimals |
| | 13: Powers |
| | 14: Square Roots |
| | 15: Measure of Central Tendency |
| 12 | 16: Ratios, Rates, and Proportions |
| | 17: Combinations |
| | 18: Permutations |
| 13 | 19: Probability of an Event |
| | 20: Perimeter and Area of Plane Figures |
| | 21: Surface Area and Volume of Solid Figures |
| 10, 11, 12 | 22: Mental Math: Multiply by 4 and 8 |
| and 13 | 23: Mental Math: Divide by 4 and 8 |
| | 24: Mental Math: Multiply with Fractions |
| | 25: Mental Math: Use Compatible Numbers |

## KEEP IN MIND

**SYNONYM**
A word or phrase that has the same or nearly the same meaning as another word

⬇

## SYNONYM QUESTIONS

### Question

Select the word or phrase whose meaning is closest to the meaning of the word in capital letters.

**AMORPHOUS**

A. unlovable
B. headless
C. muscular
D. shapeless
E. sleepwalker

**STEP 1:** Read the word and all the answer choices.

**STEP 2:** Eliminate obviously incorrect answer choices. For example, you can eliminate *sleepwalker* because it is a noun and *amorphous* and the other answer choices are all adjectives.

**STEP 3:** Think of any words you may know that have the same or similar word parts. For example, when someone *morphs* into a superhero, they "change their body or shape."

**STEP 4:** Eliminate answer choices based on your analysis. Based on the meaning of *morph*, *unlovable* and *muscular* do not seem like reasonable answers.

**STEP 5:** Select the meaning from the remaining choices. Notice that two of the remaining words end in *–less*, meaning "without." The prefix *a-* is similar because it often means "not or without."

**THINK**
*Headless* and *shapeless* seem like possible answers. But, *morph* means "body or shape."

### Answer

**D.** *Shapeless* is the best synonym for *amorphous*.

## Question

Select the word or phrase whose meaning is closest to the meaning of the word in capital letters.

**MALEDICTION**

A. an unpleasant taste
B. a masculine speaker
C. a flexible microphone
D. a burnt marshmallow
E. an evil spell or curse

## THINK

If you already know the meaning of the word, try to define it in your own words before you evaluate the answer choices.

**STEP 1: Determine if the word has any parts you know or seem reasonable.** For example, *malediction* seems to have two parts *mal* and *diction*.

**STEP 2: Identify the meaning of any parts you already know.** You probably know that *diction* has something to do with "speaking" or "words."

**STEP 3: Look at the answer choices to determine if any meaning is related to the word part you know.** Choices B, C, or E have something to do with "speaking or words."

**STEP 4: Be careful of false signals.** For example, the word *malediction* seems to begin with the word *male* meaning "man." However, the word actually begins with *mal* meaning "bad or evil." The rest of the word is formed from *edict* meaning "something spoken."

**STEP 5: Select an answer from among the remaining choices.** If you are down to two possible answers, it is worth taking a guess.

## Answer

E. "An evil spell or curse" is the best synonym for *malediction*.

## KEEP IN MIND

**VERBAL ANALOGY**
A comparison between pairs of words or phrases that is based on a logical relationship

## VERBAL ANALOGIES: ONE-WORD ANSWER CHOICES

### Question

Find the relationship for the words. Then select the answer choice that best completes the meaning of the sentence.

**Monologue is to dialogue as unicycle is to**

A. motorcycle
B. circle
C. encyclopedia
D. recycler
E. cyclone

**THINK**
You might expect to find the word *bicycle,* but it is not one of the answer choices. *Motorcycle* is the only answer that is connected with the idea of "two."

**STEP 1: Determine the meaning of the first two words.** A *dialogue* is "a conversation between two or more people." If you do not know the meaning of the word *monologue,* you can figure it out easily. The prefix *mono-* means "one." Therefore, a *monologue* is probably "a speech by one person."

**STEP 2: Determine the logical relationship between the first two words.** Ask yourself: How are the two words alike, different, or connected? For example, the difference between the two words is the *number* of people speaking.

**STEP 3: Identify the meaning of the third word in the analogy and relate it to the first word.** Use your knowledge of roots and other words. A *monologue* has one speaker and a *unicycle* has one wheel. So, the words are related by "one." Since a *dialogue* has "two" speakers, look for an answer choice that carries the idea of "two." A *motorcycle* has two wheels.

**STEP 4: Select the answer that works best.** *Motorcycle* is the logical choice.

### Answer

**A.** *Motorcycle* best completes the analogy.

## KEEP IN MIND

**SENTENCE COMPLETION**
A sentence completion question asks you to choose a word or phrase that best completes the meaning of a sentence.

## SENTENCE COMPLETION QUESTIONS

### Question

Choose the word that best fits the meaning of the sentence.

**Emptying the large house of everything seemed _____ as a task for just one person.**

A. extraneous
B. onerous
C. repugnant
D. undemanding

 **Prep Alert**

Using the following types of clues will help you successfully answer sentence completion questions.

• Logical relationships
• Complementary ideas
• Cause and effect
• Definition
• Explanation

**STEP 1: Read the sentence and look for clues about how its parts are related.** For example, you know that the house that is to be emptied is large and that it has to be emptied by one person. ***Think:*** Would this be an easy or difficult task?

**STEP 2: Use the clue words to anticipate the meaning of the answer you will look for.** Based on the clue words, you will be looking for an answer that suggests hard or difficult work.

**STEP 3: Eliminate answer choices whose meanings do not match what you are looking for.** For example, *extraneous* means "something extra or unnecessary." Therefore, you can eliminate choice A. How can you use your knowledge of the prefix *un-* to eliminate answer choice D?

**STEP 4: Select the answer choice that works best or guess from the remaining choices.** After elimination, select from the remaining answer choices.

### Answer

**B.** *Onerous* best completes the sentence.

# 4 Main Ideas

## KEEP IN MIND

**MAIN IDEA**
The main idea is the key concept of a selection. It is what the entire passage is mostly about.

## MAIN IDEA QUESTIONS

### Question

Which statement best expresses the main idea of this passage?

A. Manatees were first discovered by the explorer Christopher Columbus.

B. Manatees are large sea mammals that live in warm coastal waters.

C. Manatees are similar to dolphins and whales because of their flippers and tails.

D. Manatees feed on small fish and sea grasses.

Manatees, also known as sea cows, are a small group of mammals that live only in warm water. West Indian manatees inhabit the coastal areas and rivers of the southern United States, mainly near Florida. These creatures grow to be twelve feet long and weigh more than a thousand pounds. They are herbivores, feeding only on the sea grasses that grow in shallow waters. Like dolphins and whales, manatees move about using strong flippers and a paddle-like tail. Manatees are so friendly and human-like, ancient seafarers thought of them as mermaids. In fact, on January 9, 1493, Christopher Columbus made a diary entry about seeing three "mermaids" near present-day Haiti. As coastal waters have become polluted, the number of manatees has decreased significantly.

**STEP 1: Skim the questions before you read the passage.** This will help you focus on what to look for as you read.

**STEP 2: Look for a topic sentence that expresses the key idea.** Topic sentences often appear at the beginning or end of passages.

**STEP 3: Eliminate answer choices that merely restate specific details.** Nonfiction passages usually contain many facts about *one* topic.

**STEP 4: Select the main idea from the choices.**

### Answer

**B.** "Manatees are large sea mammals that live in warm coastal waters" is the correct answer.

## KEEP IN MIND

### DETAILS
Details are specific facts or ideas that support the main idea.

## DETAIL QUESTIONS

### Question

Which of the following is NOT a detail expressed in the passage?

A. Centuries ago sailors thought manatees were mermaids.
B. Manatees often weigh a thousand pounds or more.
C. Manatees are fast swimmers because of their flippers and tails.
D. Manatees eat only plants that grow in the water.

**STEP 1:** Skim the questions before you read the passage. This will help you focus on the details you need to answer the questions correctly.

**STEP 2:** Mark up the passage for details related to each question. Details most often appear in the middle or body of a passage.

**STEP 3:** Eliminate answers that are about the general topic and unrelated details. Remember details offer support for the main idea, but they are not themselves topic sentences.

**STEP 4:** Eliminate answer choices that are only partially supported by the passage.

**STEP 5:** Select the relevant detail from the remaining choices.

### Answer

C. "Manatees are fast swimmers because of their flippers and tails" is the correct answer.

## REMEMBER

Some detail questions may ask you to identify a fact that is *not* in the passage.

## KEEP IN MIND

**INFERENCE**
An inference is a conclusion that is formed based on evidence and reasoning. The conclusion that is inferred is *not* stated directly in the passage.

## INFERENCE QUESTIONS

### Question

From the passage you can infer that manatees

A. have powerful flippers and a tail
B. are sometimes called sea cows
C. look a lot like people that are swimming
D. are now or may soon be an endangered species

### REMEMBER

Keep track of choices you eliminate by placing a check ✔ or an ✘ before the statement or phrase.

**STEP 1:** Identify the inference question and read all answer choices. Most inference questions use the word *infer* or *conclude.*

**STEP 2:** Identify answer choices you think are directly stated in the passage and eliminate them. Remember that if a fact or detail clearly appears in a passage it is *not* something you are inferring.

**STEP 3:** Check the remaining answer choices by skimming the passage. If you cannot identify the correct answer right away, continue the elimination process.

**STEP 4:** Select the answer choice that requires you to think "beyond" the specific words in the passage. The last sentence says, "the number of manatees has decreased significantly." So, it is reasonable to infer that manatees are or will soon be "endangered."

**STEP 5:** If you cannot find an answer, review the answer choices you eliminated or guess between two reasonable choices.

### Answer

D. "Manatees are now or may soon be an endangered species" is the correct answer.

## KEEP IN MIND

You will have 25 minutes to plan and write your essay on the SSAT and 30 minutes on the ISEE.

## ESSAY WRITING PROCESS

### Prompt

You will have 25 to 30 minutes to plan and write an essay on the topic given below. You may make notes in the space provided. Write your final essay on the lined pages. Write or print neatly in blue or black ink. Your essay must be about the assigned topic.

**Topic:** No one who lives in society is truly free.

**Assignment:** Do you agree or disagree with this statement? Support your answer with examples from your own experience, the experience of others, current events, history, or literature.

**STEP 1:** **Read the writing prompt carefully. Spend 1-2 minutes on this step.** Try to say the question in the prompt in your own words.

**STEP 2:** **Brainstorm by writing words and phrases that you think will be helpful in writing your essay. Spend 5-7 minutes on this step.** Do not try to evaluate your thoughts as you first list them. Just get them down on paper as quickly as you can. Then look them over and mark those ideas you think will best support essay.

**STEP 3:** **Draft your essay. Spend 15 minutes on this step.** Try using the words in the prompt to focus your topic sentence. Select details from your notes to write the body of your essay. Include a concluding sentence or short paragraph.

**STEP 4:** **Proofread your essay. Spend 4-5 minutes on this step.** Reread your essay. Identify and correct errors in grammar, usage, spelling, and punctuation. Cross out sentences that do not support your topic sentence. Add details, if needed, to clarify your ideas.

# Order of Operations

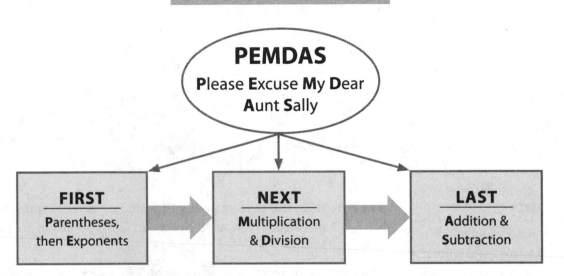

## KEEP IN MIND

**PEMDAS**

**P**lease **E**xcuse **M**y **D**ear **A**unt **S**ally

**FIRST**

Parentheses, then **E**xponents

**NEXT**

**M**ultiplication & **D**ivision

**LAST**

**A**ddition & **S**ubtraction

## Problem

Evaluate.

$2 \times 4^2 + (14 - 6) \div 4 = ?$

A. 9
B. 12
C. 34
D. 36
E. 40

**STEP 1:** Evaluate inside parentheses.

$$2 \times 4^2 + (14 - 6) \div 4 = 2 \times 4^2 + 8 \div 4$$

**STEP 2:** Evaluate exponents.

$$2 \times 4^2 + 8 \div 4 = 2 \times 16 + 8 \div 4$$

**STEP 3:** Multiply and divide from left to right.

$$2 \times 16 + 8 \div 4 = 32 + 2$$

**STEP 4:** Add and subtract from left to right.

$$32 + 2 = 34$$

## Answer

**C.** $2 \times 4^2 + (14 - 6) \div 4 = 34.$

# PROBLEMS WITH SQUARE ROOTS

## Problem

Evaluate.

$(8 - 6)^2 \times \sqrt{25} + 5 \div 5 = ?$

A. 21
B. 8
C. 4
D. 3

**REMEMBER**
The $\sqrt{25}$ equals $25^{1/2}$, so radicals are evaluated at the same time as exponents.

**STEP 1:** Evaluate inside parentheses.
$$(8 - 6)^2 \times \sqrt{25} + 5 \div 5 = (2)^2 \times \sqrt{25} + 5 \div 5$$

**STEP 2:** Evaluate exponents and radicals.
$$(2)^2 \times \sqrt{25} + 5 \div 5 = 4 \times 5 + 5 \div 5$$

**STEP 3:** Multiply and divide from left to right.
$$4 \times 5 + 5 \div 5 = 20 + 1$$

**STEP 4:** Add and subtract from left to right.
$$20 + 1$$

## Answer

**A.** $(8 - 6)^2 \times \sqrt{25} + 5 \div 5 = 21.$

# PROBLEMS WITH FRACTION BARS

## Problem

Evaluate.

$\dfrac{4 + 2^3 \times 2}{3 \times -8 + 4} = ?$

A. $-1\frac{1}{2}$

B. $-1$

C. $-\frac{1}{2}$

D. $\frac{1}{2}$

E. $1$

**THINK**
Follow the order of operations above and below the fraction bar.

**STEP 1:** Use the order of operations in the numerator.
$$\frac{4 + 2^3 \times 2}{3 \times -8 + 4} = \frac{4 + 8 \times 2}{3 \times -8 + 4} =$$
$$\frac{4 + 16}{3 \times -8 + 4} = \frac{20}{3 \times -8 + 4}$$

**STEP 2:** Use the order of operations in the denominator.
$$\frac{4 + 2^3 \times 2}{3 \times -8 + 4} = \frac{4 + 8 \times 2}{3 \times -8 + 4} = \frac{4 + 16}{-20} = \frac{20}{-20}$$

**STEP 3:** Simplify.
$$\frac{20}{-20} = -1$$

## Answer

**B.** $\dfrac{4 + 2^3 \times 2}{3 \times -8 + 4} = -1$

# Factors

## KEEP IN MIND

**Common Factors**
Factors shared by two nonzero whole numbers

**Factors**
Numbers you multiply to get another number

**Greatest Common Factor**
The greatest whole number that is a factor of two or more nonzero numbers

**Factors of 8 and 12**
8: 1, 2, 4, 8
12: 1, 2, 3, 4, 6, 12

**Factors of 30**
$2 \times 3 \times 5 = 30$
$1 \times 30 = 30$
$2 \times 15 = 30$
$3 \times 10 = 30$
$6 \times 5 = 30$

**Factors of 12 and 16**
12: 1, 2, 3, 4, 6, 12
16: 1, 2, 4, 8, 16

**T H I N K**
So, 1, 2, and 4 are common factors of 8 and 12.

**T H I N K**
So, 1, 2, 3, 5, 6, 10, 15, and 30 are factors of 30.

**T H I N K**
So, 4 is the greatest common factor of 12 and 16.

## COMMON FACTORS

### Problem

Which is *not* a common factor of 12 and 18?

A. 1
B. 2
C. 3
D. 4
E. 6

**STEP 1:** List the factors of each number.
12: **1, 2, 3, 4, 6, 12**
18: **1, 2, 3, 6, 18**

**STEP 2:** Identify the common factors.
**1, 2, 3, 6**

**STEP 3:** Identify the factor that the numbers do not have in common.

### Answer

**D.** 4 is a factor of 12, but not a factor of 18.

# GREATEST COMMON FACTOR

## Problem

What is the greatest common factor (GCF) of 16, 24, and 36?

A. 2
B. 3
C. 4
D. 12
E. 16

**STEP 1:** List the factors of each number.

> 16: 1, 2, 4, 8, 16
> 24: 1, 2, 3, 4, 6, 8, 12, 24
> 36: 1, 2, 3, 4, 9, 12, 36

**STEP 2:** Identify the common factors the numbers share.

> 1, 2, and 4, are common factors of 16, 24, and 36.

**STEP 3:** Identify the greatest common factor (CGF) all the numbers share.

### THINK

Which factor shared among 16, 24, and 36 is the greatest?

### Answer

**C. 4 is the greatest common factor (GCF) of 16, 24, and 36.**

# PRIME FACTOR TREE

## Problem

What is the greatest common factor (GCF) of 150 and 225?

A. 75
B. 50
C. 25
D. 15

**STEP 1:** Use a factor tree to find the prime factorization of each number.

**STEP 2:** Find the prime numbers in common.

> 150: 5 × 2 × 3 × 5
> 225: 5 × 5 × 3 × 3
> **Common Prime Factors: 5 × 5 × 3**

**STEP 3:** Multiply common prime factors to find the greatest common factor.

> 5 × 5 × 3 = 75

### REMEMBER

A prime number has two distinct factors, 1 and the number itself.

### Answer

**A. 75 is the greatest common factor of 150 and 225.**

# Fractions and Mixed Numbers

## KEEP IN MIND

**MULTIPLY**

### Fractions

$$\frac{3}{4} \times \frac{2}{3} = ?$$

**STEP 1:** Multiply the numerators.

$$\frac{3}{4} \times \frac{2}{3} = \frac{6}{?}$$

**STEP 2:** Then multiply the denominators.

$$\frac{3}{4} \times \frac{2}{3} = \frac{6}{12}$$

**STEP 3:** Simplify.

$$\frac{6}{12} = \frac{1}{2}$$

### Mixed Numbers

$$2\frac{1}{2} \times 3\frac{1}{3} = ?$$

**STEP 1:** Write the mixed numbers as improper fractions.

$$2\frac{1}{2} \times 3\frac{1}{3} = \frac{5}{2} \times \frac{10}{3}$$

**STEP 2:** Then multiply the numerators and denominators.

$$\frac{5}{2} \times \frac{10}{3} = \frac{50}{6}$$

**STEP 3:** Simplify. Write as a mixed number.

$$\frac{50}{6} = \frac{25}{3} = 8\frac{1}{3}$$

### Problem

$$\frac{2}{5} \times 250 = ?$$

A.  50
B.  100
C.  250
D.  1,125

### Fractions and Whole Numbers

**STEP 1:** Write the whole number as a fraction by placing it over the denominator 1.

$$\frac{2}{5} \times 250 = \frac{2}{5} \times \frac{250}{1}$$

**STEP 2:** Then multiply the numerators and denominators.

$$\frac{2}{5} \times \frac{250}{1} = \frac{500}{5}$$

**STEP 3:** Simplify.

$$\frac{500}{5} = 100$$

### Answer

**B.** $\frac{2}{5} \times 250 = 100$

# DIVIDE FRACTIONS AND WHOLE NUMBERS

## Problem

You have $\frac{2}{3}$ pound of cheese to share equally among 4 people. How much cheese will each person be served?

A. $\frac{1}{6}$

B. $\frac{3}{8}$

C. $1\frac{1}{4}$

D. $2\frac{2}{3}$

**STEP 1:** Write the problem as the division of two fractions.

$$\frac{2}{3} \div \frac{4}{1} = ?$$

**STEP 2:** Change the second fraction into its reciprocal and write the related multiplication problem.

$$\frac{2}{3} \times \frac{1}{4} = ?$$

**STEP 3:** Multiply the numerators and then the denominators.

$$\frac{2}{3} \times \frac{1}{4} = \frac{2}{12}$$

**STEP 4:** Simplify:

$$\frac{2}{12} = \frac{1}{6}$$

## Answer

C. $\frac{2}{3} \div 4 = \frac{1}{6}$.

### REMEMBER

Reciprocals are two nonzero numbers whose product is 1.

$$\frac{3}{1} \times \frac{1}{3} = \frac{3}{3} = 1$$

So, $\frac{3}{1}$ and $\frac{1}{3}$ are reciprocals.

# DIVIDE FRACTIONS AND MIXED NUMBERS

## Problem

A recipe calls for $2\frac{1}{2}$ cups of milk. You have only a $\frac{1}{4}$ cup measure. How many times must you fill the $\frac{1}{4}$ cup measure for $2\frac{1}{2}$ cups of milk?

A. 1

B. 3

C. 5

D. $5\frac{1}{2}$

E. 10

**STEP 1:** Change the mixed number into an improper fraction:

$$2\frac{1}{2} = \frac{5}{2}$$

**STEP 2:** Write the problem as the division of two fractions.

$$\frac{5}{2} \div \frac{1}{4} = ?$$

**STEP 3:** Change the second fraction into its reciprocal and write the related multiplication problem.

$$\frac{5}{2} \times \frac{4}{1} = ?$$

**STEP 4:** Solve and simplify.

$$\frac{5}{2} \times \frac{4}{1} = \frac{20}{2} = 10$$

### THINK

How many $\frac{1}{4}$'s are in $2\frac{1}{2}$?

## Answer

E. $2\frac{1}{2} \div \frac{1}{4} = 10$.

## KEEP IN MIND

**Common Multiples**
A multiple that is shared by two or more numbers

**Multiples**
The product of the number and any nonzero whole number

**Least Common Multiple**
The least multiple shared by two or more numbers

**Multiples of 3 and 4**
3, 6, 9, <u>12</u>, 15, 18, 21, <u>24</u>, …
4, 8, <u>12</u>, 16, 20, <u>24</u>, 28, …

**Multiples of 2 and 5**
2, 4, 6, 8, <u>10</u>, 12, 14, …
5, <u>10</u>, 15, 20, 25, 30, …

**Multiples of 3 and 5**
3, 6, 9, 12, <u>15</u>, 18, 21 …
5, 10, <u>15</u>, 20, 25, 30, 35 …

**THINK**
Finding multiples is like skip counting by a number.

**THINK**
So, 12 and 24 are common multiples of 3 and 4.

**THINK**
So, 15 is the least common multiple of 3 and 5.

## COMMON MULTIPLE

| **Problem** |
| --- |
| Which is not a common multiple of 2 and 3? |
| A. 6 |
| B. 8 |
| C. 12 |
| D. 18 |
| E. 24 |

**STEP 1:** List the multiples of each number.

**2: 2, 4, 6, 8, 10, 12, 14, 16, 18, 20, 24, …**
**3: 3, 6, 9, 12, 15, 18, 24, 27, 30, …**

**STEP 2:** Identify the common multiples.

**6, 12, 18, 24**

**STEP 3:** Identify the multiple that the numbers do *not* have in common.

## Answer

**B.** 8 is a not a common multiple of 2 and 3.

# LEAST COMMON MULTIPLE

## Problem

What is the least common multiple (LCM) of 12, 18, and 24?

A. 24
B. 36
C. 54
D. 72
E. 96

**STEP 1:** List the multiples of each number.

**12:** 12, 24, 36, 48, 60, 72, 84, 96, …
**18:** 18, 36, 54, 72, 90, 108, …
**24:** 24, 48, 72, 96, …

**STEP 2:** Identify the first multiple the numbers have in common. 72 is the first multiple the numbers have in common.

**STEP 3:** Identify the least common multiple (LCM) all the numbers share.

## Answer

**C.** 72 is the LCM of 12, 18, and 24.

# PRIME FACTOR TREE

## Problem

What is the least common multiple (LCM) of 60 and 40?

A. 10
B. 20
C. 120
D. 240

**STEP 1:** Use a factor tree to find the prime factorization of each number.

**STEP 2:** Find the prime numbers in common.

**Common Prime Factors: 2 × 2 × 5**

## REMEMBER

A good way to keep track of common prime factors is to loop them. Each looped pair is multiplied only once.

**STEP 3:** Multiply common prime factors once for each pair and all the other single prime factors.

$2 × 2 × 5 × 3 × 2 = 120$

## Answer

**C.** 120 is the least common multiple of 60 and 40.

# Percents, Fractions, and Decimals

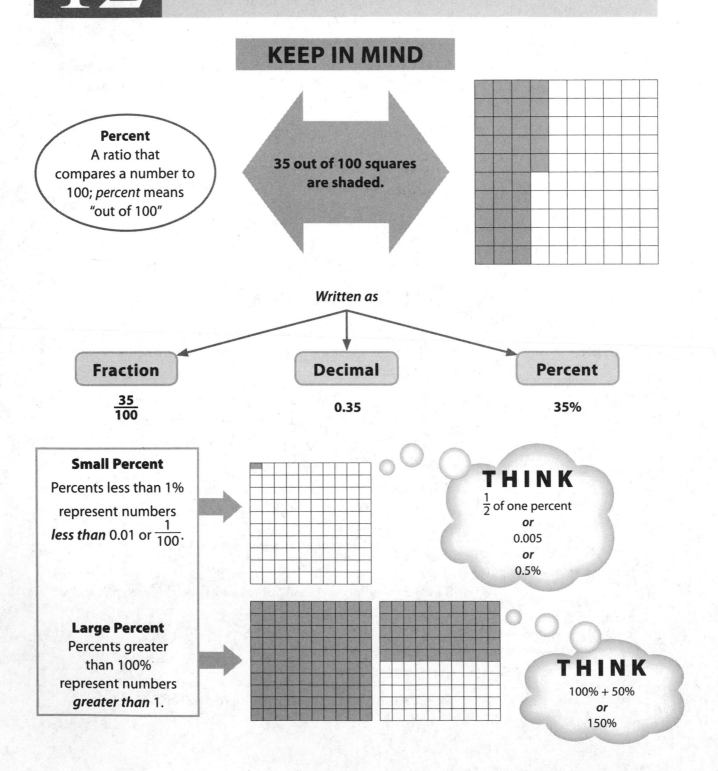

**KEEP IN MIND**

**Percent**
A ratio that compares a number to 100; *percent* means "out of 100"

35 out of 100 squares are shaded.

*Written as*

| Fraction | Decimal | Percent |
|----------|---------|---------|
| $\frac{35}{100}$ | 0.35 | 35% |

**Small Percent**
Percents less than 1% represent numbers *less than* 0.01 or $\frac{1}{100}$.

**THINK**
$\frac{1}{2}$ of one percent
*or*
0.005
*or*
0.5%

**Large Percent**
Percents greater than 100% represent numbers *greater than* 1.

**THINK**
100% + 50%
*or*
150%

# PERCENT OF A NUMBER

## Problem

Mikela hit a run 35% of the time she was at bat. She has been at bat 40 times this season. How many runs has Mikela hit?

**THINK**

**Use a Fraction**

$35\% = \frac{35}{100} = \frac{7}{20}$

$\frac{7}{20} \times 40 = \frac{280}{20} = 14$

**THINK**

**Use a Decimal**

$35\% = 0.35?$

$0.35 \times 40 = 14$

## Answer

So, Mikela has scored 14 hits at bat.

# PERCENT ONE NUMBER IS OF ANOTHER

## Problem

The Smith children picked 75 apples at a local orchard. They gave 15 of the apples to their grandmother to make apple pies. What percent of the apples the Smith children picked did they give to their grandmother?

A.  5%
B.  10%
C.  15%
D.  20%
E.  25%

**STEP 1:** Write the problem as an equation:

$15 = 75x$

**STEP 2:** Solve the problem for $x$:

$x = \frac{15}{75} = 0.20$

**STEP 3:** Write the decimal as a percent:

$0.20 = 20\%$

## Answer

D.  15 is 20% of 75.

**THINK**

**15 is what percent of 75?**

There are 5 sets of 15 in 75.

One set of 15 is $\frac{1}{5}$ of 75.

$\frac{1}{5} = 0.20 = 20\%$

## KEEP IN MIND

base    exponent

$5^3$

power

A power tells you
how many times a
base number is repeated
as a factor.

$5 \times 5 \times 5$

### Problem

$3^2 + 2^4 = ?$

A. 11
B. 14
C. 25
D. 56

### Add and Subtract with Exponents

**STEP 1:** Expand each expression with an exponent and write
it in parentheses.

$$3^2 + 2^4 = (3 \times 3) + (2 \times 2 \times 2 \times 2)$$

**STEP 2:** Evaluate each expression in parentheses.

$$(3 \times 3) + (2 \times 2 \times 2 \times 2) = (9) + (16) =$$

**STEP 3:** Perform the operation.

$$(9) + (16) = 25$$

### Answer

C. $3^2 + 2^4 = 25$

### Problem

$2^3 \times 3^2 = ?$

A. 12
B. 25
C. 36
D. 72
E. 736

### Multiply with Exponents

**STEP 1:** Expand each expression with an exponent and write
it in parentheses.

$$2^3 \times 3^2 = (2 \times 2 \times 2) \times (3 \times 3)$$

**STEP 2:** Evaluate each expression in parentheses.

$$(2 \times 2 \times 2) \times (3 \times 3) = (8) \times (9)$$

**STEP 3:** Perform the operation.

$$(8) \times (9) = 72$$

### Answer

D. $2^3 \times 2^2 = 72$

# 14 Square Roots

## KEEP IN MIND

$$\sqrt{100}$$

Say: "the square root of 100"

**Square Root**
The square root of a number $\sqrt{n}$ is another number that when multiplied by itself results in $n$.

**THINK**
What number multiplied by itself results in a product of 100?

$10 \times 10 = 100$

## EQUATIONS WITH SQUARE ROOTS

### Problem

Each member of a community garden is given a square plot of land to farm. Each plot has an area of 121 square feet. What is the length of each side of a garden plot?

A.  10
B.  11
C.  12
D.  21

**STEP 1:** Write an equation to represent the problem.
$$A = s^2$$

**STEP 2:** Substitute known values in the equation.
$$121 = s^2$$

**STEP 3:** Solve the equation.
$$s^2 = 121$$
$$s = \sqrt{121}$$
$$s = 11$$

### Answer

**B.**  Each side $s$ is 11 feet long.

**THINK**
What number multiplied by itself results in a product of 121?

$11 \times 11 = 121$

# Measures of Central Tendency

## KEEP IN MIND

**Data Set**
A collection of facts or numbers that describe something

**Jamal's Weekly Math Test Scores**

94, 91, 86, 75, 86, 90, 88, 93, 80

**Ordered Data Set**
Data arranged in some logical way, such as least to greatest

**Ordered Data Set of Jamal's Weekly Math Test Scores**

75, 80, 86, 86, 88, 90, 91, 93, 94

## Mean

The *mean,* or *average,* is the sum of the numbers divided by the number of items in the set.

$783 \div 9 = 87$

So, the mean (average) of Jamal's test scores is 87.

## Median

The *median* is the middle number in the data set when it is arranged from least the greatest.

So, the median of Jamal's test scores is 88.

## Mode

The *mode* is the number that occurs most frequently in the data set.

So, the mode of Jamal's test scores is 86.

## Range

The *range* is the difference between the greatest number and least number in the data set.

$94 - 75 = 19$

So, the range of Jamal's test scores is 19.

### Problem

What is the average high temperature in degrees Fahrenheit last week based on the data shown below?

**76, 72, 77, 71, 76, 74, 79**

A. 71
B. 75
C. 76
D. 79

**STEP 1:** Find the sum of the numbers in the data set.

**76 + 72 + 77 + 71 + 76 + 74 + 79 = 525**

**STEP 2:** Identify the number of items in the data set.

**There are 7 items in the data set**

**STEP 3:** Write a division sentence and solve.

**525 ÷ 7 = 75**

### Answer

**B.** The average high temperature was 75° F.

## MEDIAN, MODE, AND RANGE

### Problem

In which set of data is the median, mode, and the range the same?

A. 1, 2, 3, 1, 2, 3, 1
B. 1, 3, 1, 2, 3, 2, 3
C. 1, 3, 3, 3, 2, 3, 1
D. 1, 2, 3, 3, 2, 1, 2

**THINK**

All data sets use the numbers 1, 2, and 3, so the range of all sets is 2.

**STEP 1:** Order the items in each data set from least to greatest.

**A: 1, 1, 1, 2, 2, 3, 3**
**B: 1, 1, 2, 2, 3, 3, 3**
**C: 1, 1, 2, 3, 3, 3, 3**
**D: 1, 1, 2, 2, 2, 3, 3**

**STEP 2:** Find the range of each set.

**Range: 3 – 1 = 2**

**STEP 3:** Find the data sets with a median of 2.

**Median is 2: Data sets A, C, and D**

**STEP 4:** Find the data set with a mode of 2.

**Mode is 2: Only data set D**

### Answer

**D.** Only data set D has 2 as a median, mode, and range.

# Ratios, Rates, and Proportions

## KEEP IN MIND

**Rate**
A ratio that involves two quantities

**Ratio**
Relationship between two numbers

**Proportion**
An equation that states two ratios are equal

30 miles per hour
30 : 1
$\frac{30}{1}$ $\frac{miles}{hour}$

*Written as*
2 to 3
2 : 3
$\frac{2}{3}$

$\frac{2}{3} = \frac{8}{12}$

## RATIO PROBLEMS

**Problem**

The ratio of boys to girls in Ms. Rashid's Arabic class is 3 to 5. There are 48 students in the class. How many of the students are girls?

**THINK**

For every 8 students, there are 3 boys and 5 girls. But, the ratio of girls to students is 5 to 8.

**QUESTION**

There are 48 students in all. How many groups of 8 are in 48? What number times 8 equals 48?

$$\frac{5}{8} = \frac{30}{48}$$

× 6

× 6

**Answer**

**30 of the 48 students are girls.**

# PROPORTION PROBLEMS

## Problem

A wooden dowel is 21 inches long. Tanya wants to cut it into two pieces in a ratio of 2 : 5. What is the length of the longer piece?

A. 6 inches
B. 10 inches
C. 15 inches
D. 42 inches
E. 105 inches

**THINK**

For every 2 inches of the shorter pipe, there are 5 inches of longer pipe.

**STEP 1:** State the *known ratio* as a fraction:
$$\frac{2}{5}$$

**STEP 2:** State the *unknown ratio* as a fraction:
$$\frac{\textbf{Short piece}}{\textbf{Long piece}} = \frac{x}{21 - x}$$

**STEP 3:** Write a proportion. Set the two ratios equal to each other.
$$\frac{2}{5} = \frac{x}{21 - x}$$

**STEP 4:** Cross multiply and solve.

$2(21 - x) = 5x$

$42 - 2x = 5x$

$42 = 5x + 2x$

$42 = 7x$

$x = 6$

**THINK**

Let the short piece be represented by $x$.

Let the long piece be represented by the total length 21 minus $x$.

## Answer

**C.** The long piece is $21 - 6 = 15$ inches. So, the answer is C.

## ⚠ Prep Alert

When writing a proportion, both ratios must be set up in the same way.

$$\frac{\text{Part}}{\text{Whole}} = \frac{\text{Part}}{\text{Whole}}$$

$$\frac{\text{Whole}}{\text{Part}} = \frac{\text{Whole}}{\text{Part}}$$

$$\frac{\text{Part A}}{\text{Part B}} = \frac{\text{Part A}}{\text{Part B}}$$

$$\frac{\text{Part B}}{\text{Part A}} = \frac{\text{Part B}}{\text{Part A}}$$

## KEEP IN MIND

**COMBINATION**
A way of selecting several objects from a larger group, where order does not matter

## NUMBER OF COMBINATIONS

### Problem

The school cafeteria offers 4 main dishes, 3 drinks, along with 2 desserts for lunch. How many possible lunch meals are there if one of each type of item is selected?

A. 24
B. 20
C. 14
D. 9

**THINK**
How many meals consisting of a main course, a drink, and a dessert are possible?

**STEP 1:** Determine the number of choices for each group of elements in the problem.

**Main courses = 4 choices**
**Drinks = 3 choices**
**Desserts = 2 choices**

**STEP 2:** Write a multiplication sentence that uses each group of choices

$4 \times 3 \times 2 = ?$

**STEP 3:** Solve to find the product, or the number of possible combinations

$4 \times 3 \times 2 = 24$

### Answer

A. The number of possible lunch combinations is 24.

## KEEP IN MIND

### PERMUTATION
A way of organizing several objects from a larger group, where order matters

## NUMBER OF PERMUTATIONS

### Problem

How many two-digit numbers can you form using two different digits from 2, 3, 4, and 5?

A.  8
B.  10
C.  12
D.  16
E.  120

**STEP 1:** Use an organized list to arrange all possible outcomes.

**Begins with 2: 23, 24, 25**
**Begins with 3: 32, 34, 35**
**Begins with 4: 42, 43, 45**
**Begins with 5: 52, 53, 54**

**STEP 2:** Check to make sure you have included each possible outcome without any repetitions.

**STEP 3:** Count the number of possible outcomes.

**23, 24, 25, 32, 34, 35, 42, 43, 45,**
**52, 53, 54 = 12 outcomes**

### THINK

The question states that each two-digit number must be made from two different digits. So, numbers that repeat the same digit, for example, 22, 33, 44, and 55 are not acceptable.

### Answer

**C.** There are 12 different possible numbers.

# 19 Probability of Events

## KEEP IN MIND

**Possible Events**

Rolling any number:
1, 2, 3, 4, 5, or 6

**PROBABILITY**

$$\frac{\text{Number of Favorable Outcomes}}{\text{Number of Possible Outcomes}}$$

*What is the probability of rolling an even number?*

**Favorable Events**

Rolling an even number:
2, 4, or 6

**THINK**

There is an equal chance of rolling each number.

**THINK**

There are 3 chances out of 6 of rolling an even number.

$$\frac{3}{6} = \frac{1}{2}$$

## PROBABILITY OF AN INDEPENDENT EVENT

### Problem

If you make a spin on the spinner shown, what is the probability that you will land on an odd number?

A. 0

B. $\frac{1}{8}$

C. $\frac{1}{4}$

D. $\frac{1}{3}$

E. $\frac{3}{8}$

**STEP 1:** Count the number of possible outcomes.

**There are 8 possible outcomes.**

**STEP 2:** Count the number of favorable outcomes.

**There are 2 favorable outcomes.**

**STEP 3:** Write the probability as a fraction and simplify.

$$\frac{2}{8} = \frac{1}{4}$$

### Answer

**C.** So, the probability of spinning an odd number is $\frac{1}{4}$.

**THINK**

There are 8 equal of the spinner, but only 2 of them show odd numbers.

# PROBABILITY OF TWO INDEPENDENT EVENTS

## Problem

Mara rolls a standard number cube and flips a coin. What is the probability that she will roll an even number and flip heads?

A. 0

B. $\frac{1}{12}$

C. $\frac{1}{4}$

D. $\frac{1}{3}$

E. $\frac{1}{2}$

**STEP 1:** Determine the probability of the first event, spinning an even number, and simplify.

$$\frac{3}{6} = \frac{1}{2}$$

**STEP 2:** Determine the probability of the second event, flipping heads, and then simplify.

$$\frac{1}{2}$$

**STEP 3:** Multiple the two probabilities.

$$\frac{1}{2} \times \frac{1}{2} = \frac{1}{4}$$

## Answer

C. The probability of spinning an even number and flipping heads is $\frac{1}{4}$.

# PROBABILITY OF DEPENDENT EVENTS

## Problem

In a box of 10 cell phones, three are broken. Suppose 3 cell phones are randomly chosen and tested. Assume that the first and second cell phones are not replaced after testing. What is the probability that all three cell phones selected are broken?

A. $\frac{1}{9}$

B. $\frac{1}{120}$

C. $\frac{1}{150}$

D. $\frac{27}{100}$

**STEP 1:** Determine the probability of each event in the order in which the events occur.

(*P*) of Broken Cell Phone $= \frac{3}{10}$

(*P*) of Broken 1st Cell Phone $= \frac{3}{10}$

(*P*) of Broken 2nd Cell Phone $= \frac{2}{9}$

(*P*) of Broken 3rd Cell Phone $= \frac{1}{9}$

**STEP 2:** Multiply the probability of each favorable event.

$$\frac{3}{10} \times \frac{2}{9} \times \frac{1}{8} = ?$$

**STEP 3:** Solve to find the probability of the dependent events.

$$\frac{3}{10} \times \frac{2}{9} \times \frac{1}{8} = \frac{6}{720} = \frac{1}{120}$$

## Answer

C. The probability of selecting 3 broken cell phones out of 10 is $\frac{1}{120}$.

**THINK**

As each cell phone is chosen, the number of cell phones in the group gets smaller. So, the probability of the next event changes.

# Perimeter and Area of Plane Figures

## KEEP IN MIND

**PLANE FIGURES**
A closed 2-D figure having length and width but no thickness

**Perimeter/ Circumference**

The **perimeter** is the distance around a figure with sides. **Circumference** is the distance around a circle.

**Area**

The **area** is the number of square units it takes to cover the surface of a plane figure.

### Triangle

Perimeter $= a + b + c$

Area $= \frac{1}{2}bh$

Degrees $= 180°$

### Quadrilateral

Perimeter $= 2l + 2w$

Area $= l \times w$

Degrees $= 360°$

### Circle

Circumference $= 2\pi r$

Area $= \pi r^2$

Degrees $= 360°$

# FIND THE PERIMETER AND AREA OF A CIRCLE

## Problem

A circle has a circumference of $6\pi$ inches. What is the area of the circle?

A. $3\pi$
B. $6\pi$
C. $9\pi$
D. $12\pi$

**STEP 1:** Write the formula for the circumference of a circle.

$$C = 2\pi r$$

**STEP 2:** Substitute the known value.

$$6\pi = 2\pi r$$

**STEP 3:** Simplify and solve.

$$6\pi = 2\pi r$$
$$6 = 2r$$
$$r = 3$$

**STEP 4:** Substitute the value of the radius into the formula for the area of a circle.

$$A = \pi r^2$$
$$A = \pi 3^2$$

**STEP 5:** Solve.

$$A = 9\pi$$

## Answer

**C.** The area of the circle is $9\pi$ square units.

# FIND THE AREA OF A TRIANGLE

## Problem

What is the area of the triangle?

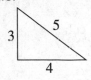

A. 6 square units
B. 7 square units
C. 12 square units
D. 15 square units
E. 20 square units

**STEP 1:** Write the formula for the area of a triangle.

$$A = \frac{1}{2}bh$$

**STEP 2:** Substitute the known value.

$$A = \frac{1}{2}(4)(3)$$

**STEP 3:** Simplify and solve.

$$A = \frac{1}{2}(12)$$
$$A = 6$$

## Answer

**A.** The area of the triangle is 6 square units.

# Surface Area and Volume of Solid Figures

## KEEP IN MIND

**SOLID FIGURES**
A 3-D figure having length, width, and height

**Surface Area**

The **surface area (SA)** of a solid figure is the sum of the areas of all of its sides.

**Volume**
The **volume (V)** of a solid figure is the amount of space it occupies in 3-dimensions.

| Cube | Rectangular Prism |
|------|-------------------|
| $SA = 6a^2$ | $SA = 2(wl + hl + hw)$ |
| $V = a^3$ | $V = w \times l \times h$ |

## FIND THE SURFACE AREA AND VOLUME OF A CUBE

### Problem

A cube has an edge that is 5 cm long. What is the surface area of the cube?

A.  30 square units
B.  150 square units
C.  600 square units
D.  750 square units

**STEP 1:** Write the formula for the surface area of a cube.

$$SA = 6a^2$$

**STEP 2:** Substitute the known values.

$$SA = 6(5)^2$$

**STEP 3:** Simplify and solve.

$$SA = 6(25)$$
$$SA = 150 \text{ square units}$$

### Answer

**B.** The surface area of the cube is 150 square units.

### Problem

What is the volume of this cube?

A.  25 cube units
B.  50 cube units
C.  125 cube units
D.  525 cube units

**STEP 1:** Write the formula for the volume of a cube.

$$V = a^3$$

**STEP 2:** Substitute the known values.

$$V = (5)^3$$

**STEP 3:** Simplify and solve.

$$V = 5 \times 5 \times 5$$
$$V = 125 \text{ cube units}$$

### Answer

**C.** The volume of the cube is 125 cubic units.

# Mental Math • Multiply by 4 and 8

## KEEP IN MIND

**MULTIPLY**

### By 4

$212 \times 4 = ?$

**STEP 1:** Double the factor you are multiplying.

$212 \times 2 = 424$

**STEP 2:** Then double the new product.

$424 \times 2 = 848$

**So,** $212 \times 4 = 848$

### By 8

$23 \times 8 = ?$

**STEP 1:** Double the factor you are multiplying.

$23 \times 2 = 46$

**STEP 2:** Then double the new product.

$46 \times 2 = 92$

**STEP 3:** Then double the last product.

$92 \times 2 = 184$

**So,** $23 \times 8 = 184$

## Problems

Use mental math to find the product of each multiplication problem.

1. $32 \times 4 = ?$
2. $45 \times 8 = ?$
3. $512 \times 4 = ?$
4. $128 \times 8 = ?$

**Answers**

**1.** 128; **2.** 360; **3.** 2,048; **4.** 1,024

**REMEMBER**

Practicing doubling numbers will sharpen your mental math skills. Use a calculator to check your work.

# Mental Math • Divide by 4 and 8

## KEEP IN MIND

**DIVIDE**

### By 4

454 ÷ 4 = ?

**STEP 1:** Think of half the dividend, or the number you are dividing.

454 ÷ 2 = 227

**STEP 2:** Then find half the new quotient.

227 ÷ 2 = 113 + 0.5

So,  454 ÷ 4 = 113.5

### By 8

568 ÷ 8 = ?

**STEP 1:** Think of half the dividend.

568 ÷ 2 = 284

**STEP 2:** Then half the new quotient.

284 ÷ 2 = 142

**STEP 3:** Then half the last quotient.

142 ÷ 2 = 71

So,  568 ÷ 8 = 71

## Problems

Use mental math to find the quotient of each division problem.

1. 86 ÷ 4 = ?
2. 184 ÷ 8 = ?
3. 768 ÷ 4 = ?
4. 2,712 ÷ 8 = ?

**Answers**

**1.** 21.5; **2.** 23; **3.** 192; **4.** 339

## REMEMBER

When the number is odd, subtract 1 to make it even. Your exact answer will be slightly larger.

# Mental Math • Multiply with Fractions

## KEEP IN MIND

**MULTIPLY**

### Unit Fractions

$\frac{1}{5} \times 65 = ?$

**STEP 1:** Think of a related division problem. Write the whole number.

65

**STEP 2:** Then divide by the denominator of the fraction. Solve.

$65 \div 5 = 13$

**So,** $\frac{3}{5} \times 65 = 13$

### Proper Fractions

$\frac{3}{5} \times 65 = ?$

**STEP 1:** Divide the whole number by the denominator of the fraction.

$65 \div 5 = 13$

**STEP 2:** Then multiply this quotient by the numerator of the fraction.

$13 \times 3 = 39$

**So,** $\frac{1}{5} \times 65 = 39$

## Problems

Use mental math to find the product of each problem.

1. $\frac{1}{3} \times 159 = ?$

2. $\frac{1}{7} \times 609 = ?$

3. $\frac{2}{5} \times 205 = ?$

4. $\frac{5}{9} \times 729 = ?$

**Answers**

**1.** 53; **2.** 87; **3.** 82; **4.** 405

## REMEMBER

A **unit fraction** has a numerator of 1. A **proper fraction** has a numerator that is less than the denominator.

# Mental Math • Use Compatible Numbers

## KEEP IN MIND

**Add & Subtract**

- Round to estimate sums and differences.
- Add or subtract to make compatible numbers.

**COMPATIBLE NUMBERS**

A pair of numbers that make it easy to complete basic math operations mentally.

**Multiply & Divide**

- Round to estimate products and quotients.
- Add or subtract to make compatible numbers.

## ADDITION & SUBTRACTION

### Problems

Solve using mental math.

$284 - 38 = ?$

Use mental math to find the quotient of each division problem.

1. $592 - 75 = ?$
2. $1,563 - 27 = ?$
3. $248 + 33 = ?$
4. $1,216 + 97 = ?$

**STEP 1:** Write the problem.

$284 - 38 = ?$

**STEP 2:** Think of a compatible number. Add it to both numbers in the original problem.

$(284 + 2) - (38 + 2) = 286 - 40$

**STEP 3:** Solve the simpler problem mentally.

$284 - 40 = 246$

**SO, 284 − 38 is 246.**

### Answers

**1.** 517; **2.** 1,536; **3.** 281; **4.** 1,313

**THINK**

What can I add to make the numbers compatible? 2

**REMEMBER**

For addition, add to make one number compatible and then subtract it from your sum.

# PART II

# STRATEGIES FOR THE VERBAL, READING, AND WRITING SECTIONS

# Strategies for Synonym Questions

Synonym questions make up one-half of the Verbal Reasoning section on both the SSAT and the ISEE. On the SSAT, synonyms account for 30 of the 60 verbal questions. On the ISEE, synonyms account for 20 of the 40 verbal questions. On both tests, synonym questions are designed to test your knowledge of word meanings.

## Format of Synonym Questions

Each synonym question consists of a word in capital letters followed by four (ISEE) or five (SSAT) words or phrases. Your task is to select the one word or phrase whose meaning is closest to the meaning of the word in capital letters.

## Sample Synonym Question Explained

Let's look at a sample question to see what's involved.

CANDOR:
(A) charm
(B) patience
(C) honesty
(D) consent
(E) caution

If you know the meaning of the word *candor*, just pick the answer choice that is closest to the word you thought of and move on to the next question. If you don't know the meaning of *candor*, think about the word itself. Have you ever heard it used? Does it look like some other word you know? Perhaps you recognize that *candor* looks a lot like *candid*. A candid photo is one that is unposed or natural. Now look at the answer choices to find one that means something like unposed or natural.

(A) *Charm* means "attractiveness" or "appeal." This is a possibility, but there is probably a better choice.

(B) *Patience* means "tolerance" or "restraint." This is not even close, so you can eliminate it.

(C) *Honesty* means "truthfulness" or "openness." This choice is closer to the idea of natural or unposed than choice A.

(D) *Consent* means "approval" or "agreement." This choice can be eliminated because it has nothing to do with candor.

(E) *Caution* means "carefulness," which has nothing to do with candor.

The answer choice that comes closest to the idea of being unposed or natural is choice C. *Candor* means "frankness," "openness," or "honesty."

## Strategies for Answering Synonym Questions

Here is a six-step strategic plan that you can use to answer synonym questions.

1. Look carefully at the capitalized word.
2. If you know what it means, think of another word that means the same and look for that word among the answer choices.
3. If you don't know the word, try to put it in context. If you remember hearing or reading the word, try to remember how it was used.
4. If context doesn't help, look at the word for clues. See if it contains a word or word part that is familiar to you.
5. Read the answer choices and select the one that comes closest to the meaning you thought of.
6. If you have no idea what the word means, eliminate any answer choices you know are not correct and then guess from among the remaining choices.

Try the six-step strategy to help you answer the synonym questions that follow. As you complete each question, compare your answer to the explanation given.

## Sample Synonym Question Set Explained

**Directions:** Each of the following questions consists of a word in capital letters followed by four (ISEE) or five (SSAT) words or phrases. Your task is to select the one word or phrase whose meaning is closest to the meaning of the word in capital letters.

---

*SSAT/ISEE Coach Says . . .*

The correct answer may not be a perfect synonym for the capitalized word, but it will be the one that is closest in meaning to the given word.

---

1. APATHY:
   (A) sorrow
   (B) ability
   (C) sickness
   (D) inconvenience
   (E) indifference

1. **E is correct.** *Apathy* is a lack of interest or concern about something, and *indifference*, choice E, is a good synonym. Word parts can help define this word. The word part *-pathy* means "feelings" or "emotions," and the prefix *a-* means "without." Thus *apathy* can be defined as "without feelings," which is nearly the same as indifference.

---

***SSAT/ISEE Coach Says . . .***
Often you can get a good idea of what a new word means by taking it apart and defining each separate piece.

---

2. REVISE:
   (A) relapse
   (B) consider
   (C) prevail
   (D) amend
   (E) reiterate

2. **D is correct.** The prefix *re-* means "again" or "back." To *revise* means to "reconsider (to consider again) and change or modify." *Amend*, which means "to make better or improve" is the best synonym.

   Don't be fooled by the fact that choices A and E both include the prefix *re-*. *Relapse* means "to fall back to a previous condition" and *reiterate* means "to repeat" or "to say again."

3. ABATE:
   (A) pretend
   (B) decrease
   (C) finalize
   (D) endanger
   (E) oppose

3. **B is correct.** *Abate* means "to reduce in amount or degree," "to lessen," or "to decrease." Perhaps you remember hearing *abate* mentioned during a weather report: "The storm is expected to abate before nightfall."

---

***SSAT/ISEE Coach Says . . .***
Try to remember where you may have heard a new word used. Just knowing the context in which the word was used can help you define it.

---

4. DECEIVE:
   (A) betray
   (B) protect
   (C) deduce
   (D) verify
   (E) disparage

4. **A is correct.** To *deceive* is to mislead, delude, or betray. If you do not know the word *deceive*, perhaps you recognize that it is a word that is used in a negative way. This fact will allow you to eliminate choices B and D since *protect* and *verify* are both positive words. *Deduce* (choice C), which means "to infer by reasoning," is neither positive nor negative. That leaves only choices A and E from which to choose. *Betray* (choice A) means "to break faith with" or "to mislead," and *disparage* (choice D) means to "discredit" or "belittle." Clearly, choice A is the best answer.

---

*SSAT/ISEE Coach Says . . .*
Many words convey either a positive or a negative feeling. You may be able to choose the right synonym simply by asking, "Is this word negative or positive?"

---

5. OBSCURE:
   (A) obtain
   (B) replace
   (C) ignore
   (D) conceal
   (E) observe

5. **D is correct.** *Obscure* can be an adjective meaning "vague" or "dark." Or it can be a verb meaning to "obliterate" or "hide." All you have to do is look at the answer choices to know which meaning you are looking for. In this case, all the answer choices are verbs. That means you are looking for a word that means the same as "hide." Choice D is the best answer.

---

*SSAT/ISEE Coach Says . . .*
Many words have different meanings, depending upon whether they are used as nouns or verbs or adjectives. If you can't tell which meaning of a word you are looking for, just look at the answer choices. They will always be the same part of speech as the capitalized word.

---

## On Your Own

Now take the time to apply what you have just learned about synonym questions to see how well you can do on Practice Set A. When you are finished, use the answer key to score your work.

- You may find that some words are easier to deal with than others. Remember that synonym questions get harder as you work through the test. On the ISEE, answer every question, even if you have to take a wild guess. On the SSAT, answer every question for which you know, or think you know, the answer. Whenever you can eliminate at least two of the answer choices as definitely incorrect, make a guess.

- Review the strategies and tips discussed above and then try Practice Set B. Remember that the more you practice with these items, the easier the questions will become for you to answer correctly.

## Practice Set A

**Directions:** Each of the following questions consists of a word in capital letters followed by five words or phrases labeled (A), (B), (C), (D), and (E). Your task is to select the one word or phrase whose meaning is closest to the meaning of the word in capital letters.

**Example:**
CANDOR:
(A) charm
(B) patience
(C) honesty
(D) consent
(E) caution

Correct Answer: C

1. PROFOUND:
   (A) deep
   (B) complex
   (C) captivating
   (D) discouraging
   (E) miraculous

2. INADEQUATE:
   (A) diminutive
   (B) subsequent
   (C) deficient
   (D) interminable
   (E) tangible

3. ADVERSARY:
   (A) proverb
   (B) opening
   (C) atrocity
   (D) opponent
   (E) desolation

4. PRESERVE:
   (A) commemorate
   (B) revere
   (C) protect
   (D) warrant
   (E) confine

5. TENTATIVE:
   (A) indefinite
   (B) hidden
   (C) sociable
   (D) critical
   (E) charming

6. CLAMOR:
   (A) mistake
   (B) mixture
   (C) package
   (D) commotion
   (E) recollection

7. CONTEMPORARY:
   (A) appropriated
   (B) current
   (C) momentary
   (D) transient
   (E) convenient

8. CAJOLE:
   (A) sneer
   (B) ridicule
   (C) peek
   (D) persuade
   (E) target

9. PRIMITIVE:
   (A) functional
   (B) wooden
   (C) basic
   (D) fragile
   (E) lowly

10. MUNDANE:
    (A) ordinary
    (B) vigorous
    (C) swollen
    (D) restful
    (E) cautious

## Answers and Explanations

1. **A is correct.** *Profound* means "thoroughgoing," "far-reaching," or "deep."
2. **C is correct.** *Inadequate* means "not adequate to fulfill a need" or "deficient."
3. **D is correct.** An *adversary* is an "enemy" or an "opponent."
4. **C is correct.** To *preserve* is to "keep from damage or harm" or to "protect."
5. **A is correct.** *Tentative* means "not fully worked out or agreed upon." To say that you have tentative plans is to say that your plans are "indefinite."
6. **D is correct.** A *clamor* is an uproar or a racket—in other words, a "commotion."
7. **B is correct.** *Contemporary* means "of or in the style of the present," "modern," or "current."
8. **D is correct.** To *cajole* is to "coax with flattery or to persuade with gentle and repeated appeals."
9. **C is correct.** *Primitive* means "not derived from something else," "primary," or "basic."
10. **A is correct.** *Mundane* means "commonplace" or "ordinary."

## Practice Set B

**Directions:** Each of the following questions consists of a word in capital letters followed by five words or phrases labeled (A), (B), (C), (D), and (E). Your task is to select the one word or phrase whose meaning is closest to the meaning of the word in capital letters.

**Example:**
ALLEVIATE:
(A) sickness
(B) fever
(C) pain
(D) help
(E) result

Correct Answer: D

1. ROBUST:
   (A) mechanical
   (B) fresh
   (C) hearty
   (D) elaborate
   (E) mindful

2. ALLOT:
   (A) research
   (B) distribute
   (C) apply
   (D) inform
   (E) ingest

3. BREVITY:
   (A) shortness
   (B) sadness
   (C) determination
   (D) insignificance
   (E) guilt

4. CHRONIC:
   (A) troublesome
   (B) secure
   (C) unknown
   (D) persistent
   (E) difficult

5. PRAISE:
   (A) ascend
   (B) abhor
   (C) aspire
   (D) bolster
   (E) commend

6. APTITUDE:
   (A) height
   (B) ability
   (C) attitude
   (D) retraction
   (E) contrast

7. WINSOME:
   (A) small
   (B) limber
   (C) quiet
   (D) charming
   (E) restless

8. APPREHENSION:
   (A) consequence
   (B) beginning
   (C) dread
   (D) dismissal
   (E) imperfection

9. ACCLAIM:
   (A) prospect
   (B) aversion
   (C) delight
   (D) approval
   (E) accessory

10. PREVAIL:
    (A) triumph
    (B) strain
    (C) assume
    (D) precede
    (E) clarify

**Answers and Explanations**

1. **C is correct.** *Robust* means "full of health and strength," "vigorous," or "hearty."
2. **B is correct.** To *allot* is to "parcel out" or to "distribute."
3. **A is correct.** *Brevity* is the quality or state of being brief in duration—in other words, shortness.
4. **D is correct.** *Chronic* means "of long duration," "continuing," or "persistent."
5. **E is correct.** To *praise* is to express approval or admiration of, to extol, or to "commend."
6. **B is correct.** *Aptitude* is a talent or natural ability.
7. **D is correct.** *Winsome* means "attractive in an engaging way," or "charming."
8. **C is correct.** *Apprehension* is an anxious feeling or foreboding or "dread."
9. **D is correct.** *Acclaim* is loud or enthusiastic praise, applause, or "approval."
10. **A is correct.** To *prevail* is to be greater in strength or influence—in other words, to "triumph."

# Strategies for Verbal Analogy Questions (SSAT Only)

Verbal analogy questions account for 30 of the 60 questions in the Verbal Reasoning section of the SSAT. There are no verbal analogy questions on the ISEE, so you can skip this chapter if you are preparing to take the ISEE.

Verbal analogy questions are designed to test your knowledge of word meanings along with your ability to understand how words relate to each other. On the ISEE, verbal analogy questions are arranged in order of difficulty from easiest to hardest.

## Format of Verbal Analogy Questions

Analogy questions come in two different formats.

- In one format the question contains three main words and each answer choice contains one word. Your task is to find the single word that is related to the third word in the question in the same way that the first two words are related.

- In the other format, each question contains one pair of main words and each answer choice contains another pair of words. You are to find the pair of words among the answer choices that is related in the same way as the pair of words in the question.

## Sample Analogy Questions Explained

Here are samples of each analogy format to give you an idea of what's involved.

1. Maintain is to preserve as magnify is to
   (A) protect.
   (B) exert.
   (C) amplify.
   (D) rectify.
   (E) restrain.

1. **C is correct.** *Maintain* and *preserve* are synonyms. Therefore the correct answer will be the word that means most nearly the same as *magnify*. *Amplify*, which means "to make larger or stronger," is a good synonym for *magnify*. Choice A is wrong because *protect* is a synonym for *maintain* and

*preserve*, not for *magnify*. Choice B is wrong because *exert* means "to put forth or use energetically," which has nothing to do with *magnify*. Choice D is wrong because *rectify* means "to correct or improve," which is not related to *magnify*. Choice E is wrong because *restrain* means "to hold back," which has no direct relationship to *magnify*.

2. Page is to book as
   (A) drama is to play.
   (B) note is to letter.
   (C) pen is to paper.
   (D) letter is to word.
   (E) arm is to hand.

2. **D is correct.** This is a part-to-whole analogy. A *book* is made up of *pages* in the same way that a *word* is made up of *letters*. Choice A is wrong because a *drama* is one type of *play*. Choice B is wrong because a *note* is a type of *letter*. Choice C is wrong because a *pen* is used to write on *paper*. Choice E is wrong because an *arm* is not part of a *hand*.

## Common Relationships Found in Analogy Questions

The majority of SSAT analogy questions fall into one of the following categories:

- Contrasts
  *Negligent is to careful*
  *Bravery is to cowardice*
- Part to whole
  *Keyboard is to computer*
  *Trunk is to car*
- Part to part
  *Keyboard is to mouse (parts of a computer)*
  *Trunk is to hood (parts of a car)*
- Activity to result
  *Heat is to warmth*
  *Rain is to flooding*
- Use
  *Pencil is to write*
  *Scissors is to cut*
- Individual to object
  *Doctor is to stethoscope*
  *Painter is to brush*

- Measurement
  *Clock is to time*
  *Decibel is to sound*
- Degree of difference or similarity
  *Cool is to frozen*
  *Breeze is to gale*

## How to Answer Analogy Questions

Here is a helpful five-step strategy for answering verbal analogy questions.

1. Figure out how the first two words are related.
2. Make up a sentence that expresses the relationship between the first pair of words.
3. Try out your sentence on the second pair of words and eliminate the ones that don't work.
4. If you find that your sentence works on more than one answer pair (or on none of the answer pairs), revise your sentence to make it more precise.
5. Choose the answer that works best.

Use the five-step strategy and what you have learned about analogy relationships to answer the practice verbal analogy questions that follow. As you complete each question, compare your answer to the explanation given.

## Sample Verbal Analogy Question Set Explained

**Directions:** The questions that follow ask you to find relationships between words. For each question, select the answer choice that best completes the meaning of the sentence.

---

*SSAT Coach Says . . .*
The key to answering an analogy question is being able to express the relationship between the words in a pair.

---

1. Reap is to sow as
   (A) suggest is to order.
   (B) send is to remit.
   (C) assemble is to disband.
   (D) furnish is to provide.
   (E) plant is to seed.

1. **C is correct.** *Reap* and *sow* are related as opposites. To *reap* is to "gather" or to "harvest," and to *sow* is to "scatter seed."
   Choice A: Is *suggest* the opposite of *order*? No. *Suggest* and *order* are different degrees of the same concept.
   Choice B: Is *send* the opposite of *remit*? No. *Send* and *remit* are synonyms.
   Choice C: Is *assemble* the opposite of *disband*? Yes. *Assemble* means "gather together," and *disband* means "separate." This appears to be the correct answer, but let's check the remaining choices to be sure.
   Choice D: Is *furnish* the opposite of *provide*? No. *Furnish* and *provide* are synonyms.
   Choice E: Is *plant* the opposite of *seed*? No. *Plant* and *seed*, in their verb forms, are synonyms.
   The best answer is definitely choice C.

2. Sprint is to runner as
   (A) slither is to snake.
   (B) gallop is to horse.
   (C) hop is to rabbit.
   (D) glide is to skater.
   (E) race is to track.

2. **B is correct.** A *sprint* is an action taken by a *runner*. This sentence eliminates choice E, but it works for choices A, B, C, and D. To arrive at one correct answer, you must go back and revise the initial sentence to make it more precise. *Sprint* is a fast action of a *runner*. This sentence eliminates choices A, C, and D, leaving choice B as the correct answer.

---

**SSAT Coach Says . . .**
If your first sentence does not work, revise it to make it more precise.

---

3. Shovel is to excavate as scissors is to
   (A) dig.
   (B) expose.
   (C) scoop.
   (D) snip.
   (E) tear.

3. **D is correct.** The relationship in this analogy is one of an object to its use. A *shovel* is used to *excavate* just as *scissors* are used to *snip*. Don't be misled by the fact that choices A, B, and C are all synonyms for the word *excavate*. The word you are looking for is a use for a *scissors*, not a synonym for *excavate*.

*SSAT Coach Says . . .*

Don't be tricked into choosing a word just because it has *some* relationship to the word in the question. In an analogy, the two word pairs must express the *same* relationship.

Examples:
*object* is to *use* as *object* is to *use*
or
*part* is to *whole* as *part* is to *whole*

4. Tree is to forest as ship is to
(A) vessel.
(B) fleet.
(C) captain.
(D) cargo.
(E) shore.

4. **B is correct.** This is a part-to-whole analogy. A *tree* is part of a *forest* just as a *ship* is part of a *fleet*.

*SSAT Coach Says . . .*

Sometimes it's easier to see a relationship if you reverse the terms. Just remember that if you reverse the terms in the first pair, you must also reverse the terms in the second pair.

5. Toe is to heel as
(A) arm is to wing.
(B) roof is to house.
(C) chair is to table.
(D) fruit is to flower.
(E) wheel is to brake.

5. **E is correct.** This is a part-to-part analogy. *Toe* and *heel* are both parts of the *foot*. In the same way, *wheel* and *brake* are both parts of a *bicycle*. No other answer pair has the same part-to-part relationship.

*SSAT Coach Says . . .*

Know the most common analogy categories. This will help you to make up a sentence that shows how the words are related.

6. Slip is to fall as drop is to
(A) break.
(B) flood.
(C) liquid.
(D) tempt.
(E) raise.

6. **A is correct.** This is an activity-to-result analogy. A *slip* may result in a *fall*. Similarly *dropping* something may result in *breaking* it.

## On Your Own

Now take the time to apply what you have just learned about verbal analogies to see how well you can do on your own. When you are finished, use the answer key to score your work.

You may find that certain types of analogies are easier for you to deal with than others. Remember that analogy questions appear in order of their difficulty, so the last few questions are likely to be tougher than the first ones. Use Practice Set A to determine which types of analogies are most difficult for you.

Review the strategies and tips discussed above and then try Practice Set B. The more you practice answering analogy questions, the easier they will become for you to answer correctly.

**Practice Set A**

**Directions:** The questions that follow ask you to find relationships between words. For each question, select the answer choice that best completes the meaning of the sentence.

**Example:**
Chapter is to book as
(A) note is to letter.
(B) scene is to play.
(C) story is to novel.
(D) writer is to director.
(E) reader is to audience.

Correct Answer: B

A *chapter* is a division of a *book* and a *scene* is a division of a *play*.

1. File is to smooth as tape is to
   (A) gouge.
   (B) record.
   (C) taper.
   (D) roll.
   (E) peel.

2. Novel is to entertain as
   (A) paper is to write.
   (B) author is to persuade.
   (C) jury is to justify.
   (D) newspaper is to inform.
   (E) editorial is to read.

3. Donkey is to bray as duck is to
   (A) waddle.
   (B) bill.
   (C) quack.
   (D) fly.
   (E) goose.

4. Core is to center as
   (A) angle is to acute.
   (B) cliff is to steep.
   (C) edge is to border.
   (D) circumference is to circle.
   (E) sharp is to dull.

5. Engine is to jet as paddle is to
   (A) swim.
   (B) reprimand.
   (C) ball.
   (D) boat.
   (E) otter.

6. Pound is to weight as
   (A) radius is to point.
   (B) diameter is to across.
   (C) height is to inch.
   (D) mile is to measure.
   (E) ounce is to volume.

7. Portray is to depict as
   (A) swindle is to cheat.
   (B) influence is to bribe.
   (C) behave is to decide.
   (D) affirm is to deny.
   (E) determine is to subvert.

8. Claw is to lobster as
   (A) callous is to hand.
   (B) paw is to bear.
   (C) tail is to monkey.
   (D) ink is to octopus.
   (E) elephant is to trunk.

9. Inquire is to ask as acquire is to
   (A) obtain.
   (B) take.
   (C) agree.
   (D) concede.
   (E) leave.

10. Wool is to sweater as
    (A) cotton is to soft.
    (B) denim is to jeans.
    (C) house is to wood.
    (D) container is to store.
    (E) leather is to rugged.

## Answers and Explanations

1. **B is correct.** The relationship presented in this sequence is one of object to use. A *file* is used to *smooth* a rough surface, just as *tape* is used to *record* audio or video signals.

2. **D is correct.** This analogy is one of usage. People read a *novel*, and other works of fiction, to be *entertained*. Similarly, people read a *newspaper* in order to be *informed* about issues and events of importance.

3. **C is correct.** Initially, the relationship in this sequence may strike you as one of part to whole. However, you will need to take the analogy one step further in order to arrive at the correct answer. *Bray* is the name given to the sound a *donkey* makes just as *quack* is the name given to the sound a *duck* makes.

4. **C is correct.** This sequence tests your knowledge of synonyms. *Core* means the same as *center* in the same way that *edge* means the same as *border*.

5. **D is correct.** This is a part-to-whole analogy. An *engine* propels a *jet* just as a *paddle* propels a *boat*. An *otter* may also use its tail as a *paddle* to navigate; however, both a jet and a boat are vehicles while an otter is an animal. This distinction makes *boat* a better answer than *otter*.

6. **E is correct.** This analogy tests your knowledge of measurement units. *Weight* is measured in *pounds* and *volume* is measured in *ounces*. Choice C is incorrect because the order is reversed.

7. **A is correct.** The analogy presented in this sequence is one of synonyms. When you *portray* someone you are *depicting* that person. Similarly, when you *swindle* someone you are *cheating* that person.

8. **B is correct.** This is a part-to-whole analogy. However, in order to arrive at the correct answer, you will have to take the comparison to a second step. A *lobster* has a *claw* for a hand just as a *bear* has a *paw* for a hand. No other choice provides a similar comparison.

9. **A is correct.** This sequence tests your knowledge of synonyms. When you *inquire* about something, you *ask* about it. Similarly, when you *acquire* an item you *obtain* it. None of the other options is a synonym for *acquire*.

10. **B is correct.** In order to arrive at the correct answer for this analogy, you will have to conclude that the relationship between the first

two words is that *sweaters* are often made out of *wool*. Similarly, you will have to recognize that *jeans* are most often made from *denim*. Choice C cannot be correct because the relationship between the two words is reversed.

## Practice Set B

**Directions:** The questions that follow ask you to find relationships between words. For each question, select the answer choice that best completes the meaning of the sentence.

**Example:**
Chapter is to book as
(A) note is to letter.
(B) scene is to play.
(C) story is to novel.
(D) writer is to director.
(E) reader is to audience.

Correct Answer: B

A *chapter* is a division of a *book* and a *scene* is a division of a *play*.

1. Card is to deck as
   (A) note is to symphony.
   (B) garden is to flower.
   (C) sun is to shine.
   (D) box is to handle.
   (E) cupboard is to dish.

2. Flicker is to blaze as
   (A) pace is to walk.
   (B) gasp is to frighten.
   (C) toss is to lob.
   (D) trickle is to flow.
   (E) crease is to fold.

3. Disinfectant is to cut as detergent is to
   (A) teeth.
   (B) hands.
   (C) sink.
   (D) dry.
   (E) laundry.

4. Clock is to time as
   (A) height is to inch.
   (B) thermometer is to temperature.
   (C) weight is to mass.
   (D) length is to width.
   (E) second is to minute.

5. Cap is to bottle as
   (A) lid is to pot.
   (B) house is to roof.
   (C) handle is to pitcher.
   (D) heat is to steam.
   (E) head is to hat.

6. Tomato is to vine as
   (A) apple is to stem.
   (B) grape is to seed.
   (C) stalk is to corn.
   (D) vanilla is to bean.
   (E) coconut is to tree.

7. Salve is to balm as
   (A) snake is to bite.
   (B) sentry is to guard.
   (C) choke is to suffocate.
   (D) thorn is to prickly.
   (E) oil is to filter.

8. Storm is to flood as fire is to
   (A) water.
   (B) food.
   (C) heat.
   (D) weapon.
   (E) attack.

9. Pedestrian is to original as
   (A) bright is to brilliant.
   (B) stable is to variable.
   (C) insolent is to rude.
   (D) foolish is to absurd.
   (E) critical is to wise.

10. Golfer is to club as
    (A) dentist is to teeth.
    (B) boxer is to ring.
    (C) teacher is to student.
    (D) carpenter is to wood.
    (E) surgeon is to scalpel.


## Answers and Explanations

1. **A is correct.** The relationship provided in this sequence is one of part to whole. A *card* is part of a *deck* just as a *note* is part of a *symphony*. Choices B and D are incorrect because the relationship in each choice is inverted—that is, the whole comes before the part.

2. **D is correct.** The comparison in this sequence is one of degrees of contrast. To *flicker* is to "burn unsteadily or fitfully," while to *blaze* is to "shine brightly." Similarly, to *trickle* is to "run slowly and unsteadily," while to *flow* is to "pour forth in a steady stream."

3. **E is correct.** The analogy presented in this question is one of object to use. *Disinfectant* is used to clean a *cut* or wound, just as *detergent* is used to clean *laundry*.

4. **B is correct.** This analogy asks you to identify a measurement and the object used to register the measurement. A *clock* measures *time* just as a *thermometer* measures *temperature*. Choice A is incorrect because the order of the comparison is reversed.

5. **A is correct.** In order to arrive at the correct answer for this part-to-whole analogy, you will have to take the comparison a step further. Several of the answer choices offer sequences that are part to whole, however, only choice A is correct. A *cap* is placed on top of a *bottle* just as a *lid* is placed on top of a *pot*. Choices B and E are incorrect because they invert the order, and choice C is incorrect because a *handle* is located on the side (rather than the top) of a pitcher.

6. **E is correct.** To answer this analogy correctly, you will need to know that a *tomato* grows on a *vine*. Of the answer choices available, only choice E is correct; a *coconut* grows on a *tree*.

7. **B is correct.** This sequence tests your knowledge of synonyms. Both *salve* and *balm* are oils or resins that are rubbed onto the skin to soothe, heal, or comfort. Likewise, both a *sentry* and a *guard* are people who are posted at a given spot to monitor activity and prevent the passage of unauthorized persons.

8. **C is correct.** The relationship in the question is one of cause and effect. A *storm* is the cause and a *flood* the effect. Similarly, *fire* is the cause and *heat* the effect.

9. **B is correct.** The relationship in this analogy is one of contrast. *Pedestrian*, which means "commonplace" or "ordinary," is the opposite of *original*, which means "fresh and new." In the same way, *stable*, which means "static" or "unchangeable," is the opposite of *variable*, which means "inconstant" or "changeable."

10. **E is correct.** This analogy is one of individual to object. The tool used by a *golfer* is a *club* just as the tool used by a *surgeon* is a *scalpel*. No other choice reflects this relationship.

# CHAPTER 7

# Strategies for Sentence Completion Questions (ISEE Only)

Sentence completion questions account for 20 of the 40 questions in the Verbal Reasoning section of the ISEE. There are no sentence completion questions on the SSAT, so you can skip this chapter if you are preparing to take the SSAT.

Sentence completion questions are designed to test your knowledge of word meanings along with your ability to understand the logical structure of a sentence. On the ISEE, sentence completion questions are arranged in order of difficulty from easiest to hardest.

## Format of Sentence Completion Questions

Each sentence completion question consists of a statement with one or two blanks. Each blank indicates a missing word. Following each sentence are four words or sets of words labeled (A), (B), (C), and (D). You are to select the word or set of words that, when inserted in the sentence, best fits the meaning of the sentence as a whole.

Often more than one pair of words among the answer choices will fit the structure of the sentence that appears in the question stem. However, in order to answer sentence completion questions correctly, you must determine which pair of words *best* completes the meaning of the sentence. To do this, you must consider both word meaning and logic.

---

**ISEE Coach Says . . .**

Sentence completion questions come after synonyms in the ISEE Verbal Reasoning section, but you can choose to do these questions first if you find them easier to answer.

---

## Sample Sentence Completion Question Explained

Let's look at a sample question to see what's involved.

Although she was habitually _____, Jenna was first in line when the concert tickets went on sale.
(A) aloof
(B) impatient
(C) tardy
(D) realistic

The word *although* provides an important clue that this sentence involves a contrast. The sentence says that Jenna did something different from her usual habit. That means you are looking for a word that is the opposite of being "first in line" for tickets. Now look at each of the answer choices to find the one that best reflects this relationship.

(A) *Aloof* means "distant" or "reserved." It could be correct, but *aloof* is not really the opposite of being "first in line," so keep looking for a better answer.
(B) *Impatient* means "eager" or "excitable," which is similar to the idea of wanting to be "first in line," so you can eliminate this choice.
(C) *Tardy* means "late." Someone who is always late is not likely to be "first in line." That makes *tardy* a better choice than *aloof*, and choice C is the best answer.
(D) *Realistic* means "practical," which has nothing to do with being "first in line."

## Strategies for Answering Sentence Completion Questions

Here is a six-step strategic plan that you can use to answer sentence completion questions.

1. Read the sentence to get the overall meaning.
2. Look for clue words that show how sentence parts are related.
3. Use the clue words to anticipate the answer based on the relationship indicated.
4. Read the answer choices and select the one that is best.
5. Check your answer by reading the sentence with your answer choice in place.
6. If you still cannot determine the correct answer, eliminate answer choices that do not make sense. Then, guess from among the remaining answer choices.

---

*ISEE Coach Says . . .*
Circle clue words in your test booklet that show relationships.

---

## Using Clue Words

Use this chart to help you determine how sentence parts are frequently related in sentence completion questions.

| Logical Relationship | Clues |
|---|---|
| Contrasting ideas<br>**Even though** the plane was late taking off, we arrived at our destination right on time. | although, but, despite, even though, however, instead of, nonetheless, not, on the contrary, rather, yet |
| Complementary ideas<br>The hurricane destroyed homes all along the coastline; **furthermore,** it knocked down power lines, leaving millions without electricity. | additionally, also, and, because, besides, consequently, for, furthermore, likewise, moreover, similarly |
| Cause and effect<br>**Because** they were so hot and thirsty after the ballgame, they could hardly wait to get a cold drink from the picnic cooler. | accordingly, because, consequently, for, hence, in order to, since, so, therefore, thus |
| Definition or explanation<br>Maria was extremely **unselfish, willing to share** even her most prized possessions with her friends. | comma, semicolon, colon |

Use the six-step strategy and what you have learned about sentence logic to answer the practice sentence completion questions that follow. Then compare your answers to the explanations given.

## Sample Sentence Completion Question Set Explained

**Directions:** Each sentence below has one or two blanks. Each blank indicates that something is missing. Following each sentence are four words or sets of words labeled (A), (B), (C), and (D). You are to select the word or set of words that, when inserted in the sentence, best fits the meaning of the sentence as a whole.

---

*ISEE Coach Says . . .*
In choosing your answer, consider both word meaning and logic.

---

1. Carl had a reputation for being a _____ because he fearlessly skied down the steepest trails.
   (A) leader
   (B) dreamer
   (C) clown
   (D) daredevil

1. **D is correct.** The word *because* is a clue that the sentence shows a cause-and-effect relationship. Skiing fearlessly down the steepest trails is likely to earn someone the reputation for being a *daredevil*. No other answer choice makes sense in this context.

**ISEE Coach Says . . .**
Remember that words such as *because, for,* and *since* often signal that a sentence completion question has a structure based on cause and effect, so look for words that express an expected causal relationship.

2. The model of _____, he displayed impeccable manners and excellent taste.
   (A) duplicity
   (B) decorum
   (C) depravity
   (D) versatility

2. **B is correct.** The comma in this sentence completion question is a clue that the missing word means the same as "impeccable manners and excellent taste." *Decorum*, which means "propriety and good taste in behavior, speech, or dress," is the best choice. Choices A, C, and D are all wrong because they have nothing to do with good manners or taste. *Duplicity* (choice A) means "cunning or deception." *Depravity* (choice C) means "corruption or wickedness." *Versatility* (choice D) means "ability to do many things."

**ISEE Coach Says . . .**
Remember that the use of a comma instead of a semicolon may signal that a sentence completion question has a structure based on definition.

3. The directions to the airport were _____; consequently we missed our flight and had to stay an extra day.
   (A) clear
   (B) convenient
   (C) confusing
   (D) expert

3. **C is correct.** This question asks you to find complementary, rather than contrasting, statements. Directions that are *confusing* are most likely to result in a missed flight.

**ISEE Coach Says . . .**
Remember that words such as *additionally, consequently, besides, so,* and *also* often signal that a sentence completion question has a structure based on complementary ideas. With these questions, look for words among the answer choices that best complete the meaning of the sentence.

4. Easy to reach by car, the house was also _____ by public transportation.
   (A) accessible
   (B) isolated
   (C) enhanced
   (D) hindered

4. **A is correct.** This question asks you to find complementary, rather than contrasting, ideas. The word *also* is a clue that the word you are looking for is a word that is similar to or supports *easy to reach*. The best choice is *accessible*, which means "approachable" or "capable of being reached."

5. The detectives believed that the fingerprint on the glass was _____ evidence; it definitely placed the defendant at the scene of the crime.
   (A) negligible
   (B) incorrigible
   (C) incriminating
   (D) inevitable

5. **C is correct.** The semicolon is a clue that the second part of the sentence describes or explains the first part of the sentence. Evidence that places someone at the scene of a crime is *incriminating*; it involves the person and makes that person look guilty.

   Choice A is wrong because *negligible* means "trifling or unimportant." Choice B is wrong because *incorrigible* means "incapable of being corrected or improved." Choice D is wrong because *inevitable* means "unavoidable."

---

**ISEE Coach Says . . .**

Remember that sentence completion questions are generally arranged in order of difficulty, from easiest to hardest. Pace yourself accordingly.

---

6. Despite our best efforts to protect the environment and keep it safe, until the problems of pollution are _____, the future of our environment seems, at best, _____.
   (A) created . . . gloomy
   (B) revoked . . . secure
   (C) solved . . . uncertain
   (D) replaced . . . revered

6. **C is correct.** *Despite* is a clue that the sentence sets up a contrast. We want to keep the environment safe, but there are problems with pollution. The first blank requires a word that tells what we want to do about the problems of pollution. The best choice is to end them or solve them as in choice C. Until those problems can be *solved*, the future of the environment is not safe, but rather it is *uncertain*.

   Choice A can be eliminated because the first word makes no sense in the first blank. Choices B and D can be eliminated because the second word does not work in the second blank.

*ISEE Coach Says . . .*

Remember that words such as *although, but, despite,* and *however* often signal that a sentence completion question has a structure based on contrast, so look for words with opposite or different meanings rather than the same or similar meanings.

7. Knowledgeable dog owners recommend obtaining a purebred dog from a _____ breeder, one who is _____ and respected by customers and breeders alike.
   (A) humble . . . feared
   (B) demanding . . . flexible
   (C) churlish . . . charming
   (D) reputable . . . admired

7. **D is correct.** The comma following the word *breeder* is a clue that the words that follow will define or explain what kind of breeder is recommended. Only choice D provides two words that can define or explain each other. A *reputable* breeder is one who is *admired* and respected.

   Choice A is wrong because a *humble* breeder is not likely to be *feared*. Choice B is wrong because a *demanding* breeder is not likely to be *flexible*. Choice C is wrong because a *churlish* (rude or boorish) breeder is not likely to be *charming*.

## On Your Own

Now take the time to apply what you have just learned about the structure and types of sentence completion questions to see how well you can use the strategies. When you are finished, use the answer key to score your work.

You may find that certain types of structure are easier for you to deal with than others. Remember that sentence completion questions appear in order of their difficulty. Use Practice Set A to determine which types of questions give you the most difficulty.

Review the strategies and clues discussed above and then try Practice Set B, focusing on the kinds of items that you found difficult. Remember that the more you practice with these items, the easier they will become for you to answer correctly.

**Practice Set A**

> **Directions:** Each sentence below has one or two blanks. Each blank indicates that something is missing. Following each sentence are four words or sets of words labeled (A), (B), (C), and (D). You are to select the word or set of words that, when inserted in the sentence, best fits the meaning of the sentence as a whole.
>
> **Example:**
> 1. Easy-to-reach by car, the house was also _____ by public transportation.
> (A) accessible
> (B) isolated
> (C) enhanced
> (D) hindered
>
> Correct Answer: A

1. Knowing that her dental appointment might run late, Donelle made _____ plans to get together with Irene afterward.
   (A) absurd
   (B) tentative
   (C) authoritative
   (D) cantankerous

2. The critic dismissed the movie as _____ because of its unlikely plot and improbable dialogue.
   (A) banal
   (B) articulate
   (C) boisterous
   (D) hallowed

3. Both _____ and _____, Mrs. Dowd is typically full of enthusiasm and enjoys being around people.
   (A) fervent . . . effervescent
   (B) outgoing . . . flippant
   (C) impervious . . . cordial
   (D) cheerful . . . extroverted

4. As a way to _____ the undefeated season, the booster club presented the coach with a plaque engraved with all of the team's winning scores.
   (A) convene
   (B) contend
   (C) ascertain
   (D) commemorate

5. The concert featured a number of _____ jazz compositions, and for fans of the music, the evening was an example of harmonic _____.
   (A) spirited . . . bile
   (B) vivacious . . . impasse
   (C) vibrant . . . bliss
   (D) choleric . . . euphoria

6. Many historians of the nineteenth century believe that the railroad was the _____ of the future, the first sign of the coming of the Industrial Revolution.
   (A) bravado
   (B) harbinger
   (C) debt
   (D) entourage

7. Despite being in training, Elise knew she would soon _____ to the temptation of her mother's freshly baked cookies.
   (A) reckon
   (B) yield
   (C) obstruct
   (D) suppress

8. Unable to _____ the jury to believe his sketchy alibi, the defendant finally acknowledged committing the crimes he stood accused of.
   (A) induce
   (B) imply
   (C) deplore
   (D) raze

9. Having achieved enormous success with his books, J. D. Salinger quit publishing his work, hid from public view, and became literature's most famous _____.
   (A) reminiscence
   (B) shanty
   (C) surrogate
   (D) recluse

10. Although at first the senator had been one of the candidate's most _____ supporters, her support waned as the candidate's _____ voting record came to light.
    (A) ardent . . . dubious
    (B) facetious . . . undependable
    (C) impassioned . . . indisputable
    (D) bereft . . . suspect

**Answers and Explanations**

1. **B is correct.** *Tentative*, meaning "not fully worked out, concluded, or agreed on," is the only choice that supports the information in the sentence that the girls' plans had not been finalized.

2. **A is correct.** Because the movie features "an unlikely plot and improbable dialogue," you should be able to conclude that the critic did not like it very much. Of the four choices, *banal* (choice A), meaning "drearily commonplace and often predictable," has the strongest negative connotation.

3. **D is correct.** This type of question is known as a vocabulary-in-context question. The key to solving this type of question is to recognize that the meanings of the words you are looking for are located in the sentence. Because Mrs. Dowd is described as "typically full of enthusiasm and enjoys being around people," you should look for words that have meanings that reflect these characteristics. *Cheerful*, meaning "happy," and *extroverted*, meaning "outgoing and interested in others," is the only word pair that works in both blanks.

4. **D is correct.** Sometimes it is helpful to come up with an answer to a sentence completion question on your own, without even looking at the answer choices. For this sentence, you might come up with *mark* or *celebrate*. Now, look at the answer choices and choose the one that is closest in meaning to the words you thought of. *Commemorate*, meaning "to serve as a memorial to," is correct.

5. **C is correct.** It is often easier to solve two-blank sentence completion questions by focusing on one of the blanks and eliminating any obviously wrong answers. Looking at the first blank, you should be able to eliminate *choleric* (choice D), meaning "easily angered or bad tempered." Choices A, B, and C all offer positive words to describe the jazz compositions. Thus the sense of the sentence requires a positive word for the second blank as well. Only choice C provides two positive words, and it is the best choice.

6. **B is correct.** The comma is a clue that the words that follow will define or explain the missing word. The word that means the same as "a sign of something to come" is *harbinger*. As used in the context of this sentence, many historians believe that the railroad was the true indication of the coming Industrial Revolution. None of the other answer choices makes sense.

7. **B is correct.** The logic of the sentence indicates that despite the fact that Elise was in training, she knew that she would soon give in to the temptation of her mother's cookies. *Yield* (choice B) meaning "to give up," "to surrender," or "to submit," is the correct answer.

8. **A is correct.** The logic of this question indicates that the defendant was unable to influence the jury or convince them to accept his weak alibi. Since neither *influence* nor *convince* is among the answer choices, you

want to try to select the word you believe comes closest in meaning. *Induce* (choice A) meaning "to lead or move, as to a course of action, by influence or persuasion," is correct.

9. **D is correct.** Knowing the definitions of the words you have to choose from will help you select the correct answer to this question. Someone who withdraws from the world to live in seclusion is a recluse. Thus, choice D is the only possible answer.

10. **A is correct.** Be on the lookout for sentences that feature words and phrases such as "although," "despite," "even though," and "in spite of." Typically, these words are a sign that the sentence contains two contrasting ideas. Starting with the first blank, you can immediately eliminate choices B and D since neither *facetious*, which means "humorous," nor *bereft*, which means "deprived" or "sorrowful," makes sense as a description of a supporter. What kind of voting record is more likely to make an ardent or an impassioned supporter withdraw that support? A *dubious* record, meaning "one that is open to doubt or suspicion," or an *indisputable* record, meaning "one that is impossible to doubt"? Clearly, *dubious* is the best answer and choice A is correct.

**Practice Set B**

**Directions:** Each sentence below has one or two blanks. Each blank indicates that something is missing. Following each sentence are four words or sets of words labeled (A), (B), (C), and (D). You are to select the word or set of words that, when inserted in the sentence, best fits the meaning of the sentence as a whole.

**Example:**
1. Despite our best efforts to protect the environment and keep it safe, until the problems of pollution are _____, the future of our environment seems, at best, _____.
   (A) created…gloomy
   (B) revoked . . . secure
   (C) solved . . . uncertain
   (D) replaced . . . revered

Correct Answer: C

1. Before she opened her boutique, Jocelyn used to _____ the jewelry she made at flea markets and bazaars.
   (A) inhibit
   (B) entice
   (C) peddle
   (D) emulate

2. The _____ of traveling to see the Aurora Borealis is that while the spectacular display is well worth the trip, it is impossible to predict whether the event will take place during your travels.
   (A) configuration
   (B) prestige
   (C) ingenuity
   (D) paradox

3. Although the manager's relationship with her assistant had never turned intolerable, it had always been _____ at best.
   (A) cordial
   (B) staunch
   (C) tempestuous
   (D) tenacious

4. Before the book was _____, references to several living people were _____.
   (A) banned . . . deleted
   (B) published . . . expunged
   (C) printed . . . informed
   (D) reviewed . . . added

5. One of the most _____ songwriters of her generation, Joni Mitchell has written and recorded over 300 songs since 1968.
   (A) regal
   (B) independent
   (C) prolific
   (D) pretentious

6. The teacher had refused to disclose what would be on the test, but as far as the students could_____, it would cover everything since the midterm.
   (A) propose
   (B) deject
   (C) grovel
   (D) surmise

7. In his prime, Muhammad Ali was a(n)_____ boxer whose ability to land a knockout punch inspired fear and commanded respect among his opponents.
   (A) scathing
   (B) ostentatious
   (C) obtuse
   (D) formidable

8. After the spelling bee's nerve-wracking final round, Sheila could only _____ at her competitor's composure.
   (A) lunge
   (B) stipulate
   (C) marvel
   (D) wander

9. The scholarly and thoughtful mayor was well known for her _____ disposition.
   (A) insurgent
   (B) judicious
   (C) lenient
   (D) kinetic

10. Although the scientist's _____ was that the results could be duplicated, the review board did not find her theory _____.
    (A) assertion . . . celestial
    (B) contention . . . plausible
    (C) enigma . . . credible
    (D) avowal . . . eminent

**Answers and Explanations**

1. **C is correct.** The message that this sentence conveys is that before Jocelyn opened her boutique, she used to travel from place to place to sell her jewelry. *Peddle* (choice C), meaning "to travel about selling wares," is correct.

2. **D is correct.** The logic of this sentence is based on the problem that it is worth traveling to see the Aurora Borealis, but you cannot predict if the spectacular display will take place during your travels. A *paradox* (choice D) is "a seemingly contradictory statement that may nonetheless be true." Therefore, choice D is correct.

3. **C is correct.** The key phrases to this question are "had never turned intolerable" and "at best." With these clues, you should be able to conclude that the word you are looking for is not as extreme as "intolerable." *Tempestuous* (choice C), meaning "tumultuous or stormy," is the correct answer.

4. **B is correct.** The key word in this sentence is "before," which sets up a logical structure for the sentence and tells you that before *this* can occur, *that* must occur. Choice A can be discounted almost immediately because names do not have to be deleted before a book is banned. Choice D is incorrect because by the time a book is reviewed, it is too late to add any material to the manuscript. Choice C is wrong because *printed* is a reference to a book that is an inanimate object and therefore cannot be informed of anything. Choice B is correct.

5. **C is correct.** The word you are looking for should reflect the information the sentence provides—that Joni Mitchell has written over 300 songs since 1968. *Prolific* (choice C), meaning "producing abundant works or results," is the choice that best fits the sentence's context.

6. **D is correct.** Sometimes supplying your own answer before looking at the options can help you determine the right choice. Perhaps you came up with the word "guess" or "infer." Even if you don't know the correct answer, you should be able to eliminate some choices that are clearly wrong. *Surmise* (choice D), meaning "to infer (something) without sufficiently conclusive evidence," is correct.

7. **D is correct.** The word you are looking for is one that means "inspired fear and commanded respect." *Formidable* (choice D), meaning "arousing fear, dread, or alarm," is the correct choice.

8. **C is correct.** *Wander* (choice D) is an attractive distracter, but don't mistake it for "wonder." *Wonder* means "to be filled with curiosity or doubt," but *wander* means "to move about without a definite destination or purpose." *Marvel* (choice C), meaning "to become filled with wonder or astonishment," is the correct answer.

9. **B is correct.** The clue to this sentence is the phrase "scholarly and thoughtful," because the correct answer will likely have a definition that supports this description of the mayor. *Judicious* (choice B), meaning "sensible," "prudent," or "wise," is correct.

10. **B is correct.** Try focusing on the second blank and eliminating any obviously wrong answers. Neither *celestial* (choice A), meaning "of or relating to the sky or the heavens," nor *eminent* (choice D), meaning "prominent" or "towering above others," seem to fit the context of the sentence, and both can be discounted. Turning your attention to the first blank, you should be able to conclude that *contention* (choice B), meaning "an assertion put forward in an argument," is a better choice than *enigma* (choice C), meaning "one that is puzzling, ambiguous, or inexplicable."

# Strategies for Reading Comprehension Questions

Reading comprehension is tested on both the SSAT and the ISEE. Each exam includes one Reading Comprehension section consisting of 40 questions based on six to eight reading passages. The passages can be as short as 100 words or as long as 500 words. They cover a variety of categories from the fields of the humanities (literature, art, biography, poetry), social studies (history, economics, sociology), and science (medicine, meteorology, zoology). Each passage is followed by four to seven questions based on its content.

## Types of Reading Comprehension Questions

Whatever the subject matter of the reading passages on your test, the questions you will have to answer will fall into one of the following major categories:

- *Main Idea Questions*—test your ability to select the main idea in the passage, to determine the purpose of the passage, or to select the best title for a passage.
- *Detail Questions*—test your ability to understand specific references or to identify specific things about a passage.
- *Inference Questions*—test your ability to see relationships between ideas or to make assumptions based on information provided by the passage.
- *Tone or Mood Questions*—test your ability to determine the tone or mood of the passage, to tell whether it is serious or humorous, formal or informal, personal or impersonal, for example.
- *Vocabulary Questions*—test your ability to determine the meaning of words based on their use in the passage.
- *Organization or Logic Questions*—test your ability to recognize how a passage is organized or to follow an author's logic.

Each question is followed by four answer choices (on the ISEE) or five answer choices (on the SSAT). Your job is to identify the best answer from among the choices presented.

## How to Answer Reading Comprehension Questions

Here's a helpful four-step plan that you can use for answering reading comprehension questions.

1. Skim the questions to focus on the information you will need. Ignore the answer choices for now.
2. Read the passage to get the big picture.
   - Ask yourself: What's this passage all about? Why did the author write it?
   - Mark up the passage or make notes in the margin as you read.
3. Read the questions with the answer choices.
   - Choose the answer if you know it.
   - If not, go back to the passage to find it.
   - Use line references to help locate information.
   - Cross out answer choices you can definitely eliminate.
4. Answer every question on the ISEE, even if you have to guess. On the SSAT, guess if you can eliminate even one or two of the answer choices.
   - Try to answer all the questions based on a reading passage the first time around.
   - If you have to go back to an unanswered question, you'll have to reread the passage, which takes valuable time.

*Remember:*

- Long passages tend to be harder than short ones, so start with the shortest passage and leave the longest one for last.
- The answer to a reading question can be found in or inferred from the passage.
- An answer choice that is true is not necessarily the correct answer. The correct choice must be both a true statement and the one that best answers the question.
- When a question refers to a numbered line, go back to the passage and read the information around the line reference. It will clarify the question and help you choose the best answer.
- Read the passage. Don't try to memorize it.

## Sample Reading Comprehension Question Set Explained

Here is a sample reading passage with questions illustrating each of the six most common types of reading questions. Read the passage first. Then answer the questions based on what is stated or implied in the passage.

Can you imagine shoppers lining up just to buy ballpoint pens? It happened at Gimbel's Department Store in New York City in October 1945. Gimbel's sold out its entire stock of 10,000 pens on the very first day ballpoint pens were sold commercially anywhere in the United States.

5     Before 1945, most people wrote with fountain pens. The biggest problem with a fountain pen is that it has to be filled, sometimes more than once a day. The ballpoint pen solved this problem. However, it took nearly 60 years for inventors to get it to work properly.

    In a ballpoint pen, the writing tip is a tiny ball that rolls as you write. Part of
10 the ball is inside the pen and picks up ink from the ink supply. As the ball rolls, the ink-covered part rolls outside. The ink then flows from the ball to the paper you are writing on.

    Inventors had been working on ballpoint pens since 1888 when John Loud, an American leather tanner, patented a marking pen with a roller ball tip.
15 Loud's rolling ball pen was never produced, nor were any of the other 350 patents for ball-type pens issued over the next 50 years. The major problem with all these pens was the ink. If the ink was too watery, the pens would leak. If the ink was too thick, it would harden inside the pen. Depending on the temperature, the ink would sometimes do both. Ballpoint pens had another
20 problem, too. Because they depended on gravity to carry the ink down to the rolling ball at the bottom of the pen, ballpoints had to be held straight up, but most people tilt a pen when they write.

    Two Hungarian brothers, Georg and Ladislas Biro, found the solution to both problems. Working as a journalist, Georg Biro noticed that newspaper ink
25 dried quickly, leaving the paper smudge-free. This gave him the idea to use this syrupy ink for pens. However, the thicker ink would not flow from a regular metal tip, so he fitted his pen with a ball bearing that acted like a sponge. The roller ball soaked up ink from the tube inside the pen. Now the pen could be held at an angle.

30     The Biro brothers filed a patent for their ballpoint pen in Paris in 1938, just after they escaped the Nazi regime in Hungary. They emigrated to Argentina and established a successful business selling pens that could "write for a year without refilling." In 1945, Milton Reynolds, a Chicago businessman, discovered the Biro brothers' invention while vacationing in Argentina. Ignoring patent rights, Reynolds
35 copied the Biro design and in less than four months the Reynolds Pen Company was manufacturing millions of ballpoint pens. Reynolds signed a deal with Gimbel's, making it the first retail store in America to sell his pens. Gimbel's took out a full-page ad in *The New York Times* to advertise the "fantastic . . . miraculous . . . guaranteed" new pens for $12.50. Five thousand people crowded the sidewalk before the store
40 opened the next day, and Gimbel's sold all 10,000 pens before the end of the day. Within a few years, the pen that took over 50 years to reach the market would become the most used pen in the world.

---

***SSAT/ISEE Coach Says . . .***
Feel free to mark up the passage as you read. Highlight main ideas, important supporting details, and words that indicate special relationships.

1. Which of the following is the best title for this selection?
   (A) A Short History of the Ballpoint Pen.
   (B) The Biro Brothers: Millions of Dollars from Millions of Pens.
   (C) Ballpoint Pens Change Writing Habits around the World.
   (D) Miraculous Writing Tool Sweeps the Nation.
   (E) How Gimbel's Sold Thousands of Ballpoint Pens.

This is a **main idea question**. A good title suggests both the topic and the purpose of a selection. In this case the topic is the ballpoint pen and the purpose is to provide a brief history of its development from the marking pen invented by John Loud in 1888, to the Biro pen patented in 1938, to the Reynolds pen sold at Gimbel's in 1945. Choice A is the best title for this selection.

Choice B is wrong because it concerns only the Biro brothers, and the one who seemed to make millions of dollars from millions of pens was Milton Reynolds.

Choice C is wrong because the article never explains how ballpoint pens changed writing habits around the world.

Choice D is wrong because the passage does not focus on how a miraculous writing tool swept the nation.

Choice E is wrong because Gimbel's is the focus of only the first and last paragraphs, not of the passage as a whole.

---

**SSAT/ISEE Coach Says . . .**
Remember that virtually every sentence in a well-written passage relates to the main idea.

---

2. From the passage you can infer that after 1945
   (A) fountain pens became cheaper and more reliable.
   (B) people spent more time writing, since they didn't have to refill their pens.
   (C) people used fewer fountain pens.
   (D) people got used to holding pens straight up when they wrote.
   (E) expensive ballpoint pens became a status symbol.

This **inference question** asks you to draw a conclusion based on the information that is given in the passage. According to the passage, before 1945 "most people wrote with fountain pens." Now, however, the ballpoint pen has become "the most used pen in the world." From this information, you can reasonably conclude that with the growing popularity of the ballpoint pen, fewer and fewer fountain pens were used in the years after 1945.

Choice C is the correct answer.

Choices A, B, and E are not supported by information in the passage.

Choice D is mentioned as one of the problems of ballpoint pens that was resolved by the Biro brothers.

*SSAT/ISEE Coach Says . . .*
Find specific words and phrases that support your answer choice.

3. According to the article, which of the statements is true about the ink used in newspaper printing compared to the ink used in fountain pens?
   (A) It is cheaper.
   (B) It is thinner.
   (C) It hardens inside the pen.
   (D) It dries mores quickly.
   (E) It smudges more easily.

This **detail question** asks you to locate a particular piece of information in the passage. Newspaper ink is mentioned in the fifth paragraph. "Working as a journalist, Georg Biro noticed that newspaper ink dried quickly, leaving the paper smudge-free." Thus choice D is the best answer.

Choice A is incorrect because the passage never mentions the cost of the ink.

Choice B is incorrect because the passage mentions that the "syrupy" newspaper ink was thicker than fountain pen ink.

Choice C is incorrect because the passage mentions that one of the problems Biro solved by using newspaper ink was the problem of the ink hardening inside the pen.

Choice E is incorrect because the passage states that the newspaper ink "dried quickly, leaving the paper smudge-free."

*SSAT/ISEE Coach Says . . .*
Locate the key words "newspaper ink" and then read the surrounding sentences to find your answer.

4. The tone of the passage indicates that the author considers the invention of the ballpoint pen to be
   (A) insignificant.
   (B) impressive.
   (C) unfortunate.
   (D) miraculous.
   (F) disappointing.

This is a **tone question**. It asks you to determine the author's attitude or point of view toward the topic. Tone is revealed by the author's choice of words and details. In this passage, phrases such as "Gimbel's sold out its entire stock of 10,000 pens on the very first day," "it took nearly 60 years for inventors to get it to work properly," "five thousand people crowded the sidewalk," and "within a few years, the pen that took over 50 years to reach the market would become the most used pen in the world" suggest that the author thought the invention of the ballpoint pen was a notable or impressive achievement. Choice B is correct.

Choices A, C, and E are incorrect because they are negative words, and the author obviously has a positive attitude toward the invention of the ballpoint pen.

Choice D reflects a positive attitude, but it is too extreme to describe this account of the history of the ballpoint pen.

---

**SSAT/ISEE Coach Says . . .**
Look carefully at the way the author uses words.

---

5. In this passage, the term "patent" refers to
   (A) a ballpoint pen.
   (B) a fountain pen.
   (C) John Loud's marking pen.
   (D) a license or exclusive right for an invention.
   (E) a pen that could write for a year without refilling.

This is a **vocabulary question**. The word *patent* appears several times in this passage: John Loud "patented a marking pen," the Biro brothers "filed a patent for their ballpoint pen," Milton Reynolds ignored "patent rights." From these uses you should be able to conclude that a patent is a license or an exclusive right for a new product or process. Choice D is correct.

---

**SSAT/ISEE Coach Says . . .**
Substituting each answer choice in the original sentences is helpful in eliminating some obviously wrong answers.

---

6. Which of the following best describes the relationship of the first paragraph to the passage as a whole?
   (A) The first paragraph presents an interesting anecdote that introduces the topic of the selection.
   (B) The first paragraph begins a chronological look at the development of the ballpoint pen.
   (C) The first paragraph identifies key developments that are explained in the rest of the selection.
   (D) The first paragraph presents a theory about ballpoint pens that is proved by the rest of the selection.
   (E) The first paragraph criticizes early attempts at the development of the ballpoint pen.

This **organization question** tests your ability to recognize how the author has organized a passage. In this case, the first paragraph tells what happened when ballpoint pens were first offered for sale in the United States. This anecdote is intended to catch the reader's interest, which it does by creating the image of thousands of people waiting in line to buy ballpoint pens, and to introduce the topic of the selection, which is the development of these pens. Choice A is correct.

Choice B is wrong because the passage begins with the successful introduction of the ballpoint pen and then goes back in time to show how the pen was developed.

Choices C and D are wrong because the paragraph is not a presentation of key developments or of a theory.

Choice E is wrong because the paragraph is not critical of early attempts to develop the ballpoint pen.

---

***SSAT/ISEE Coach Says . . .***
Go back and reread the lines referenced in the question.

---

## Vocabulary-in-Context Questions

Some reading comprehension questions ask you to define the meaning of a word as it is used in the context of the passage that you have read. Such vocabulary-in-context questions will always give you a line indicator or a paragraph reference so that you can easily find the word in the passage.

Some vocabulary-in-context questions deal with difficult words that you likely do not know. In other cases, a vocabulary-in-context question will be about an unusual meaning of an easier, familiar word. Regardless of which type of vocabulary-in-context question you are dealing with, your goal is always the same: find the meaning of the word as it is used within the context of the passage.

### Strategies for Vocabulary-in-Context Questions

Below you will find four simple strategies that will help you to answer vocabulary-in-context questions correctly.

1. Use the line reference to locate the word.
2. Read the entire sentence.
3. Try to come up with a synonym on your own, and then look for your word among the answer choices.
4. If you can't come up with a synonym, try substituting each answer choice in the original sentence to see which one makes the most sense.

### Sample Vocabulary-in-Context Questions Explained

Use the vocabulary strategies you studied earlier to answer the sample questions that follow the passage.

**Directions:** The passage below is followed by questions based on its content. Answer each question on the basis of what is stated or implied in the passage and the introductory material.

Questions 1–3 are based on the following passage.

Participation in regular physical activity—at least 30 minutes of moderate activity at least five days per week, or 20 minutes of vigorous physical activity at least three times per week—is critical to sustaining good health. Youth should strive for at least one hour of exercise a day. Regular physical
5 activity has beneficial effects on most (if not all) organ systems, and consequently it helps prevent a broad range of health problems and diseases. People of all ages, both male and female, derive substantial health benefits from physical activity.

Regular physical activity can help improve the lives of young people beyond
10 its effects on physical health. Although research has not been conducted to conclusively demonstrate a direct link between physical activity and improved academic performance, such a link might be expected. Studies have found participation in physical activity increases adolescents' self-esteem and reduces anxiety and stress. Through its effects on mental health, physical activity may
15 help increase students' capacity for learning. One study found that spending more time in physical education did not have harmful effects on the standardized academic achievement test scores of elementary school students; in fact, there was some evidence that participation in a two-year health-related physical education program had several significant favorable effects on academic
20 achievement.

1. In line 3, "critical" most nearly means
   (A) decisive.
   (B) demeaning.
   (C) dangerous.
   (D) cynical.
   (E) risky.

1. **A is correct.** "Critical" is a multiple-meaning word that can have any of the meanings offered. To determine which meaning is correct, locate the sentence in which critical is used: "Participation in regular physical activity . . . is critical to sustaining good health." Try substituting each answer choice in the original sentence and you will see that in this context only *decisive* makes sense.

2. In line 14, "stress" most nearly means
   (A) force.
   (B) emphasis.
   (C) importance.
   (D) tension.
   (E) significance.

2. **D is correct.** "Stress" can mean any of the words offered as answer choices, depending upon the context in which it is used. In this case, the word *stress* occurs in the following sentence: "Studies have found participation in physical activity increases adolescents' self-esteem and reduces anxiety and stress." If you substitute each answer choice in the sentence, you will see that the only one that makes sense is "tension."

3. In line 15, "capacity" most nearly means
   (A) commitment.
   (B) content.
   (C) aptitude.
   (D) magnitude.
   (E) creativity.

3. **C is correct.** The word *capacity* is used in this sentence: "Through its effects on mental health, physical activity may help increase students' capacity for learning." The only answer choice that makes sense in this context is "aptitude."

## On Your Own

Below you will find a variety of types of passages and questions that you encounter on the SSAT and ISEE reading tests.

- Review the strategies discussed above before you try Practice Set A. You may find that certain types of questions are easier for you to deal with than others. For example, vocabulary-in-context questions are likely to be easier to answer than inference questions.
- Focus on the kinds of items that you found difficult as you worked through the samples. Use the practice set to determine which types of questions continue to give you difficulty. Then, complete Practice Set B. Remember that the more you practice with these items, the less troublesome you are likely to find them.

**Practice Set A**

**Directions:** Each reading passage is followed by questions about it. Answer the questions that follow a passage on the basis of what is stated or implied in that passage. For each question, circle the letter of the answer you think is best.

**Nature**
As a fond mother, when the day is o'er,
Leads by the hand her little child to bed,
Half willing, half reluctant to be led,
And leave his broken playthings on the floor,
5 Still gazing at them through the open door,
Nor wholly reassured and comforted
By promises of others in their stead,

Which, though more splendid, may not please him more;
So Nature deals with us, and takes away
10 Our playthings one by one, and by the hand
Leads us to rest so gently, that we go
Scarce knowing if we wish to go or stay,
Being too full of sleep to understand
How far the unknown transcends the what we know.

Henry Wadsworth Longfellow

1. In this poem, the author compares
    (A) a mother to a child.
    (B) childhood to adulthood.
    (C) life to sleep.
    (D) death to sleep.
    (E) a mother to Mother Nature.

2. Which best describes the author's attitude toward death?
    (A) Children are not afraid of death.
    (B) Death is not to be feared.
    (C) The death of a child is a terrible thing.
    (D) A sudden death is better than a long and lingering one.
    (E) Death brings an end to illness and pain.

3. What are the "playthings" mentioned in line 10?
    (A) a child's toys
    (B) adult status symbols
    (C) the people and things that fill our lives
    (D) irritating things that happen in life
    (E) favorite activities

4. The tone of this poem is best described as
    (A) calm and reassuring.
    (B) hostile and angry.
    (C) troubled and sad.
    (D) full of fear.
    (E) troubled and uncertain.

5. In which line does the speaker switch points of view?
    (A) 2
    (B) 5
    (C) 9
    (D) 12
    (E) 14

One of the most impressive feats in nature is the ability of birds to travel hundreds or even thousands of miles to distant lands where they breed and spend the winter. Migration is not just the seasonal movement of birds each fall and spring. In every month, some percentage of the Western Hemisphere's five billion birds are in the midst of migration. Their journeys can take weeks or months to complete, depending on the species and difficulties encountered along the way.

Impending cold weather is one of a number of factors that encourage birds to migrate. The main trigger is depletion of the food supply, as when insects go into hibernation or when snow cover makes seeds inaccessible. Diminishing daylight means that there is less time to feed, and birds begin to have difficulty maintaining sufficient energy stores to cope with lower temperatures. This cause-and-effect relationship creates another signal that it is time to head south. Once the instinct to migrate is triggered, activities such as feeding, resting, and aggression are often suppressed, allowing birds to focus on little else but reaching their destination.

Most large-scale migration occurs at night when the air is cool and calm and there are few predators. Warblers, vireos, thrushes, and tanagers are all night-time flyers, as are shorebirds. Daylight migrants include ducks, geese, cranes, loons, swallows, and swifts. Soaring birds, such as hawks and vultures, migrate during the day to take advantage of the warm updrafts created by heat from the sun.

Migrating birds use mountain ranges, narrow peninsulas, and coastlines as landmarks to help them navigate. They are also known to use the setting sun and star patterns for migration, and some bird species appear to rely on the magnetic field of the Earth. Overcast or foggy nights can hamper the progress of birds that rely on the stars for navigational cues. Birds have help, however, from seasonal wind patterns that blow in the general direction they need to travel. Whatever the means of navigation, it is extraordinary that many species are capable of returning not only to their home ranges, but to their exact nesting or winter feeding sites.

6. This passage is primarily about
    (A) how and why birds migrate.
    (B) using landmarks to navigate.
    (C) reasons why birds fly at night.
    (D) locating the right nesting and feeding sites.
    (E) preparations for a long flight.

7. All of the following prefer to migrate at night EXCEPT:
    (A) thrushes.
    (B) warblers.
    (C) hawks.
    (D) shorebirds.
    (E) tanagers.

8. Which of the following best describes the author's attitude toward migration?
   (A) hostile
   (B) admiring
   (C) amused
   (D) skeptical
   (E) concerned

9. The author suggests that most large-scale migration occurs at night primarily because
   (A) there are few predators at night.
   (B) birds can fly faster at night.
   (C) birds are better able to take advantage of seasonal wind patterns at night.
   (D) birds have good night vision.
   (E) the stars make it easier for birds to navigate.

10. The instinct to migrate is triggered primarily by
   (A) longer days.
   (B) warmer temperatures.
   (C) increased activity of predators.
   (D) insufficient food supplies.
   (E) the need to hibernate.

11. According to the passage, which of the following is NOT true?
   (A) Migrations can take months to complete.
   (B) Spring and fall are the times when birds migrate.
   (C) Many species return to their exact nesting sites.
   (D) During migration, instincts such as feeding and resting may be suppressed.
   (E) Seasonal wind patterns blow in the direction birds need to travel.

There was at this time among the Onondagas a chief of high rank whose name, variously written—Hiawatha, Hayonwatha, Ayongwhata, Taoungwatha— is rendered, "he who seeks the wampum belt." He had made himself greatly esteemed by his wisdom and his benevolence. He was now past middle age.
5  Though many of his friends and relatives had perished by the machinations of Atotarho, he himself had been spared. The qualities which gained him general respect had, perhaps, not been without influence even on that redoubtable chief. Hiawatha had long beheld with grief the evils which afflicted not only his own nation, but all the other tribes about them, through the continual wars in which
10  they were engaged, and the misgovernment and miseries at home which these wars produced. With much meditation he had elaborated in his mind the scheme of a vast confederation which would ensure universal peace. In the mere plan of a confederation there was nothing new. There are probably few, if any, Indian tribes which have not, at one time or another, been members of a league or con-
15  federacy. It may almost be said to be their normal condition. But the plan which Hiawatha had evolved differed from all others in two particulars. The system which he devised was to be not a loose and transitory league, but a permanent

government. While each nation was to retain its own council and its management of local affairs, the general control was to be lodged in a federal senate,
20 composed of representatives elected by each nation, holding office during good behavior, and acknowledged as ruling chiefs throughout the whole confederacy. Still further, and more remarkably, the confederation was not to be a limited one. It was to be indefinitely expansible. The avowed design of its proposer was to abolish war altogether. He wished the federation to extend until all the tribes of
25 men should be included in it, and peace should everywhere reign. Such is the positive testimony of the Iroquois themselves; and their statement, as will be seen, is supported by historical evidence.

Horatio Hale from *Hiawatha and the Iroquois Confederation*

12. Which of the following best describes the author's attitude toward Hiawatha?
    (A) amused
    (B) dubious
    (C) hostile
    (D) respectful
    (E) unimpressed

13. It can be inferred from the passage that the Onondagas looked upon Hiawatha as
    (A) fierce and warlike.
    (B) ruthless and unsparing.
    (C) caring and wise.
    (D) old and frail.
    (E) cautious and indecisive.

14. As used in line 3, the word *rendered* most nearly means
    (A) provided.
    (B) translated.
    (C) surrendered.
    (D) handed down.
    (E) caused to become.

15. According to the passage, Hiawatha's plan for a confederation of Indian nations contained all of the following provisions EXCEPT:
    (A) It was to be a permanent government.
    (B) Each nation was to retain its own council and manage its local affairs.
    (C) Control was to be in the hands of a federal senate composed of elected representatives.
    (D) Membership in the confederation was open to all nations.
    (E) Only the head chief could declare war.

16. The author's main purpose for writing this passage is to
    (A) describe the conditions under which native peoples lived at the time.
    (B) inform readers about Hiawatha's plan for a confederacy of Indian nations.
    (C) compare Hiawatha to other chiefs of the time.
    (D) dispel myths about Hiawatha.
    (E) describe the derivation of the name Hiawatha.

17. The style of the passage is most like that found in a
    (A) personal letter.
    (B) novel about native peoples.
    (C) history textbook.
    (D) explorer's diary.
    (E) autobiography.

     Today, the U.S. Environmental Protection Agency announced the availability of an additional $10 million in grants to eligible states, territories, and tribes to monitor beach water quality. This brings the five-year total to nearly $42 million. As a critical part of the Administration's Clean Beaches Plan, this is the fifth year
5  that grants are being made available since the Beaches Environmental Assessment and Coastal Health (BEACH) Act passed in October 2000.
     "Americans want clean and healthy beaches," said EPA's Assistant Administrator for Water, Ben Grumbles. "These funds will help improve water monitoring and public information programs to alert beachgoers about the health of their beaches."
10     The grants are designed to support water monitoring, which helps to ensure that the public receives information on how to protect their health when visiting beaches. Beach water monitoring results are used to issue warnings and closures if bacteria levels are at unsafe levels and to help identify actions needed to reduce pollution.
15     In addition, as part of the Clean Beaches Plan, the EPA is developing new technology that will provide faster test results, which will enable local health agencies to more quickly determine if a beach should be open for swimming.

18. This passage is mainly about
    (A) the Environmental Protection Agency.
    (B) how to get an EPA grant.
    (C) monitoring the quality of beach water.
    (D) developing better ways to test water.
    (E) what the public can do to ensure beach safety.

19. This passage can best be described as a
    (A) news item.
    (B) textbook excerpt.
    (C) biography.
    (D) short story.
    (E) research report.

20. Beach water monitoring results are used primarily to
    (A) direct swimmers to the nearest public beaches.
    (B) close beaches that do not test water.
    (C) alert swimmers to rough surf conditions.
    (D) issue warnings when bacteria levels are too high.
    (E) make the public aware of what they can do to keep beaches clean.

21. Which of the following questions is answered by information in the passage?
    (A) What is the Environmental Protection Agency?
    (B) When was the Beaches Environmental Assessment and Coastal Health Act passed?
    (C) How much grant money is available to a particular state, territory, or tribe?
    (D) When should grants be submitted?
    (E) How many individual grants have been awarded over the past five years?

22. The tone of the passage is best described as
    (A) humorous.
    (B) cautious.
    (C) impersonal.
    (D) argumentative.
    (E) enthusiastic.


**End of Practice Set A**

**Answers and Explanations**

1. **D is correct.** The poet compares a mother leading her child to sleep in lines 1–8 to Nature leading a person to his or her final sleep (or death) in lines 9–14.

2. **B is correct.** By comparing death to a "fond mother" (line 1) leading her child to sleep, the author paints a soft image of death as a gentle rest (line 11), not something to be feared.

3. **C is correct.** The author mentions "playthings" twice in this poem. In lines 3–4, he says that the child is reluctant to "leave his broken playthings on the floor." In lines 9–10, the author says that Nature "takes away our playthings one by one" and leads us gently to rest. The first mention of playthings refers to a child's toys. The second mention of playthings refers to all the people and things that fill an adult's life and that are taken away by death.

4. **A is correct.** Tone is the author's attitude or point of view toward a topic. It is conveyed through the author's word choice. Here, the tone is calm and reassuring as evidenced by the mother and child image and the use of words such as "fond mother" and "leads us to rest so gently." The last line "How far the unknown transcends the what we know" indicates the author's belief that the afterlife will be better than the life we know.

5. **C is correct.** Lines 1–8 describe a mother leading her child to bed at the end of the day. Lines 9–14 describe Nature leading a man or woman to the final sleep at the end of life. The change is signaled by line 9 ("So nature deals with us, and takes away").

6. **A is correct.** The entire passage concerns how and why birds migrate. In contrast, choices B and D are mentioned only in paragraph 4 and choice C is mentioned only in paragraph 3. Choice E is not covered by this passage.

7. **C is correct.** The answer to this question can be found in the third paragraph: "Warblers, vireos, thrushes, and tanagers are all nighttime flyers, as are shorebirds. . . . Soaring birds, such as hawks and vultures, migrate during the day to take advantage of the warm updrafts created by heat from the sun."

8. **B is correct.** Attitude is revealed through the author's word choice. In this case, the author refers to migration as "one of the most impressive feats in nature" and later calls it "extraordinary" that many species are able to return to their exact nesting or feeding sites. This highly positive language makes it apparent that the author is admiring of the act of nature known as migration.

9. **A is correct.** The first sentence of the third paragraph lists two reasons why most large-scale migration occurs at night: "the air is cool and calm and there are few predators." Choice B is incorrect because the passage never mentions whether birds fly faster by day or by night. Choice C is incorrect because the passage states just the opposite. Choices D and E may be correct, but neither one is specifically cited in the passage as being a reason for migration to take place at night.

10. **D is correct.** This detail is found in paragraph 2, which states that the main trigger for migration "is depletion of the food supply, as when insets go into hibernation or when snow cover makes seeds inaccessible." Choice A is incorrect because migration is triggered by

"diminishing daylight," not longer days. Choice B is incorrect because "impending cold weather," not warmer weather, is a factor that encourages migration. Choice C is incorrect because it is not supported by information in the passage. Choice E is incorrect because it is the insects, not the birds, that hibernate in winter.

11. **B is correct.** As stated in the first paragraph, "Migration is *not* just the seasonal movement of birds each fall and spring. In every month, some percentage of the Western Hemisphere's five billion birds are in the midst of migration." Choice A is stated in the last sentence of paragraph 1. Choice C is stated in the last sentence of the passage. Choice D is stated in the last sentence of paragraph 2. Choice E is stated in the next-to-last sentence of the passage.

12. **D is correct.** The author uses highly positive words to describe Hiawatha: "esteemed by his wisdom and his benevolence," possessed of "qualities which gained him general respect," and capable of devising a system of government "which would ensure universal peace." Such language indicates that the author is respectful of Hiawatha.

13. **C is correct.** The first sentence describes Hiawatha as an Onondaga chief "of high rank." The next sentence goes on to say, "He had made himself greatly esteemed by his wisdom and his benevolence."

14. **B is correct.** The word *rendered* can have any of the meanings offered as choices. However, in this context the one that fits best is "translated." In other words, the name Hiawatha means "he who seeks the wampum belt."

15. **E is correct.** The aim of the confederation was "to abolish war altogether." Nowhere in the passage is there any mention of declaring war, by the head chief or by anyone else. Choice A is specifically mentioned in lines 17–18: "The system which he devised was to be not a loose and transitory league, but a permanent government." Choice B is specifically noted in line 19: "each nation was to retain its own council and its management of local affairs." Choice C is mentioned in lines 20–21: "the general control was to be lodged in a federal senate, composed of representatives elected by each nation." Choice D is mentioned in lines 23–26: "the confederation was not to be a limited one . . . . He wished the federation to extend until all the tribes of men should be included in it."

16. **B is correct.** The author's main purpose is to provide information about Hiawatha's plan for a confederacy of Indian nations and to show how this plan differed from other similar plans. Choices A and C are wrong because the passage does not describe living conditions or compare Hiawatha to other chiefs. Choice D is wrong because there is no mention of myths about Hiawatha. Choice E is wrong because the translation of the name Hiawatha is the focus of only one sentence in the passage.

17. **C is correct.** The language in this selection may seem old-fashioned, but it is actually representative of the language used in 1881 when this passage was written. Choice A is incorrect because the passage is too formal in tone for a personal letter. Choice B is wrong because the passage is fact, not fiction. Choices D and E are wrong because the passage is written in the third person (using pronouns such as *he* and *him*), not the first person (using pronouns such as *I* and *me*). The style of the passage most closely resembles that of a history textbook or historical research published in the nineteenth century.

18. **C is correct.** The entire passage concerns monitoring the quality of beach water. The aspects of the topic covered include a source of funds for testing beach water, benefits of water monitoring, new technology for faster results, where to find more information about the program, and the grants.

19. **A is correct.** The word *today* at the start of the passage is a clue that this is a timely announcement typical of a news item. The first paragraph also follows the classic news article structure by answering these questions: Who? (U.S. Environmental Protection Agency) What? (announced availability of $10 million in grants) When? (today) Why? (to monitor beach water quality as part of the Clean Beaches Plan).

20. **D is correct.** As stated in paragraph 3, "Beach water monitoring results are used to issue warnings and closures if bacteria levels are at unsafe levels and to help identify actions needed to reduce pollution." Choice A is wrong because water monitoring has nothing to do with directing swimmers to a public beach. Choice B is wrong because water monitoring results can be used to close beaches that have unsafe bacterial levels, not those that do not test their waters. Choice C is wrong because water monitoring tests for bacteria in the water, not for surf conditions. Choice E is wrong because the water monitoring results do not tell people what they can do to keep beaches clean.

21. **B is correct.** As stated in the first paragraph, the Beaches Environmental Assessment and Coastal Health Act was passed in October 2000. The passage does not provide answers for choices A, C, D, or E.

22. **C is correct.** The passage merely states the facts in a straightforward and impersonal way. Choice A is wrong because the author makes no attempt to be humorous about the topic. Choice B is wrong because the passage contains no words of caution. Choices D and E are wrong because nothing in the passage could be considered either argumentative or enthusiastic.

**Practice Set B**

**Directions:** Each reading passage is followed by questions about it. Answer the questions that follow a passage on the basis of what is stated or implied in that passage. For each question, circle the letter of the answer you think is best.

When the door below was opened, a thick stream of men forced a way down the stairs, which were of an extraordinary narrowness and seemed only wide enough for one at a time. Yet they somehow went down almost three abreast. It was a difficult and painful operation.

5　The crowd was like a turbulent water forcing itself through one tiny outlet. The men in the rear, excited by the success of the others, made frantic exertions, for it seemed that this large band would more than fill the quarters and that many would be left upon the pavements. It would be disastrous to be of the last, and accordingly men, with the snow biting their faces, writhed and twisted with their might. One

10　expected that from the tremendous pressure, the narrow passage to the basement door would be so choked and clogged with human limbs and bodies that movement would be impossible. Once indeed the crowd was forced to stop, and a cry went along that a man had been injured at the foot of the stairs. But presently the slow movement began again, and the policeman fought at the top of the flight to

15　ease the pressure on those who were going down.

A reddish light from a window fell upon the faces of the men when they, in turn, arrived at the last three steps and were about to enter. One could then note a change of expression that had come over their features. As they thus stood upon the threshold of their hopes, they looked suddenly content and compla-

20　cent. The fire had passed from their eyes and the snarl had vanished from their lips. The very force of the crowd in the rear, which had previously vexed them, was regarded from another point of view, for it now made it inevitable that they should go through the little doors into the place that was cheery and warm with light.

25　The tossing crowd on the sidewalk grew smaller and smaller. The snow beat with merciless persistence upon the bowed heads of those who waited. The wind drove it up from the pavements in frantic forms of winding white, and it seethed in circles about the huddled forms, passing in, one by one, three by three, out of the storm.

Stephen Crane from "The Men in the Storm"

1. According to the author, the men forcing their way down the stairs most closely resembled which of the following?
   (A) a swirling blizzard
   (B) a raging stream
   (C) a marching band
   (D) a roaring fire
   (E) a strong wind

2. The men are pushing their way down the stairs primarily because they want to
   (A) escape from the police.
   (B) get medical help.
   (C) find shelter from the storm.
   (D) go home.
   (E) avoid being crushed by the crowd.

3. Based on the passage, each of the following words may be used to describe the men waiting at the top of the stairs EXCEPT
   (A) frozen.
   (B) snarling.
   (C) frantic.
   (D) vexed.
   (E) complacent.

4. Which of the following caused the change of expression to come over the faces of the men when they reached the last three steps?
   (A) They knew that the snowstorm was over.
   (B) They knew that they would make it into the shelter.
   (C) They found other family members inside.
   (D) They watched in dismay as a fire broke out.
   (E) Their faces were illuminated by a red light.

5. The passage suggests that the men in the story regard the room at the foot of the stairs as a
   (A) place to be feared.
   (B) place to be avoided.
   (C) welcoming place.
   (D) prison.
   (E) place for sick people.

6. This passage can best be described as an excerpt from
   (A) a news article.
   (B) a research study.
   (C) an epic poem.
   (D) a short story.
   (E) an autobiography.

The results of a four-year study of the Arctic, conducted by an international team of 300 scientists, show that the region is warming much more rapidly than previously known. Some areas in the Arctic have warmed 10 times as fast as the world as a whole, which has warmed an average of 1 degree Fahrenheit ($\frac{5}{9}$°C)
5   over the past century. Increasing greenhouse gases from human activities are projected to make the Arctic warmer still.

At least half of the summer sea ice in the Arctic is projected to melt by the end of this century, along with a significant portion of the Greenland Ice Sheet, because the region is expected to warm an additional 7 to 13°F (4–7°C) by 2100.
10 These changes will have major global impacts. They will contribute to global sea-level rise and intensify global warming. In addition, the disappearance of summer sea ice is likely to have devastating consequences for some arctic animal species such as ice-living seals, and for local people for whom these animals are a primary food source, according to the final report of the Arctic Climate Impact
15 Assessment (ACIA).

The assessment was commissioned by the Arctic Council (a ministerial inter-governmental forum comprised of the eight Arctic countries, and six Indigenous Peoples organizations) and the International Arctic Science Committee (an international scientific organization appointed by 18 national academies of science).
20 The assessment's projections are based on a moderate estimate of future emissions of carbon dioxide and other greenhouse gases. They incorporate results from five major global climate models used by the Intergovernmental Panel on Climate Change.

"The impacts of global warming are affecting people *now* in the Arctic," says
25 Robert Corell, chair of the ACIA. "The Arctic is experiencing some of the most rapid and severe climate change on earth. The impacts of climate change on the region and the globe are projected to increase substantially in the years to come."

7. The primary purpose of this passage is to
    (A) argue the need for immediate action to halt Arctic warming.
    (B) record the impact of Arctic warming on the Greenland Ice Sheet.
    (C) illustrate the impact of global warming on the world as a whole.
    (D) relate the results of a research study of the Arctic.
    (E) compare Arctic warming with warming in the world as a whole.

8. In line 6, "projected" most nearly means
    (A) promoted.
    (B) predicted.
    (C) designed.
    (D) delegated.
    (E) prepared.

9. Which of the following best describes the Arctic Council?
    (A) an international scientific organization.
    (B) an intergovernmental forum.
    (C) an organization commissioned to study global warming.
    (D) an organization that governs Arctic nations.
    (E) an organization of Indigenous Peoples.

10. According to the passage, all of the following are true about Arctic warming EXCEPT:

(A) The Arctic is warming more rapidly than the world as a whole.

(B) Melting summer sea ice will have major global impacts.

(C) The world as a whole has warmed an average of 1 degree F ($\frac{5}{9}$ degree C) over the past century.

(D) The impacts of global warming are already affecting people in the Arctic.

(E) Climate change in the Arctic is less pronounced than it is in other parts of the world.

11. Melting sea ice will result in

I. a rise in global sea level

II. more greenhouse gases

III. intensified global warming

(A) II only

(B) III only

(C) I and III only

(D) I, II, and III

(E) Neither I, II, or III

12. According to the passage, it is reasonable to assume that

(A) Arctic warming is affected by greenhouse gases.

(B) the Greenland Ice Sheet will disappear by 2100.

(C) Arctic temperatures will return to normal by the end of this century.

(D) the impact of climate change on the Arctic will decrease over time.

(E) increasing arctic temperatures primarily affect arctic wildlife.

As president of the United States, Thomas Jefferson was responsible for one of the largest and most peaceful land transactions this country has ever known. In 1803, Jefferson purchased 828,000 square miles, an area known then as the Louisiana Territory, from France in exchange for $15 million. At the time this
5  acquisition was met with both joy and opposition. Those who praised Jefferson saw the Louisiana Territory as a vast region with unlimited natural resources and economic opportunities. Those who opposed the purchase saw the territory as nothing but a burden and a waste of money. To Jefferson, this purchase was a chance of a lifetime for both him and the country. Practically overnight, the country doubled
10 in size adding new resources to its already impressive supply. Jefferson believed that out west there was "Land enough for our descendants to the thousandth and thousandth generation." There was a potential for endless economic opportunities and new trade routes. Overall, the Louisiana Purchase provided Jefferson with an opportunity to build a strong independent nation that is founded upon democracy
15 and freedom.

Thomas Jefferson looked at the West the way people look at outer space today. For him, the West evoked the same excitement and wonder that many people feel today as they gaze at the stars and dream of traveling to other galaxies. Jefferson believed that in the West anything could exist. However, the purchase of the

20 Louisiana Territory raised many questions. At that time the Louisiana Territory extended from the Mississippi River all the way to the Rocky Mountains. Even as late as 1803 much of this territory had yet to be explored. Jefferson had heard many stories about the West from explorers and trappers. There were stories about wooly mammoths and giant seven-foot beavers, about active volcanoes and huge pillars

25 of salt. Perhaps the most intriguing story of all concerned a Northwest Passage, a body of water that extended from the Mississippi River to the Pacific Ocean. If such a passage did exist, it could speed up the country's ability to export goods. To unlock the mysteries of the West, Jefferson decided to send an expedition into this region to determine just what was out there.

13. Which of the following is the best title for this selection?
    (A) Thomas Jefferson: Third President of the United States
    (B) The Legacy of Thomas Jefferson
    (C) Double or Nothing
    (D) Thomas Jefferson and the Louisiana Purchase
    (E) Reach for the Stars

14. Which of the following best describes the author's opinion of Thomas Jefferson?
    (A) a visionary leader
    (B) a spendthrift
    (C) an impractical dreamer
    (D) unscrupulous
    (E) confused

15. All of the following were true of the Louisiana Territory at the time of its purchase EXCEPT:
    (A) It encompassed an area of 828,000 square miles.
    (B) It extended from the Mississippi River to the Pacific Ocean.
    (C) It was purchased from France.
    (D) Its purchase doubled the size of the United States.
    (E) It was largely unexplored.

16. In line 18, "gaze" most nearly means
    (A) aim.
    (B) laugh.
    (C) lunge.
    (D) stare.
    (E) exclaim.

17. Which of the following can be inferred about Jefferson's attitude toward the Louisiana Territory?
    (A) He looked upon it as more exciting than space travel.
    (B) He saw it as a land of limitless opportunity.
    (C) He expected to meet great resistance from the French.
    (D) He believed the West had little of value to offer the new country.
    (E) He feared it would be too great a drain on the treasury of the new nation.

18. Which of the following questions is NOT answered by the passage?
    (A) How much land was included in the Louisiana Purchase?
    (B) What was the cost of the Louisiana Purchase?
    (C) What was the new territory actually like?
    (D) What was the reaction of the U.S. public to the purchase?
    (E) Why did Jefferson want to purchase the Louisiana Territory?

19. The style of this passage is most like that found in
    (A) a news article.
    (B) a personal letter.
    (C) an historical novel.
    (D) an autobiography.
    (E) a history textbook.

**End of Practice Set B**

**Answers and Explanations**

1. **B is correct.** In the first sentence of the second paragraph, the author says the crowd forced its way down the narrow stairs "like a turbulent water forcing itself through one tiny outlet." The motion of the crowd is compared to a raging stream of water attempting to force itself through a tiny opening. *A swirling blizzard* (choice A) and a strong wind (choice E) are what the men are trying to escape from, but neither one describes how the men looked as they tried to force their way to shelter. Although the passage refers to the crowd as a "large band," this means only that they were a large group of men; it has nothing to do with a marching band (choice C). There is nothing to support the comparison of the crowd of men to a roaring fire (choice D).

2. **C is correct.** The aim of the men is to escape the snow that was "biting their faces" and beating "with merciless persistence" upon their heads. Their hope was to "go through the little doors into the place that was cheery and warm with light." Choice A is wrong because the only mention of the police is the policeman who fought at the top of the stairs "to ease the pressure on those who were going down." Choice B is wrong because "the difficult and painful operation" to which the author refers means only getting into the shelter, not getting medical aid. Choice D is

wrong because the men in this passage are seeking refuge from the cold and snow in a shelter, which implies that they do not have a home to go to. Choice E is wrong because, although it is possible that pushing one's way down the stairs can result in being hurt, this is certainly not the reason for the pushing.

3. **E is correct.** The passage describes the men standing at the top of the stairs with "snow biting their faces" and beating "with merciless persistence upon the bowed heads of those who waited." Thus it is reasonable to describe the men as *frozen*, or *cold*, as in choice A. When the men finally reach the last three stairs, "the snarl had vanished from their lips"; therefore, it is reasonable to assume that the men waiting to get in out of the cold are *hostile* or *snarling* with anger as in choice B. The men at the rear "made frantic exertions" to avoid being left out in the cold, so they can be described as *frantic* as in choice C. When the men reached the bottom steps, the force of the crowd "which had previously vexed them" was now regarded from a different point of view. Thus, the men at the top could be described as *worried* or *vexed*, as in choice D. Only once they reached the bottom step and it became inevitable that they would get inside, did the men look "content and complacent."

4. **B is correct.** As stated in the third paragraph, a change of expression came over the features of the men once they reached the last three steps. "As they thus stood upon the threshold of their hopes, they looked suddenly content and complacent. The fire had passed from their eyes and the snarl had vanished from their lips. The very force of the crowd in the rear, which had previously vexed them, was regarded from another point of view, for it now made it inevitable that they should go through the little doors into the place that was cheery and warm with light."

5. **C is correct.** The men in the story are pushing and shoving to get to the bottom of the stairs from which point they were assured of going through the little doors "into the place that was cheery and warm with light." Everything in the passage makes it clear that the men desperately want to get into this place. Therefore, it is not a place to be feared (choice A) or avoided (choice B). Nor is it a prison (choice D) or a hospital for treating the sick (choice E).

6. **D is correct.** The passage describes an event as seen through the eyes of the author. The vivid imagery and literary language make it more likely to be an excerpt from a short story than a news article (choice A) or a research study (choice B). The prose passage has no similarity to an epic poem (choice C); and, since it is written in the third person, rather than the first person, it is not typical of an autobiography (choice E).

7. **D is correct.** The first sentence announces that the passage will present the "results of a four-year study of the Arctic conducted by an international team of 300 scientists." The remainder of the passage covers the findings of the study and who commissioned it. Choice A is wrong because

the passage merely presents the findings without suggesting action to be taken. Choice B is wrong because the melting of the Greenland Ice Sheet is only one of the findings of the study, not its entire purpose. Choice C is wrong because the study focused on the Arctic, not the world as a whole. Choice E is wrong for the same reason as choice B; it concerns only one part of the study.

8. **B is correct.** The word *projected* is used several times in the passage: "increasing greenhouse gases from human activities are projected to make the Arctic warmer still"; "At least half of the summer sea ice in the Arctic is projected to melt by the end of this century"; "The impacts of climate change on the region and the globe are projected to increase substantially in the years to come." In each case, "projected" means "forecasted" or "predicted."

9. **B is correct.** The words in parentheses following the mention of Arctic Council define the council as "a ministerial intergovernmental forum comprised of the eight Arctic countries, and six Indigenous Peoples organizations." Choice A refers to the International Arctic Science Committee. Choice C refers to the Arctic Climate Impact Assessment. There is no mention of a single organization that governs the Arctic nations as in choice D, and choice E names only part of the makeup of the Arctic Council.

10. **E is correct.** The study shows that "the Arctic . . . is warming much more rapidly than previously known." In fact, some areas in the Arctic "have warmed 10 times as fast as the world as a whole." Thus climate change in the Arctic is more, not less, pronounced than it is in other parts of the world and choice E is false. Choice A is mentioned in the first paragraph. Choices B and C are mentioned in the first and second paragraphs. Choice D is mentioned in the last paragraph.

11. **C is correct.** The effects of melting sea ice "will contribute to global sea-level rise and intensify global warming." As noted in the first paragraph, the increase in greenhouse gases comes from human activities, not from melting sea ice.

12. **A is correct.** As stated in the first paragraph, "Increasing greenhouse gases from human activities are projected to make the Arctic warmer still." Thus, it may be assumed that greenhouse gases have an effect on Arctic warming. Choice B is incorrect because the passage says only that "a significant portion of the Greenland Ice Sheet" is projected to melt by the end of this century. Choices C and D run counter to everything in the passage, which points toward ever-increasing arctic temperatures. Choice E is incorrect because the passage specifically mentions the effect of increasing temperatures upon both "arctic animal species such as ice-living seals" and "local people for whom these animals are a primary food source."

13. **D is correct.** A good title indicates both the topic and the purpose of the selection. In this case, the selection is a straightforward expository

passage about Thomas Jefferson's purchase of the Louisiana Territory. That makes choice D the best answer. Choices A and B are too broad for this passage, which is limited to Jefferson's part in the Louisiana Purchase. Choices C and E may be catchy phrases, but they fail to name the topic of the selection and they are too informal for this textbook-type passage.

14. **A is correct.** The author's positive opinion of Jefferson is revealed in statements such as these: "Thomas Jefferson was responsible for one of the largest and most peaceful land transactions this country has ever known."; "Practically overnight, the country doubled in size adding new resources to its already impressive supply."; "Overall, the Louisiana Purchase provided Jefferson with an opportunity to build a strong independent nation that is founded upon democracy and freedom." Choice C is wrong because, although the author may have thought of Jefferson as a dreamer, there is no indication that the author thought him to be impractical. There is no support in the passage for choices B, D, or E.

15. **B is correct.** The passage states that the Louisiana Territory "extended from the Mississippi River all the way to the Rocky Mountains." It did not extend to the Pacific Ocean. Choices A and C are mentioned in lines 3–5: "Jefferson purchased 828,000 square miles, an area known then as the Louisiana Territory, from France." Choice D is mentioned in line 9: "Practically overnight, the country doubled in size." Choice E is mentioned in lines 22–23: "as late as 1803 much of this territory had yet to be explored."

16. **D is correct.** "Gaze" appears in the following sentence: "For him, the west evoked the same excitement and wonder that many people feel today as they gaze at the stars and dream of traveling to other galaxies." Try substituting each answer choice in the original sentence and you will see that choice D fits best. To "gaze" is to "look intently" or to "stare."

17. **B is correct.** The passage says the following about Jefferson's attitude toward the Louisiana Purchase: "To Jefferson, this purchase was a chance of a lifetime for both him and the country." and "There was a potential for endless economic opportunities and new trade routes." From these statements it is reasonable to infer that Jefferson saw the Louisiana Territory as a land of great opportunity, as stated in choice B. There is no support in the passage for any other answer choice.

18. **C is correct.** The only thing the passage says about what the territory was actually like is that "Jefferson decided to send an expedition into this region to determine just what was out there." Thus the passage does not say what the new territory was actually like. Choice A is answered in line 3: "Jefferson purchased 828,000 square miles." Choice B is answered in line 4: "in exchange for $15 million." Choice D is answered in line 5: "At the time this acquisition was met with both joy and opposition." Choice E is answered in lines 8–15: "To Jefferson, this purchase was a chance of a lifetime for both him and the country . . . . There was a potential for endless

economic opportunities and new trade routes. Overall, the Louisiana Purchase provided Jefferson with an opportunity to build a strong independent nation that is founded upon democracy and freedom."

19. **E is correct.** The passage is written in the straightforward expository style most likely to be used in a history textbook. Choice A is wrong because the passage has none of the timely references common to a news article. Choice B is wrong because the passage lacks the informal, chatty style of most personal letters. Choice C is wrong because the passage is fact, not fiction. Choice D is wrong because the passage is not Jefferson's own account of his life.

# CHAPTER 9 | Strategies for the Writing Section

Both the SSAT and ISEE tests include a writing section that requires you to respond to an assigned topic. Your essay is not scored. Instead a copy is sent to each of the schools that receive your score report. Schools may use your writing sample as an indication of how well you can write under controlled conditions.

## Sample SSAT Writing Prompt

The SSAT writing section is administered at the beginning of the test before the multiple-choice sections. You will have 25 minutes to plan and write your essay. Each essay question provides two choices. Choice A consists of a statement and asks you to agree or disagree with it and to explain your answer. Choice B presents the opening sentence for you to use at the beginning of your story or narrative.

Read the topics below and choose the one that interests you the most. Fill in the circle for your chosen idea. Plan and write your essay or story on the paper provided.

---

Ⓐ Never ruin an apology with an excuse.

Do you agree or disagree with the topic sentence? Support your position with examples from your personal experience, the experience of others, current events, history, or literature.

---

Ⓑ There are no foolish questions, only foolish answers. Write a story that uses this as the first sentence.

---

**Topic:** Experience is the best teacher.

**Assignment:** Do you agree or disagree with the topic statement? Support your position with one or two specific examples from your own experiences, the experiences of others, current events, history, or literature.

---

## Sample ISEE Writing Prompt

The ISEE writing section is always administered after the multiple-choice sections of the test. You will have 30 minutes for your ISEE essay. A typical ISEE essay topic will ask a question that you are expected to answer using details and examples. As with the SSAT questions, there are no right or wrong answers. Just be sure to write on the assigned topic. An essay on any other topic is unacceptable.

If you were given the power to change one thing about the way that we choose a president of the United States, what would you change and why?

## The Essay Writing Process: Steps for Success

To be successful with any project, you need the right materials, and you need to complete the steps in the right order. The same is true of writing a good essay. If you follow the four steps discussed below, you will be able to write a thoughtful, well-organized SSAT or ISEE essay.

### Step 1: Brainstorm

Prewriting, or brainstorming ideas, is essential to writing successfully. When you brainstorm you shouldn't be concerned with grammar, spelling, or usage. It's more important to let your ideas flow freely, even if you won't use them all in your writing.

- Write key words or a phrase that summarizes the topic of the essay according to the writing prompt.
- Brainstorm ideas by quickly jotting down words or phrases about the topic.

### Step 2: Organize

Once you have written down your ideas, look them over. Cross out any that you don't want to use. Then try to organize the remaining ideas in a logical order. You might organize your thoughts in time-order, by order of importance, by space-order, or any other way that makes sense.

- Organize your thoughts by numbering them or by drawing circles or lines that show the way your ideas are related to each other.
- Write a clear statement that explains your position or point of view.

### Stage 3: Draft

Remember that it is important to stick to your plan. That doesn't mean you can't make changes as you draft your essay, but it does mean that you shouldn't ignore all the work you have done so far.

- Use your prewriting notes as you draft your essay.
- Begin each paragraph with a topic sentence.
- Provide at least two supporting details or examples for each main point.
- Make sure your essay has an introduction, body, and conclusion (in other words, a beginning, middle, and an end).

## Stage 4: Revise/Proofread

Always allow a few minutes to revise and proofread your essay. Think of this as the clean-up stage of a project you have just completed. Your essay will have a more professional look if you use editing marks carefully.

- Add any important ideas that are missing. Cross out any ideas or words that are irrelevant or unnecessary.
- Correct mistakes by crossing out neatly and adding new words above the crossed out material.
- Become familiar with the common editing symbols shown below.

| Insert | ∧ | Capital letter | ≡ |
| Period | ⊙ | Lower-case letter | / |
| Comma | ⋀ | Spell correctly | ∾ |
| Quotation marks | ＂ | Delete | ℘ |
| Paragraph indent | ⌗ | Move | ⊂ |
| | | Transpose | ∽ |

## Writing Process: SSAT/ISEE Essay

Take a good look at how one student responded to the writing prompt shown below. The suggestions are intended to help you move through the various steps of the writing process.

---

**Topic:** The grass is always greener on the other side of the fence.

**Assignment:** Do you agree or disagree with the topic statement? Support your position with examples from your own experience, the experience of others, current events, history, or literature.

---

### Step 1: Brainstorm

Prewriting, or brainstorming, is the first step in the writing process. The goal of this first step is to discover and explore your ideas about a subject. There is no one right way to brainstorm. Whatever techniques help you get your ideas down on paper are good enough. Here are some tried-and-true prewriting strategies.

**Freewriting**  *Freewriting* means jotting down all the ideas that "pop" into your mind about the topic. You shouldn't worry about complete sentences, correct punctuation, spelling, or grammar. Here's an example of freewriting based on the prompt.

*The grass is always greener on the other side of the fence means that what some-
one else has is always better than what you have. Matt can be a brat sometimes.
He always wants the same things his friends have even though he won't take care
of them. He wanted a remote controlled bus but he broke it right away. He always
begged mom for the same pets that his friends had—frogs, fish, you name it, he
wants it. He finally learned that our dog Max is a good friend but I'm pretty sure
he really got the lesson.*

**Making a List**   A good way to get your ideas down on paper is to make a list of
short phrases. Here's an example of making a list based on the prompt.

*Grass is greener means you want what others have*
*Truck*
*Video games*
*Matt wants what Eric has*
*Frog*
*Fish*
*Hermit crabs*

**Clustering**   Clustering involves making a diagram that shows how your ideas are
related. Start with a circle in the middle and write your main idea there. Then write
your supporting details in smaller circles and draw lines connecting them to your
main idea. It is a good idea to group similar supporting details together as you create
your cluster. Here's an example of clustering based on the prompt.

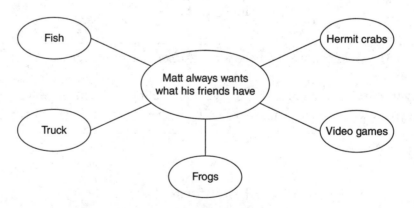

## Step 2: Organize

When you are traveling somewhere, street signs help direct you to your destination. In the same way, carefully organizing your ideas will help your readers follow what you are saying. Once you have completed the prewriting step, you should
look over what you wrote. Decide which ideas you want to use in your essay and

cross out the ideas that you won't use. Then number your remaining ideas in the order in which you want to present them. Here's an example of how to organize your prewriting ideas.

1. *Grass is greener means you want what others have*
2. *Matt wants what Eric has*
5. *Frog*
3. *Fish*
4. *Hermit crabs*

## Step 3: Draft

Once you have completed the prewriting and organizing steps, it is time to draft your essay. You should work in order from the beginning, to the middle, and finally to the end. The key to writing effectively in the allotted 25 to 30 minutes is to draft a strong opening statement and then follow your organizational plan. This strategy will speed up your writing and leave time to revise and proofread your essay. Here's an example of a draft based on the prewriting and outlining steps discussed above.

*A well-known proverb says, "The grass is always greener on the other side of the fence." This common saying means that most people are not satisfied with what they have. They think that what someone else has is better. In general, this statement is ture. My little brother Matt's ideas about pets are a perfect example of what it means to want something just because someone else has it.*

*We have a wonderful dog. Max. Max is everyones best friend. He greet us everyday when we get come from school. His tail wagging and a toy in his mouth ready to play. If you sit down on the sofa, Max will kurl up on your lap. If you lay down on the floor, he will stretch out right next to you. Was this good enough for Matt? No. Matt wants a different kind of pet, a pet like his friend Eric have.*

*First, Matt wanted a big aquarium full of exotic fish, just like the one he saw at Eric's house. Mom said he could start with a fishbowl and a few tropical fish. For a while, Matt was fascinated by the fish. He feed them and cared for them without being told to do so. Within a week, the novelty wore off. Matt forgot all about his desire for a big aquarium.*

*Next, Matt had to have hermit crabs after he saw the ones his friend Ty had. This new intest lasted for about a month. Matt visited Mike and saw Mike's pet frog. Suddenly, Matt wanted a frog too.*

*This time Mom put her foot down. No more pets for Matt. She told him he would have to make do with Max. Out of the blue Matt decided to teach Max a bunch of tricks. He got Max to walk on his hind legs and bark. Max also learned to roll a basketball with his nose. Matt put on a show for all his friends in our backyard. Max was the star. Matt understood the grass was actually greener on our side of the fence.*

## Step 4: Revise and Proofread

The final step in writing your essay is to carefully revise and proofread it. Keep the following questions in mind as you work.

- Does everything in the essay support the main idea or topic?
- Do the ideas in the essay follow naturally from one sentence to the next?
- Are the details in the essay clearly connected?
- Are ideas in the essay unnecessarily repeated?
- Is the grammar and usage of each sentence correct?
- Are punctuation marks used correctly?
- Are words capitalized correctly?
- Are words spelled correctly?

Here's an example of a revised and proofread essay.

*A well-known proverb says, "The grass is always greener on the other side of the fence." This common saying means that most people are not satisfied with what they have. They think that what someone else has is better. In general, this statement is* ~~true~~ *true. My little brother Matt's ideas about pets are a perfect example of what it means to want something just because someone else has it.*

*We have a wonderful dog.* ~~Max.~~ or *Max is everyones' best friend. He greet*s *us everyday when we get home from school,* with *His tail wagging and a toy in his mouth ready to play. If you sit down on the sofa, Max will* ~~kurl~~ curl *up on your lap. If you* ~~lay~~ lie *down on the floor, he will stretch out right next to you. Was this good enough for Matt? No. Matt want*red *a different kind of pet, a pet like his friend Eric* ~~have~~ has *.*

*First, Matt wanted a big aquarium full of exotic fish, just like the one he saw at Eric's house. Mom said he could start with a fishbowl and a few tropical fish. For a while, Matt was fascinated by the fish. He fe*e*d them and cared for them without being told to do so. Within a week, the novelty wore off. Matt forgot all about his desire for a big aquarium.*

*Next, Matt had to have hermit crabs after he saw the ones his friend Ty had. This new* ~~intest~~ interest *lasted for about a month.* Then one day *Matt visited Mike and saw Mike's pet frog. Suddenly, Matt wanted a frog too.*

*This time Mom put her foot down. No more pets for Matt. She told him he*

*would have to make do with Max. Out of the blue Matt decided to teach Max a*

*bunch of tricks. He got Max to walk on his hind legs and bark. Max also learned*

~~push~~
*to ~~roll~~ a basketball with his nose. Matt put on a show for all his friends in our*

*I laughed when I realized that for once*

*backyard. Max was the star. Matt understood the grass was actually greener on*
            ^

*our side of the fence.*

## A Sample SSAT/ISEE Final Essay

---

**Topic:** The grass is always greener on the other side of the fence.

**Assignment:** Do you agree or disagree with the topic statement? Support your position with examples from your own experience, the experience of others, current events, history, or literature.

---

*There is a well-known proverb that says, "The grass is always greener on the other side of the fence." This common saying means that most people are not satisfied with what they have. They think that what someone else has is better. In general, this statement is true. My little brother Matt's ideas about pets are a perfect example of what it means to want something just because someone else has it.*

*We have a wonderful dog. Max is everyone's best friend. He greets us everyday when we get home from school with his tail wagging and a toy in his mouth ready to play. If you sit down on the sofa, Max will curl up on your lap. If you lie down on the floor, he will stretch out right next to you.*

*Was this good enough for Matt? No. Matt wanted a different kind of pet, a pet like his friends have.*

*First, Matt wanted a big aquarium full of exotic fish, just like the one he saw at his friend Eric's house. Mom said he could start with a fishbowl and a few tropical fish. For a while, Matt was fascinated by the fish. He fed them and cared for them without being told to do so. Within a week, the novelty wore off. Matt forgot all about his desire for a big aquarium.*

*Next, Matt had to have hermit crabs after he saw the ones his friend Ty had. This new interest lasted for about a month. Then one day Matt visited Mike and saw Mike's pet frog. Suddenly, Matt wanted a frog too.*

*This time Mom put her foot down. No more exotic pets for Matt. She told him he would have to make do with Max. Out of the blue Matt decided to teach Max a bunch of tricks. He got Max to walk on his hind legs and bark. Max also learned to push a basketball with his nose. Matt put on a show for all his friends in our backyard. Max was the star. I laughed when I realized that for once Matt understood the grass was actually greener on our side of the fence.*

## Tips for Writing Excellent Essays

Here are some additional tips for writing an excellent essay for the SSAT and ISEE exams.

1. **Read the question carefully.**

   - Rephrase the question in your own words to make sure you understand what it is asking you.

2. **Answer the question.**

   - Follow all the directions and do *exactly* what you are asked to do.
   - You can be creative in your approach to the subject, but you *must* write on the topic you are assigned or you paper will be discounted.

3. **Have a plan for your essay.**

   - Allow at least 3–5 minutes to prewrite and organize your essay.
   - Write down supporting examples or details below each main idea.

4. **Write your essay.**

   - For the SSAT, allow about 15 minutes to write your essay.
   - For the ISEE, allow about 20 minutes for the writing stage.
   - As you work, write your essay as neatly and legibly as you can.
   - You MUST write in ink on the lined pages provided.
   - Revise your essay by looking for ways to make your ideas clearer.

5. **Stick to your plan.**

   - Stay focused on your topic.
   - Follow your plan.

6. **Use editing marks.**

   - Allow about five minutes to revise *and* proofread your essay.
   - You may strike through a word or phrase and change it, but remember that someone has to be able to read what you have written.
   - Make sure your changes are clear. Use editing symbols to help keep your essay as readable as possible.

   Now try an essay of your own. Use the strategies and tips you have learned to write an essay on one of the sample topics below. Set a timer for 25 minutes (for the SSAT) or 30 minutes (for the ISEE) to get a feel for how much time you will have for each step of the writing process. Write your final essay on the ruled lines on the following pages.

## On Your Own

**SSAT Essay Practice**

**SSAT Essay A**

**Directions:** You will have 25 minutes to plan and write an essay on the topic assigned below. Read the topic carefully. Make some brief notes on scratch paper and organize your thoughts before you begin to write. Write your final essay on the lined pages that follow.

**Topic:** Beauty is in the eye of the beholder.

**Assignment:** Do you agree or disagree with this statement? Support your position with examples from your own experience, the experience of others, current events, history, or literature.

**SSAT Essay B**

**Directions:** You will have 25 minutes to plan and write an essay on the topic assigned below. Read the topic carefully. Make some brief notes on scratch paper and organize your thoughts before you begin to write. Write your final essay on the lined pages that follow.

**Topic:** Experience is the best teacher.

**Assignment:** Do you agree or disagree with the topic statement? Support your position with examples from your own experience, the experience of others, current events, history, or literature.

**ISEE Essay A**

**Directions:** You will have 30 minutes to plan and write an essay on the topic assigned below. You must write on the assigned topic only. An essay on another topic will not be acceptable. You may make notes in the space provided for that purpose. Write your final essay on the lined pages that follow. Write or print legibly in blue or black ink.

How would you define courage? Give an example of a courageous man or woman and explain why you have chosen this person.

**ISEE Essay B**

**Directions:** You will have 30 minutes to plan and write an essay on the topic assigned below. You must write on the assigned topic only. An essay on another topic will not be acceptable. You may make notes in the space provided for that purpose. Write your final essay on the lined pages that follow. Write or print legibly in blue or black ink.

Do people change over time, or do their personalities stay the same? Give two or three examples based on personal experience or on the lives of real people.

# PART III

## REVIEW FOR THE MATH SECTIONS

# The Arithmetic You Need to Know

## Arithmetic on the SSAT and ISEE

Whether you are taking the SSAT or the ISEE, you will need to be familiar with the following topics in arithmetic:

**Topics**

| | |
|---|---|
| Place Value | Reducing Fractions to Lowest Terms |
| Addition | Operations with Fractions and Mixed Numbers |
| Subtraction | Operations with Decimals |
| Multiplication | Changing Decimals to Fractions |
| Division | Changing Fractions to Decimals |
| Order of Operations | Percents |
| Positive and Negative Numbers | Finding a Percent of a Number |
| Multiplying and Dividing by Zero | Finding the Percent of Increase or Decrease |
| Factors | Exponents |
| Greatest Common Factor | Scientific Notation |
| Multiples | Square Roots |
| Least Common Multiple | Units of Measure |
| Proper and Improper Fractions | |

If you are taking the upper level version of the SSAT or ISEE, you should also be familiar with the following:

- Exponents
- Roots

This chapter will give you a complete review of all of these arithmetic topics. After you study each topic, check your progress by working through the practice sets called "On Your Own." Answers for these practice sets appear at the end of the chapter.

## Arithmetic Review

### Place Value

In numbers, the *place* is the position held by a digit. *Place value* is the product of the digit multiplied by its place. Here are some examples.

42, 657, 203.123

23,456,789.247
2 (the first 2) is in the ten millions place
3 is in the millions place
4 (the first 4) is in the hundred thousands place
5 is in the 10 thousands place
6 is in the thousands place
7 (the first 7) is in the hundreds place
8 is in the tens place
9 is in the ones place
2 is in the tenths place
4 is in the hundredths place
7 is in the thousandths place

#### On Your Own—Place Value

1. For the number 98,345.47, which number is in the ones place?
2. For the number 77,456,782.09, which number is in the tenths place?
3. For the number 45,234.006, which number is in the thousandths place?

### Addition

There are two ways to show addition:

$$\begin{array}{r} 234 \\ + 123 \\ \hline \end{array} \quad \text{or} \quad 234 + 123 =$$

In either case you need to add the two numbers to get the sum. Many SSAT or ISEE problems will require you to add numbers. Practicing the skill will allow you to perform the tasks accurately and quickly.

## On Your Own—Addition

Find the answers to the following addition questions.

1.  731
    + 14

2.  16,790
    + 4,670

3.  1,677
    + 23,999

4.  18,998
    + 78,988

5.  98,068,459
    + 673,899

6.  3,450,989
    + 9,999

7.  670,369
    + 135

8.  1,700,009,856
    + 2,853,990,975

9.  1,434,209
    + 5,478,999

10.  169,801
    + 34,788,976

## Subtraction

There are also two ways to show subtraction:

     234        or       234 − 123 =
    − 123

Some SSAT or ISEE problems will ask to you subtract numbers in order to calculate the correct answer. Practicing subtraction will help you get the correct answer in a short period of time.

**Subtraction of Whole Numbers with Renaming**   Sometimes you have to "rename" numbers in order to complete subtraction.

     731
    − 465

To subtract the 5 from the 1 in the ones place, "rename" the "31" in the top number as "2 tens and 11 ones." Write "2" above the 3 in the tens place and "11" above the 1 in the ones place. Subtract 5 from 11 to get 6.

    2 11
    7̸3̸1̸
    − 465
       6

Next, you need to subtract the 6 from the (new) 2 in the tens place, so rename "72" as "6 hundreds and 12 tens." Write "6" above the 7 in the hundreds place and "12" above the 3 in the tens place. Subtract 6 from 12 to get 6. Then subtract 4 from 6 in the hundreds place to get 2, completing the subtraction.

$$
\begin{array}{r}
\overset{6\ \ 12\ \ 11}{7\cancel{3}\cancel{1}} \\
-\ 465 \\
\hline
266
\end{array}
$$

### On Your Own—Subtraction
Find the answers to the following subtraction questions.

1.  890
    − 78

2.  3,456
    − 961

3.  87,589
    − 65,178

4.  89,923
    − 34,478

5.  34,789,909
    − 23,784,498

6.  674,329
    − 84,498

7.  88,320,087
    − 3,497,698

8.  1,000,997
    − 9,809

9.  145,000,045
    − 14,409

10. 1,798
    − 1,699

## Multiplication

Multiplication is a bit more complicated in that it can be shown in various ways.

$10 \times 3 = 30$
$10\,(3) = 30$
$(10)\,3 = 30$
$10 \cdot 3 = 30$
$(10)(3) = 30$

$$
\begin{array}{r}
10 \\
\times\ 3 \\
\hline
30
\end{array}
$$

Be sure to know your multiplication tables. You should already know the answers to any numbers multiplied up to 12, but the table below is a refresher. Knowing the multiplication tables without any hesitation will help you answer many of the math items quickly and accurately. To know this table by heart will give you a bit of extra time to answer the tougher items.

| x | 0 | 1 | 2 | 3 | 4 | 5 | 6 | 7 | 8 | 9 | 10 | 11 | 12 |
|---|---|---|---|---|---|---|---|---|---|---|----|----|----|
| 0 | 0 | 0 | 0 | 0 | 0 | 0 | 0 | 0 | 0 | 0 | 0 | 0 | 0 |
| 1 | 0 | 1 | 2 | 3 | 4 | 5 | 6 | 7 | 8 | 9 | 10 | 11 | 12 |
| 2 | 0 | 2 | 4 | 6 | 8 | 10 | 12 | 14 | 16 | 18 | 20 | 22 | 24 |
| 3 | 0 | 3 | 6 | 9 | 12 | 15 | 18 | 21 | 24 | 27 | 30 | 33 | 36 |
| 4 | 0 | 4 | 8 | 12 | 16 | 20 | 24 | 28 | 32 | 36 | 40 | 44 | 48 |
| 5 | 0 | 5 | 10 | 15 | 20 | 25 | 30 | 35 | 40 | 45 | 50 | 55 | 60 |
| 6 | 0 | 6 | 12 | 18 | 24 | 30 | 36 | 42 | 48 | 54 | 60 | 66 | 72 |
| 7 | 0 | 7 | 14 | 21 | 28 | 35 | 42 | 49 | 56 | 63 | 70 | 77 | 84 |
| 8 | 0 | 8 | 16 | 24 | 32 | 40 | 48 | 56 | 64 | 72 | 80 | 88 | 96 |
| 9 | 0 | 9 | 18 | 27 | 36 | 45 | 54 | 63 | 72 | 81 | 90 | 99 | 108 |
| 10 | 0 | 10 | 20 | 30 | 40 | 50 | 60 | 70 | 80 | 90 | 100 | 110 | 120 |
| 11 | 0 | 11 | 22 | 33 | 44 | 55 | 66 | 77 | 88 | 99 | 110 | 121 | 132 |
| 12 | 0 | 12 | 24 | 36 | 48 | 60 | 72 | 84 | 96 | 108 | 120 | 132 | 144 |

### On Your Own—Multiplication
Calculate the following multiplication items.

1. $(4)(5) =$

2. $(5)(4) =$

3. $9 \times 7 =$

4. $27 \times 65 =$

5. $67 \times 98 =$

6. $899 \times 457 =$

7. $\begin{array}{r} 1,649 \\ \times\, 8,942 \\ \hline \end{array}$

8. $\begin{array}{r} 76,834 \\ \times\, 78,459 \\ \hline \end{array}$

9. $\begin{array}{r} 275,849 \\ \times\, 769,422 \\ \hline \end{array}$

10. $\begin{array}{r} 9,750,439 \\ \times\, 56,893,478 \\ \hline \end{array}$

## Division

Division can also be shown in more than one way.

$12 \div 3 = 4$

$12/3 = 4$

$\dfrac{12}{3} = 4$

Many SSAT or ISEE problems will require you to solve division problems. Division also relates to the use of fractions and the calculation of percentages.

*On Your Own—Division*

Calculate the following division items.

1. $16 \div 4 =$

2. $48 \div 4 =$

3. $90 \div 45 =$

4. $25,536 \div 56 =$

5. $121,401 \div 123 =$

6. $254,646 \div 987 =$

7. $41,536 \div 1,298 =$

8. $18,895,065 \div 899,765 =$

9. $144 \div 12 =$

10. $1,655 \div 5 =$

---

**Symbols**

$=$ is equal to

$\neq$ is not equal to

$<$ is less than

$\leq$ is less than or equal to

$>$ is greater than

$\geq$ is greater than or equal to

$\parallel$ is parallel to

$\cong$ is approximately equal to

$\approx$ is approximately

$\perp$ is perpendicular to

$| \ |$ absolute value

$\pm$ plus or minus

$\%$ percent

$a{:}b$ ratio of $a$ to $b$ or $\dfrac{a}{b}$

---

*On Your Own—Symbols*

True or False? Write "T" or "F" in the blank to indicate whether each statement below is true of false.

1. _____ $9 > 7$

2. _____ $6.99 \boxtimes 7$

3. _____ $47 \geq 47$

4. _____ $89 < 64$

5. _____ $99\%$ is 99 percent

6. _____ $7 \neq 7$

7. _____ $2:4 = \frac{2}{4}$

8. _____ $|-7| = 7$

9. _____ $8 = -8$

10. _____ $49 \le 34$

## Order of Operations

If addition, subtraction, multiplication, and division are all in the same mathematical statement, the order of operations (what you do first, second, third, etc.) is

1. Perform operations shown within **Parentheses**.
2. Attend to **Exponents** and square roots.
3. Perform **Multiplication** or **Division**, whichever comes first left to right.
4. Perform **Addition** or **Subtraction**, whichever comes first left to right.

**Order Is Important!** You almost certainly will get an SSAT or ISEE math item that will require you to know order of operations rules. You can use the sentence "**P**lease **E**xcuse **M**y **D**ear **A**unt **S**ally" to help you remember the order of operations.

### Examples

$2 + 3 \times 4 =$
$2 + 12 = 14$

$3^2 + 4(5 - 2) =$
$3^2 + 4(3) =$
$9 + 4(3) =$
$9 + 12 = 21$

$5(10 + 2) + 2 + 3 =$
$5(12) + 2 + 3 =$
$60 + 5 = 65$

$3^3(8 + 3) \times (\sqrt{9}) + (9 \times 2) - (298 + 300) =$
$27(11) \times (3) + (18) - (598) =$
$297 \times 3 + 18 - 598 =$
$891 + 18 - 598 =$
$909 - 598 = 311$

---

**ORDER OF OPERATIONS**
1. Simplify groupings inside parentheses, brackets, and braces first. Work with the innermost pair, moving outward.
2. Simplify the exponents and radicals.
3. Do the multiplication and division in order from left to right.
4. Do the addition and subtraction in order from left to right.

*On Your Own—Order of Operations*
Calculate the answers to the following.

1. $(17 + 3) + 20 =$

2. $(45 - 43) + (16 + 32) =$

3. $(12 + 3)(2 \times 3) =$

4. $14 \div 2 + 14 =$

5. $6^2 + 3 + 2 =$

6. $12 \times 12 + 2^3 =$

7. $3^2 + 4(5 - 2) =$

8. $(4 + 2)^3 + (3 \times 2) - 2^2 =$

## Positive and Negative Numbers

Positive numbers are numbers that are greater than 0, such as +6. Negative numbers are numbers that are less than 0, such as −4. Positive and negative whole numbers are called *integers*.

The *absolute value* of a number is the distance of the number from 0 on a number line. For example, the absolute value of +6 is 6. The absolute value of −4 is 4.

**Adding Positive and Negative Numbers**   *To add numbers with the same sign*, add their absolute values. The sum will have the same sign as the numbers you added.

**Examples**
Add:   −4
       $\underline{-3}$
       −7

*To add numbers with different signs*, first find their absolute values. Subtract the lesser absolute value from the greater absolute value. Give the sum the same sign as the number with the greater absolute value.

---

*SSAT/ISEE Coach Says . . .*
**Know Negative Numbers!** Be sure to practice adding, subtracting, multiplying, and dividing using negative numbers.

---

**Examples**
Add:   +4
       $\underline{-3}$
       +1

Add:   +4
       $\underline{-6}$
       −2

*On Your Own—Adding Positive and Negative Numbers*
Add the following numbers.

1. $4 + (-3) =$

2. $-10 + 3 =$

3. $75 + (-34 - 32) =$

4. $80 + (75 - 25) =$

5. $-64 + 18 - 12 =$

6. $1{,}000 - (800) =$

7. $1{,}000 - (800 - 120) =$

8. $200 - 325 =$

**Subtracting Positive and Negative Numbers**  Look again at the number line.

- When you subtract a positive number, you move *left* on the number line the distance equal to the absolute value of the number being subtracted.
- When you subtract a negative number, you move *right* on the number line the distance equal to the absolute value of the number being subtracted.

**Examples**
Subtract positive numbers (move *left* on the number line):

$$\begin{array}{r} +7 \\ -\,(+12) \\ \hline -5 \end{array}$$

$$\begin{array}{r} -7 \\ -\,(+12) \\ \hline -19 \end{array}$$

Subtract negative numbers (move *right* on the number line):

$$\begin{array}{r} 7 \\ -\,(-12) \\ \hline +19 \end{array}$$

$$\begin{array}{r} -7 \\ -\,(-12) \\ \hline +5 \end{array}$$

**Note: A simple rule is that when you subtract negative numbers, all you really need to do is change the sign of the number being subtracted from negative to positive, and then add.**

*On Your Own—Subtracting Positive and Negative Numbers*
Subtract the following numbers.

1. $12 - (4) =$
2. $12 - (-4) =$
3. $12 - (-8) =$
4. $45 - (12) =$
5. $125 - (-3)^2 =$

6. $500 - (5)^2 =$
7. $1,500 - (-10)^2 =$
8. $1,500 - (10)^2 =$
9. $42 - (45 - 5) - (-60) =$

**Absolute Value**   A number regardless of its sign (+ or −) is called the *absolute value*. The absolute value of a number is shown as the number placed between two vertical parallel lines; for example: $|-4|$ or $|4|$. In each of these cases, the absolute value of the number is 4. When using absolute values, just ignore the sign.

**Examples**
$|-x| = x$
$|-5 - 6| = |-11| = 11$
$8 + |-9| = 17$

**Multiplying and Dividing Negative Numbers**   These operations are easy if you use just one trick. To multiply or divide negative numbers, first treat all the numbers as positive and perform the operation as normal.

- If there is an *odd number of negative signs*, the answer will be a negative.
- If there is an *even number of negative signs*, the number will be positive.

**Examples**

$(-5)(+6)(+2) = -60$    This expression has 1 negative sign. Since 1 is an odd number, the result is negative.

$(-5)(-6)(+2) = +60$    This expression has 2 negative signs. Since 2 is an even number, the result is positive.

$\dfrac{-88}{-11} = +8$    This expression has 2 negative signs. Since 2 is an even number, the result is positive.

$\dfrac{-88}{+11} = -8$    This expression has 1 negative sign. Since 1 is an odd number, the result is negative.

*On Your Own—Multiplying and Dividing Negative Numbers*
Evaluate the following expressions.

1. $(-2)(-2)(-2) =$
2. $(-2)(-2)(2) =$

3. $(5)(-2)(-4) =$
4. $\dfrac{90}{-45} =$

5. $\dfrac{-90}{-45} =$

7. $(-4)(-5)(-2)(-8) =$

6. $\dfrac{-90}{45} =$

8. $(5)(-5)(2) =$

**Subtracting Numbers within Parentheses**   If there is a minus sign in front of numbers in parentheses, change the sign of all the numbers within the parentheses and then add.

**Examples**

$11 - (+3 - 5 + 2 - 8)$
changes to
$11 + (-3 + 5 - 2 + 8) =$
$11 + (-5 + 13) =$
$11 + (+8) = 19$

$20 - (-3 + 5 - 2 + 8) =$
$20 + (+3 - 5 + 2 - 8) =$
$20 + (+5 - 13) =$
$20 + (-8) = 12$

***On Your Own—Subtracting Numbers within Parentheses***
Evaluate the following expressions.

1. $200 - (90 - 10) =$

5. $1,000 - (750) =$

2. $50 - (45) =$

6. $22 - (-12 + 15) =$

3. $125 - (45 - 55) =$

7. $95 + (34 - (-22)) =$

4. $575 - (400 - 300) =$

## Multiplying and Dividing by Zero

Any number multiplied by zero = zero.
Zero divided by any number = zero.
Dividing by zero is considered to be "undefined."

**Examples**

$45 \times 0 = 0$
$1,232,456 \times 0 = 0$
$10.45399 \times 0 = 0$
$0 \div 5 = 0$
$0 \div 500 = 0$
$7 \div 0$ is undefined
$\dfrac{32}{0}$ is undefined

$\dfrac{89}{0}$ is undefined

Evaluate the following expressions.

1. $02316 \times 0 =$

2. $1,457,956,002.234 \times 0 =$

3. $4.78 \times 0 =$

4. $0 \div 6,000 =$

5. $6,000 \div 0 =$

## Factors

Factors are numbers that are multiplied together to create another number.

### Examples

$2 \times 4 = 8$ (2 and 4 are factors of 8.)
$1 \times 8 = 8$ (1 and 8 are factors of 8.)
So 1, 2, 4, and 8 are all factors of 8.

$1 \times 32 = 32$ (1 and 32 are factors of 32.)
$2 \times 16 = 32$ (2 and 16 are factors of 32.)
$8 \times 4 = 32$ (8 and 4 are factors of 32.)
So 1, 2, 4, 8, 16, and 32 are all factors of 32.

Knowing about factors will be very useful when solving equations.

**Common Factors**   Common factors are factors that are shared by two or more numbers. As shown above, 8 and 32 share the common factors 1, 2, 4, and 8.

**Greatest Common Factor**   The greatest common factor (**GCF**) of two or more nonzero whole numbers is the greatest whole number that evenly divides each of the given numbers.

### Example

What is the greatest common factor of 32 and 48?

The factors of 32 are 2, 4, 8, 16, and 32.
The factors of 48 are 2, 4, 6, 8, 12, 16, 24, and 48.
The common factors of 32 and 48 are 2, 4, 8, and 16.

Therefore the greatest common factor of 32 and 48 is 16.

*On Your Own—Greatest Common Factor*

1. What is the greatest common factor of 24 and 42?

2. What is the greatest common factor of 74 and 111?

3. What is the greatest common factor of 34 and 85?

4. What is the greatest common factor of 24 and 352?

## Multiples

Multiples of a number are found by multiplying the number by 1, 2, 3, 4, 5, 6, 7, 8, etc. So multiples of 5 are 10, 15, 20, 25, 30, 35, 40, etc.

**Common Multiples**   Common multiples are multiples that are shared by two or more numbers.

**Example**

| 2 | 4 | 6 | 8 | 10 | 12 | 14 | 16 | 18 | 20 | 22 | 24 |
|---|---|---|---|----|----|----|----|----|----|----|----|

⇕    ⇕    ⇕    ⇕

| 3 | 6 | 9 | 12 | 15 | 18 | 21 | 24 |
|---|---|---|----|----|----|----|----|

In the example above, 3 and 2 share the common multiples 6, 12, 18, and 24.

**Least Common Multiple**  The least common multiple is the smallest multiple which two numbers share. In the case of the example above, the number 6 is the least common multiple.

*On Your Own—Least Common Multiple*
What is the least common multiple of the following numbers?

1. _____ 2, 4, 8          3. _____ 9, 6, 21

2. _____ 6, 18, 54        4. _____ 8, 80

## Proper and Improper Fractions

Fractions have two numbers, a numerator and a denominator. Fractions represent portions of a whole or parts of a set.

$$\frac{3}{6} = \frac{\text{numerator}}{\text{denominator}}$$

The denominator tells how many parts something is divided into. The numerator tells how many of those parts you have. The fraction as a whole tells the *proportion* of parts you have to parts there are in all.

So if a pie is divided into 8 pieces and you take 2 of them, the fraction telling the proportion of the pie you have is $^2/_8$. The denominator (8) tells how many pieces of pie there are in all. The numerator (2) tells how many of those pieces you have.

$\frac{2}{8}$  or a proportion of 2 to 8.

Fractions can be positive or negative. A negative fraction is written like this:

$-\frac{2}{8}$    or    $\frac{-2}{8}$    or    $\frac{2}{-8}$

**Proper Fractions**  Fractions representing amounts smaller than 1 are called proper fractions. Fractions smaller than 1 have numerators that are smaller than the denominators.

**Examples**

$\frac{1}{3}$    $\frac{3}{7}$    $\frac{5}{8}$    $\frac{9}{11}$    $\frac{6}{32}$    $\frac{99}{100}$

**Improper Fractions**  Improper fractions are greater than 1. The numerator is larger than the denominator.

**Examples**

$$\frac{22}{3} \qquad \frac{3}{2} \qquad \frac{12}{5} \qquad \frac{17}{8} \qquad \frac{66}{3} \qquad \frac{11}{9}$$

**Mixed Numbers**   Expressions that include both whole numbers and fractions are called mixed numbers.

**Examples**

$$2\frac{7}{8} \qquad 3\frac{1}{2} \qquad 9\frac{2}{3} \qquad 27\frac{3}{4}$$

**Renaming an Improper Fraction as a Mixed Number**   To rename an improper fraction as a mixed number, simply divide the numerator by the denominator.

---

*SSAT/ISEE Coach Says . . .*
**You'll See These for Sure.** You will have items that require you to manipulate fractions and mixed numbers. Don't despair. Be sure to understand the procedures thoroughly and you should have no problem on your test.

---

**Examples**

$$\frac{22}{3} = 22 \div 3 = 7\frac{1}{3}$$

$$\frac{3}{2} = 3 \div 2 = 1\frac{1}{2}$$

$$\frac{12}{5} = 12 \div 5 = 2\frac{2}{5}$$

$$\frac{17}{8} = 17 \div 8 = 2\frac{1}{8}$$

*On Your Own—Changing Improper Fractions into Mixed Numbers*
Change the following improper fractions into mixed numbers.

1. $\frac{25}{2} =$

2. $\frac{7}{3} =$

3. $\frac{45}{4} =$

4. $\frac{79}{3} =$

5. $\frac{84}{5} =$

6. $\frac{77}{10} =$

**Renaming a Mixed Number as a Fraction**   To rename a mixed number as an improper fraction, simply multiply the whole number by the denominator and add the numerator. Put that number over the denominator. For example, $2\frac{1}{2}$ would be

$$2 \overset{+}{\underset{\times}{\longleftarrow}} \frac{1}{2} \quad \text{or } 2 \times 2 + 1 \text{ over the denominator} = \frac{5}{2}$$

**Examples**

$$7\frac{1}{3} = 3 \times 7 + 1 = 22$$

Put 22 over the denominator $= \dfrac{22}{3}$

$$2\frac{2}{5} = 2 \times 5 + 2 = 12$$

Put 12 over the denominator $= \dfrac{12}{5}$

***On Your Own—Renaming a Mixed Number as a Fraction***

1. $3\dfrac{1}{3} =$

2. $6\dfrac{1}{4} =$

3. $5\dfrac{11}{12} =$

4. $3\dfrac{3}{4} =$

5. $7\dfrac{2}{5} =$

**Finding Equivalent Fractions**  Two fractions are said to be equivalent (the same in value) if they use different numbers but represent the same proportion. For example, the following fractions are equivalent:

$$\frac{1}{2} \qquad \frac{4}{8} \qquad \frac{3}{6} \qquad \frac{5}{10}$$

To change a fraction into an equivalent fraction, multiply or divide the numerator and denominator by the same number.

**Examples**

$\dfrac{2 \times 3 = 6}{4 \times 3 = 12}$ so $\dfrac{2}{4}$ is equivalent to $\dfrac{6}{12}$.

$\dfrac{9 \div 3 = 3}{12 \div 3 = 4}$ so $\dfrac{9}{12}$ is equivalent to $\dfrac{3}{4}$.

***On Your Own—Finding Equivalent Fractions***

List three equivalent fractions for each of the following:

1. $\dfrac{1}{3}$

2. $\dfrac{2}{3}$

3. $\dfrac{2}{4}$

## Reducing Fractions to Lowest Terms

Fractions are commonly shown in their lowest terms, that is, the smallest numbers that still represent the original proportion. When a fraction is not in its lowest terms, you can reduce it to its lowest terms by dividing the numerator and denominator by the largest number that will divide into both evenly.

### Examples

$\frac{40}{80}$ can be divided evenly by 40 giving a fraction of $\frac{1}{2}$.

$\frac{9}{15}$ can be divided evenly by 3 giving a fraction of $\frac{3}{5}$.

$\frac{21}{28}$ can be divided evenly by 7 giving a fraction of $\frac{3}{4}$.

*On Your Own—Reducing Fractions to Lowest Terms*

1. $\frac{11}{33} =$

2. $\frac{24}{48} =$

3. $\frac{16}{64} =$

4. $\frac{108}{216} =$

5. $\frac{33}{264} =$

6. $\frac{5}{65} =$

## Operations with Fractions and Mixed Numbers

**Adding and Subtracting Fractions**   To add and subtract fractions with *like denominators*, simply add or subtract the numerators. The result is often shown in lowest terms.

### Examples

$$\frac{3}{10} + \frac{1}{10} = \frac{4}{10} = \frac{2}{5} \qquad \frac{9}{10} - \frac{1}{10} = \frac{8}{10} = \frac{4}{5}$$

To add and subtract fractions with *unlike denominators*, you first need to find equivalent fractions that all have the same denominator. To do this, you need to find the *least common denominator (LCD)*, the least common multiple of the denominators of all the fractions. Use the LCD to create new fractions equivalent to the original ones. Then add the new numerators.

### Examples

$$\frac{6}{8} + \frac{1}{2} =$$

The least common denominator is 8, so $\frac{6}{8}$ does not need to be changed. However, $\frac{1}{2}$ is changed to the equivalent fraction $\frac{4}{8}$.

$$\frac{6}{8} + \frac{4}{8} = \frac{10}{8} = 1\frac{2}{8} = 1\frac{1}{4} \text{ (reduced to lowest terms)}$$

$$\frac{1}{3} + \frac{1}{2} + \frac{7}{8}$$

Find the least common denominator. The least common multiple of 8, 3, and 2 is 24, so 24 is the least common denominator. Use the LCD to create new fractions equivalent to the original ones:

$$\frac{1}{3} + \frac{1}{2} + \frac{7}{8}$$

$$= \frac{8}{24} + \frac{12}{24} + \frac{21}{24}$$

$$= \frac{41}{24} = 1\frac{17}{24}$$

Use the same approach to add and subtract positive and negative fractions. Refer to the section earlier in this math review on adding and subtracting positive and negative numbers.

***On Your Own—Adding and Subtracting Fractions***

1. $\dfrac{1}{3} + \dfrac{6}{12} =$

2. $\dfrac{2}{3} + \dfrac{7}{8} =$

3. $\dfrac{3}{4} + \dfrac{7}{8} =$

4. $\dfrac{8}{10} - \dfrac{2}{15} =$

5. $\dfrac{4}{5} - \dfrac{1}{3} =$

**Adding and Subtracting Mixed Numbers**   Add and subtract mixed numbers by following the same rules previously outlined. Change the fractions to equivalent fractions using the least common denominator. Add or subtract the fractions. Add or subtract the whole numbers. If the fractions add up to more than a whole number, simplify and add the new whole number to the existing whole numbers.

**Example (Addition)**

$$3\frac{3}{4}$$
$$+ \ 2\frac{1}{2}$$
_____

changes to

$$3\frac{3}{4}$$
$$+ \ 2\frac{2}{4}$$
_____

Add $\frac{3}{4} + \frac{2}{4} = \frac{5}{4} = 1\frac{1}{4}$

Add 3 and 2 = 5

$5 + 1\frac{1}{4} = 6\frac{1}{4}$

**Examples (Subtraction)**

$$3\frac{3}{4}$$
$$-\ 2\frac{1}{2}$$
$$\overline{\phantom{-\ 2\frac{1}{2}}}$$

changes to

$$3\frac{3}{4}$$
$$-\ 2\frac{2}{4}$$
$$\overline{\phantom{-\ 2\frac{2}{4}}}$$

$\frac{3}{4} - \frac{2}{4} = \frac{1}{4}$

$3 - 2 = 1$

$1 + \frac{1}{4} = 1\frac{1}{4}$

$$3\frac{3}{4}$$
$$-\ 5\frac{1}{2}$$
$$\overline{\phantom{-\ 5\frac{1}{2}}}$$

changes to

$$3\frac{3}{4}$$
$$-\ 5\frac{2}{4}$$
$$\overline{\phantom{-\ 5\frac{2}{4}}}$$

*Caution*: Remember that subtraction means moving *left* on the number line. Start at $3^3/_4$ and move left $5^2/_4$ on the number line. The correct answer is $-1^3/_4$.

*On Your Own—Adding and Subtracting Mixed Numbers*

1. $1\dfrac{3}{4} + 3\dfrac{3}{4} =$

2. $6\dfrac{5}{6} + 9\dfrac{1}{3} =$

3. $12\dfrac{1}{3} + \dfrac{4}{5} =$

4. $8\dfrac{7}{8} - 4\dfrac{1}{4} =$

5. $10\dfrac{2}{3} - 3\dfrac{1}{9} =$

**Multiplying Fractions**   To multiply fractions, just multiply the numerators and multiply the denominators. Reduce the resulting fraction to lowest terms.

**Examples**

$$\dfrac{5}{12} \times \dfrac{2}{3} =$$

Multiply the numerators: $5 \times 2 = 10$
Multiply the denominators: $12 \times 3 = 36$

Result: $\dfrac{10}{36} = \dfrac{5}{18}$

$$\dfrac{4}{5} \times \dfrac{7}{8} =$$

Multiply the numerators: $4 \times 7 = 28$
Multiply the denominators: $5 \times 8 = 40$

Result: $\dfrac{28}{40} = \dfrac{7}{10}$

---

*SSAT/ISEE Coach Says . . .*

**Simplify, Simplify.** Sometimes it is possible to simplify terms before performing any math operation. Take the same example we have already completed:

$$\dfrac{4}{5} \times \dfrac{7}{8}$$

Find a number (or greatest common factor) that divides into one of the numerators and one of the denominators. In this example the number 4 divides into 4 and into 8.

$$\dfrac{\overset{1}{\cancel{4}}}{5} \times \dfrac{7}{\underset{2}{\cancel{8}}}$$

To finish the problem, multiply $1 \times 7$ and $5 \times 2$, making the final answer

$$\dfrac{7}{10}.$$

---

1. $\dfrac{3}{4} \times \dfrac{7}{10} =$

3. $\dfrac{2}{7} \times \dfrac{2}{5} =$

2. $\dfrac{12}{15} \times \dfrac{1}{5} =$

**Dividing Fractions**  To divide fractions, invert the second fraction and multiply. Reduce the result to lowest terms.

**Examples**

$$\frac{1}{2} \div \frac{1}{3} =$$

$$\frac{1}{2} \times \frac{3}{1} =$$

$$\frac{3}{2} = 1\frac{1}{2}$$

$$\frac{3}{4} \div \left(-\frac{1}{2}\right)$$

$$\frac{3}{4} \times \left(-\frac{2}{1}\right) =$$

$$-\left(\frac{6}{4}\right) = -1\frac{2}{4} = -1\frac{1}{2}$$

---

*SSAT/ISEE Coach Says . . .*

**Dividing Fractions.** Always remember that when you are dividing fractions, just invert and multiply.

---

*SSAT/ISEE Coach Says . . .*

**Dividing Fractions.** Sometimes you might see division of fractions in this format.

$$\frac{\dfrac{1}{2}}{\dfrac{1}{3}}$$

Treat it the same as

$$\frac{1}{2} \div \frac{1}{3}$$

---

*On Your Own—Dividing Fractions*

1. $\dfrac{1}{2} \div \dfrac{2}{4} =$       3. $\dfrac{8}{9} \div \dfrac{1}{3} =$

2. $\dfrac{4}{5} \div \dfrac{1}{3} =$

**Multiplying Mixed Numbers**   To multiply mixed numbers, change each mixed number to a fraction and then multiply as usual. Reduce to lowest terms.

**Examples**

$1\dfrac{1}{4} \times 2\dfrac{1}{2} =$

$\dfrac{5}{4} \times \dfrac{5}{2} =$

$\dfrac{25}{8} = 3\dfrac{1}{8}$

$3\dfrac{2}{3} \times 9\dfrac{1}{2} =$

$\dfrac{11}{3} \times \dfrac{19}{2} =$

$\dfrac{209}{6} = 34\dfrac{5}{6}$

The fraction cannot be simplified because it is already in its lowest terms.

$34\dfrac{5}{6}$

---

***SSAT/ISEE Coach Says . . .***
**Watch the Signs!** To multiply or divide negative numbers, first treat all the numbers as positive and perform the operation as normal. Then if there is an odd number of negative signs, the answer will be negative. If there is an even number of negative signs, the number will be positive.

---

*On Your Own—Multiplying Mixed Numbers*

1. $2\dfrac{2}{3} \times 7\dfrac{2}{5} =$       3. $12\dfrac{2}{3} \times 2\dfrac{1}{3} =$

2. $5\dfrac{1}{5} \times 4\dfrac{1}{2} =$

**Dividing Mixed Numbers**   To divide mixed numbers, rename the mixed numbers as fractions and then follow the rule for dividing fractions: invert the second fraction and multiply.

**Example**

$$3\frac{1}{2} \div 1\frac{1}{4} =$$

$$\frac{7}{2} \div \frac{5}{4} =$$

$$\frac{7}{2} \times \frac{4}{5} =$$

$$\frac{28}{10} =$$

$$2\frac{8}{10} =$$

Simplify the fraction

$$2\frac{4}{5}$$

*On Your Own—Dividing Mixed Numbers*

1. $12\frac{2}{3} \div 2\frac{1}{3} =$

3. $6\frac{1}{2} \div 2\frac{1}{2} =$

2. $6\frac{1}{2} \div \frac{1}{2} =$

## Operations with Decimals

A decimal is a number with one or more digits to the right of the decimal point. 0.862 and 3.12 are decimals. (Note that a zero is shown to the left of the decimal point when the decimal is between 0 and 1.)

**Adding and Subtracting Decimals**   To add or subtract decimals, line up the decimal points one above the other. Then add or subtract as you would normally. Place a decimal point in the answer beneath the other decimal points.

**Examples (Addition)**

```
    14.50
   200.32
+ 1,245.89
  1,460.71
```

```
   14.50
  200.047
   48.0075
+ 10.6
```

Add zeros in the blank decimal places to make this problem easier to tackle.

$$
\begin{array}{r}
14.5000 \\
200.0470 \\
48.0075 \\
+\ 10.6000 \\
\hline
273.1545 \\
\end{array}
$$

### Examples (Subtraction)

$$
\begin{array}{r}
475.89 \\
-\ 62.45 \\
\hline
413.44 \\
\end{array}
$$

$$
\begin{array}{r}
\overset{7\ 14}{475.8\cancel{4}} \\
-\ 62.69 \\
\hline
413.15 \\
\end{array}
$$
Since 9 is larger than 4, rename 84 as 7 tens and 14 ones.

### On Your Own—Adding and Subtracting Decimals

1.
$$
\begin{array}{r}
325.45 \\
+\ 221.12 \\
\hline
\end{array}
$$

4.
$$
\begin{array}{r}
788.99 \\
-\ 102.12 \\
\hline
\end{array}
$$

2.
$$
\begin{array}{r}
12,456.213 \\
+\ 32,114.788 \\
\hline
\end{array}
$$

5.
$$
\begin{array}{r}
5,612.12 \\
-\ 4,599.99 \\
\hline
\end{array}
$$

3.
$$
\begin{array}{r}
788.99 \\
+\ 102.12 \\
\hline
\end{array}
$$

6.
$$
\begin{array}{r}
45.00 \\
-\ 12.89 \\
\hline
\end{array}
$$

**Multiplying Decimals**   To multiply decimals, follow the usual multiplication rules. Count the number of places to the right of the decimals in each factor. Add the numbers of places. Put that many decimal places in the answer.

### Examples

12.43 (two decimal places)
× 2.4 (one decimal place)
29.832 (total of three decimal places in the answer)

6.624 (three decimal places)
× 1.22 (two decimal places)
8.08128 (total of 5 decimal places)

*On Your Own—Multiplying Decimals*

1. $\begin{array}{r} 12.89 \\ \times\,2.04 \\ \hline \end{array}$    3. $\begin{array}{r} 144.45 \\ \times\,16.23 \\ \hline \end{array}$

2. $\begin{array}{r} 56.12 \\ \times\,2.89 \\ \hline \end{array}$

**Dividing Decimals**   To divide decimals, follow the usual division rules. If the divisor (the number you are dividing by) has decimals, move the decimal point to the right as many places as necessary to make the divisor a whole number. Then move the decimal point of the dividend (the number you are dividing) that same number of places to the right. (You may have to add some zeros to the dividend to make this work.) Put the decimal point in the answer directly above the decimal point in the dividend.

**Examples**

$$12.76\overline{)58.696} = 1{,}276\overset{46}{\overline{)5{,}869.6}}$$   Note that the decimal point is moved two places to the right in each term. The decimal point in the answer is directly above the decimal point in the dividend.

$$1.25\overline{)50} = 125\overset{40}{\overline{)5{,}000}}$$   In this example the decimal point is moved two places to the right in 1.25 to make 125. The dividend 50 can also be expressed as 50.00 (adding zeros), and moving the decimal point the same number of places to the right makes 5,000. No decimal point needs to be shown in the answer because the answer is a whole number.

*On Your Own—Dividing Decimals*

1. $143.37 \div 12.15 =$    3. $62.15 \div 2.2 =$

2. $24.7 \div 20.7 =$

## Changing Decimals to Fractions

Read the decimal and then write the fraction. Reduce the fraction to its lowest terms.

**Examples**

$0.5 =$ five tenths or 5 over 10: $\dfrac{5}{10} = \dfrac{1}{2}$

$0.66 = 66$ hundredths or 66 over 100: $\dfrac{66}{100} = \dfrac{33}{50}$

$0.75 = 75$ hundredths or 75 over 100: $\dfrac{75}{100} = \dfrac{3}{4}$

$0.006 = 6$ thousandths or 6 over 1,000: $\dfrac{6}{1{,}000} = \dfrac{3}{500}$

$0.0006 = 6$ ten thousandths or 6 over 10,000: $\dfrac{6}{10{,}000} = \dfrac{3}{5{,}000}$

*On Your Own—Changing Decimals to Fractions*

1. $0.80 =$   3. $0.05 =$

2. $0.\overline{33} =$

---

**SSAT/ISEE Coach Says . . .**

**Fractions and Decimals.** All proper fractions are less than one, so the corresponding decimals will be to the right of the decimal point. Numbers to the left of the decimal point will be whole numbers.

---

## Changing Fractions to Decimals

To change a fraction to a decimal, divide the numerator by the denominator.

**Examples**

$$\frac{1}{2} = 1 \div 2 = 0.5$$

$$\frac{3}{4} = 3 \div 4 = 0.75$$

$$\frac{6}{1,000} = 6 \div 1,000 = 0.006$$

$\frac{2}{3} = 2 \div 3 = 0.6\overline{6}$ (The bar over the final 6 indicates that this is a *repeating decimal*. That means that you could keep on dividing forever and always have the same remainder.)

*On Your Own—Changing Fractions to Decimals*

1. $\frac{1}{8} =$   3. $\frac{5}{6} =$

2. $\frac{12}{36} =$

## Percents

*Percent* means "out of 100" or "per hundred." For example, "70%" is read as "70 percent," meaning 70 out of 100 equal parts. Percents are useful ways to show parts of a whole. They can also be easily changed into decimals or fractions.

**Changing Percents to Decimals**  As stated, percent means "per 100." So 70% means "70 per 100," which is 70/100 or 70 ÷ 100, which is 0.70. So to change percents to decimals, delete the percent sign and place the decimal point two places to the left. You may need to add zeros.

**Examples**

67% = 0.67

6% = 0.06 (A zero was added to the left of the 6.)

187% = 1.87

0.14% = 0.0014 (Two zeros were added to the left of the 14.)

*On Your Own—Changing Percents to Decimals*

1. 78% =                                    3. 443% =

2. 12% =

**Changing Decimals to Percents**   To change decimals to percents, merely move the decimal point two places to the right and add a percent sign. (You may need to add a zero on the right.)

**Examples**

0.67 = 67%

0.4 = 40% (A zero was added to the right of the 4.)

1.87 = 187%

28.886 = 2888.6%

0.0014 = 0.14%

*On Your Own—Changing Decimals to Percents*

1. 0.75 =                                    3. 0.4 =

2. 0.225 =

**Changing Percents to Fractions**   A percent is some number over (divided by) 100. So every percent is also a fraction with a denominator of 100. For example, 45% = 45/100. To change percents to fractions, remove the percent sign and write the number over 100. Reduce the fraction to lowest terms.

**Examples**

$$50\% \ = \ \frac{50}{100} \ = \ \frac{5}{10} \ = \ \frac{1}{2}$$

$$25\% \ = \ \frac{25}{100} \ = \ \frac{1}{4}$$

$$30\% \ = \ \frac{30}{100} \ \ \frac{3}{10}$$

*On Your Own—Changing Percents to Fractions*

1. 34% =                                    3. 99% =

2. 57% =

**Changing Fractions to Percents**  To change fractions to percents, change the
fraction to a decimal and then change the decimal to a percent.

**Examples**

$\frac{1}{2}$ = 0.5 = 50%

$\frac{1}{4}$ = 0.25 = 25%

$\frac{1}{10}$ = 0.10 = 10%

$\frac{6}{20}$ = $\frac{3}{10}$ = 0.3 = 30%

$\frac{1}{3}$ = 0.33$\overline{3}$ = 33$\frac{1}{3}$%

*On Your Own—Changing Fractions to Percents*

1. $\frac{1}{5}$ =                                 3. $\frac{3}{8}$ =

2. $\frac{2}{5}$ =

Time Savers: Fractions, Decimals, and Percents

Memorizing some of these relationships might save you some calculation time.

| Fraction(s) | = Decimal | = Percent (%) |
|---|---|---|
| $\frac{1}{100}$ | 0.01 | 1% |
| $\frac{1}{10}$ | 0.1 | 10% |
| $\frac{1}{5}$ = $\frac{2}{10}$ | 0.2 | 20% |
| $\frac{3}{10}$ | 0.3 | 30% |
| $\frac{2}{5}$ = $\frac{4}{10}$ | 0.4 | 40% |
| $\frac{1}{2}$ = $\frac{5}{10}$ | 0.5 | 50% |

(Continued)

Memorizing some of these relationships might save you some calculation time.

| Fraction(s) | = Decimal | = Percent (%) |
|---|---|---|
| $\frac{3}{5} = \frac{6}{10}$ | 0.6 | 60% |
| $\frac{4}{5} = \frac{8}{10}$ | 0.8 | 80% |
| $\frac{1}{4} = \frac{2}{8} = \frac{25}{100}$ | 0.25 | 25% |
| $\frac{3}{4} = \frac{75}{100}$ | 0.74 | 75% |
| $\frac{1}{3} = \frac{2}{6}$ | $0.33\frac{1}{3}$ | $33\frac{1}{3}\%$ |
| $\frac{2}{3}$ | $0.66\frac{2}{3}$ | $66\frac{2}{3}\%$ |
| $\frac{1}{8}$ | 0.125 | 12.5% |
| $\frac{3}{8}$ | 0.375 | 37.5% |
| $\frac{5}{8}$ | 0.625 | 62.5% |
| $\frac{1}{6}$ | $0.16\frac{2}{3}$ | $16\frac{2}{3}\%$ |
| 1 | 1.00 | 100% |
| 1.5 | 1.50 | 150% |

### Finding a Percent of a Number

The SSAT and ISEE may include problems that ask you to find a percent of a number. Problems are often worded like this: "What is 25% of 1,000?" There are two ways you can solve this kind of problem. You can start by changing the percent into a fraction, or you can change it into a decimal.

If you change 25% into a fraction, solve the problem like this:

$$\frac{25}{100} \times 1,000 = \frac{25,000}{100} = 250$$

If you change 25% into a decimal, solve the problem like this: $0.25 \times 1,000 = 250$. You should use the approach that is easiest and best for you.

Percent problems are sometimes stated in another way. For example, a problem may ask, "What percent of 200 is 25?" When you see a problem like this, make it into an equation:

$25 = x(200)$ where $x$ is the percent.

$$x = \frac{25}{200} = \frac{1}{8} = 0.125 = 12.5\%$$

**Example**
30 is what percent of 90?
$30 = x(90)$

$$\frac{30}{90} = \frac{1}{3} = 0.3\overline{3} = 33\frac{1}{3}\%$$

There is a third way in which percent problems are sometimes stated. Here is an example: "What percent of 25 is 20?"

When you see this kind of question, start by setting up a proportion:

Some unknown percent $(x\%) = \dfrac{20}{25}$

$x\%$ is really $\dfrac{x}{100}$, so the proportion becomes $\dfrac{x}{100} = \dfrac{20}{25}$.

Reduce the fraction and solve:

$$\frac{x}{100} = \frac{4}{5}$$
$5x = 400$
$x = 80$, so 20 is 80 percent of 25.

**Example**
30 is what percent of 120?

$$\frac{x}{100} = \frac{30}{120}$$

$$\frac{x}{100} = \frac{3}{12}$$

$12x = 300$

$$x = \frac{300}{12} = 25$$

$x = 25\%$

***On Your Own—Finding a Percent of a Number***

1. 25% of 125 =

2. 50% of 250 =

3. 80% of 200 =

### Finding the Percent of Increase or Decrease

You might also encounter two other types of percent problems on the SSAT or ISEE. Here is an example: "What is the percent increase in Kim's salary if she gets a raise from $12,000 to $15,000 per year?" Set this up as an equation with the following structure:

$$\frac{\text{Amount of change}}{\text{Original number}} = \text{Percent of change}$$

### Example: Percent of Increase

For the problem above about Kim's salary, the amount of change is 3,000 because Kim's salary increased by that amount. The original number is 12,000. Plug those numbers into the formula:

$$\frac{3,000}{12,000} = \frac{3}{12} = 0.25 = 25\%.$$ Kim's salary increased by 25%.

### Example: Percent of Decrease

A CD player has its price reduced from $250 to $200. What is the percent of decrease? Use the same process as with the previous problem.

$$\frac{\text{Amount of change}}{\text{Original number}} = \text{Percent of change}$$

The amount of change (decrease) is 50 (250 minus 200). The original number (original price) is $250. Plug these numbers into the formula:

$$\frac{50}{250} = \frac{5}{25} = \frac{1}{5} = 0.20.$$ The CD player price decreased by 20%.

#### *On Your Own—Finding the Percent of Increase or Decrease*

1. An iPod went on sale from $500 to $350. What is the percent decrease?
2. A house was purchased at $200,000 and sold for $350,000. What is the percent increase?
3. A car that cost $24,000 went on sale for $21,000. What is the percent decrease?

### Exponents

An *exponent* is a number that tells how many times another number is multiplied by itself. In the expression $4^3$, the 3 is an exponent. It means that 4 is multiplied by itself three times or $4 \times 4 \times 4$. So $4^3 = 64$. The expression $4^2$ is read "4 to the second power" or "4 squared." The expression $4^3$ is read "4 to the third power" or "4 cubed." The expression $4^4$ is read "4 to the fourth power." In each of these cases, the exponent is called a "power" of 4. In the expression $5^2$ ("5 to the second power" or "5 squared"), the exponent is a "power" of 5.

**Examples**

$3^5 = 3 \times 3 \times 3 \times 3 \times 3 = 243$

$6^2 = 6 \times 6 = 36$

**Negative Exponents**   Exponents can also be negative. To interpret negative exponents, follow this pattern:

$$2^{-3} = \frac{1}{2^3} = \frac{1}{8}$$

**Examples**

$$3^{-2} = \frac{1}{3^2} = \frac{1}{9}$$

$$4^{-3} = \frac{1}{4^3} \quad \text{or} \quad \frac{1}{64}$$

**Multiplying Numbers with Exponents**   To multiply numbers with exponents, multiply each number and then perform the operation.

**Examples**

$3^4 \times 2^3 = (3 \times 3 \times 3 \times 3) \times (2 \times 2 \times 2)$

$= 81 \times 8 = 648$

$2^9 \times 12^2 = (2 \times 2 \times 2 \times 2 \times 2 \times 2 \times 2 \times 2 \times 2) \times (12 \times 12)$

$= 512 \times 144 = 73,728$

*On Your Own—Multiplying Numbers with Exponents*

1.  $3^3 \times 6^2 =$ 

3.  $8^1 \times 6^3 =$ 

2.  $6^2 \times 12^2 =$ 

## Scientific Notation

A number written in scientific notation is the product of two factors. The first factor is a number greater than or equal to 1 but less than the number 10 ($1 \leq$ number $< 10$).

The second factor is 10 raised to an exponent, or power, of 10.

**Examples**

In scientific notation, the number 5,500 is written as $5.5 \times 10^3$. Remember that $10 \times 10 \times 10$ equals 1,000, and $1,000 \times 5.5$ equals 5500. A number such as $5.5 \times 10^3$ means that starting with the decimal point in 5.5, you must add zeros and move the decimal point three digits to the right. So $5.5 \times 10^3$ becomes 5,500.

When a number is less than 1, scientific notation uses negative exponents. The number 0.025 is written as $2.5 \times 10^{-2}$. The exponent is negative, so the standard form is a number less than 1. Write two zeros before the 2 in 2.5 and move the decimal point two places to the left. So $2.5 \times 10^{-2}$ becomes 0.025.

1. What is 1,200 written in scientific notation?
2. What is 0.0075 written in scientific notation?
3. What is 23,500,000 written in scientific notation?
4. What is $1.25 \times 10^5$ written in standard form?
5. What is $3.5 \ 10^{-5}$ written in standard form?

## Square Roots

The *square* of a number is the number times the number. The square of 2 is $2 \times 2 = 4$. The *square root* of a number is the number whose square equals the original number. One square root of 4 (written $\sqrt{4}$) is 2, since $2 \times 2 = 4$. Note that $-2$ is also a square root of 4 since $(-2) \times (-2) = 4$.

---

*SSAT/ISEE Coach Says . . .*
**Watch the Signs!** Remember that a negative number multiplied by itself results in a positive number.

---

### Some Examples

$\sqrt{1} = 1$ or $-1$

$\sqrt{4} = 2$ or $-2$

$\sqrt{9} = 3$ or $-3$

$\sqrt{16} = 4$ or $-4$

$\sqrt{25} = 5$ or $-5$

$\sqrt{36} = 6$ or $-6$

$\sqrt{49} = 7$ or $-7$

$\sqrt{64} = 8$ or $-8$

$\sqrt{81} = 9$ or $-9$

$\sqrt{100} = 10$ or $-10$

$\sqrt{121} = 11$ or $-11$

$\sqrt{144} = 12$ or $-12$

$\sqrt{169} = 13$ or $-13$

$\sqrt{196} = 14$ or $-14$

$\sqrt{225} = 15$ or $-15$

### On Your Own—Square Roots

1. $\sqrt{256} =$                                             3. $\sqrt{441} =$

2. $\sqrt{400} =$

## Units of Measure

If you don't know the following units of measure, you just need to memorize them to make the necessary conversions from one unit to another.

---

**UNITS OF MEASURE**

**Customary System**

**Length**

12 inches (in) = 1 foot (ft)

3 feet = 1 yard (yd)

36 inches = 1 yard

5,280 feet = 1 mile (mi)

**Area**

1 square foot ($ft^2$) = 144 square inches ($in^2$)

9 square feet = 1 square yard ($yd^2$)

**Weight**

16 ounces (oz) = 1 pound (lb)

2,000 pounds = 1 ton (ton)

**Liquid Volume**

2 cups (c) = 1 pint (pt)

2 pints = 1 quart (qt)

4 quarts = 1 gallon (gal)

**Time**

7 days = 1 week

4 weeks = 1 month

12 months = 1 year

52 weeks = 1 year

10 years = 1 decade

**Metric System**

**Length**

100 centimeters (cm) = 1 meter (m)

1,000 meters = 1 kilometer (km)

**Volume**

1,000 milliliters (mL) = 1 liter (L)

**Mass**

1,000 grams (g) = 1 kilogram (kg)

1,000 kilograms = 1 metric ton (t)

**Converting Between Systems**

1 meter ≈ 39.37 inches

1 kilometer ≈ 0.62 mile

1 centimeter ≈ 0.39 inch

1 kilogram ≈ 2.2 pounds

1 liter ≈ 1.057 quarts

1 gram ≈ 0.035 ounce

---

*On Your Own—Measurement*

1. How many yards are in 252 inches?
2. How many square feet are in 5 square yards?
3. How many tons are in 5,000 pounds?
4. How many cups are in 4 gallons?
5. How many weeks are in 10 decades?
6. How many meters are in 8 kilometers?
7. How many meters are in 600 centimeters?
8. How many liters are in 25,000 milliliters?
9. How many grams are in 1.25 kilograms?
10. How many metric tons are in 2,500 kilograms?

## Answers to "On Your Own" Practice Sets

**On Your Own—Place Value**

1. 5                    2. 0                    3. 6

**On Your Own—Addition**

| | |
|---|---|
| 1. 745 | 6. 3,460,988 |
| 2. 21,460 | 7. 670,504 |
| 3. 25,676 | 8. 4,554,000,831 |
| 4. 97,986 | 9. 6,913,208 |
| 5. 98,742,358 | 10. 34,958,777 |

**On Your Own—Subtraction**

| | |
|---|---|
| 1. 812 | 6. 589,831 |
| 2. 2,495 | 7. 84,822,389 |
| 3. 22,411 | 8. 991,188 |
| 4. 55,445 | 9. 144,985,636 |
| 5. 11,005,411 | 10. 99 |

**On Your Own—Multiplication**

| | |
|---|---|
| 1. 20 | 6. 410,843 |
| 2. 20 | 7. 14,745,358 |
| 3. 63 | 8. 6,028,318,806 |
| 4. 1,755 | 9. 212,244,289,278 |
| 5. 6,566 | 10. 554,736,386,736,842 |

## On Your Own—Division

| | |
|---|---|
| 1. 4 | 6. 258 |
| 2. 12 | 7. 32 |
| 3. 2 | 8. 21 |
| 4. 456 | 9. 12 |
| 5. 987 | 10. 331 |

## On Your Own—Symbols

| | |
|---|---|
| 1. T | 6. F |
| 2. T | 7. T |
| 3. T | 8. T |
| 4. F | 9. F |
| 5. T | 10. F |

## On Your Own—Order of Operations

| | |
|---|---|
| 1. 40 | 5. 41 |
| 2. 50 | 6. 152 |
| 3. 90 | 7. 21 |
| 4. 21 | 8. 218 |

## On Your Own—Adding Positive and Negative Numbers

| | |
|---|---|
| 1. 1 | 5. −58 |
| 2. −7 | 6. 200 |
| 3. 9 | 7. 320 |
| 4. 130 | 8. −125 |

## On Your Own—Subtracting Positive and Negative Numbers

| | |
|---|---|
| 1. 8 | 6. 475 |
| 2. 16 | 7. 1,400 |
| 3. 20 | 8. 1,400 |
| 4. 33 | 9. 62 |
| 5. 116 | |

### On Your Own—Multiplying and Dividing Negative Numbers

1. −8
2. +8
3. +40
4. −2
5. +2
6. −2
7. 320
8. −50

### On Your Own—Subtracting Numbers within Parentheses

1. 120
2. 5
3. 135
4. 475
5. 250
6. 19
7. 151

### On Your Own—Multiplying and Dividing by Zero

1. 0
2. 0
3. 0
4. 0
5. undefined

### On Your Own—Greatest Common Factor

1. 6
2. 37
3. 17
4. 8

### On Your Own—Least Common Multiple

1. 2
2. 2
3. 3
4. 2

### On Your Own—Changing Improper Fractions into Mixed Numbers

1. $12\frac{1}{2}$
2. $2\frac{1}{3}$
3. $11\frac{1}{4}$
4. $26\frac{1}{3}$
5. $16\frac{4}{5}$
6. $7\frac{7}{10}$

## On Your Own—Renaming a Mixed Number as a Fraction

1. $\dfrac{10}{3}$

2. $\dfrac{25}{4}$

3. $\dfrac{71}{12}$

4. $\dfrac{15}{4}$

5. $\dfrac{37}{5}$

## On Your Own—Finding Equivalent Fractions

1. $\dfrac{2}{6}$; $\dfrac{3}{9}$; $\dfrac{4}{12}$

2. $\dfrac{4}{6}$; $\dfrac{6}{9}$; $\dfrac{8}{12}$

3. $\dfrac{1}{2}$; $\dfrac{4}{8}$; $\dfrac{6}{12}$

## On Your Own—Reducing Fractions to Lowest Terms

1. $\dfrac{1}{3}$

2. $\dfrac{1}{2}$

3. $\dfrac{1}{4}$

4. $\dfrac{1}{2}$

5. $\dfrac{1}{8}$

6. $\dfrac{1}{13}$

## On Your Own—Adding and Subtracting Fractions

1. $\dfrac{5}{6}$

2. $1\dfrac{13}{24}$

3. $1\dfrac{5}{8}$

4. $\dfrac{2}{3}$

5. $\dfrac{7}{15}$

## On Your Own—Adding and Subtracting Mixed Numbers

1. $5\dfrac{1}{2}$

2. $16\dfrac{1}{6}$

3. $13\dfrac{2}{15}$

4. $4\dfrac{5}{8}$

5. $7\dfrac{5}{9}$

**On Your Own—Multiplying Fractions**

1. $\frac{21}{40}$
3. $\frac{4}{35}$

2. $\frac{12}{75}$

**On Your Own—Dividing Fractions**

1. 1
3. $2\frac{2}{3}$

2. $2\frac{2}{5}$

**On Your Own—Multiplying Mixed Numbers**

1. $19\frac{11}{15}$
3. $29\frac{5}{9}$

2. $23\frac{2}{5}$

**On Your Own—Dividing Mixed Numbers**

1. $5\frac{3}{7}$
3. $2\frac{3}{5}$

2. 13

**On Your Own—Adding and Subtracting Decimals**

1. 546.57
4. 686.87

2. 44,571.001
5. 1,012.13

3. 891.11
6. 32.11

**On Your Own—Multiplying Decimals**

1. 26.2956
3. 2,344.4235

2. 162.1868

**On Your Own—Dividing Decimals**

1. 11.8
3. 28.25

2. 1.19

**On Your Own—Changing Decimals to Fractions**

1. $\dfrac{4}{5}$

2. $\dfrac{1}{3}$

3. $\dfrac{1}{20}$

**On Your Own—Changing Fractions to Decimals**

1. 0.125

2. $0.\overline{3}$

3. $0.8\overline{3}$

**On Your Own—Changing Percents to Decimals**

1. 0.78

2. 0.12

3. 4.43

**On Your Own—Changing Decimals to Percents**

1. 75%

2. 22.5%

3. 40%

**On Your Own—Changing Percents to Fractions**

1. $\dfrac{17}{50}$

2. $\dfrac{57}{100}$

3. $\dfrac{99}{100}$

**On Your Own—Changing Fractions to Percents**

1. 20%

2. 40%

3. 37.5%

**On Your Own—Finding a Percent of a Number**

1. 31.25

2. 125

3. 160

**On Your Own—Finding the Percent of Increase or Decrease**

1. 30%

2. 75%

3. 12.5%

**On Your Own—Multiplying Numbers with Exponents**

1. 972

2. 5,184

3. 1,728

**On Your Own—Scientific Notation**

1. $1.2 \times 10^3$

2. $7.5 \times 10^{-3}$

3. $2.35 \times 10^7$

4. 125,000

5. 0.000035

**On Your Own—Square Roots**

1. 16

2. 20

3. 21

**On Your Own—Measurement**

1. 7 yd

2. 45 ft$^2$

3. 2 $\frac{1}{2}$ tons

4. 64 c

5. 520 weeks

6. 8,000 m

7. 6 m

8. 25 L

9. 1250 g

10. 2.5 t

# The Algebra You Need to Know

## Algebra on the SSAT and ISEE

If you are taking the lower-level version of the SSAT or the ISEE, you will need to know some very simple concepts in algebra. If you are taking the upper-level version of either test, you may need to be familiar with some more advanced algebra concepts. This chapter will review the following topics:

**Topics**

| | |
|---|---|
| Evaluating Expressions | Operations with Algebraic Expressions |
| Solving Simple Equations | Operations with Imaginary Numbers |
| Ratios, Rates, and Proportions | Sequences—Arithmetic and Geometric |

This chapter will give you a complete review of all these algebra topics. After you study each topic, check your progress by working through the practice sets called "On Your Own." Answers for these practice sets appear at the end of the chapter.

## Algebra Review

### The Language of Algebra

Algebra uses arithmetic functions and processes, but some of the numbers are replaced by letters. The letters merely represent numbers that are currently unknown or that can change in value according to circumstances. In algebra, a letter representing a number that can change in value is called a *variable*.

- An expression such as $6x$ means "6 times $x$" or "$x$ times 6."
- An expression such as $x + 7$ means "some number, currently unknown, plus 7."
- An expression such as $x - 12$ means "some number, currently unknown, less 12."
- An expression such as $\frac{x}{5}$ means "some number, currently unknown, divided by 5, or the ratio of some number and 5."

Very often verbal expressions in word problems need to be translated into algebraic expressions before they can be solved. Below are some examples of verbal expressions and their algebraic counterparts.

| Verbal Expression | Algebraic Expression |
|---|---|
| Some number plus 7 | $x + 7$ |
| Some number subtracted from 8 | $8 - x$ |
| 8 subtracted from some number | $x - 8$ |
| The product of some number and 12 | $12x$ |
| The product of 5 and the sum of $x$ and $y$ | $5(x + y)$ |
| Some number divided by 4 | $\dfrac{x}{4}$ |
| The ratio of 6 and some number | $\dfrac{6}{x}$ |
| 9 times some number plus the sum of 5 and $y$ | $9x + (5 + y)$ |
| 12 less the sum of 3 and some number | $12 - (3 + x)$ |

### On Your Own—Algebra Language
Write the following using algebraic expressions.

1. Six times some number plus four squared.
2. Twelve times the sum of six plus some number.
3. The product of $x$ and $y$ times the product of 11 plus the product of $x$ and $y$.
4. Some number divided by 40 and the product of $x$ and $y$.
5. Some number squared plus that number times 14 equals minus 21.

## Evaluating Expressions

To evaluate an algebraic expression, substitute a given value for the unknown and then perform the arithmetic as indicated.

### Examples

Evaluate $a + b + c$ if $a = 2$, $b = 4$, and $c = 3$
Substitute each value for the corresponding letter and then do the addition as indicated.

$2 + 4 + 3 = 9$

Evaluate $2x^2 + 4y + 5$ if $x = 2$ and $y = 3$

$2(2)^2 + 4(3) + 5$
$= 2(4) + 12 + 5$
$= 8 + 12 + 5 = 25$

Evaluate $\dfrac{a+b}{4} + \dfrac{a}{b+c}$ if $a = 2$, $b = 6$, and $c = 10$

$$\dfrac{2+6}{4} + \dfrac{2}{6+10}$$

$$= \dfrac{8}{4} + \dfrac{2}{16}$$

$$= 2 + \dfrac{2}{16}$$

$$= 2\dfrac{1}{8}$$

---

***SSAT/ISEE Coach Says . . .***

**Don't Forget:** Order of operations is critical!
- Simplify anything within the parentheses.
- Apply the powers or exponents.
- Multiply and divide in order from left to right.
- Add and subtract in order from left to right.

---

***On Your Own—Evaluating Expressions***
Evaluate the following:

1. $x + y + z$ if $x = 2$, $y = 6$, $z = 10$
2. $(x + y)^2 + (y - 1)$ if $x = 8$, $y = 4$
3. $6x + (y + z)^2$ if $x = 5$, $y = 2$, $z = 3$

## Solving Simple Equations

An *equation* is a mathematical statement having an equal (=) sign. When an equation contains a letter standing for an unknown number, you can use the equation to find the value of that unknown. This is called *solving the equation for the unknown*.

Think of an equation as a balanced scale. Everything to the right of the = sign has to balance with everything on the left side of the = sign.

Because an equation is balanced, it will stay in balance if you do the same thing to the numbers on both sides of the = sign. For example, the equation $10 = 10$ will stay balanced if you add 3 to both sides. The new equation will be $13 = 13$. Similarly, the equation $x + y = x + y$ will stay balanced if you subtract 10 from both sides. The new equation will be $x + y - 10 = x + y - 10$.

Likewise, the equation $x + y = a + b$ will stay balanced if you add 8 to both sides. The new equation will be $x + y + 8 = a + b + 8$.

To solve an equation and find the value of an unknown, you need to get the *unknown on one side of the equation* and all the other terms on the other side of the equation. Consider this example.

Solve: $y - 4 = 20$

Add 4 to both sides:

$y - 4 + 4 = 20 + 4$
$y = 20 + 4$
$y = 24$

---

***SSAT/ISEE Coach Says . . .***

**Another Way to Think about It.** Here is a simple way to think about using addition or subtraction to solve an equation: Just move the number you are adding or subtracting from one side of the = sign to the other and change its sign (either − to + or + to −). So in the equation shown, move the − 4 to the other side of the = sign and make it + 4. This makes the equation $y = 20 + 4$ or 24.

---

An equation will also stay balanced if you multiply or divide both sides by the same number. You can use these operations to solve equations.

**Example (Division)**

Solve: $3x = 18$

You want to get $x$ all alone on the left side of the equation, so divide $3x$ by 3. Since $\frac{3}{3} = 1$, $\frac{3x}{3} = x$. To maintain the balance, divide the right side of the equation by 3 as well:

$\frac{18}{3} = 6$.  So $x = 6$

---

***SSAT/ISEE Coach Says . . .***

**Another Way to Think about It.** Here is another way to think about using division to solve an equation. With a problem such as $3x = 18$, instead of trying to divide both sides by 3, simply move the 3 across the = sign and make it the denominator of the other side of the equation:

$3x = 18$

$x = \frac{18}{3}$

$x = 6$

---

**Example (Multiplication)**

$$\frac{x}{3} = 12$$

Multiply both sides by 3:

$$3\,\frac{x}{3} = 3(12)$$

$$x = 3(12)$$

$$x = 36$$

---

*SSAT/ISEE Coach Says . . .*

**Another Way to Think about It.** Here is another way to think about using multiplication to solve an equation: In a problem such as $x/2 = 20$, move the denominator 2 across the = sign and make it the multiplier on the other side.

$$\frac{x}{2} = 20$$

$$x = 2(20)$$

$$x = 40$$

---

**Examples**

Solve for $z$:

$$16 + z = 24$$

Subtract 16 from both sides.

$$z = 24 - 16 = 8$$

Solve for $x$:

$$\frac{x}{5} - 4 = 2$$

Add 4 to both sides.

$$\frac{x}{5} = 2 + 4$$

$$\frac{x}{5} = 6$$

Multiply each side by 5 to isolate $x$ on the left side.

$$x = 5(6) = 30$$

Solve for $a$:

$$\frac{2}{3}a - 5 = 9$$

Add 5 to both sides.

$$\frac{2}{3}a = 9 + 5$$

$$\frac{2}{3}a = 14$$

Multiply each side by $\frac{3}{2}$.

$$a = 14\left(\frac{3}{2}\right)$$

$$a = \frac{42}{2} = 21$$

---

**SSAT/ISEE Coach Says . . .**
**Divide Out Common Factors.** Another way to do this final step is to divide out common factors.

$$\frac{{}^7\cancel{14}}{1} \times \frac{3}{\cancel{2}_1} = 21$$

---

Solve for $y$:

$7y = 3y - 12$

$7y - 3y = -12$

$4y = -12$

$y = -\dfrac{12}{4}$

$y = -3$

***On Your Own—Solving Simple Equations***
Solve for the unknown in each equation.

1. $20 + z = 32$

2. $\dfrac{x}{10} - 5 = 25$

3. $\dfrac{x}{3} = -15$

4. $y - 12 = -20$

## Ratios, Rates, and Proportions

A *ratio* is a comparison of one number to another. A ratio can be represented by a fraction.

**Example**

On a certain road, there are 6 cars for every 4 trucks. The ratio is $\dfrac{6}{4}$ or $\dfrac{3}{2}$.

A *proportion* is an equation stating that two ratios are equivalent. Ratios are equivalent if they can be represented by equivalent fractions. A proportion may be written

$$\frac{a}{b} = \frac{c}{d}$$

where *a/b* and *c/d* are equivalent fractions. This proportion can be read "*a* is to *b* as *c* is to *d*."

Like any other equation, a proportion can be solved for an unknown by isolating that unknown on one side of the equation. In this case, to solve for *a*, multiply both sides by *b*:

$$(b)\frac{a}{b} = (b)\frac{c}{d}$$

$$a = \frac{bc}{d}$$

**Examples**

Solve for *c*:

$$\frac{c}{p} = \frac{h}{j}$$

Multiply both sides by *p*.

$$(p)\frac{c}{p} = (p)\frac{h}{j}$$

$$c = \frac{ph}{j}$$

Solve for *a*:

$$\frac{a}{4} = \frac{3}{6}$$

$$(4)\frac{a}{4} = (4)\frac{3}{6}$$

$$a = \frac{12}{6}$$

$$a = 2$$

A *rate* is a ratio with a unit of measure attached. If your car gets 30 miles per gallon of gas (30 mpg), how many gallons will you use if you drive 75 miles? You can solve the problem using a proportion.

$$\frac{30\ m}{1\ g} = \frac{75\ m}{x}$$

$$30x = 75$$

$$x = 2.5\ g$$

**SSAT/ISEE Coach Says . . .**

**Another Way to Solve It.** Another way to solve proportion problems is to find the cross products.

Solve for $a$:

$$\frac{a}{4} = \frac{3}{6}$$

Cross-multiply:

$a \times 6 = 4 \times 3$
$6a = 12$
$a = 2$

Solve for $k$:

$$\frac{2}{5} = \frac{8}{k}$$

$2k = 40$

$k = 20$

### On Your Own—Ratios, Rates, and Proportions

1. Solve for $m$:  $\dfrac{2}{5} = \dfrac{16}{m}$

2. Solve for $q$:  $\dfrac{2}{5} = \dfrac{q}{16}$

3. Solve for $d$:  $\dfrac{a}{b} = \dfrac{c}{d}$

4. If you type 50 words per minute, how many words will you type in 25 minutes?

## Operations with Algebraic Expressions

Study the following examples to learn how to add, subtract, multiply, and divide simple algebraic expressions.

**Adding and Subtracting Algebraic Expressions**   As long as the variables are the same, just add or subtract the numbers.

### Examples

Add:
$$\begin{array}{r} 9y \\ +11y \\ \hline 20y \end{array}$$

Subtract:
$$\begin{array}{r} 30b \\ -15b \\ \hline 15b \end{array}$$

| Add: | Subtract: |
|---|---|
| $12a^2bc$ | $12a^2bc$ |
| $+4a^2bc$ | $-4a^2bc$ |
| $16a^2bc$ | $8a^2bc$ |

**Multiplying Algebraic Expressions**   When multiplying simple algebraic expressions, multiply any numbers, then multiply unknowns. Add any exponents. Keep in mind that in a term like $x$ or $2x$, the $x$ is understood to have the exponent 1 even though the 1 is not shown.

**Examples**

$(2k)(k) = 2k^2$

$(3x)(2y) = 6xy$

$(k^2)(k^3) = k^5$

$(j^3k)(j^2k^3) = j^5k^4$

$-5(b^4c)(-3b^3c^5) = 15b^7c^6$

**Dividing Algebraic Expressions**   To divide simple algebraic expressions, divide the numbers and subtract any exponents (the exponent of the divisor from the exponent of the number being divided).

**Examples**

$$\frac{2g^5}{6g^3} = \frac{1}{3}g^2$$

$$3\frac{g^5}{g^3} = 3g^2$$

$$\frac{12a^6b^2}{3a^3b} = 4a^3b$$

$$\frac{m^5}{m^8} = m^{-3} = \frac{1}{m^3}$$

*On Your Own—Operations with Algebraic Expressions*

1. Add:

    $6a^2bc$
    $+ 3a^2bc$

2. Subtract:

    $12a^2bc$
    $- 16a^2bc$

3. Multiply:

    $5(g^4c)(-3g^3c^5)$

4. Divide:

    $$\frac{3x^3y^5}{xy^2}$$

**Operations with Imaginary Numbers**

An **imaginary number** is a number that when squared results in a negative product. The square root of $\sqrt{4}$ is $+2$ or $-2$. We know this because $2 \times 2 = 4$ and $-2 \times -2 = 4$. What would be the value of $\sqrt{-4}$? Imaginary numbers make it possible to answer this question. The imaginary unit is expressed as $i = \sqrt{-1}$, where $i^2 = -1$.

Remember, any number raised to the power of zero ($^0$) equals 1. In summary $i^0 = 1$, $i = \sqrt{-1}$, and $i^2 = -1$.

A **complex number** has the form $a + bi$, where $a$ and $b$ are real numbers and $i$ represents the imaginary unit. The number $4 + 2i$ is a complex number written in standard form. The problems you will encounter with imaginary numbers will require that you use basic operations to evaluate expressions.

**Examples**

$$\sqrt{-9} = \sqrt{9(-1)} = \sqrt{9} \times \sqrt{-1} = 3 \times i = 3i$$

$$\sqrt{-16} + \sqrt{-25} = \sqrt{16} \times \sqrt{-1} + \sqrt{25} \times \sqrt{-1} = 4 + \sqrt{-1} + 5 + \sqrt{-1} = 9 + 2i$$

$$\sqrt{-25} \times \sqrt{-25} = \sqrt{25}i \times \sqrt{25}i = (\sqrt{25} \times \sqrt{25}) \times i \times i = (\sqrt{25})^2 \times i^2$$

$$= 25 \times -1 = -25$$

$$(3 + 4i) + (2 - 2i) = (3 + 2) + (4i - 2i) = 5 + 2i$$

*On Your Own—Operations with Imaginary Numbers*

Evaluate and write in simplest form.

1. $\sqrt{-36}$
2. $\sqrt{-49} \times \sqrt{-49}$

3. $\sqrt{-16} + \sqrt{-64}$
4. $(4 - 3i) - (2 + 2i)$

## Sequences—Arithmetic and Geometric

A **sequence** is a list of numbers that follow a particular rule or pattern. There are two basic types of sequences.

In an **arithmetic sequence**, the next term is generated by adding a common difference to the preceding term.

**Examples**

Look at the arithmetic sequence shown below.

9, 10.5, 12, 13.5, 15, …

The common difference of this sequence is 1.5. To find the next term, you add 1.5 to the preceding term. So $15 + 1.5 = 16.5$; therefore the next term is 16.5. The term after that would be $16.5 + 1.5 = 18$.

The arithmetic sequence below has a more complex pattern.

3, 5, 8, 12, 17, …

The common difference of this sequence seems to change from one number to the next. However, it does contain a pattern. Notice that 2 is added to the first term to form the second term; that is, $3 + 2 = 5$. You form the third term by adding 3 to the second term, the fourth term by adding 4 to the third term, and so on. In other words, the common difference between terms keeps increasing by one, so the difference is $n + 1$, where $n$ represents the number. Therefore the next term in this sequence would be $17 + 6 = 23$.

In a **geometric sequence**, you generate the next term by multiplying the preceding term by the same number, called a common ratio.

### Examples

1, 4, 16, 64, 256, …

The common ratio of this sequence is 4. Each next term is found by multiplying the previous term by 4. The next term in this sequence is 1,024, because $256 \times 4 = 1,024$. The term after this would be $1,024 \times 4 = 4,096$.

2, 1, $^1/_2$, $^1/_4$, …

In the geometric sequence above, the common ratio is $^1/_2$. Each next term is found by multiplying the preceding term by $^1/_2$. Therefore, the next term in this sequence is 1/16.

### *On Your Own—Sequences—Arithmetic and Geometric*

1. What is the next term of this sequence below?

   3, 7, 11, 15, 19, …

2. What is the next term of this sequence below?

   46, 35, 26, 19, 14, …

3. What is the next term of this sequence below?

   1, 3, 9, 27, 81, …

4. What is the next term of this sequence below?

   9, 3, 1, $^1/_3$, $^1/_9$, …

## Answers to "On Your Own" Practice Sets

### On Your Own—Algebra Language

1. $6x + (4)^2$

2. $12(6 + x)$

3. $(xy)(11 + xy)$

4. $\dfrac{g}{40 + xy}$

5. $x^2 + 14x = -21$

**On Your Own—Evaluating Expressions**

1. 18

2. 147

3. 55

**On Your Own—Solving Simple Equations**

1. $z = 12$

2. $x = 300$

3. $x = -45$

4. $y = -8$

**On Your Own—Ratios, Rates, and Proportions**

1. $m = 40$

2. $q = 6\dfrac{2}{5}$

3. $d = \dfrac{cb}{a}$

4. 1,250 words

**On Your Own—Operations with Algebraic Expressions**

1. $9a^2bc$

2. $-4a^2bc$

3. $-15g^7c^6$

4. $3x^2y^3$

**On Your Own—Operations with Imaginary Numbers**

1. $6i$

2. $-49$

3. $12i$

4. $2 - 5i$

**On Your Own—Sequences—Arithmetic and Geometric**

1. 23

2. 11

3. 243

4. $\dfrac{1}{27}$

# CHAPTER 12

# The Geometry You Need to Know

## Geometry on the SSAT and ISEE

If you are taking the lower level version of the SSAT or the ISEE, you will need to know some very simple concepts in geometry. If you are taking the upper level version of either test, you may need to be familiar with some more advanced geometry concepts. This chapter will review the following topics:

### Topics

| | |
|---|---|
| Points, Lines, and Angles | Median of a Triangle |
| Classifying Angles | Special Right Triangles |
| Classifying Pairs of Lines | Triangle Congruence and Similarity |
| Classifying Pairs of Angles | Quadrilaterals |
| Indentifying Congruent (Equal) Angles | Circles |
| Solving Angle Problems | Perimeter and Area |
| Triangles | Three-Dimensional (Solid) Figures |
| Base and Height of a Triangle | Finding the Volume of Solid Figures |

This chapter will give you a complete review of all these geometry topics. After you study each topic, check your progress by working through the practice sets called "On Your Own." Answers for these practice sets appear at the end of the chapter.

## Geometry Review

### Points, Lines, and Angles

To work with geometry, you need to understand points, lines, and angles.

- A *point* is an exact location in space. It is represented by a dot and a capital letter.
- A *line* is a set of points that form a straight path extending in either direction without end. A line that includes points $B$ and $D$ is represented as follows: $\overline{BD}$.
- A *ray* is a part of a line that has one end point and continues without end in the opposite direction. A ray that ends at point $A$ and includes point $B$ is represented as follows: $\overline{AB}$.

- A *line segment* is a part of a ray or a line that connects two points. A line segment connecting points $A$ and $B$ is represented as follows: $\overline{AB}$.

An *angle* is a figure formed by two rays that have the same end point. That end point is called the *vertex* (plural: *vertices*) of the angle. An example is shown below.

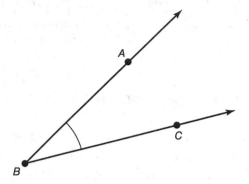

In this example, rays $BA$ and $BC$ have the same end point, which is point $B$. So point $B$ is the vertex of the angle. The two line segments $BA$ and $BC$ are called the sides of the angle. The symbol $\angle$ is used to indicate an angle.

An angle is labeled or identified in several different ways:

- By the vertex: $\angle B$
- By the letters of the three points that form it: $\angle ABC$ or $\angle CBA$. (The vertex is always the middle of the three letters.)

The measure of the size of an angle is expressed in *degrees* (°).

---

**SSAT/ISEE Coach Says . . .**
**Bisect.** You will see the word *bisect* used in some geometry problems. To *bisect* merely means to split into two equal parts.

---

## Classifying Angles

There are three types of angles that you should know for the SSAT or ISEE. They are right angles, acute angles, and obtuse angles.

**Right Angles**   A right angle measures exactly 90°. Right angles are found in squares, rectangles, and certain triangles. $\angle ABC$ is a right angle.

**Examples**

Both angles below are right angles.

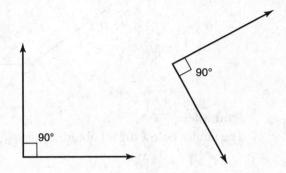

**Acute Angles**   An angle that measures less than 90° is called an acute angle. ∠*ABC* is an acute angle.

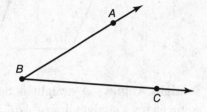

**Examples**

The angles below are all acute angles.

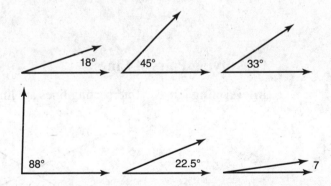

**Obtuse Angles**  An angle with a measure that is greater than 90° but less than 180° is called an obtuse angle. ∠*DEF* is an obtuse angle.

**Examples**
The angles below are all obtuse angles.

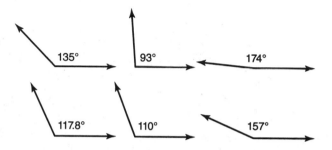

**Straight Angles**  A straight angle is one that measures exactly 180°. This kind of angle forms a straight line. ∠*ABC* is a straight angle.

## Classifying Pairs of Lines

**Intersecting Lines**  Intersecting lines are lines that meet or cross each other.

Line *DF* intersects line *GH* at point *E*.

**Parallel Lines**   Parallel lines are lines in a plane that never intersect.

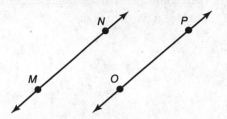

Line *MN* is parallel to line *OP*. In symbols, *MN* ∥ *OP*.

**Perpendicular Lines**   Perpendicular lines intersect to form right angles.

Line *ST* is perpendicular to line *UV*. In symbols, *ST* ⊠ *UV*.

## Classifying Pairs of Angles

**Adjacent Angles**   Adjacent angles have the same vertex and share one side. ∠*ABC* and ∠*CBD* are adjacent angles.

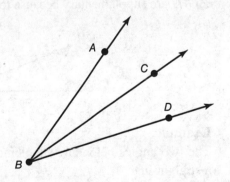

**Complementary Angles**  Two adjacent angles whose measures total 90° are called complementary angles. ∠*MNO* and ∠*ONP* are complementary. Their measures total exactly 90°.

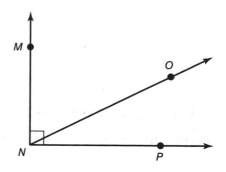

### Example
These two angles are complementary. Together they measure 90°.

**Supplementary Angles**  Two adjacent angles whose measures total 180° are called supplementary angles. Together they make a straight line. ∠*KHG* and ∠*GHJ* are supplementary because together they add to 180° or a straight line.

### Example
The two angles below are supplementary. Together they measure 180° and form a straight line.

**Vertical Angles**   Two angles formed by intersecting lines are called vertical angles if they are not adjacent. In the figure below, ∠AED and ∠BEC are vertical angles. ∠AEB and ∠DEC are also vertical angles. Vertical angles are often said to be "opposite" to each other as shown in the figure.

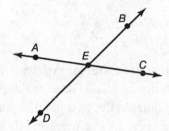

Vertical angles are *congruent*. That is, their measures are the same. ∠AED = ∠BEC and ∠AEB = ∠DEC.

**Example**

## Identifying Congruent (Equal) Angles

In the figure below, lines *AC* and *DF* are parallel. They are intersected by a third line *GH*. This third line is called a *transversal*.

This intersection creates eight angles. There are four pairs of vertical congruent angles:

∠ABH = ∠EBC
∠ABE = ∠HBC
∠DEB = ∠GEF
∠DEG = ∠BEF

**Alternate Interior Angles**    In addition, four of these angles make two pairs of alternate interior angles. These are angles that are on opposite sides of the transversal, are between the two parallel lines, and are not adjacent. When parallel lines are intersected by a transversal, alternate interior angles are congruent. The two pairs are:

$\angle ABE = \angle BEF$
$\angle DEB = \angle EBC$

**Alternate Exterior Angles**    Four of the angles also make two pairs of alternate exterior angles. These are angles that are on opposite sides of the transversal, are outside the two parallel lines, and are not adjacent. When parallel lines are intersected by a transversal, alternate exterior angles are congruent. The two pairs are:

$\angle ABH = \angle GEF$
$\angle HBC = \angle DEG$

**Corresponding Angles**    Eight of the angles also make four pairs of corresponding angles. These are angles that are in corresponding positions. When parallel lines are intersected by a transversal, corresponding angles are congruent. The four pairs are:

$\angle ABH = \angle DEB$
$\angle HBC = \angle BEF$
$\angle ABE = \angle DEG$
$\angle EBC = \angle GEF$

## Solving Angle Problems

On the SSAT or ISEE, you may be asked to use what you know about angles and angle relationships to solve problems. You may be asked to tell which angles in a figure are congruent. Or you may be given the measure of one angle and asked for the measure of an adjacent angle or some related angle in a figure.

## Examples

In the following diagram, parallel lines *MO* and *RT* are intersected by transversal *WV*.

Which angle is congruent to ∠MNW?
A. ∠MNS
B. ∠WNO
C. ∠RSV
D. ∠VST

Of the choices, the only one that is congruent to ∠MNW is ∠VST because they are alternate exterior angles.

Which angle is congruent to ∠MNS?
A. ∠RSV
B. ∠SNO
C. ∠VST
D. ∠MNW

Of the choices, the only one that is congruent to ∠MNS is ∠RSV because they are corresponding angles.

If ∠RSN measures 50°, what is the measure of ∠RSV?
A. 90°
B. 110°
C. 130°
D. 150°

∠RSN and ∠RSV are supplementary angles. That is, together they form a straight line and their measures add up to 180°. So if ∠RSN measures 50°, then ∠RSV measures 180 − 50 = 130°.

### On Your Own—Angles

1. Which of the following is an obtuse angle?

2. A straight angle has how many degrees?
3. What is the measure of ∠A in the figure below?

4. If ∠ABC is a right angle, what is the measure of ∠ABD?

5. In the figure below, if ∠AEB measures 24°, what is the measure of ∠CED?

6. In the figure above, if ∠AEB measures 24°, what is the measure of ∠AEC?

7. In the figure below, if ∠IHK measures 43°, what is the measure of ∠JBA?

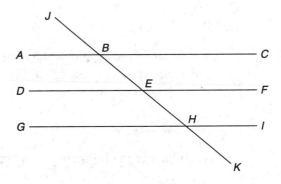

8. In the figure above, if ∠FEH measures 40°, what is the measure of ∠ABE?

9. In the figure above, if ∠FEH measures 30°, what is the measure of ∠JBC?

10. In the figure above, if ∠JBC measures 110°, what is the measure of ∠DEH?

## Triangles

A *polygon* is a closed figure that can be drawn without lifting the pencil. It is made up of line segments (sides) that do not cross. A triangle is a polygon with three sides. Every triangle has three angles that total 180°.

---

*SSAT/ISEE Coach Says . . .*

**Look for Tick Marks and Arcs.** When sides of a polygon are congruent (equal), they may be marked with an equal number of tick marks. When angles are congruent, they may be marked with an equal number of arcs.

**Example**

The tick marks indicate that sides *AB* and *AC* have the same length. The arcs indicate that ∠*ABC* has the same measure as ∠*ACB*.

If sides have different numbers of tick marks, they are not congruent. If angles have different numbers of arcs, they are not congruent.

---

*SSAT/ISEE Coach Says . . .*
All triangles have three angles that total 180°.

---

**Identifying the Longest Side of a Triangle** The longest side of a triangle is always opposite the largest angle. So, if a triangle has angles of 45°, 55°, and 80°, the side opposite the 80° angle is the longest.

There are four main types of triangles. They are *equilateral, isosceles, scalene,* and *right*. Each has special characteristics that you should know.

**Equilateral Triangle**   This kind of triangle has three congruent (equal) sides and three congruent (equal) angles. In an equilateral triangle, each angle measures 60°.

**Isosceles Triangle**   This type of triangle has at least two congruent sides, and the angles opposite the congruent sides are also congruent. In the isosceles triangle shown below, sides *AB* and *BC* are congruent. ∠*BAC* and ∠*BCA* are also congruent. In an isosceles triangle, if you know the measure of any one angle, you can calculate the measures of the other two.

**Examples**

In this isosceles triangle, if ∠1 measures 30°, what is the measure of ∠3?

Since ∠1 and ∠2 are congruent, ∠2 must also measure 30°. Together, ∠1 and ∠2 add up to 60°. Since the sum of all three angles in any triangle is 180°, ∠3 must be $180 - 60 = 120°$.

If ∠3 measures 100°, what are the measures of ∠1 and ∠2?

Since the sum of all three angles in any triangle is 180°, the sum of the measures of ∠1 and ∠2 must be $180 - 100 = 80°$. Since angles 1 and 2 are congruent, each one must measure $80° \div 2 = 40°$.

**Scalene Triangle**   This kind of triangle has no equal sides or angles.

**Right Triangle**   This kind of triangle has one angle that measures 90°. This angle is the *right angle*. It is identified in the figure by the little "box." Since the sum of all three angles in any triangle is 180°, the sum of the two remaining angles in a right triangle is $180 - 90 = 90°$.

In a right triangle, there is a special relationship among the lengths of the three sides. This relationship is described by the *Pythagorean theorem.*

In the right triangle below, $\angle C$ is the right angle. The side opposite the right angle is called the *hypotenuse* ($c$). It is always the longest side. The other two sides ($a$ and $b$) are called *legs*.

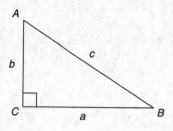

According to the Pythagorean theorem, in any right triangle, the sum of the squares of the legs equals the square of the hypotenuse. In symbols:

$$a^2 + b^2 = c^2$$

So if you know the lengths of any two sides of a right triangle, you can calculate the length of the third side.

**Examples**

If $a = 2$ and $b = 3$, what is $c$?

Following the Pythagorean theorem,

$2^2 + 3^2 = c^2$
$4 + 9 = c^2$
$13 = c^2$
$\sqrt{13} = c$

If $a = 3$ and $b = 4$, what is $c$?
$3^2 + 4^2 = c^2$
$9 + 16 = c^2$
$25 = c^2$
$5 = c$

If $a = 6$ and $c = 10$, what is $b$?
$6^2 + b^2 = 10^2$
$36 + b^2 = 100$
$b^2 = 100 - 36$
$b^2 = 64$
$b = \sqrt{64}$
$b = 8$

## Base and Height of a Triangle

Any side of a triangle can be called the *base*. The *height* is the length of a line segment that connects a base to the vertex opposite that base and is perpendicular to it.

Look at the triangle below. Dashed line $CD$ is the height. Line $CD$ is perpendicular to the base $AB$. Where line $CD$ meets base $AB$, it creates two right angles, $\angle CDA$ and $\angle CDB$.

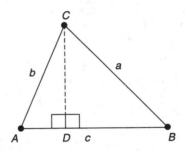

> **SSAT/ISEE Coach Says . . .**
> Sometimes you will see the word *perpendicular* represented by the symbol $\perp$. So in the triangle shown, $\overline{CD} \perp \overline{AB}$.

## Median of a Triangle

A *median* of a triangle is a line drawn from any vertex to the middle of the opposite side. This line splits the opposite side into two equal lengths.

**Example**

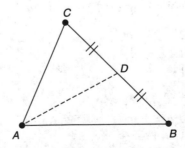

Dashed line $AD$ is a median of triangle $ABC$. It splits side $BC$ into two equal lengths, $\overline{CD}$ and $\overline{BC}$.

1. The triangle above is an equilateral triangle. What is the measure of ∠*ACB*?

2. In the triangle above, if line *AC* measures 4 inches, what is the length of line *BC*?

3. If the triangle above is an isosceles triangle and ∠*ABC* measures 100°, what is the measure of ∠*BAC*?

4. In the triangle above, if line *AB* measures 15 cm, what is the length of line *BC*?

5. In the triangle above, if ∠*ACB* measures 30°, what is the measure of ∠*CAB*?

6. In the triangle above, which side is the longest?

7. In the triangle above, if side *AC* measures 5 cm, what are the lengths of sides *AB* and *BC*?

8. In the figure above, if ∠*CBD* measures 25°, what is the measure of ∠*CAD*?

## Special Right Triangles

There are two types of right triangles that have special characteristics. If you remember these characteristics, you will save valuable time on the test and improve the accuracy of your answers.

### Examples

The first type of special right triangle is an *isosceles right triangle*, also often called a *45°–45°–90° triangle*. The definition of an isosceles triangle is that two legs are congruent, that is, the same length. Therefore, an isosceles right triangle has two legs that are the same length and a 90° angle, and the length of its hypotenuse is the length of a leg times the $\sqrt{2}$.

In the diagram above, the other leg of the triangle is also 5 cm. Therefore the length of the hypotenuse is $5\sqrt{2}$ cm.

The second type of special right triangle is a *30°–60°–90° triangle*. The short leg is opposite the 30° angle. The hypotenuse is twice the length of the short leg. The long leg of a 30°–60°–90° triangle is the length of the shorter leg times the $\sqrt{3}$.

 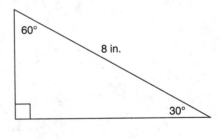

In the diagram above, the short leg is one-half the length of the hypotenuse (8), so the short leg is $\frac{1}{2} \times 8 = 4$ in. The long leg is the length of the short leg (4) times the square root of 3, so the long leg is $4 \times (\sqrt{3}) = 4\sqrt{3}$ in.

***On Your Own—Special Right Triangles***

1. In the triangle shown above, what is the length of each leg?
2. What is the length of the hypotenuse of an isosceles right triangle with legs that are 7 cm long?

3. In the triangle shown above, what is the length of the longer leg?
4. What is the length of the hypotenuse of the triangle shown above?
5. What is the length of the hypotenuse of a 30°–60°–90° triangle with a short leg of 2 cm?

## Triangle Congruence and Similarity

When you take the SSAT or ISEE, you can be certain that there will be questions on congruent or similar polygons. Two polygons are congruent if all their sides and angles are the same.

You can tell whether two triangles are congruent by looking for the following relationships.

- If the lengths of the three sides of two triangles are the same, then the triangles are congruent. Therefore the measures of the three angles are also congruent. (*Side-Side-Side* or *SSS theorem*)

- If two triangles have identical side-angle-side relationships, then the triangles are congruent. Note that the angle is in the middle and is formed by the two congruent sides. (*Side-Angle-Side* or *SAS theorem*)

- If two triangles have identical angle-side-angle relationships, then the triangles arc congruent. Note that the side is in the middle in this situation. (*Angle-Side-Angle* or *ASA theorem*)

- If two angles and a non-included side of one triangle are congruent to two angles and the corresponding non-included side of another triangle, the two triangles are congruent. (*Angle-Angle-Side* or *AAS theorem*)

Note that other relationships such as *Angle-Angle-Angle, Side-Side-Angle,* and *Angle-Side-Side* are not theorems and do *not* guarantee that triangles are congruent.

You can determine whether two triangles are similar by looking for the following two relationships. *Note:* The two triangles must exhibit both characteristics discussed below for them to be similar triangles.

- For two triangles to be similar, the three angles in the first triangle must be congruent or the same as the three angles in the second triangle.

- For two triangles to be similar, the corresponding sides of the two triangles must be in proportion to each other. The common ratio of their corresponding sides is called the ratio of similitude.

When triangles are similar, the ratio of similitude is the same for all corresponding lines. This means that not only are the sides of the triangle expressed by the same ratio, so are the altitudes, medians, angle bisectors, and perimeters.

**Examples**

Are the two triangles shown below congruent? How can you tell? Notice the tick marks on the corresponding sides and angles of the triangles. The triangles are congruent because they have identical angle-side-angle relationships. In other words, the *ASA* theorem guarantees that the triangles are congruent.

What is the length of side *XY*? What is the length of side *AC*? Both *BC* and *YZ* are 4. Since side *XY* corresponds to side *AB*, its length must be 3. Likewise, *AC* corresponds with side *XZ*. Since *XZ* is 5, *AC* must also be 5.

The figures below show two similar triangles. What is the ratio of similitude for the corresponding sides of the triangles? What is the length of side *YZ*?

The ratio of similitude can be determined by looking at the measures of the two corresponding sides for which the length is given. Sides *AB* and *XY* are corresponding sides with measures of 12 and 4. If you write the lengths of these sides as a ratio of 12:4 or 12/4, you can easily determine that the ratio of similitude is 3/1 since $12/4 = 6/2 = 3/1$. This means that for every one unit in the smaller triangle, the larger similar triangle has three units. Since *BC* and *YZ* are corresponding sides they have the same ratio of 3:1. You know from the figure that side *YZ* has a length of 6. Therefore side *BC* has a length of 18 ($6 \times 3 = 18$).

In the figure below, the two triangles are similar. What is the length of *x*, the altitude in triangle *EFG*?

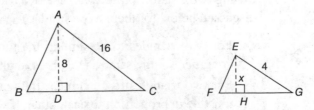

Since the triangles are similar, the altitudes will express the same ratio as the sides. You know from the diagram that side *AC* is 16 and side *EG* is 4. Therefore the ratio of similitude is 16:4 or 4:1. If line *AD*, the altitude of triangle *ABC*, is 8, then the altitude *EH* of triangle *EFG* is 2.

*On Your Own—Triangle Congruence and Similarity*

1. In the figure above, what is the length of side *RS*?
2. In the figure above, what is the perimeter of both triangles?

3. In the figure above, what is the ratio of similitude?
4. In the figure above, what is the length of altitude *AD*?

## Quadrilaterals

A *quadrilateral* is a polygon with four sides and four angles. The sum of the four angles is always 360°.

There are several different kinds of quadrilaterals. Each type is classified according to relationships among its sides and angles. The square, rectangle, parallelogram, and rhombus are all types of quadrilaterals.

**Parallelogram**   A parallelogram is a quadrilateral with both pairs of opposite sides parallel and congruent. The opposite angles are also congruent. Around the edge of the parallelogram, the pair of consecutive angles are supplementary; that is, their sum is 180°. Diagonal lines drawn from opposite vertices *bisect* each other (divide each other exactly in half), but the diagonals themselves are not equal in length.

$\angle A = \angle D$
$\angle C = \angle B$

$\angle A + \angle B = 180°$
$\angle B + \angle D = 180°$
$\angle D + \angle C = 180°$
$\angle C + \angle A = 180°$

**SSAT/ISEE Coach Says . . .**
Consecutive angles are angles that are next to each other. *Supplementary* means that the angles add to 180°.

Like triangles, quadrilaterals have bases and height. Any side of a parallelogram can be a base. The *height* is a line originating at a vertex and drawn perpendicular to the opposite base. The height forms two right angles where it meets the base.

**Rhombus**   A rhombus is a parallelogram with four congruent sides. Opposite angles are also congruent.

**SSAT/ISEE Coach Says . . .**
Watch out for questions that use parallelograms, rhomboids, or trapezoids, but involve the Pythagorean theorem. In the rhombus, for example, you might be asked to calculate the hypotenuse by knowing the length of $\overline{CE}$ and $\overline{AE}$. Notice that the hypotenuse of triangle *AEC* is also the side *AC* of the rhombus.

**Rectangle**   A rectangle is a parallelogram with four right angles. Diagonal lines drawn from opposite vertices of a rectangle bisect each other (divide each other exactly in half) and are equal in length.

**Square**   A square is a rectangle with four congruent sides. Diagonal lines drawn from opposite vertices of a rectangle bisect each other (divide each other exactly in half) and are equal in length.

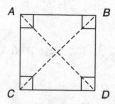

**Trapezoid**   A trapezoid is a quadrilateral with only one pair of parallel sides. Like other quadrilaterals, it has bases and height. In the example below, dashed line *CE* is the height. Sides *AB* and *CD* are parallel, but sides *AC* and *BD* are not parallel.

***On Your Own—Quadrilaterals***

1. In the square above, what is the sum of all four angles?

2. In the square above, if side *AD* measures 16 inches, what is the length of side *DC*?

3. In the rhombus above, what is the sum of all four angles?

4. In the rhombus above, if ∠*ADC* measures 60°, what is the measure of ∠*ABC*?

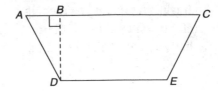

5. In the trapezoid above, what is the measure of ∠CBD?

## Circles

A circle is a closed figure having all points the same distance from a *center*. A circle with its center at point *A* is called circle *A*.

**Parts of a Circle**   A *chord* is a line segment that has end points on a circle. A *diameter* is a chord that passes through the center of a circle. A *radius* is a line segment that connects the center of a circle and a point on the circle. Its length equals half the length of the diameter. In the figure below, *A* is the center of the circle. *EF* is a chord. *BC* is a diameter of the circle. *AC*, *AB*, and *AD* are each a radius of the circle.

   An *arc* is two points on a circle and the part of the circle between the two points. In the figure below, *CD* is an arc of the circle. A *central angle* is an angle whose vertex is the center of a circle. In the figure below, ∠*CAD* is a central angle. Its measure is 50°. The sum of the measures of the central angles in a circle is 360°.

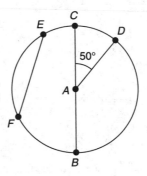

## Perimeter and Area

The *perimeter* is the distance around a closed two-dimensional figure. The *area* is the amount of surface a two-dimensional figure covers. Area is measured in square units such as square inches (in²) or square centimeters (cm²). A square inch is the area of a square with sides 1 inch long.

**Finding the Perimeter of a Polygon**   To find the perimeter of a polygon, just add the length of each side to find the total.

**Example**

$\triangle ABC$ is an isosceles triangle. If side $AB$ has a length of 25 cm and side $BC$ has a length of 15 cm, what is the perimeter?

Since $\triangle ABC$ is an isosceles triangle, side $AB$ = side $AC$. So if side $AB$ has a length of 25 cm, side $AC$ also has a length of 25 cm. Thus the perimeter is $25 + 25 + 15 = 65$ cm.

**Finding the Area of a Polygon**  There are special formulas you can use to calculate the areas of various types of polygons. You will want to memorize these as you may be asked a question about area on the SSAT or ISEE.

**Area of a Triangle**  The area ($A$) of a triangle is one-half the base ($b$) multiplied by the height ($h$), or

$$A = \frac{1}{2} bh$$

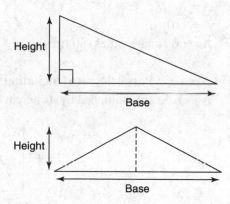

**Example**

If a triangle has a height that measures 30 cm and a base that measures 50 cm, what is its area?

$b = 50$ cm
$h = 30$ cm

$$A = \frac{1}{2} bh$$

$$A = \frac{1}{2}(50)(30)$$

$$A = \frac{1}{2} \, 1{,}500$$

$$A = 750 \text{ cm}^2$$

> **SSAT/ISEE Coach Says . . .**
> Any time you see units squared, you are dealing with area. Examples: sq inches (in²), sq centimeters (cm²), sq yards (yd²), etc.

**Area of a Square or Rectangle**  The area ($A$) of a square or rectangle is its length ($l$) multiplied by its width ($w$), or $A = lw$.

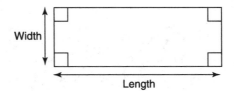

**Example**

If this rectangle is 10 miles long and 6 miles wide, what is its area?

$A = lw$
$A = (10)(6)$
$A = 60$ square miles (60 mi²)

**Area of a Parallelogram (Including the Rhombus)**  The area ($A$) of a parallelogram is its base ($b$) multiplied by its height ($h$), or $A = bh$.

**Example**

If a parallelogram has a base of 6 meters and a height of 4 meters, what is the area?

$A = bh$
$A = (6)(4)$
$A = 24$ square meters (24 m²)

**Area of a Trapezoid**  The area ($A$) of a trapezoid is one-half the height ($h$) multiplied by the sum of the two bases ($b_1$ and $b_2$), or $A = \frac{1}{2}(b_1 + b_2)h$.

Base 2

Height

Base 1

### Example

If a trapezoid has one base of 30 meters and another base of 60 meters and its height is 20 meters, what is the area?

$$A = \frac{1}{2}(b_1 + b_2)h$$

$$A = \frac{1}{2}(30 + 60)20$$

$$A = \frac{1}{2}(90)20$$

$$A = \frac{1}{2}(1,800)$$

$A = 900$ square meters ($900 \text{ m}^2$)

***On Your Own—Perimeter and Area***

1. In the triangle above, if side *AB* measures 3 inches and side *BC* measures 2 inches, what is the perimeter of the triangle?

2. In the triangle above, if line *AD* measures 6 inches and side *BC* measures 2 inches, what is the area of the triangle?

8 in

4 in

3. What is the perimeter of the rectangle above?

4. What is the area of the rectangle above?

20 cm

8 cm    10 cm

5 cm

5. What is the perimeter of the trapezoid above?

6. What is the area of the trapezoid above?

**Finding the Circumference and Area of a Circle**   The *circumference* of a circle is the distance around the circle. The circumference (*C*) divided by the diameter (*d*) always equals the number $\pi$ (pi). Pi is an irrational number, that is, a nonterminating and nonrepeating decimal. When you use it to solve problems, you can approximate $\pi$ as 3.14 or $^{22}/_7$.

To find the circumference of a circle, use the formula $C = \pi d$.

### Example

If a circle has a radius of 3 inches, what is the circumference?

Since the diameter is twice the radius (2*r*), the diameter is 6 inches.

$C = \pi d$
$C \approx 3.14(d)$
$C \approx 3.14\,(6)$
$C \approx 18.84$ in

To find the area of a circle, multiply $\pi$ times the square of the radius.

---

**SSAT/ISEE Coach Says . . .**

If you prefer working with fractions, then $\pi = \dfrac{22}{7}$.

---

### Example

If a circle has a radius of 4 centimeters, what is its area?

$A = \pi r^2$
$A = 3.14\,(4)^2$
$A = 3.14\,(16)$
$A = 50.24$ cm$^2$

1. What is the circumference of the circle above?
2. What is the area of the circle above?

## Three-Dimensional (Solid) Figures

A figure is *two-dimensional* if all the points on the figure are in the same plane. A square and a triangle are two-dimensional figures. A figure is *three-dimensional* (solid) if not all of its points lie in the same plane.

On solid figures, the flat surfaces are called *faces*. *Edges* are line segments where two faces meet. A point where three or more edges intersect is called a *vertex*.

On the SSAT or ISEE, you may see problems related to these solid figures: rectangular solid (prism), cube, cylinder, and sphere.

**Rectangular Solid (Prism)** On a rectangular solid (also called a prism), all the faces are rectangular. The top and bottom faces are called bases. All opposite faces on a rectangular solid are parallel and congruent.

**Cube** A cube is a rectangular solid on which every face is a square. All faces of a cube are congruent squares.

**Cylinder**   A cylinder is a solid figure with two parallel congruent circular bases and a curved surface connecting the boundaries of the two faces.

**Sphere**   A sphere is a solid figure that is the set of all points that are the same distance from a given point, called the center. The distance from the center to the curved surface is the radius ($r$) of the sphere.

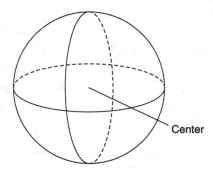

### Finding the Volume of Solid Figures

Volume is the amount of space within a three-dimensional figure. Volume is measured in cubic units such as cubic inches ($in^3$) or cubic centimeters ($cm^3$). A cubic inch is the volume of a cube with edges 1 inch long.

**Volume of a Rectangular Solid**   To find the volume ($V$) of a rectangular solid, multiply the length ($l$) times the width ($w$) times the height ($h$). The formula is $V = lwh$.

**Example**

If a rectangular solid has a length of 3 yards, a height of 1.5 yards, and a width of 1.5 yards, what is its volume?

$V = lwh$
$V = (3)(1.5)(1.5)$
$V = 6.75$ cubic yards (6.75 yd$^3$)

**Volume of a Cube**   On a cube, the length, width, and height are all the same: each one equals one side ($s$). To find the volume ($V$) of a cube, multiply the length × width × height. This is the same as multiplying side × side × side. The formula is $V = s \times s \times s = s^3$.

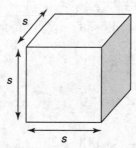

**Example**

If each side of a cube measures 9 feet, what is its volume?

$V = s^3$
$V = (9)^3$
$V = 729$ cubic feet (729 ft$^3$)

**Volume of a Cylinder**   To find the volume ($V$) of a cylinder, first find the area of the circular base by using the formula $A = \pi r^2$. Then multiply the result times the height ($h$) of the cylinder. The formula is $V = (\pi r^2)h$.

### Example

If a cylinder has a height of 7 meters and a radius of 2 meters, what is its volume?

$V = (\pi r^2)h$
$V = 3.14(2)^2(7)$
$V = 3.14(4)(7)$
$V = 87.92$ cubic meters (or 87.92 m³)

**Volume of a Sphere** To find the volume of a sphere, multiply ⁴/₃ times $\pi$ times the radius cubed. The formula is $V = \dfrac{4}{3}\pi r^3$.

### Example

If the radius of a sphere measures 12 inches, what is its volume?

$V = \dfrac{4}{3}\pi r^3$

$V = \dfrac{4}{3}\pi(12)^3$

$V = \dfrac{4}{3}(3.14)(1,728)$

$V = \dfrac{4}{3}(5,425.92)$

$V = 7,234.56$ cubic inches (7,234.56 in³)

***On Your Own—Volume***

1. What is the volume of the cube above?

2. What is the volume of the rectangular solid above?

3. What is the volume of the cylinder above?

4. What is the volume of the sphere above?

Shapes and Formulas: Summary

| Shapes | Formulas |
| --- | --- |
| Triangle diagram with sides $a$, $c$, height $h$, base $b$ | Triangle<br>Area = $\frac{1}{2}$ of the base × the height<br>$A = \frac{1}{2}bh$<br>Perimeter = $a + b + c$ |
| Square diagram with side $s$ | Square<br>Area = length × width<br>$A = lw$<br>Perimeter = side + side + side + side<br>$P = 4s$ |

(Continued)

| Shapes | Formulas |
|--------|----------|
| | **Rectangle** <br> Area = length × width <br> $A = lw$ <br> Perimeter = 2 × length + 2 × width <br> $P = 2l + 2w$ |
| | **Parallelogram and Rhombus** <br> Area = base × height <br> $A = bh$ <br> Perimeter = 2 × length + 2 × width <br> $P = 2l + 2w$ |
| | **Trapezoid** <br> Area = the sum of the two bases divided by 2 × height <br> $A = \dfrac{b_1 + b_2}{2}h$ <br><br> Perimeter = $a + b_1 + b_2 + c$ <br> $P = a + b_1 + b_2 + c$ |
| | **Circle** <br> The distance around the circle is its circumference ($C$). The length of a line segment passing through the center with end points on the circle is the diameter ($d$). The length of a line segment connecting the center to a point on the circle is the radius ($r$). The diameter is twice the length of the radius ($d = 2r$). <br> $C = \pi d = 2\pi r$ <br> $A = \pi r^2$ <br> $\pi = 3.14$ or $\dfrac{22}{7}$ |
| | **Cube** <br> Volume =.side × side × side <br> $V = s^3$ |

| Shapes | Formulas |
|---|---|
| | **Rectangular Solid**<br>Volume = length × width × height<br>$V = lwh$ |
| | **Cylinder**<br>Volume = $\pi r^2$ × height<br>$V = \pi r^2 h$ |
| | **Sphere**<br>Volume = $\frac{4}{3}\pi r^3$<br><br>$V = \frac{4}{3}\pi r^3$ |

## Answers to "On Your Own" Practice Sets

**On Your Own—Angles**

1. B
2. 180°
3. 143°
4. 74°
5. 24°

6. 156°
7. 43°
8. 140°
9. 150°
10. 110°

**On Your Own—Triangles**

1. 60°                    5. 60°

2. 4 inches               6. *AC*

3. 40°                    7. 3 cm; 4 cm

4. 15 cm                  8. 65°

**On Your Own—Special Right Triangles**

1. 4 inches               4. 28 inches

2. $7\sqrt{2}$ cm         5. 4 cm

3. $14\sqrt{3}$ inches

**On Your Own—Triangle Congruence and Similarity**

1. 3                      3. 3:2

2. 15                     4. 6

**On Your Own—Quadrilaterals**

1. 360°                   4. 60°

2. 16 inches              5. 90°

3. 360°

**On Your Own—Perimeter and Area**

1. 8 inches               4. 32 sq inches

2. 6 sq inches            5. 45 cm

3. 24 inches              6. 100 sq cm

**On Your Own—Circles: Circumference and Area**

1. 62.8 cm                2. 314 sq cm

**On Your Own—Volume**

1. 729 m$^3$              3. 226.08 in$^3$

2. 576 cm$^3$             4. 523.33 cm$^3$

# The Data Analysis and Probability You Need to Know

## Data Analysis and Probability on the SSAT and ISEE

If you are taking the lower version of the SSAT or the ISEE, you will need to know some very basic concepts in data analysis and probability. If you are taking the upper level version of either test, you will need to be familiar with some more advanced data analysis and probability concepts. This chapter will review the following topics.

### Topics

| | |
|---|---|
| Mean, Median, Mode, and Range | Box-and-Whisker Plot |
| Circle or Pie Graph | Scatter Plot and Line of Best Fit |
| Bar Graph | Probability of Simple Events |
| Histogram | Probability of Independent Events |
| Line Graph | Probability of Dependent Events |
| Pictograph | Experimental Probability |
| Stem-and-Leaf Plot | |

## Data Analysis Review

### Mean (Average)

The *mean* of a set of numbers is the average. Add the numbers and divide by the number of items.

### Examples

What is the mean of the numbers 2, 4, 7, 4, and 5?

The sum is 22. Since there are 5 numbers, divide 22 by 5 to get a mean or average of 4.4.

What is the mean of the numbers 3, 4, 2, 6, 7, 12, 56, and 104?

The sum is 194. There are 8 numbers, so divide 194 by 8 to get 24.25.

*On Your Own—Calculating the Mean*

Calculate the mean of the following numbers.

1. 2, 4, 5, 6, 7, 12, 43, 55, 78

2. 44, 67, 80, 10, 23, 23, 23, 77, 88, 100

3. 125, 334, 522, 16, 822

## Median

Order a set of numbers from least to greatest. If there is an odd number of items, the *median* is the number in the middle of that sequence of items. If there is an even number of items, the median is the mean or average of the two middle numbers.

### Examples

What is the median of the following numbers?

14, 999, 75, 102, 39, 456, 19

Reorder the numbers from least to greatest: 14, 19, 39, 75, 102, 456, 999

The middle number is 75, so that is the median.

What is the median of the following numbers?

15, 765, 65, 890, 12, 1

Reorder the numbers from least to greatest: 1, 12, 15, 65, 765, 890

Since there is an even number of items, find the average of the middle two numbers.

$15 + 65 = 80$
$80 \div 2 = 40$
40 is the median

## Mode

The *mode* of a set of numbers is the number that appears most frequently in that set.

### Example

What is the mode of the following set of numbers?

12, 14, 15, 15, 15, 17, 18

The number 15 appears most often in this set, so it is the mode of the set.

## Range

The range is the difference between the greatest number and the least number in a set of data.

**Example**

What is the range of the following set of numbers?

13, 9, 11, 17, 8, 14

First arrange the numbers in order from least to greatest.

8, 9, 11, 13, 14, 17

The greatest number is 17, and the least number is 8. The difference of 17 − 8 is 9. So the range is 9.

*On Your Own—Mean, Median, Mode, and Range*

1. What is the mean?
   3, 5, 7, 6, 4

2. What is the median?
   2, 7, 4, 19, 15, 12, 11

3. What is the mode?
   9, 3, 10, 3, 7, 13, 14

4. What is the range?
   5, 14, 7, 21, 4, 11

# Graphs

It is often helpful to represent numbers in a visual form called a *graph*. The most common graphs are circle graphs, bar graphs, and line graphs. You won't be asked to construct these graphs on your test, but you may have to interpret one or more of them.

**Circle or Pie Graph**    This kind of graph uses a circle divided into parts to show fractional or percentage relationships.

**Example**

In a survey at a local high school, students were asked to name their favorite lunch food. The results of that survey are shown in the circle graph below.

**Favorite Lunch Food of High School Students**

Questions such as the following are typical.

- Which food was most (or least) popular with the students? (most: sandwich; least: salad)
- Which two food selections of the students make up 50% of the total? (sandwich and pasta: 40% and 10% = 50%)
- What is the ratio of the students who selected sandwiches to students who selected hamburgers? (4:3)
- If the total number of students surveyed was 2,500, how many chose salad as their favorite lunch? (125; 2,500 × 0.05 = 125)

### On Your Own—Circle or Pie Graph

1. Which station was the most watched?
2. What is the ratio of NBC watchers to ESPN watchers?
3. Which was the least-watched station?

**Bar Graph**    This kind of graph uses bars to provide a visual comparison of different quantities.

### Example

The following bar graph compares the number of different types of sandwiches sold on Tuesday at a certain sandwich shop.

Questions such as the following are typical.

- Which kind of sandwich did the store sell the most of on Tuesday? (veggie)
- How many more tuna sandwiches than turkey sandwiches were sold on Tuesday? (21)
- How many tuna sandwiches and beef sandwiches were sold on Tuesday? (36)

*On Your Own—Bar Graph*

**NUMBER OF STUDENTS RATING SUBJECT AS THEIR FAVORITE**

1. According to the bar graph, which subject is the favorite of most students?
2. Which subject is the favorite of the fewest students?
3. What is the total number of students who picked their favorite subject?
4. What is the ratio of students who picked art as their favorite subject to students who picked math?

**Histogram**    A **histogram** is like a bar graph because it represents the distribution of numerical data. The following histogram shows the distribution of math test scores for Mr. Hughley's class. Notice that there is no space between the bars in this histogram. This means that the intervals are continuous with no gaps between them.

Questions such as the following are typical.

- Which range of scores did the greatest number of students achieve? (71–80)
- How many more students scored between 91–100 than scored between 61–70? (2)
- How many students scored 81 or more? (13)

*On Your Own—Histogram*

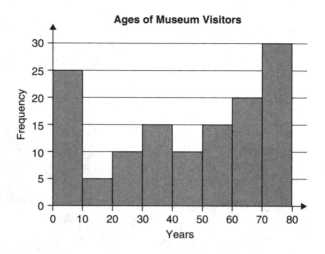

1. Which age group had the most number of visitors to the museum?
2. Which age group had the fewest number of visitors to the museum?
3. How many more visitors between the ages of 70–80 visited the museum than visitors between the ages of 20–30?
4. How many visitors 50 years or older visited the museum?

**Line Graph**   This kind of graph is generally used to show change over time.

**Example**

The following line graph shows the change in attendance at this year's football games.

Questions such as the following are typical.

- How many more people attended game 3 than game 2? (353)
- Which game had the highest attendance? (Game 5)
- How many people attended the first game of the year? (334)

*On Your Own—Line Graph*

1. Which year had the greatest rainfall?
2. Which year had the least rainfall?
3. What was the average yearly rainfall in the park during this time period?
4. How many more inches of rain fell in 2000 than in 1996?

**Pictograph**   This type of graph uses pictures or symbols to represent a given number of objects. A pictograph makes visual comparisons of different quantities or trends in data easy to read.

**Example**

Questions such as the following are typical.

- Which flavor of ice cream cone sold the least at the Jefferson School Fair? (butter pecan)
- How many more chocolate ice cream cones were sold than strawberry cones? (15)
- How many ice cream cones were sold in all during the Jefferson School Fair? (100)

### On Your Own—Pictograph

**Number of Babies Born at Madison Hospital (2008–2011)**

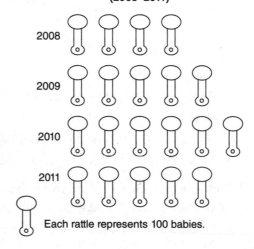

Each rattle represents 100 babies.

1. During which year were the most babies born at Madison Hospital?
2. How many babies were born during 2010 and 2011 at Madison Hospital?
3. How many more babies were born at Madison Hospital in 2010 than in 2008?

**Stem-and-Leaf Plot**   This type of graph shows a set of data in order by place value. The **leaf** is in the right column and shows the last digit of each data item. The **stem** is in the left column and shows the digits to the left of each leaf.

### Example

On a recent math test, the 15 students in Mr. Chin's class scored the following grades:

81, 79, 93, 77, 79, 86, 67, 79, 81, 90, 88, 72, 60, 91, 80

The following is a stem-and-leaf plot that displays the data.

| Stem | Leaf |
|------|-------|
| 6 | 0 7 |
| 7 | 2 7 9 9 9 |
| 8 | 0 1 1 6 8 |
| 9 | 0 1 3 |

- What number is the mode in this set of data? Since the mode is the most frequently occurring number, the mode in this set of data is 79.
- What is the median of this set of data? The median is the middle number in a set of data. This set has a total of 15 items. Therefore, the median is 80, the eighth number in this data set.

### *On Your Own—Stem-and-Leaf Plot*

The following stem-and-leaf plot shows the bowling scores that members of the Midwood High School Bowling Club received on Saturday afternoon.

| Stem | Leaf |
|------|------|
| 8 | 9 |
| 9 | 3 5 |
| 10 | 6 8 |
| 11 | 3 6 |
| 12 | 4 5 9 |
| 13 | 3 3 7 8 |
| 14 | 1 3 4 9 |
| 15 | 2 6 9 |

1. What score is the mode of this data set?
2. What is the range of this data set?
3. What is the median of this data set?

**Box-and-Whisker Plot**   This type of graph displays the median, lower quartile, upper quartile, and the minimum and maximum values of a set of data. The **median** is the middle data point in a collection of data. The **lower quartile** is the median of the lower half of the numbers in a data set. The **upper quartile** is the median of the upper half of numbers. The **interquartile range** is the difference between the upper and lower quartiles.

### Example

The data below shows the number of books owned by 15 different families with students who attend Reese Middle School. The data is arranged in order from least to greatest.

17, 25, 32, 51, 54, 58, 61, 67, 76, 81, 85, 87, 91, 95, 100

There are 15 data items in this set. The median, or middle number, is 67.

There are seven data items to the left of the median: 17, 25, 32, 51, 54, 58, 61. The middle number, or median, of the lower quartile is 51. Similarly, there are seven numbers to the right of the median of the entire data set: 76, 81, 85, 87, 91, 95, 100. Therefore, the median of the upper quartile is 87.

The interquartile range for this set of data is $87 - 51 = 36$. The interquartile range is important because it represents the middle 50% of data values and, therefore, is less influenced by the extreme values represented in the lower and upper quartiles.

Here is what a box-and-whisker plot for this data set looks like.

**Number of Books per Household**

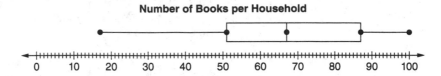

### On Your Own—Box-and-Whisker Plot

The box-and-whisker plot below shows the number of points scored by the Monroe High School basketball team during the 11 games they've played this season.

**Monroe High School Basketball Scores**

1. What is the median number of points scored by the Monroe High School basketball team?
2. What is the median of the lower quartile?
3. What is the median of the upper quartile?
4. What is the interquartile range?

**Scatter Plot and Line of Best Fit**  This type of graph relates data from two different sets. A scatter plot displays points along the *x*-axis and *y*-axis of a coordinate plane. The line of best fit is drawn along a scatter plot near the points to show the trend between two sets of data.

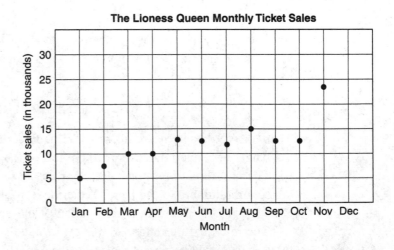

**Examples**

According to the scatter plot, about how many tickets did producers of *The Lioness Queen* sell in September?

A) 5,000

B) 10,000

C) 12,500

D) 15,000

Look along the *x*-axis until you find September. Then look up from this point to locate the dot. Check the number of ticket sales for this point along the *y*-axis. Since the point is between 10,000 and 15,000 tickets, the best answer is 12,500.

Based on the data in the scatter plot, during which three-month period were the fewest number of tickets sold to *The Lioness Queen*? To find the answer to this question, look for the three lowest points in a row on the scatter plot. It is clear that the three-month period with the lowest sales are January, February, and March. During these three months, about 22,500 tickets to *The Lioness Queen* were sold in all.

Often a line of best fit is drawn along a scatter plot near the points to show the trend between two sets of data. For the data shown in the scatter plot above, a line of best fit would look like the one shown below.

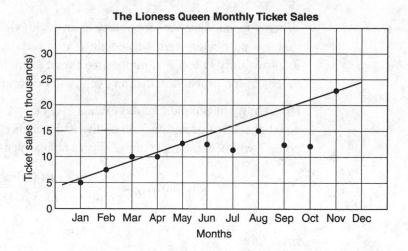

Based on the line of best fit, how many tickets would the producers of *The Lioness Queen* expect to sell in December?

Since the line of best fit rises to the right, the correlation is positive. This means that as the months go by, more tickets are sold. According to the line of best fit, the producers can expect to sell about 25,000 tickets during the month of December.

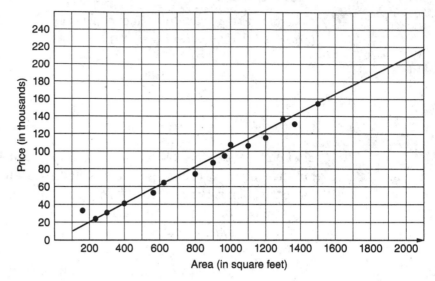

1. According to the scatter plot, about how much would a person expect to pay for a 1,600-square-foot apartment?
2. According to the line of best fit, about how much would a 750-square-foot apartment cost?

## Probability Review

When you calculate the probability of an event, you are determining the likelihood that this particular event will occur. If it is certain that an event must occur, then its probability is 1. If it is impossible for an event to occur, its probability is 0. All values of the probability that an event will occur are between 0 and 1.

**Probability of Simple Events**   When every event in a set of possible events has an equal chance of occurring, probability is the chance that a particular event (or "outcome") will occur. Simple probability is represented by the formula:

$$\text{Probability} = \frac{\text{Number of favorable outcomes}}{\text{Number of possible outcomes}}$$

**Examples**

*Solve*: Let's say you have a spinner with an arrow that spins around a circle that is divided into six equal parts. The parts are labeled from 1 to 6. When you spin the arrow, what is the probability that it will land on the part labeled 4?

Following the formula:

$$\text{Probability} = \frac{\text{Number of positive outcomes}}{\text{Number of possible outcomes}}$$

$$\text{Probability} = \frac{1}{6} \text{ or 1 in 6}$$

Let's take that same spinner. What is the probability that the arrow will land on the number 2 or the number 3 when spun? Using the formula:

$$\text{Probability} = \frac{\text{Number of positive outcomes}}{\text{Number of possible outcomes}}$$

$$\text{Probability} = \frac{2}{6} = \frac{1}{3} \text{ or 1 in 3}$$

*Solve:* A box is filled with 25 black balls, 50 white balls, and 75 red balls. If Wendell reaches into the box and picks a ball without looking, what is the probability that he will pick a black or a white ball?

### Procedure

*What must you find?* Probability that either of two events will occur.
*What are the units?* Fraction, decimal, or percent.
*What do you know?* How many of each kind of ball are in the box.
*Create an equation.*

$$\text{Probability} = \frac{\text{Number of positive outcomes}}{\text{Number of possible outcomes}}$$

Substitute values and solve.

Number of positive outcomes = number of black balls + number of white balls = 25 + 50 = 75

Number of possible outcomes = 25 + 50 + 75 = 150

$$\text{Probability} = \frac{75}{150} = \frac{1}{2} = 1:2 = 0.5 = 50\%$$

**Probability of Independent Events**   Independent events are events that have no effect on one another. The probability of independent events is represented by the formula:

$$\text{Probability } (A \text{ and } B) = \text{Probability } (A) \bullet \text{Probability } (B)$$

### Examples

If you roll two dice, what is the probability that you will roll two even numbers?

Each die has six sides with the numbers 1 to 6 on each side. Therefore, the probability of rolling an even number on the first die is $\frac{1}{2}$. Likewise, the probability of rolling an even number on the second die is also $\frac{1}{2}$. So the probability of rolling two even numbers is:

$$P(A \text{ and } B) = P(A) \bullet P(B)$$

$$P(A \text{ and } B \text{ even}) = \frac{1}{2} \bullet \frac{1}{2} = \frac{1}{4}$$

If you roll two dice, what is the probability that you will roll two 3's? The probability of rolling a 3 on the first die is 1/6, and on the second die it is also 1/6. So, the probability of rolling two 3's is:

$$P(A \text{ and } B) = P(A) \bullet P(B)$$

$$P(A \text{ and } B \text{ 3 and 3}) = \frac{1}{6} \bullet \frac{1}{6} = \frac{1}{36}$$

**Probability of Dependent Events**   Dependent events are events in which the probability on one event affects the probability of another event. The probability of dependent events is represented by the formula:

$$\text{Probability } (A \text{ or } B) = \text{Probability } (A) \bullet \text{Probability } (B \text{ following } A)$$

### Examples

If you pick two cards in a row from a deck of cards and *don't replace* the first card, what is the probability of selecting two hearts?

The probability of picking a heart on the first card is 13 out of 52, since there are 13 cards of each suit—hearts, diamonds, clubs, and spades. If you select a heart on the first draw and don't put the card back, then there are only 12 hearts in a deck of 51 cards. Therefore, the probability of picking a heart as the second card is 12 out of 51. The probability of picking two hearts in a row is:

$$\text{Probability (two hearts)} = \frac{13}{52} \bullet \frac{12}{51} = \frac{156}{2656}$$

$$= \frac{1}{17}$$

If you pick two cards in a row from a deck of cards and you *replace* the first card, what is the probability of selecting two hearts? In this case, the probability of selecting a heart on the first card is 13 out of 52. Since you put the card back in the deck, the probability of choosing a heart on the second selection remains 13 out of 52. When you replace the first card, the probability of selecting two hearts in a row is:

$$\text{Probability (two hearts)} = \frac{13}{52} \bullet \frac{13}{52} = \frac{169}{2704}$$

$$= \frac{1}{16}$$

**Experimental Probability**   Experimental probability is based on data collected through research such as surveys, questionnaires, and polls. The data collected is summarized and then used to make predictions.

### Example

The National Fruit Growers' Association is conducting a random survey asking people to tell their favorite fruit. The chart shows the results so far.

| Favorite Fruit | Number of People |
|---|---|
| Apples | 236 |
| Peaches | 389 |
| Oranges | 250 |
| Pears | 125 |

What is the probability that the next randomly selected person will say that pears are his or her favorite fruit?

### Procedure

*What must you find?* Probability that a certain event will occur.
*What are the units?* Fraction or decimal or percent.
*What do you know?* The number of people selecting each fruit as their favorite.
*Create an equation.*

$$\text{Probability} = \frac{\text{Number of positive outcomes}}{\text{Number of possible outcomes}}$$

Substitute values and solve.

Number of positive outcomes = 125 people who named pears as their favorite fruit

Number of possible outcomes = all people surveyed = 236 + 389 + 250 + 125 = 1,000

$$\text{Probability} = \frac{125}{1,000} = \frac{1}{8} = 1:8 = 0.125 = 12.5\%$$

### On Your Own—Probability

1. The local travel bureau is conducting a random survey asking people to indicate how they will spend their next vacation. The chart shows the results so far.

| Type of Vacation | Number of People |
|---|---|
| Spending time at the beach | 56 |
| Cruising the islands | 89 |
| Hiking in the mountains | 50 |
| Scuba diving | 40 |
| Visiting museums | 67 |
| Reading and relaxing | 98 |
| Total number of people surveyed | 400 |

What is the probability that the next randomly selected person will say that hiking in the mountains will be how he or she will spend his or her vacation?

2. A box is filled with 50 black balls, 75 white balls, and 25 red balls. If Marty reaches into the box and picks a ball without looking, what is the probability that he will pick a white or a red ball?

3. A drawer contains one pair of socks of each of the following colors: black, white, blue, brown, and red. The socks are rolled up so that each pair is a separate matching set. If you select a pair of socks randomly without looking, what is the probability you will select a pair of white socks?

4. Suppose you select a pair of socks from the drawer described in the previous problem. After your first selection, you put the socks back in the drawer and make a second selection. What is the probability that you will select the red socks both times?

## Answers to "On Your Own" Practice Sets

**On Your Own—Calculating the Mean**

1. 23.5

2. 53.5

3. 363.8

**On Your Own—Mean, Median, Mode, and Range**

1. 5

2. 11

3. 3

4. 17

**On Your Own—Circle or Pie Graph**

1. ESPN

2. 1:2

3. CBS

**On Your Own—Bar Graph**

1. SCIENCE
2. ART

3. 338
4. 1:2

**On Your Own—Histogram**

1. 70–80
2. 10–20

3. 20
4. 65

**On Your Own—Line Graph**

1. 2002
2. 1996

3. 43.8
4. 40 inches

**On Your Own—Pictograph**

1. 2010
2. 1100

3. 200

**On Your Own—Stem-and-Leaf Plot**

1. 133
2. 70

3. 133

**On Your Own—Box-and-Whisker Plot**

1. 38
2. 31

3. 45
4. 14

**On Your Own—Scatter Plot and Line of Best Fit**

1. $163,000

2. $80,000

**On Your Own—Probability**

1. $\frac{1}{8}$
2. $\frac{2}{3}$

3. $\frac{1}{5}$
4. $\frac{1}{25}$

# How to Solve Word Problems

## Introduction to Word Problems

What is a word problem? Basically it is a description of a real-life situation that requires a mathematical solution. To solve a word problem, you need to translate the situation into mathematical terms and then calculate the answer.

Many of the math questions on the SSAT and ISEE are word problems. To do well, you need to learn good word problem-solving skills. The following pages will show you many different kinds of word problems. For each kind, you'll learn how to translate the facts of the problem into mathematical terms. Then you'll see how to use those terms to set up an equation. Finally, you'll see how to solve that equation for the missing piece of information that you're looking for.

## How to Tackle Word Problems

Here are some helpful suggestions for dealing with word problems.

- Read the problem all the way through before you start making any calculations. That way, you will better understand what the problem is about and what you are supposed to find out.

- Be sure you understand what the problem is asking. Are you supposed to find a distance? How fast something is moving? When someone will arrive at point *A*? How much something costs? How many items you can buy if you have a certain amount of money? How much older Kim is than Kay? Draw a picture if that helps.

- List the information that the problem gives you. Note any units of measure (meters, pounds, feet per second, and the like).

- Look for key words in the problem that define relationships or indicate what mathematical operation you need to use. (See the list of key words that follows.)

- Figure out what unit of measure you must use to express your answer. Cubic meters? Centimeters per second? Dollars? Minutes? Number of items?

- Weed out unnecessary information that will not help you solve the problem.

- Use the information you have gathered to create an equation to help you solve the problem.
- Solve the equation.

## Key Words

Many word problems contain key words that tell you what mathematical operation you need to use to solve the problem. It pays to know these key words, so be sure you study the following list.

| Key Words | Example Phrases |
|---|---|
| These Key Words Tell You to ADD | |
| Increased by | If the temperature is increased by |
| More than | If the bicycle costs $75 more than |
| Sum | If the sum of the paychecks is |
| Total | The total number of payments equals |
| Added | If $a$ is added to $b$ |
| Plus | If the interest plus the principle is |
| Combined | If the volume of the cube is combined with |
| In all | How many pounds in all |
| Successive | The cost of 8 successive phone bills |
| These Key Words Tell You to SUBTRACT | |
| Less than | The interest payment was less than |
| Difference | The difference between the time it takes to |
| Are left | How many pieces of pie are left if |
| Fewer than | If there are 15 fewer scholarships this year than |
| Minus | Some number minus 36 |
| Reduced by | If the federal budget is reduced by |
| These Key Words Tell You to MULTIPLY | |
| Times | There are 3 times as many red tiles as blue tiles. |
| Product | The product of $a$ and $b$ is |
| Increased by a factor of | If the speed is increased by a factor of |
| Decreased by a factor of | If the temperature is decreased by a factor of |
| At | If you buy 12 cameras at $249 each |
| Per | If a ferry can carry 20 cars per trip, how many cars can it carry in 6 trips? |
| Total | If you spend $10 a week on movies for a total of 5 weeks |
| Twice | The house covers twice as many square feet as |

| Key Words | Example Phrases |
|-----------|-----------------|
| These Key Words Tell You to DIVIDE | |
| Quotient | What is the quotient if the numerator is 500? |
| Divided equally among | If 115 tickets are divided equally among 5 groups |
| Divided into equal groups | If the students were divided into 6 equal groups |
| Ratio of | If the ratio of oxygen to hydrogen is |
| Per | If a ferry can carry 24 cars per trip, how many trips will it take to carry 144 cars? |
| Percent | What percent of 100 is 30? |
| Half | If half the profits go to charity, then how much |
| These Key Words Tell You to Use an EQUALS SIGN | |
| Is | If the total bill is $19.35 |
| Sells for | If the car sells for $26,000 |
| Gives | If multiplying $a^2$ and $b^2$ gives $c^2$ |

*On Your Own—Key Words*
For each of the following phrases, indicate what operation is appropriate.

1. How many are left? _____
2. What is the ratio of 6 to 3? _____
3. What is the sum? _____
4. How much is twice the amount? _____
5. If it sells for _____

## Setting Up an Equation and Solving for an Unknown

Before you start tackling word problems, you need to know how to set up an equation and solve for an unknown. For each problem, you will be given certain pieces of information (*what you know*). You first need to translate this information into mathematical terms. Then you can use those terms to set up an equation. An *equation* is nothing more than a mathematical expression that indicates that one mathematical term is equal to another. The terms in an equation are shown on opposite sides of an equals sign. The missing piece of information that you are looking for (*what you need to find*) is called the *unknown*. In your equation, you can represent an unknown by a letter such as $x$ or $a$.

In the pages that follow, you will see how to set up equations for many different kinds of word problems. The process of solving an equation for an unknown is pretty simple. Work through these examples until you get perfectly comfortable with the process.

**Examples**

Solve for $x$.

$$25x = 200$$

This equation is read, "25 times some unknown number $x$ equals 200." Your task is to determine what number $x$ is. Here is how to solve this equation.

Divide both sides of the equation by 25:

$$\frac{25x}{25} = \frac{200}{25}$$

$$x = \frac{200}{25}$$

$$x = 8$$

Solve for $x$:

$$\frac{x}{5} = \frac{3}{45}$$

To solve this type of problem, cross-multiply (45 times $x$ and 3 times 5).

$$45x = 15$$

$$x = \frac{15}{45} = \frac{1}{3} = 0.3\overline{3}$$

Solve for $x$:

$$\frac{10}{x} = \frac{50}{350}$$

To solve this problem, cross-multiply (10 times 350 and 50 times $x$).

$$50x = 3{,}500$$

$$x = 70$$

To check your answer, merely substitute 70 back into the equation and see if it works.

$\dfrac{10}{70} = \dfrac{50}{350}$ Reduce the fractions to $\dfrac{1}{7} = \dfrac{1}{7}$ or cross-multiply (10 times 350 and 70 times 50) making $3{,}500 = 3{,}500$. Either way, you are correct.

## Types of Arithmetic Word Problems

In the pages that follow, you will learn about many different kinds of word problems that you are likely to see on the SSAT or ISEE test. For each kind, you will see how to use the information you are given to set up an equation. Then you will see how to solve the equation for the unknown that is the answer to the problem. The following chart shows the different kinds of word problems discussed in this chapter.

## Arithmetic Word Problem Types

| Simple Interest | Percent Change |
| --- | --- |
| Compound Interest | Numbers and Number Relationships |
| Ratio and Proportion | Age |
| Motion | Measurement |
| Percent | |

## Simple Interest

*Interest* is an amount paid for the use of money. *Interest rate* is the percent paid per year. *Principal* is the amount of money on which interest is paid. *Simple interest* is interest that is computed based only on the principal, the interest rate, and the time. To calculate simple interest, use this formula:

Interest = Principal × Rate × Time

$\quad I = prt$

## Examples

Martina has $300 in a savings account that pays simple interest at a rate of 3% per year. How much interest will she earn on that $300 if she keeps it in the account for 5 years?

## Procedure

*What must you find?* Amount of simple interest.
*What are the units?* Dollars.
*What do you know?* Rate = 3% per year; time = 5 years; principal = $300.
*Write an equation and solve.*

$I = prt$
$I = (\$300)(0.03)(5)$
$I = \$45$

Five years ago, Robin deposited $500 in a savings account that pays simple interest. She made no further deposits, and today the account is worth $750. What is the rate of interest?

## Procedure

*What must you find?* Rate of simple interest.
*What are the units?* Percent per year.
*What do you know?* Interest = $250 ($750 – $500); principal = $500; time = 5 years.
*Create an equation and solve.*

$250 = (500)(x)(5)$
$250 = 2{,}500x$
$\dfrac{250}{2{,}500} = x$
$x = \dfrac{250}{2{,}500} = 0.10 \text{ or } 10\%$

1. Sheena has $500 in a savings account that pays simple interest at a rate of 2% per year. How much interest will she earn on that $500 if she keeps it in the account for 5 years?

2. Five years ago, Kevin deposited $1,000 in a savings account that pays simple interest. He made no further deposits, and today the account is worth $1,250. What is the rate of interest?

3. Two years ago, Peggy borrowed $5,000 to purchase a car. The interest rate is 2.5%. After two years, how much interest has she paid?

## Compound Interest

*Compound interest* is the interest paid on the principal and also on any interest that has already been paid. To calculate compound interest, you can use the formula $I = prt$, but you must calculate the interest for each time period and then combine them for a total.

### Example
Ricardo bought a $1,000 savings bond that earns 5% interest compounded annually. How much interest will he earn in two years?

### Procedure
*What must you find?* Amount of compound interest.
*What are the units?* Dollars.
*What do you know?* Principal = $1,000; rate = 5%; time = 2 years.
*Create an equation and solve.*

To find the compound interest, calculate the amount earned the first year. Add that amount to the principal, then calculate the interest earned in the second year. Total the amount of interest earned in the two years.

Year 1: $I = prt$
$I = (\$1,000)(0.05)(1)$
$I = \$50$

New principal = $1,050

Year 2: $I = prt$
$I = (\$1,050)(0.05)(1)$
$I = \$52.50$

So the total compound interest paid in two years is $50 + $52.50 = $102.50.

### On Your Own—Compound Interest

1. Kerry bought a $500 savings bond that earns 8% interest compounded annually. How much will the bond be worth in two years?

2. Leo invested $10,000 in a savings account that earned 3.5% compounded annually. How much will the account be worth in 3 years?

## Ratio, Rate, and Proportion

On the SSAT or ISEE you may encounter word problems that will require you to work with ratios, rates, and proportions.

### Examples

Kim reads an average of 150 pages per week. At that rate, how many weeks will it take him to read 1,800 pages?

### *Procedure*

*What must you find?* How long it will take to read 1,800 pages.
*What are the units?* Weeks.
*What do you know?* 150 pages read each week; 1,800 pages to be read.
*Set up a proportion and solve.*

$$\frac{\text{Number of pages}}{1 \text{ week}} = \frac{\text{Number of pages}}{x \text{ weeks}}$$

Substitute values into the equation and solve.

$$\frac{150 \text{ pages}}{1 \text{ week}} = \frac{1,800 \text{ pages}}{x \text{ weeks}}$$

Cross-multiply:

$150x = 1,800$
$x = 12$ weeks

It takes 8 hours to fill a swimming pool that holds 3,500 gallons of water. At that rate, how many hours will it take to fill a pool that holds 8,750 gallons?

### *Procedure*

*What must you find?* How long it will take to fill the 8,750-gallon pool.
*What are the units?* Hours.
*What do you know?* Number of hours for 3,500 gallons.
*Set up a proportion and solve.*

$$\frac{\text{Number of gallons}}{\text{Number of hours}} = \frac{\text{Number of gallons}}{\text{Number of hours}}$$

$$\frac{3,500 \text{ gallons}}{8 \text{ hours}} = \frac{8,750 \text{ gallons}}{x}$$

Cross-multiply:

$3,500x = (8)(8,750)$
$3,500x = 70,000$
$x = 20$ hours

An airplane travels the 1,700 miles from Phoenix to Nashville in 2.5 hours. Flying at the same speed, the plane could travel the 2,550 miles from Phoenix to Boston in how many hours?

*Procedure*

*What must you find?* Time it would take to fly 2,550 miles.
*What are the units?* Hours.
*What do you know?* The plane traveled 1,700 miles in 2.5 hours.
*Set up a proportion and solve.*

$$\frac{\text{Number of miles}}{\text{Number of hours}} = \frac{\text{Number of miles}}{\text{Number of hours}}$$

Substitute values:

$$\frac{1{,}700\ \text{miles}}{2.5\ \text{hours}} = \frac{2{,}550\ \text{miles}}{x}$$

Cross-multiply:

$1{,}700x = (2.5)(2{,}550)$
$1{,}700x = 6{,}375$
$x = 3.75\ \text{hours}$

### On Your Own—Ratio, Rate, and Proportion

1. Jerry reads an average of 75 pages per week. At that rate, how many weeks will it take him to read 1,000 pages?

2. It takes 2 minutes to fill a balloon that holds 4,000 units of helium. At that rate, how many minutes will it take to fill a balloon that holds 6,000 units of helium?

3. An empty swimming pool can hold 5,000 gallons of water. If a hose can fill the pool at 250 gallons every $^{1}/_{2}$ hour, how long will it take to fill the pool?

## Motion

Motion problems deal with how long it will take to get from point *a* to point *b* if you are traveling at a certain steady rate. To solve them, use this formula:

Distance = Rate × Time or $d = rt$

## Example

If a racing boat travels at a steady rate of 80 miles per hour, how many miles could it travel in 3.5 hours?

*Procedure*

*What must you find?* Distance traveled in 3.5 hours.
*What are the units?* Miles.
*What do you know?* Rate = 80 miles per hour; time = 3.5 hours.
*Create an equation and solve.*

$d = rt$

Substitute values into the formula:

$d = (80)(3.5)$
$d = 280$ miles

### On Your Own—Motion

1. If a motorcycle travels at a steady rate of 40 miles per hour, how many miles could it travel in 4.5 hours?
2. If a jet travels at 450 miles per hour, how long will it take for the jet to travel 5,940 miles?

## Percent

There are likely to be word problems involving percent on both the SSAT and ISEE.

### Examples

Lilly's bill at a restaurant is $22.00 and she wants to leave a 15% tip. How much money should her tip be?

### Procedure

*What must you find?* Amount of tip.
*What are the units?* Dollars and cents.
*What do you know?* Total bill = $22.00; percent of tip = 15.
*Create an equation and solve.*

Tip = 15% × 22.00

Substitute and solve:

$t = (0.15)(22.00)$
$t = \$3.30$

Frederick earns $1,500 per month at his job, but 28% of that amount is deducted for taxes. What is his monthly take-home pay?

### Procedure

*What must you find?* Monthly take-home pay.
*What are the units?* Dollars and cents.
*What do you know?* Monthly pay before taxes = $1,500; percent deducted = 28%.
*Create an equation and solve.*

Take-home pay is 1,500 minus 28% × 1,500.
$T = 1,500 - (1,500 \times 0.28)$
$T = 1,500 - (420)$
$T = \$1,080$

40 is 80% of what number?

### Procedure

*What must you find?* Number of which 40 is 80%.
*What are the units?* Numbers.
*What do you know?* 40 is 80% of some larger number.
*Create an equation and solve.*

$40 = 0.8x$

$0.8x = 40$

$x = \dfrac{40}{0.8}$

$x = 50$

### On Your Own—Percent

1. If your gross monthly pay is $3,000 and 32% is removed for taxes and insurance, what is your net pay?

2. If you invest $1,000 in a mutual fund that has a 0.5% fee, how much is the fee?

## Percent Change

Some word problems may ask you to calculate the percent of change from one number or amount to another.

### Examples

Samantha now earns $300 per month working at a cosmetics store, but starting next month her monthly salary will be $375. Her raise will be what percent increase over her current salary?

### Procedure

*What must you find?* Percent change from current salary.
*What are the units?* Percent.
*What do you know?* Current pay = $300/month; pay after the raise = $375/month.
*Create an equation and solve.*

$$\text{Percent change} = \frac{\text{Amount of change}}{\text{Starting point}}$$

Substitute values and solve:

$$\text{Percent change} = \frac{(375 - 300)}{300}$$

$$\text{Percent change} = \frac{75}{300}$$

Percent change = 0.25 or 25%

On his 16th birthday, Brad was 60 inches tall. On his 17th birthday he was 65 inches tall. What was the percent increase in Brad's height during the year to the nearest whole number?

### Procedure

*What must you find?* Percent change in height.
*What is the unit?* Percent.
*What do you know?* Starting height = 60 inches; height after a year = 65 inches.
*Create an equation and solve.*

$$\text{Percent change} = \frac{\text{Amount of change}}{\text{Starting point}}$$

Substitute values and solve:

$$\text{Percent change} = \frac{5 \text{ inches}}{60 \text{ inches}}$$

Percent change = 0.08 or 8%

At a certain store, every item is discounted by 15% off the original price. If Kevin buys a CD originally priced at $15.00 and a baseball cap originally priced at $11.50, how much money will he save to the nearest cent?

### Procedure

*What must you find?* Total amount saved.
*What are the units?* Dollars and cents.
*What do you know?* Percent change = 15%; original price for two items = $15.00 + $11.50 = $26.50.
*Create an equation and solve.*

$$\text{Percent change} = \frac{\text{Amount of change}}{\text{Starting point}}$$

Substitute values and solve:

$$0.15 = \frac{x}{26.50}$$

$x = 0.15(26.50)$
$x = \$3.98$

### On Your Own—Percent Change

1. A magazine has reduced its subscription price from $15.00 per month to $13.00 per month. What is the percent reduction to the nearest whole number?

2. The tuition for college was increased from $10,000 per year to $12,500 per year. What is the percent increase?

3. A car is discounted 12% for an "end of the year" sale. The car's original price was $25,000. What is the sale price?

## Numbers and Number Relationships

Pay attention to the key words in this type of word problem.

### Examples

If the sum of two numbers is 45 and one number is 5 more than the other, what are the two numbers?

### *Procedure*

*What must you find?* Value of each number.
*What are the units?* Numbers.
*What do you know?* The sum of two numbers is 45; one number is 5 more than the other.
*Create an equation and solve.*

Let $x$ be the smaller number.

$$x + (x + 5) = 45$$

Solve for $x$:

$$x + x + 5 = 45$$
$$2x = 40$$
$$x = 20$$

## Age

Some word problems ask you to calculate a person's age given certain facts.

### Example

Jessica is 26 years old. Two years ago she was twice as old as her brother Ned. How old is Ned now?

### *Procedure*

*What must you find?* Ned's age now.
*What are the units?* Years.
*What do you know?* When Jessica was 24, she was 2 times as old as Ned.
*Create an equation and solve.*

Let $x$ = Ned's age two years ago.

$$2x = 24$$
$$x = 12$$

Ned's age two years later $= 12 + 2 = 14$ years.

1. One number is 3 times another number less 12. If the first number is 108, what is the second number?
2. Aaron is 30 years old. If his sister Angela is half his age plus 2 years, how old is Angela?

## Addition and Subtraction with Matrices

A **matrix** is a rectangular array of numbers, symbols, or expressions. The size of a matrix is based on its number of rows and columns. Remember: rows are horizontal and columns are vertical.

### Examples

2 × 2 Matrix          2 × 3 Matrix

$$\begin{bmatrix} 3 & 3 \\ 2 & -4 \end{bmatrix} \qquad \begin{bmatrix} 7 & 1 & 4 \\ -3 & 3 & 2 \end{bmatrix}$$

The numbers in matrices of the same size can be added or subtracted just like integers as long as the numbers are in the same position.

### Examples
### Addition

$$\begin{bmatrix} 3 & 3 \\ 2 & -4 \end{bmatrix} + \begin{bmatrix} 4 & -2 \\ -3 & 3 \end{bmatrix} = \begin{bmatrix} 7 & 1 \\ -1 & -1 \end{bmatrix}$$

### Subtraction

$$\begin{bmatrix} 5 & -2 \\ -3 & 4 \end{bmatrix} - \begin{bmatrix} -2 & -2 \\ 3 & 3 \end{bmatrix} = \begin{bmatrix} 7 & 0 \\ -6 & 1 \end{bmatrix}$$

*On Your Own—Addition and Subtraction of Matrices*

1.                                  2.

$$\begin{bmatrix} 3 & 3 \\ 2 & -4 \end{bmatrix} + \begin{bmatrix} 4 & -2 \\ -3 & 3 \end{bmatrix} \qquad \begin{bmatrix} -2 & 3 \\ 5 & -4 \end{bmatrix} - \begin{bmatrix} 2 & -1 \\ 3 & -2 \end{bmatrix}$$

## Geometry Word Problems

Word problems on the SSAT or ISEE may also deal with geometry concepts such as perimeter, area, and volume. To solve these problems, you may also need to use information about different units of measure. To review units of measure, see Chapter 10.

Just as with other kinds of word problems, you can solve geometry problems by following a specific procedure. In the examples that follow, pay special attention to the procedure outlined in each solution. Follow this same procedure whenever you need to solve this kind of word problem.

**Examples**

Sally is buying wood to make a rectangular picture frame measuring 11 in. × 14 in. The wood costs 25 cents per inch. How much will Sally have to pay for the wood?

**Procedure**

*What must you find?* Cost of the wood for the frame.
*What are the units?* Dollars and cents.
*What do you know?* Cost of the wood per inch, shape of the frame, measure of the frame.
*Create an equation and solve.*

Length of wood needed for rectangular frame = $2l + 2w$

Substitute values and solve:

Length of wood = $2(14) + 2(11)$
Length of wood = $28 + 22 = 50$ in.

If each inch costs 0.25, then $0.25 \times 50 = \$12.50$.

Sergei is planting rosebushes in a rectangular garden measuring 12 ft × 20 ft. Each rosebush needs 8 ft² of space. How many rosebushes can Sergei plant in the garden?

**Procedure**

*What must you find?* Number of rosebushes that can be planted in the garden.
*What are the units?* Numbers.
*What do you know?* Shape of the garden, garden length and width, amount of area needed for each rosebush.
*Create an equation and solve.*

$A = lw$

Substitute values and solve:

$A = 12 \times 20 = 240$ ft²

Each rosebush needs 8 ft² area.

$240 \div 8 = 30$

Sergei can plant 30 rosebushes in the garden.

**On Your Own—Geometry**

1. A floor is 10 feet long and 12 feet wide. Chris wants to lay tiles that are 10 inches square on the floor. How many whole tiles will he need?

2. Ian has a front lawn that is 300 feet by 120 feet. If 1 pound of fertilizer is needed for every 600 square feet, how many pounds of fertilizer are needed?

3. Gerry wants to inflate an exercise ball. The ball has a radius of 15 inches. If a pump can push 5 cubic inches of air every second, how many seconds will it take to inflate the ball?

4. A grey wolf needs 10.75 square miles of land to live. If a national park measures 20 miles by 60 miles of land, about how many grey wolves can be supported?

5. A garden is shaped like a triangle with a base of 40 feet and a height of 25 feet. If Ralph wants to plant lemon trees, each of which requires about 15 square feet of growing space, what is the maximum number of trees he can plant?

## Answers to "On Your Own" Practice Sets

**On Your Own—Key Words**

1. subtract

2. divide

3. add

4. multiply

5. equals

**On Your Own—Simple Interest**

1. $50

2. 5%

3. $250

**On Your Own—Compound Interest**

1. $583.20

2. $11,087.18

**On Your Own—Ratio, Rate, and Proportion**

1. 13.33 weeks

2. 3 minutes

3. 20 half hours or 10 hours

**On Your Own—Motion**

1. 180 miles

2. 13.2 hours

**On Your Own—Percent**

1. $2,040.00

2. $5.00

**On Your Own—Percent Change**

1. about 13%

2. 25%

3. $22,000

**On Your Own—Numbers and Number Relationships**

1. 40

2. 17

**On Your Own—Addition and Subtraction of Matrices**

1.

$$\begin{bmatrix} 7 & 1 \\ -1 & -1 \end{bmatrix}$$

2.

$$\begin{bmatrix} -4 & 4 \\ 2 & -2 \end{bmatrix}$$

**On Your Own—Geometry**

1. 173 tiles

2. 60 pounds

3. 2,826 seconds

4. about 112 wolves

5. 33 trees

# How to Solve Quantitative Comparisons (ISEE Only)

Quantitative comparisons are another type of math question that appears only on the ISEE. If you are taking the SSAT, you can skip this chapter.

On the ISEE, quantitative comparisons appear only on the upper level and middle level versions of the test. If you are taking the lower level version, you will not see this question type.

On the upper level versions of the ISEE, quantitative comparison questions appear in the Quantitative Reasoning section, where they make up 15 of the 35 total questions.

## Format of Quantitative Comparison Questions

Each quantitative comparison question consists of two mathematical quantities shown side by side, one in column A and the other in column B. Some problems present additional information relating to the two quantities that you need to consider when choosing your answer. This additional information will appear in the center, between column A and column B. Your task is to evaluate the two quantities and determine whether one quantity is greater than the other, whether the two are the same, or whether it is impossible to determine if one is greater than the other. Quantitative comparison problems may be drawn from arithmetic, algebra, or geometry.

## Sample Quantitative Comparison Question Explained

Let's look at a sample question to see what is involved. Quantitative comparison questions have their own special set of directions. Read the directions, then study the question that follows.

**Directions:** For each of the following quantities, two quantities are given—one in column A, the other in column B. Compare the two quantities and mark your answer sheet as follows:

(A) if the quantity in column A is greater
(B) if the quantity in column B is greater
(C) if the quantities are equal
(D) if the relationship cannot be determined from the information given

**Notes**

- Information concerning one or both of the compared quantities will be centered between the two columns for some items.
- Symbols that appear in both columns represent the same thing in column A and in column B.
- Letters such as $x$, $n$, and $k$ are symbols for real numbers.
- Figures are drawn to scale unless otherwise noted.

| Column A | Column B |
|----------|----------|

1.
$$3x - 4 = 2$$
$$3y + 15 = 9$$

$x$                 $y$

In the problem, you are asked to compare $x$ and $y$. The centered information tells you about $x$ and $y$. If you solve the two equations, you can find values for $x$ and $y$ as follows:

$3x - 4 = 2$
$3x = 2 + 4$
$3x = 6$
$x = 2$

$3y + 15 = 9$
$3y = 9 - 15$
$3y = -6$
$y = -2$

Now that you have values for $x$ and $y$, you can compare the two quantities. If $x = 2$ and $y = -2$, then $x$ is greater than $y$. Since $x$ is the quantity in column A, the correct answer is choice A, "The quantity in column A is greater."

## How to Solve Quantitative Comparison Questions

Here is a six-step strategic plan that you can use to solve quantitative comparison questions.

1. Look carefully at the two quantities. Ask yourself: Are they fractions or percents? Algebraic expressions? Geometric measures? Is the quantity in column A the same kind of quantity as the one in column B?
2. Look to see if there is any information centered between the two columns that might help you solve the problem. If so, how does it apply to the given quantities?
3. Think of how you might restate one or both of the quantities so that you are comparing like terms. Maybe you will need to perform an arithmetic

calculation. Maybe you will need to substitute values into an algebraic expression. Maybe you will need to find a geometric measure.

4. Carry out your plan. Restate one or both quantities so that you can compare like terms. Then compare.

5. Be sure to mark your answer correctly. Mark choice A if the quantity in column A is larger. Mark choice B if the quantity in column B is larger. Mark choice C if the two quantities are equal. Mark choice D if the relationship cannot be determined.

6. If the two quantities are algebraic expressions and values are not specified, keep in mind that your answer must be true for any values you substitute for unknowns. If the relationship between the quantities is different for different values, you must mark choice D as your answer.

Try the six-step strategy to help you answer the quantitative comparison questions that follow. Then compare your answer to the solution that follows each question.

## Sample Quantitative Comparison Question Set Explained

**Directions:** For each of the following quantities, two quantities are given—one in column A, the other in column B. Compare the two quantities and mark your answer sheet as follows:

(A) if the quantity in column A is greater
(B) if the quantity in column B is greater
(C) if the quantities are equal
(D) if the relationship cannot be determined from the information given

**Notes**

- Information concerning one or both of the compared quantities will be centered between the two columns for some items.
- Symbols that appear in both columns represent the same thing in column A and in column B.
- Letters such as $x$, $n$, and $k$ are symbols for real numbers.
- Figures are drawn to scale unless otherwise noted.

| Column A | Column B |
|---|---|
| 1. | Sequence: 100, 90, 180, 170, 340, … |
| seventh term in sequence | eighth term in sequence |

**1. A is correct.**
The sequence follows the rule: Starting with the first number, subtract 10, then double. The seventh term will be 660. The eighth term will be 650.

2.    $2^{-4}$                                          $(1/4)^2$

**2. C is correct.**

$2^{-4} = \dfrac{1}{2^4}$; $2^4 = 2 \times 2 \times 2 \times 2 = 16$; so, $\dfrac{1}{2^4} = \dfrac{1}{16}$.

$\left(\dfrac{1}{4}\right)^2 = \dfrac{1}{4} \times \dfrac{1}{4} = \dfrac{1}{16}$

3.                          $a$, $b$, and $c$ are integers.
                          $a > 0 > b > c$

         $a/b$                                        $a/c$

**3. B is correct.**

Since $a > 0$, it is a positive integer. Since and $b$ and $c$ are less than zero, they are both negative integers. The quotient of a positive integer divided by a negative integer is a negative rational number. So, $a/b$ and $a/c$ are negative rational numbers.

   Since both have the same numerator, the negative rational number that has the greater denominator will be greater.

4.

         $m \angle A$                                      $m \angle B$

**4. A is correct.**
$\angle BCA$ and $\angle BCD$ are supplementary angles.
Therefore, $m \angle BCA + m \angle BCD = 180°$.
$m \angle BCA + 145 = 180°$
$m \angle BCD = 35°$

The sum of the measures of the three angles in a triangle is equal to 180.
$m \angle A + m \angle B + m \angle C = 180°$
$m \angle A + 71° + 35° = 180°$
$m \angle A + 106° = 180°$
$m \angle A = 74°$

5.                          $x < 0 < y$

         $[x^2 - 1]$                                    $[2y + 1]$

**5. D is correct.**
A number less than 0 is a negative number. So, $x$ is a negative number. The square of a negative number is a positive number. Without knowing the absolute values of $x$ and $y$, there is insufficient information to determine the answer to this question.

6.      width of a rectangle                    length of the side of a square

         that has a perimeter of 20 feet             that has a perimeter of 24 feet

**6. D is correct.**

You can determine that the length of the side of the square is 6 ft, since $4s = 24$. However, you cannot determine the width of the rectangle, since you do not know its length.

7.

         volume of cylinder 1            volume of cylinder 2

**7. B is correct.**

Substitute values for $r$ and $h$ into the formula: $V = \pi r^2 h$.

*Cylinder 1*

$h = 8$ cm; $d = 4$ cm, so $r = 2$ cm

$V = \pi r^2 h$

$\quad = \pi(2)^2(8)$

$\quad = 32\pi$

*Cylinder 2*

$h = 4$ cm; $d = 8$ cm, so $r = 4$ cm

$V = \pi r^2 h$

$\quad = \pi(4)^2(4)$

$\quad = 64\pi$

8.                                 $y = 2x^2 + 4x + 5$

          $y$, when $x = -2$                           $y$, when $x = 0$

**8. C is correct.**

$y = 2x^2 + 4x + 5$                             $y = 2x^2 + 4x + 5$

$y = 2(-2)^2 + 4(-2) + 5$                $y = 2(0)^2 + 4(0) + 5$

$y = 8 - 8 + 5$                                $y = 0 + 0 + 5$

$y = 5$                                        $y = 5$

## On Your Own

Now take the time to apply what you have just learned about quantitative comparison questions to see how well you can do on Practice Set A. When you are finished, use the answer key to score your work.

Review the strategies and tips discussed above and then try Practice Set B. Remember that the more you practice with these items, the easier they will become for you to answer correctly.

### Practice Set A

**Directions:** For each of the following quantities, two quantities are given—one in column A, the other in column B. Compare the two quantities and mark your answer sheet as follows:

(A) if the quantity in column A is greater
(B) if the quantity in column B is greater
(C) if the quantities are equal
(D) if the relationship cannot be determined from the information given

### Notes

- Information concerning one or both of the compared quantities will be centered between the two columns for some items.
- Symbols that appear in both columns represent the same thing in column A as in column B.
- Letters such as $x$, $n$, and $k$ are symbols for real numbers.
- Figures are drawn to scale unless otherwise noted.

|  | **Column A** |  | **Column B** |
|---|---|---|---|
| 1. |  | $\dfrac{9}{a} = \dfrac{36}{8}$ |  |
|  | $\dfrac{2}{a}$ |  | $\dfrac{a}{2}$ |
| 2. |  | $x + y = 5$ |  |
|  |  | $3x + 2y = 12$ |  |
|  | $x$ |  | $y$ |
| 3. |  | $p$ is a prime number |  |
|  |  | $c$ is a composite number |  |
|  | the sum of the factors of $p$ |  | the sum of the factors of $c$ |
| 4. | percent increase from 20 to 25 |  | percent increase from 50 to 60 |
| 5. | $0.\overline{6}$ |  | $\dfrac{2}{3}$ |
| 6. |  | $-5m - 2 = 3$ |  |
|  |  | $4n + 12 = 8$ |  |
|  | $m$ |  | $n$ |

7.  A 13-foot ladder is leaning against a building. The top of the ladder reaches 12 feet up the building. The distance of the bottom of the ladder from the base of the building is *a*.

13 feet    12 feet

*a*

| *a* | 10 feet |
| --- | --- |

8.  8,047                    $(8 \times 10^2) + (4 \times 10^1) + (7 \times 10^0)$

9.  $100/\sqrt{25}$                    $2\sqrt{16}$

10. number of fluid ounces         number of hours in
    in 15 gallons                 3 weeks

**Answers and Explanations**

1. **C is correct.**

$$\frac{9}{a} = \frac{36}{8}$$

$36a = 72$

$a = 2$

$$\frac{2}{a} = \frac{2}{2} = 1 \text{ and } \frac{a}{2} = \frac{2}{2} = 1$$

2. **B is correct.**
Solve the first equation for *y*.
$x + y = 5$
$y = 5 - x$

Substitute the expression for *y* into the second equation.
$3x + 2y = 12$
$3x + 2(5 - x) = 12$

Solve for *x*.
$3x + 10 - 2x = 12$
$x + 10 = 12$
$x = 2$

Substitute the value for *x* into the first equation and solve for *y*.
$x + y = 5$
$2 + y = 5$
$y = 3$

### 3. **D is correct.**

A prime number is a whole number greater than 1 that has only two factors, the number itself and 1. A composite number is a whole number greater than 1 that has other factors besides 1 and itself. However, the size of the factors is not known, so the answer to the question posed cannot be answered.

### 4. **A is correct.**

Subtract to find amount of increase.

$25 - 20 = 5$ $\qquad\qquad\qquad\qquad$ $60 - 50 = 10$

Write the ratio comparing the amount of increase to the original amount.

$\dfrac{5}{20} = \dfrac{1}{4}$ $\qquad\qquad\qquad\qquad$ $\dfrac{10}{50} = \dfrac{1}{5}$

Express the ratio as a percent.

$\dfrac{1}{4} = 25\%$ $\qquad\qquad\qquad\qquad$ $\dfrac{1}{5} = 20\%$

### 5. **C is correct.**

Let $n = 0.\overline{6}$.

Since one digit repeats, multiply by 10. $10n = 6.\overline{6}$

Subtract the original equation.

$$10n = 6.\overline{6}$$
$$\underline{-\ n = 0.\overline{6}}$$
$$9n = 6.0$$

Solve the equation.

$9n = 6$

$n = \dfrac{6}{9} = \dfrac{2}{3}$

### 6. **C is correct.**

$-5m - 2 = 3$ $\qquad\qquad\qquad\qquad$ $4n + 12 = 8$

$-5m = 5$ $\qquad\qquad\qquad\qquad\quad$ $4n = -4$

$m = -1$ $\qquad\qquad\qquad\qquad\quad$ $n = -1$

### 7. **B is correct.**

The ladder, wall of building, and ground form a right triangle. Using the Pythagorean theorem.

$a^2 = c^2 - b^2$

$a^2 = 13^2 - 12^2$

$a^2 = 169 - 144$

$a^2 = 25$

$a = 5$ feet

### 8. **A is correct.**

$(8 \times 10^2) + (4 \times 10^1) + (7 \times 10^0)$

$= (8 \times 100) + (4 \times 10) + (7 \times 1) = 847$

**9. A is correct.**

$$\frac{100}{\sqrt{25}} = \frac{100}{5} = 20$$

$$2\sqrt{16} = 2(4) = 8$$

**10. B is correct.**

32 fl oz = 1 gal

15 × 32 = 480 fl oz in 15 gal

24 hours = 1 day

7 days = 1 week

7 × 24 = 168 hours in 1 week

3 × 168 = 504 hours in 3 weeks

**Practice Set B**

1.　　　　　　　　Parallelogram *MNPQ* is shown below.

　　length of *MN*　　　　　　　　　　　　　　　　length of *PN*

2.　　　　　　　　　　　　$10 > t > -2$

　　　$3t$　　　　　　　　　　　　　　　　　　　　　　$-4t$

3.　　　　　　　　　　　　$\dfrac{5}{12} = \dfrac{y}{144}$

　　$\dfrac{y}{2}$　　　　　　　　　　　　　　　　　　　　$90 - y$

4.　　percent decrease from 53 to 37.1　　percent decrease from 72 to 50.4

5.　　　　　　　　　　　*j* and *k* are integers

　　　　　　　　　　　　　　$j < k < 0$

　　　$j + k$　　　　　　　　　　　　　　　　　　　　$k - j$

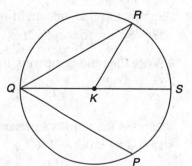

6.

　　number of different chords　　　　　number of different radii
　　drawn　　　　　　　　　　　　　　　　drawn

7. The average weight of Bertha, Sue, and Myra is 105 pounds.

the sum of Sue's and
Bertha's weights

the sum of Myra's and
Sue's weights

8.
$$d = 125\% \text{ of } 800$$
$$g = 0.2\% \text{ of } 50{,}000$$

$d$         $g$

9.
$a$, $b$, and $c$ are integers
$b > a$, and $c > a$

$a/b \times a/c$       1

10. the number of congruent
sides in an equilateral triangle

the number of congruent
angles in a right triangle

## Answers and Explanations

**1. D is correct.**
Since the figure is a parallelogram, opposite sides are congruent. So the length of $\overline{MN}$ is 10 cm. However, the length of $\overline{PN}$ cannot be determined.

**2. D is correct.**
Since $t$ could be any value from 10 to −2, it is impossible to determine which algebraic expression is greater.

**3. C is correct.**
$$\frac{5}{12} = \frac{y}{144}$$
$$12y = 5 \times 144$$
$$12y = 720$$
$$y = 60$$
$$\frac{y}{2} = \frac{60}{2} = 30$$
$$90 - y = 90 - 60 = 30$$

**4. C is correct.**
Subtract to find amount of increase.

$53 - 37.1 = 15.9$            $72 - 50.4 = 21.6$

Write the ratio comparing the amount of decrease to the original amount.

$\dfrac{15.9}{5.3}$            $\dfrac{21.6}{72}$

Express the ratio as a percent by dividing.

$15.9 \div 53 = 0.3 = 30\%$       $21.6 \div 72 = 0.3 = 30\%$

**5. B is correct.**

Since both $j$ and $k$ are integers $< 0$, they are negative integers. Since $j < k$, then $j + k$, which represents the sum of two negative integers, will always be a negative integer, and $k - j$, which represents the difference between the greater integer and the lesser integer, will always be a positive integer. All positive integers are greater than all negative integers.

**6. C is correct.**

A chord is any line segment with both end points on a circle. There are 3 chords drawn in the circle: $\overline{QP}$, $\overline{QR}$, and $\overline{QS}$.

A radius is a line segment that has one end point in the center of the circle, and another end point on the circle. There are 3 radii drawn in the circle: $\overline{KQ}$, $\overline{KR}$, and $\overline{KS}$.

**7. D is correct.**

There is no information about the weights of each girl in order to determine and compare the sum of any two girls' weights.

**8. C is correct.**

125% of 800 = 1.25 × 800 = 1,000
0.2% of 50,000 = 0.02 × 50,000 = 1,000

**9. B is correct.**

Since $b$ and $c$ are greater than $a$, the rational numbers $a/b$ and $a/c$ are each less than 1. The product of any two rational numbers, each less than 1, is less than 1.

**10. A is correct.**

There are 3 congruent sides in an equilateral triangle. A right isosceles triangle has 2 congruent 45° angles.

# PART IV

# PRACTICE TESTS FOR THE SSAT

# SSAT Practice Test I

The following practice test is designed to be just like the real SSAT. It matches the actual test in content coverage and level of difficulty. The test is in five sections: Verbal, Quantitative I, Reading Comprehension, Quantitative II, and the Essay.

This practice test will be an accurate reflection of how you'll do on test day if you treat it as the real examination. Here are some hints on how to take the test under conditions similar to those of the actual exam:

- Find a quiet place to work and set aside a period of approximately 3 hours when you will not be disturbed.
- Work on only one section at a time, and use your watch or a timer to keep track of the time limits for each test part.
- Tear out your answer sheet and mark your answers by filling in the ovals for each question.
- Write your essay on the pages provided.
- Become familiar with the directions for each part of the test. You'll save time on the actual test day by already being familiar with this information.

At the end of the test you'll find answer keys for each section and explanations for every question. Check your answers against the keys to find out how you did on each section of the test and what test topics you might need to study more. Then review the explanations, paying particular attention to the ones for the questions you answered incorrectly.

You will receive three scores, one for each of these three categories: Quantitative, Verbal, and Reading. Each category has a low score of 500 and the high score of 800, making your total score somewhere between 1500 and 2400.

The actual SSAT also provides a Percentile Score that compares your performance with that of other U.S. and Canadian students who took the test during the past three years. Your reported percentile test scores are compared to this "norm group" for each section of the test.

The writing sample is not scored, but it is included with the score reports that you send to schools. The following table shows the various sections, numbers of questions, and time allotments.

## SSAT: Structure and Time Allotments

| Section | Number of Questions | Time Allowed |
|---|---|---|
| Writing Sample | 1 (unscored) | 25 minutes |
| Break | | 5 minutes |
| Quantitative 1 | 25 | 30 minutes |
| Reading | 40 | 40 minutes |
| Break | | 5 minutes |
| Verbal | 60 | 30 minutes |
| Quantitative 2 | 25 | 30 minutes |
| Experimental | 16 (unscored) | 15 minutes |
| Totals | 167 | 3 hours, 5 minutes |

Of the 167 total questions, only 150 items are scored. The writing sample and questions on the Experimental section are *not* scored.

# SSAT Practice Test I

ANSWER SHEET

## Section 1: Quantitative I

1. Ⓐ Ⓑ Ⓒ Ⓓ Ⓔ    11. Ⓐ Ⓑ Ⓒ Ⓓ Ⓔ    21. Ⓐ Ⓑ Ⓒ Ⓓ Ⓔ
2. Ⓐ Ⓑ Ⓒ Ⓓ Ⓔ    12. Ⓐ Ⓑ Ⓒ Ⓓ Ⓔ    22. Ⓐ Ⓑ Ⓒ Ⓓ Ⓔ
3. Ⓐ Ⓑ Ⓒ Ⓓ Ⓔ    13. Ⓐ Ⓑ Ⓒ Ⓓ Ⓔ    23. Ⓐ Ⓑ Ⓒ Ⓓ Ⓔ
4. Ⓐ Ⓑ Ⓒ Ⓓ Ⓔ    14. Ⓐ Ⓑ Ⓒ Ⓓ Ⓔ    24. Ⓐ Ⓑ Ⓒ Ⓓ Ⓕ
5. Ⓐ Ⓑ Ⓒ Ⓓ Ⓔ    15. Ⓐ Ⓑ Ⓒ Ⓓ Ⓔ    25. Ⓐ Ⓑ Ⓒ Ⓓ Ⓔ
6. Ⓐ Ⓑ Ⓒ Ⓓ Ⓔ    16. Ⓐ Ⓑ Ⓒ Ⓓ Ⓔ
7. Ⓐ Ⓑ Ⓒ Ⓓ Ⓔ    17. Ⓐ Ⓑ Ⓒ Ⓓ Ⓔ
8. Ⓐ Ⓑ Ⓒ Ⓓ Ⓔ    18. Ⓐ Ⓑ Ⓒ Ⓓ Ⓔ
9. Ⓐ Ⓑ Ⓒ Ⓓ Ⓔ    19. Ⓐ Ⓑ Ⓒ Ⓓ Ⓔ
10. Ⓐ Ⓑ Ⓒ Ⓓ Ⓔ    20. Ⓐ Ⓑ Ⓒ Ⓓ Ⓔ

## Section 2: Reading Comprehension

1. Ⓐ Ⓑ Ⓒ Ⓓ Ⓔ    17. Ⓐ Ⓑ Ⓒ Ⓓ Ⓔ    33. Ⓐ Ⓑ Ⓒ Ⓓ Ⓔ
2. Ⓐ Ⓑ Ⓒ Ⓓ Ⓔ    18. Ⓐ Ⓑ Ⓒ Ⓓ Ⓔ    34. Ⓐ Ⓑ Ⓒ Ⓓ Ⓔ
3. Ⓐ Ⓑ Ⓒ Ⓓ Ⓔ    19. Ⓐ Ⓑ Ⓒ Ⓓ Ⓔ    35. Ⓐ Ⓑ Ⓒ Ⓓ Ⓔ
4. Ⓐ Ⓑ Ⓒ Ⓓ Ⓔ    20. Ⓐ Ⓑ Ⓒ Ⓓ Ⓔ    36. Ⓐ Ⓑ Ⓒ Ⓓ Ⓔ
5. Ⓐ Ⓑ Ⓒ Ⓓ Ⓔ    21. Ⓐ Ⓑ Ⓒ Ⓓ Ⓔ    37. Ⓐ Ⓑ Ⓒ Ⓓ Ⓔ
6. Ⓐ Ⓑ Ⓒ Ⓓ Ⓔ    22. Ⓐ Ⓑ Ⓒ Ⓓ Ⓔ    38. Ⓐ Ⓑ Ⓒ Ⓓ Ⓔ
7. Ⓐ Ⓑ Ⓒ Ⓓ Ⓔ    23. Ⓐ Ⓑ Ⓒ Ⓓ Ⓔ    39. Ⓐ Ⓑ Ⓒ Ⓓ Ⓔ
8. Ⓐ Ⓑ Ⓒ Ⓓ Ⓔ    24. Ⓐ Ⓑ Ⓒ Ⓓ Ⓔ    40. Ⓐ Ⓑ Ⓒ Ⓓ Ⓔ
9. Ⓐ Ⓑ Ⓒ Ⓓ Ⓔ    25. Ⓐ Ⓑ Ⓒ Ⓓ Ⓔ
10. Ⓐ Ⓑ Ⓒ Ⓓ Ⓔ    26. Ⓐ Ⓑ Ⓒ Ⓓ Ⓔ
11. Ⓐ Ⓑ Ⓒ Ⓓ Ⓔ    27. Ⓐ Ⓑ Ⓒ Ⓓ Ⓔ
12. Ⓐ Ⓑ Ⓒ Ⓓ Ⓔ    28. Ⓐ Ⓑ Ⓒ Ⓓ Ⓔ
13. Ⓐ Ⓑ Ⓒ Ⓓ Ⓕ    29. Ⓐ Ⓑ Ⓒ Ⓓ Ⓔ
14. Ⓐ Ⓑ Ⓒ Ⓓ Ⓔ    30. Ⓐ Ⓑ Ⓒ Ⓓ Ⓔ
15. Ⓐ Ⓑ Ⓒ Ⓓ Ⓔ    31. Ⓐ Ⓑ Ⓒ Ⓓ Ⓔ
16. Ⓐ Ⓑ Ⓒ Ⓓ Ⓔ    32. Ⓐ Ⓑ Ⓒ Ⓓ Ⓔ

## Section 3: Verbal

| | | |
|---|---|---|
| 1. Ⓐ Ⓑ Ⓒ Ⓓ Ⓔ | 21. Ⓐ Ⓑ Ⓒ Ⓓ Ⓔ | 41. Ⓐ Ⓑ Ⓒ Ⓓ Ⓔ |
| 2. Ⓐ Ⓑ Ⓒ Ⓓ Ⓔ | 22. Ⓐ Ⓑ Ⓒ Ⓓ Ⓔ | 42. Ⓐ Ⓑ Ⓒ Ⓓ Ⓔ |
| 3. Ⓐ Ⓑ Ⓒ Ⓓ Ⓔ | 23. Ⓐ Ⓑ Ⓒ Ⓓ Ⓔ | 43. Ⓐ Ⓑ Ⓒ Ⓓ Ⓔ |
| 4. Ⓐ Ⓑ Ⓒ Ⓓ Ⓔ | 24. Ⓐ Ⓑ Ⓒ Ⓓ Ⓔ | 44. Ⓐ Ⓑ Ⓒ Ⓓ Ⓔ |
| 5. Ⓐ Ⓑ Ⓒ Ⓓ Ⓔ | 25. Ⓐ Ⓑ Ⓒ Ⓓ Ⓔ | 45. Ⓐ Ⓑ Ⓒ Ⓓ Ⓔ |
| 6. Ⓐ Ⓑ Ⓒ Ⓓ Ⓔ | 26. Ⓐ Ⓑ Ⓒ Ⓓ Ⓔ | 46. Ⓐ Ⓑ Ⓒ Ⓓ Ⓔ |
| 7. Ⓐ Ⓑ Ⓒ Ⓓ Ⓔ | 27. Ⓐ Ⓑ Ⓒ Ⓓ Ⓔ | 47. Ⓐ Ⓑ Ⓒ Ⓓ Ⓔ |
| 8. Ⓐ Ⓑ Ⓒ Ⓓ Ⓔ | 28. Ⓐ Ⓑ Ⓒ Ⓓ Ⓔ | 48. Ⓐ Ⓑ Ⓒ Ⓓ Ⓔ |
| 9. Ⓐ Ⓑ Ⓒ Ⓓ Ⓔ | 29. Ⓐ Ⓑ Ⓒ Ⓓ Ⓔ | 49. Ⓐ Ⓑ Ⓒ Ⓓ Ⓔ |
| 10. Ⓐ Ⓑ Ⓒ Ⓓ Ⓔ | 30. Ⓐ Ⓑ Ⓒ Ⓓ Ⓔ | 50. Ⓐ Ⓑ Ⓒ Ⓓ Ⓔ |
| 11. Ⓐ Ⓑ Ⓒ Ⓓ Ⓔ | 31. Ⓐ Ⓑ Ⓒ Ⓓ Ⓔ | 51. Ⓐ Ⓑ Ⓒ Ⓓ Ⓔ |
| 12. Ⓐ Ⓑ Ⓒ Ⓓ Ⓔ | 32. Ⓐ Ⓑ Ⓒ Ⓓ Ⓔ | 52. Ⓐ Ⓑ Ⓒ Ⓓ Ⓔ |
| 13. Ⓐ Ⓑ Ⓒ Ⓓ Ⓔ | 33. Ⓐ Ⓑ Ⓒ Ⓓ Ⓔ | 53. Ⓐ Ⓑ Ⓒ Ⓓ Ⓔ |
| 14. Ⓐ Ⓑ Ⓒ Ⓓ Ⓔ | 34. Ⓐ Ⓑ Ⓒ Ⓓ Ⓔ | 54. Ⓐ Ⓑ Ⓒ Ⓓ Ⓔ |
| 15. Ⓐ Ⓑ Ⓒ Ⓓ Ⓔ | 35. Ⓐ Ⓑ Ⓒ Ⓓ Ⓔ | 55. Ⓐ Ⓑ Ⓒ Ⓓ Ⓔ |
| 16. Ⓐ Ⓑ Ⓒ Ⓓ Ⓔ | 36. Ⓐ Ⓑ Ⓒ Ⓓ Ⓔ | 56. Ⓐ Ⓑ Ⓒ Ⓓ Ⓔ |
| 17. Ⓐ Ⓑ Ⓒ Ⓓ Ⓔ | 37. Ⓐ Ⓑ Ⓒ Ⓓ Ⓔ | 57. Ⓐ Ⓑ Ⓒ Ⓓ Ⓔ |
| 18. Ⓐ Ⓑ Ⓒ Ⓓ Ⓔ | 38. Ⓐ Ⓑ Ⓒ Ⓓ Ⓔ | 58. Ⓐ Ⓑ Ⓒ Ⓓ Ⓔ |
| 19. Ⓐ Ⓑ Ⓒ Ⓓ Ⓔ | 39. Ⓐ Ⓑ Ⓒ Ⓓ Ⓔ | 59. Ⓐ Ⓑ Ⓒ Ⓓ Ⓔ |
| 20. Ⓐ Ⓑ Ⓒ Ⓓ Ⓔ | 40. Ⓐ Ⓑ Ⓒ Ⓓ Ⓔ | 60. Ⓐ Ⓑ Ⓒ Ⓓ Ⓔ |

## Section 4: Quantitative II

| | | |
|---|---|---|
| 1. Ⓐ Ⓑ Ⓒ Ⓓ Ⓔ | 11. Ⓐ Ⓑ Ⓒ Ⓓ Ⓔ | 21. Ⓐ Ⓑ Ⓒ Ⓓ Ⓔ |
| 2. Ⓐ Ⓑ Ⓒ Ⓓ Ⓔ | 12. Ⓐ Ⓑ Ⓒ Ⓓ Ⓔ | 22. Ⓐ Ⓑ Ⓒ Ⓓ Ⓔ |
| 3. Ⓐ Ⓑ Ⓒ Ⓓ Ⓔ | 13. Ⓐ Ⓑ Ⓒ Ⓓ Ⓔ | 23. Ⓐ Ⓑ Ⓒ Ⓓ Ⓔ |
| 4. Ⓐ Ⓑ Ⓒ Ⓓ Ⓔ | 14. Ⓐ Ⓑ Ⓒ Ⓓ Ⓔ | 24. Ⓐ Ⓑ Ⓒ Ⓓ Ⓔ |
| 5. Ⓐ Ⓑ Ⓒ Ⓓ Ⓔ | 15. Ⓐ Ⓑ Ⓒ Ⓓ Ⓔ | 25. Ⓐ Ⓑ Ⓒ Ⓓ Ⓔ |
| 6. Ⓐ Ⓑ Ⓒ Ⓓ Ⓔ | 16. Ⓐ Ⓑ Ⓒ Ⓓ Ⓔ | |
| 7. Ⓐ Ⓑ Ⓒ Ⓓ Ⓔ | 17. Ⓐ Ⓑ Ⓒ Ⓓ Ⓔ | |
| 8. Ⓐ Ⓑ Ⓒ Ⓓ Ⓔ | 18. Ⓐ Ⓑ Ⓒ Ⓓ Ⓔ | |
| 9. Ⓐ Ⓑ Ⓒ Ⓓ Ⓔ | 19. Ⓐ Ⓑ Ⓒ Ⓓ Ⓔ | |
| 10. Ⓐ Ⓑ Ⓒ Ⓓ Ⓔ | 20. Ⓐ Ⓑ Ⓒ Ⓓ Ⓔ | |

## SECTION 1

Time: 30 Minutes
25 Questions

**Directions:** For each of the following questions, mark the letter of your choice on the answer sheet.

---

1. If $6 + 12 + \underline{\hspace{0.5cm}} = 5 + 11 + 6$, then $\underline{\hspace{0.5cm}} =$
   (A)  2
   (B)  3
   (C)  4
   (D)  5
   (E)  6

2. $4 \times 3 \times 6 \times 2$ is equal to the product of 24 and
   (A)  6
   (B)  7
   (C)  8
   (D)  9
   (E)  11

3. If $^2/_3$ of a number is 24, then $^1/_4$ of the same number is
   (A)  20
   (B)  16
   (C)  13
   (D)  12
   (E)  9

4. A box of chocolates has 45 pieces. If 9 pieces have nuts in them, what percent of the chocolates are without nuts?
   (A)  20%
   (B)  45%
   (C)  79%
   (D)  80%
   (E)  84%

5. In the Northshore Swimming Club, 6 of 48 members are females. What is the ratio of females to all club members?
   (A)  $\dfrac{3}{16}$

   (B)  $\dfrac{1}{15}$

   (C)  $\dfrac{1}{4}$

   (D)  $\dfrac{1}{8}$

   (E)  $\dfrac{1}{12}$

6. Two numbers together add to 375. One number is twice the size of the other. What are the two numbers?
   (A)  25, 50
   (B)  50, 100
   (C)  75, 150
   (D)  95, 190
   (E)  125, 250

7. $6^3/_4\% =$
   (A)  67.5
   (B)  6.75
   (C)  0.675
   (D)  0.0675
   (E)  0.00675

**GO ON TO THE NEXT PAGE.**

8. A club collected $1,085.00. If 75% of that came from membership dues, how much money came from sources other than membership?
   (A) $271.25
   (B) $338.75
   (C) $365.75
   (D) $425.05
   (E) $442.25

9. A right angle is an angle that measures
   (A) exactly 90°
   (B) greater than 90°
   (C) less than 90°
   (D) 45°
   (E) 30°

10. In the equilateral triangle shown, what is the measure of each angle?

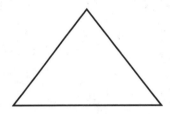

   (A) 60°
   (B) 90°
   (C) 120°
   (D) 140°
   (E) 180°

11. If $12a + 4a \boxtimes 7a = 27$, $a =$
    (A) 1
    (B) 2
    (C) 3
    (D) 4
    (E) 5

12. It costs $n$ dollars to buy 10 boxes of crackers. At the same rate, how many dollars will it cost to buy 25 boxes of crackers?
    (A) 2.5$n$
    (B) 25$n$
    (C) 2$n$/5
    (D) 5$n$/2
    (E) 250$n$

13. In the figure below, if $\angle 1$ is 33°, what is the measure of $\angle 2$?

   (A) 56°
   (B) 110°
   (C) 130°
   (D) 147°
   (E) 180°

14. Paul has a garden that is 4 meters by 7 meters. If he uses 2 ounces of fertilizer per square meter, how many ounces must he use?
    (A) 21 oz
    (B) 42 oz
    (C) 44 oz
    (D) 50 oz
    (E) 56 oz

15. Steve is measuring the growth of a tomato plant. The chart below indicates his measurements for the past five weeks. Based on the information in the chart, what should he predict will be the height of the plant at week 6?

   (A) 15 inches
   (B) 17 inches
   (C) 18 inches
   (D) 21 inches
   (E) 24 inches

16. A student buys a sandwich for 80 cents, milk for 20 cents, and pie for 30 cents. How much does the meal cost?
    (A) $1.00
    (B) $1.20
    (C) $1.30
    (D) $1.40
    (E) $1.50

**GO ON TO THE NEXT PAGE.**

17. On a test with 75 questions, Cassidy answered 45 correctly. What percent did she answer correctly?
    (A) 60%
    (B) 72%
    (C) 84%
    (D) 89%
    (E) 92%

18. Which of the following is NOT equal to a whole number?

    (A) $\dfrac{16}{4}$

    (B) $6 \times \dfrac{2}{3}$

    (C) $4 \div \dfrac{1}{4}$

    (D) $\dfrac{1}{3} \times 4$

    (E) $3 + 2$

19. Jake spent one-fifth of his life in school. If he is now 55, how many years did he spend in school?
    (A) 9
    (B) 11
    (C) 13
    (D) 15
    (E) 17

20. What is the perimeter of the following rectangle?

    11 m | 3 m

    (A) 12 m
    (B) 18 m
    (C) 24 m
    (D) 28 m
    (E) 30 m

21. Bobby's test scores for social studies are 93, 76, 91, 83, and 72. What is his average score?
    (A) 83
    (B) 87
    (C) 91
    (D) 93
    (E) 94

22. Riverside School has 150 fewer students than twice the number of students at Hillside School. If Riverside School has 500 students, how many students attend Hillside School?
    (A) 125
    (B) 150
    (C) 250
    (D) 300
    (E) 325

23. A ladder is placed against a building. If the ladder makes a 55° angle with the ground, what is the measure of the angle that the ladder makes with the building?
    (A) 25°
    (B) 30°
    (C) 35°
    (D) 40°
    (E) 45°

24. Ashley buys 48 apples. There are 12 Red Delicious apples and 16 Granny Smith apples. What fraction of the apples are not Red Delicious or Granny Smith?

    (A) $\dfrac{1}{5}$

    (B) $\dfrac{1}{4}$

    (C) $\dfrac{1}{3}$

    (D) $\dfrac{5}{12}$

    (E) $\dfrac{7}{12}$

25. What is the total cost of a $750 television, including an 8% sales tax?
    (A) $765
    (B) $784
    (C) $79,218
    (D) $810
    (E) $824

**STOP!**
If you finish before time is up, check your work on this section only.

Time: 40 Minutes
40 Questions

**Directions:** Each reading passage is followed by questions about it. Answer the questions that follow a passage on the basis of what is stated or implied in that passage. For each question, select the answer you think is best and record your choice by filling in the corresponding oval on the answer sheet.

Volcanoes are mountains, but they are very different from other mountains; they are not formed by folding and crumpling or by uplift and erosion. Instead, volcanoes are built by the accumulation of
5  their own eruptive products—lava, bombs (crusted over lava blobs), ashflows, and tephra (airborne ash and dust). A *volcano* is most commonly a conical hill or mountain built around a vent that connects with reservoirs of molten rock below the surface of the
10 Earth. The term volcano also refers to the opening or vent through which the molten rock and associated gases are expelled.

Deep within the Earth it is so hot that some rocks slowly melt and become a thick flowing substance
15 called *magma*. Because it is lighter than the solid rock around it, magma rises and collects in magma chambers. Eventually some of the magma pushes through vents and fissures in the Earth's surface and a volcanic eruption occurs. Magma that has erupted
20 is called *lava*.

Some volcanic eruptions are explosive and others are not. How explosive an eruption is depends on how runny or sticky the magma is. If magma is thin and runny, gases can escape easily from it. When
25 this type of magma erupts, it flows out of the volcano. Because they move slowly enough for people to get out of their way, lava flows rarely kill people. They can, however, cause considerable destruction to buildings in their path. If magma is thick and sticky,
30 gases cannot escape easily. Pressure builds up until the gases escape violently and explode. In this type of eruption, the magma blasts into the air and breaks apart into pieces called *tephra*. Tephra can range in size from tiny particles of ash to house-size boulders.
35 Large-sized tephra typically falls back to the ground

on or close to the volcano and progressively smaller fragments are carried away from the vent by wind. Volcanic ash, the smallest tephra fragments, can travel hundreds to thousands of kilometers downwind
40 from a volcano.

1. A primary difference between volcanoes and other mountains is in
   (A) their height
   (B) their ruggedness
   (C) their age
   (D) where they are located
   (E) how they are formed

2. A volcanic eruption is likely to be most explosive if magma
   (A) is thin and runny
   (B) is thick and sticky
   (C) rises and collects in magma chambers
   (D) pushes out through fissures in the Earth's surface
   (E) becomes lava

3. The author uses italic print primarily to
   (A) emphasize words that are used in an unusual way
   (B) indicate words that are difficult to pronounce
   (C) point out foreign words
   (D) highlight important terms that are defined in the text
   (E) indicate words that are not necessary to understanding the passage

**GO ON TO THE NEXT PAGE.**

4. All of the following can be explicitly answered by the passage EXCEPT:
   (A) What factors contribute to hot temperatures deep inside the Earth?
   (B) Why are some volcanic eruptions explosive while others are not?
   (C) As dangerous as eruptions can be, why do lava flows rarely kill people?
   (D) Why does magma rise and collect in chambers?
   (E) Why does pressure build up in magma that is thick and sticky?

5. This passage would most likely appear in
   (A) a newspaper
   (B) a science textbook
   (C) an adventure novel
   (D) a travel brochure
   (E) a safety manual

6. Which of the following statements is NOT true of tephra?
   (A) It can range in size from tiny particles of ash to huge boulders.
   (B) It can travel thousands of kilometers from a volcano.
   (C) It can be found trapped in magma.
   (D) Large tephra falls on or close to a volcano.
   (E) It is the term for rock fragments erupted into the air by volcanoes.

*The following speech was delivered by Frederick Douglass at a meeting of the Anti-Slavery Society in Pittsburgh in 1863.*

I am one of those who believe that it is the mission of this war to free every slave in the United States. I am one of those who believe that we should consent to no peace which shall not be an Abolition
5  peace. I am, moreover, one of those who believe that the work of the American Anti-Slavery Society will not have been completed until the black men of the South, and the black men of the North, shall have been admitted, fully and completely, into the body
10 politic of America. I look upon slavery as going the way of all the earth. It is the mission of the war to put it down.

I know it will be said that I ask you to make the black man a voter in the South. It is said that
15 the colored man is ignorant, and therefore he shall not vote. In saying this, you lay down a rule for the black man that you apply to no other class of

your citizens. If he knows enough to be hanged, he knows enough to vote. If he knows an honest man
20 from a thief, he knows much more than some of our white voters. If he knows enough to take up arms in defence of this Government and bare his breast to the storm of rebel artillery, he knows enough to vote.
25 All I ask, however, in regard to the blacks, is that whatever rule you adopt, whether of intelligence or wealth, as the condition of voting for whites, you shall apply it equally to the black man. Do that, and I am satisfied, and eternal justice is satisfied; liberty, fraternity,
30 equality, are satisfied, and the country will move on harmoniously.

7. According to Douglass, the mission of the Civil War is to
   (A) destroy the Confederacy
   (B) punish the rebel soldiers
   (C) end slavery
   (D) preserve the Union
   (E) create a new class of citizens

8. Douglass believes the work of the Anti-Slavery Society should not be considered complete until
   (A) slavery is abolished
   (B) black men in the South are able to vote
   (C) blacks can move freely between the South and the North
   (D) black men of the North and South have the right to vote
   (E) all conditions for voting are ended

9. What does Douglass mean by calling for black men to be admitted "fully and completely into the body politic of America"(lines 9–10)?
   (A) They must have the same rights and privileges as all other citizens.
   (B) They must be able to vote.
   (C) They must be able to run for office.
   (D) They must take up arms to defend the Government.
   (E) They must be considered a separate class of citizens.

**GO ON TO THE NEXT PAGE.**

10. The purpose of Douglass's speech was to
    (A) inform members of the society of the horrors of slavery
    (B) convince listeners to adopt fair and equal voting requirements
    (C) inform listeners of the progress of the war
    (D) convince members of the society that slavery should be ended
    (E) explain how the right to vote would create harmony

The great Pullman was whirling onward with such dignity of motion that a glance from the window seemed simply to prove that the plains of Texas were pouring eastward. Vast flats of green grass, dull-hued spaces of mesquite and cactus, little groups of frame houses, woods of light and tender trees, all were sweeping into the east, sweeping over the horizon, a precipice.

A newly married pair had boarded this coach at San Antonio. The man's face was reddened from many days in the wind and sun, and a direct result of his new black clothes was that his brick-colored hands were constantly performing in a most conscious fashion. From time to time he looked down respectfully at his attire. He sat with a hand on each knee, like a man waiting in a barber's shop. The glances he devoted to other passengers were furtive and shy.

The bride was not pretty, nor was she very young. She wore a dress of blue cashmere, with small reservations of velvet here and there and with steel buttons abounding. She continually twisted her head to regard her puff sleeves, very stiff, straight, and high. They embarrassed her. It was quite apparent that she had cooked, and that she expected to cook, dutifully. The blushes caused by the careless scrutiny of some passengers as she had entered the car were strange to see upon this plain, under-class countenance, which was drawn in placid, almost emotionless lines.

They were evidently very happy. "Ever been in a parlor-car before?" he asked, smiling with delight.

"No," she answered, "I never was. It's fine, ain't it?"

"Great! And then after a while we'll go forward to the diner and get a big layout. Finest meal in the world. Charge a dollar."

"Oh, do they?" cried the bride. "Charge a dollar? Why, that's too much—for us—ain't it, Jack?"

"Not this trip, anyhow," he answered bravely. "We're going to go the whole thing."

—Stephen Crane from
"The Bride Comes to Yellow Sky"

11. The tone of the passage suggests that the author regards the newly married couple with
    (A) embarrassment
    (B) disrespect
    (C) sympathy
    (D) sorrow
    (E) scorn

12. Which word best describes the newlywed couple?
    (A) well-to-do
    (B) sad
    (C) frightened
    (D) unsophisticated
    (E) unpleasant

13. When this passage takes place, the bride and groom are most probably
    (A) in a hotel
    (B) at a train station
    (C) on a stagecoach
    (D) in a diner
    (E) on a train

14. As it is used in line 17, the word "furtive" most nearly means
    (A) stealthy
    (B) steady
    (C) focused
    (D) friendly
    (E) unabashed

15. The narrator of this story is
    (A) the groom
    (B) the bride
    (C) a participant in the story
    (D) an outside observer
    (E) an adult looking back on his life

**GO ON TO THE NEXT PAGE.**

16. The main purpose of this passage is to
    (A) express an opinion
    (B) analyze information
    (C) introduce characters and setting
    (D) resolve a crisis
    (E) set up a conflict between two characters

17. By saying, "It was quite apparent that she had cooked, and that she expected to cook, dutifully," the author is suggesting that the bride
    (A) expects to eat out regularly
    (B) has led a life of hard work
    (C) has never eaten in a restaurant before
    (D) wants to learn more about cooking
    (E) will learn to cook her husband's favorite foods

Over two decades ago, scientists in the Agricultural Research Service Vegetable Crops Research Unit at Madison, Wisconsin, began a quest to breed carrots packed with beta-carotene—
5 an orange pigment used by the body to create vitamin A. Thanks largely to their work, today's carrots provide consumers with 75 percent more beta-carotene than those available 25 years ago.

The researchers, led by plant geneticist Philipp
10 Simon, haven't limited themselves to the color orange. They've selectively bred a rainbow of carrots—purple, red, yellow, even white. Scientists are learning that these plant pigments perform a range of protective duties in the human body.
15 Red carrots derive their color mainly from lyco-pene, a type of carotene believed to guard against heart disease and some cancers. Yellow carrots accumulate xanthophylls, pigments similar to beta-carotene that support good eye health. Purple carrots possess an
20 entirely different class of pigments—anthocyanins— which act as powerful antioxidants.

While colored carrots are unusual, they're not exactly new. "Purple and yellow carrots were eaten more than 1,000 years ago in Afghani-
25 stan and 700 years ago in western Europe," says Simon. "But the carrot-breeding process has gone on intensively for just 50 years."

In nature, different strains of carrots contain varying types and amounts of carotenoids—the pig-
30 ments responsible for orange, yellow, and red colors. To assist seed companies and growers who wish to produce nutrient-rich carrots, Simon and his lab are working to map all the genes that play a part in

synthesizing carotenoids in major carrot lines. Simon
35 now knows of 20 genes that are involved. But deter-mining a particular gene's role in generating carot-enoids is not that straightforward.

Aside from enhancing the nutritional value of carrots—as well as onions, garlic, and cucumbers—
40 researchers at Simon's laboratory also work to improve the vegetable's culinary quality and appeal.

With their compelling health benefits and a thumbs-up from taste testers, Simon's colorful car-rots will be a great addition to supermarket produce
45 aisles once consumers create a demand for them.

18. The main purpose of this passage is to
    (A) explain why carrots can be various colors
    (B) point out the health benefits of carotenoids
    (C) report on enhancements to the nutritional value of carrots
    (D) explore ways to increase carrot production
    (E) encourage people to buy carrots of various colors

19. The author's tone can best be described as
    (A) argumentative
    (B) emotional
    (C) sentimental
    (D) informative
    (E) optimistic

20. According to the passage, carrots have been bred in all of the following colors EXCEPT:
    (A) yellow
    (B) green
    (C) white
    (D) red
    (E) purple

21. The type of carotene that gives carrots a red color is
    (A) lycopene
    (B) xanthophyll
    (C) anthocyanin
    (D) beta-carotene
    (E) antioxidant

**GO ON TO THE NEXT PAGE.**

22. Which of the following is true of colored carrots?
    (A) They first appeared about 50 years ago.
    (B) They do not equal regular carrots in nutritive value.
    (C) They are not as tasty as traditional carrots.
    (D) They were first bred by scientists at the Agricultural Research Service Vegetable Crops Research Unit.
    (E) They derive their color from varying types and amounts of carotenoids.

23. This passage can best be described as
    (A) a short story
    (B) a biography
    (C) a research report
    (D) propaganda
    (E) an editorial

Georgia O'Keeffe is esteemed as one of the premiere American artists in the twentieth century. Born on a farmhouse in rural Sun Prairie, Wisconsin, in November 1887, O'Keeffe's interest in art began at
5 very young age. By the time she was ten, she had firmly decided to become an artist. O'Keeffe sought to further her penchant for painting by studying at the prestigious Art Institute of Chicago and subsequently at the Art Students League of New York.
10    In 1917, Alfred Stieglitz, a world-famous photographer, was shown ten of O'Keeffe early abstract paintings and immediately put on a solo exhibit of these works at his New York City gallery. Stieglitz encouraged O'Keeffe to move to New York, where
15 she met other well-known modernist painters. Her early work included cityscapes of New York City streets, buildings, and waterways.
      In the 1920s, O'Keeffe began painting her famous close-up flowers on large canvases. With
20 some additional encouragement by Stieglitz, with whom she now shared a life-long personal relationship, her paintings began to sell at ever-increasing prices. In 1929, O'Keeffe visited Taos, New Mexico—a place whose natural beauty trans-
25 formed her view of art. She continued to paint her exquisite flowers and soon added other parts of the Southwestern landscape including nearby mountain ranges and soaring cliffs, along with the sun-bleached skulls and other bones of animals that
30 had died in the dry, deserted landscape she now called home.

Although she lost most of her vision from macular degeneration late in life, O'Keeffe said of her blindness, "I can see what I want to paint. The thing that
35 makes you want to create is still there." With the aid of young assistants, O'Keeffe continued to paint until about two years before her death in 1986 at the age of 98. Her paintings are now revered worldwide and command prices as high as $44 million. In 1997, the
40 Georgia O'Keeffe Museum opened to house and showcase this exemplary American artist's works.

24. In line 7, "penchant" means most nearly
    (A) aversion
    (B) strong liking
    (C) prejudice
    (D) weakness
    (E) knack

25. The author's tone in this passage is best described as
    (A) persuasive
    (B) argumentative
    (C) unforeseen
    (D) laudatory
    (E) indifferent

26. O'Keeffe's statement, "I can see what I want to paint. The thing that makes you want to create is still there" indicates that
    (A) artistic vision is not just a matter of what the artist sees
    (B) making art is a matter of getting help from other people
    (C) what constitutes art always remains a mystery to the artist
    (D) illness is not something that will stop a true artist from creating
    (E) growing old only makes an artist's work more valuable

27. Which factor had the strongest influence on the subject of O'Keeffe's paintings in her middle and late years?
    (A) New York City's buildings
    (B) her career as a teacher
    (C) New Mexico's landscape
    (D) Alfred Stieglitz
    (E) her loss of sight

**GO ON TO THE NEXT PAGE.**

The Statue of Liberty was a gift to the people of the United States from the people of France in recognition of the friendship established between the two nations during the American Revolution. Over the years, the Statue of Liberty has come to symbolize freedom and democracy, as well as this international friendship.

Sculptor Frederic Auguste Bartholdi was commissioned to design a sculpture with the year 1876 in mind for completion, to commemorate the centennial of the American Declaration of Independence. Alexandre Gustave Eiffel (designer of the Eiffel Tower) was called in to address the structural issues of Bartholdi's colossal sculpture. The Statue was a joint effort between America and France and it was agreed upon that the American people would build the pedestal, and the French people would be responsible for the Statue and its assembly here in the United States. Lack of funds was a problem on both sides of the Atlantic Ocean. In France, public fees, various forms of entertainment, and a lottery were among the methods used to raise funds. In the United States, benefit theatrical events, art exhibitions, auctions and prize fights helped to provide the needed funds. When fundraising for the pedestal lagged, Joseph Pulitzer (noted for the Pulitzer Prize) used the editorial pages of his newspaper *The World* to aid in the fundraising effort. Pulitzer's campaign of harsh criticism against both the rich, who had failed to finance the pedestal construction, and the middle class, who were content to rely upon the wealthy to provide the funds, was successful in motivating the people of America to donate.

Financing for the pedestal was completed in August 1885, and pedestal construction was finished in April of 1886. The Statue was completed in France in July 1884 and arrived in New York Harbor in June, 1885, on board the French frigate *Isere*. In transit, the Statue was reduced to 350 individual pieces and packed in 214 crates. The Statue was re-assembled on her new pedestal in four months time. On October 28, 1886, in front of thousands of spectators, President Grover Cleveland accepted the Statue on behalf of the United States. She was a centennial gift ten years late.

28. According to the passage, the Statue of Liberty was intended to celebrate the
   (A) centennial of the Declaration of Independence
   (B) end of the Civil War
   (C) end of hostilities between France and the United States
   (D) start of the twentieth century
   (E) dawn of a new era of international cooperation

29. In line 13, which word can be substituted for "address" without changing the meaning of the sentence?
   (A) speak to
   (B) focus on
   (C) forward
   (D) lecture
   (E) label

30. From his actions, it can be inferred that Joseph Pulitzer's attitude toward the Statue of Liberty was
   (A) openly hostile
   (B) extremely cautious
   (C) enthusiastically supportive
   (D) completely neutral
   (E) overly critical

31. According to the passage, the Statue of Liberty symbolizes
   I. democracy
   II. freedom
   III. international friendship
   IV. a treaty between the United States and France

   (A) I only
   (B) II only
   (C) I and III only
   (D) I, II, and III only
   (E) I, II, III, and IV

**GO ON TO THE NEXT PAGE.**

32. According to the passage, all of the following are true EXCEPT:
    (A) The United States agreed to finance and build the pedestal.
    (B) Bartholdi needed help with structural issues of the statue.
    (C) Joseph Pulitzer was instrumental in raising money for the pedestal.
    (D) The designer of the Eiffel Tower was called in to help raise funds for the project.
    (E) The statue was completed in France before the pedestal was fully funded.

33. The main purpose of the passage is to
    (A) inform the reader about the history of the Statue of Liberty
    (B) describe how Bartholdi designed the Statue of Liberty
    (C) compare fundraising efforts in the United States and France
    (D) defend the use of newspaper editorials to help raise funds for the project
    (E) explain how the Statue was assembled on her pedestal

34. This passage would most likely appear in a
    (A) short story
    (B) novel
    (C) newspaper
    (D) engineering journal
    (E) textbook

At the end of what seemed a tedious while, I had managed to pack my head full of islands, towns, bars, "points," and bends; and a curiously inanimate mass of lumber it was, too. However, 5 inasmuch as I could shut my eyes and reel off a good long string of these names without leaving out more than ten miles of river in every fifty, I began to feel that I could take a boat down to New Orleans if I could make her skip those little gaps. 10 But of course my complacency could hardly get start enough to lift my nose a trifle into the air, before Mr. Bixby would think of something to fetch it down again. One day he turned on me suddenly with this settler: —

15 "What is the shape of Walnut Bend?"

He might as well have asked me my grand-mother's opinion of protoplasm. I reflected respect- fully, and then said I didn't know it had any particular shape. My gunpowdery chief went off with a bang, of course, 20 and then went on loading and firing until he was out of adjectives.

I had learned long ago that he only carried just so many rounds of ammunition, and was sure to subside into a very placable and even remorseful old smooth- 25 bore as soon as they were all gone. That word "old" is merely affectionate; he was not more than thirty-four. I waited. By and by he said, —

"My boy, you've got to know the *shape* of the river perfectly. It is all there is left to steer by on a 30 very dark night. Everything else is blotted out and gone. But mind you, it hasn't the same shape in the night that it has in the day-time."

"How on earth am I ever going to learn it, then?"

35 "How do you follow a hall at home in the dark? Because you know the shape of it. You can't see it."

"Do you mean to say that I've got to know all the million trifling variations of shape in the banks of this interminable river as well as I know the shape of the 40 front hall at home?"

"On my honor you've got to know them *better* than any man ever did know the shapes of the halls in his own house."

"I wish I was dead!"

—Mark Twain from *Life on the Mississippi*

35. When the narrator says, "my complacency could hardly get start enough to lift my nose a trifle into the air, before Mr. Bixby would think of something to fetch it down again," he means:
    (A) Whenever the narrator picked his head up, Mr. Bixby was there to tell him to keep his eyes on the river.
    (B) Just as he thought he was learning the river, Bixby would demonstrate how little the narrator actually knew.
    (C) No one can name all the islands, towns, bars, points, and bends of the Mississippi River.
    (D) No other pilot knew the river as well as Mr. Bixby did.
    (E) The narrator could never hope to know the river as well as Bixby did.

**GO ON TO THE NEXT PAGE.**

36. Why does the narrator compare Bixby's question about the shape of Walnut Bend to asking about his grandmother's opinion of protoplasm?
   (A)  Only his grandmother could answer Bixby's question.
   (B)  Both are questions that have no real answer.
   (C)  Both are questions the narrator cannot answer.
   (D)  Walnut Bend has the same shape as protoplasm.
   (E)  Bixby does not know the narrator's grandmother.

37. What is the meaning of "gunpowdery" in line 19?
   (A)  loud
   (B)  smoky
   (C)  strong
   (D)  explosive
   (E)  gritty

38. Which of the following best describes the narrator's reaction to the information that he will need to know the shape of the river perfectly even at night?
   (A)  anger
   (B)  regret
   (C)  amazement
   (D)  enthusiasm
   (E)  despair

39. The tone of this passage can best be described as
   (A)  humorous
   (B)  serious
   (C)  angry
   (D)  analytical
   (E)  tense

40. This passage can best be described as
   (A)  a news item
   (B)  propaganda
   (C)  an autobiography
   (D)  a research report
   (E)  a textbook excerpt

**STOP!**
If you finish before time is up, check your work on this section only.

Time: 30 Minutes
60 Questions

This section includes two different types of questions: synonyms and analogies. There are directions and a sample question for each question type.

**Directions:** Each of the following questions consists of a word in capital letters followed by five words. Select the one word that means most nearly the same as the word in capital letters.

Sample Question:

> ESSENTIAL:
> (A) dire
> (B) confusing
> (C) vital
> (D) expert
> (E) honest
>
> Correct Answer: C

1. NOVICE:
   (A) burden
   (B) agreement
   (C) beggar
   (D) beginner
   (E) expression

2. FABRICATE:
   (A) stitch
   (B) fasten
   (C) falsify
   (D) deter
   (E) decorate

3. FRIENDLY:
   (A) congenital
   (B) amiable
   (C) sanctimonious
   (D) ambivalent
   (E) responsive

4. GENRE:
   (A) proposal
   (B) category
   (C) purpose
   (D) principle
   (E) generation

5. SUMMIT:
   (A) conference
   (B) valley
   (C) essence
   (D) nadir
   (E) outline

6. DEFTLY:
   (A) wilfully
   (B) closely
   (C) quickly
   (D) randomly
   (E) skillfully

**GO ON TO THE NEXT PAGE.**

7. PROSPER:
   (A) accomplish
   (B) strive
   (C) affect
   (D) gather
   (E) thrive

8. SPURN:
   (A) cross
   (B) return
   (C) betray
   (D) reject
   (E) hinder

9. COMPLIMENTARY:
   (A) secondary
   (B) free
   (C) charming
   (D) attractive
   (E) matched

10. VISAGE:
    (A) encounter
    (B) station
    (C) face
    (D) bandage
    (E) wound

11. RESPITE:
    (A) pause
    (B) presumption
    (C) recluse
    (D) blockage
    (E) susceptibility

12. REGRETFUL:
    (A) bewildered
    (B) credulous
    (C) desultory
    (D) contrite
    (E) dubious

13. FRUGAL:
    (A) inadequate
    (B) shrewd
    (C) economical
    (D) balanced
    (E) equitable

14. IMPLY:
    (A) suggest
    (B) implore
    (C) greet
    (D) reminisce
    (E) appeal

15. INCITE:
    (A) insist
    (B) dispel
    (C) maintain
    (D) assert
    (E) provoke

16. MEAGER:
    (A) paltry
    (B) stunted
    (C) timid
    (D) sloppy
    (E) frigid

17. PREDICTION:
    (A) predecessor
    (B) forecast
    (C) predicament
    (D) prejudice
    (E) display

18. FACET:
    (A) goal
    (B) endeavor
    (C) tactic
    (D) aspect
    (E) ambition

19. ABSOLVE:
    (A) admonish
    (B) accede
    (C) opine
    (D) clear
    (E) affirm

20. DESTROY:
    (A) inveigh
    (B) subvert
    (C) rescind
    (D) sanction
    (E) abjure

GO ON TO THE NEXT PAGE.

21. MOURN:
    (A) replete
    (B) whimper
    (C) argue
    (D) disapprove
    (E) grieve

22. POISONOUS:
    (A) dangerous
    (B) hurtful
    (C) toxic
    (D) devious
    (E) ruthless

23. APLOMB:
    (A) omen
    (B) ascent
    (C) epitome
    (D) confidence
    (E) atonement

24. CORROBORATION:
    (A) confirmation
    (B) announcement
    (C) bulletin
    (D) tribulation
    (E) ordeal

25. ERRATIC:
    (A) mistaken
    (B) immaculate
    (C) unpredictable
    (D) opportune
    (E) inadvertent

26. CREDIBLE:
    (A) languid
    (B) believable
    (C) forthright
    (D) fallible
    (E) enviable

27. ABSCOND:
    (A) abolish
    (B) choose
    (C) leave
    (D) remove
    (E) steal

28. CALM:
    (A) rest
    (B) inspire
    (C) exalt
    (D) soothe
    (E) commend

29. IRRITABLE:
    (A) voluble
    (B) timorous
    (C) transitory
    (D) turgid
    (E) petulant

30. TRAVESTY:
    (A) disaster
    (B) mockery
    (C) misfortune
    (D) adage
    (E) opinion

**GO ON TO THE NEXT PAGE.**

**Directions:** The questions that follow ask you to find relationships between words. For each question select the answer choice that best completes the meaning of the sentence.

Sample Question:

Swim is to pool as
(A) fork is to plate
(B) sweep is to broom
(C) clean is to kitchen
(D) sleep is to bed
(E) trot is to horse

Correct Answer: D
Choice D is correct because a pool is a place to swim just as a bed is a place to sleep.

---

31. Safe is to dangerous as
    (A) taste is to smell
    (B) bland is to spicy
    (C) dry is to fire
    (D) multiplication is to divide
    (E) lazy is to exercise

32. Star is to sky as
    (A) mountain is to valley
    (B) cloud is to sun
    (C) fish is to ocean
    (D) dream is to sleep
    (E) fit is to shoe

33. Cut is to wound as
    (A) storm is to snow
    (B) brick is to building
    (C) drink is to thirst
    (D) save is to money
    (E) cry is to tears

34. Camera is to picture as
    (A) breeze is to fan
    (B) paint is to frame
    (C) brush is to hair
    (D) phone is to call
    (E) horse is to gallop

35. Lumens is to brightness as
    (A) velocity is to speed
    (B) decibel is to volume
    (C) pint is to liquid
    (D) mile is to kilometer
    (E) measure is to depth

36. Book is to writer as
    (A) needle is to doctor
    (B) cavity is to dentist
    (C) truck is to driver
    (D) crop is to farmer
    (E) script is to actor

37. Frigid is to tropical as
    (A) raw is to cooked
    (B) detergent is to clean
    (C) snow is to sunshine
    (D) sleek is to stylish
    (E) beach is to sandy

38. Los Angeles is to California as
    (A) Phoenix is to New Mexico
    (B) Philadelphia is to Pittsburgh
    (C) Houston is to Texas
    (D) state is to country
    (E) Denver is to America

39. Menu is to diner as catalog is to
    (A) cashier
    (B) order
    (C) seller
    (D) purchase
    (E) shopper

40. Cuff is to collar as mouse is to
    (A) keyboard
    (B) cheese
    (C) cat
    (D) trap
    (E) rodent

**GO ON TO THE NEXT PAGE.**

41. Snake is to belly as
    (A) monkey is to tail
    (B) bear is to hands
    (C) horse is to legs
    (D) pig is to snout
    (E) person is to feet

42. Carat is to diamond as
    (A) calorie is to heat
    (B) liquid is to volume
    (C) perimeter is to inches
    (D) unit is to measurement
    (E) gram is to pound

43. Book is to read as data is to
    (A) analyze
    (B) prove
    (C) submit
    (D) foretell
    (E) conclude

44. Burnish is to polish as
    (A) search is to find
    (B) wash is to rinse
    (C) peel is to scrape
    (D) shine is to glisten
    (E) reinforce is to strengthen

45. Fresh is to rancid as
    (A) heat is to boil
    (B) ripe is to rotten
    (C) molten is to lava
    (D) shed is to discard
    (E) cooked is to burnt

46. Fire is to heat as
    (A) cold is to snow
    (B) lamp is to light
    (C) cool is to breeze
    (D) wax is to melt
    (E) music is to listen

47. Browsing is to shopping as
    (A) skimming is to reading
    (B) nodding is to agreeing
    (C) walking is to running
    (D) hiking is to climbing
    (E) seeing is to recognizing

48. Recital is to pianist as exhibit is to
    (A) museum
    (B) clay
    (C) auction
    (D) artist
    (E) gallery

49. Song is to medley as
    (A) series is to book
    (B) collection is to displays
    (C) gumball is to machines
    (D) picture is to collage
    (E) survey is to lists

50. Exercise is to sweat as
    (A) wander is to meander
    (B) reduce is to budget
    (C) harvest is to produce
    (D) accept is to refuse
    (E) vote is to confirm

51. Stamen is to flower as
    (A) computer is to monitor
    (B) lens is to eye
    (C) socket is to cord
    (D) spiral is to notebook
    (E) pillow is to sleep

52. Map is to cartographer as
    (A) club is to golfer
    (B) book is to librarian
    (C) car is to mechanic
    (D) building is to architect
    (E) cake is to baker

53. Baby is to crawling as
    (A) rock is to skipping
    (B) trout is to fishing
    (C) frog is to jumping
    (D) parent is to driving
    (E) bird is to nesting

54. Eraser is to chalkboard as
    (A) mop is to floor
    (B) keyboard is to computer
    (C) ballpoint is to pen
    (D) towel is to soap
    (E) machine is to washing

**GO ON TO THE NEXT PAGE.**

55. Eager is to fervent as
    (A) tedious is to bored
    (B) glum is to sad
    (C) pleased is to ecstatic
    (D) enraged is to mad
    (E) remorse is to sorrow

56. Bread is to moldy as
    (A) whisker is to hairy
    (B) disease is to sickly
    (C) blood is to scab
    (D) steel is to rusty
    (E) running is to sweaty

57. Dog is to collie as lizard is to
    (A) cage
    (B) chameleon
    (C) reptile
    (D) pet
    (E) desert

58. Chisel is to carving as
    (A) thread is to sewing
    (B) clay is to sculpting
    (C) wheel is to driving
    (D) blender is to mixing
    (E) recipe is to cooking

59. Drop is to break as
    (A) spill is to tip
    (B) stumble is to fall
    (C) adorn is to decorate
    (D) stitch is to sew
    (E) drive is to crash

60. Ruby is to red as amber is to
    (A) brown
    (B) green
    (C) pink
    (D) blue
    (E) purple

**STOP!**
If you finish before time is up, check your work on this section only.

Time: 30 Minutes
25 Questions

**Directions:** For each of the following questions, mark the letter of your choice on the answer sheet.

1. What is 2% of 5,000?
   (A) 10
   (B) 80
   (C) 100
   (D) 105
   (E) 110

2. $3.5 \times 0.93 =$
   (A) 2.886
   (B) 2.965
   (C) 3.255
   (D) 3.311
   (E) 3.405

3. Which of the following is NOT equal to a whole number?
   (A) $\dfrac{32}{4}$
   (B) $4 \times \dfrac{8}{16}$
   (C) $8 \div \dfrac{1}{8}$
   (D) $\dfrac{5}{12} \times 8$
   (E) $6.4 + 11.6$

4. Which operation should be done first?
   $12 \div (9 - 6) + 4 \times 3^2$
   (A) Multiply: $3 \times 3$
   (B) Subtract: $9 - 6$
   (C) Divide: $18 \div 9$
   (D) Add: $3 + 4$
   (E) Multiply: $4 \times 3$

5. It costs $m$ dollars to buy 60 nails. At the same rate, how many dollars will it cost to buy 24 nails?
   (A) $\dfrac{m}{5}$
   (B) $\dfrac{2m}{5}$
   (C) $2m$
   (D) $5m$
   (E) $10m$

6. If $\frac{5}{12}$ of a number is 50, then $\frac{1}{2}$ of the same number is
   (A) 72
   (B) 70
   (C) 64
   (D) 60
   (E) 56

7. $4^2 + 3(2 - 6) =$
   (A) 4
   (B) 12
   (C) $-4$
   (D) $-8$
   (E) $-12$

8. What is the mean of the following numbers?
   24, 36, 18, 30, 90, 690
   (A) 48
   (B) 64
   (C) 148
   (D) 152
   (E) 160

9. If $\dfrac{2}{25} = \dfrac{n}{500}$, what is $n$?
   (A) 20
   (B) 40
   (C) 60
   (D) 80
   (E) 100

10. If $6 \times 8 \div$ _____ $= 5 \times 4 + 4$, then _____ $=$
    (A) 2
    (B) 3
    (C) 4
    (D) 5
    (E) 6

**GO ON TO THE NEXT PAGE.**

11. How many possible integer values are there for $x$ if $-3 < x < 4$?
    (A) 3
    (B) 4
    (C) 5
    (D) 6
    (E) 7

12. $2 + {}^4/_{25} =$
    (A) 2.225
    (B) 2.16
    (C) 2.24
    (D) 2.45
    (E) 2.40

13. At the amusement park, Karen uses $1/3$ of her tickets for rides and $1/6$ of her tickets for food. What fraction of her tickets is left?
    (A) $\dfrac{1}{6}$
    (B) $\dfrac{1}{4}$
    (C) $\dfrac{1}{2}$
    (D) $\dfrac{2}{3}$
    (E) $\dfrac{3}{5}$

14. $12 \div 3^3/_4 =$
    (A) $1\dfrac{4}{5}$
    (B) $2\dfrac{2}{3}$
    (C) $2\dfrac{7}{16}$
    (D) $3\dfrac{1}{5}$
    (E) $3\dfrac{9}{13}$

15. Rosa buys a blouse for $23.95. The sales tax is 6.5%. What is the total cost of the blouse, including the sales tax?
    (A) $24.35
    (B) $24.78
    (C) $25.20
    (D) $25.51
    (E) $26.92

16. Kyle can ride his bike 30 km in 2 hours. At the same rate, how far can he ride in 7 hours?
    (A) 90 km
    (B) 105 km
    (C) 125 km
    (D) 130 km
    (E) 150 km

17. The distance around a rectangular park is 1 mile. If the width of the park is 880 feet, what is its length?
    (A) 720 ft
    (B) 840 ft
    (C) 1,250 ft
    (D) 1,510 ft
    (E) 1,760 ft

18. $10 \times (0.38 + 3.5) + 5.2 =$
    (A) 15.25
    (B) 24.15
    (C) 32.40
    (D) 44
    (E) 46.5

19. Daryl rents a computer by the hour. The rental company charges $25 + $6 per hour. Which equation represents this situation?
    (A) $25 + 6h$
    (B) $6h - 25$
    (C) $6(25 + h)$
    (D) $\dfrac{6}{h} + 25$
    (E) $h + \dfrac{25}{h}$

20. The temperature at midnight was $-12°C$. It rose $2°C$ each hour. What was the temperature at 11:00 A.M.?
    (A) $-2°C$
    (B) $4°C$
    (C) $8°C$
    (D) $10°C$
    (E) $12°C$

21. Which pair of numbers has the same sum and difference?
    (A) 4 and 4
    (B) 6 and 3
    (C) 7 and 5
    (D) 8 and 0
    (E) 9 and 11

**GO ON TO THE NEXT PAGE.**

22. What is 231,000 written in scientific notation?
    (A) $2.31 \times 10^{-3}$
    (B) $2.31 \times 10^3$
    (C) $2.31 \times 10^4$
    (D) $2.31 \times 10^5$
    (E) $231 \times 10^3$

23. What is the median of the set of data shown in this box-and-whisker plot?

    (A) 22
    (B) 26
    (C) 28
    (D) 32
    (E) 36

24. What is the next term in this sequence?
    1, 4, 16, 64, . . .
    (A) 80
    (B) 128
    (C) 144
    (D) 160
    (E) 256

25. What is the mode of the set of data shown in this stem-and-leaf plot?

| Stem | Leaf |
|------|------|
| 11 | 4  4 |
| 12 | 3  6 |
| 13 | 2  3  4  7 |
| 14 |  |
| 15 | 8  9 |
| 16 | 0  5  8 |

    (A) 114
    (B) 134
    (C) 158
    (D) 158.5
    (E) 168

**STOP!**
If you finish before time is up, check your work on this section only.

## UPPER LEVEL SSAT
## Writing Sample

Time: 25 Minutes

**Directions:** Read the topics below and choose the one that interests you the most. Fill in the circle for your chosen idea. Plan and write your essay or story on the paper provided.

---

(A) Haste makes waste.

Do you agree or disagree with the topic statement? Support your position with examples from your own experience, the experience of others, current events, history, or literature.

---

(B) I couldn't believe my luck! Write a story that uses this as the first sentence.

_____

_____

_____

_____

_____

_____

_____

_____

_____

_____

_____

_____

_____

## Answer Key

### Section 1 Quantitative I

| | | | | | |
|---|---|---|---|---|---|
| 1. | C | 10. | A | 19. | B |
| 2. | A | 11. | C | 20. | D |
| 3. | E | 12. | A | 21. | A |
| 4. | D | 13. | D | 22. | E |
| 5. | D | 14. | E | 23. | C |
| 6. | E | 15. | B | 24. | D |
| 7. | D | 16. | C | 25. | D |
| 8. | A | 17. | A | | |
| 9. | A | 18. | D | | |

### Section 2 Reading Comprehension

| | | | | | |
|---|---|---|---|---|---|
| 1. | E | 15. | D | 29. | B |
| 2. | B | 16. | C | 30. | C |
| 3. | D | 17. | B | 31. | D |
| 4. | A | 18. | C | 32. | D |
| 5. | B | 19. | D | 33. | A |
| 6. | C | 20. | B | 34. | E |
| 7. | C | 21. | A | 35. | B |
| 8. | D | 22. | E | 36. | C |
| 9. | A | 23. | C | 37. | D |
| 10. | B | 24. | B | 38. | E |
| 11. | C | 25. | D | 39. | A |
| 12. | D | 26. | A | 40. | C |
| 13. | E | 27. | C | | |
| 14. | A | 28. | A | | |

## Section 3 Verbal

| | | | | | |
|-----|---|-----|---|-----|---|
| 1. | D | 21. | E | 41. | E |
| 2. | C | 22. | C | 42. | A |
| 3. | B | 23. | D | 43. | A |
| 4. | B | 24. | A | 44. | E |
| 5. | A | 25. | C | 45. | B |
| 6. | E | 26. | B | 46. | B |
| 7. | E | 27. | C | 47. | A |
| 8. | D | 28. | D | 48. | D |
| 9. | B | 29. | E | 49. | D |
| 10. | C | 30. | B | 50. | C |
| 11. | A | 31. | B | 51. | B |
| 12. | D | 32. | C | 52. | E |
| 13. | C | 33. | E | 53. | C |
| 14. | A | 34. | D | 54. | A |
| 15. | E | 35. | B | 55. | C |
| 16. | A | 36. | D | 56. | D |
| 17. | B | 37. | A | 57. | B |
| 18. | D | 38. | C | 58. | D |
| 19. | D | 39. | E | 59. | B |
| 20. | B | 40. | A | 60. | A |

## Section 4 Quantitative II`

| | | | | | |
|-----|---|-----|---|-----|---|
| 1. | C | 10. | A | 19. | A |
| 2. | C | 11. | D | 20. | D |
| 3. | D | 12. | B | 21. | D |
| 4. | B | 13. | C | 22. | D |
| 5. | B | 14. | D | 23. | C |
| 6. | D | 15. | D | 24. | E |
| 7. | A | 16. | B | 25. | A |
| 8. | C | 17. | E | | |
| 9. | B | 18. | D | | |

# Answers and Explanations

## Section 1 Quantitative I

1. **C is correct.** $5 + 11 + 6 = 22$; $6 + 12 = 18$; and $22 - 18 = 4$.

2. **A is correct.** $4 \times 3 \times 6 \times 2 = 144$; $144 \div 24 = 6$.

3. **E is correct.**
   $\frac{2}{3}x = 24$
   $\frac{1}{3}x = 12$
   $x = 36$
   $\frac{1}{4}x = 9$

4. **D is correct.** This problem needs to be completed in two steps. First, you need to determine what percent of chocolates have nuts and then subtract that from 100% to determine what percent do not have nuts. Dividing 9 by 45 gives the percent that have nuts, which is 20%. Subtracting that number from 100% gives the correct answer: 80% of the chocolates do not have nuts.

5. **D is correct.** To find the ratio of one number to another, create a fraction to show the relationship. In this problem there are 6 female club members in a total of 48 club members. The fraction that shows the relationship is $\frac{6}{48}$. This fraction can be simplified to $\frac{1}{8}$, the correct answer.

6. **E is correct.** Set this up as an equation. A number plus 2 times that number is 375.
   $x + 2x = 375$
   Solve for $x$.
   $3x = 375$
   $x = 125$
   So one number is 125 and the other is twice that, or 250.

7. **D is correct.** $6\frac{3}{4}\% = 0.0675$.

8. **A is correct.** Multiply $1,085.00 by 0.25 to get $271.25.

9. **A is correct.** By definition, a right angle is one that measures 90°.

10. **A is correct.** In an equilateral triangle, all three angles are equal. Since the sum of the angles in a triangle is 180°, each angle must be $180 \div 3 = 60°$.

11. **C is correct.** Solve the equation.
    $12a + 4a - 7a = 27$
    $16a - 7a = 27$
    $9a = 27$
    $a = 3$

12. **A is correct.** It costs $n$ dollars to buy 10 boxes. Since $25 = 2.5 \times 10$, it will cost $2.5n$ dollars to buy 25 boxes.

13. **D is correct.** A straight angle measures 180°. So if $\angle 1$ is 33°, the other angle must measure $180° - 33° = 147°$.

14. **E is correct.** Calculate the number of square meters in the garden and then determine how many ounces of fertilizer are needed. The area of a rectangle is calculated by multiplying the length × the width. So the area of the garden is $4 \times 7 = 28$ m². Paul needs 2 oz of fertilizer for every square meter, so $2 \times 28 = 56$ oz.

15. **B is correct.** According to the chart, the plant is growing 3 inches taller each week. So in week 6, it should be $14 + 3 = 17$ inches tall.

16. **C is correct.** $0.80 + $0.20 + $0.30 = $1.30.

17. **A is correct.** To calculate the percent, divide the number of items answered correctly by the total number of items. $45 \div 75 = 0.60$. To change that to a percent, move the decimal point two places to the right and add the percent sign to get 60%.

18. **D is correct.** $^{16}/_4 = 4$; $6 \times {}^2/_3 = {}^{12}/_3 = 4$; $4 \div {}^1/_4 = 4 \times {}^4/_1 = 16$; $3 + 2 = 5$. However, $^1/_3 \times 4 = {}^4/_3$, which is not a whole number.

19. **B is correct.** In this problem you need to find $^1/_5$ of 55. $55 \div 5 = 11$.

20. **D is correct.** To find the perimeter of a rectangle, add the lengths of the four sides. In this instance, 11 meters + 11 meters + 3 meters + 3 meters = 28 meters, the correct answer.

21. **A is correct.** To find the average, add the numbers and divide by the number of numbers. In this problem the numbers add to 415. Dividing that by 5 gives an average of 83.

22. **E is correct.** Create an equation:

    Riverside = 2 × Hillside −150
    $500 = 2x - 150$
    $750 = 2x$
    $325 = x$

23. **C is correct.** In this problem you know two of the three angles, one measuring 55° and the other measuring 90°, since the building forms a 90° angle with the ground. Together those two angles measure 145°. Since a triangle has a total of 180°, the third angle must measure $180° - 145° = 35°$.

24. **D is correct.** 12 Red Delicious apples + 16 Granny Smith apples = 28 apples. $48 - 28 = 20$ apples that are not Red Delicious or Granny Smith. $^{20}/_{48} = {}^5/_{12}$.

25. **D is correct.** 8% of $750 = 0.08 \times 750 = $60$. $750 + $60 = $810.

## Section 2 Reading Comprehension

1. **E is correct.** As stated in the first two sentences, "Volcanoes are mountains, but they are very different from other mountains; they are not formed by folding and crumpling or by uplift and erosion. Instead, volcanoes are built by the accumulation of their own eruptive products—lava, bombs (crusted over lava blobs), ashflows, and tephra (airborne ash and dust)."

2. **B is correct.** As stated in the third paragraph, "How explosive an eruption is depends on how runny or sticky the magma is. . . . If magma is thick and sticky, gases cannot escape easily. Pressure builds up until the gases escape violently and explode." Choice A is wrong because if magma is thin and runny, "gases can escape easily from it," and when this type of magma erupts, "it flows out of the volcano." Choices C and D are both true of magma, but neither indicates how explosive an eruption will be. Choice E is wrong because magma that has erupted is called lava, regardless of the explosiveness of the eruption.

3. **D is correct.** The words in italics are scientific terms for which the author provides definitions within the text. ("A *volcano* is most commonly a conical hill or mountain built around a vent that connects with reservoirs of molten rock below the surface of the Earth." "Magma that has erupted is called *lava*.")

4. **A is correct.** The passage states that "Deep within the Earth it is so hot that some rocks slowly melt and become a thick flowing substance called *magma*." However, the passage does not mention the factors that contribute to hot temperatures deep inside the Earth. Choice B is answered in lines 22–37. Choice C is answered in lines 26–27. Choice D is answered in lines 16–18. Choice E is answered in lines 31–33.

5. **B is correct.** This passage explains how volcanoes are formed and the nature of volcanic eruptions using the scientific terminology and strictly factual presentation typical of information presented in a science textbook. There is nothing timely about the information, so it is not likely to be from a newspaper article as in choice A. There is no evidence of a plot or characters, so you can easily eliminate choice C. The passage does not describe a particular volcano or its surroundings, so it is unlikely to be from a travel brochure as in choice D, and there is no mention of safety, so choice E cannot be correct.

6. **C is correct.** During a volcanic eruption, magma blasts into the air and breaks apart into pieces called tephra; thus choice E is true. As explained in the last paragraph, tephra can vary greatly in size (choice A), it can travel hundreds to thousands of kilometers downwind from a volcano (choice B), and large tephra typically falls back to the ground on or close to the volcano (choice D). Gases, not tephra, may be trapped in magma; therefore choice C is the only choice that is NOT true of tephra.

7. **C is correct.** Douglass makes this point in the very first sentence when he says, "I am one of those who believe that it is the mission of this war to free every slave in the United States." Choices A, B, and D might all be consequences of the Civil War, but in this speech Douglass mentions only freeing every slave in the United States as the mission of the war.

8. **D is correct.** Douglass believed that "the work of the American Anti-Slavery Society will not have been completed until the black man of the South, and the black men of the North, shall have been admitted, fully and completely, into the body politic of America." He specifically mentions that voting rights should be extended equally to all black men. He does not advocate voting rights only for black men in the South (choice B) and he does not mention that voting rights should be extended to everyone (choice E). Douglass advocates the abolition of slavery as the "mission of the war," but he believes that the work of the Anti-Slavery Society should go beyond this goal to the greater goal of setting the same conditions for voting for black men and white men.

9. **A is correct.** The *body politic* means "the people of a politically organized nation or state." To be fully and completely admitted to the body politic means to have all the rights accorded to any other citizen of the nation or state. Choices B, C, and D are rights and duties that are included in choice A. If black men were considered as a separate class of citizens, they would not be "fully and completely" admitted to the body politic.

10. **B is correct.** The passage is written in the first person and offers the views of the author on the subject of slavery and voting rights. The last paragraph makes it clear that the author is trying to convince members of the society that "whatever rule you adopt, whether of intelligence or wealth, as the condition of voting for whites, you shall apply it equally to the black man." He goes on to say that if "I am satisfied, and eternal justice is satisfied; liberty, fraternity, equality, are satisfied, and the country will move on harmoniously." As stated in the italic text at the start of the article, this speech was given at a meeting of the Anti-Slavery Society. It is unlikely that members of an Anti-Slavery Society would need to be convinced that slavery should be ended, so choice D can be eliminated. Choices A and C can also be eliminated because the passage is a statement of the author's opinions on the subject, not just an objective presentation of information about the horrors of slavery (choice A) or the progress of the war (choice C). Choice E is not correct because, while the passage mentions that granting voting rights to blacks will help the country "move on harmoniously," it does not explain how this will happen.

11. **C is correct.** The author describes the newly married pair as uncomfortable in their new clothes, unused to taking trips in a "fine" parlor-car, and embarrassed by the scrutiny of other passengers. He seems to like the unsophisticated couple and to be sympathetic toward their situation. The bride and groom may be embarrassed, but the author is not, so choice A is incorrect. Choices B, D, and E are all incorrect because nothing in the passage supports the idea that the author regards the couple with *disrespect* (meaning "discourtesy" or "rudeness"), *sorrow* (meaning "sadness"), or *scorn* (meaning "contempt" or "disdain").

12. **D is correct.** Both the bride and the groom were unaccustomed to wearing new clothes. The groom's face was "reddened from many days in the wind and sun." The bride had never traveled in a parlor car and she was clearly more used to cooking than to eating in a dining car. All of these clues point to the fact that the newlyweds were *unsophisticated* (meaning "innocent") country people. The fact that the bride thinks that a dollar is too much for them to spend on a meal indicates that the couple is not wealthy or well-to-do, so choice A is wrong. The pas-

sage mentions that the bride and groom "were evidently very happy," so choice B is wrong. Although the couple is described as being shy and embarrassed by the attention of other passengers, there is nothing to support the idea that they were either frightened (choice C) or unpleasant (choice E).

13. **E is correct.** The story takes place on a train crossing the plains of Texas. You can tell this from the fact that the groom asks his bride, "Have you ever been in a parlor-car before?" and then mentions that they will "go forward to the diner and get a big layout." Parlor-cars and dining cars are found on trains. Although the passage states that the newly married pair "had boarded this coach at San Antonio," the coach that is referred to is a car on a train, not a stage coach, so choice C is wrong. The groom mentions that "after a while we'll go forward to the diner," but, at the time this passage takes place, they have not yet gone to the diner to eat, so choice D is wrong. The couple has already boarded the train, so they cannot be in a hotel (choice A) or at a train station (choice B).

14. **A is correct.** Lines 17–18 states that "The glances he devoted to other passengers were furtive and shy." From this sentence you can tell that *furtive* must be something that goes with *shy*. Neither *friendly* nor *unabashed* (meaning "unembarrassed" or "not shy") works well with shy, so you can eliminate choices D and E. Similarly, you can eliminate choice C because *focused* means "clear and sharp," which is not commonly associated with *shy.* That leaves choice A, which is correct. A *furtive* glance is a secret or stealthy glance.

15. **D is correct.** The story is told in the third person by someone who is not a participant in the story. Therefore you can eliminate choices A, B, and C. In a story told by someone looking back on his life, the story would most likely be told in the first person (using "I" and "me" throughout). Because this story is told by someone who can see everything that is happening in the tale, but is not himself participating in the tale, it is most likely the work of an outside observer.

16. **C is correct.** This passage is actually the beginning of a short story. Its purpose is to introduce the characters and setting of the story to come. The passage is purely descriptive. There is no attempt to express an opinion (choice A), analyze information (choice B), or resolve a crisis (choice D). At this point in the story there is no conflict between the major characters. In fact, the bride and groom are described as "evidently very happy."

17. **B is correct.** If you can tell by simply looking at the bride that "she had cooked, and that she expected to cook, dutifully," then the bride most probably has the red, rough hands indicative of a life of hard work. Just looking at a person is unlikely to reveal whether that person expects to eat out regularly or has ever eaten in a restaurant before, so choices A and C are incorrect. Similarly, it is impossible to tell what a person wants to or might expect to learn about cooking by observation alone, so choices D and E are also incorrect.

18. **C is correct.** The purpose of this passage is to report on the work done by scientists to breed carrots with enhanced nutritional value. The researchers have selectively bred carrots in a rainbow of colors and studied the effects of the various plant pigments on the human body.

19. **D is correct.** The passage is intended to inform readers of developments in carrot breeding. The passage does not argue a point, nor does it contain any emotionally charged language; thus choices A and B can be eliminated. Nothing about the passage could be termed sentimental; and although the last sentence offers the opinion that colorful carrots will be a good addition to supermarket produce aisles, this is not enough to describe the entire passage as optimistic.

20. **B is correct.** As stated in lines 11–12, researchers have "selectively bred a rainbow of carrots—purple, red, yellow, even white." The only choice not mentioned is green.

21. **A is correct.** As stated in lines 16–18, "Red carrots derive their color mainly from lycopene, a type of carotene believed to guard against heart disease and some cancers." Xanthophyll (choice B) is found in yellow carrots. Anthocyanin (choice C) is the pigment found in purple carrots. Beta-carotene (choice D) is the pigment found in orange carrots. An antioxidant (choice E) is a substance that slows down oxidation and helps check deterioration.

22. **E is correct.** As stated in the passage, "In nature, different strains of carrots contain varying types and amounts of carotenoids—the pigments responsible for orange, yellow, and red colors." Choices A and D are incorrect

because the passage states that colored carrots were eaten "more than 1,000 years ago in Afghanistan and 700 years ago in western Europe." Choice B is wrong because it is contradicted by the statement that "today's carrots provide consumers with 75 percent more beta-carotene than those available 25 years ago." Choice C is wrong because the last sentence says the colorful carrots get "a thumbs-up from taste testers."

23. **C is correct.** The passage reports on the work of agricultural research scientists as they attempt to breed nutrient-rich carrots. It has no characters or plot so it cannot be a short story. It is not the story of someone's life, so it cannot be a biography. It is not written for the purpose of promoting some doctrine or cause, so it does not fall into the category of propaganda. It is not primarily an expression of the opinion of the author, so it is not an editorial.

24. **B is correct.** The passage makes it clear that O'Keeffe had a deep interest in art from a very early age. This indicates that she had a strong liking, or *penchant*, for artistic pursuits.

25. **D is correct.** Tone is the author's attitude toward a topic. It is created through details and language. The passage offers an objective presentation of facts about O'Keeffe's life and art, but it is very positive in its viewpoint of the importance of her unique artistic vision. Therefore, *praiseworthy* is the correct choice.

26. **A is correct.** In lines 32–33, O'Keeffe discusses her "vision" of what painting is about. She indicates that the desire to create is based on the realization that in blindness there is something "still there" even if it cannot be experienced in the same way a sighted person sees it.

27. **C is correct.** The passage makes it clear in lines 23–31 that the landscape of the Southwest had a profound effect on O'Keeffe's art once she visited Taos, New Mexico, in 1929.

28. **A is correct.** As stated in the second paragraph, the sculpture was commissioned to be completed in 1876, "to commemorate the centennial of the American Declaration of Independence." Choice B is incorrect because the Statue commemorated the friendship between the United States and France during the Revolutionary War, not the Civil War. Choice C is incorrect because the passage mentions only friendship between France and the United States; there is no mention of hostility between the two nations. Choice D is incorrect because the Statue was supposed to have been completed in 1876, which is 24 years before the start of the twentieth century. Choice E is wrong because there is no mention of a new era of international cooperation.

29. **B is correct.** Eiffel was called in to *attend to* or *focus on* the structural issues of the sculpture. All of the choices are synonyms for the word *address*, but only choice B fits the context of this sentence.

30. **C is correct.** When Pulitzer saw that fundraising for the pedestal was lagging, he "used the editorial pages of his newspaper *The World* to aid in the fundraising effort." He criticized the rich for failing to give enough to finance the pedestal, and he criticized the middle class for relying on the rich to provide all the funds needed for the pedestal. These actions imply that Pulitzer was enthusiastic in his support of the Statue and did his best to convince others to support it as well.

31. **D is correct.** As stated in the first paragraph, the Statue was a gift to the people of the United States "in recognition of the friendship established between the two nations during the American Revolution." Over the years, however, "the Statue of Liberty has come to symbolize freedom and democracy as well as this international friendship." There is no mention in the passage of a treaty between the United States and France.

32. **D is correct.** Alexandre Gustave Eiffel, who designed the Eiffel Tower, was called in "to address the structural issues of Bartholdi's colossal sculpture," not to help raise money for the project. Choice A is mentioned in line 17. Choice B is mentioned in lines 12–14. Choice C is mentioned in lines 27–35. Choice E can be ascertained by noting that the statue was completed in France in July 1884 and financing for the pedestal was completed in August 1885, more than a year later.

33. **A is correct.** This passage is entirely devoted to telling the history of the Statue of Liberty from design to financing to completion. It does not describe how Bartholdi designed the statue (choice B), but only tells that he did so with the help of Eiffel. It mentions fundraising in the United States and France (choice C), but is not devoted to comparing them. Likewise, it mentions how Pulitzer used newspaper editorials to increase donations (choice D), but makes no attempt to defend this practice. Only one sentence in the entire passage is devoted to assembling the statue on her pedestal (choice E).

34. **E is correct.** This informational article is most likely to be found in a textbook. Choices A and B are easily eliminated because the passage is fact, not fiction. Choice C is incorrect because the passage tells of events that happened long ago, not timely current events as would be reported in a newspaper article. The passage does not describe the engineering aspects of the Statue, so choice D is not a likely choice.

35. **B is correct.** Bixby never gave the narrator a chance to become complacent about what he had learned. There were always more twists and turns to be studied and more shapes to be learned. The narrator may have thought that Bixby knew the river better than any other pilot, but that is not the meaning of this particular quote.

36. **C is correct.** The narrator is comparing his knowledge of the shape of Walnut Bend to his knowledge of his grandmother's opinion of protoplasm. Since it is highly unlikely that the narrator knows anything about his grandmother's opinion of protoplasm (or even whether she has any such opinion), you can infer that he also knows nothing about the shape of Walnut Bend.

37. **D is correct.** In describing Bixby's response to the narrator's not knowing the shape of Walnut Bend, the author says, "My gunpowdery chief went off with a bang, of course, and then went on loading and firing until he was out of adjectives." The word that best describes something that goes off with a bang and keeps on firing until the ammunition runs out is *explosive*.

38. **E is correct.** Upon learning that he must know all the variations of shape in the banks of the river as well as he knows "the shape of the front hall at home," the narrator replies, "I wish I was dead!" This reaction can best be described as "hopelessness" or "despair."

39. **A is correct.** Tone is the writer's attitude toward a topic. It is revealed through the writer's word choice. Statements such as "a curiously inanimate mass of lumber it was" and "He might as well have asked me my grandmother's opinion of protoplasm" help to reveal the humor with which the author regards the situation.

40. **C is correct.** The passage is written in the first person and appears to describe events that occurred in the life of the author. These are characteristic of autobiographical writing.

## Section 3 Verbal

1. **D is correct.** A *novice* is a person new to a field or activity—a *beginner*.

2. **C is correct.** To *fabricate* is to concoct in order to deceive—in other words, to *falsify*.

3. **B is correct.** *Friendly* means agreeable in disposition, good-natured and likable, or *amiable*.

4. **B is correct.** A *genre* is a type or class. The choice that best fits this definition is *category*.

5. **A is correct.** A *summit* is a *conference* or meeting of high-level officials, typically called to shape a course of action.

6. **E is correct.** To do something *deftly* is to do it quickly and *skillfully*.

7. **E is correct.** To *prosper* is to be fortunate or successful, especially in terms of one's health or finances—in other words, to *thrive*.

8. **D is correct.** To *spurn* is to *reject* disdainfully or contemptuously; *scorn*.

9. **B is correct.** *Complimentary* means given *free* to repay a favor or as an act of courtesy.

10. **C is correct.** *Visage* is the *face* or facial expression of a person; *countenance*.

11. **A is correct.** A *respite* is a usually short interval of rest or relief—in other words, a *pause*.

12. **D is correct.** *Regretful* means feeling troubled, remorseful, or *contrite* for one's sins or offenses.

13. **C is correct.** *Frugal* means thrifty or *economical*.

14. **A is correct.** To *imply* is to *suggest*, express, or indicate indirectly.

15. **E is correct.** To *incite* is to *provoke* or urge on.

16. **A is correct.** *Meager* means deficient in quantity, fullness, or extent; scanty or *paltry*.

17. **B is correct.** A *prediction* is a foretelling or a *forecast*.

18. **D is correct.** A *facet* is one of numerous *aspects*, as of a subject.

19. **D is correct.** To *absolve* is to *clear* someone of guilt or blame.

20. **B is correct.** To *subvert* means to overthrow or *destroy* something.

21. **E is correct.** To *mourn* is to feel or express grief or sorrow—in other words, to *grieve*.

22. **C is correct.** *Poisonous* means capable of harming or killing by or as if by poison; venomous or *toxic*.

23. **D is correct.** *Aplomb* is self-assurance or *confidence*.

24. **A is correct.** *Corroboration* is ratification or *confirmation* that some statement or fact is true.

25. **C is correct.** Behavior that is *erratic* lacks consistency, regularity, or uniformity; in other words it is *unpredictable*.

26. **B is correct.** *Credible* means plausible or *believable*.

27. **C is correct.** To *abscond* is to *leave* quickly and secretly and hide oneself, often to avoid arrest or prosecution.

28. **D is correct.** To *calm* is to make or become calm or quiet—in other words, to *soothe*.

29. **E is correct.** *Irritable* means easily provoked, impatient, ill-tempered, or *petulant*.

30. **B is correct.** A *travesty* is a debased or grotesque likeness or a *mockery*.

31. **B is correct.** *Safe* is the opposite of *dangerous* just as *bland* is the opposite of *spicy*. Only choice B provides two adjectives that are opposite in meaning. Choices D and E cannot be correct because the words in each pair are not the same part of speech.

32. **C is correct.** A *star* is found in the *sky* in the same way that a *fish* is found in the *ocean*.

33. **E is correct.** This analogy pairs an activity with a result. Of the answer choices, only choice E has the same relationship as the original word pair: To *cut* produces a *wound* as to *cry* produces *tears*.

34. **D is correct.** This stem provides a usage sequence by pairing *camera* with *picture*. Choice A comes close to being right but reverses the order by placing *breeze* before *fan*. Only choice D follows the logic of the stem and places the words in the correct order: a *camera* is used to take a *picture* just as a *phone* is used to make a *call*.

35. **B is correct.** This sequence tests your knowledge of relationships between units of measurement. *Lumens* are a measure of *brightness* just as a *decibel* is a measure of *volume*.

36. **D is correct.** *Books* are produced by *writers* much as *crops* are produced by *farmers*. No other choice offers a product made by a particular worker. *Doctors* do not make *needles* (choice A); *dentists* do not produce *cavities* (choice B); *drivers* do not build *trucks* (choice C); and *actors* do not write *scripts* (choice E).

37. **A is correct.** *Frigid* is the opposite of *tropical*, and *raw* is the opposite of *cooked*. No other answer choice offers the proper contrast.

38. **C is correct.** This analogy tests your knowledge of places and locations. Los Angeles is a city in California just as Houston is a city in Texas. Choice A is incorrect because Phoenix is in Arizona, not New Mexico. Philadelphia and Pittsburgh (choice B) are both cities in Pennsylvania. Choice E is incorrect because it pairs a city with a country, not a state.

39. **E is correct.** The relationship in this sequence is one of individual to object. A *diner* uses a *menu* in the way that a *shopper* would use a *catalog*. One provides a list of options for the other.

40. **A is correct.** This sequence offers a part-to-part relationship. A *cuff* is a part of a shirt in the same way that a *collar* is a part of a shirt. Similarly, a *mouse* is part of a computer in the same way that a *keyboard* is part of a computer.

41. **E is correct.** Initially, this relationship in this sequence may strike you as one of part to whole. However, you will need to take the analogy one step further in order to arrive at the correct answer. The *belly* is the part of the *snake* used for traveling just as *feet* are the part of a *person* used for traveling. Don't be fooled by choice C; a *horse* travels on its feet, just like a person.

42. **A is correct.** The relationship that this sequence is testing is one of measurement units. A *diamond* is measured in *carats* and *heat* is measured in *calories*. Choices C and D provide the right descriptions, however both answer choices invert the correct order.

43. **A is correct.** This is another example of an object-to-activity analogy. People *read books* in much the same way that they *analyze data*.

44. **E is correct.** This sequence provides another example of an activity-to-result analogy. When you *burnish* an object, you *polish* it. Similarly, when you *reinforce* an object, you *strengthen* it.

45. **B is correct.** The relationship in this question is one of contrasts. *Fresh* is the opposite of *rancid*, just as *ripe* is the opposite of *rotten*. No other answer choice offers a comparable contrast.

46. **B is correct.** A *fire* produces *heat* much the same way that a *lamp* gives off *light*. Choice B is the only option that presents a similar relationship.

47. **A is correct.** The relationship in this sequence is one of degrees of contrast. *Browsing* denotes inspecting something in a leisurely and casual manner in the same way that *skimming* a book does. Both *shopping* and *reading* require a greater degree of commitment.

48. **D is correct.** The relationship presented in this sequence is one of usage. As a showcase for talent, a *recital* is used by a *pianist* in much the same way that an *exhibit* is used by an *artist*.

49. **D is correct.** This is a part-to-whole analogy. A *song* is a part of a *medley* as a *picture* is part of a *collage*. Choice A may seem correct, but the terms are reversed. A *book* can be part of a *series*, but a *series* cannot be a part of a *book*.

50. **C is correct.** The relationship in this question is one of an activity (*exercise*) and a result (*sweat*). Only choice C provides a comparable relationship.

51. **B is correct.** This analogy is one of a part to a whole. The *stamen* is a part of the *flower* in much the same way the *lens* is a part of the *eye*. Choice A is almost correct, except that it offers the whole before the part. Choice B is the only answer choice that presents a logical sequence in the right order.

52. **E is correct.** Flip the words: a *cartographer* makes *maps*. Similarly, a *baker* makes *cakes*. No other option presents the same relationship.

53. **C is correct.** A *baby* travels by *crawling* much the same way a *frog* travels by *jumping*. A *rock* only travels across the water by *skipping* (choice A) when thrown by a person. The correct answer does not rely on an outside influence.

54. **A is correct.** This analogy is one of usage. An *eraser* is used to clean a *chalkboard*, and in a similar way, a *mop* is used to clean a *floor*.

55. **C is correct.** This is an analogy of degrees of similarity. Flip the words and you will see that *fervent* is a more intense feeling than *eager* just as *ecstatic* is a more intense feeling than *pleased*. Choice D may seem correct, but the words appear in reverse order, from more intense to less intense. To be correct, *mad* would need to come before *enraged*.

56. **D is correct.** When *bread* deteriorates or gets old, it becomes *moldy*. Similarly, when *steel* becomes old or is left to deteriorate in the elements, it becomes *rusty*.

57. **B is correct.** Again, flip the words around and you will see that a *collie* is a particular type of *dog*, just as a *chameleon* is a particular type of *lizard*. Choice C is incorrect because *reptile* is too general.

58. **D is correct.** This sequence presents an object-to-activity analogy, also known as a tool-to-function analogy. A *chisel* is used for *carving* in the same way that a *blender* is used for *mixing*. No other option provides an appropriate comparison. Choices A and B are both incorrect for the same reason; they are used respectively in each activity, but are not the tool used to perform the activity. Choice C is incorrect because a car is used for driving, and choice E is incorrect because a stove or oven is used for cooking.

59. **B is correct.** This sequence is another example of an activity to a result analogy. When you *drop* something, it can *break*. Similarly, when you *stumble* you can *fall*. Choices A, C, and D are all synonyms, and choice E is too big a stretch.

60. **A is correct.** The relationship presented in this sequence is one of part to whole. *Ruby* is a shade of *red*, and *amber* is a shade of orange or *brown*. Since *orange* is not an option, choice A is the correct answer.

## Section 4 Quantitative II

1. **C is correct.** 2% is the equivalent of 0.02; $0.02 \times 5{,}000 = 100$.

2. **C is correct.**
$$\begin{array}{r} 3.50 \\ \times\, 0.93 \\ \hline 1\ 05 \\ 31\ 5\phantom{0} \\ \hline 3.255 \end{array}$$

3. **D is correct.** $^{32}/_4 = 8$; $4 \times {}^8/_{16} = {}^{32}/_{16} = 2$; $8 \div {}^1/_8 = 8 \times {}^8/_1 = 64$; $6.4 + 11.6 = 18$. However, ${}^5/_{12} \times 8 = {}^{40}/_{12} = 3\,{}^1/_3$, which is not a whole number.

4. **B is correct.** According to the order of operations (PEMDAS), operations within parentheses should be evaluated first.

5. **B is correct.** It costs $m$ dollars to buy 60 nails. 24 nails are ${}^2/_5$ of 60, so the cost of 24 nails will be ${}^2/_5 \times m = {}^{2m}/_5$ dollars.

6. **D is correct.**
$5/12 x = 50$
$1/12 x = 10$
$x = 120$
$1/2 x = 60$

7. **A is correct.** Perform operations in the parentheses first, then the exponents, and then the remaining operations.
$16 + 3(-4)$
$16 + (-12) = 4$

8. **C is correct.** When calculating the average or mean, add the numbers and then divide by the number of numbers. The sum of 24, 36, 18, 30, 90, and 690 is 888, divided by 6 is 148.

9. **B is correct.** This item is set up as a proportion. To solve for $n$, cross-multiply so that the problem becomes $25n = 1,000$. $n = 1,000 \div 25 = 40$.

10. **A is correct.** $5 \times 4 + 4 = 24$. $6 \times 8 = 48$, and $48 \div 24 = 2$.

11. **D is correct.** Integer values for $x$ are: $-2, -1, 0, 1, 2, 3$.

12. **B is correct.** $2 + 4/25 = 2.16$.
The fraction $4/25 = 16/100 = 0.16$, so $2 + 4/25 = 2.16$.

13. **C is correct.** $1/3 + 1/6 = 2/6 + 1/6 = 3/6$.
$3/6 = 1/2$, so if Karen has used $1/2$ of her tickets, $1/2$ are left.

14. **D is correct.**
$$12 \div 3\frac{3}{4} = \frac{12}{1} \div \frac{15}{4}$$
$$= \frac{12}{1} \times \frac{4}{15}$$
$$= \frac{48}{15} = 3\frac{3}{15} = 3\frac{1}{5}$$

15. **D is correct.** $\$23.95 \times 0.065 = \$1.56$. $\$23.95 + \$1.56 = \$25.51$.

16. **B is correct.** Set up a proportion:
$30/2 = n/7$
$n = 105$

17. **E is correct.** 1 mile = 5,280 ft. If the width of the park is 880 feet, then two sides of the park measure $880 + 880 = 1,760$ ft. $5,280 - 1,760 = 3,520$. The other two sides of the park must each measure one-half of 3,520 ft. $3,520 \div 2 = 1,760$ ft.

18. **D is correct.**
$10 \times (0.38 + 3.5) + 5.2$
$= (10 \times 0.38) + (10 \times 3.5) + 5.2$
$= 3.8 + 35 + 5.2$
$= 44$

19. **A is correct.** The rental company charges $25 + $6 per hour. The equation that represents this situation is $25 + 6h$ where $h = $ number of hours.

20. **D is correct.** From midnight to 11:00 A.M. there are 11 hours. If the temperature rose 2°C each hour, then it rose 22°C.
$(-12) + 22 = 10°C$

21. **D is correct.** The sum of $8 + 0 = 8$ and the difference of $8 - 0 = 8$.

22. **D is correct.**
    $2.31 \times 100000$
    $2.31 \times 10^5$

23. **C is correct.** The median is 28 and is represented by the line within the box.

24. **E is correct.** Each term is determined by multiplying the previous term by 4.
    $64 \times 4 = 256$

25. **A is correct.** The mode is the number that occurs most frequently in a data set. The number 114 occurs twice, whereas all the other numbers occur once.

# SSAT Practice Test II

The following practice test is designed to be just like the real SSAT. It matches the actual test in content coverage and level of difficulty. The test is in five sections: Verbal, Quantitative I, Reading Comprehension, Quantitative II, and the Essay.

This practice test will be an accurate reflection of how you'll do on test day if you treat it as the real examination. Here are some hints on how to take the test under conditions similar to those of the actual exam:

- Find a quiet place to work and set aside a period of approximately 3 hours when you will not be disturbed.
- Work on only one section at a time, and use your watch or a timer to keep track of the time limits for each test part.
- Tear out your answer sheet and mark your answers by filling in the ovals for each question.
- Write your essay on the pages provided.
- Become familiar with the directions for each part of the test. You'll save time on the actual test day by already being familiar with this information.

At the end of the test you'll find answer keys for each section and explanations for every question. Check your answers against the keys to find out how you did on each section of the test and what test topics you might need to study more. Then review the explanations, paying particular attention to the ones for the questions you answered incorrectly.

You will receive three scores, one for each of these three categories: Quantitative, Verbal, and Reading. Each category has a low score of 500 and the high score of 800, making your total score somewhere between 1500 and 2400.

The actual SSAT also provides a Percentile Score that compares your performance with that of other U.S. and Canadian students who took the test during the past three years. Your reported percentile test scores are compared to this "norm group" for each section of the test.

The writing sample is not scored, but it is included with the score reports that you send to schools. The following table shows the various sections, numbers of questions, and time allotments.

## SSAT: Structure and Time Allotments

| Section | Number of Questions | Time Allowed |
|---|---|---|
| Writing Sample | 1 (unscored) | 25 minutes |
| Break | | 5 minutes |
| Quantitative 1 | 25 | 30 minutes |
| Reading | 40 | 40 minutes |
| Break | | 5 minutes |
| Verbal | 60 | 30 minutes |
| Quantitative 2 | 25 | 30 minutes |
| Experimental | 16 (unscored) | 15 minutes |
| Totals | 167 | 3 hours, 5 minutes |

Of the 167 total questions, only 150 items are scored. The writing sample and questions on the Experimental section are *not* scored.

# SSAT Practice Test II

ANSWER SHEET

## Section 1: Quantitative I

1. (A) (B) (C) (D) (E)   11. (A) (B) (C) (D) (E)   21. (A) (B) (C) (D) (E)
2. (A) (B) (C) (D) (E)   12. (A) (B) (C) (D) (E)   22. (A) (B) (C) (D) (E)
3. (A) (B) (C) (D) (F)   13. (A) (B) (C) (D) (E)   23. (A) (B) (C) (D) (E)
4. (A) (B) (C) (D) (E)   14. (A) (B) (C) (D) (E)   24. (A) (B) (C) (D) (E)
5. (A) (B) (C) (D) (E)   15. (A) (B) (C) (D) (E)   25. (A) (B) (C) (D) (E)
6. (A) (B) (C) (D) (E)   16. (A) (B) (C) (D) (E)
7. (A) (B) (C) (D) (E)   17. (A) (B) (C) (D) (E)
8. (A) (B) (C) (D) (E)   18. (A) (B) (C) (D) (E)
9. (A) (B) (C) (D) (E)   19. (A) (B) (C) (D) (E)
10. (A) (B) (C) (D) (E)   20. (A) (B) (C) (D) (E)

## Section 2: Reading Comprehension

1. (A) (B) (C) (D) (E)   17. (A) (B) (C) (D) (E)   33. (A) (B) (C) (D) (E)
2. (A) (B) (C) (D) (E)   18. (A) (B) (C) (D) (E)   34. (A) (B) (C) (D) (E)
3. (A) (B) (C) (D) (E)   19. (A) (B) (C) (D) (E)   35. (A) (B) (C) (D) (E)
4. (A) (B) (C) (D) (E)   20. (A) (B) (C) (D) (E)   36. (A) (B) (C) (D) (E)
5. (A) (B) (C) (D) (E)   21. (A) (B) (C) (D) (E)   37. (A) (B) (C) (D) (E)
6. (A) (B) (C) (D) (E)   22. (A) (B) (C) (D) (E)   38. (A) (B) (C) (D) (E)
7. (A) (B) (C) (D) (E)   23. (A) (B) (C) (D) (E)   39. (A) (B) (C) (D) (E)
8. (A) (B) (C) (D) (E)   24. (A) (B) (C) (D) (E)   40. (A) (B) (C) (D) (E)
9. (A) (B) (C) (D) (E)   25. (A) (B) (C) (D) (E)
10. (A) (B) (C) (D) (E)   26. (A) (B) (C) (D) (E)
11. (A) (B) (C) (D) (E)   27. (A) (B) (C) (D) (E)
12. (A) (B) (C) (D) (E)   28. (A) (B) (C) (D) (E)
13. (A) (B) (C) (D) (E)   29. (A) (B) (C) (D) (E)
14. (A) (B) (C) (D) (E)   30. (A) (B) (C) (D) (E)
15. (A) (B) (C) (D) (E)   31. (A) (B) (C) (D) (E)
16. (A) (B) (C) (D) (E)   32. (A) (B) (C) (D) (E)

## Section 3: Verbal

| 1. Ⓐ Ⓑ Ⓒ Ⓓ Ⓔ | 21. Ⓐ Ⓑ Ⓒ Ⓓ Ⓔ | 41. Ⓐ Ⓑ Ⓒ Ⓓ Ⓔ |
|---|---|---|
| 2. Ⓐ Ⓑ Ⓒ Ⓓ Ⓔ | 22. Ⓐ Ⓑ Ⓒ Ⓓ Ⓔ | 42. Ⓐ Ⓑ Ⓒ Ⓓ Ⓔ |
| 3. Ⓐ Ⓑ Ⓒ Ⓓ Ⓔ | 23. Ⓐ Ⓑ Ⓒ Ⓓ Ⓔ | 43. Ⓐ Ⓑ Ⓒ Ⓓ Ⓔ |
| 4. Ⓐ Ⓑ Ⓒ Ⓓ Ⓔ | 24. Ⓐ Ⓑ Ⓒ Ⓓ Ⓔ | 44. Ⓐ Ⓑ Ⓒ Ⓓ Ⓔ |
| 5. Ⓐ Ⓑ Ⓒ Ⓓ Ⓔ | 25. Ⓐ Ⓑ Ⓒ Ⓓ Ⓔ | 45. Ⓐ Ⓑ Ⓒ Ⓓ Ⓔ |
| 6. Ⓐ Ⓑ Ⓒ Ⓓ Ⓔ | 26. Ⓐ Ⓑ Ⓒ Ⓓ Ⓔ | 46. Ⓐ Ⓑ Ⓒ Ⓓ Ⓔ |
| 7. Ⓐ Ⓑ Ⓒ Ⓓ Ⓔ | 27. Ⓐ Ⓑ Ⓒ Ⓓ Ⓔ | 47. Ⓐ Ⓑ Ⓒ Ⓓ Ⓔ |
| 8. Ⓐ Ⓑ Ⓒ Ⓓ Ⓔ | 28. Ⓐ Ⓑ Ⓒ Ⓓ Ⓔ | 48. Ⓐ Ⓑ Ⓒ Ⓓ Ⓔ |
| 9. Ⓐ Ⓑ Ⓒ Ⓓ Ⓔ | 29. Ⓐ Ⓑ Ⓒ Ⓓ Ⓔ | 49. Ⓐ Ⓑ Ⓒ Ⓓ Ⓔ |
| 10. Ⓐ Ⓑ Ⓒ Ⓓ Ⓔ | 30. Ⓐ Ⓑ Ⓒ Ⓓ Ⓔ | 50. Ⓐ Ⓑ Ⓒ Ⓓ Ⓔ |
| 11. Ⓐ Ⓑ Ⓒ Ⓓ Ⓔ | 31. Ⓐ Ⓑ Ⓒ Ⓓ Ⓔ | 51. Ⓐ Ⓑ Ⓒ Ⓓ Ⓔ |
| 12. Ⓐ Ⓑ Ⓒ Ⓓ Ⓔ | 32. Ⓐ Ⓑ Ⓒ Ⓓ Ⓔ | 52. Ⓐ Ⓑ Ⓒ Ⓓ Ⓔ |
| 13. Ⓐ Ⓑ Ⓒ Ⓓ Ⓔ | 33. Ⓐ Ⓑ Ⓒ Ⓓ Ⓔ | 53. Ⓐ Ⓑ Ⓒ Ⓓ Ⓔ |
| 14. Ⓐ Ⓑ Ⓒ Ⓓ Ⓔ | 34. Ⓐ Ⓑ Ⓒ Ⓓ Ⓔ | 54. Ⓐ Ⓑ Ⓒ Ⓓ Ⓔ |
| 15. Ⓐ Ⓑ Ⓒ Ⓓ Ⓔ | 35. Ⓐ Ⓑ Ⓒ Ⓓ Ⓔ | 55. Ⓐ Ⓑ Ⓒ Ⓓ Ⓔ |
| 16. Ⓐ Ⓑ Ⓒ Ⓓ Ⓔ | 36. Ⓐ Ⓑ Ⓒ Ⓓ Ⓔ | 56. Ⓐ Ⓑ Ⓒ Ⓓ Ⓔ |
| 17. Ⓐ Ⓑ Ⓒ Ⓓ Ⓔ | 37. Ⓐ Ⓑ Ⓒ Ⓓ Ⓔ | 57. Ⓐ Ⓑ Ⓒ Ⓓ Ⓔ |
| 18. Ⓐ Ⓑ Ⓒ Ⓓ Ⓔ | 38. Ⓐ Ⓑ Ⓒ Ⓓ Ⓔ | 58. Ⓐ Ⓑ Ⓒ Ⓓ Ⓔ |
| 19. Ⓐ Ⓑ Ⓒ Ⓓ Ⓔ | 39. Ⓐ Ⓑ Ⓒ Ⓓ Ⓔ | 59. Ⓐ Ⓑ Ⓒ Ⓓ Ⓔ |
| 20. Ⓐ Ⓑ Ⓒ Ⓓ Ⓔ | 40. Ⓐ Ⓑ Ⓒ Ⓓ Ⓔ | 60. Ⓐ Ⓑ Ⓒ Ⓓ Ⓔ |

## Section 4: Quantitative II

| 1. Ⓐ Ⓑ Ⓒ Ⓓ Ⓔ | 11. Ⓐ Ⓑ Ⓒ Ⓓ Ⓔ | 21. Ⓐ Ⓑ Ⓒ Ⓓ Ⓔ |
|---|---|---|
| 2. Ⓐ Ⓑ Ⓒ Ⓓ Ⓔ | 12. Ⓐ Ⓑ Ⓒ Ⓓ Ⓔ | 22. Ⓐ Ⓑ Ⓒ Ⓓ Ⓔ |
| 3. Ⓐ Ⓑ Ⓒ Ⓓ Ⓔ | 13. Ⓐ Ⓑ Ⓒ Ⓓ Ⓔ | 23. Ⓐ Ⓑ Ⓒ Ⓓ Ⓔ |
| 4. Ⓐ Ⓑ Ⓒ Ⓓ Ⓔ | 14. Ⓐ Ⓑ Ⓒ Ⓓ Ⓔ | 24. Ⓐ Ⓑ Ⓒ Ⓓ Ⓔ |
| 5. Ⓐ Ⓑ Ⓒ Ⓓ Ⓔ | 15. Ⓐ Ⓑ Ⓒ Ⓓ Ⓔ | 25. Ⓐ Ⓑ Ⓒ Ⓓ Ⓔ |
| 6. Ⓐ Ⓑ Ⓒ Ⓓ Ⓔ | 16. Ⓐ Ⓑ Ⓒ Ⓓ Ⓔ | |
| 7. Ⓐ Ⓑ Ⓒ Ⓓ Ⓔ | 17. Ⓐ Ⓑ Ⓒ Ⓓ Ⓔ | |
| 8. Ⓐ Ⓑ Ⓒ Ⓓ Ⓔ | 18. Ⓐ Ⓑ Ⓒ Ⓓ Ⓔ | |
| 9. Ⓐ Ⓑ Ⓒ Ⓓ Ⓔ | 19. Ⓐ Ⓑ Ⓒ Ⓓ Ⓔ | |
| 10. Ⓐ Ⓑ Ⓒ Ⓓ Ⓔ | 20. Ⓐ Ⓑ Ⓒ Ⓓ Ⓔ | |

Time: 30 Minutes
25 Questions

**Directions:** For each of the following questions, mark the letter of your choice on the answer sheet.

---

1. Louisa went to the grocery store and bought a package of hamburger patties for $6.16, a package of buns for $2.10, a container of mustard for $1.78, a jar of relish for $2.16, and a bag of charcoal for $5.35. What was her total bill?
   - (A) $12.64
   - (B) $14.74
   - (C) $16.15
   - (D) $17.55
   - (E) $19.65

2. A teacher has assigned 315 pages of reading. If Jessica starts reading on Monday and reads 65 pages each day, on what day will she complete the assignment?
   - (A) Wednesday
   - (B) Thursday
   - (C) Friday
   - (D) Saturday
   - (E) Sunday

3. Renee deposits $4,000 in a saving account that earns 2% simple interest per year. How much interest will she earn after 2 years?
   - (A) $100
   - (B) $160
   - (C) $165
   - (D) $180
   - (E) $195

4. Rachel flies 2,880 miles in 9 hours. What is the average speed of her airplane?
   - (A) 285 miles/hour
   - (B) 315 miles/hour
   - (C) 320 miles/hour
   - (D) 340 miles/hour
   - (E) 355 miles/hour

5. Which of the following is an obtuse angle?
   - (A) 45°
   - (B) 85°
   - (C) 100°
   - (D) 190°
   - (E) 210°

6. Al has 3 times as much money as Bill. Bill has 2 times as much money as Charlie. If Charlie has $12.55, how much money does Al have?
   - (A) $33.75
   - (B) $75.30
   - (C) $82.20
   - (D) $88.35
   - (E) $96.40

7. Alex's car gets an average of 26 miles per gallon of gas on the highway. If he drives 858 miles, how many gallons of gas will he use?
   - (A) 33 gallons
   - (B) 57 gallons
   - (C) 78 gallons
   - (D) 84 gallons
   - (E) 92 gallons

**GO ON TO THE NEXT PAGE.**

8. In the figure shown, the two outer rays form a right angle. If angle 1 measures 65°, what is the measure of angle 2?

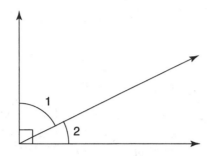

(A) 120°
(B) 90°
(C) 60°
(D) 35°
(E) 25°

9. Will has $12,444.12 in his checking account. He writes checks for $8,204.94 and $890.99. How much is left in Will's account?
(A) $989.65
(B) $2,259.30
(C) $2,867.30
(D) $2,945.60
(E) $3,348.19

10. Paula is 3 years older than Lindsey, who is 2 years younger than Dave. If Paula is 17, how old is Dave?
(A) 16
(B) 17
(C) 19
(D) 21
(E) 23

11. In a recent election, Rebecca received 14% of the votes. If 7,000 votes were cast, how many votes did Rebecca receive?
(A) 680
(B) 980
(C) 1,080
(D) 1,220
(E) 1,460

12. In the figure shown, if angle 2 measures 45°, what is the measure of angle 4?

(A) 135°
(B) 75°
(C) 45°
(D) 35°
(E) 25

13. If ¼ of a number is 12, then ⅙ of the same number is
(A) 16
(B) 15
(C) 12
(D) 9
(E) 8

14. Figure WXYZ is a parallelogram. Which of the following is NOT necessarily true?

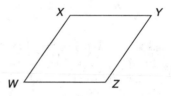

(A) Side WX is parallel to side ZY.
(B) Side XY is parallel to side WZ.
(C) ∠W has the same measure as ∠Y.
(D) Side WX is the same length as side XY.
(E) ∠X has the same measure as ∠Z.

15. Renee wants to carpet her living room. The rectangular room measures 15 feet × 18 feet. How many square yards of carpet must Renee purchase?
(A) 20 yd²
(B) 30 yd²
(C) 32 yd²
(D) 35 yd²
(E) 40 yd²

**GO ON TO THE NEXT PAGE.**

16. In an equilateral triangle, what is the measure of each angle?
    (A) 30°
    (B) 45°
    (C) 60°
    (D) 90°
    (E) 110°

17. Last month, the librarian at a certain library kept track of all books checked out. The graph below shows the results by type of book. Which type of book was checked out least?

**Number of Library Books Checked Out of Local Library**

    (A) Mysteries
    (B) Science fiction
    (C) Travel
    (D) Nonfiction
    (E) Sports

18. If $9 + 3 + $ _____ $= 8 + 6 + 4$, then ___ =
    (A) 2
    (B) 3
    (C) 4
    (D) 5
    (E) 6

19. $2 \times 3 \times 5 \times 6$ is equal to the product of 30 and
    (A) 6
    (B) 7
    (C) 8
    (D) 9
    (E) 11

20. Which of the following is NOT equal to a whole number?
    (A) $\dfrac{20}{5}$
    (B) $5 \times \dfrac{3}{4}$
    (C) $6 \div \dfrac{1}{6}$
    (D) $\dfrac{3}{5} \times 10$
    (E) $7 + 5$

21. $4\,^3/_{10}\% =$
    (A) 43
    (B) 4.3
    (C) 0.43
    (D) 0.043
    (E) 0.0043

22. It costs $d$ dollars to buy 6 granola bars. At the same rate, how many dollars will it cost to buy 15 granola bars?
    (A) $2.5d$
    (B) $25d$
    (C) $\dfrac{2d}{5}$
    (D) $\dfrac{5d}{2}$
    (E) $250d$

23. In the triangle shown, $\angle ACB$ measures 55° and $\angle CAB$ measures 65°. What is the measure of $\angle CBA$?

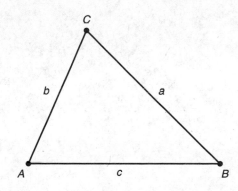

    (A) 50°
    (B) 60°
    (C) 80°
    (D) 90°
    (E) 110°

**GO ON TO THE NEXT PAGE.**

24. There are 15 black marbles and 10 white marbles in a bag. If you pick a marble from the bag without looking, what are your chances of picking a white marble?

(A) $\dfrac{1}{25}$

(B) $\dfrac{3}{25}$

(C) $\dfrac{2}{5}$

(D) $\dfrac{3}{5}$

(E) $\dfrac{4}{5}$

25. $\dfrac{3}{4} - \dfrac{5}{12} =$

(A) $\dfrac{1}{12}$

(B) $\dfrac{3}{12}$

(C) $\dfrac{1}{3}$

(D) $\dfrac{2}{3}$

(E) $\dfrac{3}{4}$

**STOP!**
If you finish before time is up, check your work on this section only.

## SECTION 2

Time: 40 Minutes
40 Questions

Each reading passage is followed by questions about it. Answer the questions that follow a passage on the basis of what is stated or implied in that passage. For each question, select the answer you think is best and record your choice by filling in the corresponding oval on the answer sheet.

At the Thirteenth Annual Convention of the National Negro Business League in 1912, no women were included on the schedule of speakers. Madam C. J. Walker, a highly successful inventor and dis-
5  tributor of hair care products for African-American women, shocked the participants when she walked up and claimed the podium from moderator Booker T. Washington:

"Surely you are not going to shut the door
10  in my face. I feel that I am in a business that is a credit to the womanhood of our race. I am a woman who started in business seven years ago with only $1.50. This year (up to the 19th day of this month . . .) I had taken in $18,000. (Prolonged applause.) This
15  makes a grand total of $63,049 made in my hair business in Indianapolis. (Applause.) I have been trying to get before you business people to tell you what I am doing. I am a woman that came from the cotton fields of the South; I was promoted from there to
20  the wash-tub (laughter); then I was promoted to the cook kitchen, and from there I promoted myself into the business of manufacturing hair goods and prepa-rations . . . I am not ashamed of my past; I am not ashamed of my humble beginning. Don't think that
25  because you have to go down in the wash-tub that you are any less a lady! (Prolonged applause.)"

1. The purpose of Madam Walker's speech was to
   (A) demonstrate her hair products to the league
   (B) lash out at Booker T. Washington for ignor-ing her
   (C) make the members of the league take notice of her business success
   (D) influence the members of the league to admit more women
   (E) encourage black women to go into business for themselves

2. As reflected in her speech, Madam Walker's atti-tude is best described as
   (A) envious
   (B) proud
   (C) reverent
   (D) cautious
   (E) fearful

3. The reaction of the members of the league to Madam Walker's speech can be described as
   (A) indifferent
   (B) angry
   (C) sad
   (D) favorable
   (E) critical

**GO ON TO THE NEXT PAGE.**

4. The reference to her promotion from the cotton fields to the wash-tub to the cook kitchen is used to
   (A) show how far she has come
   (B) establish a connection with her audience
   (C) suggest that hard work is not ladylike
   (D) debunk a myth about African-American women
   (E) make people feel sorry for her

5. What does Madam Walker means when she says, "Don't think that because you have to go down in the wash-tub that you are any less a lady" (lines 24–26)?
   (A) Ladies should not have to scrub and cook.
   (B) Getting down on your knees to scrub is hard work for a lady.
   (C) It is not ladylike to work with your hands.
   (D) Very few ladies get ahead in the business world.
   (E) There is nothing demeaning about hard work.

On March 20, 1980, a series of small earthquakes signaled the awakening of Mount St. Helens from a 123-year slumber. Over the next two months more than 10,000 earthquakes followed as magma moved
5  into the volcano, wedging the volcano apart at a rate of five feet per day. Heat from a rising plume of volcanic ash melted glacial ice creating cement-like slurries of rock and ash called mudflows. Superheated avalanches of hot gas, magma caused a visible swell-
10 ing of the volcano's north flank creating a feature that scientists called "the bulge."

Many geologists weren't surprised by Mount St. Helens' awakening. In the 1950s, geologists had begun an extensive study of the deposits around
15 Mount St. Helens. In 1975, they published a report predicting that Mount St. Helens was the volcano in the lower 48 states most likely to erupt by the end of the century.

On the morning of May 18, 1980, a magnitude
20 5.1 earthquake triggered the collapse of the summit and north flank of Mount St. Helens and formed the largest landslide in recorded history. Gas-rich magma and super-heated groundwater trapped inside the volcano were suddenly released in a powerful lateral
25 blast. In less than three minutes, 230 square miles of forest lay flattened. The hot gas and magma melted the snow and ice that covered the volcano. The resulting floodwater mixed with the rock and debris to create concrete-like mudflows that scoured river val-
30 leys surrounding the mountain.

A plume of volcanic ash and pumice billowed out of the volcano reaching a height of 15 miles and transformed day into night across Eastern Washington. Avalanches of super-heated gas and pumice,
35 called pyroclastic flows, swept down the flanks of the volcano. While the landslide and lateral blast were over within minutes, the eruption column, mudflows and pyroclastic flows continued throughout the day and following night. By the following morning
40 major eruptive activity had ceased and the landscape appeared to be a gray wasteland.

6. The primary purpose of this passage is to
   (A) offer general information about volcanoes
   (B) describe a specific volcanic eruption
   (C) offer specific advice about what to do when a volcano erupts
   (D) provide historical background about volcanoes
   (E) appeal for action to protect the environment

7. The first sentence implies that
   (A) Mount St. Helens had never before erupted
   (B) Mount St. Helens erupts every 123 years
   (C) Mount St. Helens last erupted in 1857
   (D) no records exist for eruptions that occurred more than 123 years ago
   (E) no one suspected that Mount St. Helens could erupt

8. As used in line 6, "rising" most nearly means
   (A) growing
   (B) maturing
   (C) approaching
   (D) ascending
   (E) advancing

**GO ON TO THE NEXT PAGE.**

9. The statement that "Many geologists weren't surprised by Mount St. Helens' awakening," (lines 12–13) primarily suggests that
   (A) geologists were able to predict when Mount St. Helens would erupt
   (B) the assumptions geologists had made about Mount St. Helens were being proven
   (C) the longer a volcano remains dormant, the more likely it is to become active
   (D) nothing is surprising to geologists
   (E) the heat rising from the volcanic ash had provided an important clue to the geologists

10. The author describes the events of May 18, 1980, mainly by means of
    (A) scientific analysis
    (B) detached and impartial observation
    (C) vivid language and dramatic images
    (D) presentation of facts in chronological order
    (E) presentation of details in spatial order

11. By calling the landscape "a gray wasteland" (line 41), the author implies that
    (A) the landscape was covered with a blanket of dirty snow
    (B) the landscape was littered with garbage and other waste matter
    (C) the trees were all covered with gray ash
    (D) the sun could not penetrate the forest
    (E) the landscape had been stripped bare and covered in volcanic ash

It was Paul's afternoon to appear before the faculty of the Pittsburgh High School to account for his various misdemeanors. He had been suspended a week ago, and his father had called the Principal's office and confessed his perplexity about his son. Paul entered the faculty room suave and smiling. His clothes were a trifle outgrown, and the tan velvet on the collar of his open overcoat was frayed and worn; but for all that there was something of the dandy about him, and he wore an opal pin in his neatly knotted black four-in-hand, and a red carnation in his buttonhole. This latter adornment the faculty somehow felt was not properly significant of the contrite spirit befitting a boy under the ban of suspension.

Paul was tall for his age and very thin, with high, cramped shoulders and a narrow chest. His eyes were remarkable for a certain hysterical brilliancy, and he

continually used them in a conscious, theatrical sort of way, peculiarly offensive in a boy. The pupils were abnormally large, as though he were addicted to belladonna, but there was a glassy glitter about them which that drug does not produce.

When questioned by the Principal as to why he was there Paul stated, politely enough, that he wanted to come back to school. This was a lie, but Paul was quite accustomed to lying; found it, indeed, indispensable for overcoming friction. His teachers were asked to state their respective charges against him, which they did with such a rancor and aggrievedness as evinced that this was not a usual case. Disorder and impertinence were among the offenses named, yet each of his instructors felt that it was scarcely possible to put into words the real cause of the trouble, which lay in a sort of hysterically defiant manner of the boy's; in the contempt which they all knew he felt for them, and which he seemingly made not the least effort to conceal. Once, when he had been making a synopsis of a paragraph at the blackboard, his English teacher had stepped to his side and attempted to guide his hand. Paul had started back with a shudder and thrust his hands violently behind him. The astonished woman could scarcely have been more hurt and embarrassed had he struck at her. The insult was so involuntary and definitely personal as to be unforgettable. In one way and another he had made all his teachers, men and women alike, conscious of the same feeling of physical aversion. In one class he habitually sat with his hand shading his eyes; in another he always looked out of the window during the recitation; in another he made a running commentary on the lecture, with humorous intention.

—Willa Cather from "Paul's Case: A Study in Temperament"

12. This passage can best be characterized as
    (A) an amusing story about a high school escapade
    (B) a fond remembrance of the narrator's youth
    (C) a penetrating examination of a young man's character
    (D) a polite appeal for forgiveness
    (E) an astute description of the relationship between a father and son

**GO ON TO THE NEXT PAGE.**

13. In line 9–10, the expression "there was something of the dandy about him" means that Paul
    (A) was afraid of appearing before the faculty
    (B) was in need of new clothes
    (C) did not care how he looked
    (D) paid great attention to his clothes
    (E) was hard on his clothes

14. The red carnation in Paul's buttonhole in lines 11–12 made the faculty feel that Paul
    (A) did not take his suspension seriously enough
    (B) did not really want to come back to school
    (C) was trying to impress the principal
    (D) thought he should be forgiven
    (E) was sincere in his desire to improve his behavior

15. In the eyes of the faculty, Paul's most serious offense was his
    (A) insulting remarks made in class
    (B) inability to control his temper
    (C) failure to complete his assignments
    (D) obvious contempt for his teachers
    (E) lack of attention in class

16. Which adjective best describes Paul?
    (A) contrite
    (B) funny
    (C) defiant
    (D) violent
    (E) embarrassed

17. As used in line 30, the word "rancor" means
    (A) turmoil
    (B) bitterness
    (C) remorse
    (D) resistance
    (E) dismay

18. In lines 41–42, Paul shuddered and threw his hands behind him because
    (A) his teacher had touched his hand
    (B) he could not answer the teacher's question
    (C) his teacher had hurt him
    (D) he was afraid of the teacher
    (E) he wanted to strike the teacher

The Homestead Act of 1862 has been called one the most important pieces of legislation in the history of the United States. Designed to spur Western migration, the Homestead Act culminated a twenty-year battle to distribute public lands to citizens willing to farm. Opposition to the Act came from Northern businessmen, who feared it would lower property values and reduce the supply of cheap labor, and from Southerners, who feared homesteaders would add to the voices calling for the abolition of slavery. With Southerners out of the picture in 1862, the legislation finally passed and was signed into law by Abraham Lincoln. Under this Act, 270 million acres, or 10% of the area of the United States, was claimed and settled.

A homesteader had only to be the head of a household and at least 21 years of age to claim a 160-acre parcel of land. Settlers from all walks of life, including newly arrived immigrants, farmers without land of their own from the East, single women and former slaves came to meet the challenge of "proving up" and keeping this "free land." Homesteaders were required to live on the land, build a home, make improvements, and farm for 5 years before they were eligible to "prove up." A total filing fee of $18 was the only money required, but settlers paid a big price in sacrifice and hard work.

People interested in Homesteading first had to file their intentions at the nearest Land Office where they paid a fee of $10 to claim the land temporarily, and a $2 commission to the land agent. The homesteader then returned to the land to begin the process of building a home and farming the land, both requirements for "proving up." After five years of living on and working the land, the homesteader had to find two neighbors or friends willing to vouch for the truth of his or her statements about the land's improvements and sign the "proof" document. With the successful completion of this final form and payment of a $6 fee, the homesteader received the patent (or deed) for the land, signed with the name of the current President of the United States.

**GO ON TO THE NEXT PAGE.**

19. The primary purpose of the passage is to
    (A) discuss the reasons for westward expansion in the United States
    (B) explain the provisions of the Homestead Act
    (C) point out the difficulties of homesteading
    (D) argue in favor of extending the Homestead Act
    (E) explain the importance of "proving up"

20. In line 28, "file" most nearly means
    (A) arrange in order
    (B) classify
    (C) sharpen
    (D) record
    (E) finish

21. In order to acquire land under the Homestead Act, claimants had to meet all of the following conditions EXCEPT:
    (A) be a head of household
    (B) be at least 21 years of age
    (C) be a native-born U.S. citizen
    (D) farm the land for five years
    (E) build a house on the land

22. How much U.S. land was transferred to individuals under the terms of the Homestead Act?
    (A) 160 acres per person
    (B) 320 acres per family
    (C) 1.6 million acres
    (D) 270 million acres
    (E) 30% of all U.S. land

23. The author calls the Homestead Act one of the most important pieces of legislation in United States history because it
    (A) helped settle the West
    (B) provided cheap labor
    (C) lowered land values
    (D) helped to end slavery
    (E) passed after a twenty year battle

    Manatees and dugongs, also known as sea cows, belong to the scientific order Sirenia. In ancient mythology, "siren" was a term used for monsters or sea nymphs who lured sailors and their ships to
5   treacherous rocks and shipwreck with mesmerizing songs. Throughout history, sailors sometimes thought they were seeing mermaids when they were probably seeing manatees or dugongs. With a little

10  imagination, manatees have an uncanny resemblance to human form that could only increase after long months at sea. In fact, manatees and dugongs may have helped to perpetuate the myth of mermaids. Like the mythological creatures for which they were named, all sirenians living on earth today are vulner-
15  able to extinction

    Manatees and dugongs are the only completely aquatic mammals that are herbivores. Unlike the other marine mammals (dolphins, whales, seals, sea lions, sea otters, walruses, and polar bears) sire-
20  nians eat only seagrasses and other aquatic vegetation. Unlike other marine mammals, sirenians have an extremely low metabolism and zero tolerance for cold water. Like dolphins and whales, manatees and dugongs are totally aquatic mammals that never leave
25  the water—not even to give birth. The combination of these factors means that sirenians are restricted to warm shallow coastal waters, estuaries, and rivers, with healthy ecosystems that support large amounts of seagrass and other vegetation.

30      The average adult manatee is about three meters (9.8 feet) long and weighs between 362–544 kilograms (800–1,200 pounds). It is estimated that a manatee can eat about 10–15% of its body weight in vegetation daily. So, for example, a 453-kilogram (1,000-
35  pound) manatee would probably eat between 45–68 kilograms (100–150 pounds) of sea grass and water hyacinths a day!

24. Paragraph 1 is primarily concerned with
    (A) the origin of the scientific classification Sirenia
    (B) the similarities between manatees and mermaids
    (C) how manatees cause shipwrecks
    (D) a comparison between manatees and dugongs
    (E) the imagination of manatees

25. As used in line 5–6, "mesmerizing" most nearly means
    (A) discordant
    (B) mellifluous
    (C) high pitched
    (D) hypnotic
    (E) mysterious

**GO ON TO THE NEXT PAGE.**

26. The passage supports which of the following conclusions?
    (A) Manatees are like other marine mammals in their diet.
    (B) All sirenians are endangered.
    (C) Because of their low metabolism, manatees tolerate cold water well.
    (D) Mermaids were classified as sirenians.
    (E) Manatees leave the water only to give birth.

27. The author develops paragraph 2 by presenting
    (A) two sides of an issue
    (B) a thesis followed by specific examples
    (C) a description of similarities and differences
    (D) an opinion and reasons why it is held
    (E) a hypothesis and data to prove it

28. According to the passage, manatees prefer the shallow coastal waters of Florida because of which of the following?
    I.   availability of vegetation
    II.  favorable water temperatures
    III. safety

    (A) I only
    (B) II only
    (C) III only
    (D) I and II only
    (E) I, II, and III

29. Which of the following represents the number of pounds of food an average adult manatee consumes in a day?
    (A) 10–15
    (B) 100–150
    (C) 352–544
    (D) 800–1,000
    (E) 1,000–1,200

---

Day had broken cold and gray, exceedingly cold and gray, when the man turned aside from the main Yukon trail and climbed the high earth-bank, where a dim and little-traveled trail led eastward through
5   the fat spruce timberland. It was a steep bank, and he paused for breath at the top, excusing the act to himself by looking at his watch. It was nine o'clock. There was no sun nor hint of sun, though there was not a cloud in the sky. It was a clear day, and yet

---

10  there seemed an intangible pall over the face of things, a subtle gloom that made the day dark, and that was due to the absence of sun. This fact did not worry the man.

As he turned to go on, he spat speculatively.
15  There was a sharp, explosive crackle that startled him. He spat again. And again, in the air, before it could fall to the snow, the spittle crackled. He knew that at fifty below spittle crackled on the snow, but this spittle had crackled in the air. Undoubtedly it
20  was colder than fifty below—how much colder he did not know. But the temperature did not matter. He was bound for the old claim on the left fork of Henderson Creek, where the boys were already. They had come over across the divide from the Indian Creek country,
25  while he had come the roundabout way to take a look at the possibilities of getting out logs in the spring from the islands in the Yukon.

At the man's heels trotted a dog, a big native husky, the proper wolf-dog, gray-coated and with-
30  out any visible or temperamental difference from its brother, the wild wolf. The animal was depressed by the tremendous cold. It knew that it was no time for travelling. Its instinct told it a truer tale than was told to the man by the man's judgment. It
35  experienced a vague but menacing apprehension that subdued it and made it slink along at the man's heels, and that made it question eagerly every unwonted movement of the man as if expecting him to go into camp or to seek shelter somewhere
40  and build a fire.
                        —Jack London from "To Build a Fire"

30. In the first paragraph the author establishes a mood of
    (A) promise
    (B) serenity
    (C) hostility
    (D) foreboding
    (E) regret

31. As used in line 1, "broken" most nearly means
    (A) dawned
    (B) separated
    (C) shattered
    (D) interrupted
    (E) cracked

**GO ON TO THE NEXT PAGE.**

32. The statement that "It was a steep bank, and he paused for breath at the top, excusing the act to himself by looking at his watch," (lines 5–7) suggests that the man
    (A) was worried about running late
    (B) was not accustomed to hiking in the Yukon
    (C) was disoriented by the extreme cold
    (D) had traveled farther than he thought
    (E) expected to see the sun

33. The discussion of spitting into the air (lines 14–19) serves primarily to suggest
    (A) the strangeness of the landscape
    (B) the severity of the cold
    (C) the courage of the man
    (D) the frustration of the dog
    (E) the gloom of the day

34. In lines 15–16, the author includes the detail that the sharp, explosive crackle "startled him" primarily to emphasize
    (A) the man's fragile state of mind
    (B) how eerily quiet it had become
    (C) that the temperature was dropping
    (D) the danger the man was in
    (E) that it was colder than the man thought

35. Which word best describes how the author regards the man in the story?
    (A) clever
    (B) cautious
    (C) foolish
    (D) ambitious
    (E) ruthless

36. With which of the following statements is the author most likely to agree?
    (A) The man is right to press on.
    (B) The dog is unfazed by the cold.
    (C) The man is jealous of the dog.
    (D) The dog is wiser than the man.
    (E) The sun will make the day more bearable.

Harmful algal blooms, or HABs, occur when colonies of algae—simple plants that live in the sea and freshwater—grow out of control. Algal blooms can produce toxic effects, resulting in illness and death
5   among fish, shellfish, marine mammals, and birds. The human illnesses caused by HABs, though rare, can be debilitating or even fatal.

While many people call these blooms "red tides," scientists prefer the term *harmful algal bloom*. One
10  of the best known HABs in the nation occurs nearly every summer along Florida's Gulf Coast. This bloom, like many HABs, is caused by microscopic algae that produce toxins that kill fish and make shellfish dangerous to eat. The toxins may also make
15  the surrounding air difficult to breathe. As the name suggests, the bloom of algae often turns the water red.

HABs have been reported in every U.S. coastal state, and their occurrence may be on the rise. HABs are a national concern because they affect not only
20  the health of people and marine ecosystems, but also the "health" of local and regional economies.

But not all algal blooms are harmful. Most blooms, in fact, are beneficial because the tiny plants are food for animals in the ocean. In fact, they are the
25  major source of energy that fuels the ocean food web.

A small percentage of algae, however, produce powerful toxins that can kill fish, shellfish, mammals, and birds, and may directly or indirectly cause illness in people. HABs also include blooms of nontoxic
30  species that have harmful effects on marine ecosystems. For example, when masses of algae die and decompose, the decaying process can deplete oxygen in the water, causing the water to become so low in oxygen that animals either leave the area or die.
    —National Oceanic and Atmospheric Agency (NOAA)

37. In line 4, "toxic" means most nearly
    (A) wholesome
    (B) uncommon
    (C) poisonous
    (D) harmless
    (E) murderous

38. Based on the text, which of the following statements is true?
    (A) All algal blooms are dangerous because they kill fish, sea mammals, and birds.
    (B) Most algal blooms are helpful because they provide food for ocean animals.
    (C) Algal blooms affect only the Florida's Gulf Coast during the hottest days of summer.
    (D) When algal blooms die, they may produce dangerous levels of oxygen in the ocean.
    (E) Algal blooms do not affect local and state economies in any significant way.

**GO ON TO THE NEXT PAGE.**

39. The author's attitude toward the subject of algal blooms is best described as
    (A) disapproving
    (B) persuasive
    (C) indifferent
    (D) objective
    (E) uninformative

40. According to the text, where do most algal blooms occur?
    (A) in all states that have ocean coastlines
    (B) off the Gulf Coast of Florida
    (C) in politically conservative red states
    (D) in areas where summer temperatures are high
    (E) in interior lakes and ocean coastal areas

**STOP!**
If you finish before time is up, check your work on this section only.

## SECTION 3

Time: 30 Minutes
60 Questions

This section includes two different types of questions: synonyms and analogies. There are directions and a sample question for each question type.

**Directions:** Each of the following questions consists of a word in capital letters followed by five words or phrases. Select the one word or phrase that means most nearly the same as the word in capital letters.

Sample Question:

> ESSENTIAL:
> (A) dire
> (B) confusing
> (C) vital
> (D) expert
> (E) honest
>
> Correct Answer: C

1. SHAME:
   - (A) grief
   - (B) anguish
   - (C) suffering
   - (D) remorse
   - (E) humiliation

2. TELL:
   - (A) censure
   - (B) preclude
   - (C) dissuade
   - (D) divulge
   - (E) contrive

3. CONCISE:
   - (A) clever
   - (B) brief
   - (C) small
   - (D) exclusive
   - (E) subdued

4. INQUIRY:
   - (A) testimony
   - (B) subpoena
   - (C) investigation
   - (D) verification
   - (E) statement

5. ATTITUDE:
   - (A) disposition
   - (B) dissension
   - (C) charisma
   - (D) exemption
   - (E) dispensation

6. TEDIOUSLY:
   - (A) tremendously
   - (B) delicately
   - (C) relentlessly
   - (D) fearlessly
   - (E) tiresomely

**GO ON TO THE NEXT PAGE.**

7. DEPLETE:
   (A) deride
   (B) reduce
   (C) deprecate
   (D) discredit
   (E) elicit

8. CAUTIOUS:
   (A) discreet
   (B) anxious
   (C) startled
   (D) scared
   (E) stricken

9. SPARSE:
   (A) spatial
   (B) thin
   (C) spastic
   (D) vivid
   (E) lifeless

10. AVERSION:
    (A) model
    (B) portrayal
    (C) dislike
    (D) history
    (E) arrangement

11. BENEFACTOR:
    (A) composer
    (B) contributor
    (C) agent
    (D) connoisseur
    (E) demagogue

12. DORMANT:
    (A) inactive
    (B) restful
    (C) covert
    (D) durable
    (E) arbitrary

13. MALCONTENT:
    (A) sickly
    (B) troublesome
    (C) dissatisfied
    (D) malicious
    (E) foolhardy

14. SATISFY:
    (A) please
    (B) appease
    (C) consume
    (D) imbibe
    (E) dissipate

15. MERIT:
    (A) deserve
    (B) require
    (C) necessitate
    (D) pardon
    (E) base

16. PROMINENT:
    (A) excellent
    (B) accomplished
    (C) admirable
    (D) extensive
    (E) conspicuous

17. OBJECTIVE:
    (A) interest
    (B) forbearance
    (C) observation
    (D) concern
    (E) intention

18. BREACH:
    (A) admission
    (B) representation
    (C) felony
    (D) violation
    (E) security

19. LAMENT:
    (A) remark
    (B) acknowledge
    (C) regret
    (D) explain
    (E) declare

20. RECTIFY:
    (A) start
    (B) give
    (C) examine
    (D) fix
    (E) advance

**GO ON TO THE NEXT PAGE.**

21. SUBMERGE:
    (A) submit
    (B) subscribe
    (C) immerse
    (D) subsist
    (E) clarify

22. PERMANENT:
    (A) historical
    (B) indelible
    (C) delectable
    (D) permissive
    (E) conspicuous

23. ABYSS:
    (A) island
    (B) chamber
    (C) niche
    (D) hole
    (E) division

24. ORDER:
    (A) imbroglio
    (B) judgment
    (C) decree
    (D) appraisal
    (E) verdict

25. SHREWD:
    (A) poignant
    (B) astute
    (C) copious
    (D) specious
    (E) tactile

26. CLANDESTINE:
    (A) secret
    (B) criminal
    (C) familiar
    (D) apprehensive
    (E) disgraceful

27. COERCE:
    (A) twist
    (B) mislead
    (C) perceive
    (D) chastise
    (E) compel

28. DILATE:
    (A) embellish
    (B) impede
    (C) deflate
    (D) enlarge
    (E) prevent

29. INANE:
    (A) ridiculous
    (B) deficient
    (C) practical
    (D) cumbersome
    (E) indulgent

30. PLETHORA:
    (A) quandary
    (B) resonance
    (C) excess
    (D) separation
    (E) veneer

**GO ON TO THE NEXT PAGE.**

**Directions:** The questions that follow ask you to find relationships between words. For each question select the answer choice that best completes the meaning of the sentence.

Sample Question:

Swim is to pool as
(A)   fork is to plate
(B)   sweep is to broom
(C)   clean is to kitchen
(D)   sleep is to bed
(E)   trot is to horse

Correct Answer: D
Choice D is correct because a pool is a place to swim just as a bed is a place to sleep.

31. Insult is to compliment as
    (A)   puzzle is to vex
    (B)   difficulty is to enjoy
    (C)   brood is to worry
    (D)   assure is to console
    (E)   please is to annoy

32. Wolf is to pack as
    (A)   lamb is to sheep
    (B)   kitten is to mother
    (C)   goose is to gaggle
    (D)   school is to fish
    (E)   cattle is to herd

33. Announce is to inform as
    (A)   dig is to hole
    (B)   fold is to box
    (C)   finger is to point
    (D)   wrap is to conceal
    (E)   water is to extinguish

34. Shovel is to dig as
    (A)   launch is to rocket
    (B)   blade is to cut
    (C)   sneeze is to cold
    (D)   eye is to blink
    (E)   bowling is to ball

35. Liter is to volume as
    (A)   gram is to mass
    (B)   ounce is to pound
    (C)   centimeter is to kilometer
    (D)   inches is to ruler
    (E)   radius is to diameter

36. Tourist is to sightseeing as analyst is to
    (A)   traveling
    (B)   curing
    (C)   ruins
    (D)   science
    (E)   examining

37. Whisper is to scream as
    (A)   holler is to yell
    (B)   calm is to water
    (C)   pester is to bother
    (D)   glance is to stare
    (E)   carry is to gather

38. Rock is to quarry as
    (A)   rust is to iron
    (B)   coal is to mine
    (C)   pan is to gold
    (D)   metal is to alloy
    (E)   water is to ice

39. Spider is to web as
    (A)   teller is to bank
    (B)   bird is to nest
    (C)   horse is to track
    (D)   pasture is to cow
    (E)   school is to student

40. Seat is to steering wheel as handle bar is to
    (A)   hand
    (B)   steer
    (C)   rider
    (D)   bike
    (E)   brake

**GO ON TO THE NEXT PAGE.**

41. Drive is to street as
    (A) walk is to path
    (B) run is to school
    (C) eat is to snack
    (D) fly is to bird
    (E) study is to book

42. Mile is to distance as minute is to
    (A) rate
    (B) quickness
    (C) time
    (D) hour
    (E) speed

43. Kick is to foot as
    (A) back is to float
    (B) swim is to arms
    (C) chew is to mouth
    (D) grind is to mill
    (E) content is to book

44. Feed is to nourish as
    (A) trap is to bury
    (B) giggle is to laugh
    (C) travel is to skate
    (D) water is to hydrate
    (E) throw is to fetch

45. Plum is to prune as
    (A) pear is to pineapple
    (B) hen is to rooster
    (C) cream is to milk
    (D) corn is to pop
    (E) grape is to raisin

46. Maple tree is to syrup as
    (A) coffee is to bean
    (B) orange is to juice
    (C) seed is to grass
    (D) chip is to chocolate
    (E) wheat is to bread

47. Envious is to jealous as
    (A) melancholic is to mournful
    (B) distressed is to dismayed
    (C) entertained is to amused
    (D) happy is to joyful
    (E) sorry is to regretful

48. Knitter is to needles as
    (A) teacher is to test
    (B) diver is to ocean
    (C) chef is to apron
    (D) singer is to recording
    (E) boxer is to gloves

49. Claw is to cat as
    (A) tail is to donkey
    (B) shell is to turtle
    (C) fang is to snake
    (D) talon is to eagle
    (E) hand is to clock

50. Surprise is to startle
    (A) choose is to grab
    (B) inflate is to breathe
    (C) destroy is to ruin
    (D) need is to want
    (E) mix is to bake

51. Scene is to play as
    (A) stage is to screen
    (B) projector is to movie
    (C) car is to engine
    (D) chapter is to book
    (E) award is to actor

52. Aquatic is to water as terrestrial is to
    (A) outer space
    (B) island
    (C) rocket
    (D) land
    (E) planet

53. Passenger is to bus as
    (A) cargo is to ship
    (B) pilot is to plane
    (C) bicycle is to motorist
    (D) motor is to boat
    (E) freight is to rail

54. Seed is to rind as
    (A) socket is to plug
    (B) bark is to branch
    (C) spark is to light
    (D) knob is to door
    (E) propeller is to plane

**GO ON TO THE NEXT PAGE.**

55. Malign is to disparage as
    (A) elate is to enjoy
    (B) irritate is to bother
    (C) emulate is to deprecate
    (D) ask is to say
    (E) ponder is to worry

56. Shoreline is to ocean as
    (A) horizon is to sunrise
    (B) wave is to water
    (C) lake is to river
    (D) current is to tide
    (E) border is to country

57. Shark is to hammerhead as bear is to
    (A) arctic
    (B) cub
    (C) moose
    (D) polar
    (E) paw

58. Sociologist is to behavior as
    (A) ballerina is to slipper
    (B) writer is to computer
    (C) zoologist is to tree
    (D) chef is to meal
    (E) archaeologist is to artifact

59. Hold is to grip as
    (A) jump is to bounce
    (B) jog is to sprint
    (C) drive is to fast
    (D) speak is to tell
    (E) talk is to speech

60. Player is to team as
    (A) guide is to tour
    (B) membership is to club
    (C) actor is to cast
    (D) herd is to pack
    (E) principal is to school

**STOP!**
If you finish before time is up, check your work on this section only.

**Directions:** For each of the following questions, mark the letter of your choice on the answer sheet.

1. If $16 \div 4 \times \underline{\quad} = 5 \times 8 - 16$, then $\underline{\quad} =$
   (A) 2
   (B) 3
   (C) 4
   (D) 5
   (E) 6

2. $42 \div 7 \times 8 \times 5$ is equal to the product of 12 and
   (A) 16
   (B) 20
   (C) 24
   (D) 28
   (E) 32

3. Which of the following is NOT equal to a whole number?
   (A) $\dfrac{30}{5}$

   (B) $4 \times \dfrac{12}{16}$

   (C) $16 \div \dfrac{1}{16}$

   (D) $\dfrac{5}{9} \times 8$

   (E) $10.2 + 12.8$

4. $46\frac{3}{4}\% =$
   (A) 467.5
   (B) 46.75
   (C) 4.675
   (D) 0.4675
   (E) 0.04675

5. It costs $m$ dollars to buy 48 notepads. At the same rate, how many dollars will it cost to buy 30 notepads?
   (A) $\dfrac{m}{8}$

   (B) $\dfrac{5m}{8}$

   (C) $5m$

   (D) $\dfrac{8m}{5}$

   (E) $10m$

6. If $\frac{3}{7}$ of a number is 18, then $\frac{1}{2}$ of the same number is
   (A) 32
   (B) 30
   (C) 28
   (D) 24
   (E) 21

7. 60 is approximately what percent of 90?
   (A) 30%
   (B) 33%
   (C) 45%
   (D) 67%
   (E) 70%

8. $\sqrt[3]{216} =$
   (A) 3
   (B) 5
   (C) 6
   (D) 11
   (E) 12

**GO ON TO THE NEXT PAGE.**

9. In the following figure, if ∠6 measures 90°, what is the measure of ∠1?

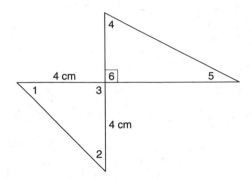

(A) 25°
(B) 35°
(C) 45°
(D) 55°
(E) 58°

10. Each edge of a cube measures 8 cm. What is the volume?
(A) 64 cm³
(B) 176 cm³
(C) 384 cm³
(D) 420 cm³
(E) 512 cm³

11. $-10 - (-5 - 4) =$
(A) $-4$
(B) $-3$
(C) $-1$
(D) 1
(E) 3

12. $^3/_4 + {}^1/_2 + {}^2/_3 - {}^5/_6 =$
(A) $1\dfrac{1}{12}$
(B) $1\dfrac{1}{3}$
(C) $1\dfrac{5}{6}$
(D) $2\dfrac{1}{6}$
(E) $2\dfrac{1}{4}$

13. Karen is driving to a town 175 miles away. If she drives at a steady speed of 50 miles per hour, how long will the trip take?
(A) 2 hours 50 minutes
(B) 3 hours
(C) 3 hours 10 minutes
(D) 3 hours 30 minutes
(E) 3 hours 50 minutes

14. The number of students who won awards at the science fair this year was 2 more than 3 times as many as last year. If 20 students won awards this year, how many won awards last year?
(A) 18
(B) 15
(C) 12
(D) 8
(E) 6

15. If $3.4a + 8.7a = 38.72$, $a =$
(A) 2.9
(B) 3.2
(C) 3.5
(D) 3.9
(E) 4.6

16. 18 is what percent of 144?
(A) 8%
(B) 12.5%
(C) 14%
(D) 16.75%
(E) 22%

17. When added, the sum of three consecutive integers is 18. What is the greatest number?
(A) 5
(B) 6
(C) 7
(D) 8
(E) 9

18. Which value of $x$ satisfies the inequality $2/5 + x < 1$?
(A) $\dfrac{2}{3}$
(B) $\dfrac{3}{4}$
(C) $\dfrac{1}{2}$
(D) $\dfrac{5}{7}$
(E) $\dfrac{7}{9}$

**GO ON TO THE NEXT PAGE.**

19. A truck travels 126 miles in 3 hours. At that speed, in how many hours will the truck reach its destination, 924 miles away?
    (A)  22 hours
    (B)  24 hours
    (C)  25.5 hours
    (D)  28 hours
    (E)  30.5 hours

20. What is $3.2 \times 10^3$?
    (A)  32
    (B)  320
    (C)  3,200
    (D)  32,000
    (E)  320,000

21. In a dresser drawer there are 3 pairs of white socks, 5 pairs of black socks, and 4 pairs of blue socks. If you pick a pair without looking, what are the chances that you will pick a blue pair?
    (A)  $\dfrac{1}{12}$
    (B)  $\dfrac{1}{6}$
    (C)  $\dfrac{1}{4}$
    (D)  $\dfrac{1}{3}$
    (E)  $\dfrac{7}{12}$

22. What is the least common multiple of 3, 4, and 18?
    (A)  18
    (B)  24
    (C)  36
    (D)  54
    (E)  72

23. What is the greatest common factor of 16, 24, 96, and 120?
    (A)  2
    (B)  4
    (C)  8
    (D)  12
    (E)  36

24. What is the length line segment $AC$ in triangle $ABC$?

    (A)  4
    (B)  $4\sqrt{2}$
    (C)  $4\sqrt{3}$
    (D)  8
    (E)  $8\sqrt{2}$

25. What is the next term in this sequence?
    2, 3, 5, 9, ...
    (A)  7
    (B)  11
    (C)  13
    (D)  15
    (E)  17

**STOP!**
If you finish before time is up, check your work on this section only.

## SECTION 5
Time: 25 Minutes

Read the topics below and choose the one that interests you the most. Fill in the circle for your chosen idea. Plan and write your essay or story on the paper provided.

(A) Every cloud has a silver lining.

Do you agree or disagree with the topic statement? Support your position with examples from your own experience, the experience of others, current events, history, or literature.

(B) Sometimes even best friends disagree. Write a story that uses this as the first sentence.

_____

_____

_____

_____

_____

_____

_____

_____

_____

_____

_____

_____

_____

_____

## SSAT Practice Test II,

## Answer Key

### Section 1 Quantitative I

| | | | | | | | |
|---|---|---|---|---|---|---|---|
| 1. | D | 10. | A | 19. | A |
| 2. | C | 11. | B | 20. | B |
| 3. | B | 12. | C | 21. | D |
| 4. | C | 13. | E | 22. | A |
| 5. | C | 14. | D | 23. | B |
| 6. | B | 15. | B | 24. | C |
| 7. | A | 16. | C | 25. | C |
| 8. | E | 17. | C | | |
| 9. | E | 18. | E | | |

### Section 2 Reading Comprehension

| | | | | | | | |
|---|---|---|---|---|---|---|---|
| 1. | C | 15. | D | 29. | B |
| 2. | B | 16. | C | 30. | D |
| 3. | D | 17. | B | 31. | A |
| 4. | A | 18. | A | 32. | B |
| 5. | E | 19. | B | 33. | B |
| 6. | B | 20. | D | 34. | E |
| 7. | C | 21. | C | 35. | C |
| 8. | D | 22. | D | 36. | D |
| 9. | B | 23. | A | 37. | C |
| 10. | C | 24. | A | 38. | B |
| 11. | E | 25. | D | 39. | D |
| 12. | C | 26. | B | 40. | A |
| 13. | D | 27. | C | | |
| 14. | A | 28. | D | | |

## Section 3 Verbal

| | | | | | |
|---|---|---|---|---|---|
| 1. | E | 21. | C | 41. | A |
| 2. | D | 22. | B | 42. | C |
| 3. | B | 23. | D | 43. | C |
| 4. | C | 24. | C | 44. | D |
| 5. | A | 25. | B | 45. | E |
| 6. | E | 26. | A | 46. | B |
| 7. | B | 27. | E | 47. | A |
| 8. | A | 28. | D | 48. | E |
| 9. | B | 29. | A | 49. | D |
| 10. | C | 30. | C | 50. | C |
| 11. | B | 31. | E | 51. | D |
| 12. | A | 32. | C | 52. | D |
| 13. | C | 33. | D | 53. | A |
| 14. | B | 34. | B | 54. | B |
| 15. | A | 35. | A | 55. | B |
| 16. | E | 36. | E | 56. | E |
| 17. | E | 37. | D | 57. | D |
| 18. | D | 38. | B | 58. | E |
| 19. | C | 39. | B | 59. | B |
| 20. | D | 40. | E | 60. | C |

## Section 4 Quantitative II

| | | | | | |
|---|---|---|---|---|---|
| 1. | E | 10. | E | 19. | A |
| 2. | B | 11. | C | 20. | C |
| 3. | D | 12. | A | 21. | D |
| 4. | D | 13. | D | 22. | C |
| 5. | B | 14. | E | 23. | C |
| 6. | E | 15. | B | 24. | B |
| 7. | D | 16. | B | 25. | E |
| 8. | C | 17. | C | | |
| 9. | C | 18. | C | | |

# Answers and Explanations

## Section 1 Quantitative I

1. **D is correct.** This is a simple addition problem. Add the amounts to get the total of $17.55.

2. **C is correct.** If Jessica has 315 pages of reading and reads 65 pages each day, on Monday she has read 65 pages, on Tuesday she has read 2(65) or 130 pages, on Wednesday she has read 3(65) or 195 pages, and on Thursday she has read 4(65) or 260 pages. On Friday, Jessica would need to read only 55 pages to complete the assignment. Another way to do this is to divide 315 by 65 to get 4.85. If Monday is 1, Tuesday is 2, Wednesday is 3, and Thursday is 4, then Friday would be 5. On Friday Jessica would complete the assignment.

3. **B is correct.** Simple interest problems use the formula $I = prt$ where $I$ is the amount of interest, $p$ is the principal or the amount saved or invested, $r$ is the rate of interest, and $t$ is the amount of time that the interest is accruing. In this problem, you are asked to find the interest, given that the principal is $4,000, the rate of interest is 2%, and the amount of time is 2 years. Substituting this information into the formula, you get $I = 4,000(0.02)(2) = \$160$ in interest.

4. **C is correct.** $2,880 \div 9 = 320$ miles per hour.

5. **C is correct.** By definition, an obtuse angle is one that measures greater than 90° and less than 180°.

6. **B is correct.** Create equations to solve this problem.
   Al = 3(Bill)
   Bill = 2(Charlie)
   Charlie = $12.55
   Solve for Al.
   Substitute what you know into the formulas.
   Bill = 2($12.55)
   Bill = $25.10
   To find Al, substitute what you know about Bill.
   Al = 3($25.10)
   Al = $75.30

7. **A is correct.** In this problem you need to calculate the number of 26-mpg units there are in 858. Do this by dividing 858 by 26.
   $858 \div 26 = 33$ gallons

8. **E is correct.** A right angle measures 90°. If angle 1 measures 65°, then angle 2 must measure 90° − 65° = 25°.

9. **E is correct.** Add the amount of the checks and subtract the total from the current amount in the checking account.
   $12,444.12 − ($8,204.94 + $890.99) = $3,348.19

10. **A is correct.** Create equations to solve this problem.
    Paula = Lindsey + 3
    Lindsey = Dave − 2
    You are told that Paula is 17. Substitute that information into the first equation.
    17 = Lindsey + 3
    Lindsey = 14
    Substitute that into the second equation.
    14 = Dave − 2
    Dave = 16

11. **B is correct.** To calculate 14% of 7,000, multiply 7,000 by 0.14.
    $7,000(0.14) = 980$ votes

12. **C is correct.** When two straight lines intersect as shown, they form opposite vertical angles. Those angles have the same measure, so if angle 2 measures 45°, then angle 4 must also measure 45°.

13. **E is correct.**
$$1/4 x = 12$$
$$x = 48$$
$$1/6 x = 8$$

14. **D is correct.** In a parallelogram, opposite sides are parallel and opposite angles are equal. However, adjacent sides are not necessarily the same length.

15. **B is correct.** The area of the room is $15 \times 18 = 270$ ft². One square yard = 9 square feet, so 270 ft² ÷ 9 = 30 yd².

16. **C is correct.** An equilateral triangle has three equal angles. A triangle has a total of 180°, so each angle must be $180° ÷ 3 = 60°$.

17. **C is correct.** According to the graph, only 150 travel books were checked out during the month. This was the fewest for any of the categories listed.

18. **E is correct.** $8 + 6 + 4 = 18$; $9 + 3 = 12$; and $18 - 12 = 6$.

19. **A is correct.** $2 \times 3 \times 5 \times 6 = 180$; $180 ÷ 30 = 6$.

20. **B is correct.** $20/5 = 4$; $6 ÷ 1/6 = 6 \times 6/1 = 36$; $3/5 \times 10 = 30/5 = 6$; $7 + 5 = 12$. However, $5 \times 3/4 = 15/4 = 3 3/4$, which is not a whole number.

21. **D is correct.** $4 3/10 \% = 0.043$.

22. **A is correct.** It costs $d$ dollars to buy 6 chocolate bars. Since $15 = 2.5 \times 6$, it will cost $2.5d$ dollars to buy 15 chocolate bars.

23. **B is correct.** The angles in a triangle total 180°. The two given angles measure $55° + 65° = 120°$. Thus the remaining angle must measure $180° - 120° = 60°$.

24. **C is correct.** There are $10 + 15 = 25$ marbles in the bag. If you pick one without looking, your chances of picking a white marble are $10/25$ or $2/5$.

25. **C is correct.** $3/4 - 5/12 = 9/12 \angle 5/12 = 4/12 = 1/3$.

## Section 2 Reading Comprehension

1. **C is correct.** As she says in lines 17–18, "I have been trying to get before you business people to tell you what I am doing." Choice A can be eliminated because Madam Walker was not trying to demonstrate her products to the members of the league, but merely to make them aware of what she was doing and how well she was doing. Choice B is wrong because Madam Walker was addressing her remarks to the entire league, not just to Booker T. Washington. Choices D and E are wrong because there is no support in the passage for either choice.

2. **B is correct.** Madam Walker came to the podium uninvited and boasted of her business success. She tells how she came from "the cotton fields" to the "wash-tub" to the "cook kitchen" and finally to head of a thriving business. She says "I am not ashamed of my past; I am not ashamed of my humble beginning." Clearly, she is proud of her accomplishments.

3. **D is correct.** The reactions of the audience are indicated in parentheses throughout the speech. The fact that the audience reacted with applause, laughter, and prolonged applause indicates that their reaction was

favorable. It is unlikely that the audience would applaud and laugh if they were indifferent (choice A), angry (choice B), sad (choice C), or critical (choice E) of the speech.

4. **A is correct**. Walker uses the reference to her promotions from farm laborer, to laundress, to cook to show just how far she has come to get to her current position as head of a company that has made more than $63,000 (a great deal of money in 1912) in only seven years.

5. **E is correct.** Madam Walker says, "I am not ashamed of my past; I am not ashamed of my humble beginning. Don't think that because you have to go down in the wash-tub that you are any less a lady!" By this she means that hard work, like washing and scrubbing, is nothing to be ashamed of. Nor does it diminish a woman's status as a lady who is entitled to be treated with respect.

6. **B is correct**. The entire passage discusses the 1980 eruption of Mount St. Helens. The information provided is specific to a particular volcano, so choices A and D are incorrect. The passage does not tell readers what to do when a volcano erupts, nor does it appeal for action to protect the environment, so choices C and E are wrong.

7. **C is correct**. A 123-year slumber means that Mount St. Helens had no eruptions going back 123 years from 1980. That puts the last eruption at 1857. Choice A is wrong because if Mount St. Helens had been "sleeping" for 123 years, it must have been active 123 years ago. Choice B is wrong because there is nothing to support the idea that Mount St. Helens erupts every 123 years. Choice D is wrong because there is no mention of when geologists began keeping records of volcanic eruptions. Choice E is wrong because if Mount St. Helens erupted 123 years ago, it could always erupt again.

8. **D is correct.** *Rising* is used in the following sentence: "Heat from a rising plume of volcanic ash melted glacial ice creating cement-like slurries of rock and ash called mudflows." Each of the answer choices is a possible meaning for *rising*. However, in context, the best meaning is *ascending*.

9. **B is correct.** The passage states that the geologists were not surprised by Mount St. Helens' awakening because they had been studying Mount St. Helens for many years and in 1975 they "published a report predicting Mount St. Helens was the volcano in the lower 48 states most likely to erupt by the end of the century." Thus, the assumptions they had made about Mount St. Helens based on extensive studies of deposits found around the volcano were proving to be correct. Choice A is wrong because the geologists predicted only that Mount St. Helens was the volcano "most likely to erupt by the end of the century." They did not predict when it would erupt, but only that it was most likely to erupt. The passage provides no information to support either choice C or choice D. Choice E describes an event leading up to the actual eruption, but it has nothing to do with why the geologists were not surprised by the volcano's awakening.

10. **C is correct.** The author's use of vivid language is illustrated by such words as "triggered," "blast," "flattened," "scoured," "billowed," and "swept." Examples of dramatic images include these: "In less than three minutes, 230 square miles of forest lay flattened," ". . . concrete-like mudflows that scoured river valleys," "A plume of volcanic ash and pumice billowed out of the volcano reaching a height of 15 miles and transformed day into night."

11. **E is correct.** A wasteland is barren land with no vegetation. The author mentions in lines 23–32 that the landslides flattened the forest and concrete-like mudflows scoured river valleys surrounding the mountain. Choice A is wrong because the landscape was covered in volcanic ash, not snow. Choice B is wrong because a wasteland is barren, not covered in waste matter. Choice C is wrong because the trees had been flattened and swept away. Choice D is wrong because the forest was no longer standing.

12. **C is correct.** The entire passage focuses on Paul's attitude and his demeanor. The red carnation in his buttonhole, the fact that he "was quite accustomed to lying," the contempt he shows for his teachers, all are evidence of the author's penetrating look at the character of the young man in question.

13. **D is correct.** A dandy is a man who is very concerned about his appearance and so pays great attention to his clothes. This description fits Paul who, even though his clothes were a trifle outgrown and the collar of his overcoat was frayed, still wore an opal pin in his necktie and a red carnation in his buttonhole.

14. **A is correct.** The faculty felt that the red carnation "was not properly significant of the contrite spirit befitting a boy under the ban of suspension." His jaunty dress made them feel that Paul was not sufficiently humbled by his suspension or sorry about his actions.

15. **D is correct.** As stated in lines 37–41, the real cause of the trouble "lay in a sort of hysterically defiant manner of the boy's; in the contempt which they all knew he felt for them, and which he seemingly made not the least effort to conceal." The insult mentioned in the passage is not a remark, but rather the way in which Paul "started back with a shudder and thrust his hands violently behind him" when his English teacher tried to guide his hand, so choice A is wrong. There is no mention of Paul's inability to control his temper or failure to complete assignments, so choices B and C are wrong. The passage mentions that Paul looked out the window during recitation, which indicates that he was inattentive in class (choice E), but this offense is minor in comparison to the obvious contempt he displayed toward his teachers.

16. **C is correct.** Paul is described as having a "defiant manner," which means he is impertinent, insolent, or boldly resistant to authority. There is no evidence in the passage that Paul is either *contrite* (remorseful) or *embarrassed* (ashamed), so choices A and E are wrong. He moves his hands violently behind him when the English teacher attempts to guide his hand, but his actions in general cannot be described as violent, so choice D is wrong. He comments on the lecture "with humorous intention," but there is no indication that others find him funny, so choice B is wrong.

17. **B is correct.** As stated in lines 31–33, the teachers stated the charges against Paul with "rancor and aggrievedness." *Rancor* means "bitterness" or "malice." Neither *turmoil*, which means "confusion," nor *resistance*, which means "opposition," makes sense in relation to stating a case, so choices A and D are wrong. *Remorse* (choice C), which means "regret;" and *dismay* (choice E), which means "discouragement" or "despair," do not fit the context of the passage.

18. **A is correct.** This story is presented as an example of the contempt which all the teachers knew Paul felt for them and which he seemed to make no effort to conceal. Paul shuddered and thrust his hands violently behind him when the English teacher attempted to guide his hand as he worked at the blackboard. "The insult was so involuntary and definitely personal as to be unforgettable. In one way and another he had made all his teachers, men and women alike, conscious of the same feeling of physical aversion." Paul's reaction had nothing to do with not being able to answer the question (choice B) or being hurt by the teacher (choice C). Likewise, there is no indication that he was afraid of the teacher (choice D) or that he wanted to strike the teacher (choice E). The passage says only that the teacher "could scarcely have been more hurt and embarrassed had he struck at her."

19. **B is correct.** This informative passage tells about the Homestead Act of 1862, including the provisions of the Act and the part it played in the settling of the American West. Choice A is wrong because the passage focuses on the Homestead Act, not on the settling of the West. Choice C is wrong because, although the passage briefly mentions the hard work and sacrifices of homesteaders, this is not the primary purpose of the entire passage. Choice D is wrong because the passage says nothing about extending the Act, and Choice E is wrong because "proving up" is just one of the provisions of the Homestead Act.

20. **D is correct.** *File* is used in the following sentence: "People interested in Homesteading first had to file their intentions at the nearest Land Office where they paid a fee of $10 to claim the land. . . ." Although each of the choices is a possible meaning for the word *file*, the one that makes sense in the context of this sentence is *record* (choice D).

21. **C is correct.** As stated in paragraph 2, "A homesteader had only to be the head of a household and at least 21 years of age to claim a 160-acre parcel of land." Also, homesteaders were required "to live on the land, build a home, make improvements, and farm for 5 years before they were eligible to 'prove up.' " There is no mention of settlers having to be native-born citizens. In fact, the passage specifically mentions "newly arrived immigrants" as would-be homesteaders.

22. **D is correct.** As stated in paragraph 1, "Under this Act, 270 million acres, or 10% of the area of the United States, was claimed and settled." Choice A is wrong because each homesteader could claim a 160-acre parcel of land, but that does not mean that every person was entitled to 160 acres of land. Choice E is wrong because the passage states that 10 percent, not 30 percent, of all U.S. lands passed into the hands of individuals.

23. **A is correct.** The Homestead Act was designed "to spur Western migration." As a result of this Act, "270 million acres, or 10% of the area of the United States, was claimed and settled." Thus the Act served its purpose of helping settle the West.

24. **A is correct.** The first paragraph tells how manatees and dugongs came to be called sirenians because of their resemblance to the sirens, or sea nymphs, of Greek mythology. Choice B is wrong because, although the passage mentions that sailors—particularly those who have spent many months at sea—may have mistaken a manatee for a mermaid, it does not provide specific similarities between manatees and mermaids. Choice C is wrong because it was the sirens of mythology who are said to have caused shipwrecks. Choice D is wrong because the passage does not compare manatees and dugongs, except to say that both are sirenians. Choice E is wrong because it is the observer of the manatee, not the manatee itself, who might imagine that the manatee looks like a mermaid.

25. **D is correct.** The second sentence of the passage tells how the sirens "lured sailors and their ships to treacherous rocks and shipwreck with mesmerizing songs." *Mesmerizing* means "captivating," "spellbinding," or "hypnotic."

26. **B is correct.** The last sentence of paragraph 1 ("Like the mythological creatures for which they were named, all sirenians living on earth today are vulnerable to extinction.") supports the idea that all sirenians are endangered. Information in the passage contradicts each of the other answer choices.

27. **C is correct.** Lines 17–27 ("Unlike . . . birth.") of the passage are devoted to listing the ways in which sirenians are different from and similar to other marine mammals.

28. **D is correct.** As stated in the passage, "sirenians eat only seagrasses and other aquatic vegetation." These grasses grow best in shallow waters where sunlight can penetrate. Additionally, "sirenians have an extremely low metabolism and zero tolerance for cold water"; therefore, they need the warmer temperatures of Florida's coastal waters. There is no mention of safety in the passage and, in fact, these very waters are also attractive to people in speedy powerboats, who pose the biggest danger to slow-moving manatees.

29. **B is correct.** The average adult manatee "weighs between 362–544 kilograms (800–1,200 pounds)" and eats "between 45–68 kilograms (100–150 pounds) of sea grass and water hyacinths a day!"

30. **D is correct.** Mood is the pervading spirit or feeling of a passage as transmitted by the author's choice of words. In this passage the day is described as "exceedingly cold and gray" with "no sun nor hint of sun, though there was not a cloud in the sky." There was "an intangible pall over the face of things, a subtle gloom that made the day dark." And yet, despite these warning signs, the man was not worried. Taken together this information imparts a sense of impending misfortune or foreboding.

31. **A is correct.** All of the choices are definitions of the word *broken*, but only choice A makes sense in context. The day was cold and gray when it came into being or dawned.

32. **B is correct.** Clearly, the facts that the man is traveling a little-used trail, is unconcerned about the extremely cold temperature, and does not notice that the dog seems almost hesitant to follow, indicate that the man is not accustomed to such activity. Choices A and D are wrong because the passage makes no mention of when the man is expected to meet the others, so it cannot be inferred that he is either behind or ahead of schedule. Choice C is wrong because, even though it is extremely cold out, there is no evidence, at this point, that the man is disoriented. Choice E is wrong, because although the passage makes note of the sun's absence, there is nothing to indicate the man expected to see it.

33. **B is correct.** The man knew that "at fifty below spittle crackled on the snow." Obviously he wanted to test the temperature of the air. When he found that this spittle "had crackled in the air," he realized that the temperature was even lower than fifty below, which indicates severe cold.

34. **E is correct.** The man was startled because he was not expecting to hear his spittle crackle before it fell to the snow. The passage goes on to say that the man knew "that at fifty below spittle crackled on the snow, but this spittle had crackled in the air. Undoubtedly it was colder than fifty below."

35. **C is correct.** The day is described as "exceedingly cold and gray." The man determines that "it was colder than fifty below," and yet he continues to travel on. Even the dog "was depressed by the tremendous cold. It knew that it was no time for traveling." Under these circumstances, the best description of the man's actions is foolish.

36. **D is correct.** As stated in lines 32–33, "The animal was depressed by the tremendous cold. It knew that it was no time for travelling. Its instinct told it a truer tale than was told to the man by the man's judgment." These statements clearly support choice D.

37. **C is correct.** The passage makes it clear that algal blooms may result in the "illness and death" of fish, shellfish, marine mammals, and birds. This indicates that such blooms are poisonous to these living creatures.

38. **B is correct.** According to lines 22–25, "Most blooms, in fact, are beneficial because the tiny plants are food for animals in the ocean."

39. **D is correct.** The author's attitude toward the topic of algal blooms is objective because it simply presents facts, even though some of the effects of algal blooms are negative.

40. **A is correct.** The passage explicitly states that HABs occur "in every U.S. coastal state."


## Section 3 Verbal

1. **E is correct.** *Shame* is a painful emotion caused by a strong sense of guilt, embarrassment, unworthiness, or disgrace. Another word for shame is *humiliation*.

2. **D is correct.** To *divulge* something is to make it known, especially something private or a secret—to *tell*.

3. **B is correct.** *Concise* is an adjective meaning expressing much in few words; clear and succinct—in other words, *brief*.

4. **C is correct.** An *inquiry* is a close examination of a matter in a search for information or truth. An *inquiry* is synonymous with an *investigation*.

5. **A is correct.** Like *disposition*, an *attitude* is a state of mind or feeling.

6. **E is correct.** To do something *tediously* is the same as doing it *tiresomely* by reason of length, slowness, dullness, or boredom.

7. **B is correct.** To *deplete* something is to decrease the fullness of it; use it up; or empty it out—in other words, to *reduce* it.

8. **A is correct.** *Cautious* describes someone who is careful, tentative, restrained, or guarded. Another way to describe such a person would be to say that she or he is *discreet*.

9. **B is correct.** *Sparse* is an adjective describing conditions that are not thick or dense. *Thin* is synonymous with *sparse*.

10. **C is correct.** An *aversion* is an avoidance of a thing, situation, or behavior because it has been associated with an unpleasant or painful stimulus. If you have an aversion to something, you have a fixed, intense *dislike* for it.

11. **B is correct.** A *benefactor* is someone who gives aid, especially financial aid—in other words, a *contributor*.

12. **A is correct.** When something is *dormant*, it is lying asleep, or as if asleep. That is, it is *inactive*.

13. **C is correct.** If someone is described as *malcontent*, he is *dissatisfied* with existing conditions.

14. **B is correct.** To *appease* means to *satisfy* or relieve.

15. **A is correct.** To *merit* means to earn or *deserve*.

16. **E is correct.** If something is *prominent*, it is immediately noticeable—in other words, *conspicuous*.

17. **E is correct.** An *objective* is something worked toward or striven for. *Intention* is synonymous with *objective*.

18. **D is correct.** A *breach* is a *violation* or infraction, as of a law, a legal obligation, or a promise.

19. **C is correct.** To *lament* is to *regret* deeply, or to express grief for or about.

20. **D is correct.** To *rectify* means to set right or correct by calculation or adjustment—in other words, to *fix*.

21. **C is correct.** To *submerge* something is to place it under water or to cover it with water. *Submerge* is synonymous with *immerse*.

22. **B is correct.** Something that is *indelible* is impossible to remove, erase, or wash away. Therefore, it is *permanent*.

23. **D is correct.** An *abyss* is an immeasurably deep chasm, depth, or void—a *hole*.

24. **C is correct.** An *order* is an authoritative indication to be obeyed; a command or direction. Similarly, a *decree* is an authoritative order having the force of law.

25. **B is correct.** A *shrewd* person is characterized by keen awareness, sharp intelligence, and often a sense of the practical. As well, a person described as *astute* has or shows discernment, awareness, and intelligence.

26. **A is correct.** *Clandestine* is an adjective meaning kept or done in *secret*, often to conceal an illicit or improper purpose.

27. **E is correct.** To *coerce* someone is to force that person to act or think in a certain way by use of pressure, threats, or intimidation. *Compel* can be used synonymously with *coerce*.

28. **D is correct.** To *dilate* something is to make it larger or wider, or to cause it to expand—in other words, to *enlarge*.

29. **A is correct.** *Inane* describes one that lacks sense or substance—*ridiculous*.

30. **C is correct.** A *plethora* is an abundance or an *excess*.

31. **E is correct.** To *insult* someone is the opposite of what you would do if you were to *compliment* someone, just as to *please* someone is the opposite of what you would do if you were to *annoy* someone. Only choice E provides two verbs that are opposite in meaning. The verbs presented in choices A, C, and D are synonymous with each other, and the words in choice B are not the same parts of speech.

32. **C is correct.** This stem provides a part-to-whole sequence by pairing a *wolf* with a *pack*, the name given to a group of wolves. Choice A is incorrect because a group of sheep is called a flock, and choice D is incorrect because the analogy is presented backward. For choice E to be correct, it would have to read "cow is to herd." Choice C is the only correct answer because a group of *geese* is often referred to as a *gaggle*.

33. **D is correct.** This question tests your knowledge of synonym pairs. *Announce* and *inform* are synonyms in much the same way that *wrap* and *conceal* are synonyms. No other answer choice offers two words that have similar meanings.

34. **B is correct.** The relationship in this sequence is one of usage. A *shovel* is used to *dig*; a *blade* is used to *cut*. Choice D is incorrect because an eye is used to see, not blink.

35. **A is correct.** This sequence tests your knowledge of relationships between units of measurement. Flip the words: *volume* can be measured in *liters*, just as *mass* can be measured in *grams*.

36. **E is correct.** This stem provides an individual-to-activity sequence by pairing *tourist* with *sightseeing*. Your task is to complete the analogy by deciding what activity an *analyst* performs. Choices C and D are easily eliminated because they are not verbs. As well, analysts aren't known for extensive traveling or curing people of ailments. Clearly, *examining* (choice E) is the only correct answer.

37. **D is correct.** This question tests your knowledge of degrees of contrast. A *whisper* is less intense than a *scream* just as a *glance* is less intense than a *stare*. The words provided in choices A and C are too close in meaning to one another, and both lack the proper contrast.

38. **B is correct.** This sequence gauges your knowledge of items to the places they are found. *Rocks* come from a *quarry*. Similarly, *coal* comes from a *mine*. No other choice represents a comparable analogy.

39. **B is correct.** This stem anaiogizes an animal or insect with its habitat. As you can see from the introduction, a *spider's* domain is its *web* just as a *bird's* domain is its *nest*. Choice D is incorrect because the sequence is inverted.

40. **E is correct.** This sentence tests your aptitude in recognizing part-to-part analogies by beginning with a *seat* and a *steering wheel,* which are both parts of a vehicle. Similarly, the correct answer (choice E) reflects that a *handle bar* and a *brake* are both parts of a bicycle.

41. **A is correct.** This is a fairly straightforward usage sequence that analogizes an activity (*driving*) to the location it takes place (*street*). You should be able to infer that a person would *drive* on the *street* just as they would *walk* on a *path*. Ask yourself: how could the other choices be made correct? You might conclude that you would substitute *track* for *school* (choice B), *snack* for *school* (choice C), *sky* for *bird* (D), and *library* for *book* (choice E).

42. **C is correct.** This is another measurement question that provides you with the stem that *miles* measure *distance*. Of all the available choices, the only one that is correct is that *minutes* measure *time* in the same way that *miles* measure *distance*.

43. **C is correct.** This sequence tests your knowledge of parts to activities. You should be able to discount choices B and D immediately because choice B uses the plural form *arms*, and choice D provides a location rather than a body part. Choice E is incorrect as well because neither word is a verb. Of the remaining choices, you could possibly make an argument for choice A except for the fact that the noun and verb are in reverse order. Choice C is correct because, like the stem, you use your *mouth* to *chew* just as you use your *foot* to *kick*.

44. **D is correct.** This stem presents an activity-to-result analogy. When you *feed* something you *nourish*. Similarly, when you *water* something you *hydrate* it. Only choice D presents this type of complementary relationship.

45. **E is correct.** To answer this analogy correctly, you will need to know that a *prune* is actually a dried *plum*. Of the answer choices available, only choice E is correct; a *raisin* is actually a dried *grape*.

46. **B is correct.** This is another type of food analogy that involves some knowledge on your part. To answer this question correctly, you will need to know that *maple trees* produce *syrup* in much the same way that *oranges* produce *juice*. That is, the product comes directly from the source. Of the choices, you should be able to conclude that coffee does not produce beans (choice A); a chip does not produce chocolate (choice D); and although wheat produces bread, bread does not come directly from this source. Similarly, choice C is incorrect because it is not a better answer than choice B. Both syrup and juice are consumed by people, while grass is typically not.

47. **A is correct.** This sequence presents another analogy in degrees of contrast. As you can see from the stem, *envious* is less extreme than *jealous* much the same way that *melancholic* is less extreme than *mournful*. All the other answer choices present word pairs that are similar in meaning to one another; however, only choice A provides enough of a contrast between the mild and more extreme.

48. **E is correct.** This analogy is one of individual to object. A *knitter* uses *needles* just as a *boxer* uses *gloves* as the tools of a trade. As well, there is the point that both of these people use these tools with their hands, and also that only choice E complements the plural *needles* with the plural *gloves;* all the other answer choices provide singular form of objects rather than plural.

49. **D is correct.** At first, this stem may appear to be a simple part-to-whole analogy, but in order to arrive at the correct answer, you will have to take it a step further. *Talon* is the name given to the claw of a predatory animal. Therefore, the correct answer is that *claw* is to *cat* as *talon* is to *eagle*. Choice C may seem correct, but it would be difficult to argue that it is a better answer than choice D.

50. **C is correct.** This is another question that tests your knowledge of synonym pairs. *Surprise* and *startle* are synonymous just as *destroy* and *ruin* are synonymous. Choice A is incorrect because you need not necessarily grab something in order to choose it, and choice D is incorrect because need and want are often easily confused with one another.

51. **D is correct.** The relationship in this sequence is one part to whole. A *scene* is part of a *play* in much the same way that a *chapter* is a part of a *book*. Choice C may seem correct; however, on closer inspection you'll notice that the relationship is inverted.

52. **D is correct.** This analogy tests your knowledge of adjectives used to describe nouns. *Aquatic* is an adjective used to describe something consisting of, relating to, or being in water. *Terrestrial* is an adjective used to describe something of, relating to, or composed of land. So the correct answer is choice D; *aquatic* is to *water* as *terrestrial* is to *land*.

53. **A is correct.** This sequence offers a part-to-whole analogy with a bit of a twist because the correct answer is a bit different from the stem. Flip the words if you have trouble discerning the right answer: a *bus* carries *passengers*. Similarly, a *ship* carries *cargo*. Keep in mind that just because the bus carries people and the ship carries things, no other option presents the relationship of a vessel carrying anything.

54. **B is correct.** The analogy presented in this stem is one of part to part. A *seed* is part of a piece of fruit in the same way that the *rind* is part of a piece of fruit. Similarly, *bark* is part of a tree just as a *branch* is part of a tree.

55. **B is correct.** This sequence presents another test of your knowledge of synonym pairs. Both *malign* and *disparage* are verbs that denote speaking unfavorably of someone, just as *irritate* and *bother* are verbs that denote annoying someone. No other choice offers a pair of words that share the same meaning.

56. **E is correct.** This part-to-whole analogy goes a step further in testing your aptitude for comparisons. A *shoreline* borders the *ocean* and separates land from water just as a *border* separates one *country* from another.

57. **D is correct.** This is another part-to-whole analogy. If you have trouble arriving at the correct response, flip the words: a *hammerhead* is a type of *shark* just as *polar* is a type of *bear*. Choice B is incorrect because a cub is a young bear, not a specific type of bear.

58. **E is correct.** This analogy asks you to make a correlation between an individual and what that individual studies. *Sociologists* study *behavior* just as an *archaeologist* would study an *artifact*. The other answers are incorrect because a ballerina does not study a slipper (choice A); a writer may use a computer but would not study one (choice B); a zoologist studies animals, not trees (choice C); and a chef prepares meals rather than studying them (choice D).

59. **B is correct.** This sequence presents an analogy of contrasts and asks you to find the degree of difference. To *hold* something denotes a less intense commitment to the object than to *grip* something does. Similarly, *jogging* denotes putting less effort into running than *sprinting* does.

60. **C is correct.** By now you should be familiar with perhaps the most easily recognizable analogy: part to whole. A *player* is part of a *team* just as an *actor* is part of a *cast*. Choice E may seem correct, because a principal is part of a school. However, both player and actor seem to imply that no special status is given to either. A principal, as we all know, is the leader of the school, and it would be difficult to argue that choice E is a better answer than choice C.

1. **E is correct.** $5 \times 8 - 16 = 24$; $16 \div 4 = 4$, and $24 \div 4 = 6$.

2. **B is correct.** $42 \div 7 \times 8 \times 5 = 6 \times 8 \times 5 = 240$; $240 \div 12 = 20$.

3. **D is correct.** $30/5 = 6$; $4 \times {}^{12}/_{16} = {}^{48}/_{16} = 3$; $16 \div {}^{1}/_{16} = 16 \times {}^{16}/_{1} = 256$; $10.2 + 12.8 = 23$. However, ${}^{5}/_{9} \times 8 = {}^{40}/_{9} = 4\,{}^{4}/_{9}$, which is not a whole number.

4. **D is correct.** $46\,{}^{3}/_{4}\% = 0.4675$.

5. **B is correct.** It costs $m$ dollars to buy 48 notepads. 30 notepads are ${}^{5}/_{8}$ of 48, so the cost of 30 notepads will be ${}^{5}/_{8} \times m = {}^{5m}/_{8}$ dollars.

6. **E is correct.**
   $${}^{3}/_{7}x = 18$$
   $${}^{1}/_{7}x = 6$$
   $$x = 42$$
   $${}^{1}/_{2}x = 21$$

7. **D is correct.** $60 = x\%$ of 90.
   $60 = 90x$ Solve for $x$.
   $$x = \frac{60}{90}$$
   $$x = \frac{6}{9}$$
   $$x = \frac{2}{3}$$ Divide 2 by 3 to get 0.6666 or 67%

8. **C is correct.** The cube root is the number that, when multiplied by itself three times, results in the original number. In this case, $6 \times 6 \times 6 = 216$, so 6 is the correct answer.

9. **C is correct.** In this problem $\angle 6$ measures 90°. Thus $\angle 3$ also measures 90° Because the two sides of the triangle are equal, it is an isosceles triangle. That makes $\angle 1$ and $\angle 2$ equal. Since $\angle 3 = 90°$, that leaves 90° to be split equally between $\angle 1$ and $\angle 2$. So each angle measures 45°.

10. **E is correct.** To find the volume, multiply length × width × height. Since the object is a cube, all these dimensions are the same.
    $8 \times 8 \times 8 = 512$ cm³

11. **C is correct.**
    $$-10 - (-5 - 4)$$
    $$= -10 - (-9)$$
    $$= -10 + 9 = -1$$

12. **A is correct.**
    $${}^{3}/_{4} + {}^{1}/_{2} + {}^{2}/_{3} - {}^{5}/_{6}$$
    $$= {}^{9}/_{12} + {}^{6}/_{12} + {}^{8}/_{12} - {}^{10}/_{12}$$
    $$= {}^{23}/_{12} - {}^{10}/_{12}$$
    $$= {}^{13}/_{12}$$
    $$= 1\,{}^{1}/_{12}$$

13. **D is correct.** Use the formula $d = r \times t$ where $d$ = distance, $r$ = rate, and $t$ = time.
    $$d = r \times t$$
    $$175 = 50 \times t$$
    $$t = {}^{175}/_{50}$$
    $$t = 3.5 \text{ hours} = 3 \text{ hours } 30 \text{ minutes}$$

14. **E is correct.** Let $n$ be the number of students who won awards last year. Set up an equation:

$3n + 2 = 20$

$3n = 18$

$n = 6$

15. **B is correct.**

$3.4a + 8.7a = 38.72$

$12.1a = 38.72$

$a = 3.2$

16. **B is correct.** Set up a proportion:

$18/144 = x/100$

$(100 \times 18) = (144 \times x)$

$1,800 = 144x$

$1,800/144 = x$

$x = 12.5$

17. **C is correct.** $5 + 6 + 7 = 18$, so 7 is the greatest integer.

18. **C is correct.**

$2/5 + x < 1$

$2/5 + 1/2 < 1$

$4/10 + 5/10 < 1$

$9/10 < 1$

19. **A is correct.** Set up a proportion:

$3/126 = x/924$

$3 \times 924 = 126x$

$2,772 = 126x$

$2,772/126 = x$

$22 = x$

20. **C is correct.**

$3.2 \times 10^3$

$3.2 \times 1000 = 3200$

21. **D is correct.** The total number of pairs in the drawer is $3 + 5 + 4 = 12$. If there are 4 pairs of blue socks, then the chances of picking a blue pair are $4/12$ or $1/3$.

22. **C is correct.** The least common multiple of a group of numbers is the least whole number (greater than 0) that is a multiple of all of the numbers. The least common multiple of 3, 4, and 18 is 36 ($3 \times 12$, $4 \times 9$, $2 \times 18$).

23. **C is correct.** The greatest common factor of a group of numbers is the largest whole number that is a factor of all the numbers. The greatest common factor of 16, 24, 96, and 120 is 8.

24. **B is correct.** This is a 45°–45°–90° triangle. Since both legs are 4, the hypotenuse $AC$ must be $4\sqrt{2}$.

25. **E is correct.** The rule for this sequence is to double the previous number and then subtract 1.

$9 \times 2 - 1 = 18 - 1 = 17$

# SSAT Practice Test III

The following practice test is designed to be just like the real SSAT. It matches the actual test in content coverage and level of difficulty. The test is in five sections: Verbal, Quantitative I, Reading Comprehension, Quantitative II, and the Essay.

This practice test will be an accurate reflection of how you'll do on test day if you treat it as the real examination. Here are some hints on how to take the test under conditions similar to those of the actual exam:

- Find a quiet place to work and set aside a period of approximately 3 hours when you will not be disturbed.

- Work on only one section at a time, and use your watch or a timer to keep track of the time limits for each test part.

- Tear out your answer sheet and mark your answers by filling in the ovals for each question.

- Write your essay on the pages provided.

- Become familiar with the directions for each part of the test. You'll save time on the actual test day by already being familiar with this information.

At the end of the test you'll find answer keys for each section and explanations for every question. Check your answers against the keys to find out how you did on each section of the test and what test topics you might need to study more. Then review the explanations, paying particular attention to the ones for the questions you answered incorrectly.

You will receive three scores, one for each of these three categories: Quantitative, Verbal, and Reading. Each category has a low score of 500 and the high score of 800, making your total score somewhere between 1500 and 2400.

The actual SSAT also provides a Percentile Score that compares your performance with that of other U.S. and Canadian students who took the test during the past three years. Your reported percentile test scores are compared to this "norm group" for each section of the test.

The writing sample is not scored, but it is included with the score reports that you send to schools. The following table shows the various sections, numbers of questions, and time allotments.

## SSAT: Structure and Time Allotments

| Section | Number of Questions | Time Allowed |
|---|---|---|
| Writing Sample | 1 (unscored) | 25 minutes |
| Break | | 5 minutes |
| Quantitative 1 | 25 | 30 minutes |
| Reading | 40 | 40 minutes |
| Break | | 5 minutes |
| Verbal | 60 | 30 minutes |
| Quantitative 2 | 25 | 30 minutes |
| Experimental | 16 (unscored) | 15 minutes |
| Totals | 167 | 3 hours, 5 minutes |

Of the 167 total questions, only 150 items are scored. The writing sample and questions on the Experimental section are *not* scored.

# SSAT Practice Test III

ANSWER SHEET

## Section 1: Quantitative I

| | | | | | | | | | | | | | | | | |
|---|---|---|---|---|---|---|---|---|---|---|---|---|---|---|---|---|
| 1. | Ⓐ | Ⓑ | Ⓒ | Ⓓ | Ⓔ | 11. | Ⓐ | Ⓑ | Ⓒ | Ⓓ | Ⓔ | 21. | Ⓐ | Ⓑ | Ⓒ | Ⓓ | Ⓔ |
| 2. | Ⓐ | Ⓑ | Ⓒ | Ⓓ | Ⓔ | 12. | Ⓐ | Ⓑ | Ⓒ | Ⓓ | Ⓔ | 22. | Ⓐ | Ⓑ | Ⓒ | Ⓓ | Ⓔ |
| 3. | Ⓐ | Ⓑ | Ⓒ | Ⓓ | Ⓔ | 13. | Ⓐ | Ⓑ | Ⓒ | Ⓓ | Ⓔ | 23. | Ⓐ | Ⓑ | Ⓒ | Ⓓ | Ⓔ |
| 4. | Ⓐ | Ⓑ | Ⓒ | Ⓓ | Ⓔ | 14. | Ⓐ | Ⓑ | Ⓒ | Ⓓ | Ⓔ | 24. | Ⓐ | Ⓑ | Ⓒ | Ⓓ | Ⓔ |
| 5. | Ⓐ | Ⓑ | Ⓒ | Ⓓ | Ⓔ | 15. | Ⓐ | Ⓑ | Ⓒ | Ⓓ | Ⓔ | 25. | Ⓐ | Ⓑ | Ⓒ | Ⓓ | Ⓔ |
| 6. | Ⓐ | Ⓑ | Ⓒ | Ⓓ | Ⓔ | 16. | Ⓐ | Ⓑ | Ⓒ | Ⓓ | Ⓔ | | | | | | |
| 7. | Ⓐ | Ⓑ | Ⓒ | Ⓓ | Ⓔ | 17. | Ⓐ | Ⓑ | Ⓒ | Ⓓ | Ⓔ | | | | | | |
| 8. | Ⓐ | Ⓑ | Ⓒ | Ⓓ | Ⓔ | 18. | Ⓐ | Ⓑ | Ⓒ | Ⓓ | Ⓔ | | | | | | |
| 9. | Ⓐ | Ⓑ | Ⓒ | Ⓓ | Ⓔ | 19. | Ⓐ | Ⓑ | Ⓒ | Ⓓ | Ⓔ | | | | | | |
| 10. | Ⓐ | Ⓑ | Ⓒ | Ⓓ | Ⓔ | 20. | Ⓐ | Ⓑ | Ⓒ | Ⓓ | Ⓔ | | | | | | |

## Section 2: Reading Comprehension

| | | | | | | | | | | | | | | | | |
|---|---|---|---|---|---|---|---|---|---|---|---|---|---|---|---|---|
| 1. | Ⓐ | Ⓑ | Ⓒ | Ⓓ | Ⓔ | 17. | Ⓐ | Ⓑ | Ⓒ | Ⓓ | Ⓔ | 33. | Ⓐ | Ⓑ | Ⓒ | Ⓓ | Ⓔ |
| 2. | Ⓐ | Ⓑ | Ⓒ | Ⓓ | Ⓔ | 18. | Ⓐ | Ⓑ | Ⓒ | Ⓓ | Ⓔ | 34. | Ⓐ | Ⓑ | Ⓒ | Ⓓ | Ⓔ |
| 3. | Ⓐ | Ⓑ | Ⓒ | Ⓓ | Ⓔ | 19. | Ⓐ | Ⓑ | Ⓒ | Ⓓ | Ⓔ | 35. | Ⓐ | Ⓑ | Ⓒ | Ⓓ | Ⓔ |
| 4. | Ⓐ | Ⓑ | Ⓒ | Ⓓ | Ⓔ | 20. | Ⓐ | Ⓑ | Ⓒ | Ⓓ | Ⓔ | 36. | Ⓐ | Ⓑ | Ⓒ | Ⓓ | Ⓔ |
| 5. | Ⓐ | Ⓑ | Ⓒ | Ⓓ | Ⓔ | 21. | Ⓐ | Ⓑ | Ⓒ | Ⓓ | Ⓔ | 37. | Ⓐ | Ⓑ | Ⓒ | Ⓓ | Ⓔ |
| 6. | Ⓐ | Ⓑ | Ⓒ | Ⓓ | Ⓔ | 22. | Ⓐ | Ⓑ | Ⓒ | Ⓓ | Ⓔ | 38. | Ⓐ | Ⓑ | Ⓒ | Ⓓ | Ⓔ |
| 7. | Ⓐ | Ⓑ | Ⓒ | Ⓓ | Ⓔ | 23. | Ⓐ | Ⓑ | Ⓒ | Ⓓ | Ⓔ | 39. | Ⓐ | Ⓑ | Ⓒ | Ⓓ | Ⓔ |
| 8. | Ⓐ | Ⓑ | Ⓒ | Ⓓ | Ⓔ | 24. | Ⓐ | Ⓑ | Ⓒ | Ⓓ | Ⓔ | 40. | Ⓐ | Ⓑ | Ⓒ | Ⓓ | Ⓔ |
| 9. | Ⓐ | Ⓑ | Ⓒ | Ⓓ | Ⓔ | 25. | Ⓐ | Ⓑ | Ⓒ | Ⓓ | Ⓔ | | | | | | |
| 10. | Ⓐ | Ⓑ | Ⓒ | Ⓓ | Ⓔ | 26. | Ⓐ | Ⓑ | Ⓒ | Ⓓ | Ⓔ | | | | | | |
| 11. | Ⓐ | Ⓑ | Ⓒ | Ⓓ | Ⓔ | 27. | Ⓐ | Ⓑ | Ⓒ | Ⓓ | Ⓔ | | | | | | |
| 12. | Ⓐ | Ⓑ | Ⓒ | Ⓓ | Ⓔ | 28. | Ⓐ | Ⓑ | Ⓒ | Ⓓ | Ⓔ | | | | | | |
| 13. | Ⓐ | Ⓑ | Ⓒ | Ⓓ | Ⓔ | 29. | Ⓐ | Ⓑ | Ⓒ | Ⓓ | Ⓔ | | | | | | |
| 14. | Ⓐ | Ⓑ | Ⓒ | Ⓓ | Ⓔ | 30. | Ⓐ | Ⓑ | Ⓒ | Ⓓ | Ⓔ | | | | | | |
| 15. | Ⓐ | Ⓑ | Ⓒ | Ⓓ | Ⓔ | 31. | Ⓐ | Ⓑ | Ⓒ | Ⓓ | Ⓔ | | | | | | |
| 16. | Ⓐ | Ⓑ | Ⓒ | Ⓓ | Ⓔ | 32. | Ⓐ | Ⓑ | Ⓒ | Ⓓ | Ⓔ | | | | | | |

## Section 3: Verbal

| | | |
|---|---|---|
| 1. (A) (B) (C) (D) (E) | 21. (A) (B) (C) (D) (E) | 41. (A) (B) (C) (D) (E) |
| 2. (A) (B) (C) (D) (E) | 22. (A) (B) (C) (D) (E) | 42. (A) (B) (C) (D) (E) |
| 3. (A) (B) (C) (D) (E) | 23. (A) (B) (C) (D) (E) | 43. (A) (B) (C) (D) (E) |
| 4. (A) (B) (C) (D) (E) | 24. (A) (B) (C) (D) (E) | 44. (A) (B) (C) (D) (E) |
| 5. (A) (B) (C) (D) (E) | 25. (A) (B) (C) (D) (E) | 45. (A) (B) (C) (D) (E) |
| 6. (A) (B) (C) (D) (E) | 26. (A) (B) (C) (D) (E) | 46. (A) (B) (C) (D) (E) |
| 7. (A) (B) (C) (D) (E) | 27. (A) (B) (C) (D) (E) | 47. (A) (B) (C) (D) (E) |
| 8. (A) (B) (C) (D) (E) | 28. (A) (B) (C) (D) (E) | 48. (A) (B) (C) (D) (E) |
| 9. (A) (B) (C) (D) (E) | 29. (A) (B) (C) (D) (E) | 49. (A) (B) (C) (D) (E) |
| 10. (A) (B) (C) (D) (E) | 30. (A) (B) (C) (D) (E) | 50. (A) (B) (C) (D) (E) |
| 11. (A) (B) (C) (D) (E) | 31. (A) (B) (C) (D) (E) | 51. (A) (B) (C) (D) (E) |
| 12. (A) (B) (C) (D) (E) | 32. (A) (B) (C) (D) (E) | 52. (A) (B) (C) (D) (E) |
| 13. (A) (B) (C) (D) (E) | 33. (A) (B) (C) (D) (E) | 53. (A) (B) (C) (D) (E) |
| 14. (A) (B) (C) (D) (E) | 34. (A) (B) (C) (D) (E) | 54. (A) (B) (C) (D) (E) |
| 15. (A) (B) (C) (D) (E) | 35. (A) (B) (C) (D) (E) | 55. (A) (B) (C) (D) (E) |
| 16. (A) (B) (C) (D) (E) | 36. (A) (B) (C) (D) (E) | 56. (A) (B) (C) (D) (E) |
| 17. (A) (B) (C) (D) (E) | 37. (A) (B) (C) (D) (E) | 57. (A) (B) (C) (D) (E) |
| 18. (A) (B) (C) (D) (E) | 38. (A) (B) (C) (D) (F) | 58. (A) (B) (C) (D) (E) |
| 19. (A) (B) (C) (D) (E) | 39. (A) (B) (C) (D) (E) | 59. (A) (B) (C) (D) (E) |
| 20. (A) (B) (C) (D) (E) | 40. (A) (B) (C) (D) (E) | 60. (A) (B) (C) (D) (E) |

## Section 4: Quantitative II

| | | |
|---|---|---|
| 1. (A) (B) (C) (D) (E) | 11. (A) (B) (C) (D) (E) | 21. (A) (B) (C) (D) (E) |
| 2. (A) (B) (C) (D) (E) | 12. (A) (B) (C) (D) (E) | 22. (A) (B) (C) (D) (E) |
| 3. (A) (B) (C) (D) (E) | 13. (A) (B) (C) (D) (E) | 23. (A) (B) (C) (D) (E) |
| 4. (A) (B) (C) (D) (E) | 14. (A) (B) (C) (D) (E) | 24. (A) (B) (C) (D) (E) |
| 5. (A) (B) (C) (D) (E) | 15. (A) (B) (C) (D) (E) | 25. (A) (B) (C) (D) (E) |
| 6. (A) (B) (C) (D) (E) | 16. (A) (B) (C) (D) (E) | |
| 7. (A) (B) (C) (D) (E) | 17. (A) (B) (C) (D) (E) | |
| 8. (A) (B) (C) (D) (E) | 18. (A) (B) (C) (D) (E) | |
| 9. (A) (B) (C) (D) (E) | 19. (A) (B) (C) (D) (E) | |
| 10. (A) (B) (C) (D) (E) | 20. (A) (B) (C) (D) (E) | |

## SECTION 1

Time: 30 Minutes

25 Questions

**Directions:** For each of the following questions, mark the letter of your choice on the answer sheet.

1. Andre had a birthday party and spent $12.98 on balloons, $47.23 on party favors, $22.97 on a cake, $14.77 on ice cream, and $15.00 on invitations. How much did Andre spend on the party?
   - (A) $87.25
   - (B) $112.95
   - (C) $125.20
   - (D) $127.30
   - (E) $131.50

2. Bob's iPod contains 800 songs. If 240 songs are either jazz or rap songs, what percent of his collection is jazz or rap?
   - (A) 12%
   - (B) 15%
   - (C) 20%
   - (D) 25%
   - (E) 30%

3. Matt took a bike trip. On the first day he rode 15 miles. On the second day he rode 35 miles, and the third day he rested. On the fourth day he rode 57 miles, and on the fifth day he rode 43 miles. What is the average number of miles that he rode per day?
   - (A) 25
   - (B) 27
   - (C) 30
   - (D) 32
   - (E) 34

4. Aaron has 256 cans of soup that he needs to pack into boxes that hold 30 cans each. How many cans of soup are left over after he fills as many boxes as he can?
   - (A) 4
   - (B) 16
   - (C) 18
   - (D) 22
   - (E) 24

5. An obtuse angle is an angle that measures
   - (A) less than 90°
   - (B) exactly 90°
   - (C) between 90° and 180°
   - (D) exactly 180°
   - (E) greater than 180°

6. Two numbers add to 1,500. One number is 4 times the size of the other. What are the two numbers?
   - (A) 300, 1,200
   - (B) 200, 1,300
   - (C) 500, 1,000
   - (D) 750, 750
   - (E) 800, 700

7. A box of laundry soap contains 200 oz. If the cost for 5 ounces is 10 cents, how much does the box of soap cost?
   - (A) $2.80
   - (B) $3.10
   - (C) $3.60
   - (D) $3.80
   - (E) $4.00

8. A computer is priced at $1,800. Next week it will be on sale for $270 less. What percent of the current price will Blythe save if she buys the computer next week?
   - (A) 10%
   - (B) 12%
   - (C) 15%
   - (D) 20%
   - (E) 25%

9. In the figure shown, lines AB and CD are parallel and ∠1 measures 120°. What is the measure of ∠2?

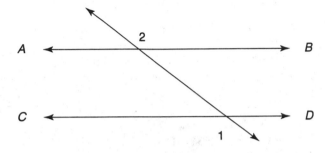

   - (A) 40°
   - (B) 60°
   - (C) 75°
   - (D) 90°
   - (E) 120°

10. High school students were asked to pick their favorite kind of birthday party. The results are shown in the chart below. Which kind of party did the fewest students pick?

   - (A) bowling
   - (B) ice skating
   - (C) laser tag
   - (D) rock climbing
   - (E) sleepover

11. It costs m dollars to buy 24 cookies. At the same rate, how many dollars will it cost to buy 6 cookies?
   - (A) $\frac{m}{4}$
   - (B) $\frac{m}{6}$
   - (C) 4m
   - (D) 6m
   - (E) 24m

12. $18 \div {}^3/_4 =$
   - (A) 3
   - (B) 6
   - (C) 12
   - (D) 24
   - (E) 30

13. A rectangular garden is 40 yards long and 15 yards wide. Darryl runs once around the edge of the garden. How far does Darryl run?
   - (A) 55 yards
   - (B) 80 yards
   - (C) 100 yards
   - (D) 110 yards
   - (E) 120 yards

14. In the figure shown, if ∠1 measures 35°, what is the measure of ∠2?

   - (A) 145°
   - (B) 95°
   - (C) 65°
   - (D) 45°
   - (E) 35°

15. If $4 \times 3 \times \underline{\hspace{1cm}} = 5 \times 4 + 4$, then $\underline{\hspace{1cm}} =$
   - (A) 2
   - (B) 3
   - (C) 4
   - (D) 5
   - (E) 6

16. If $\frac{x}{8} = 4\frac{x}{y}$, what is the value of y?
   - (A) 4
   - (B) 8
   - (C) 16
   - (D) 32
   - (E) 64

**GO ON TO THE NEXT PAGE.**

17. Which of the following is NOT equal to a whole number?

(A) $\dfrac{24}{6}$

(B) $6 \times \dfrac{8}{16}$

(C) $9 \div \dfrac{1}{9}$

(D) $\dfrac{3}{5} \times 8$

(E) $7.4 + 5.6$

18. $71\frac{1}{5}\% =$
   (A) 712
   (B) 71.2
   (C) 7.12
   (D) 0.712
   (E) 0.0712

19. In the rectangle shown, side $a$ measures 13 cm and side $b$ measures 36 cm. What is the perimeter of the rectangle?

(A) 49 cm
(B) 98 cm
(C) 196 cm
(D) 469 cm
(E) 512 cm

20. If ⅗ of a number is 18, then ½ of the same number is
   (A) 16
   (B) 15
   (C) 12
   (D) 9
   (E) 8

21. If Joanne tosses a 1–6 number cube, what is the probability that the cube number facing up will be even?

(A) $\dfrac{1}{6}$

(B) $\dfrac{1}{5}$

(C) $\dfrac{1}{4}$

(D) $\dfrac{1}{3}$

(E) $\dfrac{1}{2}$

22. A $400 television is on sale for 15% off. What is the sale price?
   (A) $390
   (B) $385
   (C) $375
   (D) $350
   (E) $340

23. In the triangle shown, side $a$ is 4 ft long, and side $b$ is 6 ft long. What is the area of the triangle?

(A) 12 ft²
(B) 18 ft²
(C) 24 ft²
(D) 36 ft²
(E) 42 ft²

**GO ON TO THE NEXT PAGE.**

24. What is the length of line segment *YZ* in triangle
    *XYZ*?

(A) 3
(B) $3\sqrt{2}$
(C) $3\sqrt{3}$
(D) 6
(E) $6\sqrt{2}$

25. Based on the scatter plot and line of best fit shown
    below, about how many years is the likely life
    expectancy for women in the United States in year
    2020?

(A) 77
(B) 79
(C) 80
(D) 85
(E) 87

**STOP!**
If you finish before time is up, check your work on this section only.

Time: 40 Minutes
40 Questions

**Directions:** Each reading passage is followed by questions about it. Answer the questions that follow a passage on the basis of what is stated or implied in that passage. For each question, select the answer you think is best and record your choice by filling in the corresponding oval on the answer sheet.

*"The President shall from time to time give to Congress information of the State of the Union and recommend to their Consideration such measures as he shall judge necessary and expedient."* Article II, Sec. 3, U.S. Constitution

On a cold January morning in 1790, George Washington personally delivered the first state of the union address to a joint meeting of the two bodies of Congress at Federal Hall in New York City, which was then the provisional capital of the United States. Since Washington's first speech to Congress, U.S. Presidents have "from time to time" given Congress an assessment of the condition of the union. Presidents have used the opportunity to present their goals and agenda through broad ideas or specific details. The annual message or "State of the Union" message's length, frequency, and method of delivery have varied from President to President and era to era.

In 1801, Thomas Jefferson discontinued the practice of delivering the address in person, regarding it as too monarchial for the new republic. Instead, Jefferson wrote out his address and sent it to Congress to be read by a clerk. This practice continued for the next 112 years. The first president to revive Washington's spoken precedent was Woodrow Wilson in 1913.

For many years, the speech was referred to as "the President's Annual Message to Congress." The term "State of the Union" did not become widely used until after 1935 when Franklin Delano Roosevelt began using the phrase.

With the advent of radio and television, the President's annual message has become not only a conversation between the President and Congress but also an opportunity for the President to communicate with the American people at the same time. Calvin Coolidge's 1923 speech was the first to be broadcast on radio. Harry S. Truman's 1947 address was the first to be broadcast on television. Lyndon Johnson's address in 1965 was the first delivered in the evening, and George W. Bush's 2002 address was the first to be broadcast live on the World Wide Web.

1. The author most likely included the quotation from the U.S. Constitution in lines 1–4 in order to
   (A) show how well the author knows the Constitution
   (B) illustrate the wording used in the Constitution
   (C) explain the reason for the State of the Union address
   (D) demonstrate how different Presidents have interpreted the same provision
   (E) point out the difference between a constitutional duty and a custom

2. The phrase "from time to time" in line 1 has been interpreted to mean
   (A) once in a while
   (B) in a timely manner
   (C) annually
   (D) at a convenient time
   (E) when time allows

**GO ON TO THE NEXT PAGE.**

3. U.S. presidents deliver State of the Union messages primarily because they
   (A) are following a tradition started by George Washington
   (B) are required to do so by the U.S. Constitution
   (C) need to fulfill campaign promises
   (D) want to thank their supporters
   (E) are trying to unify opposing factions

4. Thomas Jefferson's State of the Union address differed from Washington's address in that Jefferson
   (A) spoke first to the Senate and then to the House of Representatives
   (B) presented more frequent messages than did Washington
   (C) broadcast his message on radio
   (D) did not deliver his address in person
   (E) had his speech printed in the newspaper

5. In the first half of the twentieth century, the State of the Union address was forever changed by
   (A) the advent of radio and television
   (B) Thomas Jefferson
   (C) Lyndon Johnson
   (D) moving the site of the speech from New York to Washington, D.C.
   (E) newspaper coverage of the speech

6. Which of the following questions is answered by the information in the passage?
   (A) How many presidents have delivered spoken State of the Union messages?
   (B) When is the State of the Union message delivered?
   (C) How long is the average State of the Union message?
   (D) Why did Woodrow Wilson revive the spoken State of the Union message?
   (E) Which president delivered the first televised State of the Union message?

While they cannot be seen from the air, or felt aboard an ocean-going ship, tsunamis can cause as great a loss of life and property as their other natural disaster cousins—tornadoes and hurricanes. The tsu-
5  nami that occurred on December 26, 2004, was the worst tsunami ever recorded in terms of lives lost. Triggered by a powerful earthquake in the Indian Ocean, it ravaged the shores of Indonesia, Sri Lanka, India, and

Thailand, and even hit the east coast of Africa more
10 than 2,300 miles away.
A tsunami is a series of ocean waves generated by any rapid large-scale disturbance of the sea water. Most tsunamis are generated by earthquakes, but they may also be caused by volcanic eruptions, landslides,
15 undersea slumps, or meteor impacts. In 1963 the term "tsunami" was adopted internationally to describe this natural phenomenon. A Japanese word, it is the combination of the characters *tsu* (harbor) and *nami* (wave). Tsunamis are often mistakenly called "tidal
20 waves." However, the tides have nothing to do with the formation of tsunamis.
The waves radiate outward in all directions from the disturbance and can propagate across entire ocean basins. For example, in 1960, an earth-
25 quake in Chile caused a tsunami that swept across the Pacific to Japan. Tsunami waves are distinguished from ordinary ocean waves by their great length between peaks, often exceeding 100 miles in the deep ocean, and by the long amount of time
30 between these peaks, ranging from five minutes to an hour.
In the deep ocean, a tsunami is barely noticeable, causing only a small rising and falling of the sea surface as it passes. Only as it approaches land
35 does a tsunami become a hazard. As the tsunami approaches land and shallow water, the waves slow down and become compressed, causing them to grow in height. In the best of cases, the tsunami comes onshore like a quickly rising tide
40 and causes a gentle flooding of low-lying coastal areas.
In the worst of cases, a bore will form. A bore is a wall of turbulent water that can be several meters high and can rush onshore with great destructive power.
45 Behind the bore is a deep and fast-moving flood that can pick up and sweep away almost anything in its path. Minutes later, the water will drain away as the trough of the tsunami wave arrives, sometimes exposing great patches of the sea floor. But then the
50 water will rush in again as before, causing additional damage.
This destructive cycle may repeat many times before the hazard finally passes. Persons caught in the path of a tsunami have little chance to survive.
55 They can be easily crushed by debris or they may simply drown. Children and the elderly are particularly at risk, as they have less mobility, strength, and endurance.

**GO ON TO THE NEXT PAGE.**

7. The main purpose of this passage is to
   (A) describe the tsunami of 2004
   (B) point out the differences between tsunamis and tidal waves
   (C) explain the origin of the term "tsunami"
   (D) provide general information about tsunamis
   (E) tell how to survive a tsunami

8. The passage names all of the following as possible causes of a tsunami EXCEPT
   (A) earthquakes
   (B) volcanic eruptions
   (C) landslides
   (D) meteor impacts
   (E) tornadoes

9. The author cites the 1960 tsunami in Japan to show
   (A) how far a tsunami can reach
   (B) how devastating a tsunami can be
   (C) the importance of detecting a tsunami early
   (D) how quickly a tsunami can travel
   (E) the need for international cooperation in preventing tsunamis

10. Which of the following best describes the difference between a tsunami wave and a regular ocean wave?
    (A) Tsunami waves are more than 100 miles apart in the deep ocean, while regular ocean waves follow closely one after the other.
    (B) The length between peaks and the amount of time between peaks is greater in tsunami waves than it is in regular ocean waves.
    (C) Regular ocean waves are more harmful to young children, while tsunami waves are more likely to endanger the elderly.
    (D) Tsunami waves are more likely to affect boats in deep water than are regular ocean waves.
    (E) Tsunami waves are highest in deep water, while regular ocean waves are highest near the shore.

11. The style of the passage is most like that found in
    (A) a personal letter
    (B) an adventure novel
    (C) a weather report
    (D) a science textbook
    (E) a news article

12. A tsunami becomes a hazard as it approaches land because
    (A) the waves compress and grow higher in shallow water
    (B) the waves speed up as they approach the shore
    (C) the water drains away, exposing the sea floor
    (D) people get too close to the shore
    (E) beaches are popular with children and the elderly

13. As used in paragraph 5, the word "bore" means
    (A) hollow, cylindrical chamber
    (B) dull person
    (C) gauge
    (D) hole made by a drill
    (E) dangerous wave

---

**To an Athlete Dying Young**

The time you won your town the race
We chaired you through the market-place;
Man and boy stood cheering by,
And home we brought you shoulder-high.

5  Today, the road all runners come,
Shoulder-high we bring you home,
And set you at your threshold down,
Townsman of a stiller town.

Smart lad, to slip betimes away
10  From fields where glory does not stay,
And early though the laurel grows
It withers quicker than the rose.

Eyes the shady night has shut
Cannot see the record cut,
15  And silence sounds no worse than cheers
After earth has stopped the ears.

Now you will not swell the rout
Of lads that wore their honors out
Runners whom renown outran
20  And the name died before the man.

**GO ON TO THE NEXT PAGE.**

So set, before its echoes fade,
The fleet foot on the sill of shade,
And hold to the low lintel up
The still-defended challenge-cup.

25  And round that early-laurelled head
Will flock to gaze the strength less dead,
And find unwithered on its curls
The garland briefer than a girl's.

—A. E. Housman

14. The athlete described in this poem is most likely a
    (A) tennis player
    (B) swimmer
    (C) runner
    (D) football player
    (E) girl

15. The setting for this poem is a
    (A) victory celebration
    (B) funeral
    (C) field of laurels
    (D) rose garden
    (E) championship race

16. The "stiller town" referred to in line 8 means
    (A) old age
    (B) a country village
    (C) home
    (D) death
    (E) a quiet town

17. The author admires the athlete for
    (A) winning his race
    (B) bringing home a laurel wreath
    (C) setting a new record
    (D) returning to his hometown
    (E) dying young

18. The author is likely to agree with which of the following statements?
    I.   Glory is a fleeting thing.
    II.  It is best to die at the peak of one's fame.
    III. An athlete's fame lives on even after retirement.

    (A) I only
    (B) II only
    (C) III only
    (D) I and II only
    (E) I, II, and III

The earthquake shook down in San Francisco hundreds of thousands of dollars worth of walls and chimneys. But the conflagration that followed burned up hundreds of millions of dollars' worth of property. There is no estimating within hundreds of millions the actual damage wrought. Not in history has a modern imperial city been so completely destroyed. San Francisco is gone. Nothing remains of it but memories and a fringe of dwelling-houses on its outskirts. Its industrial section is wiped out. Its business section is wiped out. Its social and residential section is wiped out. The factories and warehouses, the great stores and newspaper buildings, the hotels and the palaces of the nabobs, are all gone. Remains only the fringe of dwelling-houses on the outskirts of what was once San Francisco.

Within an hour after the earthquake shock the smoke of San Francisco's burning was a lurid tower visible a hundred miles away. And for three days and nights this lurid tower swayed in the sky, reddening the sun, darkening the day, and filling the land with smoke.

On Wednesday morning at a quarter past five came the earthquake. A minute later the flames were leaping upward. In a dozen different quarters south of Market Street, in the working-class ghetto, and in the factories, fires started. There was no opposing the flames. There was no organization, no communication. All the cunning adjustments of a twentieth century city had been smashed by the earthquake. The streets were humped into ridges and depressions, and piled with the debris of fallen walls. The steel rails were twisted into perpendicular and horizontal angles. The telephone and telegraph systems were disrupted. And the great water-mains had burst. All the shrewd contrivances and safeguards of man had been thrown out of gear by thirty seconds' twitching of the earth-crust.

By Wednesday afternoon, inside of twelve hours, half the heart of the city was gone. At that time I watched the vast conflagration from out on the bay. It was dead calm. Not a flicker of wind stirred. Yet from every side wind was pouring in upon the city. East, west, north, and south, strong winds were blowing upon the doomed city. The heated air rising made an enormous suck. Thus did the fire of itself build its own colossal chimney through the atmosphere. Day and night this dead calm continued, and yet, near to the flames,

**GO ON TO THE NEXT PAGE.**

the wind was often half a gale, so mighty was the suck.

Wednesday night saw the destruction of the very heart of the city. Dynamite was lavishly used, and many
55 of San Francisco proudest structures were crumbled by man himself into ruins, but there was no withstanding the onrush of the flames. Time and again successful stands were made by the fire-fighters, and every time the flames flanked around on either side or came
60 up from the rear, and turned to defeat the hard-won victory.

—Jack London from
"The Story of an Eyewitness"

19. The first paragraph of the passage establishes a mood of
   (A) awe and disbelief
   (B) desperate longing
   (C) uncontrolled outrage
   (D) cautious optimism
   (E) heartfelt pity

20. The author describes the effects of the earthquake by relying on
   (A) scientific knowledge
   (B) comparisons to similar events in history
   (C) confirmed statistical data
   (D) vivid images appealing primarily to the sense of sight
   (E) insights based largely on interviews with residents

21. In line 15, "nabobs" most nearly means
   (A) knaves
   (B) wealthy persons
   (C) elected officials
   (D) native sons
   (E) descendants of royalty

22. The statement that "All the cunning adjustments of a twentieth century city had been smashed by the earthquake" (lines 30–32) suggests primarily that
   (A) the city had been reduced to a primitive existence
   (B) the earthquake destroyed many of the city's newest buildings
   (C) numerous irreplaceable mechanisms were lost during the earthquake
   (D) only necessities such as plumbing and electricity remained intact
   (E) many people died as a result of the earthquake

23. Which best describes the overall organization of the passage?
   (A) a discussion of opposing viewpoints
   (B) a description of events in spatial order
   (C) a description of events in chronological order
   (D) an enumeration of facts supported by statistical data
   (E) a statement of opinion backed up by reasons

24. The primary purpose of the passage is to
   (A) present a scientific explanation of the San Francisco earthquake
   (B) provide an eyewitness report of the San Francisco earthquake
   (C) convey the despair of San Francisco residents as they watched the destruction of their city
   (D) describe the conditions that allowed the fires to spread
   (E) praise the efforts of fire-fighters who battled bravely to put out the fires

Over 200 years ago, English physician Edward Jenner observed that milkmaids stricken with a viral disease called cowpox were rarely victims of a similar disease, smallpox. This observa-
5 tion led to the development of the first vaccine. In an experiment that was to prove a revelation, Jenner took a few drops of fluid from a pustule of a woman who had cowpox and injected the fluid into a healthy young boy who had never
10 had cowpox or smallpox. Six weeks later, Jenner injected the boy with fluid from a smallpox pustule. Miraculously, the boy remained free of the dreaded smallpox.

In those days, a million people died from small-
15 pox each year in Europe alone, most of them children. Those who survived were often left with grim reminders of their ordeals: blindness, deep scars, and deformities. When Jenner laid the foundation for modern vaccines in 1796, he started on a course
20 that would ease the suffering of people around the world for centuries to come. By the beginning of the 20th century, vaccines for rabies, diphtheria, typhoid fever, and plague were in use, in addition to the vaccine for smallpox. By 1980, an updated ver-
25 sion of Jenner's vaccine led to the total eradication of smallpox.

**GO ON TO THE NEXT PAGE.**

Since Jenner's time, vaccines have been developed against more than 20 infectious diseases such as influenza, pneumonia, whooping cough, rubella, meningitis, and hepatitis B. Due to tremendous advances in molecular biology, scientists are using novel approaches to develop vaccines against deadly diseases that still plague humankind.

Scientists use vaccines to "trick" the human immune system into producing antibodies or immune cells that protect against the real disease-causing organism. Weakened microbes, killed microbes, inactivated toxins, and purified proteins or polysaccharides derived from microbes are the most common components used in vaccine development strategies. As science advances, researchers are developing even better vaccines.

25. Which of the following best describes smallpox in the years before 1796?
(A) It struck a million people a year in Europe alone.
(B) It was common among milkmaids.
(C) It was spread by cows.
(D) It killed more than a million Europeans a year.
(E) The few who survived the disease were left unharmed.

26. According to the passage, vaccines have been developed for all of the following diseases EXCEPT:
(A) pneumonia
(B) scarlet fever
(C) typhoid fever
(D) rubella
(E) meningitis

27. According to the passage, which of the following are components used in vaccine development?
I. inactivated toxins
II. weakened microbes
III. purified proteins

(A) I only
(B) II only
(C) III only
(D) I and II only
(E) I, II, and III

28. The vaccine produced by Jenner in 1796
(A) completely eradicated smallpox
(B) was effective only against cowpox
(C) served as the basis for modern vaccines
(D) could be used against rabies
(E) wiped out typhoid fever

29. Which of the following best describes how vaccines work?
(A) They directly attack the disease-causing organism.
(B) They fool the body into producing antibodies that protect against the real disease-causing organism.
(C) They contain deadly disease-producing organisms that are injected directly into the blood stream.
(D) They contain antibodies that protect the body from deadly diseases.
(E) They cause allergic reactions in most people.

The crimson hand, which at first had been strongly visible upon the marble paleness of Georgiana's cheek, now grew more faintly outlined. She remained not less pale than ever; but the birthmark, with every breath that came and went, lost somewhat of its former distinctness. Its presence had been awful; its departure was more awful still. Watch the stain of the rainbow fading out of the sky, and you will know how the mysterious symbol passed away.

"By Heaven! It is well-nigh gone!" said Aylmer to himself, in almost irrepressible ecstasy. "I can scarcely trace it now. Success! Success! And now it is like the faintest rose color. The lightest flush of blood across her cheek would overcome it. But she is so pale!"

He drew aside the window curtain and suffered the light of natural day to fall into the room and rest upon her cheek. At the same time he heard a gross, hoarse chuckle, which he had long known as his servant Aminadab's expression of delight.

"Ah, clod! ah, earthly mass!" cried Aylmer, laughing in a sort of frenzy. "You have served me well! Matter and spirit—earth and heaven—have both done their part in this! Laugh, thing of the senses! You have earned the right to laugh."

These exclamations broke Georgiana's sleep. She slowly unclosed her eyes and gazed into the

**GO ON TO THE NEXT PAGE.**

mirror which her husband had arranged for that purpose. A faint smile flitted over her lips when she recognized how barely perceptible was now that crimson hand which had once blazed with such disastrous brilliancy as to scare away all their happiness. But then her eyes sought Aylmer's face with a trouble and anxiety that he could by no means account for.

"My poor Aylmer!" murmured she.

"Poor? Nay, richest, happiest, most favored!" exclaimed he. "My peerless bride, it is successful! You are perfect!"

"My poor Aylmer," she repeated with a more than human tenderness, "you have aimed loftily; you have done nobly. Do not repent that with so high and pure a feeling, you have rejected the best the earth could offer. Aylmer, dearest Aylmer, I am dying!"

—Nathaniel Hawthorne from "The Birthmark"

30. The birthmark on Georgiana's face had the shape of a
(A) rainbow
(B) rose
(C) hand
(D) butterfly
(E) sun

31. It can be reasonably inferred from the story that Aylmer
(A) is a poor man
(B) does not love his wife
(C) is trying to kill his wife
(D) has performed an operation on his wife
(E) is dying

32. Which of the following best describes what happens to the mark on Georgiana's cheek?
(A) It takes a new shape.
(B) It becomes very faint.
(C) It stays the same.
(D) It grows larger.
(E) It turns a deep red color.

33. Which word best describes how Aylmer regards Georgiana at the end of the passage?
(A) flawless
(B) amusing
(C) tiresome
(D) brilliant
(E) undesirable

34. Georgiana's feelings toward Aylmer could best be described as
(A) bitter
(B) angry
(C) happy
(D) tender
(E) uncaring

35. Which is the best expression of the main idea of this passage?
(A) Love is blind.
(B) Birthmarks should be removed.
(C) Perfection cannot be achieved on earth.
(D) Beauty is in the eye of the beholder.
(E) All's well that ends well.

Billions of time each day, people reach into their pockets and pull out coins to buy something they want. Before money existed, people bartered by trading goods to obtain what they required. Barter was a complex process that depended on the resources available and the needs of those doing the trading. The invention of money, especially the minting of coins, made economic transactions much easier.

When did the first money come into use? Which culture created it, and how did it become a common system of exchange? The history of money still holds some mysteries, but historians and scientists have some good ideas. In the fifth century B.C., the ancient Greek historian Herodotus mentions that the Lydians had made the first coins.

Around 650 B.C., the Lydians minted a small coin in the shape of a lion on one side with a blank back. These coins called Lydian Lions were made from a combination of silver and gold. This naturally occurring alloy, called electrum, was common in the ancient kingdom of Lydia, now part of western Syria.

According to historical records, Alyattes, King of the Lydians in the sixth century B.C., began minting coins made of electrum. On one side, each coin bore the head of a roaring lion and on the other side a punch mark, the impression made by a hammer as it forced the molten metal into the mold. The most common Lydian Lion was called a stater. Each weighed approximately 4.76 grams—a little less than an American nickel— making them easy to carry.

Lydian coins came in many sizes and weights, depending on the value. The largest was a 14-gram Lydian coin in the shape of a full lion, and the smallest was a twelfth-stater that weighed a little more than a gram.

**GO ON TO THE NEXT PAGE.**

> It did not take long before the idea of minting coins to be used in the exchange of goods caught on. Soon after the Lydican Lions were first struck, ancient Greeks, Romans, Indians, Chinese, and Middle-Eastern people were creating their own coins, and the birth of modern monetary systems had begun.

40

36. The main purpose of this passage is to
    (A) describe the way early coins were made
    (B) persuade readers of the value of Lydian coins
    (C) explain how Lydia became an important society
    (D) discuss the origins of coins in ancient Lydia
    (E) compare the ancient Lydian economy with others

37. The author describes the minting of Lydian Lions to
    (A) compare the Lydian minting process with modern methods
    (B) explain the steps in the Lydian minting process
    (C) remind collectors why Lydian Lions are valuable
    (D) compare the value of different Lydian coins
    (E) explain why gold and silver were used

38. The word *alloy* as used in line 20 most nearly means
    (A) a metal
    (B) a type of soil
    (C) a mixture
    (D) an animal
    (E) a weapon

39. According to the passage, the punch mark on the back of a stater was made
    (A) during the minting process
    (B) when mining the ore
    (C) as a royal stamp
    (D) by mistake
    (E) by conquerors

40. According to the passage, the value of a Lydian coin was based on
    (A) the type of metal in it
    (B) when it was minted
    (C) conquering armies
    (D) which king minted it
    (E) its size and weight

**STOP!**
If you finish before time is up, check your work on this section only.

## SECTION 3

Time: 30 Minutes
60 Questions

This section includes two different types of questions: synonyms and analogies. There are directions and a sample question for each question type.

**Directions:** Each of the following questions consists of a word in capital letters followed by five words or phrases. Select the one word or phrase that means most nearly the same as the word in capital letters.

Sample Question:

ESSENTIAL:
(A) dire
(B) confusing
(C) vital
(D) expert
(E) honest

Correct Answer: C

---

1. BIAS:
   (A) preference
   (B) conversion
   (C) resolution
   (D) predicament
   (E) conclusion

2. INHABIT:
   (A) continue
   (B) confirm
   (C) surround
   (D) dwell
   (E) exhibit

3. GENEROUS:
   (A) beneficial
   (B) precocious
   (C) sociable
   (D) garrulous
   (E) benevolent

4. AGGREGATE:
   (A) median
   (B) agent
   (C) organization
   (D) total
   (E) equipment

5. IMPLEMENT:
   (A) idea
   (B) detail
   (C) instrument
   (D) component
   (E) property

6. GRACIOUSLY:
   (A) gratefully
   (B) kindly
   (C) easily
   (D) comfortably
   (E) readily

**GO ON TO THE NEXT PAGE.**

7. MEANDER:
   (A) manage
   (B) exercise
   (C) review
   (D) wander
   (E) delete

8. CONCUR:
   (A) alleviate
   (B) conspire
   (C) agree
   (D) contribute
   (E) congeal

9. AGILE:
   (A) able
   (B) provocative
   (C) listless
   (D) nimble
   (E) willful

10. ADDITION:
    (A) inclusion
    (B) nucleus
    (C) origin
    (D) antecedent
    (E) inception

11. PROCLIVITY:
    (A) effulgence
    (B) inclination
    (C) finesse
    (D) resurgence
    (E) weakness

12. PERSISTENT:
    (A) intelligent
    (B) perceptible
    (C) considerable
    (D) pretentious
    (E) determined

13. TEMPERATE:
    (A) sweet
    (B) moderate
    (C) peckish
    (D) warm
    (E) memorable

14. ENCOURAGE:
    (A) foster
    (B) conduct
    (C) determine
    (D) develop
    (E) cope

15. SCOLD:
    (A) scream
    (B) incense
    (C) berate
    (D) seethe
    (E) infuriate

16. IRREGULAR:
    (A) irrelevant
    (B) eccentric
    (C) irrespective
    (D) sporadic
    (E) preternatural

17. COMMENCEMENT:
    (A) justification
    (B) beginning
    (C) announcement
    (D) experience
    (E) conclusion

18. POROUS:
    (A) confident
    (B) ruinous
    (C) soluble
    (D) permeable
    (E) clever

19. CRITICIZE:
    (A) abuse
    (B) disparage
    (C) avenge
    (D) impale
    (E) hinder

20. ACQUIRE:
    (A) abstain
    (B) prefer
    (C) taste
    (D) produce
    (E) procure

**GO ON TO THE NEXT PAGE.**

21. DELUGE:
    (A) defer
    (B) delineate
    (C) overwhelm
    (D) thrash
    (E) facilitate

22. VENERABLE:
    (A) respected
    (B) bright
    (C) varied
    (D) trivial
    (E) measured

23. OBVIOUSLY:
    (A) substantially
    (B) momentously
    (C) allegedly
    (D) comprehensively
    (E) apparently

24. CERTAINTY:
    (A) agreement
    (B) conjecture
    (C) suspicion
    (D) assurance
    (E) belief

25. INCESSANT:
    (A) annoyed
    (B) disturbed
    (C) constant
    (D) lachrymose
    (E) irrevocable

26. VAGUE:
    (A) obsolete
    (B) nebulous
    (C) precocious
    (D) vexed
    (E) ponderous

27. SIGNIFY:
    (A) indicate
    (B) dedicate
    (C) assail
    (D) ratify
    (E) imagine

28. ACQUIESCE:
    (A) compare
    (B) remit
    (C) negotiate
    (D) comply
    (E) suffer

29. DIVISIVE:
    (A) factious
    (B) contiguous
    (C) variegated
    (D) diverse
    (E) prolific

30. ACCORD:
    (A) violation
    (B) description
    (C) recognition
    (D) settlement
    (E) condition

**GO ON TO THE NEXT PAGE.**

**Directions:** The questions that follow ask you to find relationships between words. For each question select the answer choice that best completes the meaning of the sentence.

Sample Question:

---

Swim is to pool as
(A) fork is to plate
(B) sweep is to broom
(C) clean is to kitchen
(D) sleep is to bed
(E) trot is to horse

Correct Answer: D
Choice D is correct because a pool is a place to swim just as a bed is a place to sleep.

---

31. Moist is to arid as sublime is to
    (A) majestic
    (B) dull
    (C) bright
    (D) foreboding
    (E) deserted

32. Saddle is to horse as
    (A) dog is to leash
    (B) cat is to collar
    (C) car is to driver
    (D) surfer is to surfboard
    (E) cushion is to chair

33. Jazz is to music as
    (A) projector is to film
    (B) brush is to paint
    (C) sing is to perform
    (D) tap is to dance
    (E) novel is to fiction

34. Kangaroo is to hop as snake is to
    (A) rattle
    (B) bite
    (C) swallow
    (D) coil
    (E) slither

35. Bowling is to lane as
    (A) soccer is to field
    (B) tennis is to net
    (C) rink is to hockey
    (D) kitchen is to dinner
    (E) court is to basketball

36. Water is to wave as
    (A) shell is to egg
    (B) cloud is to sky
    (C) fire is to flame
    (D) galaxy is to planet
    (E) tree is to leaf

37. Brief is to time as short is to
    (A) cake
    (B) travel
    (C) stop
    (D) substantial
    (E) distance

38. Square is to cube as circle is to
    (A) sphere
    (B) pyramid
    (C) cylindrical
    (D) round
    (E) perimeter

39. Select is to choose as
    (A) accept is to deny
    (B) pardon is to excuse
    (C) smile is to laugh
    (D) rid is to leave
    (E) squander is to skimp

40. Teaspoon is to tablespoon as pint is to
    (A) measure
    (B) liter
    (C) cup
    (D) quart
    (E) volume

**GO ON TO THE NEXT PAGE.**

41. Darkness is to light as
    (A) garment is to dry
    (B) color is to contrast
    (C) gap is to hole
    (D) calm is to quiet
    (E) silence is to sound

42. Husk is to corn as
    (A) shell is to nut
    (B) stem is to apple
    (C) egg is to yolk
    (D) sunflower is to seed
    (E) drain is to water

43. Order is to sequence as
    (A) number is to line
    (B) schedule is to plan
    (C) beginning is to end
    (D) manage is to discipline
    (E) wedding is to marriage

44. Dock is to boat as
    (A) sea is to submarine
    (B) hangar is to airplane
    (C) trailer is to truck
    (D) lot is to parking
    (E) car is to garage

45. Compass is to circle as ruler is to
    (A) angle
    (B) rectangle
    (C) line
    (D) straight
    (E) measure

46. Skin is to hair as
    (A) shower is to cap
    (B) meow is to kitten
    (C) sand is to beach
    (D) stem is to petal
    (E) volume is to sound

47. Sugar is to cake as
    (A) seat is to stadium
    (B) tennis is to racket
    (C) thumb is to finger
    (D) smile is to teeth
    (E) bird is to wing

48. Chill is to freeze as giggle is to
    (A) smile
    (B) smirk
    (C) guffaw
    (D) hysterical
    (E) gasp

49. Silk is to worm as
    (A) honey is to bee
    (B) corn is to pop
    (C) bread is to wheat
    (D) egg is to chicken
    (E) frog is to croak

50. Dawn is to dusk as
    (A) shriek is to scream
    (B) start is to finish
    (C) drink is to eat
    (D) study is to learn
    (E) copy is to trace

51. Astronomer is to stars as biologist is to
    (A) earth
    (B) water
    (C) stars
    (D) rocks
    (E) life

52. Weaving is to loom as
    (A) brick is to building
    (B) diving is to swim
    (C) singing is to song
    (D) cooking is to stove
    (E) rolling is to ball

53. Celsius is to Fahrenheit as kilometer is to
    (A) distance
    (B) mile
    (C) gallon
    (D) inch
    (E) yard

54. Express is to state as
    (A) communicate is to write
    (B) restructure is to rebuild
    (C) defy is to intimidate
    (D) shorten is to abbreviate
    (E) tease is to mock

**GO ON TO THE NEXT PAGE.**

55. Hang is to dry as soak is to
    (A) vanquish
    (B) annihilate
    (C) saturate
    (D) roust
    (E) render

56. Salamander is to amphibian as kangaroo is to
    (A) pouch
    (B) land
    (C) koala
    (D) mammal
    (E) hop

57. Median is to highway as
    (A) diameter is to circle
    (B) tower is to signal
    (C) seam is to stitch
    (D) tree is to axe
    (E) razor is to beard

58. Filter is to coffeepot as
    (A) bandage is to wound
    (B) screen is to window
    (C) hole is to cover
    (D) lid is to pot
    (E) bottle is to cap

59. Stream is to drop as boulder is to
    (A) fountain
    (B) gorge
    (C) pebble
    (D) mountain
    (E) crater

60. Find is to locate as
    (A) convey is to exemplify
    (B) puzzle is to quiz
    (C) dig is to diminish
    (D) disguise is to masquerade
    (E) perceive is to interject

**STOP!**
If you finish before time is up, check your work on this section only.

**Directions:** For each of the following questions, mark the letter of your choice on the answer sheet.

---

1. If $28 \div 4 \times \underline{\hspace{1cm}} = 8 \times 9 - 16$, then $\underline{\hspace{0.5cm}} =$
   (A) 2
   (B) 3
   (C) 6
   (D) 7
   (E) 8

2. $72 \div 9 \times 6 \times 12$ is equal to the product of 18 and
   (A) 16
   (B) 20
   (C) 24
   (D) 28
   (E) 32

3. Which of the following is NOT equal to a whole number?

   (A) $\dfrac{42}{7}$

   (B) $9 \times \dfrac{7}{16}$

   (C) $14 \div \dfrac{1}{14}$

   (D) $\dfrac{8}{12} \times 9$

   (E) $22.3 + 13.7$

4. $102\frac{3}{4}\% =$
   (A) 102.75
   (B) 10.275
   (C) 1.0275
   (D) 0.10275
   (E) 0.010275

5. It costs $m$ dollars to buy 64 cans of soda. At the same rate, how many dollars will it cost to buy 48 cans?

   (A) $\dfrac{m}{4}$

   (B) $\dfrac{3m}{4}$

   (C) $3m$

   (D) $\dfrac{4m}{3}$

   (E) $5m$

6. If $\frac{7}{16}$ of a number is 42, then $\frac{1}{2}$ of the same number is
   (A) 58
   (B) 56
   (C) 52
   (D) 48
   (E) 44

7. $\frac{2}{3} \div \frac{5}{6} =$

   (A) $\dfrac{4}{5}$

   (B) $\dfrac{5}{18}$

   (C) $\dfrac{15}{6}$

   (D) $2\dfrac{1}{2}$

   (E) $3\dfrac{5}{6}$

**GO ON TO THE NEXT PAGE.**

8. If the following is a right triangle and $\angle 2$ measures 59°, what is the measure of $\angle 1$?

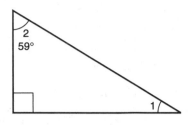

(A) 26°
(B) 31°
(C) 43°
(D) 52°
(E) 56°

9. $^1/_2 + ^1/_4 + ^3/_{16} =$

(A) $\dfrac{3}{5}$

(B) $\dfrac{5}{6}$

(C) $\dfrac{7}{8}$

(D) $\dfrac{15}{16}$

(E) $1\dfrac{1}{8}$

10. Which statement is always true?
(A) The sum of a positive and negative number is always negative.
(B) The difference of a positive and negative number is always negative.
(C) The product of two negative numbers is always positive.
(D) The quotient of two negative numbers is always negative.
(E) All of the above

11. What is the greatest common factor of 75, 90, and 120?
(A) 5
(B) 10
(C) 15
(D) 20
(E) 25

12. What is the least common multiple of 13, 26, and 2?
(A) 2
(B) 6
(C) 7
(D) 13
(E) 26

13. $^{18}/_{25} =$
(A) 0.54
(B) 0.63
(C) 0.66
(D) 0.68
(E) 0.72

14. Which pair of fractions is equivalent?

(A) $\dfrac{2}{3}, \dfrac{5}{6}$

(B) $\dfrac{9}{12}, \dfrac{5}{6}$

(C) $\dfrac{3}{4}, \dfrac{7}{8}$

(D) $\dfrac{4}{10}, \dfrac{2}{5}$

(E) $\dfrac{2}{3}, \dfrac{5}{9}$

15. A fence along a road is divided into sections that are each 5 meters long. If the fence is 0.5 kilometer long, how many sections are there?
(A) 10
(B) 50
(C) 100
(D) 250
(E) 500

16. The drama club is spending $224 to put on a play. They plan to sell tickets at $3.00 each. If they sell $n$ tickets, which of the following represents their profit after expenses?
(A) $3n - 224$

(B) $224 + \dfrac{n}{3}$

(C) $3n + 224$
(D) $224(n + 3)$

(E) $\dfrac{(n + 3)}{224}$

**GO ON TO THE NEXT PAGE.**

17. Christine spends 2 days a week painting houses and 3 days a week doing carpentry. If she earns $300 a day for painting and $240 a day for carpentry, how much does she earn in a week?
   (A) $1,280
   (B) $1,320
   (C) $1,360
   (D) $1,440
   (E) $1,460

18. The number of sixth-grade students in the Hill School is 8 more than $\frac{1}{6}$ of the whole student body. If there are 144 students in the school, how many are in sixth grade?
   (A) 26
   (B) 30
   (C) 32
   (D) 36
   (E) 40

19. One kilometer is approximately equal to 0.6 mile. How many kilometers are in 8 miles?
   (A) about 6
   (B) about 7
   (C) about 11
   (D) about 13
   (E) about 15

20. $12 + (-8) + (-9) + 6 =$
   (A) −6
   (B) −3
   (C) 0
   (D) 1
   (E) 3

21. $-36 \div (-12) =$
   (A) −12
   (B) −6
   (C) −3
   (D) 1
   (E) 3

22. At 6:00, what is the measure of the angle formed by the minute and hour hands on a clock?
   (A) 45°
   (B) 90°
   (C) 120°
   (D) 180°
   (E) 360°

23. A clock shows 2:05. What time is it when 4 hours 58 minutes have passed?
   (A) 7:03
   (B) 6:54
   (C) 6:46
   (D) 6:38
   (E) 5:50

24. A circle has a radius of 1.35 meters. Wire costs 2¢ per centimeter. How much will it cost to stretch a wire between two points on the circle if it passes through the center?
   (A) $5.40
   (B) $5.56
   (C) $5.64
   (D) $5.72
   (E) $5.80

25. If Tino rides his bike at a steady speed of 9 miles per hour, how far will he ride in 3 hours 40 minutes?
   (A) 27 miles
   (B) 33 miles
   (C) 36 miles
   (D) 39 miles
   (E) 42 miles

**STOP!**
If you finish before time is up, check your work on this section only.

## SECTION 5

Time: 25 Minutes

Read the topics below and choose the one that interests you the most. Fill in the circle for your chosen idea. Plan and write your essay or story on the paper provided.

---

Ⓐ Two heads are better than one.

Do you agree or disagree with the topic statement? Support your position with examples from your own experience, the experience of others, current events, history, or literature.

---

Ⓑ If you knew what I knew, what would you have done? Write a story that uses this as the first sentence.

_____

_____

_____

_____

_____

_____

_____

_____

_____

_____

_____

_____

_____

_____

# SSAT Practice Test III

## Answer Key

### Section 1 Quantitative I

| | | | | | |
|---|---|---|---|---|---|
| 1. | B | 11. | A | 21. | E |
| 2. | E | 12. | D | 22. | E |
| 3. | C | 13. | D | 23. | A |
| 4. | B | 14. | A | 24. | A |
| 5. | C | 15. | A | 25. | D |
| 6. | A | 16. | D | | |
| 7. | E | 17. | D | | |
| 8. | C | 18. | D | | |
| 9. | E | 19. | B | | |
| 10. | B | 20. | B | | |

### Section 2 Reading Comprehension

| | | | | | |
|---|---|---|---|---|---|
| 1. | C | 15. | B | 29. | B |
| 2. | C | 16. | D | 30. | C |
| 3. | B | 17. | E | 31. | D |
| 4. | D | 18. | D | 32. | B |
| 5. | A | 19. | A | 33. | A |
| 6. | E | 20. | D | 34. | D |
| 7. | D | 21. | B | 35. | C |
| 8. | E | 22. | A | 36. | D |
| 9. | A | 23. | C | 37. | B |
| 10. | B | 24. | B | 38. | C |
| 11. | D | 25. | D | 39. | A |
| 12. | A | 26. | B | 40. | E |
| 13. | E | 27. | E | | |
| 14. | C | 28. | C | | |

## Section 3 Verbal

| | | | | | |
|---|---|---|---|---|---|
| 1. | A | 21. | C | 41. | E |
| 2. | D | 22. | A | 42. | A |
| 3. | E | 23. | E | 43. | B |
| 4. | D | 24. | D | 44. | B |
| 5. | C | 25. | C | 45. | C |
| 6. | B | 26. | B | 46. | D |
| 7. | D | 27. | A | 47. | A |
| 8. | C | 28. | D | 48. | C |
| 9. | D | 29. | A | 49. | A |
| 10. | A | 30. | D | 50. | B |
| 11. | B | 31. | B | 51. | E |
| 12. | E | 32. | E | 52. | D |
| 13. | B | 33. | D | 53. | B |
| 14. | A | 34. | E | 54. | D |
| 15. | C | 35. | A | 55. | C |
| 16. | D | 36. | C | 56. | D |
| 17. | B | 37. | E | 57. | A |
| 18. | D | 38. | A | 58. | B |
| 19. | B | 39. | B | 59. | C |
| 20. | E | 40. | D | 60. | D |

## Section 4 Quantitative II

| | | | | | |
|---|---|---|---|---|---|
| 1. | E | 10. | C | 19. | D |
| 2. | E | 11. | C | 20. | D |
| 3. | B | 12. | E | 21. | E |
| 4. | C | 13. | E | 22. | D |
| 5. | B | 14. | D | 23. | A |
| 6. | D | 15. | C | 24. | A |
| 7. | A | 16. | A | 25. | B |
| 8. | B | 17. | B | | |
| 9. | D | 18. | C | | |

# Answers and Explanations

## Section 1 Quantitative I

1. **B is correct.** This is a simple addition problem. Add the amounts of $12.98, $47.23, $22.97, $14.77, and $15.00 to get the total of $112.95.

2. **E is correct.** To calculate the percent, divide the number of jazz and rap songs by the total number of songs. $240 \div 800 = 0.30$. To change that to a percent, move the decimal point two places to the right and add the percent sign to get the correct answer of 30%.

3. **C is correct.** To find the average, add up the numbers and divide by the number of numbers. In this instance the number of miles Matt rode adds to 150. The number of days is 5, so the average number of miles per day he rode is $150 \div 5 = 30$. Don't make the mistake of dividing by 4 because on one day Matt's number of miles was 0. That number needs to be used in calculating the average.

4. **B is correct.** If Aaron has 256 cans of soup to pack into boxes of 30, he can fill $256 \div 30 = 8$ boxes with 16 cans of soup left over.

5. **C is correct.** By definition, an obtuse angle is one that measures between 90° and 180°.

6. **A is correct.** You are told that two numbers add to 1,500 and that one of the two is 4 times the size of other. Create an equation:

   $x + 4x = 1,500$
   Solve for $x$.
   $5x = 1,500$
   $x = 300$
   $4x = 1,200$
   So the two numbers are 300 and 1,200.

7. **E is correct.** To calculate the answer, divide 200 by 5.
   $200 \div 5 = 40$

   Multiply:
   $40 \times \$0.10 = \$4.00$

8. **C is correct.** Use the following formula: $\text{Percent of change} = \dfrac{\text{Amount of change}}{\text{Starting point}}$.

   In this problem we know that the amount of change is $270 and the starting price of the computer is $1,800. Substitute that information into the formula:

   Percent of change = $270/$1,800 = 0.15.

   Change that number to a percent by moving the decimal place two places to the right and adding the percent sign.
   $0.15 = 15\%$

9. **E is correct.** Angles 1 and 2 are on opposite sides of the transversal, are outside the two parallel lines, and are not adjacent. They are therefore opposite exterior angles, which by definition have the same measure.

10. **B is correct.** According to the graph, ice skating was the least popular kind of party. It was picked by only 22 students, the fewest for any of the party types listed.

11. **A is correct.** It costs $m$ dollars to buy 24 cookies. 6 cookies are $1/4$ of 24, so the cost of 6 cookies will be $1/4 \times m = m/4$ dollars.

12. **D is correct.** $18 \div {}^3/_4 = {}^{18}/_1 \div {}^3/_4 = {}^{18}/_1 \times {}^4/_3 = {}^{72}/_3 = 24$.

13. **D is correct.** The edge of the garden is its perimeter. To find the perimeter of a rectangle, add the lengths of the sides: $40 + 15 + 40 + 15 = 110$ yards.

14. **A is correct.** The two angles together form a straight angle, which measures 180°. Therefore, $\angle 2 = 180° - 35° = 145°$.

15. **A is correct.** $5 \times 4 + 4 = 24$; $4 \times 3 = 12$; and $24 \div 12 = 2$.

16. **D is correct.** If $\frac{x}{8} = 4\frac{x}{y}$, then $xy = 32x$ and dividing by $x$, $y = 32$.

17. **D is correct.** $^{24}/_6 = 4$; $6 \times {}^8/_{16} = {}^{48}/_{16} = 3$; $9 \div {}^1/_9 = 9 \times {}^9/_1 = 81$; $7.4 + 5.6 = 13$. However, ${}^3/_5 \times 8 = {}^{24}/_5 = 4\,{}^4/_5$, which is not a whole number.

18. **D is correct.** $71{}^1/_5\% = 0.712$.

19. **B is correct.** To find the perimeter, add the lengths of the sides: $13 + 36 + 13 + 36 = 98$ cm.

20. **B is correct.**
    ${}^3/_5 x = 18$
    ${}^1/_5 x = 6$
    $x = 30$
    ${}^1/_2 x = 15$

21. **E is correct.** Of the 6 numbers on the cube, 3 are even. So the probability that the number facing up will be even is ${}^3/_6$ or ${}^1/_2$.

22. **E is correct.** 15% of $400 = 0.15 \times 400 = \$60$. $\$400 - \$60 = \$340$.

23. **A is correct.** To find the area of a triangle, use the formula $A = ({}^1/_2)bh$ where $b$ is the base of the triangle and $h$ is the height. Because the triangle shown is a right triangle, side $a$ is the height. Substituting into the formula: $A = ({}^1/_2)(6)(4) = 12$ ft².

24. **A is correct.** This is a 30°–60°–90° triangle. Line segment $YZ$ is the short leg, so it is ${}^1/_2$ the length of the hypotenuse. $6 \times {}^1/_2 = 3$

25. **D is correct.** Find 2020 along the horizontal axis and then read the number that corresponds to the vertical axis. This life expectancy is about 85 years.

## Section 2 Reading Comprehension

1. **C is correct.** The quotation shows that the president has a duty to report to Congress on the State of the Union and to recommend necessary and expedient measures. This annual message to Congress came to be known as the State of the Union. Choice A is wrong because the use of the quotation does not necessarily indicate that the author is knowledgeable about the Constitution, but only about this particular provision. Choice B is wrong because, although the quotation does illustrate the actual wording of this section of the Constitution, it is not intended to illustrate the wording of the entire Constitution. Choice D is wrong because there is no demonstration of different interpretations of this provision. The differences cited are in the form, content, and delivery method of the message, not in the need to report to Congress. Choice E is wrong because the passage does not distinguish between constitutional duty and custom. The report on the State of the Union is mandated by the Constitution.

2. **C is correct.** The Constitution requires the president to give Congress information on the state of the union "from time to time." Throughout the passage, the State of the Union message is referred to as the president's "annual message." Clearly, the phrase "from time to time" has come to mean "annually."

3. **B is correct.** This information is found in the opening quote from the U.S. Constitution, which says that presidents have a constitutional duty to "give to Congress information of the State of the Union."

4. **D is correct.** Thomas Jefferson thought Washington's oral presentation was "too monarchial for the new republic," so Jefferson "wrote out his address and sent it to Congress to be read by a clerk."

5. **A is correct.** As stated in the last paragraph, "With the advent of radio and television, the President's annual message has become not only a conversation between the President and Congress but also an opportunity for the President to communicate with the American people at the same time." Choices B and C are wrong because Thomas Jefferson was president in the nineteenth century and Lyndon Johnson in the second half of the twentieth century. Choice D is wrong because Congress moved to Washington, D.C., in 1800, and choice E is wrong because newspaper coverage of the State of the Union message began long before the start of the twentieth century.

6. **E is correct.** As stated in the last paragraph, "Harry S. Truman's 1947 address was the first to be broadcast on television." None of the other questions is answered by information in the passage.

7. **D is correct.** Since there is no mention of how to survive a tsunami, choice E can be easily eliminated. Although the passage touches upon the tsunami of 2004 (choice A), the difference between a tsunami and a tidal wave (choice B), and the origin of the word "tsunami" (choice C), each of these choices is too narrow to cover the overall purpose of the passage, which is to provide information about tsunamis in general.

8. **E is correct.** As stated in the second paragraph, "Most tsunamis are generated by earthquakes, but they may also be caused by volcanic eruptions, landslides, undersea slumps, or meteor impacts." Tornadoes are mentioned along with hurricanes, not as a cause of tsunamis, but rather as another kind of natural disaster.

9. **A is correct.** The author mentions the 1960 tsunami in Japan in the third paragraph: "The waves radiate outward in all directions from the disturbance and can propagate across entire ocean basins. For example, in 1960, an earthquake in Chile caused a tsunami that swept across the Pacific to Japan." The words "for example" indicate that the reference to Japan is intended to show how far the waves radiated from the earthquake in Chile.

10. **B is correct.** The answer to this question is found in paragraph 3 which says, "Tsunami waves are distinguished from ordinary ocean waves by their great length between peaks, often exceeding 100 miles in the deep ocean, and by the long amount of time between these peaks, ranging from five minutes to an hour." Choice A is wrong because the passage does not mention that regular waves follow closely one after the other. Choice C is wrong because it has no support in the passage. Choice D is wrong because the passage states that in deep water "a tsunami is barely noticeable, causing only a small rising and falling of the sea surface as it passes." Choice E is wrong because tsunami waves grow in height as they approach land and shallow water.

11. **D is correct.** This passage is full of the kind of strictly factual scientific information most likely to be found in a science textbook. Choice A can be eliminated because the passage has none of the folksy qualities of a personal letter. Choice B cannot be correct because the passage is clearly fact, not fiction. Choice C is wrong because the passage describes a natural disaster, not the weather, and choice E is wrong because the passage merely mentions the tsunami of 2004, but does not go on to provide the details of that particular event as a news article would.

12. **A is correct.** The answer to this question can be found in paragraph 4: "As the tsunami approaches land and shallow water, the waves slow down and become compressed, causing them to grow in height." In the best of cases the tsunami comes ashore like a rising tide causing flooding of coastal areas. In the worst of cases, a wall of turbulent water several meters high rushes ashore with great destructive power.

13. **E is correct.** All of the choices are meanings of the word "bore." However, only choice E is correct in context. As stated in the second sentence of paragraph 5, "A bore is a wall of turbulent water that can be several meters high and can rush onshore with great destructive power."

14. **C is correct.** Line 1 mentions that the athlete "won your town the race." "Runners" are also mentioned in lines 5 and 19, and line 22 mentions "the fleet foot." All of these references make it obvious that the athlete in this poem is a runner. Choice E cannot be correct because the author addresses the athlete as "Smart lad" in line 9.

15. **B is correct.** The setting is revealed in lines 5–8: "Today, the road all runners come, Shoulder-high we bring you home, And set you at your threshold down, Townsman of a stiller town." These words describe a funeral procession for a young champion being carried to his grave. Lines 1–4 describe a victory celebration that happened

at some earlier point in time. The word "today" in line 5 indicates that the poem takes place at the funeral for a young athlete.

16. **D is correct.** The second stanza describes a funeral. The athlete is carried to his gravesite, and in death becomes a "townsman of a stiller town."

17. **E is correct.** The author calls the athlete a "smart lad" to die before his glory fades (lines 9–10). Lines 17–20 praise the athlete for not becoming one of those "lads that wore their honors out," meaning an athlete who continues to compete even though he can no longer keep up.

18. **D is correct.** Lines 11–12 ("And early though the laurel grows/It withers quicker than the rose") express the poet's belief that, although the athlete's glory came early, it will not last. In other words, glory withers and dies as quickly as a rose, and statement I is correct. Statement II is confirmed by lines 9–10 ("Smart lad, to slip betimes away/From fields where glory does not stay") as well as lines 17–20 ("Now you will not swell the rout/Of lads that wore their honors out/Runners whom renown outran/And the name died before the man."). Nothing in the poem supports statement III.

19. **A is correct.** The constant repetition of "gone" and "wiped out" in lines 8–15 serves to emphasize the author's inability to believe that such devastation could possibly occur. "San Francisco is *gone* . . . Its industrial section is *wiped out*. Its business section is *wiped out*. Its social and residential section is *wiped out*. The factories and warehouses, the great stores and newspaper buildings, the hotels and the palaces of the nabobs, are all *gone*." Choices B, D, and E are wrong because there are no words in the paragraph that support a mood of desperate longing, cautious optimism, or heartfelt pity. Choice C is possible; however, the mood of the paragraph is much closer to awe and disbelief than it is to uncontrolled outrage, so choice A is a better answer.

20. **D is correct.** Here are just a few examples of the vivid images provided by the author: ". . . the smoke of San Francisco's burning was a lurid tower visible a hundred miles away . . ." "The streets were humped into ridges and depressions, and piled with the debris of fallen walls." "The steel rails were twisted into perpendicular and horizontal angles."

21. **B is correct.** A *nabob* is "a rich and important person." Choice A is wrong because *knaves* is "a rascal" or "a rogue." Choice E is wrong because although the passage mentions "the palaces of nabobs," nabobs do not have to be of royal blood. Choices C and D have nothing to do with the word "nabobs."

22. **A is correct.** The passage tells mainly of the massive destruction the San Francisco earthquake caused; roads and rail systems were destroyed, telephone and telegraph systems were "disrupted," and the "water-mains had burst." Thus, the statement conveys the idea that all modern conveniences had been lost, and the city had been reduced to living without twentieth-century amenities.

23. **C is correct.** The passage is arranged in chronological order. This is evident in the first few words of paragraphs 3, 4, and 5. Paragraph 3 starts with the words "On Wednesday morning," paragraph 4 starts with "By Wednesday afternoon," and paragraph 5 starts with "Wednesday night."

24. **B is correct.** As evidenced by lines 42–44 ("At that time I watched the vast conflagration from out on the bay."), the author was an eyewitness to the earthquake. His primary purpose for writing this passage was to report what he saw during that terrible time. Choice A is wrong because the passage provides no scientific explanation telling how earthquakes occur. Choice C is wrong because the passage describes the events of the earthquake, but does not go into the feelings of the residents. Choice D is wrong because only one paragraph of the account is devoted to the winds that helped the fire spread. Choice E is wrong because the author's praise for the firefighters' efforts is only one small part of the account, not its entire focus.

25. **D is correct.** As stated in the second paragraph, "In those days, a million people died from smallpox each year in Europe alone. . . . " Choice A is wrong because the passage states that a million people died from smallpox. Since some people did survive smallpox, it can be assumed that the disease struck many more than a million people each year. Choices B and C are wrong because milkmaids contracted cowpox, not smallpox, from the cows. Choice E is wrong because the passage states that those who survived "were often left with grim reminders of their ordeals: blindness, deep scars, and deformities."

26. **B is correct.** Choices A, D, and E are all mentioned in paragraph 3: "Since Jenner's time, vaccines have been developed against more than 20 infectious diseases such as influenza, pneumonia, whooping cough, rubella, meningitis, and hepatitis B." Choice C is mentioned in paragraph 2, "By the beginning of the 20th century, vaccines for rabies, diphtheria, typhoid fever, and plague were in use, in addition to the vaccine for smallpox." The only answer choice not mentioned is choice B, scarlet fever.

27. **E is correct.** As stated in the last paragraph, "Weakened microbes, killed microbes, inactivated toxins, and purified proteins or polysaccharides derived from microbes are the most common components used in vaccine development strategies."

28. **C is correct.** The answer to this question is found in the second paragraph, which states that "Jenner laid the foundation for modern vaccines" and "started on a course that would ease the suffering of people around the world for centuries to come." Choice A is wrong because it was not until 1980 that "an updated version of Jenner's vaccine led to the total eradication of smallpox." Choice B is wrong because Jenner used cowpox-producing organisms to make the vaccine that protected people from the more deadly smallpox. Choices D and E are wrong because although Jenner's work was the basis for the development of vaccines for rabies and typhoid fever, the vaccine Jenner produced in 1796 was for smallpox only.

29. **B is correct.** According to the last paragraph, "Scientists use vaccines to 'trick' the human immune system into producing antibodies or immune cells that protect against the real disease-causing organism." Choice A is wrong because the vaccine does not directly attack the disease-causing organism, instead it causes the body to produce antibodies against the disease-causing organism. Choice C is wrong because vaccines contain "weakened microbes, killed microbes, inactivated toxins, and purified proteins or polysaccharides derived from microbes," not deadly disease-producing organisms. Choice D is wrong because the vaccine does not contain antibodies, rather it triggers the body to produce antibodies. Choice E is wrong because although some people may have an allergic reaction to some vaccines, vaccines do not work by producing an allergic reaction.

30. **C is correct.** The first sentence describes the birthmark as a "crimson hand, which at first had been strongly visible upon the marble paleness of Georgiana's cheek." The birthmark fades like "the stain of the rainbow fading out of the sky," but it is not shaped like a rainbow, so choice A is incorrect. The birthmark fades to "the faintest rose color," but is not described as having the shape of a rose, so choice B is incorrect. There is nothing in the passage to suggest that the birthmark is shaped like a butterfly or a sun, so choices D and E are both incorrect.

31. **D is correct.** The first paragraph tells that the birthmark is fading. In the second paragraph Aylmer says, "Success! Success!" indicating that he is responsible for making the birthmark fade. Thus the most reasonable assumption is that Alymer had performed some kind of operation on his wife to remove her birthmark. The presence of a servant indicates that Aylmer is not a poor man, making choice A incorrect. Choices B and C can be eliminated because all the evidence indicates that Aylmer is striving to help his wife by removing the birthmark that "had once blazed with such disastrous brilliancy as to scare away all their happiness." Choice E is wrong because it is Georgiana, not Aylmer, who is dying.

32. **B is correct.** Georgiana gazes into the mirror and sees "how barely perceptible was now that crimson hand which had once blazed with such disastrous brilliancy as to scare away all their happiness." A mark that is barely perceptible is very faint.

33. **A is correct.** When Georgiana awakens, Alymer calls her his "peerless bride" and proclaims, "You are perfect!" The best synonym for "perfect" is "flawless."

34. **D is correct.** Even though Georgiana knows she is dying as a result of Aylmer's attempt to remove her birthmark, she speaks to Alymer "with more than human tenderness," calling him "My poor Aylmer" and "dearest Aylmer." Her words do not indicate that she is bitter (choice A) or angry (choice B). She may be happy to see that the birthmark is gone, but that does not describe her feelings toward Aylmer, so choice C is wrong. Because she is tender and loving toward her husband, she would not be described as uncaring; thus, choice E is wrong.

35. **C is correct.** Aylmer's attempt to make his wife perfect resulted in destroying her, thus illustrating the fact that perfection cannot be achieved on earth. Choice A is wrong because if love were blind Aylmer would not have attempted to remove the birthmark. Choice B is wrong because the passage proves the opposite to be true. Choice D is wrong because the effect of the birthmark was "to scare away all their happiness." Choice E is wrong because the story did not end well; it ended with Georgiana's death.

36. **D is correct.** The main purpose of the passage is to discuss the origins of coins as a part of the monetary system of ancient Lydia.

37. **B is correct.** In lines 24–27, the author describes the making of Lydian coins by explaining the key steps in the minting process.

38. **C is correct.** Line 19 of the passage explains that electrum was "a combination of silver and gold."

39. **A is correct.** According to lines 24–27 of the passage, the punch mark was an impression made by a hammer as it forced the molten metal into the mold.

40. **E is correct.** According to lines 31–35 of the passage, the value of Lydian coins depended on their size and weight.


## Section 3 Verbal

1. **A is correct.** A *bias* is a *preference* or an inclination, especially one that inhibits impartial judgment.

2. **D is correct.** To *inhabit* is to live in or reside in—in other words, to *dwell*.

3. **E is correct.** *Generous* is an adjective meaning liberal in giving or sharing. Similarly, *benevolent* is an adjective meaning characterized by or suggestive of doing good, often in regard to charity.

4. **D is correct.** *Aggregate* is a *total*, constituting or amounting to a whole.

5. **C is correct.** An *implement*, used here as a noun, is a tool or *instrument* used in doing work—for instance, *a gardening implement*.

6. **B is correct.** To behave *graciously* is to behave in a *kindly* or warm manner.

7. **D is correct.** To *meander* is to move aimlessly and idly without a fixed direction—in other words, to *wander*.

8. **C is correct.** To *concur* is to be of the same opinion—to *agree*.

9. **D is correct.** *Agile* is an adjective used to describe someone or something that is quick, light, and moves with ease. The choice that best fits this definition is *nimble*.

10. **A is correct.** *Addition* is the act or process of adding something extra to a thing; something added. Similarly, *inclusion* is the act or state of being included; something included.

11. **B is correct.** *Proclivity* is a noun meaning a natural propensity, predisposition, or *inclination*.

12. **E is correct.** When someone is *persistent*, that person refuses to give up or let go—in other words, is *determined*.

13. **B is correct.** *Temperate* is an adjective meaning *moderate* in degree or quality.

14. **A is correct.** To *encourage* is to give support to or to cultivate. Similarly, to *foster* is to promote the development and growth of.

15. **C is correct.** To *scold* is to reprimand or to criticize harshly and usually angrily—in other words, to *berate*.

16. **D is correct.** *Irregular* is an adjective used to describe something that occurs at an uneven rate, occurrence, or duration. *Sporadic* can be used synonymously with *irregular*.

17. **B is correct.** A *commencement* is a *beginning* or a start.

18. **D is correct.** *Porous* is an adjective used to describe something that permits the passage of gas or liquid through pores or small spaces. *Permeable*, meaning that which can be permeated or penetrated, especially by liquid or gases, is its synonym.

19. **B is correct.** To *criticize* is to find fault with. Similarly, to *disparage* is to speak of in a slighting or disrespectful way.

20. **E is correct.** To *acquire* is to gain possession of. *Procure*, which means to obtain or acquire, is its synonym.

21. **C is correct.** To *deluge* is to *overwhelm* with a large number or amount.

22. **A is correct.** *Venerable* is an adjective, usually used to describe a person who commands respect by virtue of age, character, dignity, or position. A person who is described as venerable could similarly be described as *respected*.

23. **E is correct.** *Obviously* is defined as easily perceived or understood. *Apparently*, its synonym, is defined as readily understood.

24. **D is correct.** A *certainty* is something that is clearly established or assured—in other words, an *assurance*.

25. **C is correct.** *Incessant* describes something that continues without interruption—something that is *constant*.

26. **B is correct.** *Vague*, like *nebulous*, describes something that is not clearly expressed or is inexplicit.

27. **A is correct.** To *signify* is to make known, as with a sign or word—in other words, to *indicate*.

28. **D is correct.** To *acquiesce* is to consent or to *comply* passively or without protest.

29. **A is correct.** *Divisive* is an adjective used to describe something creating dissension or discord. Similarly, *factious* describes something of, relating to, produced by, or characterized by internal dissension.

30. **D is correct.** An *accord* is a *settlement* or compromise of conflicting opinions.

31. **B is correct.** The relationship in this question is one of contrasts. *Moist* is the opposite of *arid* just as *sublime* (meaning "inspiring awe" or "impressive") is the opposite of *dull*. Only choice B provides an adjective that is opposite in meaning.

32. **E is correct.** This sequence presents an analogy of part to whole, but it also wants you to take the comparison a step further and consider usage when discerning the right answer. A *saddle* sits atop a *horse* in much the same way that a *cushion* sits atop a *chair*.

33. **D is correct.** This stem provides another part-to-whole analogy. *Jazz* is a style of *music* just as *tap* is a style of *dance*. No other answer choice offers a specific style of a thing paired with a broader reference to that thing.

34. **E is correct.** This is a fairly straightforward usage sequence that analogizes an activity (hop) to the animal that performs it. A *kangaroo hops* from one place to another just as a *snake slithers* from one place to another. *Coil* (choice D) is incorrect because it is the activity the snake performs in order to sleep or rest.

35. **A is correct.** This is a fairly straightforward usage sequence that analogizes an event (bowling) to the location it takes place (lane). You should be able to infer that *bowling* occurs on a *lane* just as *soccer* occurs on a *field*.

36. **C is correct.** Flip the words if you have trouble understanding this stem: *wave* is to *water* as *flame* is to *fire*. No other choice pairs a noun with another noun that suggests its form and motion. *Fire* takes the form of a *flame*; similarly, *water* can take the form of a *wave*.

37. **E is correct.** This sequence tests your familiarity of adjectives used to describe levels of contrast with nouns. A *brief* amount of *time* describes a short duration just as a *short distance* describes an abbreviated trip. No other answer choice matches the context of the stem with regard to describing a term of measurement.

38. **A is correct.** A *square* represented in three-dimensional form takes the shape of a *cube* just as a *circle* represented in three-dimensional form takes the shape of a *sphere*. Choice C is incorrect because *cylindrical* is an adjective which describes something of, relating to, or having the shape of a cylinder, not a noun.

39. **B is correct.** This is another question that tests your knowledge of synonym pairs. *Select* and *choose* are synonymous just as *pardon* and *excuse* are synonymous. Choice C is incorrect because, although both words denote pleasure or happiness, they are not synonymous. Choice E is incorrect because *squander* means "to fail to take advantage of," and *skimp* means "to provide for or supply inadequately."

40. **D is correct.** To answer this measurement analogy correctly, it will help you to know that an amount consisting of a *teaspoon* is less than an amount consisting of a *tablespoon*. So, following the pattern the stem establishes,

you will need to know which choice represents a greater measure than a *pint*. Choice B is incorrect because, although a liter is greater than *a pint*, this is a metric measurement. The other three measurements the stem provides are U.S. Customary measurements; therefore choice B is not a better answer than choice D. Choice C is incorrect because a cup is a measurement which is less than a pint, not more.

41. **E is correct.** This question provides another example of an analogy that tests your knowledge of contrasts of degrees. *Darkness* is the absence of *light* just as *silence* is the absence of *sound*. None of the other relationships offers a combination that defines one word by the absence of another; *garment* is not the absence of *dry* (choice A); *color* is not the absence of *contrast* (choice B); *gap* is not the absence of *hole* (C); and *calm* is not the absence of *quiet* (choice D).

42. **A is correct.** The relationship presented in this sequence is one of part to whole; however, this analogy goes a step further, and you will need to discern how in order to arrive at the correct answer. The *husk* is the outer covering of an ear of *corn* just as a *shell* is the outer covering of a *nut*. Therefore, choice A is correct. No other option presents this type of part-to-whole relationship.

43. **B is correct.** This sequence provides another example of an analogy involving words that are synonymous with one another. After reading the stem you should realize that *order* and *sequence* are synonyms. In order to select the correct answer, you will have to choose the option that also contains two words with similar meanings. *Schedule is to plan* is the only correct answer.

44. **B is correct.** Flip the words if you have difficulty with this sequence. A *boat* is kept at a *dock*, and similarly, a *plane* is kept in a *hangar*. Choice E may seem correct, but be careful; a closer look will reveal that this choice has *car* and *garage* in the incorrect order.

45. **C is correct.** This type of sequence is known as a usage analogy. Typically with this type of comparison, the stem will provide an instrument and a function of that instrument. You should be able to infer from the stem that a *compass* is used to draw a *circle*. Similarly, a *ruler* is used to draw a *line*.

46. **D is correct.** This question presents a part-to-part analogy. *Skin* and *hair* are both parts of the human body just as both *stem* and *petal* are parts of a flower. No other option presents two pieces that are part of a whole.

47. **A is correct.** The relationship presented in this sequence is one of part to whole. *Sugar* is one ingredient (part) of a *cake* just as a *seat* is one part of a *stadium*. Choice E is incorrect because, as it is written, the whole (bird) precedes the part (wing).

48. **C is correct.** This question tests your knowledge of degrees of contrast. To *chill* something is less extreme than to *freeze* it. Similarly, to *giggle* is less extreme than to *guffaw* (meaning "to laugh heartily and boisterously").

49. **A is correct.** By now, you have seen several types of analogies involving objects or individuals and activities. There is the object-to-activity analogy (*chisel* is to *carve*), as well as the individual-to-activity analogy (*tourist* is to *sightsee*). The sequence presented here is another variation, this time involving insects. To answer this question correctly, you will need to know that *worm* and *silk* appear in the stem because silk is produced by a species of worm. Similarly, *honey* is produced by *bees*.

50. **B is correct.** This question tests your knowledge of opposites. *Dawn* represents the beginning of daylight just as *dusk* represents the end of daylight. Only choice B offers a comparable contrast.

51. **E is correct.** This analogy asks you to make a correlation between an individual and what that individual studies. An *astronomer* studies the *stars* just as a *biologist* studies *life*.

52. **D is correct.** This is another usage sequence that analogizes an activity (weaving) to the apparatus used in that activity (loom). So choice D is correct because a *stove* is used for *cooking* just as a *loom* is used for *weaving*. No other option pairs an activity with an object used in that activity.

53. **B is correct.** This is a type of measurement question that compares metric measurements with U.S. Customary measurements. *Celsius* is how temperature is measured within the metric system just as *Fahrenheit* is how temperature is measured within the U.S. Customary system. Similarly, *kilometers* are how long distances are measured within the metric system just as *miles* are how long distances are measured within the U.S. Customary system.

54. **D is correct.** To *state* something is to *express* it just as to *shorten* something is to *abbreviate* it. No other option provides a pair of words with meanings that are synonymous.

55. **C is correct.** This type of sequence is referred to as an activity-to-result analogy. One way to dry something (clothes, for instance) is by hanging them. Therefore, *hang* is the activity and *dry* is the result. Similarly, when you *soak* something in water (say, a towel) the result is that you *saturate* it.

56. **D is correct.** To have a better chance at answering this part-to-whole analogy correctly, it will help if you know that a salamander is scientifically classified as an amphibian (meaning it can live on land or in water). Indeed, knowing this should make it easier for you to conclude that if a *salamander* is an *amphibian* then a *kangaroo* must be a *mammal*.

57. **A is correct.** A *median* divides two sides of the *highway*. In a similar sense, a *diameter* divides two sides of a *circle*.

58. **B is correct.** The *filter* in a *coffeepot* allows the liquid coffee to pass through but keeps out the coffee grounds. Similarly, a *screen* on a *window* allows air to pass through while keeping out larger pieces of debris, such as leaves.

59. **C is correct.** This sequence presents a relationship that is one of degree, with the first word being much larger than the second. A *stream* is a much larger body of water than a single *drop*. As well, a *boulder* is a much larger rock than a *pebble*.

60. **D is correct.** The analogy in this sentence is one of similarities. When you *find* an item you are looking for, you have *located* it. Likewise, when you *masquerade*, you *disguise* yourself as someone else. No other option offers a pair of words that share a similar meaning.

## Section 4 Quantitative II

1. **E is correct.** $8 \times 9 - 16 = 56$; $28 \div 4 = 7$; and $56 \div 7 = 8$.

2. **E is correct.** $72 \div 9 \times 6 \times 12 = 576$; $576 \div 18 = 32$.

3. **B is correct.** $\frac{42}{7} = 6$; $14 \div \frac{1}{14} = 14 \times \frac{14}{1} = 196$; $\frac{8}{12} \times 9 = \frac{72}{12} = 6$. $22.3 + 13.7 = 36$. However, $9 \times \frac{7}{16} = \frac{63}{16} = 3\frac{15}{16}$, which is not a whole number.

4. **C is correct.** $102\frac{3}{4}\% = 1.0275$.

5. **B is correct.** It costs $m$ dollars to buy 64 cans of soda. 48 cans are $\frac{3}{4}$ of 64, so the cost of 48 cans of soda will be $3/4 \times m = 3m/4$ dollars.

6. **D is correct.**
$$\frac{7}{16}x = 42$$
$$\frac{1}{16}x = 6$$
$$x = 96$$
$$\frac{1}{2}x = 48$$

7. **A is correct.** When dividing fractions, invert and multiply. See if you can simplify the fractions.
$$\frac{2}{3} \div \frac{5}{6}$$
$$= \frac{2}{3} \times \frac{6}{5} \quad \text{Multiply}$$
$$= \frac{12}{15} \quad \text{Simplify}$$
$$= \frac{4}{5}$$

8. **B is correct.** A right triangle has one angle that measures 90°. If a second angle measures 49°, that accounts for 139° of the total 180° in the triangle. $180° - 139° = 31°$

9. **D is correct.** Convert to equivalent expressions: $^{1}/_{2} = {}^{8}/_{16}$; $^{1}/_{4} = {}^{4}/_{16}$; $^{8}/_{16} + {}^{4}/_{16} + {}^{3}/_{16} = {}^{15}/_{16}$

10. **C is correct.** The product of two negative numbers is always positive.

11. **C is correct.** The greatest common factor of a group of numbers is the greatest whole number that is a factor of all the numbers. The greatest common factor of 75, 90, and 120 is 15.

12. **E is correct.** The least common multiple of a group of numbers is the least whole number, greater than 0, that is a multiple of all of the numbers. The least common multiple of 13, 26, and 2 is 26.

13. **E is correct.** $^{18}/_{25} = {}^{72}/_{100} = 0.72$.

14. **D is correct.** $^{4}/_{10}$ can be simplified to $^{2}/_{5}$.

15. **C is correct.** 0.5 km = 500 meters; $500 \div 5 = 100$.

16. **A is correct.** If the club sells $n$ tickets at $3.00 each, the amount they will earn is $3n$. Their profit after paying $224 in expenses is $3n - 224$.

17. **B is correct.** $(2 \times \$300) + (3 \times \$240) = \$600 + \$720 = \$1,320$

18. **C is correct.** Set up an equation. If $x$ = number of students in sixth grade,
$$x = \frac{144}{6} + 8$$
$$x = 24 + 8$$
$$x = 32$$

19. **D is correct.** $8 \div 0.6 = 13.33$, so there are about 13 kilometers in 8 miles.

20. **D is correct.** $12 + (-8) + (-9) + 6 = 4 + (-9) + 6 = -5 + 6 = 1$.

21. **E is correct.** $-36 \div (-12) = 3$. Check: $3 \times (-12) = -36$.

22. **D is correct.** At 6:00, the minute hand points straight up and the hour hand points straight down. Together, they form a straight angle that measures 180°.

23. **A is correct.** When 4 hours have passed, the time is 6:05. After another 58 minutes the time is 7:03.

24. **A is correct.** A wire stretched between two points on a circle and passing through the center will form a diameter of the circle. Diameter = radius × 2. If the radius is 1.35 m, the diameter = 2(1.35) = 2.7 m = 270 cm. If wire costs 2¢/cm, the cost of the wire stretching across the circle will be 270 × 2¢ = 540¢ = $5.40.

25. **B is correct.** Use the formula $r \times t = d$ where $r$ = rate, $t$ = time, and $d$ = distance.
3 hours 40 minutes = $3^{2}/_{3}$ hours.
$r \times t = d$
$9 \times 3^{2}/_{3} = 33$ miles

# PART V

# PRACTICE TESTS FOR THE ISEE

# ISEE Practice Test I

**(Lower Level: For Candidates for Grades 5 and 6)**

The following practice test is designed to be just like the real ISEE that you will take if you are applying for admission to grades 5 or 6. It matches the actual test in content coverage and level of difficulty. The test is in five sections: Verbal Reasoning, Quantitative Reasoning, Reading Comprehension, Mathematics Achievement, and the Essay.

This practice test will be an accurate reflection of how you'll do on test day if you treat it as the real examination. Here are some hints on how to take the test under conditions similar to those of the actual exam:

- Find a quiet place to work and set aside a period of approximately 2 hours and 20 minutes when you will not be disturbed.

- Work on only one section at a time, and use your watch or a timer to keep track of the time limits for each test part.

- Tear out your answer sheet and mark your answers by filling in the ovals for each question.

- Write your essay on the pages provided.

- Become familiar with the directions for each part of the test. You'll save time on the actual test day by already being familiar with this information.

At the end of the test you'll find answer keys for each section and explanations for every question. Check your answers against the keys to find out how you did on each section of the test and what test topics you might need to study more. Then review the explanations, paying particular attention to the ones for the questions that you answered incorrectly.

You will receive four scaled scores, one for each of these four categories: Verbal Reasoning, Quantitative Reasoning, Reading Comprehension, and Mathematics Achievement. Each section has a low scaled score of 760 and the high scaled score of 940.

The ISEE also provides a percentile score that compares your performance with that of other U.S. and Canadian students who took in the past three years. Your reported percentile test scores are compared to this "norm group" for each section of the test. In addition, the ISEE provides a stanine score which is an abbreviated version of your percentile scores based on 9 groupings rather than 99.

The writing sample is not scored, but it is included with the score reports that you send to schools. The following table shows the various sections, numbers of questions, and time allotments.

## ISEE: Structure and Time Allotments

| Section | Number of Questions | Time Allowed |
|---|---|---|
| Verbal Reasoning | 34 | 20 minutes |
| Quantitative Reasoning | 38 | 35 minutes |
| Break | | 5 minutes |
| Reading Comprehension | 25 | 25 minutes |
| Mathematics Achievement | 30 | 30 minutes |
| Break | | 5 minutes |
| Writing Sample | 1 (unscored) | 30 minutes |
| Totals | 128 | 2 hours, 30 minutes |

# ISEE Practice Test I

ANSWER SHEET

**Note:** If there are more answer lines than there are questions in a section, leave the extra answer lines blank.

## Section 1: Verbal Reasoning

| | | |
|---|---|---|
| 1. Ⓐ Ⓑ Ⓒ Ⓓ | 13. Ⓐ Ⓑ Ⓒ Ⓓ | 25. Ⓐ Ⓑ Ⓒ Ⓓ |
| 2. Ⓐ Ⓑ Ⓒ Ⓓ | 14. Ⓐ Ⓑ Ⓒ Ⓓ | 26. Ⓐ Ⓑ Ⓒ Ⓓ |
| 3. Ⓐ Ⓑ Ⓒ Ⓓ | 15. Ⓐ Ⓑ Ⓒ Ⓓ | 27. Ⓐ Ⓑ Ⓒ Ⓓ |
| 4. Ⓐ Ⓑ Ⓒ Ⓓ | 16. Ⓐ Ⓑ Ⓒ Ⓓ | 28. Ⓐ Ⓑ Ⓒ Ⓓ |
| 5. Ⓐ Ⓑ Ⓒ Ⓓ | 17. Ⓐ Ⓑ Ⓒ Ⓓ | 29. Ⓐ Ⓑ Ⓒ Ⓓ |
| 6. Ⓐ Ⓑ Ⓒ Ⓓ | 18. Ⓐ Ⓑ Ⓒ Ⓓ | 30. Ⓐ Ⓑ Ⓒ Ⓓ |
| 7. Ⓐ Ⓑ Ⓒ Ⓓ | 19. Ⓐ Ⓑ Ⓒ Ⓓ | 31. Ⓐ Ⓑ Ⓒ Ⓓ |
| 8. Ⓐ Ⓑ Ⓒ Ⓓ | 20. Ⓐ Ⓑ Ⓒ Ⓓ | 32. Ⓐ Ⓑ Ⓒ Ⓓ |
| 9. Ⓐ Ⓑ Ⓒ Ⓓ | 21. Ⓐ Ⓑ Ⓒ Ⓓ | 33. Ⓐ Ⓑ Ⓒ Ⓓ |
| 10. Ⓐ Ⓑ Ⓒ Ⓓ | 22. Ⓐ Ⓑ Ⓒ Ⓓ | 34. Ⓐ Ⓑ Ⓒ Ⓓ |
| 11. Ⓐ Ⓑ Ⓒ Ⓓ | 23. Ⓐ Ⓑ Ⓒ Ⓓ | |
| 12. Ⓐ Ⓑ Ⓒ Ⓓ | 24. Ⓐ Ⓑ Ⓒ Ⓓ | |

## Section 2: Quantitative Reasoning

| | | |
|---|---|---|
| 1. Ⓐ Ⓑ Ⓒ Ⓓ | 14. Ⓐ Ⓑ Ⓒ Ⓓ | 27. Ⓐ Ⓑ Ⓒ Ⓓ |
| 2. Ⓐ Ⓑ Ⓒ Ⓓ | 15. Ⓐ Ⓑ Ⓒ Ⓓ | 28. Ⓐ Ⓑ Ⓒ Ⓓ |
| 3. Ⓐ Ⓑ Ⓒ Ⓓ | 16. Ⓐ Ⓑ Ⓒ Ⓓ | 29. Ⓐ Ⓑ Ⓒ Ⓓ |
| 4. Ⓐ Ⓑ Ⓒ Ⓓ | 17. Ⓐ Ⓑ Ⓒ Ⓓ | 30. Ⓐ Ⓑ Ⓒ Ⓓ |
| 5. Ⓐ Ⓑ Ⓒ Ⓓ | 18. Ⓐ Ⓑ Ⓒ Ⓓ | 31. Ⓐ Ⓑ Ⓒ Ⓓ |
| 6. Ⓐ Ⓑ Ⓒ Ⓓ | 19. Ⓐ Ⓑ Ⓒ Ⓓ | 32. Ⓐ Ⓑ Ⓒ Ⓓ |
| 7. Ⓐ Ⓑ Ⓒ Ⓓ | 20. Ⓐ Ⓑ Ⓒ Ⓓ | 33. Ⓐ Ⓑ Ⓒ Ⓓ |
| 8. Ⓐ Ⓑ Ⓒ Ⓓ | 21. Ⓐ Ⓑ Ⓒ Ⓓ | 34. Ⓐ Ⓑ Ⓒ Ⓓ |
| 9. Ⓐ Ⓑ Ⓒ Ⓓ | 22. Ⓐ Ⓑ Ⓒ Ⓓ | 35. Ⓐ Ⓑ Ⓒ Ⓓ |
| 10. Ⓐ Ⓑ Ⓒ Ⓓ | 23. Ⓐ Ⓑ Ⓒ Ⓓ | 36. Ⓐ Ⓑ Ⓒ Ⓓ |
| 11. Ⓐ Ⓑ Ⓒ Ⓓ | 24. Ⓐ Ⓑ Ⓒ Ⓓ | 37. Ⓐ Ⓑ Ⓒ Ⓓ |
| 12. Ⓐ Ⓑ Ⓒ Ⓓ | 25. Ⓐ Ⓑ Ⓒ Ⓓ | 38. Ⓐ Ⓑ Ⓒ Ⓓ |
| 13. Ⓐ Ⓑ Ⓒ Ⓓ | 26. Ⓐ Ⓑ Ⓒ Ⓓ | |

## Section 3: Reading Comprehension

1. Ⓐ Ⓑ Ⓒ Ⓓ    6. Ⓐ Ⓑ Ⓒ Ⓓ    11. Ⓐ Ⓑ Ⓒ Ⓓ
2. Ⓐ Ⓑ Ⓒ Ⓓ    7. Ⓐ Ⓑ Ⓒ Ⓓ    12. Ⓐ Ⓑ Ⓒ Ⓓ
3. Ⓐ Ⓑ Ⓒ Ⓓ    8. Ⓐ Ⓑ Ⓒ Ⓓ    13. Ⓐ Ⓑ Ⓒ Ⓓ
4. Ⓐ Ⓑ Ⓒ Ⓓ    9. Ⓐ Ⓑ Ⓒ Ⓓ    14. Ⓐ Ⓑ Ⓒ Ⓓ
5. Ⓐ Ⓑ Ⓒ Ⓓ    10. Ⓐ Ⓑ Ⓒ Ⓓ    15. Ⓐ Ⓑ Ⓒ Ⓓ

16. Ⓐ Ⓑ Ⓒ Ⓓ    21. Ⓐ Ⓑ Ⓒ Ⓓ
17. Ⓐ Ⓑ Ⓒ Ⓓ    22. Ⓐ Ⓑ Ⓒ Ⓓ
18. Ⓐ Ⓑ Ⓒ Ⓓ    23. Ⓐ Ⓑ Ⓒ Ⓓ
19. Ⓐ Ⓑ Ⓒ Ⓓ    24. Ⓐ Ⓑ Ⓒ Ⓓ
20. Ⓐ Ⓑ Ⓒ Ⓓ    25. Ⓐ Ⓑ Ⓒ Ⓓ

## Section 4: Mathematics Achievement

1. Ⓐ Ⓑ Ⓒ Ⓓ    11. Ⓐ Ⓑ Ⓒ Ⓓ    21. Ⓐ Ⓑ Ⓒ Ⓓ
2. Ⓐ Ⓑ Ⓒ Ⓓ    12. Ⓐ Ⓑ Ⓒ Ⓓ    22. Ⓐ Ⓑ Ⓒ Ⓓ
3. Ⓐ Ⓑ Ⓒ Ⓓ    13. Ⓐ Ⓑ Ⓒ Ⓓ    23. Ⓐ Ⓑ Ⓒ Ⓓ
4. Ⓐ Ⓑ Ⓒ Ⓓ    14. Ⓐ Ⓑ Ⓒ Ⓓ    24. Ⓐ Ⓑ Ⓒ Ⓓ
5. Ⓐ Ⓑ Ⓒ Ⓓ    15. Ⓐ Ⓑ Ⓒ Ⓓ    25. Ⓐ Ⓑ Ⓒ Ⓓ
6. Ⓐ Ⓑ Ⓒ Ⓓ    16. Ⓐ Ⓑ Ⓒ Ⓓ    26. Ⓐ Ⓑ Ⓒ Ⓓ
7. Ⓐ Ⓑ Ⓒ Ⓓ    17. Ⓐ Ⓑ Ⓒ Ⓓ    27. Ⓐ Ⓑ Ⓒ Ⓓ
8. Ⓐ Ⓑ Ⓒ Ⓓ    18. Ⓐ Ⓑ Ⓒ Ⓓ    28. Ⓐ Ⓑ Ⓒ Ⓓ
9. Ⓐ Ⓑ Ⓒ Ⓓ    19. Ⓐ Ⓑ Ⓒ Ⓓ    29. Ⓐ Ⓑ Ⓒ Ⓓ
10. Ⓐ Ⓑ Ⓒ Ⓓ    20. Ⓐ Ⓑ Ⓒ Ⓓ    30. Ⓐ Ⓑ Ⓒ Ⓓ

## SECTION 1

Time: 20 Minutes
34 Questions

This section includes two different types of questions: synonyms and sentence completions. There are directions and a sample question for each question type.

**Part One**

**Directions:** Each of the following questions consists of a word in capital letters followed by four words labeled (A), (B), (C), and (D). Select the one word that means most nearly the same as the word in capital letters.

**Sample Question:**

> ESSENTIAL
> (A)  dire
> (B)  confusing
> (C)  vital
> (D)  expert
>
> Correct Answer: C

1. NOVICE:
   (A)  burden
   (B)  beggar
   (C)  beginner
   (D)  expression

2. FABRICATE:
   (A)  stitch
   (B)  falsify
   (C)  deter
   (D)  decorate

3. FRIENDLY:
   (A)  amiable
   (B)  insincere
   (C)  indecisive
   (D)  responsive

4. GENRE:
   (A)  proposal
   (B)  category
   (C)  purpose
   (D)  generation

5. SUMMIT:
   (A)  conference
   (B)  valley
   (C)  essence
   (D)  outline

6. DEFTLY:
   (A)  wilfully
   (B)  closely
   (C)  quickly
   (D)  skillfully

7. PROSPER:
   (A)  strive
   (B)  affect
   (C)  gather
   (D)  thrive

8. SPURN:
   (A)  cross
   (B)  betray
   (C)  reject
   (D)  hinder

9. TARDY:
   (A)  early
   (B)  late
   (C)  timely
   (D)  ancient

**GO ON TO THE NEXT PAGE.**

10. RESPITE:
    (A) pause
    (B) uproar
    (C) solitary
    (D) blockage

11. REGRETFUL:
    (A) believable
    (B) aimless
    (C) contrite
    (D) dubious

12. INCITE:
    (A) insist
    (B) dispel
    (C) assert
    (D) provoke

13. ABSOLVE:
    (A) criticize
    (B) agree
    (C) clear
    (D) affirm

14. CORROBORATE:
    (A) confirm
    (B) announce
    (C) convince
    (D) punish

15. ERRATIC:
    (A) mistaken
    (B) unpredictable
    (C) timely
    (D) accidental

16. IRRITABLE:
    (A) unimportant
    (B) cheerful
    (C) irregular
    (D) annoyed

17. LENIENT:
    (A) strict
    (B) uncaring
    (C) easygoing
    (D) tilted

**GO ON TO THE NEXT PAGE.**

**Part Two**

**Directions:** Each sentence below has one blank. Each blank indicates that a word or phrase is missing. Following each sentence are four words labeled (A), (B), (C), and (D). Select the word or set of words that, when inserted in the sentence, best fits the meaning of the sentence as a whole.

**Sample Question:**

Due to the fact that the stray kitten was so _____, Ethan's mother allowed him to keep it.

(A) tardy
(B) humid
(C) disobedient
(D) adorable

Correct Answer: D

---

18. Due to the strong odor of onions _____ through the kitchen, Jason suddenly found himself with tears in his eyes.
    (A) submitting
    (B) surpassing
    (C) wafting
    (D) impeding

19. Always _____ and outgoing, Maria could liven up any event just by walking through the door.
    (A) graceful
    (B) uneasy
    (C) sociable
    (D) solitary

20. Although her upbringing had been humble, Tonya now lived in the most _____ neighborhood in the county.
    (A) broken-down
    (B) affluent
    (C) oppressive
    (D) ordinary

21. Clearly annoyed with their lack of progress, Mr. Ramirez scolded the members of the orchestra for their _____ attitude to practicing outside of school.
    (A) fervid
    (B) hostile
    (C) exemplary
    (D) disinterested

22. Faced with the loss of his blistering fastball, the baseball team's owner finally _____ to the pitcher's demand for a guaranteed contract.
    (A) alluded
    (B) sequestered
    (C) dissented
    (D) acceded

23. Carlos knew his goals were not easily attainable but he also knew he had the determination to _____.
    (A) reconsider
    (B) relinquish
    (C) persevere
    (D) disregard

24. Perhaps the country's most renowned female artist, Georgia O'Keeffe's paintings _____ landscapes in the American West.
    (A) obscure
    (B) depict
    (C) conceal
    (D) absorb

25. An _____ test taker, Theo studied hard and seemed to have a knack for always selecting the correct answer.
    (A) uncaring
    (B) incompetent
    (C) impulsive
    (D) astute

26. An _____ chef, every meal Andre prepared for his friends left them begging for more.
    (A) adept
    (B) expedient
    (C) affable
    (D) acrid

27. Ultimately, the activists' efforts to preserve the historic building proved _____ and it was soon demolished.
    (A) futile
    (B) successful
    (C) intolerable
    (D) manageable

28. Unwilling to compromise his _____, Marlo quit the disreputable corporation and started his own consulting business.
    (A) representation
    (B) integrity
    (C) purpose
    (D) motivation

29. A devoted fan, Maria showed her _____ for the actor by leading the ovation applause during his curtain call.
    (A) scorn
    (B) reluctance
    (C) reverence
    (D) contempt

**GO ON TO THE NEXT PAGE.**

30. Always the _____, Martin realized that he would have to start studying soon in order to do well on the test next week.
    (A) pragmatist
    (B) expert
    (C) rival
    (D) detractor

31. Many historians agree that the Civil Rights movement _____ in Montgomery, Alabama, in 1955 when Rosa Parks refused to give up her seat on a bus.
    (A) originated
    (B) terminated
    (C) persisted
    (D) preceded

32. Due to the _____ weather, the principal decided to postpone tonight's open house until next Tuesday.
    (A) serene
    (B) inclement
    (C) moderate
    (D) humid

33. The scout troop was excited because the money generated by their fund-raiser had _____ even the most generous estimates.
    (A) compensated
    (B) suppressed
    (C) supported
    (D) exceeded

34. After several hours of negotiating, the two sides finally reached an _____ and were able to move beyond their disagreement.
    (A) exception
    (B) accord
    (C) ambiguity
    (D) extension

**STOP!**
If you finish before time is up, check your work on this section only.

**Directions:** For each of the following questions, mark the letter of your choice on the answer sheet.

1. Which of the following is closest to 2?
   (A) 2.4
   (B) 1.8
   (C) 1.0
   (D) 0.3

2. $4 \times 3 \times 6 \times 2$ is equal to the product of 24 and
   (A) 6
   (B) 7
   (C) 8
   (D) 9

3. One-quarter of 10,000 =
   (A) 2,500
   (B) 2,000
   (C) 1,500
   (D) 1,000

4. $6\frac{3}{4}\% =$
   (A) 67.5
   (B) 6.75
   (C) 0.675
   (D) 0.0675

5. If $6 + 12 + \_\_\_ = 5 + 11 + 6$, then $\_\_\_ =$
   (A) 2
   (B) 3
   (C) 4
   (D) 5

6. Which fractions are equivalent?
   (A) $\frac{2}{3}, \frac{5}{6}$
   (B) $\frac{9}{12}, \frac{5}{6}$
   (C) $\frac{3}{4}, \frac{7}{8}$
   (D) $\frac{4}{10}, \frac{2}{5}$

7. What is the least common multiple of 3, 4, and 18?
   (A) 18
   (B) 24
   (C) 36
   (D) 54

8. Which of the following is NOT equal to a whole number?
   (A) $\frac{16}{4}$
   (B) $6 \times \frac{2}{3}$
   (C) $4 \div \frac{1}{4}$
   (D) $\frac{1}{3} \times 4$

9. $10 \times (0.38 + 3.5) + 5.2 =$
   (A) 15.25
   (B) 24.15
   (C) 32.40
   (D) 44

10. Order from least to greatest: $\frac{3}{5}, 1\frac{1}{2}, 0.8$
    (A) $\frac{3}{5}, 0.8, 1\frac{1}{2}$
    (B) $0.8, 1\frac{1}{2}, \frac{3}{5}$
    (C) $1\frac{1}{2}, \frac{3}{5}, 0.8$
    (D) $0.8, \frac{3}{5}, 1\frac{1}{2}$

11. A student buys a sandwich for $1.75, milk for 75 cents, and pie for $1.25 cents. How much does the meal cost?
    (A) $3.50
    (B) $3.70
    (C) $3.75
    (D) $3.85

12. The temperature at midnight was −12°F. It rose 2°F each hour. What was the temperature at 11:00 A.M.?
    (A) −2°F
    (B) 4°F
    (C) 8°F
    (D) 10°F

13. Will has $12,444.12 in his checking account. He writes checks for $8,204.94 and $890.99. How much is left in Will's account?
    (A) $3,348.19
    (B) $2,945.60
    (C) $2,867.30
    (D) $2,259.30

14. Rachel flies 2,880 miles in 9 hours. What is the average speed of her airplane?
    (A) 285 miles/hour
    (B) 315 miles/hour
    (C) 320 miles/hour
    (D) 340 miles/hour

15. Jake spent one-fifth of his life in school. If he is now 55, how many years did he spend in school?
    (A) 9
    (B) 11
    (C) 13
    (D) 15

**GO ON TO THE NEXT PAGE.**

16. Which of the following is NOT equal to a whole number?
    (A) $\frac{30}{5}$
    (B) $4 \times \frac{12}{16}$
    (C) $16 \div \frac{1}{16}$
    (D) $\frac{5}{9} \times 8$

17. What is the greatest common factor of 16, 24, 96, and 120?
    (A) 2
    (B) 4
    (C) 8
    (D) 12

18. Aaron has 256 cans of soup that he needs to pack into boxes that hold 30 cans each. How many cans of soup are left over after he fills as many boxes as he can?
    (A) 4
    (B) 16
    (C) 18
    (D) 22

19. $-10 - (-5 - 4) =$
    (A) −4
    (B) −3
    (C) −1
    (D) 1

20. Alex's car gets an average of 26 miles per gallon of gas on the highway. If he drives 858 miles, how many gallons of gas will he use?
    (A) 33 gallons
    (B) 57 gallons
    (C) 78 gallons
    (D) 84 gallons

21. $2 + \frac{4}{25} =$
    (A) 2.225
    (B) 2.16
    (C) 2.24
    (D) 2.45

22. $2 \times 3 \times 5 \times 6$ is equal to the product of 30 and
    (A) 6
    (B) 7
    (C) 8
    (D) 9

23. $12 + (-8) + (-9) + 6 =$
    (A) −6
    (B) −3
    (C) 0
    (D) 1

24. On a test with 75 questions, Cassidy answered 45 correctly. What percent did she answer correctly?
    (A) 60%
    (B) 72%
    (C) 84%
    (D) 89%

25. $11\frac{1}{2} - 9\frac{3}{4} =$
    (A) $2\frac{1}{8}$
    (B) 2
    (C) $1\frac{7}{8}$
    (D) $1\frac{3}{4}$

26. $\frac{3}{4} + \frac{1}{2} + \frac{2}{3} - \frac{5}{6} =$
    (A) $1\frac{1}{12}$
    (B) $1\frac{1}{3}$
    (C) $1\frac{5}{6}$
    (D) $2\frac{1}{6}$

27. $42 \div 7 \times 8 \times 5$ is equal to the product of 12 and
    (A) 16
    (B) 20
    (C) 24
    (D) 28

28. If $4 \times 3 \times \_\_\_ = 5 \times 4 + 4$, then $\_\_\_ =$
    (A) 2
    (B) 3
    (C) 4
    (D) 5

29. A box of laundry soap contains 200 oz. If the cost for 5 ounces is 10 cents, how much does the box of soap cost?
    (A) $3.10
    (B) $3.60
    (C) $3.80
    (D) $4.00

30. Bob's i-Pod contains 800 songs. If 240 songs are either jazz or rap songs, what percent of his collection is jazz or rap?
    (A) 15%
    (B) 20%
    (C) 25%
    (D) 30%

31. Two numbers add to 1,500. One number is 4 times the size of the other. What are the two numbers?
    (A) 300, 1,200
    (B) 200, 1,300
    (C) 500, 1,000
    (D) 300, 1200

32. What is the value of $\sqrt{-25}$?
    (A) 25
    (B) 5
    (C) −5
    (D) 5*i*

33. $71\frac{1}{5}\% =$
    (A) 712
    (B) 71.2
    (C) 7.12
    (D) 0.712

34. The number of sixth-grade students in the Hill School is 8 more than $\frac{1}{6}$ of the whole student body. If there are 144 students in the school, how many are in sixth grade?
    (A) 26
    (B) 30
    (C) 32
    (D) 36

35. $62\frac{1}{2}\% =$
    (A) 625
    (B) 62.5
    (C) 6.25
    (D) 0.625

36. Which number shows 4 in the tens and thousandths place?
    (A) 1,774.482
    (B) 2,241.654
    (C) 3,847.142
    (D) 4,504.241

**GO ON TO THE NEXT PAGE.**

37. Mr. Zakos drives 8 miles in 10 minutes. He drives another half hour at the same speed. How many miles did he drive in the last 20 minutes?
   (A) 10
   (B) 12
   (C) 16
   (D) 24

38. Rashid has 32 baseball cards. Tina has four more than twice as many cards as Rashid. How many baseball cards does Tina have?
   (A) 36
   (B) 60
   (C) 64
   (D) 68

**STOP!**
If you finish before time is up, check your work on this section only.

## SECTION 3

Time: 25 Minutes
25 Questions

**Directions:** Each reading passage is followed by five questions about it. Answer the questions based on what is stated or implied in that passage. For each question, select the answer you think is best and record your choice on the answer sheet. You may write in this test booklet.

Questions 1–6

Volcanoes are mountains, but they are very different from other mountains; they are not formed by folding and crumpling or by uplift and erosion.
5 Instead, volcanoes are built by the accumulation of their own eruptive products—lava, bombs (crusted over lava blobs), ashflows, and tephra (airborne ash and dust). A *volcano* is
10 most commonly a conical hill or mountain built around a vent that connects with reservoirs of molten rock below the surface of the Earth. The term volcano also refers to the opening
15 or vent through which the molten rock and associated material flow. It is so hot that some rocks slowly melt and become a thick flowing substance called *magma*. Because it is
20 lighter than the solid rock around it, magma rises and collects in magma chambers. Eventually some of the magma pushes through vents and fissures in the Earth's surface and
25 a volcanic eruption occurs. Magma that has erupted is called *lava*.

Some volcanic eruptions are explosive and others are not. How explosive an eruption is depends on
30 how runny or sticky the magma is. If magma is thin and runny, gases can escape easily from it. When this type of magma erupts, it flows out of the volcano. Because they move
35 slowly enough for people to get out of their way, lava flows rarely kill

people. They can, however, cause considerable destruction to buildings in their path. If magma is thick
40 and sticky, gases cannot escape easily. Pressure builds up until the gases escape violently and explode. In this type of eruption, the magma blasts into the air and breaks apart
45 into pieces called *tephra*. Tephra can range in size from tiny particles of ash to house-size boulders. Large-sized tephra typically falls back to the ground on or close to the
50 volcano and progressively smaller fragments are carried away from the vent by wind. Volcanic ash, the smallest tephra fragments, can travel hundreds to thousands of kilometers
55 downwind from a volcano.

1. A primary difference between volcanoes and other mountains is in
   (A) their height
   (B) their age
   (C) where they are located
   (D) how they are formed

2. A volcanic eruption is likely to be most explosive if magma
   (A) is thin and runny
   (B) is thick and sticky
   (C) rises and collects in magma chambers
   (D) pushes out through fissures in the Earth's surface

3. The author uses italic print primarily to
   (A) emphasize words that are used in an unusual way
   (B) indicate words that are difficult to pronounce
   (C) highlight important terms that are defined in the text
   (D) indicate words that are not necessary to understanding the passage

4. All of the following can be explicitly answered by the passage EXCEPT:
   (A) What factors contribute to hot temperatures deep inside the Earth?
   (B) Why are some volcanic eruptions explosive while others are not?
   (C) Why does magma rise and collect in chambers?
   (D) Why does pressure build up in magma that is thick and sticky?

5. This passage would most likely appear in
   (A) a newspaper
   (B) a science textbook
   (C) an adventure novel
   (D) a safety manual

**GO ON TO THE NEXT PAGE.**

*The following speech was delivered by Frederick Douglass at a meeting of the Anti-Slavery Society in Pittsburgh in 1863.*

I am one of those who believe that it is the mission of this war to free every slave in the United States. I am one of those who believe that
5 we should consent to no peace which shall not be an Abolition peace. I am, moreover, one of those who believe that the work of the American Anti-Slavery Society will not have been
10 completed until the black men of the South, and the black men of the North, shall have been admitted, fully and completely, into the body politic of America. I look upon slav-
15 ery as going the way of all the earth. It is the mission of the war to put it down. I know it will be said that I ask you to make the black man a voter in the South. It is said that the coloured
20 man is ignorant, and therefore he shall not vote. In saying this, you lay down a rule for the black man that you apply to no other class of your citizens. If he knows enough to be
25 hanged, he knows enough to vote. If he knows an honest man from a thief, he knows much more than some of our white voters. If he knows enough to take up arms in
30 defence of this Government and bare his breast to the storm of rebel artillery, he knows enough to vote.

All I ask, however, in regard to the blacks, is that whatever rule
35 you adopt, whether of intelligence or wealth, as the condition of voting for whites, you shall apply it equally to the black man. Do that, and I am satisfied, and eternal justice is satisfied; liberty, fraternity, equality, are satisfied, and the country will move on harmoniously.

6. According to Douglass, the mission of the Civil War is to
   (A) destroy the Confederacy
   (B) punish the rebel soldiers
   (C) preserve the Union
   (D) end slavery

7. Douglass believes the work of the Anti-Slavery Society should
40 not be considered complete until
   (A) slavery is abolished
   (B) blacks can move freely between the South and the North
   (C) black men of the North and South have the right to vote
   (D) all conditions for voting are ended

8. What does Douglass mean by calling for black men to be admitted "fully and completely into the body politic of America" (lines 13–14)?
   (A) They must have the same rights and privileges as all other citizens.
   (B) They must be able to vote.
   (C) They must be able to run for office.
   (D) They must take up arms to defend the Government.

9. What does the word *consent* mean as it is used in the following sentence from the passage?

   I am one of those who believe that we should <u>consent</u> to no peace which shall not be an Abolition peace.
   (A) agree
   (B) disagree
   (C) understand
   (D) remember

10. The purpose of Douglass' speech was to
    (A) inform members of the society of the horrors of slavery
    (B) convince listeners to adopt fair and equal voting requirements
    (C) inform listeners of the progress of the war
    (D) convince members of the society that slavery should be ended

The great Pullman was whirling onward with such dignity of motion that a glance from the window seemed simply to prove that the
5 plains of Texas were pouring eastward. Vast flats of green grass, dull-hued spaces of mesquite and cactus, little groups of frame houses, woods of light and tender trees, all were
10 sweeping into the east, sweeping over the horizon, a precipice.

A newly married pair had boarded this coach at San Antonio. The man's face was reddened from many days
15 in the wind and sun, and a direct result of his new black clothes was that his brick-colored hands were constantly performing in a most conscious fashion. From time to
20 time he looked down respectfully at his attire. He sat with a hand on each knee, like a man waiting in a barber's shop. The glances he devoted to other passengers were
25 furtive and shy.

The bride was not pretty, nor was she very young. She wore a dress of blue cashmere, with small reservations of velvet here and there
30 and with steel buttons abounding. She continually twisted her head to regard her puff sleeves, very stiff, straight, and high. They embarrassed her. It was quite apparent
35 that she had cooked, and that she expected to cook, dutifully. The blushes caused by the careless scrutiny of some passengers as she had entered the car were strange to
40 see upon this plain, under-class countenance, which was drawn in placid, almost emotionless lines. They were evidently very happy. "Ever been in a parlor-car before?" he asked, smil-
45 ing with delight.

"No," she answered, "I never was. It's fine, ain't it?"

"Great! And then after a while we'll go forward to the diner and
50 get a big layout. Finest meal in the world. Charge a dollar."

"Oh, do they?" cried the bride. "Charge a dollar? Why, that's too much—for us—ain't it, Jack?"

**GO ON TO THE NEXT PAGE.**

55 "Not this trip, anyhow," he answered bravely. "We're going to go the whole thing."

—Stephen Crane from "The Bride Comes to Yellow Sky"

11. The tone of the passage suggests that the author regards the newly married couple with
    (A) embarrassment
    (B) disrespect
    (C) sympathy
    (D) scorn

12. When this passage takes place, the bride and groom are most probably
    (A) in a hotel
    (B) on a stagecoach
    (C) in a diner
    (D) on a train

13. As it is used in line 24, the word "furtive" most nearly means
    (A) stealthy
    (B) steady
    (C) focused
    (D) unabashed

14. The narrator of this story is
    (A) the groom
    (B) the bride
    (C) an outside observer
    (D) an adult looking back on his life

15. By saying, "It was quite apparent that she had cooked, and that she expected to cook, dutifully," the author is suggesting that the bride
    (A) expects to eat out regularly
    (B) has led a life of hard work
    (C) has never eaten in a restaurant before
    (D) wants to learn more about cooking

Questions 16–20

Over two decades ago, scientists in the Agricultural Research Service Vegetable Crops Research Unit at Madison, Wisconsin, began a quest 5 to breed carrots packed with beta-carotene—an orange pigment used by the body to create vitamin A. Thanks largely to their work, today's carrots provide consumers with 10 75 percent more beta-carotene than those available 25 years ago.

The researchers, led by plant geneticist Philipp Simon, haven't limited themselves to the color orange. 15 They've selectively bred a rainbow of carrots—purple, red, yellow, even white. Scientists are learning that these plant pigments perform a range of protective duties in the 20 human body.

Red carrots derive their color mainly from lycopene, a type of carotene believed to guard against heart disease and some cancers. 25 Yellow carrots accumulate xanthophylls, pigments similar to beta-carotene that support good eye health. Purple carrots possess an entirely different class of pigments— 30 anthocyanins—which act as powerful antioxidants. While colored carrots are unusual, they're not exactly new. "Purple and yellow carrots were eaten more than 1,000 years ago 35 in Afghanistan and 700 years ago in western Europe," says Simon. "But the carrot-breeding process has gone on intensively for just 50 years."

In nature, different strains of 40 carrots contain varying types and amounts of carotenoids—the pigments responsible for orange, yellow, and red colors. To assist seed companies and growers who 45 wish to produce nutrient-rich carrots, Simon and his lab are working to map all the genes that play a part in synthesizing carotenoids in major carrot lines. Simon now knows of 20 genes 50 that are involved. But determining a particular gene's role in generating carotenoids is not that straightforward. Aside from enhancing the nutritional value of carrots—as well 55 as onions, garlic, and cucumbers—researchers at Simon's laboratory

also work to improve the vegetable's culinary quality and appeal.

With their compelling health ben-60 efits and a thumbs-up from taste testers, Simon's colorful carrots will be a great addition to supermarket produce aisles once consumers create a demand for them.

16. The main purpose of this passage is to
    (A) report on enhancements to the nutritional value of carrots
    (B) point out the health benefits of carotenoids
    (C) explain why carrots can be various colors
    (D) encourage people to buy carrots of various colors

17. The author's tone can best be described as
    (A) emotional
    (B) sentimental
    (C) optimistic
    (D) informative

18. According to the passage, carrots have been bred in all of the following colors EXCEPT:
    (A) yellow
    (B) green
    (C) red
    (D) purple

19. The type of carotene that gives carrots a red color is
    (A) lycopene
    (B) xanthophyll
    (C) anthocyanin
    (D) beta-carotene

20. This passage can best be described as
    (A) a biography
    (B) a research report
    (C) propaganda
    (D) an editorial

**GO ON TO THE NEXT PAGE.**

Questions 21–25

Georgia O'Keeffe is esteemed as one of the premiere American artists of the twentieth century. Born in a farmhouse in rural Sun Prairie, Wisconsin, in November 1887, O'Keeffe's interest in art began at very young age. By the time she was ten, she had firmly decided to become an artist. O'Keeffe sought to further her penchant for painting by studying at the prestigious Art Institute of Chicago and subsequently at the Art Students League of New York.

In 1917, Alfred Stieglitz, a world-famous photographer, was shown ten of O'Keeffe early abstract paintings and immediately put on a solo exhibit of these works at his New York City gallery. Stieglitz encouraged O'Keeffe to move to New York, where she met other well-known modernist painters. Her early work included cityscapes of New York City streets, buildings, and waterways.

In the 1920s, O'Keeffe began painting her famous close-up flowers on large canvases. With some additional encouragement by Stieglitz, with whom she now shared a life-long personal relationship, her paintings began to sell at ever-increasing prices. In 1929, O'Keeffe visited Taos, New Mexico—a place whose natural beauty transformed her view of art. She continued to paint her exquisite flowers and soon added other parts of the Southwestern landscape including nearby mountain ranges and soaring cliffs, along with the sun-bleached skulls and other bones of animals that had died in the dry, deserted landscape she now called home.

Although she lost most of her vision from macular degeneration late in life, O'Keeffe said of her blindness, "I can see what I want to paint. The thing that makes you want to create is still there." With the aid of young assistants, O'Keeffe continued to paint until about two years before her death in 1986 at the age of 98. Her paintings are now revered worldwide and command prices as high as $44 million. In 1997, the Georgia O'Keeffe Museum opened to house and showcase this exemplary American artist's works.

21. In line 11, "penchant" means most nearly
   (A) strong liking
   (B) prejudice
   (C) weakness
   (D) knack

22. The author's tone in this passage is best described as
   (A) persuasive
   (B) scholarly
   (C) praiseworthy
   (D) indifferent

23. How did Alfred Stieglitz help O'Keeffe's early career?
   (A) He exhibited her early paintings.
   (B) He took photographs of her work.
   (C) He took her on a trip to New Mexico.
   (D) He gave her painting lessons.

24. Which factor had the strongest influence on the subject of O'Keeffe's paintings in her middle and late years?
   (A) New York City's buildings
   (B) New Mexico's landscape
   (C) Alfred Stieglitz
   (D) her loss of sight

25. O'Keeffe's statement, "I can see what I want to paint. The thing that makes you want to create is still there," indicates that
   (A) artistic vision is not just a matter of what the artist sees
   (B) making art is a matter of getting help from other people
   (C) what constitutes art always remains a mystery to the artist
   (D) illness is not something that will stop a true artist from creating

**STOP!**
If you finish before time is up, check your work on this section only.

## SECTION 4
Time: 30 Minutes
30 Questions

**Directions:** For each of the following questions, mark the letter of your choice on the answer sheet.

1. $\frac{2}{3} \div \frac{5}{6} =$
    (A) $\frac{4}{5}$
    (B) $\frac{5}{18}$
    (C) $\frac{15}{6}$
    (D) $2\frac{1}{2}$

2. If $9 + 3 + \underline{\quad} = 8 + 6 + 4$, then $\underline{\quad} =$
    (A) 3
    (B) 4
    (C) 5
    (D) 6

3. $12 + (-6) \times 3 =$
    (A) 21
    (B) 6
    (C) -6
    (D) -12

4. Ashley buys 48 apples. There are 12 Red Delicious applies and 16 Granny Smith apples. What fraction of the apples are not Red Delicious or Granny Smith?
    (A) $\frac{1}{5}$
    (B) $\frac{1}{4}$
    (C) $\frac{1}{3}$
    (D) $\frac{5}{12}$

5. $12 \div 3\frac{3}{4} =$
    (A) $2\frac{2}{3}$

    (B) $2\frac{7}{16}$
    (C) $3\frac{5}{8}$
    (D) $3\frac{1}{5}$

6. Andre had a birthday party and spent $12.98 on balloons, $47.23 on party favors, $22.97 on a cake, $14.77 on ice cream, and $15.00 on invitations. How much did Andre spend on the party?
    (A) $87.25
    (B) $112.95
    (C) $125.20
    (D) $127.30

7. Christine spends 2 days a week painting houses and 3 days a week doing carpentry. If she earns $300 a day for painting and $240 a day for carpentry, how much does she earn in a week?
    (A) $1,280
    (B) $1,320
    (C) $1,360
    (D) $1,440

8. $102\frac{3}{4}\% =$
    (A) 102.75
    (B) 10.275
    (C) 1.0275
    (D) 0.10275

9. If $16 \div 4 \times \underline{\quad} = 5 \times 8 - 16$, then $\underline{\quad} =$
    (A) 6
    (B) 5

    (C) 4
    (D) 3

10. $23.4 \div 6 =$
    (A) 39
    (B) 3.9
    (C) 0.39
    (D) 0.039

11. A teacher has assigned 315 pages of reading. If Jessica starts reading on Monday and reads 65 pages each day, on what day will she complete the assignment?
    (A) Wednesday
    (B) Thursday
    (C) Friday
    (D) Saturday

12. What is 2% of 5,000?
    (A) 10
    (B) 80
    (C) 100
    (D) 105

13. Louisa went to the grocery store and bought a package of hamburger patties for $6.16, a package of buns for $2.10, a container of mustard for $1.78, a jar of relish for $2.16, and a bag of charcoal for $5.35. What was her total bill?
    (A) $12.64
    (B) $14.74
    (C) $16.15
    (D) $17.55

**GO ON TO THE NEXT PAGE.**

14. A $400 television is on sale for 15% off. What is the sale price?
(A) $340
(B) $350
(C) $375
(D) $385

15. Riverside School has 150 fewer students than twice the number of students at Hillside School. If Riverside School has 500 students, how many students attend Hillside School?
(A) 325
(B) 300
(C) 250
(D) 150

16. If $12a + 4a - 7a = 27$, $a =$
(A) 1
(B) 2
(C) 3
(D) 4

**Answer question 17 and 18 based on information in the table below.**

| Day/Time | Adult Price | Child Price |
| --- | --- | --- |
| Weekday Afternoon | $10 | $6 |
| Weekday Evening | $12 | $7 |
| Weekend Afternoon | $12 | $8 |
| Weekend Evening | $15 | $10 |

17. How much will it cost a family of two adults and two children to go to the movies on a Wednesday evening?
(A) $19
(B) $26
(C) $34
(D) $38

18. How much more will it cost a family of two adults and three children to go to the movies on a Saturday evening than it would on a Thursday evening?
(A) $3
(B) $10
(C) $15
(D) $25

19. Kyle can ride his bike 30 km in 2 hours. At the same rate, how far can he ride in 7 hours?
(A) 90 km
(B) 105 km
(C) 125 km
(D) 130 km

20. A rectangular garden is 40 yards long and 15 yards wide. Darryl runs once around the edge of the garden. How far does Darryl run?
(A) 55 yards
(B) 80 yards
(C) 100 yards
(D) 110 yards

21. $25\frac{3}{5} \times 1\frac{1}{2} =$
(A) $38\frac{2}{5}$
(B) $35\frac{1}{3}$
(C) $32\frac{2}{3}$
(D) $30\frac{5}{3}$

22. $18 \div \frac{3}{4} =$
(A) 3
(B) 6
(C) 12
(D) 24

23. $46\frac{3}{4}\% =$
(A) 467.5
(B) 46.75
(C) 4.675
(D) 0.4675

24. What is the greatest common factor of 75, 90, and 120?
(A) 5
(B) 10
(C) 15
(D) 20

25. In the Northshore Swimming Club, 6 of 48 members are females. What is the ratio of females to males?
(A) $\frac{3}{16}$
(B) $\frac{1}{15}$
(C) $\frac{1}{4}$
(D) $\frac{1}{7}$

26. Karen is driving to a town 175 miles away. If she drives at a steady speed of 50 miles per hour, how long will the trip take?
(A) 2 hours 50 minutes
(B) 3 hours
(C) 3 hours 10 minutes
(D) 3 hours 30 minutes

27. If $3.4a + 8.7a = 38.72$, $a =$
(A) 2.9
(B) 3.2
(C) 3.5
(D) 3.9

28. What is the perimeter of the following rectangle?

(A) 12 m
(B) 18 m
(C) 24 m
(D) 28 m

29. 60 is approximately what percent of 90?
(A) 30%
(B) 33%
(C) 45%
(D) 67%

30. Rosa buys a blouse for $23.95. The sales tax is 6.5%. What is the total cost of the blouse, including the sales tax?
(A) $24.35
(B) $24.78
(C) $25.51
(D) $25.75

**STOP!**
If you finish before time is up, check your work on this section only.

## SECTION 5
### Time: 30 Minutes

**Directions:** You will have 30 minutes to plan and write an essay on the topic given below. You must write on the assigned topic only. An essay on another topic will not be acceptable. You may make notes in the space provided for that purpose.

Write your final essay on the two lined pages of your answer sheet. Write or print legibly in blue or black ink. A copy of your essay will be sent to each school that will be receiving your test results.

---

What invention do you think has most changed people's lives? Explain why you have chosen this advance.

---

USE THIS SPACE FOR NOTES

WRITE YOUR ESSAY ON THIS PAGE AND THE NEXT. WRITE IN BLUE OR BLACK INK.

## Answer Key

### Section 1 Verbal Reasoning

| | | | | | |
|---|---|---|---|---|---|
| 1. | C | 13. | C | 25. | D |
| 2. | B | 14. | A | 26. | A |
| 3. | A | 15. | B | 27. | A |
| 4. | B | 16. | D | 28. | B |
| 5. | A | 17. | C | 29. | C |
| 6. | D | 18. | C | 30. | A |
| 7. | D | 19. | C | 31. | A |
| 8. | C | 20. | B | 32. | B |
| 9. | B | 21. | D | 33. | D |
| 10. | A | 22. | D | 34. | B |
| 11. | C | 23. | C | | |
| 12. | D | 24. | B | | |

### Section 2 Quantitative Reasoning

| | | | | | |
|---|---|---|---|---|---|
| 1. | B | 14. | C | 27. | B |
| 2. | A | 15. | B | 28. | A |
| 3. | A | 16. | D | 29. | D |
| 4. | D | 17. | D | 30. | D |
| 5. | C | 18. | C | 31. | A |
| 6. | D | 19. | C | 32. | D |
| 7. | C | 20. | A | 33. | D |
| 8. | D | 21. | B | 34. | C |
| 9. | D | 22. | A | 35. | D |
| 10. | A | 23. | D | 36. | B |
| 11. | C | 24. | A | 37. | C |
| 12. | D | 25. | D | 38. | D |
| 13. | A | 26. | A | | |

## Section 3 Reading Comprehension

| | | | | | |
|---|---|---|---|---|---|
| 1. | D | 10. | B | 19. | A |
| 2. | B | 11. | C | 20. | B |
| 3. | C | 12. | D | 21. | B |
| 4. | A | 13. | A | 22. | D |
| 5. | B | 14. | C | 23. | A |
| 6. | D | 15. | B | 24. | C |
| 7. | C | 16. | A | 25. | A |
| 8. | A | 17. | D | | |
| 9. | A | 18. | B | | |

## Section 4 Mathematics Achievement

| | | | | | |
|---|---|---|---|---|---|
| 1. | A | 13. | D | 25. | D |
| 2. | D | 14. | A | 26. | D |
| 3. | C | 15. | A | 27. | B |
| 4. | D | 16. | C | 28. | D |
| 5. | D | 17. | D | 29. | D |
| 6. | B | 18. | C | 30. | C |
| 7. | B | 19. | B | | |
| 8. | C | 20. | D | | |
| 9. | A | 21. | A | | |
| 10. | B | 22. | D | | |
| 11. | C | 23. | D | | |
| 12. | C | 24. | C | | |

# Answers and Explanations

## Section 1 Verbal Reasoning

1. **C is correct.** A *novice* is a person new to a field or activity—a *beginner*.

2. **B is correct.** To *fabricate* is to concoct in order to deceive—in other words, to *falsify*.

3. **A is correct.** *Friendly* means agreeable in disposition, good-natured and likeable, or *amiable*.

4. **B is correct.** A *genre* is a type or class. The choice that best fits this definition is *category*.

5. **A is correct.** A *summit* is a *conference* or meeting of high-level officials, typically called to shape a course of action.

6. **D is correct.** To do something *deftly* is to do it quickly and *skillfully*.

7. **D is correct.** To *prosper* is to be fortunate or successful, especially in terms of one's health or finances—in other words, to *thrive*.

8. **C is correct.** To *spurn* is to reject disdainfully or contemptuously; *scorn*.

9. **B is correct.** To be *tardy* is to be late for an appointment or event.

10. **A is correct.** A *respite* is a usually short interval of rest or relief—in other words, a *pause*.

11. **C is correct.** *Regretful* means feeling troubled, remorseful, or *contrite* for one's sins or offenses.

12. **D is correct.** To *incite* is to *provoke* or urge on.

13. **C is correct.** To *absolve* is to *clear* someone of guilt or blame.

14. **A is correct.** *Corroboration* is ratification or *confirmation* that some statement or fact is true.

15. **B is correct.** Behavior that is *erratic* lacks consistency, regularity, or uniformity; in other words, it is *unpredictable*.

16. **D is correct.** *Irritable* means easily provoked, impatient, or annoyed.

17. **C is correct.** Someone who is *lenient* does not require that rules must be strictly followed and is, therefore, *easy-going*.

18. **C is correct.** The clue to this sentence is the phrase "the kitchen." Try thinking of a word on your own. Maybe you came up with *hanging* or *floating*. Don't be fooled by *surpassing* (choice B), as that means "going beyond the limit." The correct answer is *wafting*, meaning "to send floating through the air or over water."

19. **C is correct.** In this sentence you are looking for a word that works well with someone described as *outgoing*. *Gregarious*, meaning "sociable or seeking and enjoying the company of others," is the only possible correct choice.

20. **B is correct.** "Although" is another one of the words you may see on the test that signals a contrast within a two-blank sentence. When you come across words or phrases such as "despite," "although," or "even though," keep in mind that the words you are looking for are likely to have opposite meanings. Of the choices available, only *humble . . . affluent* (choice B) offers sufficient contrast.

21. **D is correct.** Since all of the first blank answers are synonymous with each other, turn your attention to the second blank. Of the choices available, only a *lackadaisical* approach (meaning "lacking spirit, liveliness, or interest") to practicing outside of school is likely to lead their instructor to have admonished them.

22. **D is correct.** The logic of this sentence implies that the owner agreed to the pitcher's demands for a guaranteed contract. *Acceded*, meaning "to give one's consent often at the insistence of another; concede," is the correct answer.

23. **C is correct.** Often when you encounter a two-blank question, a good strategy is to try and fill in one of the blanks first so that you can eliminate some of the incorrect answer choices. If you begin with the second blank of this question, you will see that you are able to eliminate choices B and D almost immediately. Now, ask yourself: which sounds better, the fact that Carlos knew his goals were not easily *attainable* or easily *deplorable*? Choice C is correct.

24. **B is correct.** The word *depict* (meaning to "represent in a picture or a sculpture") is clearly the best choice and fits the context of the sentence.

25. **D is correct.** *Astute* (meaning "having or showing shrewdness or discernment") is the best word of the choices to describe someone who studies hard and seems to have a knack for doing well on tests.

26. **A is correct.** Another way of describing a person who is highly skilled or an expert at something is to say that he is *adept* at it. *Expedient* means "fast," *affable* means "friendly," and *acrid* means "unusually sharp, unpleasant, or bitter to the taste or smell."

27. **A is correct.** Because it's unlikely that activists would try to destroy a building that was ultimately torn down, you can eliminate choice D. *Inextricable* means "so entangled as to make escape impossible," and *flagrant* means "conspicuously bad, offensive, or reprehensible." *Futile* means "having no useful result" and best fits the context of the sentence.

28. **B is correct.** "Disreputable" is a key word in this sentence, and you should look for a word that does not fit well with it. *Integrity* means "a strict adherence to a moral or ethical code," and because Mario felt his integrity was being compromised by working for a disreputable corporation, he decided to quit.

29. **C is correct.** *Reverence* (meaning "a feeling of profound awe and respect and often love") is the only word that fits the context here. Since Maria is a devoted fan, she would probably not show her *reluctance* or *disparagement* when the actor came out for his curtain call. *Ascension*, meaning "the act or process of rising," is incorrect as well.

30. **A is correct.** A *pragmatist* is a person who takes a practical approach to problems and is concerned primarily with the success or failure of her actions. This is the best answer to the question.

31. **A is correct.** After reading the sentence, you can probably figure out the word you are looking for means "started or began." *Originated*, meaning "to bring into being or to create," is the only appropriate answer.

32. **B is correct.** This sentence seems to be saying that the open house was rescheduled due to bad weather. *Inclement*, meaning "stormy," is the correct answer.

33. **D is correct.** If results go beyond your expectations, you might say that they *exceeded* your expectations. This is the only answer that fits the context of the scouts' fundraising efforts.

34. **B is correct.** An *accord* is an agreement, or a settlement or compromise of conflicting opinions. Choice B is the correct answer.

## Section 2 Quantitative Reasoning

1. **B is correct.** $2.4 - 2 = 0.4$; $2 - 1.8 = 0.2$; $2 - 1.0 = 1.0$; $2 - 0.3 = 1.7$. Of the choices, the closest to 2 is 1.8.

2. **A is correct.** $4 \times 3 \times 6 \times 2 = 144$; $144 \div 24 = 6$.

3. **A is correct.** $^1/_4 \times 10,000 = {}^{10,000}/_4 = 2,500$.

4. **D is correct.** $6^3/_4\% = 0.0675$.

5. **C is correct.** $5 + 11 + 6 = 22$; $6 + 12 = 18$; and $22 - 18 = 4$.

6. **D is correct.** $^4/_{10}$ can be simplified to $^2/_5$.

7. **C is correct.** The least common multiple of a group of numbers is the least whole number (greater than 0) that is a multiple of all of the numbers. The least common multiple of 3, 4, and 18 is 36 ($3 \times 12$, $4 \times 9$, $2 \times 18$).

8. **D is correct.** $^{16}/_4 = 4$; $6 \times ^2/_3 = {}^{12}/_3 = 4$; $4 \div ^1/_4 = 4 \times ^4/_1 = 16$. However, $^1/_3 \times 4 = ^4/_3$, which is not a whole number.

9. **D is correct.**
   $10 \times (0.38 + 3.5) + 5.2$
   $= (10 \times 0.38) + (10 \times 3.5) + 5.2$
   $= 3.8 + 35 + 5.2$
   $= 44$

10. **A is correct.** Convert to equivalent expressions. $^3/_5 = ^6/_{10}$; $0.8 = ^8/_{10}$; $1^1/_2 = 1^5/_{10} = ^{15}/_{10}$. $^6/_{10} < ^8/_{10} < ^{15}/_{10}$.

11. **C is correct.** $\$1,75 + \$0.75 + \$1.25 = \$3.75$

12. **D is correct.** From midnight to 11:00 A.M. there are 11 hours. If the temperature rose 2°F each hour, then it rose 22°F.
    $(-12) + 22 = 10°F$

13. **A is correct.** Add the amount of the checks and subtract the total from the current amount in the checking account.
    $\$12,444.12 - (\$8,204.94 + \$890.99) = \$3,348.19$

14. **C is correct.** $2,880 \div 9 = 320$ miles per hour.

15. **B is correct.** In this problem you need to find $^1/_5$ of 55; $55 \div 5 = 11$.

16. **D is correct.** $^{30}/_5 = 6$; $4 \times ^{12}/_{16} = ^{48}/_{16} = 3$; $16 \div ^1/_{16} = 16 \times ^{16}/_1 = 256$. However, $^5/_9 \times 8 = ^{40}/_9 = 4^4/_9$, which is not a whole number.

17. **C is correct.** The greatest common factor of a group of numbers is the largest whole number that is a factor of all the numbers. The greatest common factor of 16, 24, 96, and 120 is 8.

18. **B is correct.** If Aaron has 256 cans of soup to pack into boxes of 30, he can fill $256 \div 30 = 8$ boxes with 16 cans of soup left over.

19. **C is correct.**
    $-10 - (-5 - 4)$
    $= -10 - (-9)$
    $= -10 + 9 = -1$

20. **A is correct.** In this problem you need to calculate the number of 26-mpg units there are in 858. Do this by dividing 858 by 26.
    $858 \div 26 = 33$ gallons

21. **B is correct.** $2 + ^4/_{25} = 2.16$.

22. **A is correct.** $2 \times 3 \times 5 \times 6 = 180$. $^{180}/_{30} = 6$.

23. **D is correct.** $12 + (-8) + (-9) + 6 = 4 + (-9) + 6 = -5 + 6 = 1$.

24. **A is correct.** To calculate the percent, divide the number of items answered correctly by the total number of items. $45 \div 75 = 0.60$. To change that to a percent, move the decimal point two places to the right and add the percent sign to get 60%.

25. **D is correct.**
$11\frac{1}{2} - 9\frac{3}{4} = 11\frac{2}{4} - 9\frac{3}{4}$
$= 10\frac{6}{4} - 9\frac{3}{4}$
$= 1\frac{3}{4}$

26. **A is correct.**
$\frac{3}{4} + \frac{1}{2} + \frac{2}{3} - \frac{5}{6}$
$= \frac{9}{12} + \frac{6}{12} + \frac{8}{12} - \frac{10}{12}$
$= \frac{23}{12} - \frac{10}{12}$
$= \frac{13}{12}$
$= 1\frac{1}{12}$

27. **B is correct.** $42 \div 7 \times 8 \times 5 = 240$; $240 \div 12 = 20$.

28. **A is correct.** $5 \times 4 + 4 = 24$; $4 \times 3 = 12$; and $24 \div 12 = 2$.

29. **D is correct.** To calculate the answer, divide 200 by 5.
$200 \div 5 = 40 \times 0.10 = \$4.00$

30. **D is correct.** To calculate the percent, divide the number of jazz and rap songs by the total number of songs. $240 \div 800 = 0.30$. To change that to a percent, move the decimal point two places to the right and add the percent sign to get the correct answer of 30%.

31. **A is correct.** You are told that two numbers add to 1,500 and that one of the two is 4 times the size of other. Create an equation:
$x + 4x = 1,500$
Solve for $x$.
$5x = 1,500$
$x = 300$
$4x = 1,200$
So the two numbers are 300 and 1,200.

32. **D is correct.** $\sqrt{-25} = \sqrt{25} \bullet \sqrt{-1} = 5i$.

33. **D is correct.** $71\frac{1}{5}\% = 0.712$.

34. **C is correct.** Set up an equation. If $x =$ number of students in sixth grade,
$x = \frac{144}{6} + 8$
$x = 24 + 8$
$x = 32$

35. **D is correct.** $62\frac{1}{2}\% = 0.625$.

36. **B is correct.** Moving left from the decimal point the places are tens, hundreds, and thousands. Moving right from the decimal point the places are tenths, hundredths, and thousandths.

37. **C is correct.** If Mr. Zakos drives at a uniform speed of 8 miles per hour, then $2 \times 8 = 16$.

38. **D is correct.** $(2 \times 32) + 4 = 64 + 4 = 68$.

## Section 3 Reading Comprehension

1. **D is correct.** As stated in the first two sentences, "Volcanoes are mountains, but they are very different from other mountains; they are not formed by folding and crumpling or by uplift and erosion. Instead, volcanoes are built by the accumulation of their own eruptive products — lava, bombs (crusted over lava blobs), ashflows, and tephra (airborne ash and dust)."

2. **B is correct.** As stated in the second paragraph, "How explosive an eruption is depends on how runny or sticky the magma is.... If magma is thick and sticky, gases cannot escape easily. Pressure builds up until the gases escape violently and explode." Choice A is wrong because if magma is thin and runny, "gases can escape easily from it," and when this type of magma erupts, "it flows out of the volcano." Choices C and D are both true of magma, but neither indicates how explosive an eruption will be.

3. **C is correct.** The words in italics are scientific terms for which the author provides definitions within the text. ("A *volcano* is most commonly a conical hill or mountain built around a vent that connects with reservoirs of molten rock below the surface of the Earth." "Magma that has erupted is called *lava*.")

4. **A is correct.** The passage states that "Deep within the Earth it is so hot that some rocks slowly melt and become a thick flowing substance called *magma*." However, the passage does not mention the factors that contribute to hot temperatures deep inside the Earth. Choice B is answered in lines 27–30. Choice C is answered in lines 19–22. Choice D is answered in lines 39–42.

5. **B is correct.** This passage explains how volcanoes are formed and the nature of volcanic eruptions using the scientific terminology and strictly factual presentation typical of information presented in a science textbook. There is nothing timely about the information, so it is not likely to be from a newspaper article as in choice A. There is no evidence of a plot or characters, so you can easily eliminate choice C. There is no mention of safety, so choice D cannot be correct.

6. **D is correct.** Douglass makes this point in the very first sentence when he says, "I am one of those who believe that it is the mission of this war to free every slave in the United States." Choices A, B, and C might all be consequences of the Civil War, but in this speech Douglass mentions only freeing every slave in the United States as the mission of the war.

7. **C is correct.** Douglass believed that "the work of the American Anti-Slavery Society will not have been completed until the black men of the South, and the black men of the North, shall have been admitted, fully and completely, into the body politic of America." He specifically mentions that voting rights should be extended equally to all black men. He does not mention that voting rights should be extended to everyone (choice D). Douglass advocates the abolition of slavery as the "mission of the war," but he believes that the work of the Anti-Slavery Society should go beyond this goal to the greater goal of setting the same conditions for voting for black men and white men.

8. **A is correct.** The *body politic* means "the people of a politically organized nation or state." To be fully and completely admitted to the body politic means to have all the rights accorded to any other citizen of the nation or state. Choices B, C, and D are rights and duties that are included in choice A.

9. **A is correct.** *To consent* means *to agree*. This meaning fits the context of the sentence since Douglass agrees with the idea of abolition.

10. **B is correct.** The passage is written in the first person and offers the views of the author on the subject of slavery and voting rights. The last paragraph makes it clear that the author is trying to convince members of the society that "whatever rule you adopt, whether of intelligence or wealth, as the condition of voting for whites, you shall apply it equally to the black man." He goes on to say that if they do that "I am satisfied, and eternal justice is satisfied; liberty, fraternity, equality, are satisfied, and the country will move on harmoniously." As stated in the italic text at the start of the article, this speech was given at a meeting of the Anti-Slavery Society. It is unlikely that members of an Anti-Slavery Society would need to be convinced that slavery should be ended, so choice D

can be eliminated. Choices A and C can also be eliminated because the passage is a statement of the author's opinions on the subject, not just an objective presentation of information about the horrors of slavery (choice A) or the progress of the war (choice C).

11. **C is correct.** The author describes the newly married pair as uncomfortable in their new clothes, unused to taking trips in a "fine" parlor-car, and embarrassed by the scrutiny of other passengers. He seems to like the unsophisticated couple and to be sympathetic toward their situation. The bride and groom may be embarrassed, but the author is not, so choice A is incorrect. Choices B and D are incorrect because nothing in the passage supports the idea that the author regards the couple with *disrespect* (meaning "discourtesy" or "rudeness") or *scorn* (meaning "contempt" or "disdain").

12. **D is correct.** The story takes place on a train crossing the plains of Texas. You can tell this from the fact that the groom asks his bride, "Have you ever been in a parlor-car before?" and then mentions that they will "go forward to the diner and get a big layout." Parlor-cars and dining cars are found on trains. Although the passage states that the newly married pair "had boarded this coach at San Antonio," the coach that is referred to is a car on a train, not a stage coach, so choice B is wrong. The groom mentions that "after a while we'll go forward to the diner," but at the time this passage takes place, they have not yet gone to the diner to eat, so choice C is wrong. The couple has already boarded the train, so they cannot be in a hotel (choice A).

13. **A is correct.** Lines 23–24 state that "The glances he devoted to other passengers were furtive and shy." From this sentence you can tell that a *furtive glance* must be something that goes with a *shy glance*. *Unabashed* (meaning "unembarrassed" or "not shy") is the opposite of shy, so you can eliminate choice D. Similarly, you can eliminate choice C because *focused* means "clear and sharp," which is not commonly associated with *shy*. That leaves choice A, which is correct. A *furtive* glance is a secret or stealthy glance.

14. **C is correct.** The story is told in the third person by someone who is not a participant in the story. Therefore you can eliminate choices A and B. A story told by someone looking back on his life would most likely be told in the first person (using "I" and "me" throughout). Because this story is told by someone who can see everything that is happening in the tale, but is not himself participating in the tale, it is most likely the work of an outside observer.

15. **B is correct.** If you can tell by simply looking at the bride that "she had cooked, and that she expected to cook, dutifully," then the bride most probably has the red, rough hands indicative of a life of hard work. Just looking at a person is unlikely to reveal whether that person expects to eat out regularly or has ever eaten in a restaurant before, so choices A and C are incorrect. Similarly, it is impossible to tell what a person wants to or might expect to learn about cooking by observation alone, so choice D is also incorrect.

16. **A is correct.** The purpose of this passage is to report on the work done by scientists to breed carrots with enhanced nutritional value. The researchers have selectively bred carrots in a rainbow of colors and studied the effects of the various plant pigments on the human body.

17. **D is correct.** The passage is intended to inform readers of developments in carrot breeding. The passage does not contain any emotionally charged language; thus choice A can be eliminated. Nothing about the passage could be termed sentimental; and, although the last sentence offers the opinion that colorful carrots will be a good addition to supermarket produce aisles, this is not enough to describe the entire passage as optimistic.

18. **B is correct.** As stated in lines 15–17, researchers have "selectively bred a rainbow of carrots—purple, red, yellow, even white." The only choice not mentioned is green.

19. **A is correct.** As stated in lines 21–24, "Red carrots derive their color mainly from lycopene, a type of carotene believed to guard against heart disease and some cancers." Xanthophyll (choice B) is found in yellow carrots. Anthocyanin (choice C) is the pigment found in purple carrots. Beta-carotene (choice D) is the pigment found in orange carrots.

20. **B is correct.** The passage reports on the work of agricultural research scientists as they attempt to breed nutrient-rich carrots. It is not the story of someone's life, so it cannot be a biography. It is not written for the purpose of promoting some doctrine or cause, so it does not fall into the category of propaganda. It is not primarily an expression of the opinion of the author, so it is not an editorial.

21. **A is correct.** The passage makes it clear that O'Keeffe had a deep interest in art from a very early age. This indicates that she had a strong liking, or *penchant*, for artistic pursuits.

22. **C is correct.** Tone is the author's attitude toward a topic. It is created through details and language. The passage offers an objective presentation of facts about O'Keeffe's life and art, but it is very positive in its viewpoint of the importance of her unique artistic vision. Therefore, *praiseworthy* is the correct choice.

23. **A is correct.** The passage is explicit that Stieglitz was so impressed by the first O'Keefe paintings he saw that he gave her a solo exhibition in his prestigious gallery.

24. **B is correct.** In lines 34–45, the passage states that the landscape of the Southwest had a profound effect on O'Keeffe's art when she visited Taos, New Mexico, in 1929.

25. **A is correct.** In lines 46–49, O'Keeffe discusses her "vision" of what painting is about. She indicates that the desire to create is based on the realization that in blindness there is something "still there" even if it cannot be experienced in the same way a sighted person sees it.

## Section 4 Mathematics Achievement

1. **A is correct.** When dividing fractions, invert and multiply. See if you can simplify the fractions.

   $\frac{2}{3} \div \frac{5}{6} = \frac{2}{3} \times \frac{6}{5}$ Multiply

   $= \frac{12}{15}$ Simplify

   $= \frac{4}{5}$

2. **D is correct.** $8 + 6 + 4 = 18$; $9 + 3 = 12$; and $18 - 12 = 6$.

3. **C is correct.**

   $12 + -6 \times 3$

   $= 12 + (-18)$

   $= -6$

4. **D is correct.** 12 Red Delicious apples + 16 Granny Smith apples = 28 apples. $48 - 28 = 20$ apples that are not Red Delicious or Granny Smith. $20/48 = 5/12$.

5. **D is correct.**

   $12 \div 3\frac{3}{4} = \frac{12}{1} \div \frac{15}{4}$

   $= \frac{12}{1} \cdot \frac{4}{15}$

   $= \frac{48}{15} = 3\frac{3}{15} = 3\frac{1}{5}$

6. **B is correct.** This is a simple addition problem. Add the amounts of $12.98, $47.23, $22.97, $14.77, $15.00 to get the total of $112.95.

7. **B is correct.** $(2 \times \$300) + (3 \times \$240) = \$600 + \$720 = \$1,320$.

8. **C is correct.** $102\frac{3}{4}\% = 1.0275$.

9. **A is correct.** $5 \times 8 - 16 = 24$; $16 \div 4 = 4$; and $24 \div 4 = 6$.

10. **B is correct.**
    $23.4 \div 6 = 3.9$

11. **C is correct.** If Jessica has 315 pages of reading and reads 65 pages each day, on Monday she has read 65 pages, on Tuesday she has read 2(65) or 130 pages, on Wednesday she has read 3(65) or 195 pages, and on Thursday she has read 4(65) or 260 pages. On Friday, Jessica would need to read only 55 pages to complete the assignment. Another way to do this is to divide 315 by 65 to get 4.85. If Monday is 1, Tuesday is 2, Wednesday is 3, and Thursday is 4, then Friday would be 5. On Friday Jessica would complete the assignment.

12. **C is correct.** 2% is the equivalent of 0.02. $0.02 \times 5{,}000 = 100$.

13. **D is correct.** This is a simple addition problem. Add the amounts to get the total of $17.55.

14. **A is correct.** 15% of $400 = 0.15 \times 400 = \$60$; $\$400 - \$60 = \$340$.

15. **A is correct.** Create an equation:
    Riverside = 2 × Hillside −150
    $500 = 2x - 150$
    $750 = 2x$
    $325 = x$

16. **C is correct.** Solve the equation.
    $12a + 4a - 7a = 27$
    $16a - 7a = 27$
    $9a = 27$
    $a = 3$

17. **D is correct.** $2 \times \$12 + 2 \times \$7 = \$24 + \$14 = \$38$

18. **C is correct.**
    Saturday Evening: $2 \times \$15 + 3 \times \$10 = \$30 + \$30 = \$60$;
    Wednesday Evening: $2 \times \$12 + 3 \times \$7 = \$24 + \$21 = \$45$; therefore, $\$60 - \$45 = \$15$

19. **B is correct.** Set up a proportion:
    $30/2 = n/7$
    $n = 105$

20. **D is correct.** The edge of the garden is its perimeter. To find the perimeter of a rectangle, add the lengths of the sides: $40 + 15 + 40 + 15 = 110$ yards.

21. **A is correct.**
    $25\tfrac{3}{5} \times 1\tfrac{1}{2}$
    $= \tfrac{128}{5} \times \tfrac{3}{2}$
    $= \tfrac{384}{10} = 38\tfrac{4}{10} = 38\tfrac{2}{5}$

22. **D is correct.** $18 \div \tfrac{3}{4} = \tfrac{18}{1} \div \tfrac{3}{4} = \tfrac{18}{1} \times \tfrac{4}{3} = \tfrac{72}{3} = 24$.

23. **D is correct.** $46\tfrac{3}{4}\% = 0.4675$.

24. **C is correct.** The greatest common factor of a group of numbers is the greatest whole number that is a factor of all the numbers. The greatest common factor of 75, 90, and 120 is 15.

25. **D is correct.** To find the ratio of one number to another, create a fraction to show the relationship. In this problem there are 6 female club members in a total of 48 club members. Thus, there are 42 males ($48 - 6 = 42$). The fraction that shows the ratio of females to males is, $\tfrac{6}{42}$. This fraction can be simplified to $\tfrac{1}{7}$, the correct answer.

26. **D is correct.** Use the formula $d = r \times t$ where $d$ = distance, $r$ = rate, and $t$ = time.

$d = r \times t$

$175 = 50 \times t$

$t = {}^{175}/_{50}$

$t = 3.5$ hours = 3 hours 30 minutes

27. **B is correct.**

$3.4a + 8.7a = 38.72$

$12.1a = 38.72$

$a = 3.2$

28. **D is correct.** To find the perimeter of a quadrilateral, add the lengths of the four sides. In this instance, 11 meters + 11 meters + 3 meters + 3 meters = 28 meters, the correct answer.

29. **D is correct.** $60 = x\%$ of 90

$60 = 90x$     Solve for $x$.

$x = \dfrac{60}{90}$

$x = \dfrac{6}{9}$

$x = \dfrac{2}{3}$     Divide 2 by 3 to get 0.6666 or 67%

30. **D is correct.** $\$23.95 \times 0.065 = \$1.56$; $\$23.95 + \$1.56 = \$25.51$.

# ISEE Practice Test II

## (Middle Level: For Candidates for Grades 7 and 8)

The following practice test is designed to be just like the real ISEE that you will take if you are applying for admission to grades 7 or 8. It matches the actual test in content coverage and level of difficulty. The test is in five sections: Verbal Reasoning, Quantitative Reasoning, Reading Comprehension, Mathematics Achievement, and the Essay.

This practice test will be an accurate reflection of how you'll do on test day if you treat it as the real examination. Here are some hints on how to take the test under conditions similar to those of the actual exam:

- Find a quiet place to work and set aside a period of approximately 3 hours when you will not be disturbed.
- Work on only one section at a time, and use your watch or a timer to keep track of the time limits for each test part.
- Tear out your answer sheet and mark your answers by filling in the ovals for each question.
- Write your essay on the pages provided.
- Become familiar with the directions for each part of the test. You'll save time on the actual test day by already being familiar with this information.

At the end of the test you'll find answer keys for each section and explanations for every question. Check your answers against the keys to find out how you did on each section of the test and what test topics you might need to study more. Then review the explanations, paying particular attention to the ones for the questions that you answered incorrectly.

You will receive four scaled scores, one for each of these four categories: Verbal Reasoning, Quantitative Reasoning, Reading Comprehension, and Mathematics Achievement. Each section has a low scaled score of 760 and the high scaled score of 940.

The ISEE also provides a percentile score that compares your performance with that of other U.S. and Canadian students who took in the past three years. Your reported percentile test scores are compared to this "norm group" for each section of the test. In addition, the ISEE provides a stanine score which is an abbreviated version of your percentile scores based on 9 groupings rather than 99.

The writing sample is not scored, but it is included with the score reports that you send to schools. The following table shows the various sections, numbers of questions, and time allotments.

## ISEE: Structure and Time Allotments

| Section | Number of Questions | Time Allowed |
|---|---|---|
| Verbal Reasoning | 40 | 20 minutes |
| Quantitative Reasoning | 37 | 35 minutes |
| Break | | 5 minutes |
| Reading Comprehension | 36 | 35 minutes |
| Mathematics Achievement | 47 | 40 minutes |
| Break | | 5 minutes |
| Writing Sample | 1 (unscored) | 30 minutes |
| Totals | 161 | 2 hours, 50 minutes |

# ISEE Practice Test II

## ANSWER SHEET

**Note:** If there are more answer lines than there are questions in a section, leave the extra answer lines blank.

### Section 1: Verbal Reasoning

| | | |
|---|---|---|
| 1. Ⓐ Ⓑ Ⓒ Ⓓ | 17. Ⓐ Ⓑ Ⓒ Ⓓ | 33. Ⓐ Ⓑ Ⓒ Ⓓ |
| 2. Ⓐ Ⓑ Ⓒ Ⓓ | 18. Ⓐ Ⓑ Ⓒ Ⓓ | 34. Ⓐ Ⓑ Ⓒ Ⓓ |
| 3. Ⓐ Ⓑ Ⓒ Ⓓ | 19. Ⓐ Ⓑ Ⓒ Ⓓ | 35. Ⓐ Ⓑ Ⓒ Ⓓ |
| 4. Ⓐ Ⓑ Ⓒ Ⓓ | 20. Ⓐ Ⓑ Ⓒ Ⓓ | 36. Ⓐ Ⓑ Ⓒ Ⓓ |
| 5. Ⓐ Ⓑ Ⓒ Ⓓ | 21. Ⓐ Ⓑ Ⓒ Ⓓ | 37. Ⓐ Ⓑ Ⓒ Ⓓ |
| 6. Ⓐ Ⓑ Ⓒ Ⓓ | 22. Ⓐ Ⓑ Ⓒ Ⓓ | 38. Ⓐ Ⓑ Ⓒ Ⓓ |
| 7. Ⓐ Ⓑ Ⓒ Ⓓ | 23. Ⓐ Ⓑ Ⓒ Ⓓ | 39. Ⓐ Ⓑ Ⓒ Ⓓ |
| 8. Ⓐ Ⓑ Ⓒ Ⓓ | 24. Ⓐ Ⓑ Ⓒ Ⓓ | 40. Ⓐ Ⓑ Ⓒ Ⓓ |
| 9. Ⓐ Ⓑ Ⓒ Ⓓ | 25. Ⓐ Ⓑ Ⓒ Ⓓ | |
| 10. Ⓐ Ⓑ Ⓒ Ⓓ | 26. Ⓐ Ⓑ Ⓒ Ⓓ | |
| 11. Ⓐ Ⓑ Ⓒ Ⓓ | 27. Ⓐ Ⓑ Ⓒ Ⓓ | |
| 12. Ⓐ Ⓑ Ⓒ Ⓓ | 28. Ⓐ Ⓑ Ⓒ Ⓓ | |
| 13. Ⓐ Ⓑ Ⓒ Ⓓ | 29. Ⓐ Ⓑ Ⓒ Ⓓ | |
| 14. Ⓐ Ⓑ Ⓒ Ⓓ | 30. Ⓐ Ⓑ Ⓒ Ⓓ | |
| 15. Ⓐ Ⓑ Ⓒ Ⓓ | 31. Ⓐ Ⓑ Ⓒ Ⓓ | |
| 16. Ⓐ Ⓑ Ⓒ Ⓓ | 32. Ⓐ Ⓑ Ⓒ Ⓓ | |

### Section 2: Quantitative Reasoning

| | | |
|---|---|---|
| 1. Ⓐ Ⓑ Ⓒ Ⓓ | 14. Ⓐ Ⓑ Ⓒ Ⓓ | 27. Ⓐ Ⓑ Ⓒ Ⓓ |
| 2. Ⓐ Ⓑ Ⓒ Ⓓ | 15. Ⓐ Ⓑ Ⓒ Ⓓ | 28. Ⓐ Ⓑ Ⓒ Ⓓ |
| 3. Ⓐ Ⓑ Ⓒ Ⓓ | 16. Ⓐ Ⓑ Ⓒ Ⓓ | 29. Ⓐ Ⓑ Ⓒ Ⓓ |
| 4. Ⓐ Ⓑ Ⓒ Ⓓ | 17. Ⓐ Ⓑ Ⓒ Ⓓ | 30. Ⓐ Ⓑ Ⓒ Ⓓ |
| 5. Ⓐ Ⓑ Ⓒ Ⓓ | 18. Ⓐ Ⓑ Ⓒ Ⓓ | 31. Ⓐ Ⓑ Ⓒ Ⓓ |
| 6. Ⓐ Ⓑ Ⓒ Ⓓ | 19. Ⓐ Ⓑ Ⓒ Ⓓ | 32. Ⓐ Ⓑ Ⓒ Ⓓ |
| 7. Ⓐ Ⓑ Ⓒ Ⓓ | 20. Ⓐ Ⓑ Ⓒ Ⓓ | 33. Ⓐ Ⓑ Ⓒ Ⓓ |
| 8. Ⓐ Ⓑ Ⓒ Ⓓ | 21. Ⓐ Ⓑ Ⓒ Ⓓ | 34. Ⓐ Ⓑ Ⓒ Ⓓ |
| 9. Ⓐ Ⓑ Ⓒ Ⓓ | 22. Ⓐ Ⓑ Ⓒ Ⓓ | 35. Ⓐ Ⓑ Ⓒ Ⓓ |
| 10. Ⓐ Ⓑ Ⓒ Ⓓ | 23. Ⓐ Ⓑ Ⓒ Ⓓ | 36. Ⓐ Ⓑ Ⓒ Ⓓ |
| 11. Ⓐ Ⓑ Ⓒ Ⓓ | 24. Ⓐ Ⓑ Ⓒ Ⓓ | 37. Ⓐ Ⓑ Ⓒ Ⓓ |
| 12. Ⓐ Ⓑ Ⓒ Ⓓ | 25. Ⓐ Ⓑ Ⓒ Ⓓ | |
| 13. Ⓐ Ⓑ Ⓒ Ⓓ | 26. Ⓐ Ⓑ Ⓒ Ⓓ | |

## Section 3: Reading Comprehension

1. (A) (B) (C) (D)   13. (A) (B) (C) (D)   25. (A) (B) (C) (D)
2. (A) (B) (C) (D)   14. (A) (B) (C) (D)   26. (A) (B) (C) (D)
3. (A) (B) (C) (D)   15. (A) (B) (C) (D)   27. (A) (B) (C) (D)
4. (A) (B) (C) (D)   16. (A) (B) (C) (D)   28. (A) (B) (C) (D)
5. (A) (B) (C) (D)   17. (A) (B) (C) (D)   29. (A) (B) (C) (D)
6. (A) (B) (C) (D)   18. (A) (B) (C) (D)   30. (A) (B) (C) (D)
7. (A) (B) (C) (D)   19. (A) (B) (C) (D)   31. (A) (B) (C) (D)
8. (A) (B) (C) (D)   20. (A) (B) (C) (D)   32. (A) (B) (C) (D)
9. (A) (B) (C) (D)   21. (A) (B) (C) (D)   33. (A) (B) (C) (D)
10. (A) (B) (C) (D)   22. (A) (B) (C) (D)   34. (A) (B) (C) (D)
11. (A) (B) (C) (D)   23. (A) (B) (C) (D)   35. (A) (B) (C) (D)
12. (A) (B) (C) (D)   24. (A) (B) (C) (D)   36. (A) (B) (C) (D)

## Section 4: Mathematics Achievement

1. (A) (B) (C) (D)   17. (A) (B) (C) (D)   33. (A) (B) (C) (D)
2. (A) (B) (C) (D)   18. (A) (B) (C) (D)   34. (A) (B) (C) (D)
3. (A) (B) (C) (D)   19. (A) (B) (C) (D)   35. (A) (B) (C) (D)
4. (A) (B) (C) (D)   20. (A) (B) (C) (D)   36. (A) (B) (C) (D)
5. (A) (B) (C) (D)   21. (A) (B) (C) (D)   37. (A) (B) (C) (D)
6. (A) (B) (C) (D)   22. (A) (B) (C) (D)   38. (A) (B) (C) (D)
7. (A) (B) (C) (D)   23. (A) (B) (C) (D)   39. (A) (B) (C) (D)
8. (A) (B) (C) (D)   24. (A) (B) (C) (D)   40. (A) (B) (C) (D)
9. (A) (B) (C) (D)   25. (A) (B) (C) (D)   41. (A) (B) (C) (D)
10. (A) (B) (C) (D)   26. (A) (B) (C) (D)   42. (A) (B) (C) (D)
11. (A) (B) (C) (D)   27. (A) (B) (C) (D)   43. (A) (B) (C) (D)
12. (A) (B) (C) (D)   28. (A) (B) (C) (D)   44. (A) (B) (C) (D)
13. (A) (B) (C) (D)   29. (A) (B) (C) (D)   45. (A) (B) (C) (D)
14. (A) (B) (C) (D)   30. (A) (B) (C) (D)   46. (A) (B) (C) (D)
15. (A) (B) (C) (D)   31. (A) (B) (C) (D)   47. (A) (B) (C) (D)
16. (A) (B) (C) (D)   32. (A) (B) (C) (D)

This section includes two different types of questions: synonyms and sentence completions. There are directions and a sample question for each question type.

**Part One**

**Directions:** Each of the following questions consists of a word in capital letters followed by four words labeled (A), (B), (C), and (D). Select the one word that means most nearly the same as the word in capital letters.

**Sample Question:**

> ESSENTIAL
> (A) dire
> (B) confusing
> (C) vital
> (D) expert
>
> Correct Answer: C

1. SHAME:
   (A) grief
   (B) anguish
   (C) remorse
   (D) humiliation

2. TELL:
   (A) censure
   (B) preclude
   (C) dissuade
   (D) divulge

3. CONCISE:
   (A) clever
   (B) brief
   (C) small
   (D) subdued

4. INQUIRY:
   (A) testimony
   (B) subpoena
   (C) investigation
   (D) verification

5. ATTITUDE:
   (A) disposition
   (B) dissension
   (C) charisma
   (D) dispensation

6. TEDIOUSLY:
   (A) delicately
   (B) relentlessly
   (C) fearlessly
   (D) tiresomely

7. DEPLETE:
   (A) deride
   (B) reduce
   (C) deprecate
   (D) discredit

8. CAUTIOUS:
   (A) discreet
   (B) anxious
   (C) scared
   (D) stricken

9. SPARSE:
   (A) spatial
   (B) thin
   (C) vivid
   (D) lifeless

10. AVERSION:
    (A) model
    (B) portrayal
    (C) dislike
    (D) arrangement

11. DORMANT:
    (A) inactive
    (B) restful
    (C) covert
    (D) arbitrary

12. MALCONTENT:
    (A) sickly
    (B) troublesome
    (C) dissatisfied
    (D) malicious

**GO ON TO THE NEXT PAGE.**

13. MERIT:
    (A) deserve
    (B) require
    (C) necessitate
    (D) pardon

14. PROMINENT:
    (A) excellent
    (B) accomplished
    (C) admirable
    (D) conspicuous

15. OBJECTIVE:
    (A) interest
    (B) observation
    (C) intention
    (D) concern

16. PERMANENT:
    (A) historical
    (B) indelible
    (C) permissive
    (D) conspicuous

17. SHREWD:
    (A) poignant
    (B) astute
    (C) copious
    (D) tactile

18. CLANDESTINE:
    (A) secret
    (B) criminal
    (C) apprehensive
    (D) disgraceful

19. COERCE:
    (A) twist
    (B) mislead
    (C) perceive
    (D) compel

20. PLETHORA:
    (A) quandary
    (B) resonance
    (C) excess
    (D) veneer

**GO ON TO THE NEXT PAGE.**

**Part Two**

**Directions:** Each sentence below has one or two blanks. Each blank indicates that a word or phrase is missing. Following each sentence are four words or sets of words labeled (A), (B), (C), and (D). You are to select the word or set of words that, when inserted in the sentence, best fits the meaning of the sentence as a whole.

**Sample Question:**

Due to the fact that the stray kitten was so _____, Ethan's mother allowed him to keep it.
(A) tardy
(B) humid
(C) disobedient
(D) adorable

Correct Answer: D

---

21. History has shown that two of the most _____ patriots of the Revolutionary War were Samuel Adams and John Hancock.
   (A) destitute
   (B) covert
   (C) spontaneous
   (D) eminent

22. Knowing that the bonuses being offered were not easily _____, the union decided not to _____ the new contract.
   (A) attainable . . . ratify
   (B) reachable . . . nullify
   (C) restricted . . . validate
   (D) obtainable . . . repudiate

23. For _____ results with the product, the manufacturer advised customers to carefully read the manual or download the _____ tutorial from its website.
   (A) superior . . . abbreviated
   (B) unparalleled . . . selective
   (C) optimum . . . comprehensive
   (D) conventional . . . extensive

24. Although the effects of the tornado were _____, it brought the town together through a sense of _____.
   (A) beneficial . . . disgust
   (B) destructive . . . solidarity
   (C) minor . . . helplessness
   (D) significant . . . despair

25. After staying up all night and working interminably to finish the project, Gerard finally let himself _____ to sleep.
   (A) posture
   (B) succumb
   (C) dissent
   (D) regress

26. Despite her _____ temper, the actress typically displayed a _____ demeanor.
   (A) modest...humble
   (B) caustic...maniacal
   (C) explosive...timid
   (D) manageable...courteous

27. The ending of the play was so _____ that many questions the audience had were left unanswered.
   (A) derivative
   (B) lucid
   (C) explicit
   (D) equivocal

28. The supervisor forced his workers to _____ his every whim, lest they find themselves _____ from his good graces.
   (A) display . . . garnered
   (B) indulge . . . exiled
   (C) ignore . . . abetted
   (D) misunderstood . . . incited

29. Citing overwhelming evidence, many believed the judge would _____ justice by not reversing her earlier decision.
   (A) impel
   (B) hasten
   (C) impede
   (D) gratify

30. Much of Langston's Hughes' poetry tries to _____ the rhythms of blues music, the music he _____ to be the true expression of his spirit.
   (A) emulate . . . believed
   (B) capture . . . doubted
   (C) forgo . . . considered
   (D) mollify . . . maintained

**GO ON TO THE NEXT PAGE.**

31. Perhaps the best known constellation in the sky, Orion is occasionally visible throughout the Northern Hemisphere and _____ with the naked eye.
    (A) imperceptible
    (B) audible
    (C) discernible
    (D) diminished

32. Initially standing by his _____ alibi, the main suspect in the scandal later retracted it and agreed to cooperate with the prosecution.
    (A) feasible
    (B) incontrovertible
    (C) tenuous
    (D) furtive

33. The mayor's suggestion to raise property taxes in order to subsidize a new stadium was met with an _____ response from homeowners.
    (A) exuberant
    (B) affable
    (C) illustrious
    (D) ambivalent

34. The girls were often _____ at camp for their _____ behavior and willingness to comfort the younger children, many of whom were away from home for the first time.
    (A) praised . . . commendable
    (B) unnerved . . . exemplary
    (C) reviled . . . meritorious
    (D) recognized . . . contemptible

35. Due to the fact that she could often be seen carting away boxfuls of books from rummage sales, one could say that Ms. Tompkins had a _____ for accumulation.
    (A) consortium
    (B) propensity
    (C) chagrin
    (D) prospect

36. Having suffered numerous injuries over the course of her career, the gymnast demonstrated her _____ by overcoming adversity and winning the gold medal.
    (A) consternation
    (B) viscosity
    (C) dexterity
    (D) resilience

37. One would think that the _____ bear, fresh from months of hibernation, would eat everything in sight, but he is surprisingly picky.
    (A) hirsute
    (B) ravenous
    (C) fastidious
    (D) lethargic

38. At the hotel, the couple behaved rather _____ after being informed by the manager that their reservation had been _____ once the payment did not clear.
    (A) angrily . . . canceled
    (B) morosely . . . approved
    (C) extraneously . . . acknowledged
    (D) lavishly . . . confirmed

39. Even though the architect's designs were _____ to the surrounding buildings, she had to _____ them because of the impending deadline.
    (A) disproportionate . . . submit
    (B) comparable . . . deliver
    (C) excessive . . . affirm
    (D) consistent . . . present

40. By noon, the newspaper staff had been _____ by phone calls about the power outage, and by evening, it seemed as though the _____ would continue.
    (A) exhausted . . . reduction
    (B) overwhelmed . . . dearth
    (C) harassed . . . spate
    (D) inundated . . . deluge

**STOP!**
If you finish before time is up, check your work on this section only.

## SECTION 2

Time: 35 Minutes
37 Questions

This section includes two different types of questions: multiple-choice math questions and quantitative comparisons. Follow the directions for each question type.

**Part One**

**Directions:** For each of the following questions, mark the letter of your choice on the answer sheet.

---

1. $48 \div 6 \times 8 \times 8$ is equal to the product of 16 and
   - (A) 16
   - (B) 24
   - (C) 28
   - (D) 32

2. Paula is 3 years older than Lindsey, who is 2 years younger than Dave. If Paula is 17, how old is Dave?
   - (A) 16
   - (B) 17
   - (C) 19
   - (D) 21

3. $3/4 - 5/12 =$
   - (A) $\dfrac{1}{12}$
   - (B) $\dfrac{3}{12}$
   - (C) $\dfrac{1}{3}$
   - (D) $\dfrac{2}{3}$

4. 20 is approximately what percent of 80?
   - (A) 20%
   - (B) 25%
   - (C) 30%
   - (D) 60%

5. A fence along a road is divided into sections that are each 5 meters long. If the fence is 0.5 kilometers long, how many sections are there?
   - (A) 10
   - (B) 50
   - (C) 100
   - (D) 250

6. Which pair of fractions are equivalent?
   - (A) $\dfrac{6}{12}, \dfrac{3}{12}$
   - (B) $\dfrac{2}{8}, \dfrac{1}{4}$
   - (C) $\dfrac{4}{8}, \dfrac{2}{16}$
   - (D) $\dfrac{3}{9}, \dfrac{5}{9}$

7. What is the least common multiple of 9, 2, and 5?
   - (A) 45
   - (B) 60
   - (C) 90
   - (D) 180

8. Bobby's test scores for social studies are 93, 76, 91, 83, and 72. What is his average score?
   - (A) 83
   - (B) 87
   - (C) 91
   - (D) 93

9. At the amusement park, Karen uses $1/3$ of her tickets for rides and $1/6$ of her tickets for food. What fraction of her tickets is left?
   - (A) $\dfrac{1}{6}$
   - (B) $\dfrac{1}{4}$
   - (C) $\dfrac{1}{2}$
   - (D) $\dfrac{2}{3}$

10. If $6 \times 8 \div \_\_\_ = 5 \times 4 + 4$, then $\_\_\_ =$
    - (A) 2
    - (B) 3
    - (C) 4
    - (D) 5

11. Which of the following is NOT equal to a whole number?
    - (A) $\dfrac{32}{4}$
    - (B) $4 \times \dfrac{8}{16}$
    - (C) $8 \div \dfrac{1}{8}$
    - (D) $\dfrac{5}{12} \times 8$

**GO ON TO THE NEXT PAGE.**

12. The distance around a rectangular park is 1 mile. If the width of the park is 880 feet, what is its length?
 (A) 1,760 ft
 (B) 1,510 ft
 (C) 1,250 ft
 (D) 840 ft

13. If ¼ of a number is 12, then ⅙ of the same number is
 (A) 8
 (B) 9
 (C) 12
 (D) 15

14. A truck travels 126 miles in 3 hours. At that speed, in how many hours will the truck reach its destination, 924 miles away?
 (A) 22 hours
 (B) 24 hours
 (C) 25.5 hours
 (D) 28 hours

15. $5/6 - 2/3 - 1/12$
 (A) $\dfrac{1}{12}$
 (B) $\dfrac{1}{6}$
 (C) $\dfrac{1}{4}$
 (D) $\dfrac{1}{3}$

16. What is the mean of the following numbers?
 24, 36, 18, 30, 90, 690
 (A) 48
 (B) 64
 (C) 148
 (D) 152

17. It costs $12.00 dollars to buy 24 cookies. At the same rate, how many dollars will it cost to buy 6 cookies?
 (A) $3.00
 (B) $2.00
 (C) $48.00
 (D) $72.00

18. In the product shown below, what digit does □ represent?
 $(4\square5)(3) = 1,275$
 (A) 1
 (B) 2
 (C) 3
 (D) 4

19. Which of the following is NOT equal to a whole number?
 (A) $\dfrac{20}{5}$
 (B) $5 \times \dfrac{3}{4}$
 (C) $6 \div \dfrac{1}{6}$
 (D) $\dfrac{3}{5} \times 10$

20. What is the difference of
$$\begin{bmatrix} 2 & -1 \\ -3 & 2 \end{bmatrix} - \begin{bmatrix} 1 & -3 \\ -2 & 2 \end{bmatrix}?$$
 (A) $\begin{bmatrix} 3 & -4 \\ -5 & 4 \end{bmatrix}$
 (B) $\begin{bmatrix} 1 & -4 \\ -1 & 0 \end{bmatrix}$
 (C) $\begin{bmatrix} 1 & 2 \\ -1 & 0 \end{bmatrix}$
 (D) $\begin{bmatrix} 1 & 4 \\ 1 & 0 \end{bmatrix}$

**Part Two**

**Directions:** For each of the following questions, two quantities are given—one in column A, the other in column B. Compare the two quantities and mark your answer sheet as follows:

(A) if the quantity in Column A is greater
(B) if the quantity in Column B is greater
(C) if the quantities are equal
(D) if the relationship cannot be determined from the information given

**Notes**

• Information concerning one or both of the compared quantities will be centered above the two columns for some items.
• Symbols that appear in both columns represent the same thing in Column A as in Column B.
• Letters such as *x*, *n*, and *k* are symbols for real numbers.
• Figures are drawn to scale unless otherwise noted.

**GO ON TO THE NEXT PAGE.**

|  | **Column A** | **Column B** |
|---|---|---|
| 21. | 7,542 – 1,036 | 10,308 – 4,036 |
| 22. | 75% of 120 | 50% of 160 |
| 23. | 3(c + 2) | 3c + (3 • 2) |

| | | |
|---|---|---|
| 24. | m ∠ DFE | m ∠ AFC |

Janet walks 125 yards in 3 minutes.
Victoria walks 206 yards in 5 minutes.

| | | |
|---|---|---|
| 25. | The average number of yards Janet walks in a minute. | The average number of yards Victoria walks in a minute. |
| 26. | $\sqrt{150}$ | 15 |

Jeff reaches, without looking, into this box filled with letter blocks,
and picks out one block.

| | | |
|---|---|---|
| 27. | The probability of picking a vowel | The probability of picking an L or a T |

**GO ON TO THE NEXT PAGE.**

28.    The perimeter of a square having an area of 64 ft².          The perimeter of a rectangle having an area of 48 ft².

29.    $4^2/_5 \div {}^3/_{10}$                                      $7^1/_2 \div {}^2/_3$

30.    $-|4|$                                           $|-4|$

$$x + 1 = 15$$
$$y - 7 = 7$$

31.    $x$                                             $y$

Figure 1                            Figure 2

32.    Surface Area of Figure 1                 Surface Area of Figure 2

33.    The greatest common factor of 56, 96, and 200.       The greatest common factor of 27, 81, and 189.

34.    $2.76 \times 2.57$                           $21.4 \times 0.53$

35.    8 quarts 1 cup                          264 fluid ounces

36.    $0.4^2$                                $4.0^2$

37.    Petra rolls a 6-sided die with faces numbered 1 through 6.

      The probability she rolls an odd number.            The probability she rolls a prime number.

**STOP!**
If you finish before time is up, check your work on this section only.

## SECTION 3
Time: 35 Minutes
36 Questions

**Directions:** Each reading passage is followed by questions about it. Answer the questions that follow a passage on the basis of what is stated or implied in that passage. For each question, select the answer you think is best and record your choice by filling in the corresponding oval on the answer sheet.

---

### Questions 1–6

*At the Thirteenth Annual Convention of the National Negro Business League in 1912, no women were included on the schedule of*
5 *speakers. Madam C. J. Walker, a highly successful inventor and distributor of hair care products for African-American women, shocked the participants when she walked*
10 *up and claimed the podium from moderator Booker T. Washington:*

"Surely you are not going to shut the door in my face. I feel that I am in a business that is a credit to the wom-
15 anhood of our race. I am a woman who started in business seven years ago with only $1.50 . . . this year (up to the 19th day of this month . . . ) I had taken in $18,000. (Prolonged
20 applause.) This makes a grand total of $63,049 made in my hair business in Indianapolis. (Applause.) I have been trying to get before you business people to tell you what I am
25 doing. I am a woman that came from the cotton fields of the South; I was promoted from there to the wash-tub (laughter); then I was promoted to the cook kitchen, and from there
30 I promoted myself into the business of manufacturing hair goods and preparations. . . . I am not ashamed of my past; I am not ashamed of my humble beginning. Don't think that
35 because you have to go down in the wash-tub that you are any less a lady!" (Prolonged applause.)

1. The purpose of Madam Walker's speech was to
   (A) demonstrate her hair products to the league
   (B) lash out at Booker T. Washington for ignoring her
   (C) make the members of the league take notice of her business success
   (D) influence the members of the league to admit more women

2. As reflected in her speech, Madam Walker's attitude is best described as
   (A) envious
   (B) proud
   (C) reverent
   (D) cautious

3. The reaction of the members of the league to Madam Walker's speech can be described as
   (A) indifferent
   (B) angry
   (C) favorable
   (D) critical

4. The reference to her promotion from the cotton fields to the wash-tub to the cook kitchen is used to
   (A) show how far she has come
   (B) establish a connection with her audience
   (C) debunk a myth about African-American women
   (D) make people feel sorry for her

5. What is the meaning of *prolonged* as used in line 19?
   (A) loud
   (B) lengthy
   (C) unexpected
   (D) unusual

6. What does Madam Walker mean when she says, "Don't think that because you have to go down in the wash-tub that you are any less a lady" (lines 34-37)?
   (A) Ladies should not have to scrub and cook.
   (B) Getting down on your knees to scrub is hard work for a lady.
   (C) It is not ladylike to work with your hands.
   (D) There is nothing demeaning about hard work.

**GO ON TO THE NEXT PAGE.**

Questions 7–12

On March 20, 1980, a series of small earthquakes signaled the awakening of Mount St. Helens from a 123-year slumber. Over the next
5 two months more than 10,000 earthquakes followed as magma moved into the volcano, wedging the volcano apart at a rate of five feet per day. Heat from a rising plume of volcanic
10 ash melted glacial ice, creating cement-like slurries of rock and ash called mudflows. Superheated avalanches of hot gas, magma caused a visible swelling of the volcano's
15 north flank creating a feature that scientists called "the bulge."

Many geologists weren't surprised by Mount St. Helens' awakening. In the 1950's, geologists had begun
20 an extensive study of the deposits around Mount St. Helens. In 1975, they published a report predicting that Mount St. Helens was the volcano in the lower 48 states most
25 likely to erupt by the end of the century.

On the morning of May 18, 1980, a magnitude 5.1 earthquake triggered the collapse of the summit and north
30 flank of Mount St. Helens and formed the largest landslide in recorded history. Gas-rich magma and superheated groundwater trapped inside the volcano were suddenly released
35 in a powerful lateral blast. In less than three minutes, 230 square miles of forest lay flattened. The hot gas and magma melted the snow and ice that covered the volcano. The
40 resulting floodwater mixed with the rock and debris to create concrete-like mudflows that scoured river valleys surrounding the mountain.

A plume of volcanic ash and
45 pumice billowed out of the volcano reaching a height of 15 miles and transformed day into night across Eastern Washington. Avalanches of super-heated gas and pumice,
50 called pyroclastic flows, swept down the flanks of the volcano. While the landslide and lateral blast were over within minutes, the eruption column, mudflows and pyroclastic
55 flows continued throughout the day

and following night. By the following morning major eruptive activity had ceased and the landscape appeared to be a gray wasteland.

7. The primary purpose of this passage is to
   (A) offer general information about volcanoes
   (B) describe a specific volcanic eruption
   (C) offer specific advice about what to do when a volcano erupts
   (D) provide historical background about volcanoes

8. The first sentence implies that
   (A) Mount St. Helens had never before erupted
   (B) Mount St. Helens erupts every 123 years
   (C) Mount St. Helens last erupted in 1857
   (D) no one suspected that Mount St. Helens could erupt

9. As used in line 9, "rising" most nearly means
   (A) ascending
   (B) approaching
   (C) maturing
   (D) advancing

10. The statement that "Many geologists weren't surprised by Mount St. Helens' awakening," (lines 17–18) primarily suggests that
   (A) geologists were able to predict when Mount St. Helens would erupt
   (B) the assumptions geologists had made about Mount St. Helens were being proven
   (C) the longer a volcano remains dormant, the more likely it is to become active
   (D) nothing is surprising to geologists

11. The author describes the events of May 18, 1980, mainly by means of
   (A) scientific analysis
   (B) detached and impartial observation
   (C) vivid language and dramatic images
   (D) presentation of facts in chronological order

12. By calling the landscape "a gray wasteland" (line 59), the author implies that
   (A) the landscape was covered with a blanket of dirty snow
   (B) the landscape was littered with garbage and other waste matter
   (C) the trees were all covered with gray ash
   (D) the landscape had been stripped bare and covered in volcanic ash

Questions 13–18

It was Paul's afternoon to appear before the faculty of the Pittsburgh High School to account for his various misdemeanors. He had been
5 suspended a week ago, and his father had called at the Principal's office and confessed his perplexity about his son. Paul entered the faculty room suave and smiling. His
10 clothes were a trifle outgrown, and the tan velvet on the collar of his open overcoat was frayed and worn; but for all that there was something of the dandy about him, and he wore
15 an opal pin in his neatly knotted black four-in-hand, and a red carnation in his buttonhole. This latter adornment the faculty somehow felt was not properly significant of the
20 contrite spirit befitting a boy under the ban of suspension.

Paul was tall for his age and very thin, with high, cramped shoulders and a narrow chest. His eyes were
25 remarkable for a certain hysterical brilliancy, and he continually used them in a conscious, theatrical sort of way, peculiarly offensive in a boy.

**GO ON TO THE NEXT PAGE.**

The pupils were abnormally large,
30 as though he were addicted to
belladonna, but there was a glassy
glitter about them which that drug
does not produce.

When questioned by the Principal
35 as to why he was there Paul stated,
politely enough, that he wanted to
come back to school. This was a lie,
but Paul was quite accustomed to
lying; found it, indeed, indispensable
40 for overcoming friction. His teachers
were asked to state their respective
charges against him, which they did
with such a rancor and aggrievedness as evinced that this was not
45 a usual case. Disorder and impertinence were among the offenses
named, yet each of his instructors
felt that it was scarcely possible to
put into words the real cause of the
50 trouble, which lay in a sort of hysterically defiant manner of the boy's; in
the contempt which they all knew he
felt for them, and which he seemingly made not the least effort to
55 conceal. Once, when he had been
making a synopsis of a paragraph
at the blackboard, his English
teacher had stepped to his side and
attempted to guide his hand. Paul
60 had started back with a shudder
and thrust his hands violently behind
him. The astonished woman could
scarcely have been more hurt and
embarrassed had he struck at her.
65 The insult was so involuntary and
definitely personal as to be unforgettable. In one way and another
he had made all his teachers, men
and women alike, conscious of the
70 same feeling of physical aversion. In
one class he habitually sat with his
hand shading his eyes; in another
he always looked out of the window
during the recitation; in another he
75 made a running commentary on the
lecture, with humorous intention.
—Willa Cather from "Paul's
Case: A Study in Temperament"

13. This passage can best be
characterized as
(A) an amusing story about
a high school escapade
(B) a fond remembrance of
the narrator's youth
(C) a polite appeal for
forgiveness
(D) a penetrating examination of a young man's
character

14. In lines 13–14, the expression
"there was something of the
dandy about him" means that
Paul
(A) was afraid of appearing
before the faculty
(B) paid great attention to
his clothes
(C) did not care how he
looked
(D) was in need of new
clothes

15. The red carnation in Paul's
buttonhole in lines 16–17 made
the faculty feel that Paul
(A) did not take his suspension seriously enough
(B) did not really want to
come back to school
(C) was trying to impress the
principal
(D) was sincere in his desire
to improve his behavior

16. In the eyes of the faculty,
Paul's most serious offense
was his
(A) inability to control his
temper
(B) failure to complete his
assignments
(C) obvious contempt for his
teachers
(D) lack of attention in class

17. Which adjective best describes
Paul?
(A) contrite
(B) defiant
(C) violent
(D) embarrassed

18. In lines 60–62, Paul shuddered
and threw his hands behind
him because
(A) his teacher had touched
his hand
(B) he could not answer the
teacher's question
(C) he was afraid of the
teacher
(D) he wanted to strike the
teacher

Questions 19–24

Manatees and dugongs, also
known as sea cows, belong to the
scientific order Sirenia. In ancient
mythology, "siren" was a term
5 used for monsters or sea nymphs
who lured sailors and their ships to
treacherous rocks and shipwreck
with mesmerizing songs. Throughout
history, sailors sometimes thought
10 they were seeing mermaids when
they were probably seeing manatees
or dugongs. With a little imagination,
manatees have an uncanny resemblance to human form that could only
15 increase after long months at sea.
In fact, manatees and dugongs may
have helped to perpetuate the myth
of mermaids. Like the mythological
creatures for which they were named,
20 all sirenians living on earth today are
vulnerable to extinction.

Manatees and dugongs are the
only completely aquatic mammals
that are herbivores. Unlike the other
25 marine mammals (dolphins, whales,
seals, sea lions, sea otters, walruses,
and polar bears) sirenians eat only
seagrasses and other aquatic vegetation. Unlike other marine mam-
30 mals, sirenians have an extremely
low metabolism and zero tolerance
for cold water. Like dolphins and
whales, manatees and dugongs
are totally aquatic mammals that
35 never leave the water—not even to
give birth. The combination of these
factors means that sirenians are
restricted to warm shallow coastal
waters, estuaries, and rivers, with
40 healthy ecosystems that support
large amounts of seagrass and
other vegetation.

**GO ON TO THE NEXT PAGE.**

The average adult manatee is about three meters (9.8 feet) long and
45 weighs between 362–544 kilograms (800–1,200 pounds). It is estimated that a manatee can eat about 10–15% of its body weight in vegetation daily. So, for example, a 453-kilogram
50 (1,000-pound) manatee would probably eat between 45–68 kilograms (100–150 pounds) of sea grass and water hyacinths a day!

19. Paragraph 1 is primarily concerned with
    (A) the origin of the scientific classification Sirenia
    (B) the similarities between manatees and mermaids
    (C) how manatees cause shipwrecks
    (D) a comparison between manatees and dugongs

20. As used in line 8, "mesmerizing" most nearly means
    (A) discordant
    (B) high pitched
    (C) hypnotic
    (D) mysterious

21. The passage supports which of the following conclusions?
    (A) Manatees are like other marine mammals in their diet.
    (B) Manatees leave the water only to give birth.
    (C) Because of their low metabolism, manatees tolerate cold water well.
    (D) All sirenians are endangered.

22. The author develops paragraph 2 by presenting
    (A) two sides of an issue
    (B) a thesis followed by specific examples
    (C) a description of similarities and differences
    (D) an opinion and reasons why it is held

23. According to the passage, manatees prefer the shallow coastal waters of Florida because of which of the following?
    I.   Availability of vegetation
    II.  Favorable water temperatures
    III. Safety

    (A) I only
    (B) I and II only
    (C) II only
    (D) I, II, and III

24. Which of the following represents the number of pounds of food an average adult manatee consumes in a day?
    (A) 10–15
    (B) 100–150
    (C) 352–544
    (D) 800–1,000

Questions 25–30

Day had broken cold and gray, exceedingly cold and gray, when the man turned aside from the main Yukon trail and climbed the high
5 earth-bank, where a dim and little-travelled trail led eastward through the fat spruce timberland. It was a steep bank, and he paused for breath at the top, excusing the act
10 to himself by looking at his watch. It was nine o'clock. There was no sun nor hint of sun, though there was not a cloud in the sky. It was a clear day, and yet there seemed
15 an intangible pall over the face of things, a subtle gloom that made the day dark, and that was due to the absence of sun. This fact did not worry the man.
20 As he turned to go on, he spat speculatively. There was a sharp, explosive crackle that startled him. He spat again. And again, in the air, before it could fall to the snow, the
25 spittle crackled. He knew that at fifty below spittle crackled on the snow, but this spittle had crackled in the air. Undoubtedly it was colder than fifty below — how much colder he did
30 not know. But the temperature did not matter. He was bound for the old claim on the left fork of Henderson Creek, where the boys were already. They had come over across the
35 divide from the Indian Creek country, while he had come the roundabout way to take a look at the possibilities of getting out logs in the spring from the islands in the Yukon.
40 At the man's heels trotted a dog, a big native husky, the proper wolf-dog, gray-coated and without any visible or temperamental difference from its brother, the wild wolf. The
45 animal was depressed by the tremendous cold. It knew that it was no time for traveling. Its instinct told it a truer tale than was told to the man by the man's judgment . . . It experi-
50 enced a vague but menacing apprehension that subdued it and made it slink along at the man's heels, and that made it question eagerly every unwonted movement of the man as
55 if expecting him to go into camp or to seek shelter somewhere and build a fire.

—Jack London from "To Build a Fire"

25. In the first paragraph the author establishes a mood of
    (A) promise
    (B) serenity
    (C) hostility
    (D) foreboding

26. The statement that "It was a steep bank, and he paused for breath at the top, excusing the act to himself by looking at his watch" (lines 7–10) suggests that the man
    (A) was worried about running late
    (B) was not accustomed to hiking in the Yukon
    (C) was disoriented by the extreme cold
    (D) had traveled farther than he thought

**GO ON TO THE NEXT PAGE.**

27. The discussion of spitting into the air (lines 20–27) serves primarily to suggest
    (A) the strangeness of the landscape
    (B) the gloom of the day
    (C) the frustration of the dog
    (D) the severity of the cold

28. In line 22, the author includes the detail that the sharp, explosive crackle "startled him" primarily to emphasize
    (A) the man's fragile state of mind
    (B) how eerily quiet it had become
    (C) that it was colder than the man thought
    (D) the danger the man was in

29. Which word best describes how the author regards the man in the story?
    (A) clever
    (B) cautious
    (C) ambitious
    (D) foolish

30. With which of the following statements is the author most likely to agree?
    (A) The dog is wiser than the man.
    (B) The dog is unfazed by the cold.
    (C) The man is jealous of the dog.
    (D) The man is right to press on.

Questions 31–36

Harmful algal blooms, or HABs, occur when colonies of algae— simple plants that live in the sea and freshwater—grow out of control. Algal
5 blooms can produce toxic effects, resulting in illness and death among fish, shellfish, marine mammals, and birds. The human illnesses caused by HABs, though rare, can be debilitat-
10 ing or even fatal.

While many people call these blooms "red tides," scientists prefer the term *harmful algal bloom*. One of the best known HABs in the
15 nation occurs nearly every summer along Florida's Gulf Coast. This bloom, like many HABs, is caused by microscopic algae that produce toxins that kill fish and make shell-
20 fish dangerous to eat. The toxins may also make the surrounding air difficult to breathe. As the name suggests, the bloom of algae often turns the water red.
25 HABs have been reported in every U.S. coastal state, and their occurrence may be on the rise. HABs are a national concern because they affect not only the health of people
30 and marine ecosystems, but also the "health" of local and regional economies.

But not all algal blooms are harmful. Most blooms, in fact, are benefi-
35 cial because the tiny plants are food for animals in the ocean. In fact, they are the major source of energy that fuels the ocean food web.

A small percentage of algae,
40 however, produce powerful toxins that can kill fish, shellfish, mammals, and birds, and may directly or indirectly cause illness in people. HABs also include blooms of nontoxic
45 species that have harmful effects on marine ecosystems. For example, when masses of algae die and decompose, the decaying process can deplete oxygen in the water,
50 causing the water to become so low in oxygen that animals either leave the area or die.

–National Oceanic and Atmospheric Agency (NOAA)

31. In line 5, "toxic" means most nearly
    (A) wholesome
    (B) uncommon
    (C) poisonous
    (D) harmless

32. According to the passage, HABs are called "red tides" because
    (A) they turn the ocean water red
    (B) they turn fish and sea mammals red
    (C) they appear only at high tide
    (D) they occur in politically conservative states

33. Based on the text, which of the following statements is true?
    (A) All algal blooms are dangerous because they kill fish, sea mammals, and birds.
    (B) Most algal blooms are helpful because they provide food for ocean animals.
    (C) Algal blooms affect only the Florida's Gulf Coast during the hottest days of summer.
    (D) When algal blooms die, they may produce dangerous levels of oxygen in the ocean.

34. According to the text, where do most algal blooms occur?
    (A) in all states that have ocean coastlines
    (B) off the Gulf Coast of Florida
    (C) in areas where summer temperatures are high
    (D) in interior lakes and major rivers

35. A reader is most likely to find the information in this article
    (A) in a history textbook
    (B) at a government website
    (C) in an encyclopedia
    (D) in an atlas

36. The author's attitude toward the subject of algal blooms is best described as
    (A) disapproving
    (B) persuasive
    (C) indifferent
    (D) objective

**STOP!**
If you finish before time is up, check your work on this section only.

**Directions:** For each of the following questions, mark the letter of your choice on the answer sheet.

1. If 6 is added to the product of 9 and 5, the result is
   - (A)  20
   - (B)  25
   - (C)  38
   - (D)  51

2. It costs $48.00 dollars to buy 64 cans of soda. At the same rate, how many dollars will it cost to buy 48 cans?
   - (A)  $12.00
   - (B)  $9.00
   - (C)  $36.00
   - (D)  $64.00

3. $32 \div (2 + 6) - 4$
   - (A)  0
   - (B)  4
   - (C)  8
   - (D)  10

4. In a dresser drawer there are 3 pairs of white socks, 5 pairs of black socks, and 4 pairs of blue socks. If you pick a pair without looking, what are the chances that you will pick a blue pair?
   - (A)  $\dfrac{1}{12}$
   - (B)  $\dfrac{1}{6}$
   - (C)  $\dfrac{1}{4}$
   - (D)  $\dfrac{1}{3}$

5. $6 \div {}^{2}\!/_{3} =$
   - (A)  3
   - (B)  4
   - (C)  6
   - (D)  9

6. Maleka had a birthday party and spent $4.68 on balloons, $35.32 on party favors, $17.77 on a cake, $16.35 on ice cream, and $18.00 on invitations. How much did Maleka spend on the party?
   - (A)  $89.75
   - (B)  $92.12
   - (C)  $95.20
   - (D)  $103.10

7. 35% of 70 =
   - (A)  65
   - (B)  50
   - (C)  35
   - (D)  24.5

8. If Tino rides his bike at a steady speed of 9 miles per hour, how far will he ride in 3 hours 40 minutes?
   - (A)  27 miles
   - (B)  33 miles
   - (C)  36 miles
   - (D)  39 miles

9. Ashley practiced the piano for 1³/₄ hours on Monday and for 45 minutes on Tuesday. For how many hours did she practice on the two days together?
   - (A)  2
   - (B)  $2\dfrac{1}{4}$
   - (C)  $2\dfrac{1}{2}$
   - (D)  $2\dfrac{3}{4}$

10. Donna is *d* years old. Frank is *f* years old. Frank is 4 years younger than Donna. Which equation represents the relationship between Donna's and Frank's age?
    - (A)  $d = \dfrac{f}{4}$
    - (B)  $d = 4 - f$
    - (C)  $f = d - 4$
    - (D)  $f = 4 - d$

11. Matt took a bike trip. On the first day he rode 15 miles. On the second day he rode 35 miles, and on the third day he rested. On the fourth day he rode 57 miles, and on the fifth day he rode 43 miles. What is the average number of miles that he rode per day?
    - (A)  25
    - (B)  27
    - (C)  30
    - (D)  32

12. One kilometer is approximately equal to 0.6 mile. How many kilometers are in 8 miles?
    - (A)  about 6
    - (B)  about 7
    - (C)  about 11
    - (D)  about 13

**GO ON TO THE NEXT PAGE.**

13. A snowstorm started on Tuesday at 2:12 P.M. and ended on Wednesday at 5:46 A.M. How long did it snow in hours and minutes?
    (A) 15 hours, 24 minutes
    (B) 15 hours, 34 minutes
    (C) 16 hours, 14 minutes
    (D) 16 hours, 44 minutes

14. In a group of 9 hikers, each person carries $3/4$ of a pound of trail mix. How much trail mix do they carry all together?
    (A) $6\frac{3}{4}$ lb
    (B) 7 lb
    (C) $7\frac{1}{4}$ lb
    (C) $7\frac{1}{2}$ lb

15. $0.4 \times 0.5 =$
    (A) 0.02
    (B) 0.20
    (C) 2
    (D) 20

16. Which lists all the common factors of 27 and 45?
    (A) 3
    (B) 3, 5
    (C) 3, 5, 9
    (D) 1, 3, 9

17. $7/21$ is equivalent to the fractions in which list?
    (A) $\frac{2}{6}, \frac{3}{9}, \frac{9}{27}$
    (B) $\frac{6}{10}, \frac{15}{25}, \frac{30}{50}$
    (C) $\frac{2}{3}, \frac{14}{28}, \frac{24}{40}$
    (D) $\frac{3}{4}, \frac{9}{12}, \frac{24}{32}$

18. On Monday, $x$ people took buses to work. There were 6 buses with an equal number in each bus. Which expression shows the number of people in each bus?
    (A) $6x$
    (B) $\frac{x}{6}$
    (C) $x + 6$
    (D) $x - 6$

19. Barbara is filling two pots with water. Each pot holds 4 liters. How many milliliters do the two pots hold?
    (A) 80
    (B) 800
    (C) 8,000
    (D) 80,000

20. Karen hiked 23.62 miles. Anthony hiked 19.8 miles. How much farther did Karen hike than Anthony?
    (A) 2.46 miles
    (B) 2.98 miles
    (C) 3.46 miles
    (D) 3.82 miles

21. At 4:00 A.M. on a winter morning the temperature was −11°F. Every hour after that the temperature rose by 3°F. What was the temperature at 11:00 A.M.?
    (A) −2°F
    (B) 9°F
    (C) 10°F
    (D) 13°F

22. $9^{3}/_{5} + 2^{1}/_{4} =$
    (A) $11\frac{17}{20}$
    (B) $11\frac{9}{10}$
    (C) $12\frac{3}{20}$
    (D) $12\frac{1}{10}$

23. $12 \div 3^{1}/_{4} =$
    (A) $2\frac{11}{12}$
    (B) $3\frac{1}{6}$
    (C) $3\frac{2}{3}$
    (D) $3\frac{9}{13}$

24. If $8y + 5 = 41$, $y =$
    (A) 4.2
    (B) 4.5
    (C) 5.1
    (D) 5.5

25. $(8 + 2)^2 - 2^3 \times (5 - 3) =$
    (A) 84
    (B) 86

(C) 92
(D) 104

26. What is the value of the expression $85.1 - a$ for $a = 26.3$?
    (A) 63.1
    (B) 61.4
    (C) 60.2
    (D) 58.8

27. The melting point of oxygen is −218°C. Its boiling point is only 35°C higher. What is the boiling point of oxygen?
    (A) −253°C
    (B) −183°C
    (C) 183°C
    (D) 253°C

28. $3^0 =$
    (A) −3
    (B) −1
    (C) 1
    (D) 3

29. Marlene bought a hat and a scarf. The hat cost $5.96 more than the scarf. The total for the two items, before tax, was $63.94. What was the cost of the hat?
    (A) $26.39
    (B) $26.99
    (C) $28.99
    (D) $34.95

30. Order from least to greatest: $-1^{2}/_{5}, -1^{3}/_{5}, -1^{1}/_{3}$
    (A) $-1\frac{2}{5}, -1\frac{1}{3}, -1\frac{3}{5}$
    (B) $-1\frac{3}{5}, -1\frac{2}{5}, -1\frac{1}{3}$
    (C) $-1\frac{3}{5}, -1\frac{1}{3}, -1\frac{2}{5}$
    (D) $-1\frac{1}{3}, -1\frac{2}{5}, -1\frac{3}{5}$

31. $1/4 - 2/3 \times 3/4 =$
    (A) $1\frac{1}{6}$
    (B) $\frac{7}{12}$
    (C) $\frac{-1}{12}$
    (D) $\frac{-1}{4}$

**GO ON TO THE NEXT PAGE.**

32. Hideki drove the 81 miles from Glendale to Roseville in $1\frac{1}{2}$ hours. What was his average speed?
   (A)   54 mph
   (B)   56 mph
   (C)   57 mph
   (D)   58 mph

33. The half–life of a radioactive element is 1 second. If you start with 32 grams of it, how much will be left in 4 seconds?
   (A)   2 g
   (B)   4 g
   (C)   8 g
   (D)   16 g

34. Keisha rides an elevator up 2 floors and down 11 floors and gets off. She is on floor 3. Where did she get on?
   (A)   floor 4
   (B)   floor 7
   (C)   floor 10
   (D)   floor 12

35. The difference between 4 times a number and 16 is 4. What is the number?
   (A)   5
   (B)   6
   (C)   8
   (D)   9

36. The distance around a running track is 440 yards. How many times must you run around the track to run 3 miles?
   (A)   8
   (B)   9
   (C)   12
   (D)   14

37. A rectangular playground is 200 yd long and 120 yd wide. What is the length in yards of a fence all around the edge of the playground?
   (A)   620 yd
   (B)   640 yd
   (C)   660 yd
   (D)   680 yd

38. $\frac{x}{4} = \frac{45}{36}$. $x =$
   (A)   3
   (B)   4
   (C)   5
   (D)   6

39. Jorge hiked 45 miles in 3 days. If he hikes at the same rate, how many miles can he hike in 2 weeks?
   (A)   180 mi
   (B)   195 mi
   (C)   205 mi
   (D)   210 mi

40. Which shows $\frac{3}{8}$ written as a percent?
   (A)   37.5%
   (B)   40%
   (C)   44.5%
   (D)   45%

41. What percent of 144 is 108?
   (A)   65%
   (B)   68%
   (C)   72%
   (D)   75%

42. What is the total cost of a $450 television set, including an 8.5% sales tax?
   (A)   $476.75
   (B)   $488.25
   (C)   $492.50
   (D)   $494.75

43. What is 231,000 written in scientific notation?
   (A)   $2.31 \times 10^3$
   (B)   $2.31 \times 10^4$
   (C)   $2.31 \times 10^5$
   (D)   $231 \times 10^3$

44. What is the median of the set of data shown in this box?

   | 36, 22, 32, 28, 24 |
   | --- |

   (A)   26
   (B)   28
   (C)   32
   (D)   36

45. What is the next term in this sequence?

   $$1, 4, 16, 64, \ldots$$

   (A)   128
   (B)   144
   (C)   160
   (D)   256

46. If $\frac{1}{8x} = 20$, then $\frac{1}{2x} = ?$
   (A)   40
   (B)   60
   (C)   80
   (D)   120

47. When added, the sum of three consecutive integers is 18. What is the greatest number?
   (A)   5
   (B)   6
   (C)   7
   (D)   8
   (E)   9

**STOP!**
If you finish before time is up, check your work on this section only.

## SECTION 5

Time: 30 Minutes

**Directions:** You will have 30 minutes to plan and write an essay on the topic given below. You must write on the assigned topic only. An essay on another topic will not be acceptable. You may make notes in the space provided for that purpose.

Write your final essay on the two lined pages of your answer sheet. Write or print legibly in blue or black ink. A copy of your essay will be sent to each school that will be receiving your test results.

---

If you could meet one famous person from the present or the past, who would it be? Explain why you have chosen this person.

---

USE THIS SPACE FOR NOTES

## Answer Key

### Section 1 Verbal Reasoning

| | | | | | |
|---|---|---|---|---|---|
| 1. | D | 15. | C | 29. | C |
| 2. | D | 16. | B | 30. | A |
| 3. | B | 17. | B | 31. | C |
| 4. | C | 18. | A | 32. | C |
| 5. | A | 19. | D | 33. | D |
| 6. | D | 20. | C | 34. | A |
| 7. | B | 21. | D | 35. | B |
| 8. | A | 22. | A | 36. | D |
| 9. | B | 23. | C | 37. | B |
| 10. | C | 24. | B | 38. | A |
| 11. | A | 25. | B | 39. | A |
| 12. | C | 26. | C | 40. | D |
| 13. | A | 27. | D | | |
| 14. | D | 28. | B | | |

### Section 2 Quantitative Reasoning

| | | | | | |
|---|---|---|---|---|---|
| 1. | D | 14. | A | 27. | C |
| 2. | A | 15. | A | 28. | D |
| 3. | C | 16. | C | 29. | A |
| 4. | B | 17. | A | 30. | B |
| 5. | C | 18. | B | 31. | C |
| 6. | B | 19. | B | 32. | A |
| 7. | C | 20. | C | 33. | B |
| 8. | A | 21. | A | 34. | B |
| 9. | C | 22. | A | 35. | C |
| 10. | A | 23. | C | 36. | B |
| 11. | D | 24. | B | 37. | A |
| 12. | A | 25. | A | | |
| 13. | A | 26. | B | | |

## Section 3 Reading Comprehension

| | | | | | |
|---|---|---|---|---|---|
| 1. | C | 13. | D | 25. | D |
| 2. | B | 14. | B | 26. | B |
| 3. | C | 15. | A | 27. | D |
| 4. | A | 16. | C | 28. | C |
| 5. | B | 17. | B | 29. | D |
| 6. | D | 18. | A | 30. | A |
| 7. | B | 19. | A | 31. | C |
| 8. | C | 20. | C | 32. | A |
| 9. | A | 21. | D | 33. | B |
| 10. | C | 22. | C | 34. | A |
| 11. | D | 23. | B | 35. | B |
| 12. | D | 24. | B | 36. | D |

## Section 4 Mathematics Achievement

| | | | | | |
|---|---|---|---|---|---|
| 1. | D | 17. | A | 33. | A |
| 2. | C | 18. | B | 34. | D |
| 3. | A | 19. | C | 35. | A |
| 4. | D | 20. | D | 36. | C |
| 5. | D | 21. | C | 37. | B |
| 6. | B | 22. | A | 38. | C |
| 7. | D | 23. | D | 39. | D |
| 8. | B | 24. | B | 40. | A |
| 9. | C | 25. | A | 41. | D |
| 10. | C | 26. | D | 42. | B |
| 11. | C | 27. | B | 43. | C |
| 12. | D | 28. | C | 44. | B |
| 13. | B | 29. | D | 45. | D |
| 14. | A | 30. | B | 46. | C |
| 15. | B | 31. | D | 47. | C |
| 16. | D | 32. | A | | |

# Answers and Explanations

## Section 1 Verbal Reasoning

1. **D is correct.** *Shame* is a painful emotion caused by a strong sense of guilt, embarrassment, unworthiness, or disgrace. Another word for shame is *humiliation*.

2. **D is correct.** To *divulge* something is to make it known, especially something private or a secret—to *tell*.

3. **B is correct.** *Concise* is an adjective meaning expressing much in few words; clear and succinct—in other words, *brief*.

4. **C is correct.** An *inquiry* is a close examination of a matter in a search for information or truth. An *inquiry* is synonymous with an *investigation*.

5. **A is correct.** Like *disposition*, an *attitude* is a state of mind or feeling.

6. **D is correct.** To do something *tediously* is the same as doing it *tiresomely* by reason of length, slowness, dullness, or boredom.

7. **B is correct.** To *deplete* something is to decrease the fullness of it; use it up; or empty it out—in other words, to *reduce* it.

8. **A is correct.** *Cautious* describes someone who is careful, tentative, restrained, or guarded. Another way to describe such a person would be to say that she is *discreet*.

9. **B is correct.** *Sparse* is an adjective describing conditions that are not thick or dense. *Thin* is synonymous with sparse.

10. **C is correct.** An *aversion* is an avoidance of a thing, situation, or behavior because it has been associated with an unpleasant or painful stimulus. If you have an aversion to something, you have a fixed, intense *dislike* for it.

11. **A is correct.** When something is *dormant* it is lying asleep, or as if asleep. That is, it is *inactive*.

12. **C is correct.** If someone is described as *malcontent*, he is *dissatisfied* with existing conditions.

13. **A is correct.** To *merit* means to earn or *deserve*.

14. **D is correct.** If something is *prominent*, it is immediately noticeable—in other words, *conspicuous*.

15. **C is correct.** An *objective* is something worked toward or striven for. *Intention* is synonymous with *objective*.

16. **B is correct.** Something that is *indelible* is impossible to remove, erase, or wash away. Therefore, it is *permanent*.

17. **B is correct.** A *shrewd* person is characterized by keen awareness, sharp intelligence, and often a sense of the practical. As well, a person described as *astute* has or shows discernment, awareness, and intelligence.

18. **A is correct.** *Clandestine* is an adjective meaning kept or done in *secret*, often to conceal an illicit or improper purpose.

19. **D is correct.** To *coerce* someone is to force that person to act or think in a certain way by use of pressure, threats, or intimidation. *Compel* can be used synonymously with *coerce*.

20. **C is correct.** A *plethora* is an abundance or an *excess*.

21. **D is correct.** Ask yourself: Which choice best reflects a description of two famous (rather than infamous) historical figures? *Eminent* (choice D) denotes a person of prominence or high ranking. This is the only choice that fits the context of the sentence and thus it is the correct answer.

22. **A is correct.** Since choices A, B, and D all have similar first-blank meanings, you can discount choice C and focus on the second-blank choices. Of the three, *ratify* (meaning "to approve or confirm") is the best choice and works well with the idea that the sentence is trying to convey.

23. **C is correct.** By focusing on the first blank, you can almost immediately discount choice D by logically inferring that a product manufacturer would likely want a consumer to achieve better than "conventional" results with its product. Now, you will find that one of the three remaining answer choices clearly makes more sense than the other two, because it is unlikely that a tutorial would be *abbreviated* or *selective*. *Optimum . . . comprehensive* is the correct answer.

24. **B is correct.** "Although" is one of the words you may see on the test that signals a contrast within a two-clause sentence. When you come across words or phrases such as "despite," "although," or "even though," keep in mind that the word you are looking for is likely to contrast with another point the sentence makes. Of the choices available, only *destructive* and *solidarity* offers sufficient contrast to a tornado that had ruinous effects and the mutual support of the people affected by it.

25. **B is correct.** *Succumb*, meaning "to submit to an overpowering force or yield to an overwhelming desire; to give up or give in," is the correct answer.

26. **C is correct.** By noticing the "despite" construction, you are given a clue that the pair of words you are looking for will have a contrast in meaning. *Explosive . . . timid* is the only choice that offers the proper contrast.

27. **D is correct.** *Equivocal*, meaning "open to two or more interpretations and often intended to mislead," is the only possible correct answer. *Equivocal* can be used synonymously with *ambiguous*.

28. **B is correct.** The words *indulge* and *exiled* form the only answer that explains the effects of not giving someone in authority what they demand.

29. **C is correct.** The logic of this sentence suggests that many people do not agree with an earlier decision the judge made. *Impede*, meaning "to hinder or obstruct the process of," is the correct answer. Don't be fooled by the similar-looking *impel*, which means "to urge to action through moral pressure," or "to drive."

30. **A is correct.** This question is made much easier if you are able to discount choices C and D because you know that *forgo* means "to abstain from," and *mollify* means "to calm in temper or soothe." Logic tells you that it is unlikely Langston Hughes doubted blues music to be the true expression of his soul. *Emulate . . . believed* is the correct answer (*emulate* meaning "to strive to equal or excel, especially through imitation").

31. **C is correct.** *Discernible*, meaning "perceptible as by the faculty of vision or intellect," is the correct answer. *Imperceptible* (choice A) is an antonym. Pay attention to prefixes and be aware how they alter the meaning of the words you may be looking for.

32. **C is correct.** "Initially" is a key word in this sentence as it conveys the logic that the main suspect later changed his mind and agreed to cooperate with the prosecution. Indeed, had his alibi been foolproof, solid, or *feasible* (choice A), he likely would have stuck to his original story. So, the word you are looking for is *tenuous*, meaning "flimsy or having little substance."

33. **D is correct.** Logically you can infer that property owners would not be *exuberant* (choice A) over the mayor's proposal to raise property taxes in order to fund a new stadium. As well, because *exuberant* has connotations similar to *illustrious* (choice C), you should be able to eliminate both answer choices. *Ambivalent* (choice D), meaning "characterized by a mixture of opposite meanings or attitudes," is correct.

34. **A is correct.** Because this sentence lacks words or phrases that signal contrast, you should be looking for a pair of words that will complement one another. From the choices you are given, you can see that only choice A, *praised . . . commendable*, fits this criteria. All of the other choices are word pairs that have conflicting meanings.

35. **B is correct.** Seemingly, Ms. Tompkins favors collecting books. Therefore, you could say that she has a *propensity* (meaning "an innate inclination or tendency") for accumulation.

36. **D is correct.** *Resilience* (choice D) is the ability to recover quickly from illness, change, or misfortune. *Dexterity* (choice C), meaning "skill and grace in physical movement," is an attractive distracter, but the focus of the sentence is that the gymnast was able to overcome injuries. Choice D is the best answer.

37. **B is correct.** *Fastidious* (choice C) is incorrect because its meaning is similar to *picky*, which is contradicted by the conjunction "but." *Ravenous* (choice B), meaning "extremely hungry," conveys the meaning of the sentence, which is that you would expect the bear to be extremely hungry when in fact he is rather picky. *Hirsute* means "covered in hair."

38. **A is correct.** If you are unsure of the correct word pair in a two-blank question, try focusing on one of the blanks or the relationship between the two words. The idea that a couple whose hotel reservation was canceled would react angrily shows a logical relationship of ideas.

39. **A is correct.** *Comparable* (choice B) and *consistent* (choice D) do not fit the "even though" construction of this sentence. *Excessive* fits the first blank, though *affirm* (meaning "to declare positively" or "maintain to be true") makes no sense in the second blank. *Disproportionate . . . submit* (choice A) is the correct answer.

40. **D is correct.** This sentence is another example of a two-blank question in which the correct choice of words will complement, rather than contrast with, one another. Because both choice A and choice B are pairs that offer contrasting meanings, you can eliminate them. Focusing on the two remaining pairs, you can conclude that the newspaper was unlikely to be responsible for the power outage, and therefore *harassed* is an inappropriate answer. *Inundated . . . deluge* (choice D) is correct.

## Section 2 Quantitative Reasoning

1. **D is correct.** $48 \div 6 \times 8 \times 8 = 512$; $512 \div 16 = 32$.

2. **A is correct.** Create equations to solve this problem.
   Paula = Lindsey + 3
   Lindsey = Dave – 2
   You are told that Paula is 17. Substitute that information into the first equation.
   17 = Lindsey + 3
   Lindsey = 14
   Substitute that into the second equation.
   14 = Dave – 2
   Dave = 16

3. **C is correct.** $3/4 - 5/12 = 9/12 - 5/12 = 4/12 = 1/3$.

4. **B is correct.** $20 = x\%$ of 80.
   $20 = 80x$     Solve for $x$.
   $x = 20/80$
   $x = 2/8$
   $x = 1/4$     Divide 1 by 4 to get 0.25 or 25%

5. **C is correct.** 0.5 km = 500 meters; $500 \div 5 = 100$.

6. **B is correct.** $2/8$ can be simplified to $1/4$.

7. **C is correct.** The least common multiple of a group of numbers is the least whole number (greater than 0) that is a multiple of all of the numbers. The least common multiple of 9, 2 and 5 is 90 ($9 \times 10$, $2 \times 45$, $5 \times 18$).

8. **A is correct.** To find the average, add the numbers and divide by the number of numbers. In this problem the numbers add to 415. Dividing that by 5 gives an average of 83.

9. **C is correct.** $1/3 + 1/6 = 2/6 + 1/6 = 3/6$.
$3/6 = 1/2$, so if Karen has used $1/2$ of her tickets, $1/2$ are left.

10. **A is correct.** $5 \times 4 + 4 = 24$; $6 \times 8 = 48$; and $48 \div 24 = 2$.

11. **D is correct.** $32/4 = 8$; $4 \times 8/16 = 32/16 = 2$; $8 \div 1/8 = 8 \times 8/1 = 64$. However, $5/12 \times 8 = 40/12 = 3\frac{1}{3}$, which is not a whole number.

12. **A is correct.** 1 mile = 5,280 ft. If the width of the park is 880 ft, then two sides of the park measure $880 + 880 = 1,760$ ft. $5,280 - 1,760 = 3,520$. The other two sides of the park must each measure one-half of 3,520 ft. $3,520 \div 2 = 1,760$ ft.

13. **A is correct.**
$1/4 x = 12$
$x = 48$
$1/6 x = 8$

14. **A is correct.** Set up a proportion:
$3/126 = x/924$
$3 \times 924 = 126x$
$2,772 = 126x$
$2,772/126 = x$
$22 = x$

15. **A is correct.**
$5/6 - 2/3 - 1/12$
$= 10/12 - 8/12 - 1/12$
$= 2/12 - 1/12$
$= 1/12$

16. **C is correct.** When calculating the average or mean, add the numbers and then divide by the number of numbers. The sum of 24, 36, 18, 30, 90, and 690 is 888, divided by 6 is 148.

17. **A is correct.** It costs $12.00 dollars to buy 24 cookies. 6 cookies are 1/4 of 24, so the cost of 6 cookies will be $1/4 \times \$12.00 = \$3.00$ dollars.

18. **B is correct.** $3 \times 425 = 1,275$.

19. **B is correct.** $20/5 = 4$; $6 \div 1/6 = 6 \times 6/1 = 36$; $3/5 \times 10 = 30/5 = 6$; However, $5 \times 3/4 = 15/4 = 3\frac{3}{4}$, which is not a whole number.

20. **C is correct.** $\begin{bmatrix} 1 & 2 \\ -1 & 0 \end{bmatrix}$ Remember, the subtraction sign before the second matrix changes the sign of all numbers in this matrix.

21. **A is correct.** This is a quantitative-comparison question in which you are asked to compare two whole number differences. Did you notice that the last 3 digits in the numbers being subtracted are the same? The last 3 digits in the number you are subtracting from is greater in Column A than in Column B.

22. **A is correct.**
$75\% = 3/4$ and $25\% = 1/4$.
Column A: 75% of 120 = $3/4 \times 120 = 90$
Column B: 50% of 160 = $1/2 \times 160 = 80$

23. **C is correct.**
The distributive property states that $a(b + c) = (a \bullet b) + (a \bullet c)$
Use the distributive property to simplify the expression in Column A:
$3(c + 2) = (3 \bullet c) + (3 \bullet 2)$

Simplify the quantity in Column A as follows: $(3 \bullet c) + (3 \bullet 2) = 3c + 6$
Simplify the quantity in Column B as follows: $3c + (3 \bullet 2) = 3c + 6$

24. **B is correct.**
The vertex of both angles is at the center of the protractor.
Ray *FE* of ∠*DFE* passes through the zero mark on the inner scale of the protractor.
Ray *FD* of ∠*DFE* passes through 65 on the inner scale.
$m \angle DFE = 65°$
Ray *AF* of ∠*AFC* passes through the zero mark on the outer scale of the protractor.
Ray *FC* of ∠*AFC* passes through 70 on the outer scale.
$m \angle AFC = 70°$

25. **A is correct.**
To find the average number of yards per minute, divide the total number of yards walked by the number of minutes it took to walk them.
Column A: Divide the total number of yards Janet walked (125) by the number of minutes it took her to walk this distance (3). $125 \div 3 = 41^2/_3$
Column B: Divide the total number of yards Victoria walked (206) by the number of minutes it took her to walk this distance (5). $205 \div 5 = 41^1/_5$
$41^2/_3 > 41^1/_5$

26. **B is correct.**

$\sqrt{150}$ is the number whose square is 150.

$\sqrt{150}$ is a number between 12 and 13, since $12 \times 12 = 144$ and $13 \times 13 = 169$.

27. **C is correct.**
The probability of an event is the ratio of favorable outcomes to possible outcomes. This ratio can be written as a fraction.
The number of possible outcomes equals the number of letter blocks, which is 15.
Column A: Find the number of favorable outcomes by counting all the blocks that contain vowels. This includes As (3) and Es (1), for a total of 4 favorable outcomes.
Column B: Find the number of favorable outcomes by counting all the blocks that contain Ts (2) or Ls (2), for a total of 4 favorable outcomes.
$^4/_{15} = ^4/_{15}$

28. **D is correct.**
The perimeter of a rectangle is $p = 2l + 2w$. The perimeter of a square is $p = 4s$.
The area of a rectangle is $A = l \times w$. The area of a square is $A = s^2$.
Column A: Since you were given the area as 64 ft², find *s* by finding $\sqrt{64} = 8$, and then find *p*, the perimeter = $4 \times 8 = 32$ ft.
Column B: If the area is 48 ft², there are many different whole number values *l* and *w* can equal. For example, $6 \times 8 = 48$, $3 \times 16 = 48$, $2 \times 24 = 48$, and $1 \times 48 = 48$.
Use these various values for *l* and *w* to find the perimeter of the rectangle.
Some values will result in perimeters less than 32 ft, such as $l = 6$ and $w = 8$, $p = 2(6) + 2(8) = 28$. Some values will result in perimeters greater than 32, such as $l = 3$, $w = 16$, $p = 2(3) + 2(16) = 38$. Thus the relationship between the two quantities cannot be determined from the information given.

29. **A is correct.**
Column A: Rewrite $4^2/_5$ as $^{22}/_5$.
Column B: Rewrite $7^1/_2$ as $^{15}/_2$.
Rewrite the division as multiplication by first finding the reciprocal of the divisor, and then multiplying the dividend by the reciprocal of the divisor.
Column A: Rewrite $4^2/_5 \div ^3/_{10}$ as $^{22}/_5 \times ^{10}/_3$.
$^{22}/_5 \times ^{10}/_3 = ^{220}/_{15} = 14^{10}/_{15} = 14^2/_3$
Column B: Rewrite $7^1/_2 \div ^2/_3$ as $^{15}/_2 \times ^3/_2$.
$^{15}/_2 \times ^3/_2 = ^{45}/_4 = 11^1/_4$
$14^2/_3$ is greater than $11^1/_4$.

30. **B is correct.**

The absolute value is the distance from a number line to zero.
The absolute value of any number is a positive number.
Column A: Since |4| = 4, then –|4| = –4
Column B: |–4| = 4

31. **C is correct.**

Column A: Solve the equation for $x$ using the subtraction property:
$x + 1 = 15$; $x + 1 – 1 = 15 – 1$; $x = 14$
Column B: Solve the equation for $y$ using the addition property:
$y – 7 = 7$; $y – 7 + 7 = 7 + 7$; $y = 14$

32. **A is correct.**

The figures are rectangular prisms. The formula for finding the surface area of a prism is $SA = 2lw + 2lh + 2wh$
Column A: $SA = 2(3 \times 3) + 2(3 \times 8) + 2(3 \times 8) = 18 + 48 + 48 = 114$ cm²
Column B: $SA = 2(6 \times 2) + 2(6 \times 4) + 2(2 \times 4) = 24 + 48 + 16 = 88$ cm²

33. **B is correct.**

Column A: List all the factors for 56, 96, and 200:
56: 1, 2, 4, 7, 8, 14, 28, 56
96: 1, 2, 3, 4, 6, 8, 12, 16, 24, 32, 48, 96
200: 1, 2, 4, 5, 8, 10, 20, 25, 50, 100, 200
The factors that are common to all three numbers are 1, 2, 4, and 8, and 8 is the largest of these factors.
Column B: List all the factors for 27, 81, and 189:
27: 1, 3, 9, 27
81: 1, 3, 9, 27, 81
189: 1, 3, 7, 9, 21, 27, 63, 189
The factors that are common to all three numbers are 1, 3, 9, and 27, and 27 is the largest of these factors.

34. **B is correct.**

Column A: Estimate by rounding each decimal factor to its leading digit: $2.76 \times 2.57 \rightarrow 3 \times 3 = 9$
The actual product is *less than 9*, since your estimate used numbers greater than the actual factors.
Column B: Estimate by rounding each decimal factor to its leading digit: $21.4 \times 0.53 \rightarrow 20 \times 0.5 = 10$
The actual product is *greater than 10*, since your estimate used numbers less than the actual factors.

35. **C is correct.**

1 qt = 32 fl oz., and 1 c = 8 fl oz
Column A: 8 qt 1 c = $(8 \times 32) + (1 \times 8) = 256 + 8 = 264$ fl oz.
The quantity in Column A is equal to the quantity in Column B.

36. **B is correct.**

16 > 0.16

37. **C is correct.**

There are three odd numbers (1, 3, 5) and three prime numbers (2, 3, 5).

## Section 3 Reading Comprehension

1. **C is correct.** As she says in lines 22–25, "I have been trying to get before you business people to tell you what I am doing." Choice A can be eliminated because Madam Walker was not trying to demonstrate her products to the members of the league, but merely to make them aware of what she was doing and how well she was doing. Choice B is wrong because Madam Walker was addressing her remarks to the entire league, not just to Booker T. Washington. Choice D is wrong because there is no support in the passage for this choice.

2. **B is correct.** Madam Walker came to the podium uninvited and boasted of her business success. She tells how she came from "the cotton fields" to the "wash-tub" to the "cook kitchen" and finally to head a thriving business.

She says "I am not ashamed of my past; I am not ashamed of my humble beginning." Clearly, she is proud of her accomplishments.

3. **C is correct.** The reactions of the audience are indicated in parentheses throughout the speech. The fact that the audience reacted with applause, laughter, and prolonged applause indicates that their reaction was favorable. It is unlikely that the audience would applaud and laugh if they were indifferent (choice A), angry (choice B), or critical (choice D) of the speech.

4. **A is correct.** Walker uses the reference to her promotions from farm laborer, to laundress, to cook to show just how far she has come to get to her current position as head of a company that has made more than $63,000 (a great deal of money in 1912) in only seven years.

5. **D is correct.** Madam Walker says, "I am not ashamed of my past; I am not ashamed of my humble beginning. Don't think that because you have to go down in the wash-tub that you are any less a lady!" By this she means that hard work, like washing and scrubbing, is nothing to be ashamed of. Nor does it diminish a woman's status as a lady who is entitled to be treated with respect.

6. **B is correct.** The entire passage discusses the 1980 eruption of Mount St. Helens. The information provided is specific to a particular volcano, so choices A and D are incorrect. The passage does not tell readers what to do when a volcano erupts, so choice C is wrong.

7. **C is correct.** A 123-year slumber means that Mount St. Helens had no eruptions going back 123 years from 1980. That puts the last eruption at 1857. Choice A is wrong because if Mount St. Helens had been "sleeping" for 123 years, it must have been active 123 years ago. Choice B is wrong because there is nothing to support the idea that Mount St. Helens erupts every 123 years. Choice D is wrong because if Mount St. Helens erupted 123 years ago, it could always erupt again.

8. **A is correct.** *Rising* is used in the following sentence: "Heat from a rising plume of volcanic ash melted glacial ice creating cement-like slurries of rock and ash called mudflows." Each of the answer choices is a possible meaning for *rising*. However, in context, the best meaning is *ascending*.

9. **B is correct.** The passage states that the geologists were not surprised by Mount St. Helens' awakening because they had been studying Mount St. Helens for many years and in 1975 they "published a report predicting Mount St. Helens was the volcano in the lower 48 states most likely to erupt by the end of the century." Thus, the assumptions they had made about Mount St. Helens based on extensive studies of deposits found around the volcano were proving to be correct. Choice A is wrong because the geologists predicted only that Mount St. Helens was the volcano "most likely to erupt by the end of the century." They did not predict when it would erupt, but only that it was most likely to erupt. The passage provides no information to support either choice C or choice D.

10. **C is correct.** The author's use of vivid language is illustrated by such words as "triggered," "blast," "flattened," "scoured," "billowed," and "swept." Examples of dramatic images include these: "In less than three minutes, 230 square miles of forest lay flattened," . . . "concrete-like mudflows that scoured river valleys," "A plume of volcanic ash and pumice billowed out of the volcano reaching a height of 15 miles and transformed day into night."

11. **D is correct.** A wasteland is barren land with no vegetation. The author mentions in lines 31–43 that the landslides flattened the forest and concrete-like mudflows scoured river valleys surrounding the mountain. Choice A is wrong because the landscape was covered in volcanic ash, not snow. Choice B is wrong because a wasteland is barren, not covered in waste matter. Choice C is wrong because the trees had been flattened and swept away.

12. **D is correct.** The entire passage focuses on Paul's attitude and his demeanor. The red carnation in his buttonhole, the fact that he "was quite accustomed to lying," and the contempt he shows for his teachers are both evidence of the author's penetrating look at the character of the young man in question.

13. **B is correct.** A dandy is a man who is very concerned about his appearance and so pays great attention to his clothes. This description fits Paul who, even though his clothes were a trifle outgrown and the collar of his overcoat was frayed, still wore an opal pin in his necktie and a red carnation in his buttonhole.

14. **A is correct.** The faculty felt that the red carnation "was not properly significant of the contrite spirit befitting a boy under the ban of suspension." His jaunty dress made them feel that Paul was not sufficiently humbled by his suspension or sorry about his actions.

15. **C is correct.** As stated in lines 50–55, the real cause of the trouble "lay in a sort of hysterically defiant manner of the boy's; in the contempt which they all knew he felt for them, and which he seemingly made not the least effort to conceal." There is no mention of Paul's inability to control his temper or failure to complete assignments, so choices A and B are wrong. The passage mentions that Paul looked out the window during recitation, which indicates that he was inattentive in class (choice D), but this offense is minor in comparison to the obvious contempt he displayed toward his teachers.

16. **B is correct.** Paul is described as having a "defiant manner," which means he is impertinent, insolent, or boldly resistant to authority. There is no evidence in the passage that Paul is either *contrite* (remorseful) or *embarrassed* (ashamed), so choices A and D are wrong. He moves his hands violently behind him when the English teacher attempts to guide his hand, but his actions in general cannot be described as *violent*, so choice C is wrong.

17. **B is correct.** As stated in lines 43–44, the teachers stated the charges against Paul with "rancor and aggrievedness." *Rancor* means "bitterness" or "malice." *Turmoil*, which means "confusion," does not make sense in relation to stating a case, so choice A is wrong. *Remorse* (choice C), which means "regret," and *dismay* (choice D), which means "discouragement" or "despair," do not fit the context of the passage.

18. **A is correct.** This story is presented as an example of the contempt which all the teachers knew Paul felt for them and which he seemed to make no effort to conceal. Paul shuddered and thrust his hands violently behind him when the English teacher attempted to guide his hand as he worked at the blackboard. "The insult was so involuntary and definitely personal as to be unforgettable. In one way and another he had made all his teachers, men and women alike, conscious of the same feeling of physical aversion." Paul's reaction had nothing to do with not being able to answer the question, so choice B is incorrect. Likewise, there is no indication that he was afraid of the teacher (choice C) or that he wanted to strike the teacher (choice D). The passage says only that the teacher "could scarcely have been more hurt and embarrassed had he struck at her."

19. **D is correct.** This informative passage tells about the Homestead Act of 1862, including the provisions of the Act and the part it played in the settling of the American West. Choice A is wrong because the passage focuses on the Homestead Act, not on the settling of the West. Choice B is wrong because the passage says nothing about extending the Act. Choice C is wrong because although the passage briefly mentions the hard work and sacrifices of homesteaders, this is not the primary purpose of the entire passage.

20. **A is correct.** *File* is used in the following sentence: "People interested in Homesteading first had to file their intentions at the nearest Land Office where they paid a fee of $10 to claim the land . . . ." Although each of the choices is a possible meaning for the word *file*, the one that makes sense in the context of this sentence is *record* (choice A).

21. **B is correct.** As stated in paragraph 2, "A homesteader had only to be the head of a household and at least 21 years of age to claim a 160-acre parcel of land." Also, homesteaders were required "to live on the land, build a home, make improvements, and farm for 5 years before they were eligible to 'prove up'." There is no mention of settlers' having to be native-born citizens. In fact, the passage specifically mentions "newly arrived immigrants" as would-be homesteaders.

22. **C is correct.** As stated in paragraph 1, "Under this Act, 270 million acres, or 10% of the area of the United States, was claimed and settled." Choice A is wrong because each homesteader could claim a 160-acre parcel of land, but that does not mean that every person was entitled to 160 acres of land. Choice D is wrong because the passage states that 10 percent, not 30 percent, of all U.S. lands passed into the hands of individuals.

23. **A is correct.** The Homestead Act was designed "to spur Western migration." As a result of this Act, "270 million acres, or 10% of the area of the United States, was claimed and settled." Thus the Act served its purpose of helping settle the West.

24. **A is correct.** The first paragraph tells how manatees and dugongs came to be called sirenians because of their resemblance to the sirens, or sea nymphs, of Greek mythology. Choice B is wrong because although the

passage mentions that sailors—particularly those who have spent many months at sea—may have mistaken a manatee for a mermaid, it does not provide specific similarities between manatees and mermaids. Choice C is wrong because it was the sirens of mythology who are said to have caused shipwrecks. Choice D is wrong because the passage does not compare manatees and dugongs, except to say that both are sirenians.

25. **C is correct.** The second sentence of the passage tells how the sirens "lured sailors and their ships to treacherous rocks and shipwreck with mesmerizing songs." *Mesmerizing* means "captivating," "spellbinding," or "hypnotic."

26. **D is correct.** The last sentence of paragraph 1 ("Like the mythological creatures for which they were named, all sirenians living on earth today are vulnerable to extinction.") supports the idea that all sirenians are endangered. Information in the passage contradicts each of the other answer choices.

27. **C is correct.** Lines 29–35 ("Unlike . . . birth.") of the passage are devoted to listing the ways in which sirenians are different from and similar to other marine mammals.

28. **B is correct.** As stated in the passage, "sirenians eat only seagrasses and other aquatic vegetation." These grasses grow best in shallow waters where sunlight can penetrate. Additionally, "sirenians have an extremely low metabolism and zero tolerance for cold water"; therefore, they need the warmer temperatures of Florida's coastal waters. There is no mention of safety in the passage, and in fact, these very waters are also attractive to people in speedy powerboats, who pose the biggest danger to slow-moving manatees.

29. **B is correct.** The average adult manatee "weighs between 362–544 kilograms (800–1,200 pounds)" and eats "between 45–68 kilograms (100–150 pounds) of sea grass and water hyacinths a day!"

30. **D is correct.** Mood is the pervading spirit or feeling of a passage as transmitted by the author's choice of words. In this passage the day is described as "exceedingly cold and gray" with "no sun nor hint of sun, though there was not a cloud in the sky." There was "an intangible pall over the face of things, a subtle gloom that made the day dark." And yet, despite these warning signs, the man was not worried. Taken together, this information imparts a sense of impending misfortune or foreboding.

31. **C is correct.** The passage makes it clear that algal blooms may result in the "illness and death" of fish, shellfish, marine mammals and birds. This indicates that such blooms are *poisonous* to these living creatures.

32. **A is correct.** According to lines 22–24, "As the name suggests, the bloom of algae often turns the water red."

33. **B is correct.** According to lines 34–36, "Most blooms, in fact, are beneficial because the tiny plants are food for animals in the ocean."

34. **A is correct.** The passage explicitly states that HABs occur "in every U.S. Coastal State."

35. **B is correct.** The information in the selection is current and the source is listed as National Oceanic and Atmospheric Agency, a government agency.

36. **D is correct.** The author's attitude toward the topic of algal blooms is objective because it simply presents facts, even though some of the effects of algal blooms are negative.

## Section 4 Mathematics Achievement

1. **D is correct.** $9 \times 5 = 45$; $45 + 6 = 51$.

2. **C is correct.** It costs $48.00 to buy 64 cans of soda. 48 cans are $3/4$ of 64, so the cost of 40 cans of soda will be $3/4 \times \$48.00 = \$36.00$.

3. **A is correct.** $6 + 2 = 8$; $32 \div 8 = 4$; $4 - 4 = 0$.

4. **D is correct.** The total number of pairs in the drawer is $3 + 5 + 4 = 12$. If there are 4 pairs of blue socks, then the chances of picking a blue pair are $4/12$ or $1/3$.

5. **D is correct.** $6 \div {}^2/_3 = {}^6/_1 \div {}^2/_3 = {}^6/_1 \times {}^3/_2 = {}^{18}/_2 = 9$.

6. **B is correct.** This is a simple addition problem. Add the amounts of $4.68, $35.32, $17.77, $16.35, and $18.00 to get the total of $92.12.

7. **D is correct.** 35% can be rewritten as 0.35; $0.35 \times 70 = 24.5$.

8. **B is correct.** Use the formula $r \times t = d$ where $r$ = rate, $t$ = time, and $d$ = distance.
    3 hours 40 minutes = $3^2/_3$ hours.
    $r \times t = d$
    $9 \times 3^2/_3 = 33$ miles

9. **C is correct.** 45 minutes = $^3/_4$ hour; $1^3/_4 + {}^3/_4 = 1^6/_4 = 2^2/_4 = 2^1/_2$.

10. **C is correct.** If Frank is 4 years younger than Donna, then the relationship between their two ages can be expressed by the equation $f = d - 4$.

11. **C is correct.** To find the average, add up the numbers and divide by the number of items. In this instance the number of miles Matt rode sums to 150. The number of days is 5, so the average number of miles per day he rode is $150 \div 5 = 30$. Don't make the mistake of dividing by 4 because on one day Matt's number of miles was 0. That number needs to be used in calculating the average.

12. **D is correct.** $8 \div 0.6 = 13.33$, so there are about 13 kilometers in 8 miles.

13. **B is correct.** The storm started at 2:12 P.M. on Tuesday and ended at 5:46 A.M. on Wednesday. From 2:12 P.M. to 5:12 A.M. the next day is 15 hours. From 5:12 to 5:46 is 34 minutes. The storm lasted 15 hours, 34 minutes.

14. **A is correct.** $^3/_4 \times 9 = {}^{27}/_4 = 6^3/_4$.

15. **B is correct.** $0.4 \times 0.5 = 0.20$.

16. **D is correct.** The common factors of 27 and 45 are 1, 3, and 9.

17. **A is correct.** $^{14}/_{21} = {}^1/_3$; $^2/_6$, $^3/_9$, and $^9/_{27}$ all also equal $^1/_3$.

18. **B is correct.** There were $x$ people, divided evenly among 6 buses. So the number of people in each bus was $x/6$.

19. **C is correct.** 1 liter = 1,000 milliliters. The two pots together hold 8 liters. 8 liters = 8,000 milliliters.

20. **D is correct.** 23.62 miles − 19.8 miles = 3.82 miles.

21. **C is correct.** The length of time from 4:00 A.M. to 11:00 A.M. is 7 hours. $7 \times 3 = 21$, so during that time the temperature rose by 21 °F. The starting point was −11 °F, so −11 + 21 = 10 °F.

22. **A is correct.** $9^3/_5 + 2^1/_4 = 9^{12}/_{20} + 2^5/_{20} = 11^{17}/_{20}$.

23. **D is correct.** $12 \div 3^1/_4 = {}^{12}/_1 \div {}^{13}/_4$
    $= {}^{12}/_1 \times {}^4/_{13} = {}^{48}/_{13} = 3^9/_{13}$.

24. **B is correct.** $8y + 5 = 41$, so $8y = 41 - 5 = 36$.
    $y = {}^{36}/_8 = 4^4/_8 = 4^1/_2 = 4.5$

25. **A is correct.** Follow the order of operations:
    $(8 + 2)^2 - 2^3 \times (5 - 3) = (10)^2 - 2^3 \times (2)$
    $= 100 - 8 \times 2$
    $= 100 - 16 = 84$

26. **D is correct.** If $a = 26.3$, then $85.1 - a = 85.1 - 26.3$
    $= 58.8$.

27. **B is correct.** −218 °C + 35 °C = −183 °C.

28. **C is correct.** Any number with 0 as an exponent equals 1.

29. **D is correct.** Hat + scarf = $63.94; hat = scarf + 5.96
    $x + (x + 5.96) = 63.94$
    $2x = 57.98$
    $x = 28.99$
    hat = 28.99 + 5.95 = $34.95

30. **B is correct.** $-1\frac{2}{5}, -1\frac{3}{5}, -1\frac{1}{3} = -1\frac{12}{30}, -1\frac{15}{30}, -1\frac{10}{30}$
    Ordering from least to greatest: $-1\frac{15}{30}, -1\frac{12}{30}, -1\frac{10}{30}$
    $= -1\frac{3}{5}, -1\frac{2}{5}, -1\frac{1}{3}$.

31. **D is correct.** $\frac{1}{4} - \frac{2}{3} \times \frac{3}{4} = \frac{1}{4} - \frac{6}{12}$
    $= \frac{1}{4} - \frac{1}{2}$
    $= \frac{1}{4} - \frac{2}{4}$
    $= -\frac{1}{4}$

32. **A is correct.** 81 ÷ 1.5 = 54 mph.

33. **A is correct.** If the element has a half-life of 1 second, one-half of its mass decays each second. If you start with 32 g, after 1 second, $\frac{32}{2} = 16$ g are left. After 2 seconds, $\frac{16}{2} = 8$ g are left. After 3 seconds, $\frac{8}{2} = 4$ g are left. After 4 seconds, $\frac{4}{2} = 2$ g are left.

34. **D is correct.** $x + 2 - 11 = 3$.
    $x - 9 = 3$
    $x = 12$

35. **A is correct.** Let $x$ be the unknown number.
    $4x - 4 = 16$
    $4x = 20$
    $x = 5$

36. **C is correct.** 1 mile = 1,760 yards; 3 miles = 1,760 × 3 = 5,280 yd;
    5,280 ÷ 440 = 12.

37. **B is correct.** The playground measures 200 yd × 120 yd. A fence around the perimeter would measure 200 + 120 + 200 + 120 = 640 yd.

38. **C is correct.** $\frac{x}{4} = \frac{45}{36}$.
    $x = 4(45/36)$
    $x = 1(45/9)$
    $x = 5$

39. **D is correct.** Jorge hiked 45 miles in 3 days. $\frac{45}{3} = 15$ mi per day. 2 weeks = 14 days. 14 × 15 = 210 mi.

40. **A is correct.** $\frac{3}{8} = 0.375 = 37.5\%$.

41. **D is correct.** $\frac{x}{100} \times 144 = 108$.
    $\frac{144x}{100} = 108$
    $1.44x = 108$
    $x = \frac{108}{1.44}$
    $= 75\%$

42. **B is correct.** On a $450 television set, the 8.5% sales tax = $450 × 0.085
    = $38.25; $450 + $38.25 = $488.25.

43. **C is correct.**
    $2.31 \times 100000$
    $2.31 \times 10^5$

44. **B is correct**. The median is 28 and is represented by the line within the box.

45. **D is correct.** Each term is determined by multiplying the previous term by 4.
    $64 \times 4 = 256$

46. **C is correct.** Cross multiply and simplify.
    If $\frac{x}{8} = \frac{20}{1}$, then $x = 160$ and $\frac{x}{2} = \frac{160}{2} = 80$.

47. **C is correct.** $5 + 6 + 7 = 18$, so 7 is the greatest integer.

# ISEE Practice Test III

**(Upper Level: For Candidates for Grades 9–12)**

The following practice test is designed to be just like the real ISEE that you will take if you are applying for admission to grades 9 through 12. It matches the actual test in content coverage and level of difficulty. The test is in five sections: Verbal Reasoning, Quantitative Reasoning, Reading Comprehension, Mathematics Achievement, and the Essay.

This practice test will be an accurate reflection of how you'll do on test day if you treat it as the real examination. Here are some hints on how to take the test under conditions similar to those of the actual exam:

- Find a quiet place to work and set aside a period of approximately 3 hours when you will not be disturbed.
- Work on only one section at a time, and use your watch or a timer to keep track of the time limits for each test part.
- Tear out your answer sheet and mark your answers by filling in the ovals for each question.
- Write your essay on the pages provided.
- Become familiar with the directions for each part of the test. You'll save time on the actual test day by already being familiar with this information.

At the end of the test you'll find answer keys for each section and explanations for every question. Check your answers against the keys to find out how you did on each section of the test and what test topics you might need to study more. Then review the explanations, paying particular attention to the ones for the questions that you answered incorrectly.

You will receive four scaled scores, one for each of these four categories: Verbal Reasoning, Quantitative Reasoning, Reading Comprehension, and Mathematics Achievement. Each section has a low scaled score of 760 and the high scaled score of 940.

The ISEE also provides a percentile score that compares your performance with that of other U.S. and Canadian students who took in the past three years. Your reported percentile test scores are compared to this "norm group" for each section of the test. In addition, the ISEE provides a stanine score which is an abbreviated version of your percentile scores based on 9 groupings rather than 99.

The writing sample is not scored, but it is included with the score reports that you send to schools. The following table shows the various sections, numbers of questions, and time allotments.

## ISEE: Structure and Time Allotments

| Section | Number of Questions | Time Allowed |
|---|---|---|
| Verbal Reasoning | 40 | 20 minutes |
| Quantitative Reasoning | 37 | 35 minutes |
| Break | | 5 minutes |
| Reading Comprehension | 36 | 35 minutes |
| Mathematics Achievement | 47 | 40 minutes |
| Break | | 5 minutes |
| Writing Sample | 1 (unscored) | 30 minutes |
| Totals | 161 | 2 hours, 50 minutes |

# ISEE Practice Test III

ANSWER SHEET

**Note:** If there are more answer lines than there are questions in a section, leave the extra answer lines blank.

## Section 1: Verbal Reasoning

| | | | |
|---|---|---|---|
| 1. Ⓐ Ⓑ Ⓒ Ⓓ | 17. Ⓐ Ⓑ Ⓒ Ⓓ | 33. Ⓐ Ⓑ Ⓒ Ⓓ | |
| 2. Ⓐ Ⓑ Ⓒ Ⓓ | 18. Ⓐ Ⓑ Ⓒ Ⓓ | 34. Ⓐ Ⓑ Ⓒ Ⓓ | |
| 3. Ⓐ Ⓑ Ⓒ Ⓓ | 19. Ⓐ Ⓑ Ⓒ Ⓓ | 35. Ⓐ Ⓑ Ⓒ Ⓓ | |
| 4. Ⓐ Ⓑ Ⓒ Ⓓ | 20. Ⓐ Ⓑ Ⓒ Ⓓ | 36. Ⓐ Ⓑ Ⓒ Ⓓ | |
| 5. Ⓐ Ⓑ Ⓒ Ⓓ | 21. Ⓐ Ⓑ Ⓒ Ⓓ | 37. Ⓐ Ⓑ Ⓒ Ⓓ | |
| 6. Ⓐ Ⓑ Ⓒ Ⓓ | 22. Ⓐ Ⓑ Ⓒ Ⓓ | 38. Ⓐ Ⓑ Ⓒ Ⓓ | |
| 7. Ⓐ Ⓑ Ⓒ Ⓓ | 23. Ⓐ Ⓑ Ⓒ Ⓓ | 39. Ⓐ Ⓑ Ⓒ Ⓓ | |
| 8. Ⓐ Ⓑ Ⓒ Ⓓ | 24. Ⓐ Ⓑ Ⓒ Ⓓ | 40. Ⓐ Ⓑ Ⓒ Ⓓ | |
| 9. Ⓐ Ⓑ Ⓒ Ⓓ | 25. Ⓐ Ⓑ Ⓒ Ⓓ | | |
| 10. Ⓐ Ⓑ Ⓒ Ⓓ | 26. Ⓐ Ⓑ Ⓒ Ⓓ | | |
| 11. Ⓐ Ⓑ Ⓒ Ⓓ | 27. Ⓐ Ⓑ Ⓒ Ⓓ | | |
| 12. Ⓐ Ⓑ Ⓒ Ⓓ | 28. Ⓐ Ⓑ Ⓒ Ⓓ | | |
| 13. Ⓐ Ⓑ Ⓒ Ⓓ | 29. Ⓐ Ⓑ Ⓒ Ⓓ | | |
| 14. Ⓐ Ⓑ Ⓒ Ⓓ | 30. Ⓐ Ⓑ Ⓒ Ⓓ | | |
| 15. Ⓐ Ⓑ Ⓒ Ⓓ | 31. Ⓐ Ⓑ Ⓒ Ⓓ | | |
| 16. Ⓐ Ⓑ Ⓒ Ⓓ | 32. Ⓐ Ⓑ Ⓒ Ⓓ | | |

## Section 2: Quantitative Reasoning

| | | |
|---|---|---|
| 1. Ⓐ Ⓑ Ⓒ Ⓓ | 14. Ⓐ Ⓑ Ⓒ Ⓓ | 27. Ⓐ Ⓑ Ⓒ Ⓓ |
| 2. Ⓐ Ⓑ Ⓒ Ⓓ | 15. Ⓐ Ⓑ Ⓒ Ⓓ | 28. Ⓐ Ⓑ Ⓒ Ⓓ |
| 3. Ⓐ Ⓑ Ⓒ Ⓓ | 16. Ⓐ Ⓑ Ⓒ Ⓓ | 29. Ⓐ Ⓑ Ⓒ Ⓓ |
| 4. Ⓐ Ⓑ Ⓒ Ⓓ | 17. Ⓐ Ⓑ Ⓒ Ⓓ | 30. Ⓐ Ⓑ Ⓒ Ⓓ |
| 5. Ⓐ Ⓑ Ⓒ Ⓓ | 18. Ⓐ Ⓑ Ⓒ Ⓓ | 31. Ⓐ Ⓑ Ⓒ Ⓓ |
| 6. Ⓐ Ⓑ Ⓒ Ⓓ | 19. Ⓐ Ⓑ Ⓒ Ⓓ | 32. Ⓐ Ⓑ Ⓒ Ⓓ |
| 7. Ⓐ Ⓑ Ⓒ Ⓓ | 20. Ⓐ Ⓑ Ⓒ Ⓓ | 33. Ⓐ Ⓑ Ⓒ Ⓓ |
| 8. Ⓐ Ⓑ Ⓒ Ⓓ | 21. Ⓐ Ⓑ Ⓒ Ⓓ | 34. Ⓐ Ⓑ Ⓒ Ⓓ |
| 9. Ⓐ Ⓑ Ⓒ Ⓓ | 22. Ⓐ Ⓑ Ⓒ Ⓓ | 35. Ⓐ Ⓑ Ⓒ Ⓓ |
| 10. Ⓐ Ⓑ Ⓒ Ⓓ | 23. Ⓐ Ⓑ Ⓒ Ⓓ | 36. Ⓐ Ⓑ Ⓒ Ⓓ |
| 11. Ⓐ Ⓑ Ⓒ Ⓓ | 24. Ⓐ Ⓑ Ⓒ Ⓓ | 37. Ⓐ Ⓑ Ⓒ Ⓓ |
| 12. Ⓐ Ⓑ Ⓒ Ⓓ | 25. Ⓐ Ⓑ Ⓒ Ⓓ | |
| 13. Ⓐ Ⓑ Ⓒ Ⓓ | 26. Ⓐ Ⓑ Ⓒ Ⓓ | |

## Section 3: Reading Comprehension

| | A B C D | | A B C D | | A B C D |
|---|---|---|---|---|---|
| 1. | Ⓐ Ⓑ Ⓒ Ⓓ | 13. | Ⓐ Ⓑ Ⓒ Ⓓ | 25. | Ⓐ Ⓑ Ⓒ Ⓓ |
| 2. | Ⓐ Ⓑ Ⓒ Ⓓ | 14. | Ⓐ Ⓑ Ⓒ Ⓓ | 26. | Ⓐ Ⓑ Ⓒ Ⓓ |
| 3. | Ⓐ Ⓑ Ⓒ Ⓓ | 15. | Ⓐ Ⓑ Ⓒ Ⓓ | 27. | Ⓐ Ⓑ Ⓒ Ⓓ |
| 4. | Ⓐ Ⓑ Ⓒ Ⓓ | 16. | Ⓐ Ⓑ Ⓒ Ⓓ | 28. | Ⓐ Ⓑ Ⓒ Ⓓ |
| 5. | Ⓐ Ⓑ Ⓒ Ⓓ | 17. | Ⓐ Ⓑ Ⓒ Ⓓ | 29. | Ⓐ Ⓑ Ⓒ Ⓓ |
| 6. | Ⓐ Ⓑ Ⓒ Ⓓ | 18. | Ⓐ Ⓑ Ⓒ Ⓓ | 30. | Ⓐ Ⓑ Ⓒ Ⓓ |
| 7. | Ⓐ Ⓑ Ⓒ Ⓓ | 19. | Ⓐ Ⓑ Ⓒ Ⓓ | 31. | Ⓐ Ⓑ Ⓒ Ⓓ |
| 8. | Ⓐ Ⓑ Ⓒ Ⓓ | 20. | Ⓐ Ⓑ Ⓒ Ⓓ | 32. | Ⓐ Ⓑ Ⓒ Ⓓ |
| 9. | Ⓐ Ⓑ Ⓒ Ⓓ | 21. | Ⓐ Ⓑ Ⓒ Ⓓ | 33. | Ⓐ Ⓑ Ⓒ Ⓓ |
| 10. | Ⓐ Ⓑ Ⓒ Ⓓ | 22. | Ⓐ Ⓑ Ⓒ Ⓓ | 34. | Ⓐ Ⓑ Ⓒ Ⓓ |
| 11. | Ⓐ Ⓑ Ⓒ Ⓓ | 23. | Ⓐ Ⓑ Ⓒ Ⓓ | 35. | Ⓐ Ⓑ Ⓒ Ⓓ |
| 12. | Ⓐ Ⓑ Ⓒ Ⓓ | 24. | Ⓐ Ⓑ Ⓒ Ⓓ | 36. | Ⓐ Ⓑ Ⓒ Ⓓ |

## Section 4: Mathematics Achievement

| | A B C D | | A B C D | | A B C D |
|---|---|---|---|---|---|
| 1. | Ⓐ Ⓑ Ⓒ Ⓓ | 17. | Ⓐ Ⓑ Ⓒ Ⓓ | 33. | Ⓐ Ⓑ Ⓒ Ⓓ |
| 2. | Ⓐ Ⓑ Ⓒ Ⓓ | 18. | Ⓐ Ⓑ Ⓒ Ⓓ | 34. | Ⓐ Ⓑ Ⓒ Ⓓ |
| 3. | Ⓐ Ⓑ Ⓒ Ⓓ | 19. | Ⓐ Ⓑ Ⓒ Ⓓ | 35. | Ⓐ Ⓑ Ⓒ Ⓓ |
| 4. | Ⓐ Ⓑ Ⓒ Ⓓ | 20. | Ⓐ Ⓑ Ⓒ Ⓓ | 36. | Ⓐ Ⓑ Ⓒ Ⓓ |
| 5. | Ⓐ Ⓑ Ⓒ Ⓓ | 21. | Ⓐ Ⓑ Ⓒ Ⓓ | 37. | Ⓐ Ⓑ Ⓒ Ⓓ |
| 6. | Ⓐ Ⓑ Ⓒ Ⓓ | 22. | Ⓐ Ⓑ Ⓒ Ⓓ | 38. | Ⓐ Ⓑ Ⓒ Ⓓ |
| 7. | Ⓐ Ⓑ Ⓒ Ⓓ | 23. | Ⓐ Ⓑ Ⓒ Ⓓ | 39. | Ⓐ Ⓑ Ⓒ Ⓓ |
| 8. | Ⓐ Ⓑ Ⓒ Ⓓ | 24. | Ⓐ Ⓑ Ⓒ Ⓓ | 40. | Ⓐ Ⓑ Ⓒ Ⓓ |
| 9. | Ⓐ Ⓑ Ⓒ Ⓓ | 25. | Ⓐ Ⓑ Ⓒ Ⓓ | 41. | Ⓐ Ⓑ Ⓒ Ⓓ |
| 10. | Ⓐ Ⓑ Ⓒ Ⓓ | 26. | Ⓐ Ⓑ Ⓒ Ⓓ | 42. | Ⓐ Ⓑ Ⓒ Ⓓ |
| 11. | Ⓐ Ⓑ Ⓒ Ⓓ | 27. | Ⓐ Ⓑ Ⓒ Ⓓ | 43. | Ⓐ Ⓑ Ⓒ Ⓓ |
| 12. | Ⓐ Ⓑ Ⓒ Ⓓ | 28. | Ⓐ Ⓑ Ⓒ Ⓓ | 44. | Ⓐ Ⓑ Ⓒ Ⓓ |
| 13. | Ⓐ Ⓑ Ⓒ Ⓓ | 29. | Ⓐ Ⓑ Ⓒ Ⓓ | 45. | Ⓐ Ⓑ Ⓒ Ⓓ |
| 14. | Ⓐ Ⓑ Ⓒ Ⓓ | 30. | Ⓐ Ⓑ Ⓒ Ⓓ | 46. | Ⓐ Ⓑ Ⓒ Ⓓ |
| 15. | Ⓐ Ⓑ Ⓒ Ⓓ | 31. | Ⓐ Ⓑ Ⓒ Ⓓ | 47. | Ⓐ Ⓑ Ⓒ Ⓓ |
| 16. | Ⓐ Ⓑ Ⓒ Ⓓ | 32. | Ⓐ Ⓑ Ⓒ Ⓓ | | |

This section includes two different types of questions: synonyms and sentence completions. There are directions and a sample question for each question type.

**Part One**

**Directions:** Each of the following questions consists of a word in capital letters followed by four words or phrases labeled (A), (B), (C), and (D). Select the one word or phrase that means most nearly the same as the word in capital letters.

**Sample Question:**

> ESSENTIAL
> (A) dire
> (B) confusing
> (C) vital
> (D) expert
>
> Correct Answer: C

1. BIAS:
   (A) preference
   (B) conversion
   (C) resolution
   (D) conclusion

2. INHABIT:
   (A) confine
   (B) surround
   (C) dwell
   (D) exhibit

3. GENEROUS:
   (A) radiant
   (B) precocious
   (C) sociable
   (D) benevolent

4. AGGREGATE:
   (A) median
   (B) organization
   (C) total
   (D) equipment

5. IMPLEMENT:
   (A) idea
   (B) detail
   (C) instrument
   (D) component

6. GRACIOUSLY:
   (A) gratefully
   (B) kindly
   (C) easily
   (D) comfortably

7. MEANDER:
   (A) manage
   (B) exercise
   (C) review
   (D) wander

8. CONCUR:
   (A) alleviate
   (B) agree
   (C) conspire
   (D) contribute

9. AGILE:
   (A) able
   (B) listless
   (C) willful
   (D) nimble

10. ADDITION:
    (A) inclusion
    (B) origin
    (C) antecedent
    (D) inception

11. PERSISTENT:
    (A) perceptible
    (B) considerable
    (C) pretentious
    (D) determined

12. ENCOURAGE:
    (A) foster
    (B) conduct
    (C) develop
    (D) cope

**GO ON TO THE NEXT PAGE.**

13. SCOLD:
    (A) scream
    (B) incense
    (C) berate
    (D) infuriate

14. COMMENCEMENT:
    (A) justification
    (B) beginning
    (C) announcement
    (D) conclusion

15. CRITICIZE:
    (A) abuse
    (B) disparage
    (C) avenge
    (D) hinder

16. OBVIOUSLY:
    (A) substantially
    (B) momentously
    (C) allegedly
    (D) apparently

17. INCESSANT:
    (A) annoyed
    (B) disturbed
    (C) constant
    (D) irrevocable

18. ACQUIRE:
    (A) abstain
    (B) prefer
    (C) produce
    (D) procure

19. VENERABLE:
    (A) respected
    (B) bright
    (C) varied
    (D) measured

20. PROCLIVITY:
    (A) inclination
    (B) finesse
    (C) resurgence
    (D) weakness

**GO ON TO THE NEXT PAGE.**

**Part Two**

**Directions:** Each sentence below has one or two blanks. Each blank indicates that a word or phrase is missing. Following each sentence are four words or phrases labeled (A), (B), (C), and (D). You are to select the word or phrase that, when inserted in the sentence, best fits the meaning of the sentence as a whole.

**Sample Question:**

Due to the fact that the stray kitten was so _____, Ethan's mother allowed him to keep it.
(A)  tardy
(B)  humid
(C)  disobedient
(D)  adorable

Correct Answer: D

21.  Wary of defeat, the rebel factions _____ into a single army to fight the approaching invaders.
(A)  consolidated
(B)  diffused
(C)  fragmented
(D)  appealed

22.  According to the editorial, the most _____ error the governor made was _____ the public's trust in him by trying to cover up the scandal.
(A)  grievous . . . appeasing
(B)  defenseless . . . gleaning
(C)  abhorrent . . . placating
(D)  egregious . . . breaching

23.  Lacking any interesting qualities, the _____ movie featured cheap special effects, an unlikely plot, and ridiculously bad acting.
(A)  insipid
(B)  hilarious
(C)  optimistic
(D)  uproarious

24.  Despite the player's occasionally _____ play, he recently signed a _____ contract.
(A)  stellar . . . covert
(B)  negligent . . . reticent
(C)  sloppy . . . nebulous
(D)  shaky . . . lucrative

25.  The company's hope was to _____ short-term sales expectations in order to reward investors and properly _____ the staff.
(A)  suspend . . . compensate
(B)  exceed . . . remunerate
(C)  surpass . . . determine
(D)  attest . . . compromise

26.  On the last weekend of summer break at the seashore, the roads were jammed with traffic as the beach _____ with vacationers.
(A)  dispersed
(B)  maintained
(C)  deprecated
(D)  teemed

27.  Reports of the senator's _____ displays of wealth have done little to _____ her standing among working-class families or help her bid for reelection.
(A)  flagrant . . . undermine
(B)  reserved . . . solidify
(C)  grandiose . . . curtail
(D)  flamboyant . . . propel

28.  Although the tone of the play was _____, the subject matter was rather _____.
(A)  farcical . . . sobering
(B)  ominous . . . morbid
(C)  grave . . . pensive
(D)  solemn . . . bleak

29.  Because she had recorded the fastest official time, Cheryl was given _____ from the qualifying races and automatically entered in the state finals.
(A)  an occurrence
(B)  an emulsion
(C)  a quandary
(D)  an exemption

30.  Faced with the _____ of babysitting Friday night or going to the movies, Angela _____ she would rather earn money than spend money.
(A)  endeavor . . . promised
(B)  predicament . . . decided
(C)  dismay . . . relented
(D)  principle . . . suspected

31.  After the band failed to _____ the audience or sell many tickets, the offer for an extended engagement was _____.
(A)  overcome . . . negated
(B)  impress . . . revoked
(C)  accept . . . approved
(D)  inspire . . . established

**GO ON TO THE NEXT PAGE.**

32. After a series of argumentative negotiations, both sides seemed ready for _____ so they could get back to the task at hand.
    (A) an admonition
    (B) an abatement
    (C) a reconciliation
    (D) a validation

33. _____ even from a distance, Mount Everest is the highest mountain in the world, and certainly one of nature's wonders.
    (A) Monumental
    (B) Glacial
    (C) Gilded
    (D) Speculative

34. The fact that the developer's plans for the land no longer included space for a public park was a _____ of his earlier proposal.
    (A) presumption
    (B) progression
    (C) detriment
    (D) contradiction

35. Despite being mistakenly _____ for leaving the gate open, Derrick was _____ once the puppy crawled out from underneath the couch.
    (A) lectured . . . responsible
    (B) punished . . . amended
    (C) chastised . . . exonerated
    (D) criticized . . . atoned

36. The benching of the star midfielder was largely seen as an act of _____ after she skipped the team meeting.
    (A) probation
    (B) annihilation
    (C) peculiarity
    (D) retribution

37. When the owner provided a _____ certificate of authenticity, the art historian declared the painting a forgery.
    (A) legitimate
    (B) spurious
    (C) turgid
    (D) precocious

38. _____ by his _____ lifestyle, King Henry I habitually indulged his every whim until he died of food poisoning in 1135.
    (A) Strengthened . . . gratuitous
    (B) Undeterred . . . gluttonous
    (C) Fortified . . . permissive
    (D) Befallen . . . durable

39. After losing for the sixth time in a row, the basketball team hoped they had reached the _____ of their season.
    (A) nadir
    (B) malady
    (C) pinnacle
    (D) conclusion

40. Largely due to the _____ drought, there has been a _____ of fresh produce available at the farmer's market this summer.
    (A) unforeseen . . . beacon
    (B) rapid . . . sustenance
    (C) prolonged . . . dearth
    (D) shortened . . . confluence

**STOP!**
If you finish before time is up, check your work on this section only.

## SECTION 2
Time: 35 Minutes
37 Questions

This section includes two different types of questions: multiple-choice math questions and quantitative comparisons. There are directions for each question type.

**Part One**

**Directions:** For each of the following questions, mark the letter of your choice on the answer sheet.

---

1. What is the next number in the sequence 5, 8, 11, 14, 17, . . .
   - (A)  18
   - (B)  20
   - (C)  21
   - (D)  23

2. On a hike, Kurt saw 3 times as many sparrows as finches. He saw 12 birds of these two species in all. If $s$ is the number of sparrows Kurt saw, which number sentence can be used to find out how many birds of each species he saw?
   - (A)  $s + \dfrac{s}{3} = 12$
   - (B)  $s - 3s = 12$
   - (C)  $\dfrac{3s}{12} = s$
   - (D)  $s + 3s = 12$

3. Gary scored a total of 27 points in two games. He scored twice as many points in the second game as in the first. What were his scores in each game?
   - (A)  game 1: 5; game 2: 22
   - (B)  game 1: 6; game 2: 21
   - (C)  game 1: 7; game 2: 20
   - (D)  game 1: 9; game 2: 18

4. Jen bought 10 apples at $1.20 per pound. The apples weighed a total of 5.75 lb. What did she pay for all 10 apples?
   - (A)  $6.90
   - (B)  $7.20
   - (C)  $8.14
   - (D)  $9.55

5. Maria earns $9 per hour on weekdays and $12 per hour on weekends. This week she worked 8 hours on Tuesday, 6 hours on Thursday, 7 hours on Friday, and 9 hours on Saturday. How much did she earn?
   - (A)  $214
   - (B)  $279
   - (C)  $297
   - (D)  $312

6. Which of the following is greater than 1.2 but less than 1.3?
   - (A)  1.196
   - (B)  1.268
   - (C)  1.302
   - (D)  1.375

7. Smoke alarms in a house require 27 batteries. Batteries come in packs of 4. How many packs should you buy if you want 2 complete packs left over?
   - (A)  6
   - (B)  7
   - (C)  8
   - (D)  9

8. Jamal has $1.85 in quarters and dimes only. He has a total of 11 coins. How many of each coin does he have?
   - (A)  5 quarters, 6 dimes
   - (B)  4 quarters, 7 dimes
   - (C)  3 quarters, 8 dimes
   - (D)  2 quarters, 9 dimes

9. The mean of Mark's, Linda's, and Karen's ages is 18. Mark is 20 years old. Linda is 18 years old. How old is Karen?
   - (A)  16
   - (B)  17
   - (C)  18
   - (D)  19

**GO ON TO THE NEXT PAGE.**

10. A prescribed diet makes a dog lose 0.33 lb each month. After 4 months, the dog weighs 37.18 lb. What was its original weight?
    (A)   38.5 lb
    (B)   38.33 lb
    (C)   38.12 lb
    (D)   37.67 lb

11. In a survey of 950 people, 46% of them said they listened to jazz. How many people in the group did not say they listened to jazz?
    (A)   437
    (B)   478
    (C)   502
    (D)   513

12. A television set is on sale at a 25% discount. Its original price was $650. The sales tax is 12%. What will Beth pay, including tax, for the television set?
    (A)   $524
    (B)   $546
    (C)   $589
    (D)   $610

13. In a group of friends, 17 people are on the chess team, 13 people are in the band, and 8 people are both in the band and on the chess team. How many people are in the group of friends?
    (A)   18
    (B)   19
    (C)   22
    (D)   24

14. A clock is showing 6:00. What is the measure of the angle formed by the hour and minute hands?
    (A)   180°
    (B)   120°
    (C)   100°
    (D)   90°

15. A rectangular play area measures 20 yards by 15 yards. What would be the perimeter if the length and width were doubled?
    (A)   70 yd
    (B)   140 yd
    (C)   300 yd
    (D)   1,200 yd

16. A poster measures 2 feet 4 inches by 3 feet 8 inches. What length of framing is needed to frame it?
    (A)   10 ft
    (B)   10 ft 8 in
    (C)   11 ft 6 in
    (D)   12 ft

17. How many 4-in² squares fit inside a rectangle that measures 4 by 6 inches?
    (A)   4
    (B)   6
    (C)   8
    (D)   10

18. In 28 mi² there are 560 houses. What is the average number of houses per square mile?
    (A)   20
    (B)   24
    (C)   28
    (D)   32

19. What is the length of line segment AC in triangle ABC?

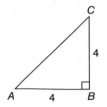

    (A)   4
    (B)   $4\sqrt{2}$
    (C)   $4\sqrt{3}$
    (D)   8

20. What is the next term in this sequence?

    2, 3, 5, 9, . . .

    (A)   11
    (B)   13
    (C)   15
    (D)   17

GO ON TO THE NEXT PAGE.

## Part Two

**Directions:** For each of the following quantities, two quantities are given—one in column A, the other in column B. Compare the two quantities and mark your answer sheet as follows:

(A)  if the quantity in column A is greater
(B)  if the quantity in column B is greater
(C)  if the quantities are equal
(D)  if the relationship cannot be determined from the information given

### Notes

- Information concerning one or both of the compared quantities will be centered above the two columns for some items.
- Symbols that appear in both columns represent the same thing in column A as in column B.
- Letters such as *x*, *n*, and *k* are symbols for real numbers.
- Figures are drawn to scale unless otherwise noted.

| Column A | Column B |
|---|---|

**21.**

The original price of a shirt was $40. During a sale, the price was reduced by 25% and then the reduced price was reduced by another 20%.

| Column A | Column B |
|---|---|
| The price of the shirt after the two reductions. | $23 |

**22.** $(4 \times 10^3) + (6 \times 10^2) + (2 \times 10^0)$        4,620

**23.**

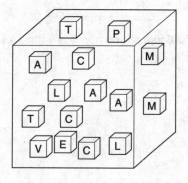

| The probability of picking a vowel. | The probability of picking a C or a T. |
|---|---|

**24.**    The radius of a circle.                  A chord in the same circle.

**25.**    The median of 40, 50, 60, 70.       The mean of 40, 50, 60, 70.

**26.**    $\sqrt{64} + \sqrt{36}$                       $\sqrt{100}$

**GO ON TO THE NEXT PAGE.**

27.

Number of vertices + 2. | Number of edges – 2.

28.             City A is 30 miles due east of City B, and City C is 40 miles due south of City B.

The shortest distance between City A and City C. | 45 miles

29.                                    *g* is an integer

*g* | –*g*

30.             Frank's weight is $1\frac{1}{4}$ of Bill's weight.

Jason's weight is $\frac{4}{5}$ of Frank's weight.

Jason's weight | Bill's weight

31.

The figure shown above is a trapezoid.

*m∠x* | *m∠y*

32.    0.02 | $1\frac{3}{4}\%$

33.                                $3 < x < 9$
                                $2 \le y \le 8$

*x* | *y*

**GO ON TO THE NEXT PAGE.**

34.

The navigator of a submarine kept track of the submarine's depth during a dive. The graph below tracks the depth over time during the entire dive.

Submarine dive

| Depth change from 10 P.M. to 12 A.M. | Depth change from 1 A.M. to 2:30 A.M. |

35.

$$\frac{m}{6} = \frac{32}{48}$$

$$\frac{100}{50} = \frac{70}{n}$$

8*m*

*n* − 1

36. $\dfrac{1}{3} + \dfrac{5}{6} + \dfrac{7}{12}$          $\dfrac{3}{4} + \dfrac{5}{8} + \dfrac{13}{16}$

37. Set A = {3, 9, 12, 19, 5, 1, 13, 9}
The mode of the set.          The median of the set.

**STOP!**
If you finish before time is up, check your work on this section only.

**Directions:** Each reading passage is followed by questions about it. Answer the questions that follow a passage on the basis of what is stated or implied in that passage. For each question, select the answer you think is best and record your choice by filling in the corresponding oval on the answer sheet.

---

Questions 1–6

*"The President shall from time to time give to Congress information of the State of the Union and recommend to their Consideration such*
5 *measures as he shall judge necessary and expedient."* Article II, Sec. 3, U.S. Constitution

On a cold January morning in 1790, George Washington person-
10 ally delivered the first State of the Union address to a joint meeting of the two bodies of Congress at Federal Hall in New York City, which was then the provisional capital of
15 the United States. Since Washington's first speech to Congress, U.S. Presidents have "from time to time" given Congress an assessment of the condition of the union. Presidents
20 have used the opportunity to present their goals and agenda through broad ideas or specific details. The annual message or "State of the Union" message's length, frequency,
25 and method of delivery have varied from President to President and era to era.

In 1801, Thomas Jefferson discontinued the practice of delivering
30 the address in person, regarding it as too monarchial for the new republic. Instead, Jefferson wrote out his address and sent it to Congress to be read by a clerk. This practice
35 continued for the next 112 years. The first president to revive Washington's spoken precedent was Woodrow Wilson in 1913.

For many years, the speech was
40 referred to as "the President's Annual Message to Congress." The term "State of the Union" did not become widely used until after 1935 when Franklin Delano Roosevelt began
45 using the phrase.

With the advent of radio and television, the President's annual message has become not only a conversation between the President
50 and Congress but also an opportunity for the President to communicate with the American people at the same time. Calvin Coolidge's 1923 speech was the first to be broadcast on radio.
55 Harry S. Truman's 1947 address was the first to be broadcast on television. Lyndon Johnson's address in 1965 was the first delivered in the evening, and George W. Bush's 2002 address
60 was the first to be broadcast live on the World Wide Web.

1. The author most likely included the quotation from the U.S. Constitution in lines 1–6 in order to
   (A) illustrate the wording used in the Constitution
   (B) explain the reason for the State of the Union address
   (C) demonstrate how different Presidents have interpreted the same provision
   (D) point out the difference between a constitutional duty and a custom

2. The phrase "from time to time" in lines 1–2 has been interpreted to mean
   (A) once in a while
   (B) in a timely manner
   (C) annually
   (D) when time allows

3. U.S. Presidents deliver State of the Union messages primarily because they
   (A) are following a tradition started by George Washington
   (B) are required to do so by the U.S. Constitution
   (C) need to fulfill campaign promises
   (D) are trying to unify opposing factions

4. Thomas Jefferson's State of the Union address differed from Washington's address in that Jefferson
   (A) spoke first to the Senate and then to the House of Representatives
   (B) broadcast his message on radio
   (C) did not deliver his address in person
   (D) had his speech printed in the newspaper

**GO ON TO THE NEXT PAGE.**

5. In the first half of the twentieth century, the State of the Union address was forever changed by
   (A) the advent of radio and television
   (B) Thomas Jefferson
   (C) Lyndon Johnson
   (D) newspaper coverage of the speech

6. Which of the following questions is answered by the information in the passage?
   (A) How many presidents have delivered spoken State of the Union messages?
   (B) When is the State of the Union message delivered?
   (C) Why did Woodrow Wilson revive the spoken State of the Union message?
   (D) Which president delivered the first televised State of the Union message?

Questions 7–12

While they cannot be seen from the air, or felt aboard an ocean-going ship, tsunamis can cause as great a loss of life and property as their other
5 natural disaster cousins—tornadoes and hurricanes. The tsunami that occurred on December 26, 2004, was the worst tsunami ever recorded in terms of lives lost. Triggered by a
10 powerful earthquake in the Indian Ocean, it ravaged the shores of Indonesia, Sri Lanka, India, and Thailand, and even hit the east coast of Africa more than 2,300 miles away.
15 A tsunami is a series of ocean waves generated by any rapid large-scale disturbance of the sea water. Most tsunamis are generated by earthquakes, but they may
20 also be caused by volcanic eruptions, landslides, undersea slumps or meteor impacts. In 1963 the term "tsunami" was adopted internationally to describe this natural phenom-
25 enon. A Japanese word, it is the combination of the characters *tsu* (harbor) and *nami* (wave). Tsunamis

are often mistakenly called "tidal waves." However, the tides have
30 nothing to do with the formation of tsunamis.

The waves radiate outward in all directions from the disturbance and can propagate across entire ocean
35 basins. For example, in 1960, an earthquake in Chile caused a tsunami that swept across the Pacific to Japan. Tsunami waves are distinguished from ordinary ocean waves
40 by their great length between peaks, often exceeding 100 miles in the deep ocean, and by the long amount of time between these peaks, ranging from five minutes to an hour.
45 In the deep ocean, a tsunami is barely noticeable, causing only a small rising and falling of the sea surface as it passes. Only as it approaches land does a tsunami
50 become a hazard. As the tsunami approaches land and shallow water, the waves slow down and become compressed, causing them to grow in height. In the best of cases, the
55 tsunami comes onshore like a quickly rising tide and causes a gentle flooding of low-lying coastal areas.

In the worst of cases, a bore will
60 form. A bore is a wall of turbulent water that can be several meters high and can rush onshore with great destructive power. Behind the bore is a deep and fast-moving flood
65 that can pick up and sweep away almost anything in its path. Minutes later, the water will drain away as the trough of the tsunami wave arrives, sometimes exposing great patches
70 of the sea floor. But then the water will rush in again as before, causing additional damage.

This destructive cycle may repeat many times before the hazard finally
75 passes. Persons caught in the path of a tsunami have little chance to survive. They can be easily crushed by debris or they may simply drown. Children and the elderly are par-
80 ticularly at risk, as they have less mobility, strength and endurance.

7. The main purpose of this passage is to
   (A) describe the tsunami of 2004
   (B) point out the differences between tsunamis and tidal waves
   (C) explain the origin of the term "tsunami"
   (D) provide general information about tsunamis

8. The author cites the 1960 tsunami in Japan to show
   (A) how devastating a tsunami can be
   (B) how far a tsunami can reach
   (C) the importance of detecting a tsunami early
   (D) how quickly a tsunami can travel

9. Which of the following best describes the difference between a tsunami wave and a regular ocean wave?
   (A) Tsunami waves are more than 100 miles apart in the deep ocean, while regular ocean waves follow closely one after the other.
   (B) The length between peaks and the amount of time between peaks is greater in tsunami waves than it is in regular ocean waves.
   (C) Regular ocean waves are more harmful to young children, while tsunami waves are more likely to endanger the elderly.
   (D) Tsunami waves are more likely to affect boats in deep water than are regular ocean waves.

10. The style of the passage is most like that found in
    (A) an adventure novel
    (B) a weather report
    (C) a science textbook
    (D) a news article

**GO ON TO THE NEXT PAGE.**

11. A tsunami becomes a hazard as it approaches land because
    (A) the waves compress and grow higher in shallow water
    (B) the waves speed up as they approach the shore
    (C) the water drains away, exposing the sea floor
    (D) people get too close to the shore

12. As used in paragraph 5, the word "bore" means
    (A) hollow, cylindrical chamber
    (B) gauge
    (C) hole made by a drill
    (D) dangerous wave

Questions 13–18

The earthquake shook down in San Francisco hundreds of thousands of dollars worth of walls and chimneys. But the conflagration that
5  followed burned up hundreds of millions of dollars' worth of property. There is no estimating within hundreds of millions the actual damage wrought. Not in history has a modern
10 imperial city been so completely destroyed. San Francisco is gone. Nothing remains of it but memories and a fringe of dwelling-houses on its outskirts. Its industrial section
15 is wiped out. Its business section is wiped out. Its social and residential section is wiped out. The factories and warehouses, the great stores and newspaper buildings, the hotels
20 and the palaces of the nabobs, are all gone. Remains only the fringe of dwelling houses on the outskirts of what was once San Francisco.
    Within an hour after the earth-
25 quake shock the smoke of San Francisco's burning was a lurid tower visible a hundred miles away. And for three days and nights this lurid tower swayed in the sky, red-
30 dening the sun, darkening the day, and filling the land with smoke.
    On Wednesday morning at a quarter past five came the earthquake. A minute later the flames

35 were leaping upward. In a dozen different quarters south of Market Street, in the working-class ghetto, and in the factories, fires started. There was no opposing the flames.
40 There was no organization, no communication. All the cunning adjustments of a twentieth century city had been smashed by the earthquake. The streets were humped into ridges
45 and depressions, and piled with the debris of fallen walls. The steel rails were twisted into perpendicular and horizontal angles. The telephone and telegraph systems were disrupted.
50 And the great water-mains had burst. All the shrewd contrivances and safeguards of man had been thrown out of gear by thirty seconds' twitching of the earth-crust.
55     By Wednesday afternoon, inside of twelve hours, half the heart of the city was gone. At that time I watched the vast conflagration from out on the bay. It was dead calm. Not a
60 flicker of wind stirred. Yet from every side wind was pouring in upon the city. East, west, north, and south, strong winds were blowing upon the doomed city. The heated air rising
65 made an enormous suck. Thus did the fire of itself build its own colossal chimney through the atmosphere. Day and night this dead calm continued, and yet, near to the flames, the
70 wind was often half a gale, so mighty was the suck.
    Wednesday night saw the destruction of the very heart of the
75 city. Dynamite was lavishly used, and many of San Francisco's proudest structures were crumbled by man himself into ruins, but there was no withstanding the onrush of the flames. Time and again successful stands
80 were made by the fire-fighters, and every time the flames flanked around on either side or came up from the rear, and turned to defeat the hard-won victory.
        —Jack London from "The Story of an Eyewitness"

13. The first paragraph of the passage establishes a mood of
    (A) awe and disbelief
    (B) desperate longing
    (C) cautious optimism
    (D) heartfelt pity

14. The author describes the effects of the earthquake by relying on
    (A) scientific knowledge
    (B) comparisons to similar events in history
    (C) vivid images appealing primarily to the sense of sight
    (D) confirmed statistical data

15. In line 20, "nabobs" most nearly means
    (A) elected officials
    (B) wealthy persons
    (C) native sons
    (D) descendants of royalty

16. The statement that "All the cunning adjustments of a twentieth century city had been smashed by the earthquake" (lines 41–43) suggests primarily that
    (A) the city had been reduced to a primitive existence
    (B) the earthquake destroyed many of the city's newest buildings
    (C) numerous irreplaceable mechanisms were lost during the earthquake
    (D) only necessities such as plumbing and electricity remained intact

17. Which best describes the overall organization of the passage?
    (A) a description of events in spatial order
    (B) a description of events in chronological order
    (C) an enumeration of facts supported by statistical data
    (D) a statement of opinion backed up by reasons

**GO ON TO THE NEXT PAGE.**

18. The primary purpose of the passage is to
   (A) present a scientific explanation of the San Francisco earthquake
   (B) convey the despair of San Francisco residents as they watched the destruction of their city
   (C) provide an eyewitness report of the San Francisco earthquake
   (D) describe the conditions that allowed the fires to spread

Questions 19–24

Over 200 years ago, English physician Edward Jenner observed that milkmaids stricken with a viral disease called cowpox were rarely
5 victims of a similar disease, smallpox. This observation led to the development of the first vaccine. In an experiment that was to prove a revelation, Jenner took a few drops
10 of fluid from a pustule of a woman who had cowpox and injected the fluid into a healthy young boy who had never had cowpox or smallpox. Six weeks later, Jenner injected the
15 boy with fluid from a smallpox pustule. Miraculously, the boy remained free of the dreaded smallpox.
   In those days, a million people died from smallpox each year in
20 Europe alone, most of them children. Those who survived were often left with grim reminders of their ordeals: blindness, deep scars, and deformities. When Jenner laid the founda-
25 tion for modern vaccines in 1796, he started on a course that would ease the suffering of people around the world for centuries to come. By the beginning of the 20th cen-
30 tury, vaccines for rabies, diphtheria, typhoid fever, and plague were in use, in addition to the vaccine for smallpox. By 1980, an updated version of Jenner's vaccine led to the
35 total eradication of smallpox.
   Since Jenner's time, vaccines have been developed against more than 20 infectious diseases such as influenza, pneumonia, whooping
40 cough, rubella, meningitis, and hepatitis B. Due to tremendous advances in molecular biology, scientists are using novel approaches to develop vaccines against deadly diseases
45 that still plague humankind.
   Scientists use vaccines to "trick" the human immune system into producing antibodies or immune cells that protect against the real dis-
50 ease-causing organism. Weakened microbes, killed microbes, inactivated toxins, and purified proteins or polysaccharides derived from microbes are the most common
55 components used in vaccine development strategies. As science advances, researchers are developing even better vaccines.

19. Which of the following best describes smallpox in the years before 1796?
   (A) It struck a million people a year in Europe alone.
   (B) It was common among milkmaids.
   (C) It was spread by cows.
   (D) It killed more than a million Europeans a year.

20. According to the passage, vaccines have been developed for all of the following diseases EXCEPT:
   (A) pneumonia
   (B) scarlet fever
   (C) typhoid fever
   (D) rubella

21. According to the passage, which of the following are components used in vaccine development?
   I. inactivated toxins
   II. weakened microbes
   III. purified proteins

   (A) I only
   (B) II only
   (C) I and II only
   (D) I, II, and III

22. The vaccine produced by Jenner in 1796
   (A) completely eradicated smallpox
   (B) was effective only against cowpox
   (C) served as the basis for modern vaccines
   (D) wiped out typhoid fever

23. What is the meaning of "eradication" in line 35?
   (A) elimination
   (B) spread
   (C) revival
   (D) understanding

24. Which of the following best describes how vaccines work?
   (A) They directly attack the disease-causing organism.
   (B) They fool the body into producing antibodies that protect against the real disease-causing organism.
   (C) They contain deadly disease-producing organisms that are injected directly into the blood stream.
   (D) They contain antibodies that protect the body from deadly diseases.

Questions 25–30

The crimson hand, which at first had been strongly visible upon the marble paleness of Georgiana's cheek, now grew more faintly outlined. She remained not less pale
5 than ever; but the birthmark, with every breath that came and went, lost somewhat of its former distinctness. Its presence had been awful; its departure was more awful
10 still. Watch the stain of the rainbow fading out of the sky, and you will know how the mysterious symbol passed away.
   "By Heaven! It is well-nigh gone!"
15 said Aylmer to himself, in almost irrepressible ecstasy. "I can scarcely trace it now. Success! Success! And now it is like the faintest rose color.

**GO ON TO THE NEXT PAGE.**

The lightest flush of blood across her cheek would overcome it. But she is so pale!"

He drew aside the window curtain and suffered the light of natural day to fall into the room and rest upon her cheek. At the same time he heard a gross, hoarse chuckle, which he had long known as his servant Aminadab's expression of delight.

"Ah, clod! ah, earthly mass!" cried Aylmer, laughing in a sort of frenzy. "You have served me well! Matter and spirit—earth and heaven—have both done their part in this! Laugh, thing of the senses! You have earned the right to laugh."

These exclamations broke Georgiana's sleep. She slowly unclosed her eyes and gazed into the mirror which her husband had arranged for that purpose. A faint smile flitted over her lips when she recognized how barely perceptible was now that crimson hand which had once blazed with such disastrous brilliancy as to scare away all their happiness. But then her eyes sought Aylmer's face with a trouble and anxiety that he could by no means account for.

"My poor Aylmer!" murmured she.

"Poor? Nay, richest, happiest, most favored!" exclaimed he. "My peerless bride, it is successful! You are perfect!"

"My poor Aylmer," she repeated with a more than human tenderness, "you have aimed loftily; you have done nobly. Do not repent that with so high and pure a feeling, you have rejected the best the earth could offer. Aylmer, dearest Aylmer, I am dying!"

—Nathaniel Hawthorne from "The Birthmark"

25. The birthmark on Georgiana's face had the shape of a
    (A)  rainbow
    (B)  rose
    (C)  hand
    (D)  butterfly

26. It can be reasonably inferred from the story that Aylmer
    (A)  is a poor man
    (B)  does not love his wife
    (C)  is trying to kill his wife
    (D)  has performed an operation on his wife

27. Which of the following best describes what happens to the mark on Georgiana's cheek?
    (A)  It takes a new shape.
    (B)  It becomes very faint.
    (C)  It grows larger.
    (D)  It turns a deep red color.

28. Which word best describes how Aylmer regards Georgiana at the end of the passage?
    (A)  flawless
    (B)  amusing
    (C)  tiresome
    (D)  brilliant

29. Georgiana's feelings toward Aylmer could best be described as
    (A)  bitter
    (B)  angry
    (C)  happy
    (D)  tender

30. Which is the best expression of the main idea of this passage?
    (A)  Love is blind.
    (B)  Birthmarks should be removed.
    (C)  Perfection cannot be achieved on earth.
    (D)  Beauty is in the eye of the beholder.

Questions 31–36

Billions of time each day, people reach into their pockets and pull out coins to buy something they want. Before money existed, people bartered by trading goods to obtain what they required. Barter was a complex process that depended on the resources available and the needs of those doing the trading. The invention of money, especially the minting of coins, made economic transactions much easier.

When did the first money come into use? Which culture created it, and how did it become a common system of exchange? The history of money still holds some mysteries, but historians and scientists have some good ideas. In the fifth century B.C., the ancient Greek historian Herodotus mentions that the Lydians had made the first coins.

Around 650 B.C., the Lydians minted a small coin in the shape of a lion on one side with a blank back. These coins called Lydian Lions were made from a combination of silver and gold. This naturally occurring alloy, called electrum, was common in the ancient kingdom of Lydia, now part of western Syria.

According to historical records, Alyattes, King of the Lydians in the sixth century B.C., began minting coins made of electrum. On one side, each coin bore the head of a roaring lion and on the other side a punch mark, the impression made by a hammer as it forced the molten metal into the mold. The most common Lydian Lion was called a stater. Each weighed approximately 4.76 grams—a little less than an American nickel—making them easy to carry.

Lydian coins came in many sizes and weights, depending on the value. The largest was a 14-gram Lydian coin in the shape of a full lion, and the smallest was a twelfth stater that weighed a little more than a gram.

It did not take long before the idea of minting coins to be used in the exchange of goods caught on. Soon after the Lydican Lions were first struck, ancient Greeks, Romans, Indians, Chinese, and Middle-Eastern people were creating their own coins, and the birth of modern monetary systems had begun.

**GO ON TO THE NEXT PAGE.**

31. The main purpose of this passage is to
    (A) describe the way early coins were made
    (B) persuade readers of the value of Lydian coins
    (C) explain how Lydia became an important society
    (D) discuss the origins of coins in ancient Lydia

32. The author describes the minting of Lydian Lions to
    (A) compare the Lydian minting process with modern methods
    (B) explain the steps in the Lydian minting process
    (C) remind collectors why Lydian Lions are valuable
    (D) compare the value of different Lydian coins

33. The word *alloy* as used in line 29 most nearly means
    (A) a metal
    (B) a type of soil
    (C) a mixture
    (D) a weapon

34. According to the passage, the punch mark on the back of a stater was made
    (A) during the minting process
    (B) when mining the ore
    (C) as a royal stamp
    (D) by mistake

35. The creation of Lydian coins led to each of the following EXCEPT
    (A) ancient Lydia's superiority in war
    (B) the decline of bartering for goods
    (C) other cultures making their own coins
    (D) the rise of modern monetary systems

36. According to the passage, the value of a Lydian coin was based on
    (A) the amount of metal in it
    (B) its size and weight
    (C) when it was minted
    (D) which king minted it

**STOP!**
If you finish before time is up, check your work on this section only.

## SECTION 4
Time: 40 Minutes
47 Questions

**Directions:** For each of the following questions, mark the letter of your choice on the answer sheet.

---

1. What value of $x$ will make the expression $(x+7)/4x$ equal to 2?
   (A) 1
   (B) 2
   (C) 3
   (D) 4

2. If $4/a = b/6$, which of the following must be true?
   (A) $\dfrac{4}{b} = \dfrac{6}{a}$
   (B) $4a = 6b$
   (C) $\dfrac{a}{b} = \dfrac{6}{4}$
   (D) $ab = 24$

3. $39.9 + 57.3 = (39.9 + 0.1) + (57.3 - x)$
   $x =$
   (A) 0.01
   (B) 0.1
   (C) 1.0
   (D) 1.1

4. $3,000 \times 0.002 =$
   (A) 0.6
   (B) 6
   (C) 60
   (D) 600

5. In the equilateral triangle shown, what is the measure of each angle?

   (A) 60°
   (B) 90°
   (C) 120°
   (D) 140°

6. $y \div 72 = 21.4$
   $y =$
   (A) 1,260.1
   (B) 1,384.6
   (C) 1,460.25
   (D) 1,540.8

7. It costs $n$ dollars to buy 10 boxes of crackers. At the same rate, how many dollars will it cost to buy 25 boxes of crackers?
   (A) $2.5n$
   (B) $25n$
   (C) $\dfrac{2n}{5}$
   (D) $\dfrac{5n}{2}$

8. In the figure below, if $\angle 1$ is 33°, what is the measure of $\angle 2$?

   (A) 56°
   (B) 110°
   (C) 130°
   (D) 147°

9. Large ice cream cones cost twice as much as small ones. Linda bought 3 large cones and 3 small cones for $13.50. How much does a small cone cost?
   (A) $0.75
   (B) $1.00
   (C) $1.25
   (D) $1.50

10. $7.426 \div 1,000 =$
    (A) 0.0007426
    (B) 0.007426
    (C) 0.07426
    (D) 0.7426

11. Paul has a garden that is 4 meters by 7 meters. If he uses 2 ounces of fertilizer per square meter, how many ounces must he use?
    (A) 42 oz
    (B) 44 oz
    (C) 50 oz
    (D) 56 oz

**GO ON TO THE NEXT PAGE.**

12. Steve is measuring the growth of a tomato plant. The chart below indicates his measurements for the past five weeks. Based on the information in the chart, what should he predict will be the height of the plant at week 6?

(A) 15 inches
(B) 17 inches
(C) 18 inches
(D) 21 inches

13. What digit is in the thousandths place in 5,624.03917?
(A) 5
(B) 3
(C) 9
(D) 1

14. A ladder is placed against a building. If the ladder makes a 55° angle with the ground, what is the measure of the angle that the ladder makes with the building?
(A) 25°
(B) 30°
(C) 35°
(D) 40°

15. If $\dfrac{2}{25} = \dfrac{n}{500}$, what is $n$?
(A) 20
(B) 40
(C) 60
(D) 8

16. Each edge of a cube measures 5 in. What is the volume?
(A) 10 in³
(B) 25 in³
(C) 100 in³
(D) 125 in³

17. Renee deposits $4,000 in a savings account that earns 2% simple interest per year. How much interest will she earn after 2 years?
(A) $100
(B) $160
(C) $165
(D) $180

18. In the figure shown, the two outer rays form a right angle. If angle 1 measures 65°, what is the measure of angle 2?

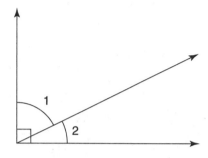

(A) 90°
(B) 60°
(C) 35°
(D) 25°

19. Which of the following numbers is evenly divisible by 4?
(A) 8,376,014
(B) 3,027,690
(C) 7,616,550
(D) 5,921,728

20. In the figure shown, if angle 2 measures 45°, what is the measure of angle 4?

(A) 135°
(B) 75°
(C) 45°
(D) 35°

21. Which if the following is divisible only by itself and 1?
(A) 61
(B) 81
(C) 171
(D) 207

22. Figure WXYZ is a parallelogram. Which of the following is NOT necessarily true?

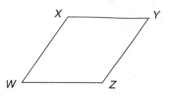

(A) Side WX is parallel to side ZY.
(B) Side XY is parallel to side WZ.
(C) ∠W has the same measure as ∠Y.
(D) Side WX is the same length as side XY.

23. Renee wants to carpet her living room. The rectangular room measures 15 feet × 18 feet. How many square yards of carpet must Renee purchase?
(A) 20 yd²
(B) 30 yd²
(C) 32 yd²
(D) 35 yd²

24. Last month, the librarian at a certain library kept track of all books checked out. The graph below shows the results by category of book. In the two most popular categories, how many books were checked out last month?

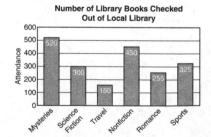

(A) 520
(B) 750
(C) 970
(D) 1,300

**GO ON TO THE NEXT PAGE.**

25. In the triangle shown, ∠ACB measures 55° and ∠CAB measures 65°. What is the measure of ∠CBA?

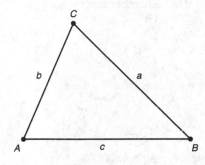

(A) 50°
(B) 60°
(C) 80°
(D) 90°

26. What are all the common factors of 24 and 36?
(A) 1, 2, 3, 12, 18
(B) 1, 2, 4, 12, 18, 24
(C) 1, 2, 12, 18, 24, 36
(D) 1, 2, 3, 4, 6, 12

27. Which fraction is in simplest form?
(A) $\dfrac{15}{18}$

(B) $\dfrac{99}{100}$

(C) $\dfrac{56}{133}$

(D) $\dfrac{45}{72}$

28. In the following figure, if ∠6 measures 90°, what is the measure of ∠1?

(A) 25°
(B) 35°
(C) 45°
(D) 55°

29. High school students were asked to pick their favorite kind of birthday party. The results are shown in the chart below. What percent of students chose either ice skating or sleepover?

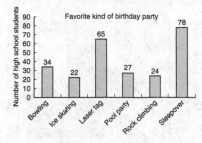

(A) 40%
(B) 45%
(C) 50%
(D) 60%

30. If Joanne tosses a 1–6 number cube, what is the probability that the cube number facing up will be even?
(A) $\dfrac{1}{2}$

(B) $\dfrac{1}{3}$

(C) $\dfrac{1}{4}$

(D) $\dfrac{1}{5}$

31. In the triangle shown, side a is 4 ft long and side b is 6 ft long. What is the area of the triangle?

(A) 12 ft²
(B) 18 ft²
(C) 24 ft²
(D) 36 ft²

32. Donna is d years old. Frank is f years old. Frank is 4 years younger than Donna. Which equation represents the relationship between Donna's and Frank's age?

(A) d = f/4
(B) d = 4 – f
(C) f = d – 4
(D) f = 4 – d

33. The drama club is spending $224 to put on a play. They plan to sell tickets at $3.00 each. If they sell n tickets, which of the following expressions represent their profit after expenses?
(A) 3n – 224
(B) 224 + n/3
(C) 3n + 224
(D) 224(n + 3)

34. A circle has a radius of 1.35 meters. Wire costs 2¢ per centimeter. How much will it cost to stretch a wire between two points on the circle if it passes through the center?
(A) $5.40
(B) $5.56
(C) $5.64
(D) $5.72

35. Order from least to greatest:
²/₈, ²/₃, ²/₉
(A) $\dfrac{2}{8}, \dfrac{2}{9}, \dfrac{2}{3}$

(B) $\dfrac{2}{9}, \dfrac{2}{8}, \dfrac{2}{3}$

(C) $\dfrac{2}{9}, \dfrac{2}{3}, \dfrac{2}{8}$

(D) $\dfrac{2}{3}, \dfrac{2}{8}, \dfrac{2}{9}$

36. 2.004 =
(A) $2\dfrac{4}{100}$

(B) $2\dfrac{2}{1{,}000}$

(C) $2\dfrac{1}{250}$

(D) $2\dfrac{1}{200}$

37. Order from least to greatest:
2⁴/₅, 2.4, ¹⁰/₄
(A) $2.4, \dfrac{10}{4}, 2\dfrac{4}{5}$

(B) $2\dfrac{4}{5}, \dfrac{10}{4}, 2.4$

(C) $\dfrac{10}{4}, 2.4, 2\dfrac{4}{5}$

(D) $\dfrac{10}{4}, 2\dfrac{4}{5}, \dfrac{10}{4}$

**GO ON TO THE NEXT PAGE.**

38. Adrinda is 8 years older than Marsha. Daryl is 3 years older than Marsha. Which equation correctly relates Adrinda's age (*a*) and Daryl's age (*d*)?
(A)  $d = a - 5$
(B)  $d = a + 5$
(C)  $d = a - 3$
(D)  $d = a + 3$

39. $5\frac{5}{8} \times 2\frac{2}{5} =$
(A)  $10\frac{3}{4}$
(B)  $13\frac{1}{2}$
(C)  $15\frac{17}{20}$
(D)  $18\frac{4}{5}$

40. $5 \times 6 \div (2 + 1) =$
(A)  15
(B)  14
(C)  11
(D)  10

41. A rule is used to generate the following sequence: 12, 17, ___, ___, 32, 37. Which are the missing numbers?
(A)  19, 28
(B)  21, 31
(C)  22, 27
(D)  24, 28

42. The graph below shows scores Mr. Smith's history class received on the mid-term exam.

How many students scored 80 or above?
(A)  8
(B)  6
(C)  4
(D)  2

43. $24 \div (-4\frac{2}{3}) =$
(A)  $-4\frac{1}{6}$
(B)  $4\frac{1}{3}$
(C)  $5\frac{5}{6}$
(D)  $-5\frac{1}{7}$

44. Cara spins a spinner divided into equal spaces numbered 1 through 12. What is the probability that the spinner will land on a number that is less than 5?
(A)  $\frac{1}{6}$
(B)  $\frac{1}{4}$
(C)  $\frac{1}{3}$
(D)  $\frac{1}{2}$

45. A map scale reads "1 in = 40 km." $6\frac{7}{8}$ inches on the map equals how many kilometers?
(A)  275 km
(B)  278 km
(C)  280 km
(D)  286 km

46. If $x = y + 3$, what is the value of $3x + 2$?
(A)  $y - 3$
(B)  $3y + 6$
(C)  $3y + 9$
(D)  $3y + 11$

47. The sum of two consecutive prime numbers
(A)  is always an even number
(B)  is always an odd number
(C)  may be an even or an odd number
(D)  is always a prime number

**STOP!**
If you finish before time is up, check your work on this section only.

## SECTION 5
Time: 30 Minutes

**Directions:** You will have 30 minutes to plan and write an essay on the topic given below. You must write on the assigned topic only. An essay on another topic will not be acceptable. You may make notes in the space provided for that purpose.

Write your final essay on the two lined pages of your answer sheet. Write or print legibly in blue or black ink. A copy of your essay will be sent to each school that will be receiving your test results.

---

If you could change one thing about your school, what would you change and why?

---

USE THIS SPACE FOR NOTES

## Answer Key

### Section 1 Verbal Reasoning

| | | | | | |
|---|---|---|---|---|---|
| 1. | A | 15. | B | 29. | D |
| 2. | C | 16. | D | 30. | B |
| 3. | D | 17. | C | 31. | B |
| 4. | C | 18. | D | 32. | C |
| 5. | C | 19. | A | 33. | A |
| 6. | B | 20. | A | 34. | D |
| 7. | D | 21. | A | 35. | C |
| 8. | B | 22. | D | 36. | D |
| 9. | D | 23. | A | 37. | B |
| 10. | A | 24. | D | 38. | B |
| 11. | D | 25. | B | 39. | A |
| 12. | A | 26. | D | 40. | C |
| 13. | C | 27. | C | | |
| 14. | B | 28. | A | | |

### Section 2 Quantitative Reasoning

| | | | | | |
|---|---|---|---|---|---|
| 1. | B | 14. | A | 27. | C |
| 2. | D | 15. | B | 28. | A |
| 3. | D | 16. | D | 29. | D |
| 4. | A | 17. | B | 30. | C |
| 5. | C | 18. | A | 31. | B |
| 6. | B | 19. | B | 32. | A |
| 7. | D | 20. | D | 33. | D |
| 8. | A | 21. | A | 34. | C |
| 9. | A | 22. | B | 35. | B |
| 10. | A | 23. | B | 36. | B |
| 11. | D | 24. | D | 37. | C |
| 12. | B | 25. | C | | |
| 13. | C | 26. | A | | |

## Section 3 Reading Comprehension

| | | | | | | |
|---|---|---|---|---|---|
| 1. | B | 13. | A | 25. | C |
| 2. | C | 14. | C | 26. | D |
| 3. | B | 15. | B | 27. | B |
| 4. | C | 16. | A | 28. | A |
| 5. | A | 17. | B | 29. | D |
| 6. | D | 18. | C | 30. | C |
| 7. | A | 19. | D | 31. | D |
| 8. | B | 20. | B | 32. | B |
| 9. | B | 21. | D | 33. | C |
| 10. | C | 22. | C | 34. | A |
| 11. | A | 23. | A | 35. | A |
| 12. | D | 24. | B | 36. | B |

## Section 4 Mathematics Achievement

| | | | | | | |
|---|---|---|---|---|---|
| 1. | A | 17. | B | 33. | A |
| 2. | D | 18. | D | 34. | A |
| 3. | B | 19. | D | 35. | B |
| 4. | B | 20. | C | 36. | C |
| 5. | A | 21. | A | 37. | A |
| 6. | D | 22. | D | 38. | A |
| 7. | A | 23. | B | 39. | B |
| 8. | D | 24. | C | 40. | D |
| 9. | D | 25. | B | 41. | C |
| 10. | B | 26. | D | 42. | A |
| 11. | D | 27. | B | 43. | D |
| 12. | B | 28. | C | 44. | C |
| 13. | C | 29. | A | 45. | A |
| 14. | C | 30. | A | 46. | D |
| 15. | B | 31. | A | 47. | C |
| 16. | D | 32. | C | | |

# Answers and Explanations

## Section 1 Verbal Reasoning

1.  **A is correct.** A *bias* is a *preference* or an inclination, especially one that inhibits impartial judgment.

2.  **C is correct.** To *inhabit* is to live in or reside in—in other words, to *dwell*.

3.  **D is correct.** *Generous* is an adjective meaning liberal in giving or sharing. Similarly, *benevolent* is an adjective meaning characterized by or suggestive of doing good, often in regard to charity.

4.  **C is correct.** *Aggregate* is a *total*, constituting or amounting to a whole.

5.  **C is correct.** An *implement*, used here as a noun, is a tool or *instrument* used in doing work—for instance, a gardening implement.

6.  **B is correct.** To behave *graciously* is to behave in a *kindly* or warm manner.

7.  **D is correct.** To *meander* is to move aimlessly and idly without a fixed direction—in other words, to *wander*.

8.  **B is correct.** To *concur* is to be of the same opinion—to *agree*.

9.  **D is correct.** *Agile* is an adjective used to describe someone or something that is quick, light, and moves with ease. The choice that best fits this definition is *nimble*.

10.  **A is correct.** *Addition* is the act or process of adding something extra to a thing; something added. Similarly, *inclusion* is the act or state of being included; something included.

11.  **D is correct.** When someone is *persistent*, she refuses to give up or let go—in other words, she is *determined*.

12.  **A is correct.** To *encourage* is to give support to or to cultivate. Similarly, to *foster* is to promote the development and growth of.

13.  **C is correct.** To *scold* is to reprimand or to criticize harshly and usually angrily—in other words, to *berate*.

14.  **B is correct.** A *commencement* is a *beginning* or a start.

15.  **B is correct.** To *criticize* is to find fault with. Similarly, to *disparage* is to speak of in a slighting or disrespectful way.

16.  **D is correct.** *Obviously* is defined as easily perceived or understood. *Apparently*, its synonym, is defined as readily understood.

17.  **C is correct.** *Incessant* describes something that continues without interruption—something that is *constant*.

18.  **D is correct.** To *acquire* is to gain possession of. *Procure*, which means "to obtain," is its synonym.

19.  **A is correct.** *Venerable* is an adjective, usually used to describe a person who commands respect by virtue of age, character, dignity, or position. A person who is described as venerable could similarly be described as *respected*.

20.  **A is correct.** *Proclivity* is a noun meaning a natural *inclination*, predisposition, or propensity.

21.  **A is correct.** *Consolidated*, meaning "to have united into one system or whole; to have combined," is the only choice that effectively conveys the meaning of the sentence.

22.  **D is correct.** Since all of the first-blank choices seem to fit, you might do better by focusing on the second blank. Because choices A and C are so similar in meaning, you can discount both of them. *Gleaning* (choice B) means

"gathering or collecting bit by bit" and makes no sense in the context of the sentence. *Breaching* (choice D) means "breaking or violating, especially an agreement," and is clearly the best answer.

23. **A is correct.** The key to this question is the phrase "lacking any interesting qualities." Of the four choices, only *insipid* has enough of a negative connotation to set it apart from the other choices. In fact, the key phrase in the sentence is essentially the definition of *insipid*, which means "lacking qualities that excite, stimulate, or interest."

24. **D is correct.** "Despite" is one of the words you may see on the test that signals a contrast within a two-clause sentence. When you come across words or phrases such as "despite," "although," or "even though," keep in mind that the words you are looking for are likely to contrast with each other. Of the choices available, only *shaky . . . lucrative* (choice D) offers the sufficient contrast needed to properly convey the logic of the "despite" construction.

25. **B is correct.** Logically, you can assume that a company would not hope to suspend short-term sales expectations, thus, you can eliminate choice A. Choice D can be eliminated as well, as *attest* makes no sense in the context of the sentence. Of the remaining choices, both choice B and choice C offer appropriate first-blank options; however, it is unlikely that the company had to "properly determine the staff." *Remunerate* (choice B), meaning "to pay a person a suitable equivalent in return for goods provided, services rendered, or losses incurred," is the correct answer.

26. **D is correct.** Knowing the definitions of the words you have to choose from will help you select the correct answer to this question. Neither *dispersed* (choice A) nor *maintained* (choice B) fits the context of the sentence, and both can be eliminated. *Deprecated* (choice C), meaning "to have expressed disapproval," is incorrect as well. *Teemed* (choice D), meaning "to have been full of things, abounded, or swarmed," is the only possible correct answer.

27. **C is correct.** *Reserved* (choice B) is easily eliminated as a first-blank choice, and you should notice that the second-blank options for choices A and D are too alike to be distinguishable from each other. That leaves choice C, *grandiose . . . curtail*; this is the only pair of words that properly conveys the meaning of the sentence.

28. **A is correct.** By now you should be able to recognize that words such as "although" and "despite" (along with the phrase "even though") signal that a two-clause sentence is likely to contain a contrast from one clause to the next. Notice that choices B, C, and D all contain pairs of words that lack the proper contrast to correctly convey the meaning of the "although" construction. Choice A, however, pairs *sobering* (meaning "marked by seriousness, gravity, or solemnity of conduct or character") with *farcical* (meaning "ludicrous or ridiculously funny").

29. **D is correct.** An *exemption* is a release from an obligation granted by or as if by an authority. Therefore, choice D is the correct answer and the only choice that fits the context of the sentence. An *emulsion* (choice B) is "a suspension of one liquid in a second liquid with which the first will not mix" (oil and water for instance), and a *quandary* (choice C) is "a state of uncertainty or perplexity; a predicament."

30. **B is correct.** Initially, you may believe that *endeavor* (choice A), which means "a purposeful or industrious activity," is the correct answer. However, keep in mind that the problem Angela faces is whether she should babysit or go to the movies on Friday night. Knowing she can only do one or the other, you can logically conclude that Angela needs to make a choice. *Predicament* (choice B), meaning a "situation that requires a choice between two options that are or seem equally unfavorable or mutually exclusive," is the correct answer.

31. **B is correct.** The easiest way to solve a two-blank question is by eliminating choices from one of the blanks based on the fact that one answer in the word pair is obviously wrong. Neither *overcome* (choice A) nor *accept* (choice C) seems appropriate for the first blank, and thus, they can be discounted. Focusing on the second blank, you can conclude that the band's offer for an extended engagement would likely not be *established* (choice D) by their failure to inspire the audience. That leaves *impress . . . revoked* (choice B) as the only remaining choice, and this is the correct answer.

32. **C is correct.** The key to this question is the phrase "after a series of argumentative negotiations." Logically, you can conclude that the two sides are ready to move past their differences "so they could get back to the task at hand." A *reconciliation* (choice C) is a "agreement" and this is the correct answer. An *admonition* (choice A) is "a warning or cautionary advice," and an *abatement* (choice B) is "a reduction."

33. **A is correct.** The answer to this question is actually revealed by the phrase "the highest mountain in the world." *Monumental* (choice A), meaning "impressively large, sturdy, or enduring," is correct.

34. **D is correct.** The logic of this question indicates that the developer's plan for the land originally included space for a public park but no longer does. Therefore, he has first said one thing and then changed his mind to say another. *Contradiction* (choice D), meaning "an inconsistency or a discrepancy," is the correct answer choice.

35. **C is correct.** This sentence contains another example of the "despite" construction. Keep in mind that, when you encounter a sentence such as this one, the correct answer will likely be a pair of words with meanings that contrast with one another. *Chastised . . . exonerated* (choice C) offers the best choice of words with contrasting meanings, and this is the correct answer. *Chastised* means "punished or criticized severely," and *exonerated* means "freed from blame."

36. **D is correct.** It may seem an act of *peculiarity* (choice C) for the star midfielder to be benched, but a better answer is that it was an act of *retribution* (choice D), meaning "something given or demanded in repayment, especially punishment."

37. **B is correct.** Likely, you can conclude that if the owner had provided a *legitimate* (choice A) certificate of authenticity, the art historian would not have declared the painting a forgery. As well, *turgid* (choice C) means "swollen," or "excessively ornate or complex in style or language," and does not fit the context of the sentence. *Precocious* (choice D) means "characterized by unusually early development or maturity" and is also wrong. *Spurious* (choice B), meaning "not genuine" or "lacking authenticity or validity," is correct.

38. **B is correct.** If you are unsure of the correct word pair in a two-blank question, try focusing on one of the blanks first. Focusing on the first blank, it is unlikely that a person who died of food poisoning would be described as "strengthened" or "fortified" by a lifestyle that "indulged his every whim." *Befallen* (choice D) is a good first-blank match, however *durable* does not fit well in the second blank. *Undeterred . . . gluttonous* (meaning "indulging in something to excess") is correct.

39. **A is correct.** Chances are that a team would not consider a six-game losing streak to be the *pinnacle* (meaning "the highest point") of their season. As well, *conclusion* (choice D) can be eliminated as the team would likely know when their season was over. *Nadir* (choice A), meaning "the lowest point" or "the time of greatest depression or adversity," is the correct answer.

40. **C is correct.** Knowing the definitions of the answer choices will help you solve this question. A *beacon* (choice A) is "a signaling or guiding device, such a light"; *sustenance* (choice B) is "something, usually food, which sustains life or health"; a *dearth* (choice C) is "a scarce supply or a lack"; and a *confluence* is "a gathering, meeting, or flowing together at one juncture or point." *Dearth* (choice C) is correct.

## Section 2 Quantitative Reasoning

1. **B is correct.** Each number in the sequence is 3 more than the preceding number. $17 + 3 = 20$.

2. **D is correct.** If Kurt saw $s$ sparrows, 3 times as many finches, and 12 birds of both species in all, you can find out how many birds of each species he saw by using the number sentence $s + 3s = 12$.

3. **D is correct.** Gary scored 27 points in the two games, and he scored twice as many in game 2 as in game 1. Let $p$ = number of points Gary scored in game 1. Write an equation:
$p + 2p = 27$
$3p = 27$
$p = 9$
So in game 1, Gary scored 9 points, and in game 2 he scored $2(9) = 18$ points.

4. **A is correct.** $5.75 \text{ lb} \times \$1.20/\text{lb} = \$6.90$.

5. **C is correct.** Maria earns $9 per hour on weekdays and $12 per hour on weekends. For 8 hours of work on Tuesday she earned $8 \times \$9 = \$72$. For 6 hours of work on Thursday she earned $6 \times \$9 = \$54$. For 7 hours of work on Friday she earned $7 \times \$9 = \$63$. For 9 hours of work on Saturday she earned $9 \times \$12 = \$108$. $\$72 + \$54 + \$63 + \$108 = \$297$.

6. **B is correct.** 1.268 is greater than 1.2 but less than 1.3.

7. **D is correct.** 27 batteries $= {}^{27}/_4 = 7$ packs with 1 battery left over. If you want 2 complete packs left over, you must buy 9 packs.

8. **A is correct.** 5 quarters $= \$1.25$; 6 dimes $= \$0.60$; $\$1.25 + \$0.60 = \$1.85$.

9. **A is correct.** Let $x =$ Karen's age. $\dfrac{(20 + 18 + x)}{3} = 18$.

    $\dfrac{(38 + x)}{3} = 18$
    $(38 + x) = 54$
    $x = 16$

10. **A is correct.** In 4 months the dog loses $4 \times 0.33 = 1.32$ lb; $37.18 + 1.32 = 38.5$ lb.

11. **D is correct.** If 46% of 950 people said that they listened to jazz, 54% did not say they listened to jazz. 54% of $950 = 0.54 \times 950 = 513$.

12. **B is correct.** 25% of $\$650 = 0.25 \times 650 = \$162.50$, so the sale price of the television set is $\$650.00 - \$162.50 = \$487.50$. The tax is 12%, so Beth will pay $\$487.50 + (\$487.50 \times 0.12) = \$487.50 + \$58.50 = \$546$.

13. **C is correct.** 8 people are both on the chess team and in the band. That means that there are $17 - 8 = 9$ additional chess players and $13 - 8 = 5$ additional band members. $8 + 9 + 5 = 22$ people in the group.

14. **A is correct.** At 6:00 the hour and minute hands on a clock form a straight angle, which measures 180°.

15. **B is correct.** If the length and width were doubled, the new dimensions would be 40 yards by 30 yards. Perimeter $= 40 + 30 + 40 + 30 = 140$ yd.

16. **D is correct.** The poster measures 2 feet 4 inches by 3 feet 8 inches. Convert to inches: 2 feet 4 inches $= 28$ inches; 3 feet 8 inches $= 44$ inches. Perimeter $= 28 + 44 + 28 + 44 = 144$ inches $= 12$ feet.

17. **B is correct.** The rectangle has an area of $4 \times 6 = 24$ in²; $24 \div 4 = 6$.

18. **A is correct.** $560 \div 28 = 20$.

19. **B is correct.** This is a 45°–45°–90° triangle. Since both legs are 4, the hypotenuse $AC$ must be $4\sqrt{2}$.

20. **D is correct.** The rule for this sequence is to double the previous number and then subtract 1.
    $9 \times 2 - 1 = 18 - 1 = 17$

21. **A is correct.**
    25% of $\$40 = \$10$; $\$40 - \$10 = \$30$;
    20% of $\$30 = \$6$; $\$30 - \$6 = \$24$

22. **B is correct.**
    $(4 \times 10^3) + (6 \times 10^2) + (2 \times 10^0) =$
    $(4 \times 1{,}000) + (6 \times 100) + (2 \times 1) =$
    $4{,}602$

23. **B is correct.**
    There are 3 As and 1 E, so P (vowel) $= {}^4/_{15}$.
    There are 3 Cs and 2 Ls, so P (C or T) $= {}^5/_{15}$.

24. **D is correct.**
The radius could be less than, equal to, or greater than the chord.

25. **C is correct.**
Mean = $(40 + 50 + 60 + 70) \div 4 =$
$220 \div 4 = 55$
Median = mean of two middle numbers
$= (50 + 60) \div 2 = 110 \div 2 = 55$

26. **A is correct.**
$\sqrt{64} + \sqrt{36} = 8 + 6 = 14$

$\sqrt{100} = 10$

27. **C is correct.**
A rectangular prism has 8 vertices and 12 edges.
$8 + 2 = 10; 12 - 2 = 10$

28. **A is correct.**
Cities A, B, and C form a right triangle. Using the Pythagorean theorem, the distance
between City A and City $C = \sqrt{(30^2 + 40^2)} = \sqrt{(900 + 1{,}600)} = \sqrt{2{,}500} = 50$ miles.

29. **D is correct.**
If $g > 0$, then $g$ is greater.
If $g < 0$, then $-g$ is greater.
If $g = 0$, then $g$ and $-g$ are equal.

30. **C is correct.**
Let $w$ = Frank's weight
Jason's weight = $^5/_4 w$
Bill's weight = $^4/_5 (^5/_4) w = w$

31. **B is correct.**
Since $ABDC$ is a trapezoid, $\overline{AB} \parallel \overline{CD}$.
Since $\angle A$ is a right angle, $\angle C$ is a right
angle. So, $m\angle x = 90°$.

The sum of the angles in a quadrilateral is equal to 360°.
$90° + 90° + 75° + m\angle y = 360°$
$255° + m\angle y = 360°$
$m\angle y = 105°$

32. **A is correct.**
$1^3/_4\% = 1.75\% = 0.0175$

33. **D is correct.**
$x$ and $y$ can take on values to make either one greater, or to make them equal.

34. **C is correct.**
At 10 P.M., ship is a sea level, 0 depth.
At 12 A.M., ship is 500 ft below sea level, −500 depth.
Depth change: $0 - (-500) = 500$.

At 1 A.M., ship is 200 ft below sea level, −200 depth.
At 2:30 A.M., ship is 700 feet below sea level, −700 depth.
Depth change: $-200 - (-700) = 500$.

35. **B is correct.**

$$\frac{m}{6} = \frac{32}{48} \qquad\qquad \frac{100}{50} = \frac{70}{n}$$

$$48m = 6(32) \qquad\quad 100n = 70(50)$$

$$48m = 192 \qquad\qquad 100n = 3{,}500$$

$$m = 4 \qquad\qquad\qquad n = 35$$

$$8m = 32 \qquad\qquad\quad n - 1 = 34$$

36. **B is correct.**

$$\frac{1}{3} + \frac{5}{6} + \frac{7}{12} = \frac{4}{12} + \frac{10}{12} + \frac{7}{12} = \frac{21}{13} = 1\frac{3}{4};$$

$$\frac{3}{4} + \frac{5}{8} + \frac{13}{16} = \frac{12}{16} + \frac{10}{16} + \frac{13}{16} = \frac{35}{16} = 2\frac{3}{16}$$

37. **C is correct.**
Organize the set from least to greatest:
{1, 3, 5, 9, 9, 12, 13, 19}. The fourth and fifth items in the array are the median (9), and the most frequently appearing number (9 again) is the mode.

## Section 3 Reading Comprehension

1. **B is correct.** The quotation shows that the President has a duty to report to Congress on the State of the Union and to recommend necessary and expedient measures. This annual message to Congress came to be known as the State of the Union. Choice A is wrong because although the quotation does illustrate the actual wording of this section of the Constitution, it is not intended to illustrate the wording of the entire Constitution. Choice C is wrong because there is no demonstration of different interpretations of this provision. The differences cited are in the form, content, and delivery method of the message, not in the need to report to Congress. Choice D is wrong because the passage does not distinguish between constitutional duty and custom. The report on the State of the Union is mandated by the Constitution.

2. **C is correct.** The Constitution required the president to give Congress information on the state of the union "from time to time." Throughout the passage, the State of the Union message is referred to as the president's "annual message." Clearly, the phrase "time to time" has come to mean "annually."

3. **B is correct.** This information is found in the opening quote from the U.S. Constitution, which says that presidents have a constitutional duty to "give to Congress information of the State of the Union."

4. **C is correct.** Thomas Jefferson thought Washington's oral presentation was "too monarchial for the new republic." Jefferson "wrote out his address and sent it to Congress to be read by a clerk."

5. **A is correct.** As stated in the last paragraph, "With the advent of radio and television, the President's annual message has become not only a conversation between the President and Congress but also an opportunity for the President to communicate with the American people at the same time." Choices B and C are wrong because Thomas Jefferson was president in the nineteenth century and Lyndon Johnson in the second half of the twentieth century. Choice D is wrong because newspaper coverage of the State of the Union message began long before the start of the twentieth century.

6. **D is correct.** As stated in the last paragraph, "Harry S. Truman's 1947 address was the first to be broadcast on television." None of the other questions is answered by information in the passage.

7. **A is correct.** As stated in the second paragraph, "Most tsunamis are generated by earthquakes, but they may also be caused by volcanic eruptions, landslides, undersea slumps or meteor impacts." Tornadoes are mentioned along with hurricanes, not as a cause of tsunamis, but rather as another kind of natural disaster.

8. **B is correct.** The author mentions the 1960 tsunami in Japan in the third paragraph: "The waves radiate outward in all directions from the disturbance and can propagate across entire ocean basins. For example, in 1960, an earthquake in Chile caused a tsunami that swept across the Pacific to Japan." The words "for example" indicate that the reference to Japan is intended to show how far the waves radiated from the earthquake in Chile.

9. **B is correct.** The answer to this question is found in paragraph 3 which says, "Tsunami waves are distinguished from ordinary ocean waves by their great length between peaks, often exceeding 100 miles in the deep ocean, and by the long amount of time between these peaks, ranging from five minutes to an hour." Choice A is wrong because the passage does not mention that regular waves follow closely one after the other. Choice C is wrong because it has no support in the passage. Choice D is wrong because the passage states that in deep water "a tsunami is barely noticeable, causing only a small rising and falling of the sea surface as it passes."

10. **C is correct.** This passage is full of the kind of strictly factual scientific information most likely to be found in a science textbook. Choice A cannot be correct because the passage is clearly fact, not fiction. Choice D is wrong because the passage merely mentions the tsunami of 2004, but does not go on to provide the details of that particular event as a news article would.

11. **A is correct.** The answer to this question can be found in paragraph 4: "As the tsunami approaches land and shallow water, the waves slow down and become compressed, causing them to grow in height." In the best of cases, the tsunami comes ashore like a rising tide causing flooding of coastal areas. In the worst of cases, a wall of turbulent water several meters high rushes ashore with great destructive power.

12. **D is correct.** All of the choices are meanings of the word "bore." However, only choice (D) is correct in context. As stated in the second sentence of paragraph 5, "A bore is a wall of turbulent water that can be several meters high and can rush onshore with great destructive power."

13. **A is correct.** The constant repetition of "gone" and "wiped out" in lines 11–21 serves to emphasize the author's inability to believe that such devastation could possibly occur. "San Francisco is *gone*. . . . Its industrial section is *wiped out*. Its business section is *wiped out*. Its social and residential section is *wiped out*. The factories and warehouses, the great stores and newspaper buildings, the hotels and the palaces of the nabobs, are all *gone*." Choices B, C, and D are wrong because there are no words in the paragraph that support a mood of desperate longing, cautious optimism, or heartfelt pity.

14. **C is correct.** Here are just a few examples of the vivid images provided by the author: ". . . the smoke of San Francisco's burning was a lurid tower visible a hundred miles away . . . " "The streets were humped into ridges and depressions, and piled with the debris of fallen walls." "The steel rails were twisted into perpendicular and horizontal angles."

15. **B is correct.** A *nabob* is "a rich and important person." Choice D is wrong because although the passage mentions "the palaces of nabobs," a nabob does not have to be of royal blood. Choices A and C have nothing to do with the word "nabob."

16. **A is correct.** The passage tells mainly of the massive destruction the San Francisco earthquake caused; roads and rail systems were destroyed, telephone and telegraph systems were "disrupted," and the "water-mains had burst." Thus, the statement conveys the idea that all modern conveniences had been lost, and the city had been reduced to living without twentieth-century amenities.

17. **B is correct.** The passage is arranged in chronological order. This is evident in the first few words of paragraphs 3, 4, and 5. Paragraph 3 starts with the words "On Wednesday morning," paragraph 4 starts with "By Wednesday afternoon," and paragraph 5 starts with "Wednesday night."

18. **C is correct.** As evidenced by lines 57–59 ("At that time I watched the vast conflagration from out on the bay."), the author was an eyewitness to the earthquake. His primary purpose for writing this passage was to report what he saw during that terrible time. Choice A is wrong because the passage provides no scientific explanation telling how earthquakes occur. Choice B is wrong because the passage describes the events of the earthquake, but does not go into the feelings of the residents. Choice D is wrong because only one paragraph of the account is devoted to the winds that helped the fire spread.

19. **D is correct.** As stated in the second paragraph, "In those days, a million people died from smallpox each year in Europe alone. . . . " Choice A is wrong because the passage states that a million people died from smallpox. Since some people did survive smallpox, it can be assumed that the disease struck many more than a million people each year. Choices B and C are wrong because milkmaids contracted cowpox, not smallpox, from the cows.

20. **B is correct.** Choices A and D are both mentioned in paragraph 3: "Since Jenner's time, vaccines have been developed against more than 20 infectious diseases such as influenza, pneumonia, whooping cough, rubella, meningitis, and hepatitis B." Choice C is mentioned in paragraph 2, "By the beginning of the 20th century, vaccines for rabies, diphtheria, typhoid fever, and plague were in use, in addition to the vaccine for smallpox." The only answer choice not mentioned is choice B, scarlet fever.

21. **D is correct.** As stated in the last paragraph, "Weakened microbes, killed microbes, inactivated toxins, and purified proteins or polysaccharides derived from microbes are the most common components used in vaccine development strategies."

22. **C is correct.** The answer to this question is found in the second paragraph, which states that "Jenner laid the foundation for modern vaccines" and "started on a course that would ease the suffering of people around the world for centuries to come." Choice A is wrong because it was not until 1980 that "an updated version of Jenner's vaccine led to the total eradication of smallpox." Choice B is wrong because Jenner used cowpox-producing organisms to make the vaccine that protected people from the more deadly smallpox. Choice D is wrong because although Jenner's work was the basis for the development of a vaccine for typhoid fever, the vaccine Jenner produced in 1796 was for smallpox only.

23. **A is correct.** The previous details about Jenner's original vaccine for smallpox and the final sentence make it clear that *eradication* means "elimination."

24. **B is correct.** According to the last paragraph, "Scientists use vaccines to 'trick' the human immune system into producing antibodies or immune cells that protect against the real disease-causing organism." Choice A is wrong because the vaccine does not directly attack the disease-causing organism, instead it causes the body to produce antibodies against the disease-causing organism. Choice C is wrong because vaccines contain "weakened microbes, killed microbes, inactivated toxins, and purified proteins or polysaccharides derived from microbes," not deadly disease-producing organisms. Choice D is wrong because the vaccine does not contain antibodies, rather it triggers the body to produce antibodies.

25. **C is correct.** The first sentence describes the birthmark as a "crimson hand, which at first had been strongly visible upon the marble paleness of Georgiana's cheek." The birthmark fades like "the stain of the rainbow fading out of the sky," but it is not shaped like a rainbow, so choice A is incorrect. The birthmark fades to "the faintest rose color," but is not described as having the shape of a rose, so choice B is incorrect. There is nothing in the passage to suggest that the birthmark is shaped like a butterfly, so choice D is incorrect.

26. **D is correct.** The first paragraph tells that the birthmark is fading. In the second paragraph Aylmer says, "Success! Success!" indicating that he is responsible for making the birthmark fade. Thus the most reasonable assumption is that Alymer had performed some kind of operation on his wife to remove her birthmark. The presence of a servant indicates that Aylmer is not a poor man, making choice A incorrect. Choices B and C can be eliminated because all the evidence indicates that Aylmer is striving to help his wife by removing the birthmark that "had once blazed with such disastrous brilliancy as to scare away all their happiness."

27. **B is correct.** Georgiana gazes into the mirror and sees "how barely perceptible was now that crimson hand which had once blazed with such disastrous brilliancy as to scare away all their happiness." A mark that is barely perceptible is very faint.

28. **A is correct.** When Georgiana awakens, Alymer calls her his "peerless bride" and proclaims, "You are perfect!" The best synonym for "perfect" is "flawless."

29. **D is correct.** Even though Georgiana knows she is dying as a result of Aylmer's attempt to remove her birthmark, she speaks to Alymer "with more than human tenderness," calling him "My poor Aylmer" and "dearest Aylmer." Her words do not indicate that she is bitter (choice A) or angry (choice B). She may be happy to see that the birthmark is gone, but that does not describe her feelings toward Aylmer, so choice C is wrong.

30. **C is correct.** Aylmer's attempt to make his wife perfect resulted in destroying her, thus illustrating the fact that perfection cannot be achieved on earth. Choice A is wrong because if love were blind Aylmer would not have attempted to remove the birthmark. Choice B is wrong because the passage proves the opposite to be true. Choice D is wrong because the effect of the birthmark was "to scare away all their happiness."

31. **D is correct.** The main purpose of the passage is to discuss the origins of coins as a part of the monetary system of ancient Lydia.

32. **B is correct.** In lines 34–40, the author describes the making of Lydian coins by explaining the key steps in the minting process.

33. **C is correct.** Lines 26–29 of the passage explains that electrum was "a combination of silver and gold."

34. **A is correct.** According to lines 38–40 of the passage, the punch mark was an impression made by a hammer as it forced the molten metal into the mold.

35. **A is correct.** The passage does not mention Lydia's superiority in warring.

36. **B is correct.** According to lines 46–51 of the passage, the value of Lydian coins depended on their size and weight.

## Section 4 Mathematics Achievement

1. **A is correct.** If $x = 1$, the numerator is 8 $(1 + 7)$ and the denominator is 4 $(4 \times 1)$, and $8/4 = 2$.

2. **D is correct.**
$$\frac{4}{a} = \frac{b}{6}$$
$$(6)(4/a) = (6)(b/6)$$
$$\frac{24}{a} = b$$
$$24 = ab$$

3. **B is correct.**
$$39.9 + 57.3 = (39.9 + 0.1) + (57.3 - x)$$
$$39.9 + 57.3 = (40) + (57.3 - x)$$
$$97.2 = 40 + (57.3 - x)$$
$$57.2 = 57.3 - x$$
$$x = 0.1$$

4. **B is correct.** $3{,}000 \times 0.002 = 6$.

5. **A is correct.** In an equilateral triangle, all three angles are equal. Since the sum of the angles in a triangle is 180°, each angle must be $180 \div 3 = 60°$.

6. **D is correct.**
$$y \div 72 = 21.4$$
$$y = 21.4 \times 72$$
$$y = 1{,}540.8$$

7. **A is correct.** It costs $n$ dollars to buy 10 boxes. Since $25 = 2.5 \times 10$, it will cost $2.5n$ dollars to buy 25 boxes.

8. **D is correct.** A straight angle measures 180°. So if $\angle 1$ is 33°, the other angle must measure $180° - 33° = 147°$.

9. **D is correct.** Let $x$ = cost of small cone. $2x$ = cost of large cone.
3 small cones + 3 large cones = $13.50
$$3x + 3(2x) = \$13.50$$
$$3x + 6x = \$13.50$$
$$9x = \$13.50$$
$$x = \$1.50$$

10. **B is correct.** Count the zeros in the divisor and move the decimal point to the left that many places.
$$7.426 \div 1{,}000 = 0.007426$$

11. **D is correct.** Calculate the number of square meters in the garden and then determine how many ounces of fertilizer are needed. The area of a rectangle is calculated by multiplying the length × the width. So the area of the garden is $4 \times 7 = 28$ m². Paul needs 2 oz of fertilizer for every square meter, so $2 \times 28 = 56$ oz.

12. **B is correct.** According to the chart, the plant is growing 3 inches taller each week. So in week 6, it should be $14 + 3 = 17$ inches tall.

13. **C is correct.** The thousandths place is three places to the right of the decimal point.

14. **C is correct.** In this problem you know two of the three angles, one measuring $55°$ and the other measuring $90°$ since the building forms a $90°$ angle with the ground. Together those two angles measure $145°$. Since a triangle has a total of $180°$, the third angle must measure $180° - 145° = 35°$.

15. **B is correct.** This item is set up as a proportion. To solve for $n$, cross-multiply so that the problem becomes $25n = 1,000$. $n = 1,000 \div 25 = 40$.

16. **D is correct.** Find the volume by multiplying length $\times$ width $\times$ height. Since all of the dimensions on a cube are the same, multiply:
$5 \times 5 \times 5 = 125$ in³

17. **B is correct.** Simple interest problems use the formula $I = prt$ where $I$ is the amount of interest, $p$ is the principle or the amount saved or invested, $r$ is the rate of interest, and $t$ is the amount of time that the interest is accruing. In this problem, you are asked to find the interest, given that the principle is \$4,000, the rate of interest is 2%, and the amount of time is 2 years. Substituting this information into the formula, you get $I = 4,000(0.02)(2) = \$160$ in interest.

18. **D is correct.** A right angle measures $90°$. If angle 1 measures $65°$, then angle 2 must measure $90° - 65° = 25°$.

19. **D is correct.** A number is evenly divisible by 4 if the number formed by the last two digits is divisible by 4.

20. **C is correct.** When two straight lines intersect as shown, they form opposite vertical angles. Those angles have the same measure, so if angle 2 measures $45°$, then angle 4 must also measure $45°$.

21. **A is correct.** 61 is divisible only by itself and 1. $81 \div 9 = 9$; $171 \div 9 = 19$; $207 \div 9 = 23$.

22. **D is correct.** In a parallelogram, opposite sides are parallel and opposite angles are equal. However, adjacent sides are not necessarily the same length.

23. **B is correct.** The area of the room is $15 \times 18 = 270$ ft². One square yard = 9 square feet, so $270$ ft² $\div 9 = 30$ yd².

24. **C is correct.** According to the graph, the two most popular categories were Mysteries and Nonfiction. The number of books in those categories checked out last month was $520 + 450 = 970$.

25. **B is correct.** The angles in a triangle total $180°$. The two given angles measure $55° + 65° = 120°$. Thus the remaining angle must measure $180° - 120° = 60°$.

26. **D is correct.** A common factor of two numbers is a whole number that is a factor of both numbers. The common factors of 24 and 36 are 1, 2, 3, 4, 6, and 12.

27. **B is correct.** Only $^{99}/_{100}$ is in simplest form. $^{15}/_{18} = {}^5/_6$; $^{56}/_{133} = {}^8/_{19}$; $^{45}/_{72} = {}^5/_8$.

28. **C is correct.** In this problem $\angle 6$ measures $90°$. Thus $\angle 3$ also measures $90°$. Because the two sides of the triangle are equal, it is an isosceles triangle. That makes $\angle 1$ and $\angle 2$ equal. Since $\angle 3 = 90°$, that leaves $90°$ to be split equally between $\angle 1$ and $\angle 2$. So each angle measures $45°$.

29. **A is correct.** The number of students polled was $34 + 22 + 65 + 27 + 24 + 78 = 250$. The number who preferred ice skating or sleepover was $22 + 78 = 100$. $100 \div 250 = 40\%$.

30. **A is correct.** Of the 6 numbers on the cube, 3 are even. So the probability that the number facing up will be even is $^3/_6$ or $^1/_2$.

31. **A is correct.** To find the area of a triangle, use the formula $A = (^1/_2)bh$ where $b$ is the base of the triangle and $h$ is the height. Because the triangle shown is a right triangle, side $a$ is the height. Substituting into the formula:
$A = (^1/_2)(6)(4) = 12$ ft².

32. **C is correct.** If Frank is 4 years younger than Donna, then the relationship between their two ages can be expressed by the equation $f = d - 4$.

33. **A is correct.** If the club sells $n$ tickets at \$3.00 each, the amount they will earn is $3n$. Their profit after paying \$224 in expenses is $3n - 224$.

34. **A is correct.** A wire stretched between two points on a circle and passing through the center will form a diameter of the circle. Diameter = radius × 2. If the radius is 1.35 m, the diameter = 2(1.35) = 2.7 m = 270 cm. If wire costs 2¢/cm, the cost of the wire stretching across the circle will be 270 × 2¢ = 540¢ = \$5.40.

35. **B is correct.** Convert to equivalent fractions using the lowest common denominator: $^2/_9 = {}^{16}/_{72}$, $^2/_8 = {}^{18}/_{72}$, $^2/_3 = {}^{48}/_{72}$.

36. **C is correct.** $2.004 = 2^4/_{1,000} = 2^1/_{250}$.

37. **A is correct.** $2.4 = 2^4/_{10} = 2^8/_{20}$; ${}^{10}/_4 = {}^{50}/_{20} = 2^{10}/_{20}$; $2^4/_5 = 2^{16}/_{20}$.

38. **A is correct.** If Adrinda is 8 years older than Marsha and Daryl is 3 years older than Marsha, then Daryl must be 5 years younger than Adrinda. So $d = a - 5$.

39. **B is correct.**
$5^5/_8 = {}^{45}/_8$
$2^2/_5 = {}^{12}/_5$
$$\frac{45}{8} \cdot \frac{12}{5} = \frac{540}{40} = 13.5 = 13\frac{1}{2}$$

40. **D is correct.** Follow the order of operations:
$5 \times 6 \div (2 + 1)$
$= 5 \times 6 \div 3$
$= 30 \div 3 = 10$

41. **C is correct.** The rule of the sequence is that each number is 5 more than the one before. So the missing numbers are $17 + 5 = 22$ and $22 + 5 = 27$.

42. **A is correct.** Two students scored between 80–90 and six scored between 90–100. $2 + 6 = 8$

43. **D is correct.**
$24 \div (-4^2/_3)$
$= 24 \div ({}^{-14}/_3)$
$= 24 \times ({}^{-3}/_{14})$
$= {}^{-72}/_{14} = -5^2/_{14} = -5^1/_7$

44. **C is correct.** There are four numbers less than 5: 1, 2, 3, and 4. The probability that the spinner will land on one of these four numbers is 4 in 12 or $^4/_{12} = {}^1/_3$.

45. **A is correct.** If 1 in = 40 km, 6 in = 240 km, and $^7/_8$ in = $^7/_8 \times 40 = 35$ km; $240 + 35 = 275$ km.

46. **D is correct.** $3x + 2 = 3(y + 3) + 2 = 3y + 9 + 2 = 3y + 11$

47. **C is correct.** The number 2 is the only even prime number. The consecutive primes $2 + 3$ have a sum of 5. All other pairs of consecutive primes sum to an even number since both are odd.